Theories of economic growth

THEORIES OF ECONOMIC GROWTH

By Bert F. Hoselitz, Joseph J. Spengler, J. M. Letiche, Erskine McKinley, John Buttrick, and Henry J. Bruton

Bert F. Hoselitz, EDITOR

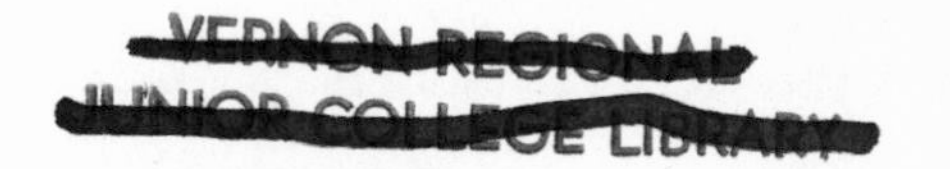

THE FREE PRESS, *New York*

COLLIER-MACMILLAN LIMITED, *London*

A DIVISION OF THE MACMILLAN COMPANY

Printed in the United States of America

Collier-Macmillan Canada, Ltd., Toronto, Ontario

Library of Congress Catalog Card Number: 60-10898

printing number
3 4 5 6 7 8 9 10

PREFACE

ALL BUT ONE of the papers included in this volume are the result of a seminar held at Dartmouth College in July and August of 1956, under the auspices of the Social Science Research Council. When it was found that the classical school's theory of economic growth appeared to be "under-represented," in that the volume lacked a comprehensive treatment of classical growth theory, the editor requested an additional essay on this topic from Dr. Erskine McKinley, who has devoted much time and study to this subject. Dr. McKinley did not participate in the Dartmouth seminar, but we feel that his contribution effectively supplements the other papers included in this volume.

In accordance with the procedure we had agreed upon, each participant at the seminar presented a first draft of his paper. This draft was then discussed by the whole group for several days; thus the final version of each paper incorporates many additional points suggested by other members of the group. The participants in the seminar were Henry Bruton, now with ICA in Iran; John A. Buttrick, University of Minnesota; Evsey D. Domar, Massachusetts Institute of Technology; Alexander Erlich, Columbia University; J. M. Letiche, University of California, Berkeley; Joseph J. Spengler, Duke University; and myself. The discussions were lively and stimulating, and I am sure that I am expressing the unanimous opinion of the group when I say that we found the experience a very profitable one.

Our thanks should be expressed, above all, to the Social Science Research Council, and especially to its Committee on Economic Growth. The Committee made the seminar possible, encouraged our efforts on this volume, and helped us to prepare it for publication. We are also grateful to Dartmouth College for making offices and a conference room available for our use. The editor wishes to express his personal appreciation to the Center for Advanced Study in the Behavioral Sciences at Stanford, California, where most of the work on his own paper was done. He also wishes to express his gratitude to Mrs. Georgianna March, who not only typed a large part of the final draft of this book, but also helped with a good deal of the editorial work. Mr. Jeremiah Kaplan of the Free Press has, by his patience and good humor, made the work of an occasionally frantic editor much more pleasant and effective.

Bert F. Hoselitz

THE UNIVERSITY OF CHICAGO

CONTENTS

Theories of economic growth

MERCANTILIST AND PHYSIOCRATIC GROWTH THEORY*

By Joseph J. Spengler

The ideas of economists and political philosophers, both when they are right and when they are wrong, are more powerful than is commonly understood.

J. M. Keynes, in *General Theory*

We, who know what followed, cannot help transferring back the image of it to the beginning.

Henri Bergson, in *The Two Sources of Morality and Religion*

MY CONCERN is the theory of economic growth, as found in the writings of mercantilists and physiocrats. It is in these writings that the contours and elements of a theory of economic growth first appear. Considerable and sustained economic progress took place in Europe before the fourteenth century, and some writers discussed those factors which they believed to be conducive to the improvement in man's material welfare. Yet, the basic elements of a dynamic theory of economic growth

*I am particularly indebted to a number of persons for their assistance in the preparation of this essay: to B. F. Hoselitz, J. M. Letiche, and Simon Kuznets for many helpful suggestions; to Mrs. Margaret Huntley for preparing several typescripts; and, above all, to Dr. Irene Butter and Dr. Robert M. Will for many weeks of careful assistance in the canvassing of the literature and the translation of its contents. I have had financial assistance from the Rockefeller and the Ford Foundations.

are not to be found in the economic literature of the Middle Ages; nor are they to be discovered in what was written during the interval of transition between the medieval and the mercantile periods. The climate of opinion and the regnant system of values did not favor growth. The degree of improvement in man's material lot that was considered desirable and to be expected was quite limited. Hence, until the composition of the value system had undergone considerable change, economic development could not be stressed.

The change took place under the combined influence of a series of events: the Renaissance; the alteration of man's attitudes toward the individual; the relaxation of ethical and other restraints upon the sovereign's exercise of power; new discoveries and the consequent quickening of the tempo of life; and the acceleration of the development and spread of capitalism in the wake of the Reformation. The Age of Mercantilism may thus be looked upon as a prolonged transitional period, in the course of which medieval unity was shattered; the medieval scheme of things underwent gradual dissolution; self-interest and the importance of material values were increasingly stressed; communal and other curbs upon man's striving after material achievement were reduced; and conditions prerequisite to the rise of politico-economic liberalism were established.[1]

Although the physiocrats also stressed wealth and contributed to the transformation of the value system, the advent of physiocracy—like Smithianism, which followed—amounted to much more than an interlude. For, whereas mercantilism emphasized the strategic character and the "causal" priority of external trade and/or industry, the importance of positive intervention by the state in economic affairs, the formulation of specific policies, and the subordination of the interests of some elements in a nation's population to the supposed purposes of state, physiocracy stressed the strategic character of agriculture, the limitedness of the positive role of the state, and the need for policy-makers to give adequate weight to the effects of policy on the welfare of lower income groups, as well

1. E.g., see R. Gonnard, "Quelques considerations sur le mercantilisme," *Revue d'économie politique,* XXXIV, 1920, pp. 428*ff*.; K. W. Deutsch, "Medieval Unity and the Economic Conditions for an International Civilization," *Canadian Journal of Economics and Political Science,* X, 1944, pp. 18-35; F. H. Knight, "Historical and Theoretical Issues in the Problem of Modern Capitalism," *Journal of Economic and Business History,* I, 1928-29, pp. 119-36; P. C. G. Walker, "Capitalism and the Reformation," *Economic History Review,* VIII, 1937, pp. 1-19; W. Roscher, *Geschichte der Nationaloekonomik in Deutschland,* Munich, 1874, esp. pp. 32-183. See also footnote 2, below. The new approach to poor relief, with its emphasis on prohibition of mendicancy and on provision of employment for the able-bodied, is well represented, in *De subventione pauperum* (Lyons, 1532), by the humanist, J. L. Vives. The mercantilists set much store by putting the idle to work and eliminating mendicancy. In earlier periods, mendicancy was less generally condemned, even though St. Thomas Aquinas and others disapproved of idleness and begging on the part of able-bodied persons. See Alfred O'Rahilly, *Aquinas versus Marx,* Oxford, 1948, pp. 12-14. It is customary to describe the medieval world as a unified one; this unity was by no means complete, however. See G. Barraclough, *History in a Changing World,* Oxford, 1955, pp. 128*ff*.

as to its impact on the more well-to-do. Physiocratic literature, furthermore, was more analytic and less common-sense in character than was mercantilist literature.

This paper is divided into two parts and is supplemented by an Appendix (at the back of this volume). The first section, which is concerned with the mercantilists (with whom the Cameralists[2] are grouped), presents a précis of their opinions with respect to economic growth. In the second section, the growth theory of the physiocrats is outlined. The Appendix contains fairly detailed summaries of the views of representative mercantilists from a number of countries; it is in part upon these summaries that my own précis is based.

Throughout this discussion much more space is given the mercantilists than the physiocrats. This division of space was prompted by a number of factors: mercantilist opinion was less homogeneous and less systematized than was physiocratic opinion; the mercantilists were more numerous and nationally diverse than were the physiocrats; the time-span during which mercantilism was in vogue embraced perhaps three centuries, whereas the period of ascendancy of physiocracy encompassed less than half a century; and finally, the mercantilists were concerned with many countries and divers situations, whereas the physiocrats dealt predominantly with eighteenth-century France. Since physiocratic theory received expression primarily in the works of a small number of authors, who differed little among themselves regarding the principles of economic growth, there was little possibility that significant repositories of this theory might have been disregarded. But it was necessary to be selective regarding

2. The Cameralists are usually distinguished from the mercantilists on various grounds: e.g., they put more stress on politico-economic philosophy, the role of the state, public finance, and the augmentation of revenue, and less stress on economic analysis. They lived, as a rule, in those parts of Europe which were less advanced economically; they were not businessmen as frequently as were mercantilist writers (at least outside of Spain); and so on. Some Cameralists were, however, interested in economic development and in concepts and instruments pertaining thereto. For this reason, and because we are not specifically concerned with the place of Cameralism in the history of economic thought, we do not distinguish between mercantilists and Cameralists as such. Concerning distinctions between the two groups, see E. F. Heckscher, *Mercantilism*, New York, rev. 2nd ed., 1955, II, pp. 263*ff*.; A. W. Small, *The Cameralists, The Pioneers of German Social Policy*, Chicago, 1909, pp. 54, 153, 246, 590-94; J. A. Schumpeter, *History of Economic Analysis*, New York, 1954, Part II, chap. 3; E. Cannan, *A Review of Economic Theory*, London, 1930, pp. 6-19; Roscher, *op.cit.* Edward Baumstark's *Kameralistische Encyclopaedie* (Heidelberg, 1835) contains little theory. See also K. Zielenziger, *Die alten deutschen Kameralisten*, Jena, 1914; Louise Sommer, *Die österreichischen Kameralisten*, Vienna, 1920; A. Tautscher, *Staatswirtschaftslehre der Kameralismus*, Bern, 1947; Axel Nielsen, *Die Enstehung der deutschen Kameralwissenschaft in 17 Jahrhundert*, Jena, 1911; W. Focke, *Die Lehrmeinungen der Kamerilisten ueber den Handel, 1650-1750*, Erlangen, 1926; W. Stieda, *Die Nationaloekonomie als Universitaetswissenschaft*, Leipzig, 1906; S. Gargas, *Volkswirtschaftliche Ansichten in Polen im XVII Jahrhundert*, Innsbruck, 1905. According to Nielsen *(op.cit.)*, the theories of the earlier Cameralists, at least, reflected the intellectual climate in which they lived, a climate infiltrated with Roman law, Greek philosophy, Aristotle's *Politics*, Bodin's political theory, and Renaissance humanism (cf. footnote 5, below). It seems agreed that little answering to the description of mercantilism was to be found in the ancient world.

mercantilist opinion. This opinion found expression in specific statutes, in administrative orders and judicial decisions, and in preambles to legislation, as well as in pamphlets, books, and tomes. My discussion, nonetheless, is confined largely to writings in which development theory finds expression. Only passing attention is devoted to implicit growth theory of the sort found in legislative, administrative, and judicial documents, which incorporated much of mercantilist achievement. I have organized my approach to the mercantilists and the physiocrats along somewhat different lines, in part for reasons already suggested, and in part because mercantilist theory never attained the status of an autonomous, self-sustaining system of ideas, as did scholastic economics, or as physiocracy almost did in the course of its short, but intellectually intensive, life. I have not dwelt upon contributions to economic tool-making because policy, rather than the fashioning of tools, was the principal concern of the mercantilists, and probably of the physiocrats as well. While my interest has focused on growth-oriented mercantilist theories, rather than mercantilist practice, it has not always been easy to distinguish these theories from theories on political strategy or the establishment of favorable market situations.[3]

Only some of the issues with which the historian of growth theory ought to concern himself will be considered. The theory of causation, present in the works under review will be neglected, since this theory usually was implicit, rather than explicit, particularly in the writings of the mercantilists. The significance of changes in the conception of man's psychological makeup will be explored, but I will not discuss the impact of these changes upon the theory of social causation. Those persons the mercantilists considered crucial decision-makers will be noted, but the

3. The meaning economists and others have assigned to "mercantilism" has continued to vary since Smith emphasized the machinations of merchants and manufacturers, and, a century later, Schmoller emphasized state-building. See C. Wilson, "'Mercantilism': Some Vicissitudes of an Idea," *Economic History Review*, X, 1957, pp. 181-88. E. F. Heckscher employed it as "simply a convenient term for summarising a phase of economic policy and economic ideas" *(ibid.*, VII, 1936-37, p. 54). According to E. Lipson *(The Economic History of England*, London, 4th ed., 1947, pp. xciv, lxxvi), mercantilism did not identify money and wealth; its achievements are found in "mercantilistic" statutes and decrees. D. C. Coleman describes mercantilism as a confusing label for economic policy; it gives "a false unity to disparate events," conceals the "close-up reality of particular times and particular circumstances," and blots out "the vital intermixture of ideas and preconceptions, of interests and influences, political and economic, and of the personalities of men." Mercantilist arguments and legislation, he believes, reflected ideas less and concrete situations (e.g., financial needs, state of trade) more than Heckscher supposed. See Coleman, "Eli Heckscher and the Idea of Mercantilism," *Scandinavian Economic History Review*, V, 1957, pp. 3-25; but cf. A. W. Coats, "In Defense of Heckscher and the Idea of Mercantilism," *ibid.*, VI, 1958, pp. 175-87. It is fairly easy to distinguish between mercantilist theory and mercantile system; but it is not possible to define the latter unarbitrarily, since it may denote "imperial economy" (thus C. R. Fay, *English Economic History Mainly Since 1700*, Cambridge, 1940, pp. 9-10), or more. See my discussion under (B) below; also A. V. Judges, "The Idea of a Mercantile State," *Transactions of the Royal Historical Society*, XXI, 1939, pp. 41-69. On physiocratic concern with policy, see Georges Weulersse, *Le mouvement physiocratique en France de 1756 à 1770*, Paris, 1910, and *La Physiocratie sous les ministères de Turgot et de Necker (1774-1781)*, Paris, 1950.

universe(s) in which they supposedly operated will neither be described nor analyzed. The allocation process, together with the arrangements counted upon to bring about an appropriate distribution of resources among uses, will be treated.

I

The Mercantilists

My discussion of mercantilist theory is based almost entirely upon opinions expressed by British, French, German (including Austrian), Italian, and Spanish (including Portuguese) writers.[4] Furthermore, attention

4. Of necessity, many writers are mentioned only by name. Concerning these, see such works as R. N. I. Palgrave's *Dictionary of Political Economy*, London, 1925; Roscher, *op.cit.;* Heckscher, *Mercantilism;* D. M. Colmeiro, *Biblioteca De Los Economistas Españoles de Los Siglos XVI, XVII Y XVIII* (1880), reprinted in Mexico City, 1942; or treatises, such as Etienne Laspeyres, *Geschichte der volkswirtschaftlichen Anschauungen der Niederländer und ihrer Litteratur zur Zeit der Republik,* Leipzig, 1863, and P. W. Buck, *The Politics of Mercantilism,* New York, 1942.

Mercantilist opinions were expressed in countries other than those considered in this paper. For example, mercantilist opinions and policy had some vogue in Russia. (See forthcoming monograph by J. M. Letiche; also E. Pernet, *La politique économique de Pierre de Grand,* Paris, 1913; W. Leontief, "Peter der Grosse; sein Wirtschaftspolitik und sein angeblicher Merkantilismus," *Jahrbücher für Geschichte Osteuropas,* II, 1937, pp. 234-71.) Swedish mercantilist literature did not differ essentially from that of other countries. Before the eighteenth century, it consisted largely of legislative and administrative materials; in the eighteenth century it included books, pamphlets, and several periodicals. Swedish mercantilist literature apparently stressed the role of the state less than did the Cameralists, and the role of science and technology more perhaps than did many non-Swedish mercantilists. (See Heckscher, *Mercantilism,* and *An Economic History of Sweden,* Cambridge, 1954, pp. 65-68, 112-15, 130-32, 194-208.) K. V. R. Aiyangar *(Indian Cameralism,* Madras, 1949) finds traces of mercantilism in the *Arthas'astra.* On Poland, see Gargas, *op.cit.*

Although Dutch policies often were mercantilist in character, mercantilist ideas had less vogue in Holland than in other leading European countries, particularly before the eighteenth century. Various circumstances were responsible for this. Freedom of commerce had the support of the merchant class, as well as that of economic writers (e.g., Grotius, Graswinckel, and Salmasius, defender of interest-taking). Protectionism found its proponents principally in the manufacturing class. Holland faced no serious economic problems in the seventeenth century, and hence was not compelled to reassess its position and perhaps intensify state intervention. Moreover, she was free of invasion during much of the seventeenth century (1609-72) and this condition may have affected Dutch theory and policy, much as England's immunity to invasion affected English theory and policy. Most continental states had continually to seek protection against invasion and occupation, forces to which Italian and other city-states finally succumbed. See A. Toynbee, *A Study of History,* London, 1935-54, II, pp. 262-64, 268, III, pp. 344-63; J. U. Nef, *War and Human Progress,* Cambridge, 1952, chap. 1 and *passim;* G. N. Clark, *The Seventeenth Century,* Oxford, 2nd ed., 1950, *passim.* On Dutch mercantilism, see especially Heckscher, *Mercantilism,* I, pp. 351-73, II, pp. 263, 274, 305*ff.;* Laspeyres, *op.cit.,* pp. 109-10, 132-36, 143, 149, 155-58. See also E. Baasch, *Hollaendische Wirtschaftsgeschichte,* Jena, 1927, p. 355; E. Beins, *Die Wirtschaftsethik der calvinistchen Kirche der Niederlande 1565-1650,* The Hague, 1931; J. W. Horrocks, *A Short History of Mercantilism,* London, 1925, pp. 109*ff.*

Typical of the best seventeenth-century Dutch "liberal" thought (which, of course, was less liberal than Smithian and post-Smithian liberal thought) are the views of Pieter de la Court (Van den Hove), as set forth in his *Intrest van Holland,* Amsterdam, 1662. In the preface of this volume the importance of political stability and of security against external attack is stressed. The author traces Holland's strength as a trading nation

is devoted primarily to writers who flourished in the seventeenth and early eighteenth centuries, when mercantilist thought was ascendant. Some consideration will be given, however, to pre-seventeenth-century mercantilist views and to the fact that medieval opinion was intermixed with mercantilist opinion, especially during and before the sixteenth century.[5] For greater clarity, this section is divided into two parts. In part (A) organizational considerations are examined; in (B) attention is given to the

to Dutch skill in buying and re-selling, the lowness of the interest rate, the activities of the East India Company, the diligence of the Dutch people, and the flourishing state of the fishing industry (by which manufacturing and complementary activities were stimulated). Among the causes of the industry of the Dutch people, he mentions the coldness of the climate and the fact that they had to work hard to earn enough to pay the high taxes imposed and to support the large families which were common in Holland. Freedom of religion and freedom to work, which attracted fresh-spirited foreigners, also helped to account for Holland's prosperity. He adds, however, that still more freedom is necessary, since monopolistic guilds and trading companies hinder industry and improvement, since competition for the consumer's custom is the most effective guarantee the consumer can have of quality and satisfactory prices, and since high import and export duties interfere with trade and manufacture. See *ibid.*, pp. 11-16, 35-45, 52, and pp. 63, 70, 146, and 246, where the advantages of peace are extolled and a monarchical government is described as much more disposed to go to war than is a government of the type found in Holland.

It is not clear from available secondary studies to what degree mercantilist principles infiltrated Dutch economic thought in the seventeenth century. It is inferable from Laspeyres *(op.cit.)* and from O. Van Rees *(Geschiedenis Der Staathuishoudkunde In Nederland,* Utrecht, 1865, I, pp. 285, 304, 396) that these principles had more support in the eighteenth than in the seventeenth century. Even in the nineteenth century, when liberalism began to be given much less-qualified expression, a mercantilist policy was pursued by William I after 1813, in that he employed state subsidies, required state agencies to consume domestic products, utilized export prohibitions and privileges, subjected capital-export to restrictive controls, and sought for Holland a preferred position in her colonial import and export markets. Industrial development was a primary objective of this moderate mercantilism. See I. J. Brugmans, "Koning Willem I als Neo-Mercantilist," in *Welvaart en Historie,* The Hague, 1950, pp. 38-51.

5. Medieval opinions, having long been systematically formulated and integrated, gave way very slowly to mercantilist opinion, just as they gave way slowly to such of the newer humanist opinion as entered into the composition of mercantilism. In fact, scholastic influence persisted into the eighteenth century, though in greater degree in some countries than in others; and mercantilism, many of whose policy proposals ran counter to the ethical norms of scholasticism, was compelled to accommodate itself to this influence. Scholastic influence is also to be found in the physiocratic literature. Medieval opinions persisted in greatest measure in Spanish economic literature, and in somewhat greater measure in Italian and (apparently) French economic literature than in that of England and Germany (but see footnote 2, above, on Aristotle's influence in Germany). Differences in the persistence of scholastic views reflect, in part, differences in the professional backgrounds of authors and in the impact of the Reformation. See T. P. Neill, "The Physiocrats's Concept of Economics," *Quarterly Journal of Economics,* LXIII, 1949, pp. 532-53; Raymond de Roover, "Scholastic Economics: Survival and Lasting Influence from the Sixteenth Century to Adam Smith," *ibid.*, LXIX, 1955, esp. pp. 177-90; Cynthia T. Morris, "Some Neglected Aspects of Sixteenth Century Economic Thought," *Explorations in Entrepreneurial History,* IX, 1957, pp. 160-71; H. M. Robertson, *Aspects of the Rise of Economic Individualism,* Cambridge, 1933, chaps. 4-6 and *passim;* E. Lipson, *op.cit.*, esp. p. lxxv; Heckscher, *Mercantilism, passim.* See also, e.g., A. B. Ferguson, "Renaissance Realism in the 'Commonwealth' Literature of Early Tudor England," *Journal of the History of Ideas,* XVI, 1955, pp. 287-305; and E. W. Tillyard, *The Elizabethan World Picture,* New York, 1944. P. Zagorin believes that not until the seventeenth century was "the critical stage" reached in "the shift from the medieval to the distinctly modern way of comprehending the world." See *A History of Political Thought in the English Revolution,* London, 1954, p. 3; also G. R. Potter, ed., *The New Cambridge Modern History,* Cambridge, 1957, I, chap. 1.

economic relationships deemed critical by the mercantilists, together with their proposals for manipulating these relationships. While the implications of these policies will be pointed out occasionally, their effects will not be assessed, since our primary concern is with mercantilist ideas, not economic history.

(A) ORGANIZATIONAL CONSIDERATIONS

Because of its heterogeneous character, at least when viewed superficially, the treatment of mercantilism presents classificatory and related problems. First, disagreement persists with respect to the policy objectives of mercantilism, particularly as to whether mercantilism had power or plenty as its over-riding objective. The resolution of this dispute has been rendered somewhat difficult by a variety of circumstances: avowed objectives varied in time and place, and, on occasion, were somewhat contradictory; essentially private objectives were sometimes described as if they were public objectives; liberal views, many of medieval origin, cropped up in mercantilist writings; mercantilists were interested in specific and practical aspects of governmental operations and policy (e.g., external economic relations and internal economic balance), rather than in general issues of political theory.[6] Moreover, legislation might resemble mercantilist legislation in content and effect, even when it was not set in a mercantilist frame of reference; and the importance attached by writers to the capacity of the state to modify the course of economic events varied in time and space. Furthermore, mercantilism was encountered in both absolute and constitutional states (variously intermixed with feudal notions and practices), and in both those countries that had, and those that had not, become economically unified states; and countries differed with respect to the nature and the amount of difficulty that attended the conversion of their political and economic institutions into those of a national state.

6. On contradictions, see Heckscher, *Mercantilism, passim;* Lipson, *op.cit.*, III, pp. 3*ff.;* A. Smith, *Wealth of Nations,* IV, chap. 8. On liberal elements in mercantilism, see De Roover, *op.cit.* and *Gresham on Foreign Exchange,* Cambridge, 1949; W. D. Grampp, "The Liberal Elements in English Mercantilism," *Quarterly Journal of Economics,* LXVI, 1952, pp. 465-501. On the political theory of the English mercantilists, see P. W. Buck, *op.cit.*, chap. 4. His findings, though apparently applicable also to Dutch mercantilist literature (Laspeyres, *op.cit.*, pp. 134*ff.*), are not descriptive of Cameralist literature, in much of which an organismic theory of the state is encountered. See A. W. Small, *op.cit.;* Tautscher, *op.cit.;* Nielsen, *op.cit.*, pp. 118*ff.* Some of the Cameralists expressed themselves in terms of a welfare state, as did some of the mercantilists, and as had various medieval political theorists. Even in the England of the Tudors, a welfare-state philosophy and policy are encountered. E.g., see S. T. Bindoff, *Tudor England,* Harmondsworth, 1951, pp. 289-94; W. G. Zeeveld, "Social Equalitarianism in a Tudor Crisis," *Journal of the History of Ideas,* VII, 1946, pp. 35-55, and *Foundations of Tudor Policy,* Cambridge, 1948. On a forerunner of Colbert, see R. Gandilhon, *Politique économique de Louis XI,* Rennes, 1940.

Finally, "mercantilist" practices were resorted to by various of the Italian city-states before the larger national states had come into being.[7]

It makes no difference, for the purpose of this discussion, whether the end of mercantilism was power or wealth, so long as power was sought through instrumentalities that tended to be strongly wealth-increasing. The evidence seems to bear out Viner's conclusion that mercantilist theorists not only looked upon wealth and power as the principal objectives of mercantilist policy, but believed these ends to be in long-run harmony, in that realization of the one fostered realization of the other. The belief that power depended upon wealth seems to have become stronger as time passed, perhaps because of the patently adverse effects of a too exclusive pursuit of dynastic or other political objectives (for example, in France and Spain, in contrast with England). Even so, many administrators probably continued to esteem power above wealth. The belief (e.g., of Montaigne and Bacon) that one nation's gain was another's loss, together with the importance mercantilists attached to war and to the supposedly exploitative character of much of trade, seems to have had its origin in part in an assumption that was not relaxed until European trade and industry

7. E.g., see G. Schmoller, *The Mercantile System*, New York, 1895; Small, *op.cit.;* Schumpeter, *op.cit.*, p. 144, and *Economic Doctrine and Method* (1912), London, 1954, pp. 32-34; Buck, *op.cit.*, pp. 113-22; J. Calmette and E. Déprez, *Les premières grands puissances*, in G. Glotz, ed., *Histoire de moyen age*, Paris, 1939, VII, Part 2; and Heckscher, *Mercantilism*, II, Part 2, and pp. 14-16, where the "state" is represented as the unifying agency before 1600, when nationalism supposedly was not yet strong. E. Silberner (in *La guerre dans la pensée économique du xvie aux viiie siècle*, Paris, 1939, pp. 11, 94-127, 262-66) describes mercantilism, above all the mercantilism of the seventeenth century, as shot through with bellicism; and L. Stone ("State Control in Sixteenth-century England," *Economic History Review*, XVII, 1947, p. 110) writes that sixteenth-century mercantilism amounted to "a system of economic nationalism," which had its origin in "the relentless pressure of war and the fear of war." However, J. Viner emphasizes the diversity of the mercantilist countries (in "Power versus Plenty as Objectives of Foreign Policy in the Seventeenth and Eighteenth Centuries," *World Politics*, I, 1948, esp. p. 2.) Yet, it is not inaccurate to say, with C. R. Fay, that rivalry furnished the key to England's trade policy during the mercantilist period. England contested with Spain and Portugal in the sixteenth century for access to the high seas and the New World; with Holland in the seventeenth for the carrying trade, a struggle that resulted in the navigation code; and with France in the eighteenth century for "an overseas empire, conceived as a source" of raw materials for manufacture and as a market for British products. See Fay's *Imperial Economy*, Oxford, 1934, and his "Adam Smith, America, and the Doctrinal Defeat of the Mercantile System," *Quarterly Journal of Economics*, XLVIII, 1934, pp. 304*ff*. It was in the possibilities of a young, free, and developing America, with which he hoped England would enter into imperial partnership, that Smith found a realistic answer, or alternative, to mercantilism (*ibid.*, pp. 314-16). Prior to the Age of Discovery in Italy (in and before the fifteenth century), commercial rivalry gave rise to market-protecting policies and sometimes to war, Venice in particular seeking to monopolize the Levant trade. See Heckscher, *Mercantilism*, II, pp. 139*ff.;* G. R. Potter, ed., *op.cit.*, I, Chaps. 10, 16; H. Baron, "Towards a More Positive Evaluation of the Fifteenth-Century Renaissance," *Journal of the History of Ideas*, IV, 1943, p. 26; G. Mattingly, *Renaissance Diplomacy*, London, 1955, pp. 58*ff*. On the commercially inspired struggles of the Hansa, and on the inability of this medieval creation to convert itself into a territorial state, see also M. M. Postan and H. J. Habakkuk, eds., *Cambridge Economic History Of Europe*, Cambridge, II, 1952, pp. 223-56, and J. R. Tanner, *et al.*, eds., *Cambridge Medieval History*, Cambridge, VII, 1949, chap. 8. C. M. Andrews ("Anglo-French Commercial Rivalry, 1700-1750: The Western Phase," *American Historical Review*, XX, 1915, pp. 538-56, 761-80) treats the New World phase.

began to respond to the stimuli of applied science and new opportunities in Asia, Africa, and the New World. Until then, it was assumed, as in the Middle Ages, that the world's stock of accessible resources was essentially fixed and that economies were relatively static.[8]

The mercantilists cannot be said to have assessed carefully whether the pursuit of power (wealth) as an end might conflict with the pursuit of wealth (power), although, apparently, some did recognize that the pursuit of power had checked, or might check, the growth of wealth. They neglected the possibility of conflict between the movement of aggregate and that of per capita indicators (e.g., of income, wealth, power), because their concern was with aggregates, or because they supposed, or pretended to suppose, that individual and aggregate indicators tended to move together.[9]

Mercantilist writers may also be classified in terms of space and time, both as to the economic variables which they considered generally significant and as to those whose manipulation they advocated, and in terms of the methods whereby they hoped to manipulate strategic variables. They might be further classified in terms of how they interrelated the economic variables which they considered important or manipulable, or in terms of the detailed objectives they sought. Of course, if writers are classified on the basis of their use of economic variables, they may be further subdivided with regard to time and/or space. For the present, our discussion proceeds in terms of space and time.

While it may be true that all, or nearly all, of the countries in which mercantilism had currency were poor, essentially agrarian, economically underdeveloped, and ill-equipped, even with small-scale manufactures, it

8. On this controversy, see Viner, *op.cit.*, pp. 1-29; Schumpeter, *op.cit.*, pp. 346-47; Heckscher, *Mercantilism*, II, pp. 23-30, 359-63; Potter, ed., *op.cit.*, chap. 16; Joseph J. Spengler, *French Predecessors of Malthus*, Durham, 1942, *passim;* Violet Barbour's comment on prevalence of gain-loss belief, in her paper in E. M. Carus-Wilson, ed., *Essays in Economic History*, London, 1954, p. 253; Coleman, *op.cit.*, pp. 18-21; P. W. Bamford, "Entrepreneurship in Seventeenth and Eighteenth Century France . . . ," *Explorations in Entrepreneurial History*, IX, 1957, pp. 204-13. J. P. Ludewig (1670-1743) had made military power depend upon economic policy (see Roscher, *op.cit.*, pp. 357-59). Political philosophers, too, became increasingly aware of the dependence of political power upon economic power, but their concern was primarily with the degree to which the intra-state distribution of political power depended upon that of economic power, together with the significance of this dependence for the specification of conditions of political stability. Harrington (e.g., in *Oceana)* found the origin of different types of government in different property systems, a condition that, in his opinion, Hobbes had overlooked. However, Machiavelli, codifier of the philosophy of the Renaissance state (cf. Robertson, *op.cit.*, p. 58), seems to have set more store by power than by liquid wealth *(The Discourses,* I, chaps. 4-5, 35, II, chap. 10), even though he noted (in *The Prince*, chaps. 14, 17, 21) the significance of princely parsimony and individual economic self-interest and stressed (in *The History of Florence*, II, chap. 1) the importance of colonial expansion, together with the pressures and prospects that induce men to develop new territory. Hobbes devoted chapter 24 of his *Leviathan* to the economic base of the commonwealth.

9. That the pursuit of power, or of wealth in the aggregate, might adversely affect the pursuit of individual welfare was recognized by Hobbes *(Leviathan* [Everyman ed. 1914], chaps. 11-13, p. 372), and Cantillon, *Essai sur la nature du commerce en général*, A. Sauvy, ed., Paris, 1952, Part II, chap. 15.

is also true that selected regions of some of these countries were relatively advanced. Of greater importance is the fact that these countries differed appreciably in area, population, population growth, state of economic and political development, class structure, favorableness of transfer and trading relations, extent and exploitability of colonial and quasi-colonial holdings, and so on.[10] These differences, particularly those which affected what were the bases of power at the time, accounted largely for inter-country differences in policies advocated or adopted, in attitudes toward the regulation of trade, and in capacity to carry out particular programs. Of these bases, size of population and degree of political or national unity were especially important. Thus, smallness of population eventually set limits to Dutch and Portuguese accomplishments, while political disunity counterbalanced the large population of Germany and Italy. Comparative largeness of number contributed to the determination with which the English, French, and Iberian peoples were able, despite varying political disunity, to pursue large-scale, external efforts.[11]

10. A comparative view of conditions at the close of the Middle Ages is provided in *The Cambridge Economic History of Europe*, Cambridge, 1941, 1952, I and II, and in *The New Cambridge Modern History*, Cambridge, 1957, I. See also F. Braudel, *La Méditerranée et le monde méditerranéen à l'époque de Philippe II*, Paris, 1949. Schumpeter stresses the agrarian character of these countries (*History*, pp. 149-50), and states (*ibid.*, pp. 78-79, 143-48), as does Braudel (*op.cit.*, pp. 616-42), that economic planning for war was fostered by the influx of precious metals and by the increase of the power of the aristocratic class (at least in Germany, France, and Spain) in the sixteenth and seventeenth centuries and at the expense of the bourgeosie, whose power had increased in the fifteenth century only to decline thereafter. Of the various countries that attempted colonization, only four were able to establish and retain control of extensive colonial holdings in the Western Hemisphere: Portugal in Brazil, Spain primarily in the rest of Latin America, and England and France in North America and parts of the Caribbean world. In Asia, Spain and Portugal established trading colonies, only to lose some of these to the Dutch, who had also established trading posts in South Asia and the East Indies. British interest eventually centered in India, whence they virtually excluded other European powers. An exploitable population lived, or was introduced in some of these colonies (e.g., in Latin America, the West Indies, and Asia), whereas in others (e.g., much of the North American mainland) numbers were sparse and not amenable to intensive exploitation. The factory or trading type predominated in Asia; the plantation type, involving relatively intensive use of resources, and dependent upon the availability of capital and exploitable labor, was found principally in the Americas; the province type, involving the exploitation of the provinces as such, was found chiefly in Asia and in the Spanish possessions. The factory system of colonization was the earliest, having been prosecuted by Venice, Genoa, and Portugal even before the discovery of America; but it had a kind of antecedent in the type of "colony" established for the purpose of maintaining military control of a conquered nation (cf. Machiavelli, *The Prince*, chap. 3). Spanish and Portuguese colonial practice was influenced by Italy's experience in the Levant and along the Black Sea in the Middle Ages. See C. Verlinden, "Italian Influence in Iberian Colonization," *Hispanic American Historical Review*, XXXIII, 1953, pp. 192-211.

11. Around 1600, France's population approximated 16 million; Spain's, 8; the United Kingdom's 6.5, of which 4.5 lived in England and Wales; that of the dominions of the Austrian Hapsburgs, about 5.5. Disunited Italy numbered 13 million (of which less than 2 lived in Venice), or 114 per square mile; disunited Germany (including the Hapsburg dominion), 20 million, or 73 per square mile. Elsewhere, population density ranged from 104 per square mile in the Netherlands, through 88 and 78 in France and England, to 44 in Spain and Portugal, and 5 in Scandinavia. (In 1950 corresponding densities in Michigan, Vermont, and New Mexico approximated 112, 41, and 6.) The populations of Portugal and Scandinavia numbered only about 2 million each; that of the Netherlands, less than 3. Between 1600 and 1700 population declined in some countries and increased in others; in Spain and Portugal it fell from about 10 to perhaps 7.3; in Italy,

We may conceive of a representative mercantile state as comprising three parts: (a) comparatively developed or industrialized regions or centers; (b) a domestic hinterland, whence produce and raw materials may be had; and (c) an external hinterland, where domestic products may be marketed and various goods, especially those which are complementary to domestic factors or products, may be obtained. The mercantilists sought the expansion of (a) and the development of (b) at a rate sufficient at least to sustain the growth of (a). When (b) was comparatively small, and of but limited exploitability, mercantilist policy advocated recourse to (c), either through the medium of more or less regulated trade, or through the medium of occupation and exploitation. And yet, this last course entailed something of a dilemma, since the capacity of a small nation to pursue it, even after the manner of the Dutch, was limited, and since the capacity of a large nation to pursue it would be reduced if this nation diverted too much of its potential productive power from (a) and (b) to (c).[12] Only England, France, and Spain proved themselves able to develop a colonial hinterland, though the capacity of France and Spain to do so was diminished by their expenditure of resources in continental war. The Dutch could exploit, but could not settle effectively. Of the German states, only Austria and what became Prussia manifested a capacity to expand into

---

from 13 to perhaps 11.3. Meanwhile, France's population rose to 19 million; the United Kingdom's and that of the Hapsburg dominions, to about 7.5 each. The population of the Low Countries did not change greatly. Between 1700 and 1750, population increased about 14-15 per cent in Italy and the United Kingdom; around 25 per cent in Prussia and Spain (including Portugal); about 22 in the other German states; about 32 in the Low Countries; only about 5 in France. The figures for 1600 and 1700 are based upon A. P. Usher, "The History of Population and Settlement in Eurasia," *Geographical Review*, XX, 1930, Tables III-IV, and G. N. Clark, *op.cit.*, chap. 2. See also Braudel, *op.cit.*, pp. 268-77, 347-59. The percentages for 1700-1750 are based upon W. Bowden, M. Karpovich, and A. P. Usher, *An Economic History of Europe Since 1750*, New York, 1937, pp. 3, 13-21. I have reported percentages rather than absolute figures because the absolute figures given by Bowden, Karpovich, and Usher for 1700 are higher than those given in Usher's earlier work and in Clark's work. The data presented represent the trends and the relevant orders of magnitude; only careful studies of each country would reveal more. In most countries the rate of growth was higher in 1750-1800 than in 1700-1750. As early as the Middle Ages, there were manifestations of nationalism, a unifying force that served to dissolve some forms of local particularism; it developed gradually, especially after the Reformation and growth in the use of native languages. See C. G. Coulton, "Nationalism in the Middle Ages," *Cambridge Historical Journal*, V (1), 1935, pp. 13-40; H. Kohn, *The Idea of Nationalism*, New York, 1948, pp. 104-83. By the late fifteenth century, England, France, and Spain were united under strong monarchies. See Potter, ed., *op.cit.*, p. 50, also Heckscher, *Mercantilism*, II, pp. 14-16, who makes the state, not nationalism, the unifying force in 1500-1700.

12. Not many mercantilist writers would have subscribed to Toynbee's view *(op.cit.*, III, pp. 134, 140, 150*ff.)* that geographical expansion tends to slow down internal development; and many believed that the development of external hinterlands intensified internal development (cf. B. Franklin's argument, described in J. Spengler, "Malthusianism in Eighteenth Century America," *American Economic Review*, XXV, 1935, pp. 693-98). Some implied, however, that investment of men and resources in external development beyond a certain rate would entail a less than optimal distribution of men and resources between (c), on the one hand, and (a) and (b), on the other. Fay *(English Economic History*, pp. 9-10, 13) restricts mercantilism to (c), to overseas imperial economy, of which Holland and England were the leading representatives. See also R. Pares, "The Economic Factors in the History of the Empire," *Economic History Review*, VII, 1937, pp. 119-44.

contiguous territory; neither developed overseas colonies or trading centers after the Dutch manner. Nor were any of the Italian or other small European states able to do so outside the Mediterranean world. It is only in the literature of some countries, therefore, that colonies occupied an important place in mercantilist theory. In the others it is (a) and (b) that are emphasized; under (c), only external trade and some expansion into contiguous territory are possible.

Inter-country variation in economic fortune is likely to be accompanied by inter-country variation in problems and issues and hence by inter-country differences in the progress of economic analysis. For economic change may intensify old problems and give rise to new problems for which solutions are sought; and the search for solutions, while conditioned by the current state of economic theory and its analytical tools, will greatly affect what portions of economic theory are used, and, when these portions prove wanting, determine both what branches of theory are subjected to reassessment and modification and in what directions the body of theory is extended. Of course, if many countries simultaneously undergo similar experiences, their economic policies are likely to be noticeably similar. Thus, in times of arrested economic development and/or economic contraction (e.g, throughout much of the fourteenth, fifteenth, and seventeenth centuries) "mercantilist" ideas and policies (e.g., market-protecting and market-creating policies; partial closure of entry into trades, industries, and commercial sectors; exchange control) will have a much greater vogue than in periods of economic expansion (e.g., from the tenth to the early fourteenth century, in parts of the sixteenth century, and in the eighteenth century), when it is comparatively easy for a large fraction of the population to sell a growing output of goods and services on favorable terms. A careful comparison of variations in the content of economic ideas and policies with variations in the state of trade should reveal a significant positive correlation and account in part for the vicissitudes of protectionist policy.

Inter-country variation in economic fortune always characterized Western and Southern Europe to some degree, but apparently this variation did not become pronounced until after the middle of the sixteenth century. The nations comprising these regions participated almost as a whole in both the stagnation of 1325-1460 and the remarkable expansion of industry and trade from 1470 to 1540. Thereafter, these countries differed with respect to both progress and decline; some suffered more than others from the retardation or decline of growth that began in or before the seventeenth century and characterized much of this period; some benefited more than others from the expansion that followed, and dominated the eighteenth century. Thus, England and Holland, together with Sweden and Switzerland, suffered less from adverse movements in the seventeenth century than did Spain, Germany, and Italy.[13] Between 1600 and the late seven-

13. Because quantitative data are incomplete, estimates of trends and inter-country differences are subject to error throughout the period covered by this essay; and, as P. Mathias observes (in "The Social Structure in the Eighteenth Century: A Calculation by Joseph Massie," *Economic History Review,* X, 1957, pp. 46*ff.),* even when considerable quantitative data are available, they need to be interpreted with care. For careful assessments of the evidence see Nef, *op.cit.*, chaps. 1, 8, 15, and Postan and Rich, eds., *Cambridge Economic History,* II, pp. 155-256, 289-354, 387-428, 456-73; also P. A. Sorokin's synthetic summaries for France and Germany (in *Social and Cultural Dynamics,* III, New York, 1937, pp. 236-47). E. J. Hobsbawm describes the seventeenth century as one of retrogression and crisis, in the course of which the social structure of society was transformed from one dominated by feudal and guild relationships to one favorable to the development of a competitive and expanding capitalism. See "The General Crisis of the European Economy in the 17th Century," *Past and Present,* No. 5, May, 1954, pp. 33-53; No. 6, November, 1954, pp. 44-65. That climatic changes may have contributed significantly to these economic variations is argued by G. Utterström, "Climatic Fluctuations and Population Problems in Early Modern History," *Scandinavian Economic History Review,* III, 1955, pp. 3-47.

That declines in England and Holland were less pronounced, and for shorter periods, is reflected in contemporary economic literature. See J. D. Gould, "The Trade Crisis of the Early 1620's and English Economic Thought," *Journal of Economic History,* XV, 1955, pp. 121-33, and "The Trade Depression of the Early 1620's," *Economic History Review,* VII, 1954, pp. 81-90; also R. W. K. Hinton, "The Mercantile System in the Time of Thomas Mun," *ibid.*, VII, 1955, pp. 277-90, esp. pp. 284-88. Elizabethan exports, completely dominated by cloth and textiles (much as English commerce had been dominated by wool two hundred years earlier), remained quantitatively almost static. See L. Stone, "Elizabethan Overseas Trade," *ibid.*, II, 1949, pp. 30-58. In fact, the character of British trade did not change significantly until the second half of the seventeenth century, a period marked, unlike that of which Mun wrote, by great optimism in economic matters. See R. Davis, "English Foreign Trade, 1660-1700," *ibid.*, VII, 1954, pp. 150-66, and K. G. Davies, "Joint-Stock Investment in the Later Seventeenth Century," *ibid.*, IV, 1952, esp. pp. 283-85. F. J. Fisher observes that while agricultural and industrial output increased in England in the sixteenth and seventeenth centuries, most of the progress experienced was confined to the later seventeenth century, and that even this progress was not of a nature and magnitude to alter the class and occupational structure enough to prompt writers to use non-medieval social categories; these were introduced in the eighteenth century. See his "The Sixteenth and Seventeenth Centuries: The Dark Ages in English Economic History," *Economica,* XXIV, 1957, pp. 6, 15-17, and "Commercial Trends and Policy in Sixteenth-Century England," *Economic History Review,* X, 1940, pp. 95-117, dealing with England's response to the post-1650 collapse of her textile-exports boom; also L. Stone's comments ("State Control . . . ," *loc.cit.*, pp. 106*ff.).*

According to Laspeyres *(op.cit.*, pp. 104, 132-38, 143, 149, 155-59), Dutch proposals for import restrictions did not appear until the second half of the seventeenth century, at which time A. Tollenaer and J. Voetius (both admirers of Colbert) were writing, and there was concern lest Dutch trade be adversely affected by intensified French competition and by the impact of the British navigation acts, themselves in part a response to revived Dutch competition. See R. W. K. Hinton, "Dutch Entrepot Trade at Boston, Lincs., 1600-1640," *Economic History Review,* IX, 1957, pp. 467-71. In the eighteenth century there appeared many treatises on the decline of Dutch trade and the means of reviving it; in the 1730's there were even demands for the protection of long-established industries. Charles Wilson *(Anglo-Dutch Commerce and Finance in the Eighteenth Century,* Cambridge, 1941, chap. 1) reports no serious decline in Dutch trade until around 1730, adding that the post-1648 contraction was eventually succeeded by the post-1680 expansion. He indicates, however, that the character of Dutch foreign economic operations changed, at least in the eighteenth century, increasing attention being given to the provision of financial services to Europe and to the facilitation of foreign investment. Dutch foreign and colonial investment increased substantially after 1749 (see Alice Carter, "Dutch Foreign Investment, 1738-1800," *Economica,* XX, 1953, pp. 330, 337-40), with some of the richest capitalists investing as much as two-fifths of their wealth abroad, a portion of it in the English public debt. (Miss Carter estimates the fraction held by Dutch investors as of 1777 at not more than one-sixth in her article, "The Dutch and the English Public Debt in 1777," *ibid.*, p. 161.) Even so, home investment remained high, since the average propensity to save was high (a banker in 1791 implied it to be 25-37 per cent). In 1688 Dutch savings may have amounted to 11 per cent of income (see footnote 83, below).

teenth century, the industrial structure of Italy collapsed, largely because it could not meet rising Dutch, French, and English competition, and because its Spanish and German markets contracted. (In 1600 Italy was still one of the most advanced of the industrial areas of Western Europe, despite its having been a battleground in the sixteenth century.)[14] Apparently, the Spanish economy began to decline just before 1600, experiencing diminutions of about 25 and 75 per cent, respectively, in population and shipping in the century that followed–a decline that was not interrupted until the first quarter of the eighteenth century.[15] After 1550, output in Germany declined, her population diminishing about one-third by 1650; this decline was accentuated in those regions which were particularly affected by the Thirty Years' War. Meanwhile, output increased notably between 1540 and 1640 in Sweden, Denmark, Scotland, the United Provinces (after 1580), and, above all, in England, where heavy industries flourished; it increased less rapidly in France and Switzerland where, as in Italy, progress was largely confined to artistic and luxury industries. During the century succeeding the Thirty Years' War, however, output grew relatively more rapidly in Germany than in England, France, and Holland, where economic progress was not so marked as it had been in the preceding century.[16]

14. See Nef, *op.cit.*, pp. 7-9, 18-19; and C. M. Cipolla, "The Decline of Italy: The Case of a Fully Matured Economy," *Economic History Review,* V, 1952, pp. 178-87. Trade between the Mediterranean ports and Western Europe increased in the sixteenth century, only to decline in the seventeenth (G. R. Potter, ed., *op.cit.*, I, p. 447). In some respects, Italy's experience confirms T. Veblen's thesis *(Imperial Germany and the Industrial Revolution,* New York, 1915, chap. 7) that unfavorable internal institutional developments tend to decelerate the rate of growth of an initially innovating and expanding economy and cause it to lose its position of superiority to other economies which, because their advance began later, have not yet become subject to growth-restricting institutional changes. It is not necessary to accept the sequence of changes which Veblen thought he had found in the British economy, or, for that matter, to suppose that the sequences will vary little from country to country. It is necessary only to show that changes consequent upon growth tend to produce increasingly effective growth-restricting institutional changes. The mercantilists were not interested in this problem, though a late contemporary, G. Vico (in *Principii di una Scienza Nuova,* 1725), sought to show that societies recurrently passed through three successive stages. See also H. M. Robertson, "Panaceas, Past and Present," *South African Journal of Economics,* XII, 1944.

15. See E. J. Hamilton, "The Decline of Spain," *Economic History Review,"* VIII, 1938, pp. 168-78, and *War and Prices in Spain 1651-1800,* Cambridge, 1947, chaps. 2-4, 12. Among the causes of the decline mentioned by Hamilton, one finds the economic effects of costly wars engaged in by a series of incompetent rulers (under the illusion perhaps that the influx of American treasure had made Spain prosperous and strong), together with "alternate monetary inflation and deflation." The supposed exodus of the Moors did not produce effects so marked as was believed at one time. Even in the sixteenth century, Mexico's population decreased by about four-fifths, only to remain nearly stationary in the seventeenth century. In consequence, Spain's ability to derive profit from Mexico was reduced. See W. W. Borah, *New Spain's Century of Depression,* Berkeley, 1951. On Spain's rise and fall, see R. Trevor Davies, *The Golden Century of Spain,* London, 1939, and *Spain in Decline 1621-1700,* London, 1951; M. Schwarzmann, "Background Factors in Spanish Decline," *Explorations in Entrepreneurial History,* III, 1951, pp. 221-47.

16. See Nef, *op.cit.*, chaps. 1, 8, 15, esp. pp. 7, 19, 35; also R. Ludloff, "Industrial Development in 16th-17th Century Germany," *Past and Present,* No. 12, November, 1957, pp. 58-75, wherein the sixteenth and eighteenth centuries are described as periods of expansion, and the seventeenth as one of

(B) MERCANTILIST THEORIES AND INSTITUTIONAL INSTRUMENTALITIES

I use the expression "theories" because my concern is with ideas and proposals, rather than practice, and because the mercantilists, unlike the scholastics or the physiocrats or the classical economists, did not systematize into a highly unified body of economic thought the many particular theories to which they gave expression and upon which their policy recommendations and proposed institutional instrumentalities were based. It is commonly held that the mercantilists were poor theorists, even at the implicit (as distinguished from the explicit) level on which most of their formulations are encountered. There is much truth in this contention. However, it is distorting, nonetheless; for the mercantilists brought into the arena of discourse many issues that had tended to escape critical examination as long as economic theorizing was concerned largely with questions of commutative and related justice, and as long as ethical preconceptions tended to place divers matters outside the bounds of discussion and controversy.[17] The mercantilists therefore played an important part in determining the scope and concerns of classical economic analysis and in drawing attention to problems which the classical writers later ignored.[18]

Having reviewed differences in the conditions and fortunes of those countries whence came representative mercantilist theorists,[19] in this section I shall identify, classify, and attempt to systematize the main growth-oriented views found in mercantilist writings. Only when these views varied significantly in time or space will such variation be noticed; otherwise, I shall assume, as was commonly the case, that roughly similar views were widely held. Mercantilist views will be examined under eight headings: (1) socio-psychological and causative theory and presuppositions; (2) allocative mechanisms; (3) occupational structure; (4) agents of produc-

---

decline and/or of decelerating growth. The glass-making industry is described as one that developed without the stimulus of mercantilist policies. Cf. J. H. Clapham's account ("Charles Louis, Elector Palatine, 1617-1680. An Early Experiment in Liberalism," *Economica*, VII, 1940, pp. 381-96) of the recovery of prosperity in the Palatinate after 1652, under a Dutch-inspired program of liberalism, and its subsequent loss under the impact of war after 1680. Between 1550 and 1650 Germany's population may have declined by one-third.

17. On the concerns of scholastic writers see E. Gilson, *The Christian Philosophy of St. Thomas Aquinas*, New York, 1956, pp. 271*ff*., 306*ff*.; B. W. Dempsey, *Interest and Usury*, Washington, 1943; J. T. Noonan, Jr., *The Scholastic Analysis of Usury*, Cambridge, 1957; see also works cited in footnote 24, below.

18. Lord Keynes accredits the mercantilists with recognizing the importance of various determinants of investment; with not supposing that the rate of interest tends automatically to move to an appropriate level; with being aware of the danger of excessive competition, scarcity of money, and surpluses of goods; and with being alert to the nationalistic character of their policies. See *The General Theory of Employment, Interest and Money*, New York, 1936, pp. 336-49, 358-62.

19. The views of many of these are summarized in the Appendix; from these detailed summaries the reader may form an impression of how individual mercantilists proposed to solve the problems they considered important.

tion, their supply, and their degree of use; (5) the role of money; (6) external economic relations; (7) the role of the state and other institutions; (8) miscellaneous matters, such as the role of science and innovation, education, technical training of workers, etc. These views will be examined insofar as they comprise elements of what may be called the mercantilist theory of economic growth. That there is a modern "ring" about the subjects with which the mercantilists were concerned is evident in a discussion and contrast of some of their views, as provided by W. A. Lewis in his representative volume on *The Theory of Economic Growth* (Homewood, Ill., 1955). Lewis concerns himself with man's desire to work, consume, and save; with the roles of knowledge, government, and capital; with economic institutions (e.g., reward systems, trade and specialization, economic freedom, localized organizations and relations) and institutional change; with population and resources; and with the means by which growth may be achieved. Among the mercantilists, many writers may be found who touched upon several or more of these matters, sometimes in conjunction with the advocacy of protectionist and related counsel, which was likely to be growth-retarding. Individual mercantilists did not, of course, question whether economic development, as they envisaged it, was good; but some of their critics did, among them the physiocrats.

(1) *Socio-psychological and causative theory and presuppositions.* Interpretations entailing causal analysis of economic and social behavior are generally socially conditioned; at least inasmuch as the percepts, concepts, socio-analytical vocabulary, logical rules, categories, etc. with which students' works are conditioned by the state of social science and by the suggestiveness of the social environment. Whether or not man's experience is deemed important, to a great degree it determines the orientation of his thinking.[20] Of all this, mercantilist literature offers evidence. The rise of Renaissance humanism was accompanied by the ascent of new ethical themes, by a shift in the focus and context of speculation from the theologico-metaphysical to the social and the individual, and, eventually, by the development of approaches which sought over-riding causes and functional relations that were subject to manipulation.[21] The social changes

20. This tendency is reflected even in ordinary language, much of which "is built of dead metaphors" (F. L. Lucas, *Style*, London, 1955, p. 193), and so gives evidence of the impact of past experience on man's ideas. Furthermore, "categories are developed in response to events." See J. S. Bruner, *et al.*, *A Study of Thinking*, New York, 1956, pp. 232-33.

21. E.g., see Ferguson, *op.cit.*, pp. 292-301; also P. O. Kristeller, *Studies in Renaissance Thought and Letters*, Rome, 1956, pp. 25*ff.*, 283*ff.*, 307. With the development of commerce in the cities of northern Italy, "a secular and largely non-theological philosophy" had gained currency in the universities. See Kristeller and J. H. Randall, Jr., "The Study of the Philosophies of the Renaissance," *Journal of the History of Ideas*, II, 1941, p. 491. Overemphasis on the impact of the Renaissance must be avoided, however; it was not particularly favorable to science, whereas improvements in medieval science were gradually modifying man's point of view and methods of thought. See *ibid.*, p. 491; A. C. Crombie, *Augustine to Galileo*, Cambridge, 1953, *passim.*

taking place, together with the problems to which they gave origin, reenforced these ideational and ideological shifts.

Because it had not yet been systematized (as was scholasticism), the newer approach was congenial to the student's examination of the social world in terms of machines and mechanical operations currently in existence, or undergoing discovery and development, in the world of natural science and engineering. Thus, the mechanism of the clock (which came into use in Europe in the thirteenth century), and not the static notion of a "body politic," furnished Hales with a conception of the social mechanism, just as the mechanics of blood circulation (finally described by Harvey in 1628) inspired mercantilists with a conception of the supposedly dynamic role of money flow.[22] More complicated conceptions, such as those of competition and of a system of interdependent and mutually-determined prices, were not as easily inferable from the then world of mechanics, and hence were formulated later. But it was inferable that cause and effect ruled in the realm of economic relations, just as it did in mechanics, for example, and that some variables were more crucial than others, because they dominated outcomes, or because they were susceptible to manipulation. As a rule, the relationships inferred (usually with the assistance of intuition) were initially deemed to be simpler than experience would ultimately reveal them to be; this, in fact, was a likely outcome of an approach, such as Hales's, which sought a principal cause and tended to ignore important ancillary causes and conditions. Yet, as Keynes observed, mercantilists often "hit upon maxims of practical wisdom," even when they did not understand their theoretical foundations. Of even greater importance, they did not accept the socio-economic world and its problems as given and immutable; they believed that conditions could be changed; and they supposed, albeit naively at times, that the state could become an agent of salutary change.[23]

The mercantilists adopted a relatively new approach to motivation and

22. E.g., see J. Viner, *Studies in the Theory of International Trade*, New York, 1937, pp. 37*ff*.; John Hales, *A Discourse of the Common Weal of this Realm of England* (1565), E. Lamond, ed., Cambridge, 1929, p. 98; E. Zilsel, in *International Encyclopedia of Unified Science*, II, No. 8, Chicago, 1941, pp. 53-69; A. R. Hall, *The Scientific Revolution, 1500-1800*, New York, 1954, *passim;* H. Höffding, *A History of Modern Philosophy*, New York, I, 1955, I, chaps. 1, 2, 4; Crombie, *op.cit.* The theory of causation, particularly in its relation to nonhuman affairs, is dealt with in *ibid.;* in L. Brunschvig, *L'expérience humaine et la causalité physique*, Paris, 1922; its origins are treated by H. Kelsen, in *Society and Nature*, Chicago, 1943. Students of inter-individual relations were very slow to make use of the concepts of mechanics. Thus, although thirteenth-century concepts might have been utilized, it was not until four or more centuries later that the usefulness of mechanical concepts began to be appreciated by analysts of society.

23. For Keynes's observation, see *General Theory*, p. 340. As late as the sixteenth century, J. W. Allen observes *(English Political Thought, 1603-1660*, I, London, 1938, pp. 59*ff*.), Englishmen had great faith in the capacity of a strong prince and his government to accomplish given objectives, a faith that experience in time helped to undermine. See Fisher, "Commercial Trends . . . ," *loc.cit.*, pp. 114-17. This faith in part reflected the confidence of craftsmen, etc., regarding their social status in the "commonwealth." E.g., see

to the mobilization of human motives. Moreover, they contributed to a redefinition of what constitutes achievement, and thus to the establishment of new social forces in European culture. Human psychology being what it is, it was essential that the passions and appetites which drive man, of whose force Christian thought had made men highly conscious, not be suppressed but be allowed free play. Otherwise, producers would not behave as effectively as they might. It was necessary, however, as is disclosed in (7) below, that man's appetites and drives, his desire for gain and private advantage, be allowed free play only within a regulative institutional framework, a framework that so channeled his behavior as to cause it, under the conditions laid down, to subserve the public interest as well.

The development of this view, associated with the Renaissance and its successor world and the growth of commerce, entailed suppression of the *Weltanschauung* of the medieval world. The importance of religious motives declined, and worldly virtues took their place alongside religious ones. With the advent of the Reformation, men of affairs grew less inclined to subject their conduct to the relatively complete "supervision and guidance of a single authority," even though this authority was becoming more favorable to the businessman and his objectives. For this ecclesiastical authority continued to look upon commerce as an activity which, because it afforded so many temptations to avarice and dishonesty, "must be carefully scrutinized and kept within due bounds."[24]

Increased emphasis was placed on the thesis that entrepreneurial drive was most powerful when undertakers were free to seek their private advantage, at least under given conditions, as man came to be viewed, not as an essentially rational being, but as one subject to the sway of appetites and passions and under the empire of universal egoism. This view was

---

G. W. Kuehn, "The Novels of Thomas Deloney as Source for 'Climate of Opinion' in Sixteenth-Century Economic History," *Journal of Political Economy*, XLVIII, 1940, pp. 865-76; also S. T. Bindoff, *op.cit.*, chaps. 4, 6.

24. See George O'Brien, *An Essay on the Economic Effect of the Reformation*, London, 1923, pp. 171-72, and *An Essay on Medieval Economic Teaching*, London, 1920, pp. 142-53, 154; also R. G. Collingwood, *The Idea of History*, New York, 1956, p. 57. There is not space to consider the relevant literature inspired by Max Weber's analysis of the supposed influence of Protestantism on the content of achievement. Concerning the views of Thomas Aquinas, which epitomize medieval thought and which were substantially displaced by mercantilist views, see Gilson, *op.cit.;* J. J. Reardon, *Selfishness and the Social Order*, Washington, 1943, esp. chaps. 1-2; and Mary F. Niemeyer, *The One and the Many in the Social Order According to Saint Thomas Aquinas*, Washington, 1951. On the impact of experience with commerce, see C. B. Hoover, "Economic Forces in the Evolution of Civil and Canon Law," *Southwestern Political and Social Science Quarterly*, X, 1929, pp. 1-14; H. M. Robertson, "European Economic Developments in the 16th Century," *South African Journal of Economics*, XVIII, 1950, pp. 47-48; Dempsey, *op.cit.;* F. Gilbert, "The Humanist Concept of the Prince and *The Prince* of Machiavelli," *Journal of Modern History*, XI, 1939, pp. 449-89, esp. pp. 461-64. According to F. Meinecke *(Machiavellism*, London, 1957, chap. 1), the early fifteenth century witnessed the beginnings of that *raison d'état* Machiavelli expressed later.

given expression first by Machiavelli,[25] and subsequently supplied with a systematic psychological foundation by Thomas Hobbes[26] and with a friendly philosophy by Francis Bacon when he made utility the end of knowledge, and thereby gave it an individual as well as a public orientation.[27] It was put in persuasive form by Mandeville when he declared, on essentially psychological premises, that "Private Vices by the dextrous Management of a skilful Politician may be turned into" what, by utilitarian standards, are "Publick Benefits," since sociability, employment, and "all Arts and Sciences" have their origin in private vices.[28] Of course, Mandeville was giving expression to an anti-rationalism that had been anticipated by La Rochefoucauld, Pascal, Fontenelle, Bayle, Montaigne, Spinoza, Gassendi, and others,[29] and to a belief in man's egoism that rose to

25. See *The Prince*, chaps. 15, 17, 21; and *The Discourses*, I, chaps. 2, 4. Earlier, France's Machiavellian Louis XI (1461-83), anxious to develop industry and commerce, had counted upon the bourgeoisie and their desire for gain to carry through his program. See C. W. Previté-Orton and Z. N. Brooke, eds., *Cambridge Medieval History*, Cambridge, VIII, 1936, chap. 8, esp. pp. 300-305. That base motives actuate men probably was widely held in Italy in Machiavelli's day. E.g., see *Aphorisms Civill And Militare*, London, 1613, by his contemporary, F. Guicciardini (1483-1540). Christian writers had long stressed drives and impulses of the sort noticed by St. Augustine when he said that "even among those who are skilled in the arts, you will rarely find a man who does not practice his own art for the purpose of pecuniary gain" (*The City of God*, VII, chap. 3). But they did not propose to build a society upon egoism. Instead, they recommended that man curb his impulses and bridle his appetites, though they recognized that doing so was more difficult than the Stoics and others had supposed. See Collingwood, *op.cit.*, p. 57; also G. S. Brett, *A History of Psychology*, London, 1921, II, pp. 168-75. For later views, see H. W. Sams, "Self-Love and the Doctrine of Work," *Journal of the History of Ideas*, IV, 1943, pp. 320-32. The values and attitudes of the fourteenth-century Italian merchant are described by I. Origo in *The Merchant of Prato*, London, 1957.

26. E.g., see his *Leviathan*, Part I. Hobbes's social psychology reflects the influence of Aristotle's *Rhetoric* and (as did Machiavelli's philosophy) Thucydides's egoistic interpretations (Brett, *op.cit.*, pp. 220-22). In his *Ethics*, Spinoza deals with appetites and the role of utility. See also H. Sidgwick, *Outlines of the History of Ethics*, London, 1939, chaps. 3-4.

27. Lord Macaulay wrote, "Two words form the key of the Baconian doctrine, Utility and Progress." See "Lord Bacon," in *The Works of Lord Macaulay*, Lady Trevelyan, ed., New York, 1866, VI, p. 204; also J. B. Bury, *The Idea of Progress*, London, 1932, chap. 2. See also Crombie, *op.cit.*, pp. 387-97. Bacon's works are cited below. Hales (*op.cit.*, pp. 22*ff.*) had indicated the practical utility of learning. Utility had been emphasized by Roger Bacon in the thirteenth century (Crombie, *op.cit.*, pp. 37-38), but his emphasis did not enter ethical philosophy.

28. See *The Fable of the Bees: Or, Private Vices, Publick Benefits*, edited with commentary by F. B. Kaye, Oxford, 1924, I, p. 369, also pp. xlvi-li; II, p. 452. Volume I appeared in nearly final form in 1723, and Volume II in 1728. According to Kaye, Mandeville, having found, in effect, that the private actions whence flowed useful public results were not unselfish and dispassionate (as are virtuous actions), deduced that these actions must be the result of selfishness and hence vicious, i.e., not compatible with both the ascetic and the rational criteria of virtue. Hence, his paradox: private vices, public benefits; and his inference that, although not all vice is publicly beneficial, all benefits are based on actions, which, according to his definition of virtue, are vicious. See *ibid.*, I, pp. xlvii, lxxv-lxxvi. Mandeville's approach, therefore, prompted critics to develop a utilitarian system of ethics. See *ibid.*, pp. cxxx*ff.* See also Spengler, "Veblen and Mandeville Contrasted," *Weltwirtschaftliches Archiv*, Band 82, Heft 1, 1959, pp. 35-65.

29. *Ibid.*, I, pp. lxxix-lxxxvi, ciii-cxiii. See also W. Hasbach, "Larochefoucault und Mandeville," *Jahrbuch für Gesetzgebung, Verwaltung und Volkswirtschaft*, XIV, Nos. 1-2, 1890, pp. 1-43; W. Deckelmann, *Untersuchungen zur Bienenfabel Mandeville's und zu ihrer Enstehungsgeschichte im Hinblick auf die Bienenfabelthese*, Hamburg, 1933.

prominence in the seventeenth century.[30] The increasing acceptance of the opinion that entrepreneurs function best when actuated by private advantage, and the particular form given it by Mandeville and his disciples, led to increasing acceptance of the view that public advantage is best served when private advantage may be freely sought, the unqualified adoption of which view would entail rejection of mercantilist interventionism.[31]

The mercantilists did not apply to all classes the maxim that men work best within a given framework, when they can serve their own interests, together with its corollary, i.e., that the output of effort is positively associated with the level of remuneration. It was widely held that the worker's subjective standard of living was virtually constant, in consequence of which it was inferred (within nonspecified limits) that the prices of wage-goods being given, an increase of money wages would evoke less work, and a decrease, more work. Accordingly, a low money-wage policy was indicated. This view began to undergo modification around the beginning of the eighteenth century, or soon thereafter, but apparently in much greater measure in England and France than in the German states. A few writers (non-mercantilists among them) recognized that, since the subjective standard of living was expansible, workers of whom this was true would do more work for somewhat higher wages. Some writers also began to appreciate the importance of the internal market, together with the fact that aggregate demand, just as did the demand for certain luxuries, depended in part upon the expenditures of workers.[32] Until the middle of the eighteenth century, however, the majority of the mercantilists endorsed

30. Kaye lists a number of forerunners of Mandeville: Hobbes, Locke, Erasmus, Spinoza, La Rochefoucauld, Pascal, Esprit, and others. See *ibid.*, pp. lxxxvii-xciii, ciii-cxiii, also index under "Anticipations." He credits Bayle with anticipating the doctrine that private vices are public benefits. See *ibid.*, I, pp. civ-cv. Erasmus's treatment of the passions (in his *Praise of Folly*) does not characterize his unmachiavelli-like *The Education of a Christian Prince*. The contribution of Pascal, a Puritan, was indirect, much as was the contribution of anti-rational medieval mysticism to the eventual rise of a laissez faire ideology (a contribution I expect to treat in a later essay).

31. On the growing recognition of the role of self-interest, or self-love, see Robertson, *Rise of Economic Individualism*, esp. chap. 3; A. F. Chalk, "Natural Law and the Rise of Economic Individualism in England," *Journal of Political Economy*, LIX, 1951, pp. 332-47, esp. 333-37; Clark, *op.cit.*, pp. 19*ff.*; Schumpeter, *op.cit.*, pp. 130-34, 171-73, 374, 376-77; Heckscher, *Mercantilism*, II, pp. 254-55, 308-14, 383-85; F. B. Kaye, *op.cit.*, I, pp. lxxvii-cxlvi, and *passim*. In Montaigne's hands, Höffding contends, the argument against the circumscription of man's behavior becomes an argument for laissez faire, founded on the notion that a wise Nature gives the best answers (*op.cit.*, I, Bk. I, chap. 4; see also Montaigne's *Essays*, Modern Library Edition, 1933, I, p. 25; II, pp. 12, 23; III, p. 13). Although Montaigne contributed significantly to the use of introspection as a source of knowledge of man's behavioral tendencies, the validity of Höffding's interpretation remains to be settled. On the Graeco-Roman origin of Renaissance and later views with respect to "Follow Nature," the transformation of this precept, and the impact of Montaigne's approach upon later writers, see A. Tilley, *Studies in the French Renaissance*, Cambridge, 1922, pp. 233-58, and A. M. Boase, *The Fortunes of Montaigne*, London, 1935.

32. Mention may be made of Cantillon, Melon, Berkeley, Cary, Defoe, Steuart, Mandeville, and others, as well as of such non-mercantilists as North and Boisguillebert, and possibly of some of the defenders of luxury. See Heckscher, *Mercantilism*, II, pp. 165-71, 208-09, 230, 291; D. C. Coleman, "Labour in the English Economy of the Seventeenth Century," *Economic History Re-*

an economy of low wages, believing that then laborers would have to work long and hard, and goods could therefore be produced cheaply; but in the third quarter of the eighteenth century an increasing number of writers came to favor improvement in the worker's pay and condition.

(2) *Allocative mechanisms.* The mercantilists can hardly be said to have conceived of a price system, its allocative and distributive roles, and its toughness and resiliency. For not even the much simpler notion of a self-regulating mechanism of specie distribution, though anticipated a century earlier, received expression until almost the beginning of the eighteenth century. Furthermore, categories suitable to describe the process of competition had not yet been formulated, even though competition had been effective in the Middle Ages.[33] Among other things, this is evident from the meanings assigned to the term "competition" and its close synonyms in French, German, Spanish, and English literature in and before the early eighteenth century. The term is used to signify a rivalry of sorts, but not the price-modifying rivalry of the market place. Competition, in the sense of unrestricted pursuit of individual self-interest, seems to have been understood; and it was taken for granted that individuals—at least merchants, bankers, and producers—respond positively (negatively) to relatively favorable (unfavorable) prices and price changes.[34] Mercantilist

---

view, VIII, 1956, pp. 280-82; Buck, *op-cit.,* pp. 47, 88, 91-96, 212-13; E. S. Furniss, *The Position of the Laborer in a System of Nationalism,* New York, 1920, *passim;* T. E. Gregory, "The Economics of Employment in England, 1660-1713," *Economica,* I, 1921, pp. 37-51; Viner, *Studies,* pp. 26-30, 55, 90-91; Lipson, *op.cit.,* III, chap. 5, secs. ii, iv; Sams, *op.cit.,* p. 329; also A. Duncan-Jones, *Butler's Moral Philosophy,* Harmondsworth, 1952, chaps. 2, 4. See also (4) below. A. W. Coats includes among those who favored or advocated higher wages between 1725 and 1750, Defoe, Vanderlint, Bishop Berkeley, and Hume. High wages would stimulate men to put forth effort and develop skill, and would swell demand; this argument was elaborated after 1750. See Coats, "Changing Attitudes to Labour in the Mid-Eighteenth Century," *Economic History Review,* XI, 1958, pp. 35-51.

33. See E. E. Hirshler, "Medieval Economic Competition," *Journal of Economic History,* XIV, 1954, pp. 52-58; on specie distribution, see Viner, *Studies,* pp. 74*ff.*

34. The impact of competition was described as follows by Guicciardini in a supplement to his *Ricordi,* translated by N. H. Thompson, New York, 1949; "Trades and Industries are at their best when they are not generally understood to be profitable. When seen by all to be so, they fall off; because, from many resorting to them, the competition prevents them from being any longer lucrative. In all things it profits to be up betimes" (i.e., "el concorso fa che non sono piú sí buone; però el levarsi a buon'ora è vantaggio grande in tutte le case") *(ibid.,* par. 178, p. 254). Sarabia de la Calle used the word "concurrir" in 1542 to refer to a cost-reducing concurrence of complementary activities when he said (in *Instrucción de Mercaderes,* Madrid, 1949, p. 56) that "the price is lowered if many of these things are combined [or joined] in one person, such as peddlar and worker . . . ," but he does not seem to have had a competitive process in mind. Antoyne de Montchrétien appreciated the role of self-interest and of price regulation by "concurrence" *(Traicté de l'oeconomie politique* [1615], Th. Funck-Brentano, ed., Paris, 1889, pp. 37-40, as did some sixteenth-century Italian churchmen, who believed that competition tended to bring about just prices. See H. R. Sewall, *The Theory of Value Before Adam Smith,* in *Publications of the American Economic Association,* II, 1901, pp. 35-36, 52. The role of prices, together with their supposed imperviousness to regulation, was recognized, not only by some of these Italian writers, but also by later English writers. Thus, Sir Dudley North, having observed that men always consult their own immediate interest (even when they identify it with the public interest), declared "that no Laws can set Prizes in Trade, the Rates of which, must and will make themselves," and that when

policy was made up largely of discouraging penalties and taxes and encouraging privileges and subsidies, all aimed primarily at entrepreneurs engaged in trade or industry; these penalties and privileges modified prices and set up substitution effects in favor of some purchases and activities and against others. It was but necessary to change the dimensions of gain and loss sufficiently; "the love of gain," the poet Petrarch remarked, "would stimulate the human mind" to do the rest.[35] The pattern of stimuli was more inclusive, of course; above all, efforts were made to establish economic and social environments favorable to industry and trade in general, and hence complementary to specific conditions favorable to specific activities.

(3) *Occupational structure*. Whether they emphasized wealth or power, mercantilists rejected the older hierarchies of industry and occupation, in which agriculturalists and the clergy were ranked well above traders and manufacturers. In the new hierarchy a relatively high rank was assigned to merchants, above all to those engaged in foreign trade, and nearly as high a rank to successful industrialists and manufacturers. The alteration in esteem in which these occupations actually were held by the population at large proceeded unevenly and slowly, however;[36] for, as has been suggested, it reflected a change both in the ethical standards by which the economic conduct of man was bound and in the values and objectives which underlay the ordering of good and bad. It also reflected the beginnings of a more Faustian outlook,[37] with which commerce and manufacture were more compatible than was agriculture. It even reflected growing acceptance of the mercantilist belief that trade and/or manufacture constituted the dynamic and strategic sector(s) of economies, the

such laws are attempted, "it is so much Impediment to Trade, and therefore prejudicial." See his *Discourses upon Trade* (1691), preface, recently attributed to Roger North by W. Letwin *(Economica*, XVIII, 1951, pp. 35*ff*.). N. Barbon pointed to the role of cost in price formation, but made price depend on the conditions of supply and demand. He described "the Market" as the "best Judge of Value; for by the Concourse of Buyers and Sellers, the Quantity of Wares, and the Occasion for them, are best known." See *A Discourse of Trade* (1690), J. H. Hollander, ed., Baltimore, 1903, pp. 15-16. Montesquieu wrote in 1748 (in *Esprit des lois*, XX, chap. 9): "C'est la concurrence qui met un prix juste aux marchandises, et qui etablit les vrais rapports entre elles." The role of competition was appreciated by the physiocrats and by their critic, Forbonnais.

35. Cited by Eileen Power in *Medieval People*, Garden City, 1954, p. 193. Petrarch is describing the power that drives Venetians to trade everywhere.

36. In her introduction to William Scott's *Essay of Drapery* (1635), Cambridge, 195? p. 1, Sylvia L. Thrupp refers to it as "th first substantial piece of writing known i English that exalts business as a career." I apparently was not a success, possibly b cause it was too learned, but in part beca early seventeenth-century readers remair more interested in how to behave as gent men than in how to cope with problems o business ethics. A businessman was more exalted at this time in Holland, as has been noted, and in Italy than in England. The comparative disfavor in which a business career was held is evidenced in the continual flow of successful businessmen, or their sons, out of the class comprising persons thus engaged into the class made up of affluent landowners. E.g., see G. R. Potter, ed., *op.cit.*, I, p. 55; Braudel, *op.cit.*, pp. 622*ff*.; Gandilhon, *op.cit.*, p. 111; and footnote 52, below.

37. See Oswald Spengler, *The Decline of the West*, New York, 1939, I, p. 183; II, pp. 292, 309.

source whence came salutary change and solutions for current economic problems, and that agriculture, being dependent upon trade or manufacture for progressive stimulus, would improve as trade and manufacturing expanded. It may also have reflected acceptance of the mercantilist belief that men engaged in some occupations produce little or nothing that contributes to the growth and power of a society, and the later inference (e.g., of Petty and others) that, because income per head is higher in some occupations, such as trade and industry, than in others, such as agriculture and some services, national income might be increased by transference of workers from low-income to high-income occupations. Mercantilists urged that honorific and other suitable symbols of high social esteem be conferred upon merchants and manufacturers, so that these occupations would continue to recruit and retain their able practitioners; this was particularly necessary in backward, feudal, nobility-ridden, agricultural economies (e.g., Austria and petty German states).

Agricultural activities were considered important—for agriculture furnished subsistence—but not strategic. It was desirable that victuals be low-priced, so that industrial money wages, which supposedly provided workers with little, if anything, beyond support for themselves and their dependents, might remain relatively low and thus make for low-cost production. Agriculture also furnished all the raw materials used in industry and trade, other than those derived from the sea or through mining. Agriculture was not, however, considered a source of dynamic economic *élan,* even by writers (especially in England, Germany, and Spain) who stressed its importance, and in some instances advocated its protection; *élan* would have to come from trade and industry. Some writers supposed, furthermore, that the market for industrial products was more extensible than that for agricultural products, and that incomes and productivity were higher ouside than inside agriculture. Mercantilists, especially when they were indulging in florid expression, or were attempting to influence agricultural interests, often claimed, of course, that pursuit of their policies would improve the situation of agriculture, for example, by stimulating employment and population growth, and thus increasing the demand for produce, or by reducing interest rates and elevating the value of land. Mercantilist opinion seems to have been less homogeneous with respect to agricultural policies than it was with respect to policies for industry and trade, at least in England; but it invariably stressed the importance of agricultural activities for the success of industry and trade.[38] However, one

38. E.g., see S. J. Brandenburg, "The Place of Agriculture in British National Economy Prior to Adam Smith," *Journal of Political Economy,* XXXIX, 1931, pp. 281-320; Lipson, *op.cit.,* II, chap. 3; Heckscher, *Mercantilism, passim;* Buck, *op.cit.,* pp. 48-52, 201. The mercantilists were not interested in pursuing policies which, in their opinion, would injure domestic agriculture.

does not encounter in the literature Pareto's argument that the creation of wealth is favored by policies which discriminate in favor of industry and trade and against agriculture, on the premise that the "residues" of merchants and industrialists are more likely to make for wealth-creating activities than are those of agriculturalists; and yet, on occasion, mercantilists may have had something like this in mind.[39] They must have supposed the capacity for economic serendipity to be higher among merchants and industrialists than among agriculturalists.

(4) *Agents of production, their supply, and their degree of use.* Section (8) below deals with some of the circumstances involved, according to mercantilist writers, in transforming a rural, village-centered, labor force into one adapted to industry.[40] In this section I shall limit my discussion to the mercantilists' treatment of the role of productive agents in economic growth. As will be indicated, they assigned primary importance to labor, secondary importance to land, and tertiary importance to capital. Despite their stress on labor, mercantilist writers did not anticipate Marx's theory of "primitive accumulation," or his emphasis on the contribution of enclosures (i.e., "expropriation of the agricultural population from the land") to the formation of a nonagricultural wage-earning class.[41]

Labor being by far the most important of the factors of production, according to mercantilist theory, the growth of production depended primarily upon the growth of the labor force (i.e., of the population, since at that time its age structure was correctly implied to be virtually constant) and upon setting the members of this labor force to work. The growth of

39. See J. Spengler, "Pareto on Population," *Quarterly Journal of Economics*, LIX, 1944, pp. 128-29.

40. For comparison of pre-eighteenth-century situations with those encountered in present-day underdeveloped areas, see W. E. Moore, *Industrialization and Labor*, Ithaca, 1951; J. H. Boeke, *Oriental Economics* (mimeographed), New York, 1947; R. Bendix, *Work and Authority in Industry*, New York, 1956, Part I. For accounts of English village communities, see G. C. Homans, *English Villagers of the Thirteenth Century*, Cambridge, 1942; Lipson, *op.cit.*, I-II; C. G. Coulton, *The Medieval Village*, Cambridge, 1925.

41. "Primitive accumulation" entailed "divorcing the producer from the means of production," initially through "expropriation of the agricultural producer . . . from the soil," and diverting a part of the resulting "surplus-value" to the "accumulation" of capital. See Karl Marx, *Capital* (Kerr edition), Chicago, 1906, I, Part 8, esp. chaps. 26-27. The mercantilists, Marx believed, did not apprehend the process of capital formation because they stressed "circulation," rather than "production," and hence overlooked the significance of "surplus-value." See *ibid.*, III, p. 396; *Theories of Surplus Value*, translated by G. A. Bonner and E. Burns, New York, 1952, pp. 24-25, 55. For an application of Marx's theory, see V. M. Lavrovsky, "Expropriation of the English Peasantry in the Eighteenth Century," *Economic History Review*, IX, 1956, pp. 271-82. On the tendency of English mercantilists to look upon land and labor as almost the only factors of production, see Johnson, *Predecessors*, chap. 12; also Furniss, *op.cit.*, pp. 15*ff*., 28, 35-36. Raw materials and labor constituted the mercantilists' main factors of production, according to Heckscher (*Mercantilism*, II, pp. 145-68). John Locke suggested that under primitive conditions, 90-99 per cent of output was attributable to labor; but he did not make clear to what extent this proportion would change with the progress of settlement (*Of Civil Government*, 1690, II, chap. 5, pars. 40-43). He and others seem to have had in mind both direct and indirect labor, stock being looked upon as largely the product of labor; clearly they believed that direct labor played a major part in production.

the nonagricultural labor force depended upon these same conditions and upon another condition whose potentially augmentative influence was appreciated only slowly, particularly while societal organization remained feudal, namely, enclosure, technical progress in agriculture, and other circumstances that displaced labor out of agriculture and made it potentially available in nonrural communities and for nonagricultural activities. Two conditions re-enforced the mercantilists in their disposition to emphasize growth of the labor force as a whole. First, they were usually concerned with aggregate output, rather than with output per head, often conceiving of the state or nation as an entity or organism. Second, they saw about them little evidence of improvement in output per head. Poverty was widespread; its victims embraced 25-50 per cent of the population, even in late seventeenth-century England—after the situation of the working class had improved somewhat.[42] They presumed that, with average

---

42. In England in 1500-1550, even before continuing population growth had ceased to reduce real wages, "about a third of the occupied population . . . were wage-earners." (See E. H. Phelps Brown and Sheila V. Hopkins, "Wages and Prices: Evidence for Population Pressure in the Sixteenth Century," *Economica*, XXIV, 1957, p. 299.) At various times, of course, unemployment and poverty rose above the average level (whatever that was), because of business fluctuations, effects of war, loss of markets, etc.; and at such times measures intended to protect the domestic market, and thus increase employment, were likely to be proposed and even introduced. E.g., see Heckscher, *Mercantilism*, II, pp. 121-24; P. Boissonnade, *Le socialisme d'état*, Paris, 1927, pp. 307-308: C. W. Cole, *French Mercantilism 1683-1700*, New York, 1943, pp. 186, 212-18; Sir John Clapham, *A Concise Economic History of Britain*, Cambridge, 1951, pp. 178, 251-52; F. J. Fisher's paper in Carus-Wilson, ed., *op.cit.*, esp. pp. 171-72. Of primary concern for the above discussion, however, are the extent of chronic unemployment, output trends, and beliefs concerning these matters. As noted earlier, F. J. Fisher ("The Sixteenth and Seventeenth Centuries . . . ," *loc.cit.*, pp. 6-8, 15) believes that total output increased in the sixteenth and seventeenth centuries, but apparently finds little evidence of improvement in the average lot until the later seventeenth century; yet "by the end of the seventeenth century the poor may have constituted a larger proportion of the population than at the beginning of the sixteenth," when Sir Thomas More complained of the widespread poverty and of the fact that the wages of many purchased only the barest subsistence. Brown and Hopkins *(op.cit.*, pp. 294-99) find that real wages fell greatly between 1451-1475 and 1600 in Southern England, France, and Alsace; they moved above the 1600 level in the middle third of the seventeenth century. M. J. Elsas's study suggests that a somewhat similar movement took place in Germany. (See *Umriss einer Geschichte der Preise und Löhne in Deutschland von ausgehenden Mittelalter bis zum Beginn des neunzehnten Jahrhunderts*, Leiden, 1949, II. E. J. Buckatzsch found that the geographical distribution of wealth changed little until near 1700; the great changes came in the eighteenth century, especially in comparatively nonagricultural counties. See "The Geographical Distribution of Wealth in England. 1086-1843," *Economic History Review*, III, 1950, pp. 180-202. The estimates of the extent of poverty in England given in the text above are those of D. C. Coleman ("Labour in the English Economy," *loc.cit.*, pp. 283-92). Coleman finds poverty was so great because so many did not work at all, or worked very irregularly, or worked only a small part of the year. E. Perroy reports that wages in Toulouse were low even in 1365-1371, with laborers working no more than one hundred fifty days per year ("Wage Labor in France in the Later Middle Ages," *Economic History Review*, VIII, 1955, pp. 237-38). See also T. S. Ashton, *An Economic History of England: The Eighteenth Century*, London, 1955, chap. 7; Lipson, *op.cit.*, III, pp. 294*ff.*, 410*ff.* In the early 1530's, Clement Armstrong commented on the extent of idleness in England (R. H. Tawney and E. Power, eds., *Tudor Economic Documents*, London, 1924, III, pp. 115-16). A little later (1549) an anonymous author remarked on the "great nombre" who worked little in summer and were more than half-idle the rest of the year, "besides theme which be always Idell" (see *ibid.*, p. 322; the work is entitled "Polices to Reduce the Realm of Englande Unto A Prosperous Wealthe And Estate"). John Law's model, designed to il-

output remaining virtually constant, total output would increase only as a result of an increase in the working labor force. Very few remarked, as did Cantillon, that an increase in population might be accompanied by a decline in average output.[43] Writers, such as Melon, who believed it likely that man's wants would increase were more likely to anticipate increases in wage and income levels than were writers who believed man's wants to be almost constant and who favored a regime of low wages.

Output could be increased in the shorter run by pursuit of two policies: (a) Because most mercantilists supposed that a considerable part of the labor force was unemployed or underemployed, they made many proposals (some of which are discussed in [5] and [6] below), the main presumptive purpose of which was to make use of this unutilized labor power. (b) Alongside this unutilized labor power, mercantilists observed various kinds of labor shortages for which they sought relief. Particular occupations and particular industries, situated in particular centers, might require either technicians who could be drawn only from other countries, or local labor, which, however, would have to be recruited from outside the immediate vicinity. In some respects, of course, the problems arising under (b) were of the sort encountered in transportation-short economies whenever a tradition-bound, predominantly rural, labor force is being transformed into one that is more modern, less rural, and industry-oriented (cf. [8] below).[44] Immigration was looked upon as a part of this transforming process. For immigrants often brought with them capital, new industries, better methods, and preferred value attitudes. Thus, their coming was encouraged, except when ecclesiastical or short-sighted balance of

---

lustrate the salutary influence of an increase in the stock of money, included the postulate that 30 per cent of the population would live on charity (Coleman, "Labour in the English Economy," *loc.cit.*, p. 289). The Venetian, G. Ortes (1713-1790), supposed that average income tends to be constant and that only half the labor force finds employment. Some of the Cameralists supposed the social structure would remain constant (Small, *op.cit.*, p. 590).

43. *Essai sur la nature du commerce en général*, A. Sauvy, ed., Paris, 1952, close of chap. 15 in Part I.

44. While much work remains to be done on labor mobility and recruitment, and on the development of labor forces in the Age of Mercantilism, the data suggest that mobility was greater in England than on the continent. See Heckscher, *Mercantilism*, I, pp. 147*ff*., 215, 224-33, and passim. During the first half of the eighteenth century, wars (which mobilized somewhat less than 5 per cent of the male population) created no labor problem and may have accelerated English economic development (A. H. John, "War and the English Economy, 1700-1763," *Economic History Review*, VII, 1955, pp. 341-44). On English experience (which reveals considerable mobility, but most of it short-distance, and not enough to eliminate wage differentials), see E. W. Gilboy, *Wages in Eighteenth Century England*, Cambridge, 1934; G. Chapman, *Culture and Survival*, London, 1940, pp. 27-32; R. Bendix, *Work and Authority*, pp. 34-73; W. E. Minchinton, "The Diffusion of Tinplate Manufacture," *Economic History Review*, IX, 1956, pp. 349-58; E. J. Buckatzsch, "Places of Origin of a Group of Immigrants into Sheffield, 1624-1799," *ibid.*, II, 1950, pp. 303-307; E. E. Rich, "The Population of Elizabethan England," *ibid.*, pp. 261-64; Buckatzsch, "The Constancy of Local Populations and Migration in England before 1800," *Population Studies*, V, 1951, pp. 62-69. See also Dorothy Marshall's paper in Carus-Wilson, ed., *op.cit.*, pp. 298*ff*. D. V. Glass cites many studies of populationism and international migration relating to 1600-1800 in "Population Controversy in Eighteenth Century England," *Population Studies*, VI, 1952, pp. 69-91.

trade considerations stood in the way. Skilled minorities were particularly welcome, and the establishment of recruiting agencies was advocated and implemented. While emigration was sanctioned when it was deemed likely to benefit the country of emigration, it was usually opposed, since it entailed the loss of population, and possibly of technological information and skill, to foreign lands. Underlying the proposals and efforts to stimulate net immigration and natural increase in the seventeenth and eighteenth centuries were evidences of depopulation, some real and some fancied (e.g., war losses, emigration, high mortality), and the fear that numbers had declined.[45]

Because long-run population growth largely governed that of output, together with other objectives (e.g., military, fiscal) involving inputs of population, the majority of the mercantilists favored policies supposedly suited to increase the rate of population growth. These policies consisted of: (a) measures intended to reduce mortality; (b) measures intended to reduce age at marriage, increase the proportion of the married population, and augment natality; (c) measures intended to reduce or prevent emigration and to induce immigration. The measures were made up principally of financial, occupational, and other penalties, disabilities, aids, and privileges, together with schemes to increase employment and to render opinion and social environment more favorable to population growth. While the rationale underlying mercantilist populationism is not always clear, several types of advantage were anticipated from increases in numbers and density. Given the fact that the new increments were employed, aggregate output would increase and, with it, the size of the favorable balance, the volume of tax revenues, the strength and security of the nation, its capacity to colonize and extend political sway, and so on. Since it could hardly be expected that increasing returns would be experienced in agriculture, and since the massive inventions that made increasing returns possible after the industrial revolution did not become effective until the last quarter of the eighteenth century, such expectations of increasing returns as may have been held at the time must have had other sources. While it is not so stated by writers, it is possible that a few assumed (as

45. See the papers by M. M. Postan and W. C. Scoville, "Spread of Techniques," *Journal of Economic History*, Supplement, XI, 1951, pp. 339-60; E. Taube, "German Craftsmen in England during the Tudor Period," *Economic History*, III, 1939, pp. 167-78; W. C. Scoville, "The Huguenots and the Diffusion of Technology," *Journal of Political Economy*, LX, 1952, pp. 294*ff*., 392*ff*. Phyllis Deane ("The Implications of Early National Income Estimates," *Economic Development and Cultural Change*, IV, 1955, p. 10) reports an influx of about 50,000 refugees, many of them skilled, and £3 million from France after 1685. See also reports on early French attempts to attract immigrants: R. Eberstadt, *Das Franzoesische Gewerberecht uns die Schaffung staatlicher Gesetzgebung und Verwaltung in Frankrich vom dreizehnten Jahrhundert bis 1581, Leipzig*, 1899, pp. 310, 316-317, 312, 336; Gandilhon, *op.cit.*, pp. 108-10, 401-402. Glass discusses Spanish, French, and German losses consequent on persecution and war in 1600-1800 and efforts to redress them (*op.cit.*, pp. 83-88). See also footnote 15, above.

Petty seems to have done) that population growth would give rise to urbanization and the better manning of urban industry; as a result specialization and social differentiation would increase and circumstances would become more favorable to technological progress and the extension of markets. It was supposed that population growth would increase rivalry and competition among workers and operate to keep down money wages. Petty is quite clear on some of the points touched upon; he supposed that the overhead cost per capita of government and church would fall, and that there might be some tendency to increasing return. Serra had said that manufacturing costs per unit of output tended to decrease with the volume of business. Some writers may have believed that methods of production might improve and increase the population-carrying capacity of countries. While populationism seemingly had greater currency in Spain and Germany, both of which had experienced depopulation, than in England and even France, where apprehension at overpopulation, as well as at underpopulation, was sometimes expressed, or than in more densely populated and economically declining Italy, it lost much of its support in the last half of the eighteenth century. At this time the view that the growth of subsistence governs that of numbers won wide acceptance, with the result that those who were still populationists usually emphasized augmentation of subsistence and growth of employment. In Germany and Austria, however, populationism continued in vogue in the eighteenth century.[46]

Attitudes toward labor and wages underwent some change during the Age of Mercantilism. During and after the sixteenth century, labor lost some of its dignity and romance, and working people were treated less sympathetically than formerly.[47] Mercantilists assumed that the costs of

46. See C. H. Hull, *The Economic Writings of Sir William Petty*, London, 1899, I, pp. 21-22, 34, 255, 286, also pp. lxix*ff*.; H. Martin (see footnote 77 below), *Considerations on the East India Trade* (1701), reprinted in J. R. McCulloch, ed., *Early English Tracts on Commerce, London*, 1856, chaps. 11-12. See also K. Schünemann, *Osterreichs Bevolkerungspolitik unter Maria Theresa*, Berlin, 1935; Furniss, *op.cit.*, pp. 133-43; Colmeiro, *Economia Politica*, II, chaps. lii-lvi, lxxviii; J. Spengler, *French Predecessors* and "Richard Cantillon: First of the Moderns," *Journal of Political Economy*, LXII, 1954, pp. 281*ff*., 406*ff*.; Heckscher, *Mercantilism*, II, pp. 44*ff*., 157-63; C. E. Stangeland, *Pre-Malthusian Doctrines of Population*, New York, 1904; O. Jolles, "Die Ansichten der deutschen nationalökonomischen Schriftsteller des sechtzehnten und siebenzehnten Jahrhunderts über Bevölkerungswesen," *Jahrbücher für Nationalökonomie und Statistik*, XLVII, 1886, pp. 193-224; E. Frohneberg, *Bevölkerungslehre und Bevölkerungspolitik des Merkantilismus*, Gelnhausen, 1930; M. B. Amzalak, *As doutrinas da populaçao em Portugal nos seculos XVII e XVIII*, Lisbon, 1947; R. S. Smith's paper on pre-Malthusian Spanish population theory, in *Teachers of History: Essays in Honor of Laurence Bradford Packard*, Ithaca, 1954, pp. 231-57; Schumpeter, *History*, chap. 5. Europe's population grew more in 1750-1800 (49 million) than in 1650-1750 (41 million).

47. In the seventeenth century there was still present a strong tendency to look upon poverty as usually the result of unavoidable misfortune; but in the eighteenth century it was viewed as the result of indolence. See Bendix, *op.cit.*, pp. 60-69. See also Clark, *op.cit.*, pp. 75-81; Nef, *op.cit.*, pp. 228-34, and his paper in M. Postan and E. E. Rich, eds., *The Cambridge Economic History of Europe*, II, pp. 473-80; P. Boissonnade, *Le socialisme d'état*, Paris, 1927, I, chap. 10, II, chap. 11, esp. p. 126; C. Loyseau, *Traité des ordres*, Chateaudun, 1610; E. Levasseur, *Histoire des classes ouvrières et de l'industrie*

goods, and hence the prices at which they could profitably be sold abroad, depended very largely upon the money cost of labor. For this reason, and because they believed that goods must be sold cheaply in foreign markets, they favored wage policies which made for low labor costs. Moreover, they usually assumed that the worker's wants were virtually constant, or might be kept from increasing. They inferred, therefore, that, with his budget of wants fixed, the wage-earner would have to work more hours per week if his money wages were low than if they were high; or that, if his money wages were fixed, he would work more when food prices were high than when they were low. Studies were even undertaken to determine how much a worker required to meet his own simple needs and those of his dependents.[48] A few writers, only some of whom followed the mercantilist tradition, believed that the worker's wants would or ought to increase, that he would work harder if his wages sufficed to supply some of these additional wants, and that higher wages would swell the domestic demand for wage goods. It is not clear whether these writers counted upon increased effort to offset these higher wages, or whether, as John Cary has suggested, they expected improvements in methods to reduce labor input. That higher wages might improve the worker's health and living situation, and thus increase his productivity, was seldom if ever specifically considered.[49]

Land, after labor, was the most important factor, being the source of produce, of labor's sustenance, and of the raw materials that were worked up by manufacturers and craftsmen. It was essential, therefore, that unutilized land be brought into use, that better use be made of land already in use, that the cost of produce and other wage goods be kept down, and that mineral resources be inventoried and effectively exploited. Recommendations to this end were common. Access to good fishing grounds, so essential to the sustenance of the strategically important fishing industry, was in effect treated as a resource somewhat comparable to land.[50]

---

en France avant 1789, Paris, 1901, pp. 964-69; Heckscher, *Mercantilism*, II, pp. 165*ff*.; Furniss, *op.cit.*, chap. 6.

48. For low-wage arguments see Heckscher, *Mercantilism*, II, pp. 152-68; Lipson, *op.cit.*, III, pp. 118, 131, 134, 169-72, 180, 248-73; Furniss, *op.cit.*, chaps. 5-7, pp. 227-35; Gilboy, *op.cit.*, pp. xx, xviii-xxiii, 228-32. Whereas some writers believed that taxes on wage goods would make laborers work longer, others thought that such taxes would increase money wages and labor costs.

49. See Heckscher, *Mecantilism*, II, pp. 168*ff*.; Gilboy, *op.cit.*, pp. 231-36; Lipson, *op.cit.*, III, pp. 273-78; Furniss, *op.cit.*, pp. 125-27, 176-80; Gregory, "The Economics . . . ," *loc.cit.*; Viner, *Studies*, pp. 56-57. Viner believes that there was more opposition to the low-wages doctrine than Furniss and Gregory supposed. Most of the proponents of high wages appear to have been English. In France, Melon and the physiocrats were among the defenders of high or rising wages. Adam Smith later asserted that when wages exceeded subsistence, workers were healthier, stronger, and more disposed to supply effort. See *Wealth Of Nations*, Modern Library Edition, 1937, pp. 81*ff*.

50. Appreciation of the existence of zero-product margins was extremely rare in the literature, though they may have been recognized by some of those engaged in enterprise. Petty stated that the rental yield of land fell off as its situation worsened, but he did not observe that the physical yield of agricultural land was subject to diminishing return. See

While the mercantilists appreciated the importance of both fixed and circulating capital, they did not analyze and emphasize its role as they did that of labor. They did not distinguish sharply between kinds of capital, or between working capital and money. In consequence, they tended to make the interest rate depend upon the money supply much more than upon the amount of capital available and its rate of growth, though the non-mercantilist, D. North, made it depend upon the nation's "stock." They inferred from the experience of Holland that low interest rates gave a country a competitive advantage over other countries. Accordingly, they stressed the importance of certain circumstances highly conducive to capital formation, since, despite their emphasis on money, they supposed that increased saving would lower interest. One of these circumstances involved the set of habits represented by the term frugality, with which thrift or parsimony was associated. This was good, so long as nonconsumption resulted, not in hoarding, but in additions to the nation's riches. The second, apparently, was the magnitude of the surplus out of which savings or capital had to arise, namely, profit or rent, since most mercantilists believed that workers enjoyed little, if any, margin above their needs out of which to accumulate capital. Petty, Davenant, and King stand out among those who noted the importance of the surplus; King believed that the portion available for savings consisted principally of the profits of trade. It is not evident that the mercantilists fully appreciated the stimulus given to capital formation by the rise in prices and the consequent profit inflation experienced variously in the sixteenth, seventeenth, and eighteenth centuries, although they were aware of the favorable environment created by the influx of treasure. In fact, they should have so interpreted the course of events, since they usually postulated the existence of unemployed and underemployed labor to which increments in the money supply might give work without appreciably affecting money wages, and since some of them must have been aware that, in certain lines at least, inelasticity of supply was sufficiently great to make great profits probable, given an upswing of demand.[51]

Hull, *op.cit.*, pp. 48-49, 249, 286-87. Demand elasticity was appreciated by some (e.g., by Mun).

51. See the papers by E. J. Hamilton and J. U. Nef, in F. C. Lane and J. C. Riemersma, eds., *Enterprise and Secular Change*, Homewood, 1953; and Hamilton, "Prices as a Factor in Business Growth," *Journal of Economic History*, XII, 1952, pp. 325-49. Nef finds that the influx of specie and rising prices had a stimulating effect in France and England, though not so great a one as Hamilton's studies have suggested. Recently, Hamilton's thesis has been questioned by D. Felix, "Profit Inflation and Industrial Growth . . . ," *Quarterly Journal of Economics*, LXX, 1956, pp. 141-63, and by R. A. Kessel, "Inflation-Caused Wealth Redistribution," *American Economic Review*, XLVI, 1956, pp. 128-41. Around 1688, England's rate of capital formation was that of an underdeveloped country in the state of potential growth, about 4 per cent of income; but very little of this was absorbed by population increase which was very low at that time. See Phyllis Deane, "The Industrial Revolution and Economic Growth . . . ," *Economic Development and Cultural Change*, V, 1957, p. 161. Mercantilist views on capital are discussed here and there in the works of Lipson, Johnson, Heck-

Mercantilist writers did not treat the service of enterprise, a form of activity clearly identified by the early 1400's, as coordinate with those of labor, land, and capital. But, as has been indicated in (3), they attached great importance to the entrepreneurial role. The enterpriser was the dynamic agent, the source of economic *élan;* upon his effectiveness largely depended the rate at which a rural or an underdeveloped economy could be industrialized or otherwise improved. They did not, however, appreciate his role as a generator of profits, and hence of capital, and they did not define his functions in detail (a task first accomplished by Cantillon). Still, one may infer from the writings of the mercantilists that they saw in the enterpriser the symbol of the Age of Mercantilism, even as earlier writers had considered the Knight and the Priest the symbols of the medieval period. The mercantilists were generally agreed, moreover, that efforts must be made to provide an environment in which the entrepreneur could operate effectively, to encourage increase in his numbers, and to discourage successful enterprisers and their children from moving out of the entrepreneurial class into that of the landed gentry, the nobility, etc.[52]

(5) *The role of money.* Money was conceived to play a most important facilitating role in economic development at all times, and a dynamic role when other circumstances were propitious. The importance of the role assigned money was not greatly reduced until the latter part of the eight-

scher, and Suviranta (see footnote 54); in Davies' paper, cited in footnote 13; and in Viner, *Studies*, pp. 26-30, 45*ff*., 89. The Age of Mercantilism witnessed the partial dissolution of anti-usury argument and practice. E.g., see E. von Böhm-Bawerk, *Capital and Interest*, New York, 1922; J. C. Riemersma, "Usury Restrictions in a Mercantile Economy," *Canadian Journal of Economics and Political Science*, XVIII, 1952, pp. 17-26; De Roover, *Gresham;* Tawney, Introduction to Wilson, *Discourse;* Robertson, *Rise of Economic Individualism, passim.* On elasticity, see Appendix, footnote 67.

52. On some aspects of early entrepreneurial theory see B. F. Hoselitz, "The Early History of Entrepreneurial Theory," *Explorations in Entrepreneurial History*, III, 1951, pp. 193-220. While mercantilist writers were concerned about the recruitment of entrepreneurs, they lacked data and theory in terms of which to analyze this process, or the associated process, whereby successful entrepreneurial families are absorbed into non-business cadres. They could not, of course, attempt a typology of entrepreneurs. Long after the entrepreneur had come into his own, many failed to find a business career sufficiently attractive. Thus in the eighteenth century (and even in the early nineteenth century) sons of businessmen, upon attending Cambridge or a similar university, tended to avoid business careers. See H. Jenkins and D. C. Jones, "Social Class of Cambridge University Alumni of the Eighteenth and Nineteenth Centuries," *British Journal of Sociology*, I, 1950, pp. 93-116. Entry into agriculture was advantageous to industry when it resulted in the rationalization and de-traditionalizing of agriculture and in the displacement of potential urban workers out of agriculture. Defoe represented the attitude of the businessman toward the landlords (who held industry and commerce in contempt) when he reported that businessmen, in virtue of their own hard-earned success, were buying up estates formerly held by the gentry or nobility. See Bendix, *op.cit.*, pp. 30-31; also footnote 36, above. At various times, of course, business was engaged in or supported by members of the nobility, aristocrats, and landed gentry. E.g., see P. G. Ohlin, "Entrepreneurial Activities of the Swedish Aristocracy," *Explorations in Entrepreneurial History*, IV, 1954, pp. 147-62, together with the five papers making up *ibid.*, No. 2, pp. 77-130; also V. Niitemaa, "Entrepreneurial Activities of the Livonian Nobility in the Middle Ages," *ibid.*, VIII, 1955, pp. 35-39, and W. Kirchner, "Entrepreneurial Activity in Russian-Western Trade Relations during the Sixteenth Century," *ibid.*, pp. 245-51; also the papers by L. Stone, W. E. Minchinton, and P. Mathias, in M. M. Postan and H. J. Habakkuk, eds., *The Entrepreneur*, Cambridge, 1957.

eenth century, when economic liberalism and a more rigidly defined quantity theory were becoming ascendant. Initially, when the mercantilists had hard money in mind, their discussions focused on the balance of trade or payments (discussed in [6]); later it evolved around land-based or other paper money.

In mercantilist literature one encounters at least three grounds for asserting that a country's stock of money must be ample and enabled to grow at a sufficient rate: (a) Economic development can proceed effectively only if the interest rate is low (as it was in Holland); and interest, being the price of money's use, can be low only if the supply of money is adequate.[53] (b) At the time when the mercantilists were writing, complaint of the "scarcity of money" was frequent, at least in England and Holland, since price-income structures did not respond speedily to recurring outflows of the media in circulation; and much consideration was given to means whereby this scarcity might be alleviated. In general, the mercantilists held that there must be enough money to satisfy the convenience, finance, liquidity, and related requirements of the business community, and to permit enough expenditure and investment to generate full employment. Labor and other agents of production would be fully employed only if the money supply were adequate and grew as these factors grew, or grew rapidly enough to employ domestic factors and, in addition, to attract labor and perhaps raw materials from abroad. So long as agents of production were unemployed or underemployed or inefficiently employed, increases in the quantity of money would augment their employment and the effectiveness with which they were used. (c) Deflation must be averted because falling prices are unfavorable to economic development. Aversion of falling prices, rather than the attainment of rising prices, was emphasized. Although some writers seem to have believed that prices should be high enough to make the terms of trade comparatively favorable, they did not favor raising prices when, given an elastic foreign demand, so doing entailed the loss of foreign sales.

Among the ambiguities running through the relevant mercantilist literature, two are particularly conspicuous. First, the mercantilists did not address themselves to the bottleneck problem (common then, just as it is in present-day underdeveloped countries), arising out of shortages of particular agents of production in short and inelastic supply. Indeed, they

53. E.g., see Heckscher, *Mercantilism*, II, pp. 198-206; Viner, *Studies*, pp. 31-32, 45-49. Thomas Manley (in *Usury at 6 per cent Examined*, 1669) was one of the very few to favor high interest rates. Few of the later seventeenth-century writers who believed a low rate of interest to be desirable favored attempting "to reduce it by purely administrative means." So doing "would be harmful and ineffective. Interest was a natural phenomenon determined by natural forces." See J. M. Low, "The Rate of Interest: British Opinion in the Eighteenth Century," *The Manchester School of Economic and Social Studies*, XXII, 1954, pp. 115-16.

wrote as if most factors were in elastic supply, or would flow freely from foreign and/or domestic sources into international trade and other strategic sectors as investment and other expenditure rose. Second, they failed to specify the conditions under which further increases in money would push up prices rather than augment employment. Whereas Petty and Cantillon attempted to estimate how much money was required under given conditions, many others seem to have been content to assume that more was required as long as there was unemployment or underemployment or the prospect of immigration. In time, however, partly as a result of experience and the rise of liberalism, a more rigid quantity theory came into vogue.[54]

(6) *External economic relations.* Although mercantilist writers rarely distinguished explicitly between open and closed economies (Cantillon being an exception), they conceived of their policies within the context of a more or less open economy (as, of course, did most of their critics). Even exponents of autarky sought advantage through externally oriented economic activities. As the mercantilists saw it, a country's economic milieu could be enlarged by extending its boundaries (usually a process that was too costly, even when possible); by establishing colonies and quasi-colonies; or by entering into trade relations with other countries. Trade, whether with colonies or with other countries, might bring in produce, specie, and raw materials, thus enlarging the stock of factors with which labor could be combined and making possible further employment or growth of the labor force. The labor force could also be enlarged through immigration, and its quality improved through the influx of persons possessing scarce or needed skills, information, etc.[55] The representative mercantilist was greatly interested, therefore, in enlarging the economic

54. See Viner, *Studies*, pp. 31-40, 47-48, 87-90; Tautscher, ". . . Dynamische Kredittheorie . . . ," *loc.cit.;* W. Dreissig, *Die Geld- und Kreditlehre des deutchen Merkantilismus*, Berlin, 1939; Heckscher, *Mercantilism*, II, pp. 95, 208, 220, 224-31, 248*ff.;* Angell, *International Prices*, chaps. 2, 8; Chi-yuen Wu, *An Outline of International Price Theories*, London, 1932, chap. 2. Sweden's unfortunate experience with bank-note financing of manufactures sponsored by mercantilists in the eighteenth century, is described by Heckscher in his *Sveriges Ekonomiska Historia*, Stockholm, 1939, II. On views regarding scarcity of money, and on scarcity of money as such, see B. E. Supple, "Currency and Commerce in the Early Seventeenth-Century," *Economic History Review*, X, 1957, pp. 239-55; J. C. Riemersma, "Monetary Confusion as a Factor in the Economic Expansion of Europe (1150-1650)," *Explorations in Entrepreneurial History*, V, 1952, pp. 61-74; Br. Suviranta, *The Theory of the Balance of Trade in England*, Helsingfors, 1923, pp. 77-96; L. J. Presnell, *Country Banking in the Industrial Revolution*, Oxford, 1956, pp. 15-21; also W. A. Shaw, *Select Tracts and Documents Illustrative of English Monetary History 1626-1730*, London, 1935, *passim*, and R. D. Richards, *The Early History of Banking in England*, London, 1929. In 1775 Campomanes listed Spain's freedom from paper-money inflation as one of her advantages. See *Apéndice à la Educacion Popular*, Madrid, 1775, pp. xxxvi*ff.*, cited by E. J. Hamilton, in "War and Inflation in Spain, 1780-1800," *Quarterly Journal of Economics*, LIX, 1944, pp. 36-37.

55. Although Aristotle still enjoyed considerable vogue, one encounters almost no reference to eugenic quality. However, De Béthune (p. 327 of work cited in footnote 10, Appendix) did remark: "Good Men come from good"; etc.

milieu of his own country, and consequently dealt with aspects of growth theory.[56]

Mercantilist concern with the balance of trade, whether based on fear of deflation or other factors,[57] resulted in concern with economic development. A country bent upon making its trade or payments balance favorable, must sell more goods and/or services than it purchases, importing the surplus as specie or utilizing it abroad to extend its foreign trade (and, less frequently, to build up foreign investment). Some mercantilists advocated resort to austerity and nonimportation of luxuries and other dispensable foreign goods, assuming that the resulting savings would flow in as specie; but this was opposed by those who believed that sumptuary and similar legislation clogged the channels of trade and reduced the incentive to work. It was widely accepted, however, that a sufficiently large balance could not be realized unless a country increased its gross output, thereby providing more goods and services for sale abroad, as well as domestic substitutes for needed wares theretofore imported. Increasing gross production thus entailed fuller and more skilled use of a country's human and natural resources: getting rid of unemployment and underemploy-

56. Presumably, increase in the size and/or efficiency of the sailing ship (for centuries the most effective energy converter at man's disposal [F. Cottrell, *Energy and Society*, New York, 1955, pp. 48-51]) in the seventeenth and eighteenth centuries enlarged the size of the milieu the mercantilists envisaged.

57. The anti-deflationist stand of mercantilists is evident in their discussion of a state emergency reserve, which continued to be mentioned long after it had lost importance around the close of the fifteenth century. If too much specie were sequestered, they said, it would depress employment just as hoarding did. See Viner, *Studies*, pp. 22-30, 45-51; Heckscher, *Mercantilism*, II, pp. 209-16; A. E. Monroe, *Monetary Theory Before Adam Smith*, Cambridge, 1923, pp. 277-80; K. E. Knorr, *British Colonial Theories 1570-1850*, Toronto, 1944, pp. 13-15; R. Ashton, "Deficit Finance in the Reign of James I," *Economic History Review*, X, 1957, pp. 15-29. It is widely held that influx of specie was often the over-riding object of mercantilist policy (see Viner, *Studies*, pp. 15-22; Buck, *Politics of Mercantilism*, pp. 22*ff*.; Heckscher, *Mercantilism*, II, Part IV, chap. 2, and "Multilateralism, Baltic Trade, and the Mercantilists," *Economic History Review*, III, 1950, pp. 219-28; Charles Wilson, "Treasure and Trade Balances: The Mercantilist Problem," *ibid*., II, 1949, pp. 152-61, and "Treasure and Trade Balances: Further Evidence," *ibid*., IV, 1951, pp. 231-42; however, a number of writers (e.g., Lord Keynes, *General Theory*, chap. 23) do not support this view. See Lipson *op.cit*., II, pp. lxxvi*ff*.; W. Focke, *op.cit*.; Small, *op.cit*., pp. 592-93; Suviranta, *op.cit*., pp. 114-26. See also Clara G. Muschweck, *Das Problem des Reichtums in der vorwirtschaftswissenschaftlichen Zeit, insbesondere in Merkantilismus*, Wurzburg, 1935; J. Niehans, *Der Gedanke der Autarke im Merkantilismus von einst und im Neomerkantilismus von gestern*, Zurich, 1945. Johnson (*Predecessors*, p. 275) believes that Adam Smith's British predecessors were concerned primarily with "the creation of effective factors of production," and that "not ten per cent of early British economic literature was devoted to the . . . balance of trade." When estimates were made of the national wealth (e.g., by Petty, G. King, Davenant, and others), it became evident that specie constituted a very small fraction of a country's wealth. Mercantilists did not closely correlate the magnitude of the favorable balance supposedly required from year to year with the incremental rate of growth of national product. In 1688 King's estimate (see Deane, "The Implications . . . ," *loc.cit*., p. 8) of the favorable balance (= foreign lending) was 1.34 per cent of national product. See also C. Davenant's comment in his *Works* (C. Whitworth, ed., London, 1771, I, pp. 375-76) on trade's doubling the nation's capital in thirty years under suitable conditions. On early French emphasis upon making the trade-balance favorable, see Gandilhon, *op. cit*., pp. 320-23.

ment;[58] bringing within the orbit of use land, mineral and other resources, etc., that had formerly remained idle, in part because there had been insufficient labor time to combine therewith; introducing more efficient methods of production; and diverting workers from less into more productive activities. Gross product and the size of the favorable balance would then grow in the longer run, as population and the labor force grew.

The growth-augmenting changes, whatever their sources, that took place in the seventeenth century, together with other circumstances conducive to belief in progress, contributed to the partial replacement of the comparatively static and nondynamic view of society and its prospects, characteristic of the medieval and early mercantilistic period, by a much more dynamic and optimistic view.[59] With this shift, and with the subsequent increase in the rate of growth of markets, there was associated a shift in economic expectation which helped bring about replacement of pre-1700 autarkism by post-1776 free-tradeism. For, if an economy is assumed to be expanding, corollary assumptions are likely to be accepted: that costs of progress and the burden of adjusting to changing circumstances will become lighter; that adverse substitution effects will be swamped by salutary expansionist effects; and that (contrary to the views of Bacon, Montaigne, and their contemporaries) one man's, or one country's, gain will not necessarily be at the expense of another.[60]

The mercantilists's conception of the role of the favorable balance gradually changed with changes in monetary practice and theory, and also with increase in the importance of invisible items (e.g., Britain's merchandise balance usually was negative as early as 1800, if not earlier). As long as hard money was used to perform monetary functions, mercantilists in countries that lacked mines at home or in their colonies emphasized the importance of increasing the stock of money through maintenance of a favorable balance of trade (or payments). By the later 1600's, however, it was widely accepted that paper money could perform some of the functions theretofore performed by hard money; and that recourse to

58. "The full employment of all Hands in the Nation, is the surest Way and Means to bring BULLION into the Kingdom," wrote F. Brewster, in *New Essays on Trade*, London, 1702, p. 45. Trade, especially colonial trade, asserted J. Cary, who believed trade and manufacture were more productive than agriculture, would generate needed employment. See *An Essay on Trade*, Bristol, 1695, pp. 68*ff*., 91*ff*., 100*ff*. What was needed, Cary, Petty, and others urged, was removal of the causes of unemployment, rather than legislation. See Heckscher, *Mercantilism*, II, p. 314.

59. Hinton ("The Mercantile System," *loc.cit.*, p. 286), apparently referring to early seventeenth-century mercantilists, says that they "did not believe in Progress," but were spurred to action by fear of "Degeneration." Johnson (*Predecessors*, pp. 21, 96) specifically includes Hales, Bacon, and Petty among the believers in progress. See also Heckscher, *Mercantilism*, II, p. 126; Clark, *Seventeenth Century*, pp. 284*ff*.; J. B. Bury, *Idea of Progress*.

60. Cf. Heckscher, *Mercantilism*, II, pp. 25-26, 112*ff*.; H. M. Robertson, "European Economic Developments . . . ," *loc.cit.*, p. 46; Coleman, "Eli Heckscher and the Idea of Mercantilism," *loc.cit.*, pp. 20-23.

the use of token money might sometimes partially replace variation of the exchange rate as a means of checking the loss of silver or gold.[61] The importance attached to a favorable balance diminished, therefore, with the establishment of banks empowered to supply these substitutes,[62] and with the development, especially in the eighteenth century, of a system of international credit, together with multilateral payments. It also declined in countries where experience had been unfavorable (especially Spain), and everywhere under the impact of criticism which, particularly during and after the late seventeenth century, found pursuit of a favorable balance at variance with a nation's true economic interests and with the developing quantity theory and its corollary, a self-regulating mechanism of specie distribution.[63]

61. On exchange-rate variation see Supple, *op.cit.;* Riemersma, "Monetary Confusion . . . ," *loc.cit.;* W. A. Shaw, *op.cit.* See C. M. Cipolla's summary of the defense of the use of token money by G. Montanari, G. A. Thesauro, and A. Serra (in *Money, Prices and Civilization in the Mediterranean World,* Princeton, 1956, pp. 28-31); also Monroe, *op.cit.,* pp. 96-98, and W. W. Carlile, *The Evolution of Modern Money,* London, 1901, pp. 143-48. That the coinage of token money must be suitably monopolized to insure limitation of its supply was slow to be appreciated. Mercantilists differed respecting the extent to which paper money might be used, some (e.g., J. Pollexfen, *A Discourse of Trade,* 1697) looking on it as a supplement to coin rather than as a substitute for hard money. On paper money mercantilism, see Heckscher, *Mercantilism,* II, pp. 231-37. In 1698 C. Davenant (who emphasized the importance of maintaining monetary circulation) estimated at 5 to 4 the ratio of assignable credit instruments to coinage *(Works,* I, pp. 161-62; also Davies, "Joint-Stock Investment in the Later Seventeenth Century," *loc. cit.,* pp. 277-78).

62. Bishop George Berkeley advocated, as a means to supply Ireland with money, not a favorable balance of trade, but the establishment of a national bank and use of paper money. Given the resulting increase in money, the interest rate would be reduced, to the advantage of enterprise; employment and wealth would increase to the limits set by the "natural appetites" of men; and the surplus productive power (above needs) thereby mobilized could be used to improve capital, above all utilities and furniture. Money beyond the amount expedient for these purposes would be "hurtful . . . to the State." See J. Johnston, "The Monetary Theories of Berkeley," *Economic History,* III, 1938, pp. 21-24. This paper is based on the *Querist,* first published in 1735. Whereas the first edition was dominated by the project of a national bank, most queries relating thereto were omitted from later editions, though not because of a decline in Berkeley's own interest in the project. See A. A. Luce and T. E. Jessop, *The Works of George Berkeley* (London, 1953, VI, pp. 91*ff.)* concerning Berkeley and Ireland's plight. In "An Essay Towards Preventing The Ruin of Great Britain" (1721) (in *Works,* VI, pp. 63-85), Berkeley stated that work and industry constitute the "sure way to wealth"; that making it possible to acquire means without work retards economic development; that industries using domestic raw materials should be encouraged; that luxury should be restricted by sumptuary laws and reduction of imports; that invention and improvement, for which there is room in most art and trade, should be encouraged with premiums; that population, being a means and a motive to industry, should be stimulated by premiums, etc.; that navigation, frugality, and simplicity of manners should be encouraged; and that some products presently imported should be supplied domestically. On the development of English banking and paper money, see Richards, *op.cit.* According to I. D. Ward, Bishop Berkeley was one of the first to undertake an analysis of "the problems of an underdeveloped economy." See "George Berkeley: Precursor of Keynes or Moral Economist on Underdevelopment," *Journal of Political Economy,* XLVII, 1959, pp. 31-40.

63. It is essential to distinguish between short-run and long-run views respecting the balance of trade (or payments), its determinants, and measures suited to influence it. Much of the literature has to do with short-run imbalance originating in exchange-rate manipulation, and must be assessed accordingly. See Supple, *op.cit.,* and works cited. On literature relating to trade-balance theory, see Viner, *op.cit.,* pp. 74*ff.;* Appendix; I. Gervaise, *The System or Theory of the Trade of the World* (1720), Baltimore, 1954, edited by J. M. Letiche (who discusses the role of smuggling and retaliation [pp. viii-xii]); and Letiche, "Isaac Gervaise on the

Most of the mercantilists strongly endorsed measures, such as the navigation acts, suited to build up demand for their shipping and related services; measures intended to expand foreign markets, which apparently were long considered more extensible and more important than domestic markets; discriminatory and protectionist measures designed to foment the growth of industrial and other preferred domestic activities; measures favorable to the re-export trade; and measures intended to prevent the loss of bullion. More specifically, the mercantilists proposed duties and other burdens on raw-material exports and foreign imports, especially manufactures and luxuries; disabilities on domestic industries whose growth would retard that of favored activities; and bounties, principally on some exports. In some instances prohibition of particular imports, exports, and activities was advocated. Because of fear of smuggling and retaliation, however, prohibitions and prohibitive burdens were not often recommended.

Although, initially, all these measures had as their principal objective the realization of a favorable balance, they also had as their objective (exclusive of the bullion controls) the development of the industrial and other preferred sectors of the nation's economy. The latter objective became paramount after the control of bullion ceased to be considered important. In a sense, however, the primary purpose finally became the importation of a surplus of "matter," or landed products (i.e., produce, raw materials, and some specie), and the exportation of a surplus of work in the form of labor-embodying wrought goods. Imported produce helped to support a country's population, and imported raw materials furnished additional stuff to work up into wrought forms, with the result that a part of this population could be said to exist on the landed products of other countries. This type of argument, nicely stated by Cantillon and given final form by Steuart, had been anticipated as early as the fourteenth, fifteenth, and sixteenth centuries, and was further developed in the seventeenth. It had a

---

International Mechanism of Adjustment," *Journal of Political Economy*, LX, 1952, pp. 34-44. On the extent to which the need for specie was increased, for a time, by the failure of multilateralism to grow as rapidly as trade, see papers by Wilson and Heckscher, cited in footnote 57, above. Inspired by this controversy, J. H. Dales has argued, on the following grounds, that the demand for bullion increased after the discoveries that: (a) the volume of trade increased; (b) a considerable part of the increase took place, not in parts where the trading systems were multilateral, and most of the accounts could be cleared, but in parts (e.g., Indian trade) where the trading systems were bilateral, and hence specie was required for settling balances. Insofar as this is a correct representation of the facts, Dales concludes, the mercantilists' belief that more specie was needed reflected their experience. See "The Discoveries and Mercantilism," *Canadian Journal of Economics and Political Science*, XXI, 1955, pp. 141-53. On the drain of bullion to the East, see Robertson, *Rise of Economic Individualism*, pp. 185*ff*. Even a partial breakdown of a multilateral system, it might be shown, could, by interrupting multilateral settlement, produce the effect described by Dales. On retaliation, see Lipson, *Economic History*, III, pp. 17-19. Smuggling greatly reduced the effectiveness of the various curbs put on trade. E.g., see *ibid., passim,* and Ramsay, *op.cit., passim,* also M. W. Beresford, "The Common Informer, the Penal Statutes and Economic Regulation," *Economic History Review*, X, 1957, pp. 221-38.

bellicose orientation, in that it represented one country as living off the primary products of others, and thereby preventing the full development of the population of any country specializing in raw materials. While this approach, with its emphasis upon maximizing a kind of population aggregate, appears to have evolved in terms of power, it seems to have had its origin and much of its support in the continuing belief that a country's labor force was not likely to be fully employed unless a portion of that labor force served foreign markets and derived support from foreign raw materials—unless, in short, exports continued in a volume sufficient to insure full employment.

While the protectionist philosophy described in the two preceding paragraphs included the recommendation of policies that might stimulate economic growth, it was not formulated in terms of growth theory. Thus, while the infant industry argument appeared as early as the seventeenth century, it was rarely used by the mercantilists, even though it may be presumed that many of them expected that protectionism would transform economies. Furthermore, although a number of writers appreciated the role of international division of labor, and a few came fairly close to recognizing its comparative advantage, mercantilists disregarded the implications of these matters for mercantilist theory, perhaps because their belief in the existence of considerable unemployment made these matters seem less important.[64]

Colonial theory was most highly developed in England. In its outlines, however, English theory did not differ greatly from that found in other countries. Sixteenth-century colonial theory was formulated in part in the light of Britain's attempts to treat Ireland as a colony and subject it to the usual restrictions.[65] The eventual objective of England's Old Colonial

64. See Viner, *Studies*, pp. 58-74, 103-10; Furniss, *op.cit.*, chap. 2; Heckscher, *Mercantilism*, II; Buck, *op.cit.;* J. Morini-Combi, *Mercantilisme et protectionisme*, Paris, 1930; and, on the "export of work" and related argument, Johnson, *Predecessors*, chaps. 11-12, 14-15. The "export of work" argument is not in the factoral-proportion tradition developed by B. Ohlin in his *Interregional and International Trade* (Cambridge, 1933). For, whereas in the Ohlin model, labor-embodying goods predominate only among the exports of labor-long countries, in the Steuart model a similar situation does not come to prevail until policies of the sort recommended by Steuart bring about a labor-long model; therefore, it is policy, not factoral proportion, that supposedly gives rise at first to wrought-goods exports, though just how this end is to be achieved is not made clear.

65. On the origins of English colonial theory, see D. B. Quinn, "Sir Thomas Smith (1513-1577) and the Beginnings of English Colonial Theory," *Proceedings of the American Philosophical Society*, LXXXIX, 1945, pp. 543-60; also H. M. Jones, *Ideas in America*, Cambridge, 1944, chap. 4; and *Tudor Economic Documents*, Tawney, ed., II, pp. 1-89. Ireland was to be restricted to agriculture and, because Irish produce, unlike that of distant America, might compete with English produce, the Irish were to be restricted to forms of agriculture not competitive with the British (Pares, *op.cit.*, pp. 121-23). Francis Bacon applied his theory of colonization to Ireland. Among the factors prerequisite to the success of such colonial ventures were profitability to their private undertakers; freedom to export commodities produced, and to import custom-free goods required by colonies, and compactness of settlement to assure easy defense; a secure and regular supply of provisions, etc.; and ready access to employment and economies of cooperation. ("If they set up together in a place, one of them will better supply the

System, to the development of which various mercantilists contributed (e.g., Malynes, Mun, Gee, etc.), was the creation of an economically self-sufficient empire—with colony and mother country carrying on different, but complementary and mutually beneficial, activities. Development of the mother country was paramount, development of the colonies took place in response to that of the mother country. In the case of Britain, expansion was dominated by the desire of the mother country for certain commodities (tobacco, sugar, timber, and fish in the seventeenth century; tea, coffee, cocoa, slave-trade profits in the eighteenth).[66] The argument was not effectively developed, however, that within this empire release would be given to the force of increasing return.

Of the economic arguments advanced in support of colonies by British writers before 1660, only a few were of major importance. Among these were arguments concerning the importance of transatlantic fisheries and the importance of the contribution colonial trade could make to the increase of seamen and a merchant marine; arguments that the colonies would provide an outlet for surplus population, and might prove a repository for criminals and undesirables (though this was a secondary consideration);[67] arguments that the colonies would provide new sources whence raw materials might derive and, though in lesser measure, controlled markets for British goods. After 1660, the role of the colonies as a nursery for seamen continued to be stressed, and strategic and naval considerations were given somewhat more weight than previously. Colonies

---

wants of another: work-folks of all sorts will be the more continually set a-work without loss of time, when if work fail in one place they have it fast by"; there will be better transport "and infinite other helps and easements"; there will not be difficulty and waste as when "every man must have a cornucopia in himself for all things he must use".) It was essential also that socio-economic overhead capital (i.e., "whatsoever is public, as building of churches, walling of towns, town-houses, bridges, causies, or highways, and the like") be supplied by the state ("come from the public estate of this kingdom"). See J. Spedding, *The Letters and the Life of Francis Bacon*, London, 1868, IV, pp. 120-25; also *The Works of Francis Bacon*, Spedding, *et al.*, eds., Boston, 1864, XII, pp. 194-98. See also footnote 69, below.

66. See L. Knowles, *The Economic Development of the British Overseas Empire*, London, 2nd ed., 1928, I, pp. 67-69; Lipson, *Economic History*, III, pp. 154-97; references cited in footnote 68, below; Pares, *op.cit.*, pp. 121-26. Colonies which could supply the mother country with needed produce and raw materials could also absorb her manufactures. Hence staple-producing colonies (e.g., the sugar islands) were deemed valuable, whereas colonies engaging in general agriculture (e.g., New England) were considered of little worth and, because they might enter into competition with the mother country (as had India), had to be denied permission to supply what the mother country produced. See *ibid.*, pp. 121, 125-28, 144. Three centuries later, a British economist was to argue that the income-expanding effect of colonial industrialization could outweigh its substitution effect with respect to Britain and increase the latter's exports. See P. Ady, "Colonial Industrialisation and British Employment," *Review of Economic Studies*, XI, 1943, pp. 42-51.

67. The argument that colonies would relieve the mother country of a surplus, and of essentially unemployed, population, thereby reducing the costs of public relief, was partly propagandistic in character and intended to build up support for colonial development. See Knorr, *op.cit.*, pp. 41-42, who endorses E. A. Johnson's comment to this effect. That the colonies depopulated the mother country was a contention of both Spanish (See Appendix, pp. 311-316) and Portuguese mercantilists (see A. Ferreira, *Unbekannte Portugiesische Merkantilisten*, Bern, 1952, pp. 43-48, 82, 103-104).

continued to be viewed as sources of raw materials and as important markets for metropolitan products, from which foreign competition could be excluded; as a result wrought goods could be exchanged for raw materials, and the volume of employment attainable within the mother country could be increased. After 1660, with intensification of the view that a large population was advantageous, colonies often were conceived of as competing with the mother country for its population, and thereby diminishing the advantages (e.g., low wages and a greater domestic market, especially for corn) derivable from greatness and density of population. Some authors asserted that the colonies actually operated to depopulate the mother country; others suggested immigration as a corrective measure for underpopulation accentuated by emigration. However, the majority view was that while the development of colonies temporarily cost the mother country population, thereby providing justification for the monopolizing of colonial trade, in the longer run, by providing raw materials and markets for exports and shipping services, colonial expansion operated to increase the metropolitan population and labor force.[68] Some authors, for example, Davenant, indicated that the gains sought by the mother country would prove attainable only if excessive colonial expansion were avoided, and boundaries were set to the colonial area open to settlement and exploitation.[69] Some authors completely rejected the view that the colonies were advantageous to England and found them disadvantageous on both economic and political grounds, noting in effect that several of the advantages supposedly to be derived from ownership of the colonies did not exist in reality or would be obtained more economically were the colonies free.[70]

(7) *The role of the state and other institutions.* Mercantilists believed in the necessity of both state intervention in the conduct of economic affairs and the establishment of institutions supposedly suited to achieve the state's aims. In this concept the mercantilists did not differ in principle from theorists of other ages; they merely assigned a relatively major role to the state. The degree of intervention proposed and/or achieved varied with each country for a number of reasons; it was relatively great in coun-

68. This summary is based upon Knorr's excellent account (*op.cit.*, chaps. 2-3). See also H. A. Edgerton, *A Short History of British Colonial Policy, 1606-1909*, London, ninth ed. (revised by A. P. Newton), 1932, pp. 3-176; G. L. Beer, *The Origins of the British Colonial System* (1908), New York, 1933, esp. chaps. 2-3, 8-9, and *The Old Colonial System, 1660-1754* (1912), New York, 1933, I, chaps. 1-2, 5. British colonies were not valued as outlets for capital; they diverted capital from domestic industry and were partly responsible for the fact that England was a capital importer (Pares, *op.cit.*, pp. 127-301).

69. See Davenant, *Works*, II, pp. 1*ff.*; Knorr, *op.cit.*, pp. 106-109; cf. J. S. Mill's account of E. G. Wakefield's proposal for limiting settlement, *Principles of Political Economy*, W. J. Ashley, ed., Philadelphia, 1921, pp. 120*ff.* See footnote 65, above.

70. See Knorr, *op.cit.*, pp. 105-25. E.g., see W. Petyt, *Brittania Languens* (1680), in McCulloch, *Early English Tracts on Commerce*, pp. 370, 380, 412-15; R. L. Schuyler, ed., *Josiah Tucker, a Selection from His Economic and Political Writings*, New York, 1931, pp. 30-39, 331*ff.* Tucker's argument against the colonies developed as he adopted an increasingly liberal philosophy.

tries with dynastic or territorial aims (e.g., France and Spain) and in comparatively backward countries (e.g., Austria and Prussia); it was less pronounced in some countries in which the power of the central government was relatively weak, the business community was relatively strong, and economic life was relatively advanced (e.g., Italy, and, especially after 1640, Holland and England.[71] The scope of intervention was conditioned by the particular nature of the problems confronting a country, by its class and interest-group composition, and by the degree to which rising nationalistic sentiments were dissolving particularistic loyalties and attachments. Scope and degree were also affected by the frequency of a country's involvement in war, by its size and geographical structure, and by prevailing conceptions of the role of state and secular society. The effectiveness of state intervention was conditioned by the stage of development of a country's civil service and by limitations arising from the nature of its terrain, its size and shape, distances between important points, and other determinants of communication.[72]

The achievement of mercantilist objectives required state intervention because neither individuals nor small groups would or could accomplish these objectives. In the absence of princely discipline and the guiding hand of the state, harmony would not prevail among the diverse groups and interests comprising the state, or between individual and collective aims. Hence, unrestricted private enterprise could not be relied upon; yet, pursuit of private advantage could be counted upon, provided that undertakers had to seek it within a suitable framework of regulatory conditions, privileges, rewards, and penalties. For this reason, and because the entrepreneurial capacity of the state bureaucracy was limited, mercantilists were disposed to urge state operation of enterprise (i.e., the hiring and combining of factors, transforming them into output, and marketing or otherwise disposing of output) only under unusual conditions (e.g., if the state were the main user of a product), or when it was believed that private enterprise could not accomplish the desired result under existing conditions. Otherwise, private enterprise was indicated. The problem then became one

71. Spain is not a very clear-cut case. There, as in Germany, France, and Austria, internal barriers to trade were slow to be removed (Heckscher, *Mercantilism*, I, Part 2). In Spain, too, a combination of circumstances (e.g., a multiplicity of powerful interests; persistence of pre-mercantilist norms; etc.) served to weaken the crown. See Schwarzmann, *op.cit.* Yet, because of dynastic considerations, the weakness of the Spanish economy, etc., governmental interventionism was marked.

72. On these determinants, see Mattingly, *op.cit.*, pp. 58-63, 122-31; Braudel, *op.cit.*, pp. 309-24, 541-45; J. H. Herz, "Rise and Demise of the Territorial State," *World Politics*, IX, 1957, pp. 477-84. On nationalism, see Mattingly, *op. cit.*, pp. 162*ff.*; G. R. Potter, ed., *The New Cambridge Modern History*, I, pp. 88-89, 194; footnote 11, above. On the development of the civil service in absolutist seventeenth-century France (where its economic regulatory duties strengthened it), in Prussia, and in a freer England, see Ernest Barker, *The Development of Public Services in Western Europe, 1660-1930*, London, 1945, chap. 1; also H. Rosenberg, *Bureaucracy, Aristocracy and Autocracy*, Cambridge, 1958.

of specifying a suitable and fomenting regulative framework (i.e., disabilities, rewards, prohibitions), together with an environment generally favorable to trade and industry (e.g., satisfactory commercial law, adequate monetary and banking conditions, suitable tax structure, a developed transport and shipping system, etc.). Elements entering into the composition of this framework were noted earlier in part I and are touched upon in the Appendix to this contribution.[73]

However, other than in Holland where the state, while it promoted commercial ends, did not participate in enterprise as such, and in England, where the resources of enterprise were almost entirely of private origin, direct state intervention was much greater than our account of mercantilist theory implies. For rulers and governmental officials, as distinguished from theoreticians, apparently looked on direct action as providing relatively easy, even if not the most economical, solutions to particular problems. States did not, therefore, confine their activities to indirect intervention, such as providing transport and utilities; loans, subsidies, tariffs; some technical education; police, military and naval protection; etc. They intervened and participated directly. The Portuguese state carried on trade; the Spanish crown, originally following the example of the Portuguese state, later limited itself largely to supplying large amounts of capital to closely regulated traders. Many state factories were established in Prussia, Russia, Austria, and other German states in the eighteenth century. In France the state both created and gave support to factories and ventures.[74]

---

73. See cited works by Heckscher, Stone, Buck, and Small; works summarized in the Appendix; A. Tautscher, *Staatswirtschaftslehre des Kameralismus;* and, on taxation, F. K. Mann, *Steuerpolitische Ideale,* Jena, 1937, Parts I-II, *passim.* In his *A Planned Economy or Free Enterprise* (London, 1944, chap. 4), Lipson describes the period 1558-1660 in England as one of struggle between the forces of "stability" (institutionalized in the corporate system) and those of progress (represented by the rising manufacturing class, the mercantile class having already been made free of the control of trading companies). The period 1660-1800 is described as one during which "the doctrine of economic freedom" gained increasing hold "over the minds of the governing body." Presumably, the extent to which restrictive statutes were enforced diminished, as attitudes favorable to industrial growth and laissez faire gathered strength. E.g., see M. G. Davies' account of the enforcement of the Statute of 1563, originally intended to check the spread of rural manufactures, in her volume, *The Enforcement of English Apprenticeship: A Study in Applied Mercantilism, 1563-1642,* Cambridge, 1956. See also R. K. Kelsall, *Wage Regulation Under the Statute of Artificers,* London, 1938. In England and France after the sixteenth century, Hoselitz finds ("The Early History of Entrepreneurial Theory," *loc.cit.,* pp. 197-204), the individual thought of as an enterpreneur was one who contracted with the government to carry on its projects.

74. See Heckscher, *Mercantilism,* I, pp. 326-455, II, pp. 273-85; J. C. Riemersma, "Economic Enterprise and Political Powers after the Reformation," *Economic Development and Cultural Change,* III, 1956, pp. 297-308, and "Government Influence on Company Organization in Holland and England (1550-1650)," in *Journal of Economic History,* Supplement, X, 1950, pp. 31-39; D. C. Coleman, "Naval Dockyards Under the Later Stuarts," *Economic History Review,* VI, 1953, pp. 134-55; F. C. Lane, "Force and Enterprise in the Creation of Oceanic Commerce," *ibid.,* pp. 19-31; Potter, ed., *op.cit.,* chaps. 15-16; J. F. Bright, *Maria Theresa,* London, 1897, pp. 74-76; S. K. Padover, *The Revolutionary Emperor,* London, 1934, chaps. 1, 5; K. Pribram, *Geschichte der Oest. Gewerbepolitik 1740-1860,* Vienna, 1907, I; Max Adler, *Die Anfänge der merkantilistischen Gewerbepolitik in Osterreich,* Leipzig, 1903; B. F. Hoselitz, "Patterns of Economic

Among the development-stimulating arrangements established to carry out mercantilist objectives, grants of exclusive privilege to manufacture particular new products, or to carry on commerce in newly opened areas, were often employed. For, despite the persistent objection to the practice of monopoly, so strong in the medieval period, domestic monopolies were granted at times in certain countries, and monopolies in foreign trading became common. During and after the sixteenth century, the regulated company gave way to the joint stock company, with exclusive foreign trading rights, a form largely of private origin in England and Holland, but more commonly of essentially government origin in France. It was felt that the uncertainties and expenses associated with opening up colonial and similar trade were so great that no private individual would undertake its development, and that no capital would be available for such undertakings, unless safeguarded, at least temporarily, by exclusive privilege. At the same time, the state might rest assured that the company would regulate its members and conform to navigation acts and similar protectionist measures. It was felt, furthermore, that the resulting foreign trade would be a source of capital for investment, as well as of increments to the money supply. Even among the mercantilists, however, there was opposition to the extension of exclusive trading and other privileges; and this opposition became stronger in the eighteenth century, after the risks of trade had decreased, after the importance of manufactures and domestic markets had increased, and perhaps because foreign trade was no longer looked upon as the most important source of new capital. It may be that, frequently, exclusive privileges often were granted because of the fiscal and administrative difficulties attendant upon the use of subsidies (but not upon that of tariffs), and because the activities favored were complementary to the home economy and did not immediately entail competition with domestic activities.[75]

Growth," *Canadian Journal of Economics and Political Science*, XXI, 1955, pp. 428-29 and his essay in *Capital Formation and Economic Growth*, M. Abramovitz, ed., Princeton, 1955, pp. 291-337; Cole, *Colbert;* Boissonnade, *Le socialisme d'état* and *Colbert, le triomphe de l'étatisme, la fondation de la suprematie industrielle de la France, la dictature du travail (1661-1683)*, Paris, 1932; Levasseur, *Histoire des classes ouvrières*, II, pp. 195-98, VI, chaps. 2-4; J. U. Nef, *Industry and Government in France and England 1540-1640*, Philadelphia, 1940; Leontief, *op.cit.;* P. I. Lyashchenko, *History of the National Economy of Russia*, New York, 1949, chaps. 16, 18, 24, 26; A. Gerschenkron's account in B. F. Hoselitz, ed., *The Progress of Underdeveloped Areas*, Chicago, 1952, pp. 14-21; N. J. G. Pounds's paper in *The State and Economic Growth*, Hugh Aitken, ed., New York, 1959. It is of interest to note that Joseph the Second of Austria combined physiocratic and mercantilist practices. He abolished serfdom, made industry tax-free, and replaced other taxes with a physiocratic single tax of 30 per cent on the gross income of peasants, out of which came governmental revenue, tithes, and manorial rents (see Padover, *op.cit.*, p. 285). It may be that favoritism of intervention along mercantilist lines persisted longer among administrators than among theoreticians. Cf. P. H. Beik, *A Judgment of the Old Regime*, New York, 1944, pp. 29-30, and pp. 160*ff*., 105*ff*., 183*ff*., 268-76, on the mercantilist views of Parliament of Provence in the 1760's.

75. Privileges, etc., are discussed here and there in Cole's *Colbert*, Heckscher's *Mercantilism*, and Buck's *Politics of Mercantilism*. See also Lipson, *Economic History*, III, pp.

Mercantilists proposed, and mercantilistic administrators were interested in creating, what Buck calls a "rudimentary bureaucracy of economic control" which might perform various functions, and even assume the form of bureaus which approximated modern development corporations more closely than modern boards of trade. These bureaus were designed to give organization and impetus to economic development, especially in the field of trade. Such a proposal was made by various English mercantilists, some of whom also suggested the creation of semi-public bodies (e.g., banks to create and manage credit, etc.; colleges of industry designed to keep the poor at work; courts to develop and administer an adequate body of mercantile law; trading companies; etc.). Among the functions sometimes assigned such a council or bureau of commerce were promotion of trade at home and abroad and removal of obstacles to its conduct; employing the poor; guarding against dearth of subsistence; reduction of interest, fomenting and improving the exploitation of natural resources and fisheries; the conduct of manufactures, etc.[76] While many mercantilists sought needed simplification and improvement of the tax system, apparently, this need was not espoused by bureaus of commerce.

(8) *Miscellaneous matters: science, innovation, technical education, etc.* In every country mercantilists stressed the importance of invention and technological improvements and the need to introduce them speedily

352*ff.*; pp. 284-85 of Davies' paper; and pp. 288-90 of Hinton's "The Mercantile System . . . ," both cited in footnote 13; and, on medieval opinions, De Roover, "Monopoly Theory Prior to Adam Smith: A Revision," *Quarterly Journal of Economics*, LXV, 1951, pp. 492-524. That anti-monopoly opinion was strong as early as 1600 is suggested by John Wheeler's *A Treatise of Commerce* (1601), edited with introduction by G. B. Hotchkiss, New York, 1931. See also D. O. Wagner, "Coke and the Rise of Liberalism," *Economic History Review*, VI, 1935-36, pp. 30-34, and "The Common Law and Free Enterprise: An Early Case of Monopoly," *ibid.*, VII, 1936-37, pp. 217-20. The monopolistic privileges available for extension to particular groups constituted a part of the system of encroachments upon private initiative which reached its peak in the seventeenth century. See Nef, *War and Human Progress*, pp. 212-21, where it is shown that in some countries even the privileged enterpriser was entangled in restrictions and lacking in prestige. For a defense of the possible use of monopoly in the industrialization of an underdeveloped country, of which England and other Northern countries were imperfect examples in the early modern period, however, see G. C. Allen, "A Note on Monopoly and Economic Progress," *Economica*, XX, 1953, pp. 359-61. That grants of monopoly contributed greatly to the development of European empire in the East before 1800, and that they originally stimulated development in the New World, is suggested by E. J. Hamilton's excellent paper, "The Role of Monopoly in the Overseas Expansion and Colonial Trade of Europe Before 1800," *American Economic Review*, XXXVIII, 1948, pp. 39-53. Colonial monopolies constituted a device by which naval and developmental costs of expansion were defrayed, though not necessarily in accordance with accepted canons of taxation, the costs being too high and not properly distributed, and the source of excessive income to the beneficiaries of these monopolies. Moreover, the monopolies were continued for too long a time. That the effects of these monopolies finally became adverse might be demonstrated in detail, as might the adverse effects of domestic monopolies and privileges; this conclusion is suggested by the fact that colonial policy and trade were more successful in the English than in the French or the Spanish colonies.

76. Cole, *Colbert*, I, pp. 357-63, 424, 470; Lipson, III, *Economic History*, pp. 310, 335; Heckscher, *Mercantilism*, I, pp. 84, 152, 213*ff.*, 340-51, II, pp. 326*ff.*; Buck, *Politics of Mercantilism*, pp. 132-42. In Austria, under Maria Theresa, a commercial council was set up.

and effectively into industry. This was particularly true in England and in Holland, whence England drew technological, as well as commercial, aids and practices, especially before the eighteenth century. While the concern of mercantilists, not yet equipped with a "Say's Law," to avert unemployment at times made them oppose the introduction of labor-saving devices when an increase in unemployment was threatened, they were generally favorably disposed to the introduction of such methods. Mercantilist theory, of course, clearly pointed to this conclusion; for, if increase in the supply of labor available for employment was the principal potential source of increase in gross product, then whatever process served to swell this supply was useful and a prospective source of increase in output. Mercantilists thus could endorse and participate in a movement that involved the development of empirical science and its application, not only to the solution of military problems, but also to the solution of mining, transport, and other problems of economic import. The Age of Mercantilism was a period of considerable invention, discovery, and patenting (in England and Western Europe), and it witnessed the development of the temporary patent monopoly (especially in England, after this form of monopoly was distinguished from other forms in 1624) as a device to encourage invention and induce disclosure of new technical discoveries.[77] The resulting improvements in applied technology increased the demand for fixed capital, thus intensifying a capital shortage of which some

77. In England, even after the legislation of 1624, which supposedly approved only patent and trading company monopolies, domestic monopolies continued to develop in the guise of patent monopolies until their revocation in 1639, and the subsequent adoption of a policy less conducive to monopoly. On mercantilism and labor-saving improvements, see Heckscher, *Mercantilism*, II, pp. 126*ff.*; G. N. Clark, *Science and Social Welfare in the Age of Newton*, London, 1949. That the hands displaced by these improvements could be set to doing other needed work was sometimes asserted; for example, by Thomas Pratt (*The History of the Royal Society*, London, 1667, pp. 399-402) and by the author of *Considerations on the East India Trade* (1701) (probably Henry Martin, according to M. Arkin in "A Neglected Forerunner of Adam Smith," *South African Journal of Economics*, XXIII, 1955, pp. 299-314). The latter (see *ibid.*, pp. 579-89, 594-95, of the McCulloch edition, cited in footnote 46, above) comes close to formulating Say's Law in relatively dynamic terms. See also A. P. Wadsworth and Julia De Lacy Mann, *The Cotton Trade and Industrial Lancasshire 1600-1780*, Manchester, 1931, pp. 100*ff.*, 353, 451*ff.* on opposition to machinery, and pp. 417-19 for John Wyatt's careful argument, advanced in 1735, that displaced labor would be re-employed. On the frequency of invention, patents, etc., see P. A. Sorokin, *op.cit.*, II, pp. 150-53, 167-68; R. K. Merton, "Science, Technology and Society in Seventeenth Century England," *Osiris*, IV, 1938, pp. 360-632. According to Dewey Anderson, major industrial inventions numbered 50, 15, 17, 43, and 108 in the fifteenth, sixteenth, seventeenth, eighteenth, and nineteenth centuries, respectively (*Final Report* of the Executive Secretary to the Temporary National Economic Committee on the Concentration of Economic Power in the United States, Washington, 1941, p. 105). On progress in science and on conditions affecting invention, see Merton, *loc.cit.*, pp. 567-97; A. P. Usher, *A History of Mechanical Inventions*, Cambridge, 1954; H. T. Pledge, *Science Since 1500*, London, 1939; A. R. Hall, *The Scientific Revolution 1500-1800;* D. C. Coleman, "Technology and Economic History, 1500-1700," *Economic History Review*, XI, 1959, pp. 506-14. Kings and rulers granted inventors and innovators exclusive rights to "practice their new arts or skills" as early as the fourteenth century. "Probably the first 'patent law' in the sense of a general promise of exclusive rights to inventors, was enacted in 1474 by the Republic of Venice." See Fritz Machlup, *An Economic Review of the Patent System*, Washington, 1958, p. 2.

mercantilists were aware. The practical application of science received continuing stimulus from mercantilist Francis Bacon's endorsement of innovation and gradual change and from his philosophy of utility. Bacon made the test of a thing's goodness its utility, asserted that the art of invention "would procure all other arts," and pointed out that science would not progress satisfactorily unless its practitioners were suitably rewarded.[78] Because the importance of invention was recognized by many English mercantilists (e.g., Grew and Petty), some under the influence of Bacon, by French mercantilists (especially Colbert), and by various others, they looked with favor upon the establishment of academies and schools to promote and diffuse science and its application.[79]

78. See *The Physical And Metaphysical Works of Lord Bacon*, J. Devey, ed., London, 1911, p. 183; the *Novum Organum* (1620), in which Bacon develops his conception of science and its role, and the allegorical *The New Atlantis* (1627), in which the application of science to the problems of a hypothetical society is illustrated. The importance of Bacon's contribution to the replacement of traditional by progressive views, and to the formulation of the scope and role of modern science is stressed by G. K. Chalmers in "Sir Thomas Browne, True Scientist," *Osiris*, II, 1936, pp. 38, 65. On the increasingly utilitarian role of science in and after Bacon's time, see Crombie, *op.cit.*, pp. 387-403 and Merton, *loc.cit.*, pp. 435*ff.* The role of innovation was conceived by Bacon in terms of a quasi-static state; but in England, as well as in Germany, the role underwent reformulation until (e.g., in Postlethwayt's treatment) it had become adapted to the needs of a dynamic society. See F. Redlich, "The Role of Innovation in a Quasi-Static World: Francis Bacon and His Successors," *Explorations in Entrepreneurial History*, VII, 1954, pp. 12-25. In *The Essayes* Bacon included usury, "parsimony," and invention among the sources of individual wealth (cf. "Riches"), and he proposed (cf. "Of Usury") to regulate usury through a dual market system which would enable merchants to borrow at rates in excess of 5 per cent. Britain's "true greatness," he said (*Works*, Spedding, *et al.*, eds., Boston, 1864, XIII, pp. 233, 246-50), consisted in the fitness of her situation and in the quantity and the quality of her population; it did not depend predominantly on her "largeness of territory," her "treasure or riches," and the fruitfulness of her soil. Her wealth could be effectively used because it "resteth in the hands of merchants, burghers, tradesmen, freeholders, farmers in the country, and the like," and not principally in the hands of a small and wasteful nobility. Petty's contemporary, Samuel Hartlib, is remindful of Bacon, in that he did much to publicize improvements in agriculture, banking, etc., and wrote of a Utopia in which fishery, colonies, and emigration, but not industry as such, are stressed (*Macaria*, 1641). M. R. Cohen believes Bacon's contributions have been exaggerated. See "The Myth About Bacon and the Inductive Method," *Scientific Monthly*, XXIII, 1926, pp. 504-508.

79. Johnson (see *Predecessors*, chaps. 12-13, and articles on improvements listed on pp. 387*ff.*) suggests that it was the multiplication of the effectiveness of labor, the principal agent of production, that appealed to the English mercantilists. Subsidies, tariffs, etc., were employed to encourage invention and new industry (Buck, *op.cit.*, pp. 34-37, 80-83, 199-200; Heckscher, *Mercantilism*, I, pp. 172, 265*ff.*, II, pp. 126*ff.*). For a list of technical discoveries, see W. F. Waffenschmidt, *Technik und Wirtschaft*, Jena, 1928, pp. 6-16. There was much less awareness on the continent (exclusive of Holland) than in England of the utility of natural science and technical invention and of its applicability to the increase of man's material welfare. See Nef's paper in *Essays*, Carus-Wilson, ed., pp. 88-107; his "A Comparison of Industrial Growth in France and England from 1540 to 1640," *Journal of Political Economy*, XLIV, 1936, pp. 289*ff.*, 505*ff.*, 643*ff.*, esp. p. 666; and his *War and Human Progress*, chaps. 3, 10-11, also pp. 297*ff.* It was in the north of Europe, above all in England, that heavy industries, adapted to supplying widely consumed goods, began to flourish; French, Italian, and other industry catered to more specialized and artistic demands (*ibid.*, pp. 6-8). The improvements which transformed the British textile industry from one emphasizing luxury goods to one supplying a mass demand for relatively cheap goods reflected both the greater English emphasis on the utilitarian and the practical and the fall in prices in the seventeenth century. See Clark, *Science and Social Welfare*, pp. 55-57, who reports also that technical progress was greatest in industries subject to international competition. Representative of the interest of English writers in "projects," are Defoe, Yarranton, and Petty.

A problem of great concern to mercantilists, as well as to others, was that of creating and maintaining a labor force equipped with the kinds of skill a slowly, but steadily, evolving set of industries required. Efforts to deal with this problem were made both at national and at subnational levels. Much reliance was placed upon attracting skilled immigrants from other countries, a resource limited by legal and other barriers to emigration. Of much greater importance was the transformation of children into sufficiently trained, productive workers of good habits, a transformation long accomplished for many by the apprenticeship system. This system did not normally afford training to all who stood to benefit by it, and it became increasingly unsuitable as tasks lying outside the environs of craft became more numerous, and as the system itself became much more restrictive than facilitative of industrial progress. However, although many of the mercantilists touched upon the inculcation of skills into the labor force, they usually dealt with the subject in the context of prescribing for idleness and unemployment, of setting and keeping children at work as had long been the wont, and, in general, of rendering the poor and the lower orders useful. It was widely accepted, moreover, that workhouses, or similar institutions, were needed to keep employed those who might otherwise be without work (transplantation and more severe remedies were reserved for the more difficult cases). Accordingly, in England, especially after 1650, much attention was given to utilizing such institutions to provide industrial training, together with some schooling, for the children of the poor, and "breed" them "up to work" and the requirements of "virtue." This system proved unsuccessful for various reasons, among them, the failure to provide suitable supervision and a resulting tendency of the work conducted to prove uneconomical and "uneducational." "Charity schools," established to provide the poor with elementary education, were opposed by mercantilists and other writers on the ground that the education provided might make the lower orders dissatisfied with their stations in life and deplete their ranks. From the dilemma involved, that of creating a working class which would be both docile and possessed of adequate and mobilizable technical knowledge, writers in the mercantilist tradition could not escape.[80]

E.g., see E. G. Jacob, *Daniel Defoe's Essay on Projects* (1697), Leipzig, 1929; and Andrew Yarranton, *England's Improvement by Sea and Land* (London, 1677), a book concerned also with setting the poor to work, increasing the supply of money, establishing a land register, improving the transportation system, etc. For a detailed account of the impact of rationalism, science, and invention in France, see James E. King, *Science and Rationalism in the Government of Louis XIV, 1661-1683*, Baltimore, 1949.

80. Perhaps the most interesting treatment of the problem of training the poor and their children is that provided by the Bristol merchant, John Cary, who believed that low wages gave rise to beggary and who described and sought to generalize the experience of Bristol. See *A Discourse on Trade*, London, 1745 (published initially without appendices, etc., in 1695 as *An Essay on the State of England*, etc.), esp. pp. 98-104, 107*ff*., 114-19, 124, 137, 147*ff*., 164-65. While a good diet is described as essential to health, health is not specifically described as a source of increased productivity (pp. 159-60). Colonies

Conclusion

This conclusion is intended to serve three purposes: (1) to contrast the mercantilist countries with present-day underdeveloped countries; (2) to delineate the mercantilist theory of growth; (3) to touch upon the weaknesses in this theory, together with some of the origins of these weaknesses. No attempt will be made, however, to assess the adverse effects of mercantilist policy, since such attempt would entail a detailed historico-economic analysis of the impact of mercantilist policies and, in many instances, a more careful specification of the conditions giving rise to effects than may be derived from the data available. This much may be said, however: it was not so much state intervention, or even unfortunate state intervention, that produced the worst effects. Rather, it was circumstances such as the following: the excessive continuation of policies (e.g., protectionist arrangements), whether initially defensible or not; measures that froze particular sets of conditions, and prevented essential adjustments to exogenous and other change; undue circumscription of decision-making on the part of creative entrepreneurs; the destructiveness of military activities, the frequent occurrence of which was somewhat connected with the mercantilist ethos.[81]

(1) The countries in which mercantilism flourished resemble present-day underdeveloped countries in some respects, and differ from them in others.[82] England and Western Europe were better equipped with resources

---

are described as an outlet for surplus labor (pp. 48, 111-12). See also Matthew Hale, *Discourse Touching Provision for the Poor* (1683); and chap. 2 of Josiah Child's *New Discourse of Trade*, discussed in the Appendix; also Mandeville, *op.cit.*, Kaye, ed., I, pp. 253*ff.*, on charity schools. Yarranton (*op.cit.*, Part I, p. 47, Part II, chaps. 8-9) pointed to the example of German industrial schools which taught young girls to spin. On Jonathan Swift's satire on political arithmetic, and on the tendency of his contemporaries "to regard people as commodities," see G. Wittowsky, "Swift's Modest Proposal: The Biography of an Early Georgian Pamphlet," *Journal of the History of Ideas*, IV, 1943, pp. 75-104. On the problems of educating the poor, setting the unemployed to work, etc., see Sidney and Beatrice Webb, *English Local Government: English Poor Law History: Part I. The Old Poor Law*, London, 1927, esp. chaps. 2-4; M. G. Jones, *The Charity School Movement*, Cambridge, 1938, pp. 85-96, 110-34; Heckscher, *Mercantilism*, II, pp. 154-57, 162, 166*ff.*, 184, 187*ff.*, 233, 258, 298, 323; Furniss, *The Position of the Laborer*, pp. 147-50; Lipson, *Economic History*, II, pp. 62, 167, 181*ff.*, III, 11, 56-61, 159-67, 279*ff.*, 375, 416-17, 425, 430-31, 435-39, 467-84; Cole, *Colbert*, II, pp. 472*ff.*; M. G. Davies, *op.cit.*; Kelsall, *op.cit.*, chaps. 3, 6. By the eighteenth century, enclosure was contributing effectively to the formation of a wage-earning class, through its displacement of workers from the land and denial to them of supplementary sources of income (e.g., use of waste or unoccupied land). Hence, vitality was lost by the system of wage regulation that had been generalized under the Statute of Artificers to prevent the bidding up of wages and the accentuation of local labor shortages. See *ibid.*, pp. 100-107.

81. See Quincy Wright, *A Study of War*, Chicago, 1942, I, chap. 9; and, on the adverse effects of "planning," H. M. Robertson's instructive "Panaceas, Past and Present . . . ," *South African Journal of Economics*, XII, 1944, pp. 251-62.

82. Attempts at comparison are handicapped by the fact that while we have considerable information on England in the late seventeenth and the eighteenth centuries, by then in the vanguard along with Holland, we have much less on backward areas, such as Prussia and Austria, or even on areas

per head than are many present-day underdeveloped countries, especially the crowded ones. The man-land ratio was more favorable, population was growing much more slowly, and savings formed as large a percentage of national income as it does today in some backward countries.[83] International lending was less important then than it is today, however, and there was less international transfer of scientific findings and skill, in part because some of the countries of Western Europe were primarily responsible for advances in technology, whereas at present underdeveloped countries may borrow heavily from technologically advanced countries. Then, perhaps even more than there is today in underdeveloped countries, there was a great deal of unemployment and underemployment, together with less organization on the part of workers; and there was much emphasis on setting the unemployed to work, whereas today the emphasis is upon utilizing unemployed labor to create capital. However, at that time the obstacles to the modernization of the labor force were much greater: Transport, together with communication, was much less satisfactory, and geographical mobility was lower; social mobility was lower, for societies were more stratified, and the ruling classes approved this stratification and opposed provision of as much education as was required, lest the ranks of the lower orders be unduly depleted; the aspiration levels of the working classes were low, even by the then prevailing standards, and relatively static; educational facilities were very inadequate, and their essentiality to economic progress was not as well appreciated. Economically unfavorable joint family farms, of the type found in many present-day underdeveloped countries, were not common in Western Europe, however, in the Age of Mercantilism. The occupational structure of European countries varied greatly; in countries like England and Holland there were comparatively fewer agriculturalists than there are in some present-day underdeveloped countries, but in the more backward European countries the relative number was comparably large. Only after detailed study would comparison of the role of external trade then and now be practicable; it is clear, however, that international transfer relations are much better in many underdeveloped countries today, and that trade plays a more important role presently than it did in England in 1688, at which time the value of exports approximated 10 per cent of

that did not lag so far behind England. Phyllis Deane presents a great deal of quantitative information for England in her papers cited in footnotes 45 and 51, above. S. Kuznets presents quantitative data on present-day developed and underdeveloped countries in "Quantitative Aspects of the Economic Growth of Nations," Parts I and II of which appeared as supplements to *Economic Development and Cultural Change,* V, 1956-57.

83. G. King's figures suggest a rate of 4-5 per cent for England in 1688. The per capita figures given by King suggest rates of about 11 per cent for Holland, about 6 for France, and about 4 for England, at a time when per capita income in England was slightly (about 2 per cent), and in France was appreciably (about 24 per cent), below the Dutch level. See Deane, "The Implications . . . ," *loc.cit.,* pp. 9, 12. See also B. F. Hoselitz, "Population Pressure, Industrialization and Social Mobility," *Population Studies,* XI, 1957, pp. 124-27.

national income, but with manufactures completely dominating the exports and primary products completely dominating the imports. In our contemporary society far more importance is attached to health and diet, and far more can be done to realize improvements in these areas, even in the face of very low incomes. Currently, underdeveloped countries can draw on much more advanced technologies and on a much better developed body of economic (i.e., tax, fiscal, monetary, etc.) and social theory and tools than could countries in the Age of Mercantilism. Furthermore, the state's role with respect to creation of a satisfactory politico-economic environment and provision of economic and social overhead capital is better understood and, as a rule, better carried out, though at times at the cost of reducing the rate at which more productive capital is formed.

(2) Any attempt to reduce the growth-oriented theories and proposals of writers representative of the Age of Mercantilism to terms of an elementary theory of economic development would entail what Roger Bacon called "forced harmonization." It has even been argued that "the highest common factor" in the concepts and policies summarized by Heckscher is "a belief in official intervention as a corrective to evils," and that detailed researches are not likely to yield conclusions compatible "with the canons of an imaginary system conceived by economists for purposes of theoretical exposition."[84] There is much sense in this observation; and yet, there is considerable overlap in time and space between what was thought or recommended in one country and what was conceived or proposed in another, especially if allowance is made for the fact that political power was much more concentrated in some countries than in others, and that the evils to be corrected, whether real or imagined, were particular as to time and place. The over-riding objective of the mercantilists, insofar as development theory is concerned, was acceleration of the rate of growth of aggregate, rather than average, output. This objective was to be realized immediately through full, skillful, and efficient use of the available factors of production (particularly labor), and ultimately through augmentation of the stock of these factors and the technological and economic skill with which they were used. Because this twin objective supposedly would not be realized under conditions of unrestricted free enterprise, it was deemed necessary for the state to intervene, both directly and indirectly, through the establishment of particular conditions designed to remove particular evils or to strengthen particular situations, and through the creation of general conditions (such as satisfactory money, banking, tax, legal, and transport facilities,) conducive to economic development. Because foreign trade and manufacturing sectors were considered strategic, in that supposedly favorable developments therein would give rise to favorable de-

84. See A. V. Hodges, "The Idea of a Mercantile State," *loc.cit.*, pp. 64, 67-68.

velopments in agricultural and other less strategic or more dependent sectors, mercantilists directed most of their attention to fostering manufacturing and commercial activities, with the state both assisting undertakers and performing divers entrepreneurial functions.

(3) Many of the weaknesses of mercantilist growth theory were of a sort common to every branch of economic theory in its earlier stages, namely, the failure to define concepts (e.g., economic productivity, capital, interest, money) with precision; or to describe specifically processes or stages (e.g., saving, investment, division of labor and increasing returns, behavior of costs); or to indicate the nature of supposedly important functional connections (e.g., between population growth and its determinants, between increments of population [or labor] and increments of output, etc.).

Perhaps the outstanding weakness of mercantilist theory was its neglect of the alternate use-value of money and productive factors, a neglect that had its origin partly in the assumption that there existed a great deal of unemployment and underemployment of labor. This neglect was manifested in much of the defense of protectionism, and probably accounted for the mercantilists' disregard of the law of comparative advantage. The assumption of unemployment must have given considerable support to protectionism and the belief that manufacturing would develop as it might only if private enterprise had assistance from the state, for the protectionist argument rested upon the assumption that protectionism would increase the demand for labor, and probably increase the supply of complements to domestic labor, by stimulating capital formation and the inflow of immigrants possessing skills in short supply. The protectionist argument was weakened by its failure to emphasize explicitly either the infant-industry principle or the infant-stage-of-development principle, though one might make a case for the proposition that many writers had acceleration of development in mind.

Almost as important as the mercantilists' neglect of opportunity cost were the shortcomings in their treatment of the response of employment to increases in the stock of money. They tended to disregard the immobilities and bottlenecks characteristic of all economies in the Age of Mercantilism. This disregard, together with their seeming supposition that increases in money would attract resources from ouside an economy, must have been responsible in large part for the persistence of so many in overlooking the antinomy between the balance of trade theory and the quantity theory, the essence of which was recognized quite early.

Closely associated with the imperfections in their treatment of the impact of money on prices and factor-use were the shortcomings in their analyses of the aggregate demand for labor and their disposition to underestimate the role of domestic consumption and the part played therein by working-class consumption. These defects probably had their origin in part in the fact that many mercantilists overemphasized a particular "investment" component of aggregate demand while underestimating other investment components, together with "consumption." For, so long as the balance of trade theory held sway, the mercantilists wrote as if the demand for specie were perfectly elastic, with the result that all increments in productive power and income, beyond what was needed to supply the basic requirements of the state and its population, became, or might become, increments in demand for a unique category of investment goods, namely, specie.[85]

The "export of work" thesis might have been transformed into a factoral-proportion analysis of international trade, along the lines later followed by Ohlin, together with an inquiry into the effect of trade upon factor movements and of factor immobility upon trade. This thesis was associated, however, with the assumption of unemployment, and it was utilized principally to describe a policy designed to increase population and aggregate (rather than average) output, with the result that the relationship between resource-structure, factor-price structure, and trade were passed over. Had average output been emphasized, these relationships might have been examined.

While the mercantilist interest theory had the merit of recognizing the role of money, it exaggerated this role and underestimated the role of "real" factors; thus, it accentuated the inflationary impact of other of their views regarding the role of money, especially paper money, in economic development.

II

The Physiocrats[86]

The approach of the physiocrats to the problem of economic growth may be described, much as may Book III of Smith's *Wealth of Nations*, as representing a reaction to the approach and theory of the mercantilists. Whereas the mercantilists had looked upon the nonagricultural sector as

85. It is of interest, in this connection, to note J. Rueff's argument (see "The Fallacies of Lord Keynes's General Theory," *Quarterly Journal of Economics*, LXI, 1947, pp. 343-67, esp. pp. 346-47) that Keynes was guilty of a similar error.

86. My discussion is based principally upon the physiocratic publications included in E. Daire, ed., *Physiocrates*, Paris, 1846; upon A. Oncken, ed., *Oeuvres, économiques et philosophiques de F. Quesnay*, Paris, 1888; and upon the following works: Carl Friedrich, Margrave of Baden, *Abrégé des principes de l'économie politique* (Carlsruhe), Paris, 1772 (also included in Daire, *op.cit.*, and there attributed in part to Dupont); Marquis of Mirabeau, *Philosophie rurale*, Paris, 1763, and *Les Économiques*, Paris, 1769; and various issues of the *Ephémérides du citoyen*, 1767-1772. In addition to my

being most strategic, and the sector potentially most responsive to developmental stimuli of governmental origin, the physiocrats found the agricultural sector to be the most strategic, and a regime of competition to be the one whereunder this sector would be most likely to flourish. They supposed that the nonagricultural sectors of an agrarian economy would grow at an optimal rate and in sympathy with, and in response to, the growth of the agricultural sector, so long as there was an absence of governmental intervention, of special privilege and monopoly, and of other interferences with the competitive process. The physiocrats agreed with the mercantilists, however, in supposing that most men were prone to do what gave promise of being to their private advantage; hence they too stressed the importance of self-interest as a motivating factor. I shall treat the writings of the physiocrats as if they were homogeneous in content; for, although some of Quesnay's disciples (other than Mirabeau) differed with him in respect to methodological and related issues, these differences did not make for heterogeneity of treatment of the issues and theories under consideration herein.

The over-riding concern of the physiocrats was the establishment of economic and political conditions which would make for the full realization of France's agricultural, and hence her nonagricultural, potential. In Ques-

French Predecessors, a paper by Neill (cited in footnote 5) and Weulersse's works (cited in footnote 3), A. I. Bloomfield, "Foreign Trade Doctrines of the Physiocrats," *American Economic Review,* XXVIII, 1938, pp. 716-35; H. Woog, *The Tableau Économique of François Quesnay,* Bern, 1950; A. Labrouquère, *Les idées coloniales des physiocrates,* Paris, 1927; M. Einaudi, *The Physiocratic Doctrine of Judicial Control,* Cambridge, 1938; and my "The Physiocrats and Say's Law of Markets," *Journal of Political Economy,* LIII, 1945, pp. 193*ff.*, 317*ff.* A new edition of Quesnay's works, under the editorship of A. Sauvy, has been published in Paris in 1958. Marx was the first outstanding economist to appreciate the contributions of the physiocrats, above all their treatment of capital, of net product (which resembles surplus value), and of circular flow. E.g., see *Capital* (Kerr edition), I, pp. 182, 213, 351*ff.*, 559, 647*ff.*, II, pp. 149, 215-44, 414*ff.*, III, pp. 910*ff.*; and *Theories of Surplus Value,* pp. 44-104. I have not included Turgot among the physiocrats because he subscribed only to some of their views; his treatment of capital and its function was more advanced than theirs. I have based my discussion entirely on French literature (even the *Abrégé* of the Margrave of Baden is but a précis of French publications), since no significant additions to physiocratic theory seem to have been made outside France, even though physiocratic ideas became current in England, Germany, Poland, and other continental countries, and the physiocratic approach to taxation exercised considerable influence. On the physiocratic theory of taxation, see Mann, *op.cit.*, esp. chap. 12; Georg Hambloch, *Der physiokratische Lehre von Reinertrag und Einheitssteuer,* Bonn, 1905. For illustrations of physiocratic influence outside France, see, besides the writings of the Margrave of Baden, J. B. Marchlewski, *Der Physiokratismus in Polen,* Zurich, 1897; R. L. Meek, "Physiocracy and the Early Theories of Under-Consumption," *Economica,* XVIII, 1951, pp. 229-69, and "Physiocracy and Classicism in Great Britain," *Economic Journal,* LXI, 1951, pp. 26-47; my "The Physiocrats . . . ," *loc.cit.;* and Joseph Dorfman, *The Economic Mind in American Civilization,* New York, 1946, I-II, *passim.* Elsewhere (see my paper in D. K. Jackson, ed., *American Studies in Honor of William Kenneth Boyd,* Durham, N. C., 1940, pp. 8-9) I have indicated that, contrary to some opinion, Thomas Jefferson did not adopt physiocratic views. It is of interest that Alexis de Tocqueville attributes to the physiocrats an *étatistic* philosophy that makes the impersonal "State" all powerful. See his *The Old Regime and the French Revolution,* New York, 1955, Part 3, chap. 3. I follow, in the text, Baudeau's terminology and classification of expenditures; his treatment is clearer than Quesnay's, particularly as found in Quesnay's earlier writings.

nay's opinion, French agriculture was depressed, its decline having been accompanied by a decline in population, from 24 million in 1660 to 16 in 1760. French agriculture had been deprived of both necessary capital and an adequate market for produce by the industry-favoring policies identified with the name of Colbert. It was subject, therefore, to increasing return to capital inputs, which made possible the use of more efficient technological methods, instruments, and scales of production. The physiocrats recognized, however, that eventually, because of the presence of physical constraints (e.g., scarcity of land), agricultural output could no longer be made to expand even as rapidly as investment in agriculture; but they did not elaborate this inference, nor did they take account of it in their models (or tableaux). Quesnay utilized his *Tableau Economique* to isolate and/or to illustrate the conditions requisite for agricultural and general economic development in an agrarian economy with a large agricultural base; and he based on this table many of his maxims of economic government, compliance with which would bring about economic development. His abbreviated table has been translated into terms of a simple Leontief model by A. Phillips; this model, reproduced as Table I below, is used for the sake of expositive convenience.[87]

Table 1

Transactions Table for the Tableau Economique (Value of Real Goods in Milliards)

Producing Industry	Purchasing Industry I Farmers	II Proprietors	III Artisans	Total Production
I Farmers	2	1	2	5
II Proprietors	2	0	0	2
III Artisans	1	1	0	2
Total Purchases	5	2	2	9

From Table 1 it is evident that the population is divisible into three classes: productive, sterile, and proprietary. The *productive* class includes land-renting farmers and other persons engaged in agriculture, fishing, and (according to some) mining; this class, which comprises about one-half of the population, is so described because it alone is capable of producing a *net product*. The *sterile* class includes manufacturers, artisans, distributors of commodities, artists, and members of the liberal professions, together with their servants, and forms about one-fourth of the population. The

87. A. Phillips, "The Tableau Économique as a Simple Leontief Model," *Quarterly Journal of Economics,* LXIX, 1955, pp. 137-44, Table II. This is the model Baudeau and (usually) Quesnay used. Even though the dimensions were modified, the principles emphasized would remain the same. On France's population, see P. E. Vincent, "French Demography in the Eighteenth Century," *Population Studies,* I, 1947, pp. 44-71.

proprietary class includes landed proprietors and others paid or supported immediately out of proprietary revenue (i.e., religious personnel and the sovereign, together with administrative, military, and other personnel directly or indirectly in the service of state or church), and makes up about one-fourth of the population. It is also evident that the farmers (the principal entrepreneurs in Quesnay's economy) are responsible for the production of 5 of the 9 milliards of (essentially) Gross National Product, and the *sterile* class (labeled artisans in the table) for 2. It is inferred that those included in the proprietary class also contribute 2 milliards, since they receive 2 milliards for their own consumption from the productive and the sterile classes (in exchange for 2 milliards of money rent [i.e., net product], originally contributed by the productive class in exchange for use of the land which is owned by the proprietary class); supposedly they are duty-bound to provide various services which, however, were not given a quantitative value (as in our model) by the physiocrats. The role of the land-owners was particularly important with respect to agriculture; they were not thought of as absentee owners (since absenteeism was not desirable), but as owners whose continuing investment, counsel, etc., operated to increase the gross and the net productivity of their lands. Not all of the gross product is accounted for in abbreviated tables of the sort on which our Table 1 is based; thus, from his abbreviated *Tableau,* Quesnay omitted 1.37 milliards of produce that was utilized to feed work animals and meet "expenses of commerce."

The distribution of the annual output of goods and services proceeded as follows: The farmers produce 5 milliards (hereinafter sometimes called reproduction), which they dispose of in this way: 2 milliards to the proprietary class in the form of rent, and which, when competition is effective, approximates the net product in value; 2 milliards retained as annual advances (i.e., subsistence, and other forms of working capital); and 1 milliard transferred to the sterile class in exchange for 1 milliard of its products, and representing a kind of replacement and insurance return on primitive advances, described below. The proprietary class exchanges its rental income for 1 milliard of agricultural produce and 1 milliard of the products of the sterile class. The sterile class obtains from the productive class 2 milliards of produce, of which it consumes 1; the other is worked up into services and wrought goods with a value of 3 milliards, of which 1 is returned to the productive class, 1 is sold to the proprietary class, and 1 is consumed by the sterile class. Aggregate consumption is thus envisioned as follows: the productive class, 2 milliards of produce and 1 milliard of the products of the sterile class; the proprietary class, 1 milliard of produce and 1 milliard of the products of the sterile class; the sterile class, 1 milliard of produce and 1 milliard of the products of the sterile class; the fifth milliard of produce has been transformed into wrought goods by the sterile class and is consumed in that form, as indicated; the 2 milliards of services supposedly supplied by the proprietary class may be said to have been consumed by the three classes, considered as a whole.

The productive equipment and inputs employed by each of the three classes may be described as follows: The equipment of the sterile class is not specifically identified by Quesnay and his followers; it is merely supposed that the 2 milliards received annually by this class suffice to support it and to sustain its equipment, but do not bring into being a net product (or surplus) out of which growth may be financed. The sterile class, together with its equipment, expands in response to increases in annual reproduction and net product. This class, it is implied, utilizes little or no fixed capital; it merely uses up working capital which is replaced in the course of the current production period (as is outlay for the support of its members and their dependents), out of the proceeds of the sale of its goods and services. As Turgot suggested, the advances of this class, therefore, resemble closely the *avances annuelles* which are also replaced during the current period of production. Since the land is owned by the proprietors, they are responsible for the maintenance of the *avances foncières,* which consist of investments made in the past by present and previous owners, to prepare the land for cultivation (e.g., clearing, leveling, drainage, plantations, hedges, buildings), and which require attention and supplementation from year to year. Baudeau fixed at one-third of the proprietors's net product (i.e., at 0.67 milliards in our model) the annual amount that ought to be devoted to the maintenance, renewal, and amelioration of the *avances foncières;* these advances do not, however, appear in the table. Social and economic overhead capital (e.g., highways, canals, rivers, bridges, ports, etc.)—designated as *avances souveraines* by Baudeau—is also provided (ultimately) out of the sovereign's share. The productive class is responsible for (a) *avances annuelles,* or working capital (i.e., outlays for the preparation of the soil, for seed, planting, cultivation, and harvesting, for the shelter and subsistence of domestic animals [not otherwise provided], and for the support of those engaged in agriculture), amounting to 2 milliards, and (b) *avances primitives,* or fixed capital (maintenance of durable instruments of production in agriculture—tools, machinery, cattle, work animals, etc.), amounting to 1 milliard per year and representing (essentially) a 10 per cent replacement return on the aggregate stock of *avances primitives.*

Maintenance of agricultural reproduction at the level of 5, and hence of gross national product at a level of 9 (as in our model), presupposes three ratios: reproduction to annual advances, 5:2; reproduction to yearly primitive advances, 5:1; reproduction to annual investment in *avances foncières,* something like 5:0.67. Maintenance of reproduction at this level, therefore, further presupposes that annual advances will amount to 2, primitive advances to 1, and *avances foncières* to something like 0.67, since each of these forms of advance conditions the response of output to the others. Usually, however, the physiocratic argument is presented in terms of annual advances, the other advances being taken for granted, and it is assumed that reproduction exceeds, approximates, or falls short of 5, accordingly, as annual advances exceed, approximate, or fall short of 2.

In our model a self-sustaining circular flow persists so long as annual advances approximate 2 milliards, given the stipulated amounts of *avances primitives* and *avances foncières*. Should annual advances fall short of 2, reproduction would diminish, and the economy would contract. If growth be desired, the rate of annual advances must be increased above 2, possibly even at the cost of a short-run contraction in outlays upon the products of the sterile class. In the longer run, however, the resultant increase in reproduction would be succeeded by an increase in both the net product, representing the income of the proprietary class, and in the outlay made upon products of the sterile class by members of the productive and the proprietary classes. Whether the precise proportions postulated in Quesnay's model would continue to hold, depends on what rates of return and what functional connections would obtain. It was recognized that there was a limit to the growth of an economy, since there was a limit to the degree to which gross and net agricultural output could be increased. When the limit was reached, the best that could be hoped for was continuance of the maximum circular flow compatible with this limit. Quesnay's abbreviated table may be interpreted as describing the circular flow at this limit and as supposing average output to be at the attainable maximum under given technological conditions.

Thus, in physiocratic theory, the growth of the entire economy is governed by the progress of annual reproduction, and this in turn is governed by the rates at which advances are made. In a sense, then, the agricultural surplus is the dynamic, growth-generating factor, to which other branches of the economy accommodate themselves. In mercantilist theory, by contrast, the agricultural surplus is at most a limiting factor that sets bounds to the extent to which a dynamic commerce and manufacture could expand the economy, though these bounds might well be extended under the stimuli of increased demand and the technological and related improvements that accompanied the expansion of commerce and manufacture.

Usually, a state of constant returns is supposed in the abbreviated expositive tables (or models) used by the physiocrats, with a unit of annual advances giving rise to 2.5 units of reproduction. However, it was possible for the physiocrats to accept a contention, such as that of

Turgot (who was not a physiocrat), that the ratio of reproduction to annual advances might rise; remain constant, as in the models; or even eventually decline, until the marginal yield of the annual advances just approximated the incremental outlay in the form of annual advances. It was recognized, of course, but it was not always made clear, that the response of output to increments of working capital was conditioned by past and current investment in various forms of fixed capital. It was usually assumed, in the models used, that *"grande,"* or *"bonne,"* *"culture"* (i.e., large-scale, relatively capital-intense, and technologically-advanced agriculture) was being practiced; and the physiocrats' supposition of increasing return in agriculture rested largely on this assumption. The substitution of *"grande culture"* for inefficient *"petite culture,"* it was assumed, would eventually be accompanied by increasing returns to capital, with both reproduction and net product increasing faster than advances, as long as physical constraints–above all, scarcity of land–did not become operative.

Continuation of economic growth presupposed continuation of expenditure on agricultural products at an adequately increasing rate, and this in turn presupposed the existence of a set of economic and political conditions that permitted, or were conducive to, such adequacy of expenditure. Suppose, for example, that the proprietary class diminished its expenditure with the productive class by 3/6 of a milliard, and simultaneously increased its expenditure with the sterile class by the same amount. Then, apart from any lags in expenditure, net outlays upon agricultural products would be reduced by 2/6 milliard, since produce constituted only one-third of the value of the products of the sterile class. Given a converse shift of expenditure, outlay upon agricultural products would increase by 2/6 milliard. If all of this 2/6 were employed as annual advances, annual reproduction in the succeeding year would decrease (increase), in this example, by about 2.5 times 2/6, or 0.83 milliard. The immediate problem thus became one of preventing diminutions and of occasioning increases in expenditure with the productive class. If a diminution ensued, less efficient methods of cultivation would replace more efficient methods, and the economy would undergo contraction; if an increase ensued, the economy would expand. On the whole, however, these magnitudes were illustrative of the French situation, since the underlying theory was considered generally applicable to large economies; other magnitudes might be encountered in other, different situations.

Physiocratic theory suggests that it is upon capital formation, more than upon anything else, that economic development depends, although the importance of applied science and technological improvements is recognized, as is the importance of good institutions. Such improvements presumably follow in the wake of increasing investment. However, it was only in agriculture that capital and applied science had important roles to play. Certainly, their roles in other sectors of the economy were not described as important, nor was the availability of a goodly supply of wrought goods and services said to be essential, in that men are motivated to work by the prospect of being able to purchase such goods and services. While the physiocrats were in agreement in their stress on the paramount role of capital in agriculture, and in their view of the net product as the source of public and private capital, they failed to appreciate fully the function of either capital or the entrepreneur in the economy as a whole. Several physiocrats, particularly Quesnay and Mirabeau, apprehensive lest competition prove inadequate, and current fiscal and banking practices push the interest rate above its natural level (i.e., the return on investment in agriculture) and thus diminish the flow of capital into agriculture, favored setting a legal limit to the rate of interest that might be charged. But the younger physiocrats, confident of the efficacy of competition, even in the monetary realm, did not endorse this view. It remained for Turgot, essentially a non-physiocrat, as mentioned earlier, to clarify some of the issues involved.[88]

Quesnay and his followers called attention to conditions that served to increase or decrease annual reproduction and gross national product. (a) As has been noted, any increase in the rate of investment in advances, above all in the annual advances, served to increase reproduction and total output. (b) Price changes which were compatible with competition might increase annual reproduction and total output. An increase in the prices of farm products, whether because of improvement in their quality or for other reasons, would have this effect. So might a price increase consequent on the introduction of freedom of trade in agricultural products, since it would improve the terms of trade and might decrease the real tax burden. Contraction of the economy might also be brought about in various ways. (a) Contraction would ensue if the tax burden should increase beyond a certain level. This might occur because taxes were too high, or because their collection was too expensive, as tended to be the case when taxes were not collected immediately out of the net product, whence they ulti-

---

88. See his *Réflexions sur la Formation et la Distribution des Richesses* (1766). Cf. selections from Dupont, Le Trosne, etc., in Daire, ed., *Physiocrates*, e.g., pp. 343*ff*., 375-77, 664*ff*., 928*ff*. Le Trosne (*ibid*., pp. 928*ff*.) observed that at any given time there existed a fund of wealth, the result of past accumulation; it had issued out of past annual reproduction, but was independent of current annual reproduction. He did not, however, specify the conditions of the fund's maintenance, presumably because he supposed that it would normally be added to every year out of net product. Hoselitz contrasts the entrepreneurial role, as envisaged by the physiocrats in their agrarian capitalism, with that formulated by later writers ("The Early History . . . ," *loc.cit*., pp. 206*ff*.). For a detailed account of the Physiocratic view of profit, see R. L. Meek, "The Physiocratic Concept of Profit," *Economica*, XXVI, 1959, pp. 39-53.

mately came under all circumstances (since wages and salaries merely sufficed to defray the living and related costs of a worker and his dependents, and since the prices of nonagricultural goods and services merely covered their labor and material costs). The share of the sovereign ought not to exceed something like one-third of the net product; or the combined share of the sovereign and the tithe-owners ought not to exceed three-sevenths of the net revenue. When the sovereign's share was excessive, and the proprietors' share descended below something like four-sevenths, annual advances and/or *avances foncières* tended to decline, and therewith annual reproduction. (b) The flow of money abroad as a result of an unfavorable balance of trade, or its diversion into hoards and into circuits not connected with reproduction, also tended to reduce economic activity. (c) A switching of expenditure from *luxe de subsistance* (i.e., farm produce) to *luxe de décoration* (i.e., wrought goods, etc., turned out by the sterile class) also operated to contract an economy; a diversion in the opposite direction resulted in expansion, as long as the limits of agricultural production had not yet been reached.[89]

The physiocrats, besides assigning a very important role to capital and its formation and making agricultural expansion the source, rather than the consequence, of growth elsewhere in the economy, interpreted differently from the mercantilists a number of conditions affecting economic growth:

(1) As has been indicated, they placed major stress upon the internal market for products, looking with favor upon the increase of per capita real income, the growth of which, they recognized, might be checked by undue population growth (which responded to changes in economic conditions, though with some variability).

(2) As critics of monopoly in its various forms, they found in a competitive regime the system that would give rise to the best set of prices, including suitable prices for agricultural products, and that would conciliate the diverse economic interests of individuals and groups.

(3) While they noted the importance (as did the mercantilists) of noninterruption by hoarders and others of the circular flow of money through the economy, they rejected mercantilist emphasis on the importance of specie and on the necessity of continually increasing the quantity of money; for they viewed money as a means of exchange, as pecuniary rather than real wealth, and they adhered to a primitive form of the quan-

89. On luxury, see N. Baudeau, *Principes de la science morale et politique sur le luxe et les lois somptuaires* (1767), A. Dubois, ed., Paris, 1912; my "Richard Cantillon . . . ," *loc.cit.*, pp. 290-92; K. Landauer, *Die Theorien der Merkantilisten und der Physiokraten über die oekonomische Bedeutung des Luxus*, Munich, 1915. Many unabbreviated models, designed to show expansive and contractile effects, are presented in Mirabeau's *Philosophie rurale*, Amsterdam, 1763, and in his *L'Ami des hommes*, Hamburg, 1760, Part VII.

tity theory. They differed regarding how much money was needed, some putting it at 25 and others at as much as 100 per cent of the net product. So long as this amount was available, a country's supply was adequate, particularly if the country was wealthy, and credit could fulfill some of the functions formerly performed by specie.

(4) The physiocrats did not attach much importance to external economic relations when a country was large and essentially self-contained (as was France, in contradistinction to small, nonagrarian, trading states); they regarded trade as sterile, though promotive of increases in utility. Nonetheless, under existing conditions, and given the supposedly depressed state of demand for French produce, they favored external, as well as internal, freedom of trade, and, above all, unrestricted freedom to export grain, since such exportation would stimulate French agriculture and economic growth generally. They looked with disfavor upon efforts to maintain a favorable balance of trade; for they believed that such efforts were likely to fail, since purchases usually tended to approximate sales in money value, and since specie movements might affect comparative prices, and they feared that real wealth might be exchanged for that which was less important at the time, namely, specie. In keeping with these views, they did not, as did the mercantilists, attach great importance to a colonial empire and to protected colonial markets. (Of course, France had lost much of its colonial empire by the time the physiocratic school had attained its zenith.)

(5) The physiocrats rejected the populationist tenets and objectives of the mercantilists; they believed, as did some of their contemporaries, that the tendency of any population to grow was powerful, with numbers usually tending to keep pace with agricultural output, and sometimes growing even faster. Hence, although Quesnay noted that colonies might serve as outlets for excessive population, he and his followers recommended the increase of agricultural output and net product, and not the increase of numbers, as the proper objective.

(6) Whereas, in the writings of both the physiocrats and the mercantilists, there is considerable emphasis on the role of technology, the physiocrats devoted their attention primarily to the introduction and diffusion of improved methods of agricultural production and the establishment of conditions conducive thereto (e.g., long-term leases that gave tenant-farmers greater incentive).[90] Because they subscribed to the principle that input per unit of output should be minimized, the physiocrats were ready to approve any and all input-economizing inventions, improvements, etc.

90. E.g., see Weulersse, *Le mouvement physiocratique*, I, pp. 80-82, also pp. 374-78, and II, pp. 151-203, on the many measures advocated and/or taken to improve agricultural methods. It was supposed that the force of competition and the desire for gain pressed agricultural entrepreneurs to introduce better methods, when available.

(7) The physiocrats postulated a much stronger tendency on the part of individual and collective interests to harmonize than did the mercantilists.

While the physiocrats assigned only a minor economic role to the state, believing in the efficacy and welfare-producing power of private enterprise and free and untrammeled competition, they supposed that an economy could progress only if its positive laws, as expressed by the sovereign, paralleled the underlying natural order and the natural laws to which the behavior of men everywhere must conform if their societies were to flourish. The physiocrats stressed, not a possible contrast between state and society, but the dangers consequent upon a lack of harmony between the positive laws of a society and the underlying natural order. Among the economic institutions and practices required by this natural order were respect for private property, together with its security; freedom to buy and sell, to produce what seemed profitable, to import and export, to initiate or withdraw from trade and industry, to choose one's occupation, etc.; a system of taxation under which taxes were made immediately incident upon the net product, were collected economically, in moderate amount, and in a manner that did not interrupt the circular flow of money, goods, and services. In sum, while the physiocrats assigned a more important role (than did the classical school) to the state regarding the legal expression to be given the underlying natural order, their political philosophy resembled that of the classical school in that it was liberal with respect to economic matters.[91] Above all, perhaps, they stressed the importance of capital and its formation, of private enterprise, and of the impelling power of self-interest; and they gave attention to growth per capita, as well as to growth in the aggregate.

91. The classical economists rejected the physiocratic emphasis on agriculture, even though some saw in agriculture a major source of growth-fostering capital.

ADAM SMITH AND DAVID RICARDO ON ECONOMIC GROWTH

By J. M. Letiche

THE CLASSICAL ECONOMISTS were concerned primarily with the problems of economic growth. But their writings have been grossly and systematically misinterpreted, and their characters maligned. They have always had great influence and a bad press—modern times are no exception. Their works, and their personalities as well, are still being distorted and caricatured, a practice which adds tinder to the massive walls of misunderstanding and distrust between peoples of more, and less, developed economies. I shall endeavor in this paper to present and appraise the salient views on economic growth of Adam Smith and David Ricardo.

I

Adam Smith

Implicitly, Adam Smith made an important contribution to the analysis of economic growth by discussing it in terms of general economic principles, rather than in terms of *a* theory of economic growth. It is conditions, he wrote, that bring about systems of political economy, although he doubtless believed that advances in political economy could also bring about changes in conditions.[1] His well-known presentation of hunting deer and beaver is a landmark in interpretive, as compared with predictive, economic analysis. First, he delineated the limits of what it is possible, and impossible, for a country to produce within a certain period of time with *given* technology and resources. By introducing the restraint of given tastes, he then formulated in simple terms the nature of all problems of economic maximization.

Furthermore, in his discussion on the division of labor, in his digressions on silver, the accumulation of capital, and the progress of opulence in various nations, he dealt with *changes* in wants, resources, and technology. Smith considered such problems with a sense of the uniqueness of human experience. They belonged to the high theme of "historical" or "evolutionary" economics.[2] In his emphasis of the importance of specialization, to a greater degree than had ever been done previously, Smith imputed to it, not only the improvement of skill, dexterity, and judgment, as well as the saving of time, but virtually all of technological progress, and even the expansion of new investment. It will be recalled that he attributed division of labor to a certain propensity in human nature "to truck, barter, and exchange one thing for another," and its development to the gradual expansion of markets.[3] Primarily because of its geographical dispersion, seasonality, and the perishability of its products, he considered the nature of agricultural production to be less conducive to division of labor than the production of manufactures. However, for economic development to occur at all, Smith believed that the production of an agricultural surplus to support the non-farm population was a primary requisite. He conjectured that the process of economic development must have been somewhat as follows.[4]

1. "The different progress of opulence in different ages and nations," observed Smith, "has given occasion to two different systems of political economy, with regard to enriching the people. The one may be called the system of commerce, the other that of agriculture." Adam Smith, *The Wealth of Nations*, E. Cannan, ed., New York, 1937, p. 397, Cf. also p. lix. The two different systems to which Smith referred were mercantilism, although he never used the term, and physiocracy.

2. Smith appreciated the fact that economic growth deals with qualitative and quantitative changes in wants, resources, and technology. It is in no way analogous to the problems dealt with in theoretical mechanics, from which the terms economic "statics" and "dynamics" were derived. Dynamics in the field of theoretical mechanics deals with motion, rather than organic change. The term "economic dynamics" is therefore misleading when applied to the phenomenon of economic growth. Cf. Frank H. Knight, *On the History and Method of Economics*, Chicago, 1956, p. 55, note 21.

3. Smith, *op.cit.*, p. 13, chaps. 1 and 2 *passim*. Cf. also G. A. Elliot, "The Impersonal Market," *Canadian Journal of Economics and Political Science*, XXIV, 1958, pp. 453-57.

4. Smith, *op.cit.*, esp. pp. 65, 126-64, 192-250, 356-59. Smith spoke in parables when he referred to an earlier golden age when land rent and interest could be neglected. History records no such golden age. Both Smith and Ricardo used this device as an ancient form of the method of successive approximations, assuming very simple models first and then introducing various complications into them. Cf. Paul A. Samuelson, "A Modern Treatment of the Ricardian

Given an extremely favorable labor-resource ratio, clothing and housing were at first free goods. As population grew, they became scarce and yielded a "rent." This induced technical improvements, and these improvements were applied to agriculture. A smaller proportion of the labor force was thus required to produce food. Consequently, workers were freed for other occupations.

. . . When by the improvement and cultivation of land the labour of one family can provide food for two, the labour of half the society becomes sufficient to provide food for the whole. The other half, therefore, or at least the greater part of them, can be employed in providing other things, or in satisfying the other wants and fancies of mankind.[5]

It was the creation of an agricultural surplus that produced the demand for other goods and services, which could be purchased with the excess supply of agricultural products. Manufacturing industries developed to supply this growing demand. Interdependently, the rising urban population required more food and had to produce an increased supply of manufactures to pay for it.

Those, therefore, who have the command of more food than they themselves can consume, are always willing to exchange the surplus . . . for gratifications of this other kind [manufactures]. What is over and above satisfying the limited desire, is given for the amusement of those desires which cannot be satisfied, but seem to be altogether endless. The poor, in order to obtain food, exert themselves to gratify those fancies of the rich, and to obtain it more certainly, they vie with one another in the cheapness and perfection of their work.[6]

Smith observed that the richest nations generally excelled all their neighbors in agriculture as well as in manufacturing (but ordinarily they were more distinguished by virtue of their superiority in manufacturing). Their lands, he noted, were better cultivated in general. However, this superiority was usually only in direct proportion to the superiority of their labor resources and the greater expense incurred on these lands. It was the impossibility of complete specialization in agriculture that explained this phenomenon; in effect, the productivity of labor in agriculture rose more slowly than in industry.

The number of workmen, Smith wrote, increased with the growing improvement and cultivation of the lands. As the nature of manufacturing business "admits of the utmost subdivisions of labour," the quantity of materials which they could work up increased in a much greater proportion

Economy: II Capital and Interest Aspects of the Pricing Process," *Quarterly Journal of Economics*, LXXIII, 1959, p. 217. The method also utilizes the process of stages in economic growth. See Bert F. Hoselitz, "Theories of Stages of Economic Growth," pp. 193-238, below.

5. Smith, *op.cit.*, p. 163.

6. *Ibid.*, p. 164.

than their numbers. Hence, a demand arose for every sort of material which human invention could employ, either useful or ornamental, "in building, dress, equipage, or household furniture; for the fossils and minerals contained in the bowels of the earth, the precious metals, and the precious stones."[7]

Foreshadowing the nineteenth-century belief of decreasing returns in agriculture and increasing returns in industry, Smith reached the Ricardian conclusion that landowners would benefit directly as a result of economic progress for two reasons: the real value of agricultural products would rise, and the landowners would receive a larger share of them. Landowners would also benefit indirectly because of the fall in the real price of manufactures. Labor would benefit because their wages would rise, and the price of part of the commodities they bought would fall. Merchants and master manufacturers would suffer, however, because increasing competition between increasing capitals would have a tendency to lower the rate of profit (interest?), and thereby check capital formation–a tendency which would have to be averted if continued economic growth were to be achieved.[8]

Smith writes as though he actually believed that if only the obstacles to economic progress were removed, the propensity to "truck and barter" would be sufficiently powerful to engender ever-increasing specialization, improvement in technology, and expansion of markets. These forces of economic progress would then counteract the tendency toward reduced capital-formation and economic decline.

But it was extremely important that the obstacles to economic progress be removed. Although Smith emphasized the role of impersonal factors of the market in achieving economic growth, he stressed the role of personal drives as well, and devoted attention to programs of reform, the adoption of which was indispensable for the successful operation of both sets of forces. He deemed ambition of the rising merchant class in the eighteenth century to be a potent catalyst in the economic development of England. It may have played no less significant a role than that of the innovator during the Industrial Revolution and thereafter. Many new operators of shops and of shipping, entrepreneurs in manufacturing, brokers, and traders became engulfed in the ambition to acquire wealth, prestige, and power. They sacrificed much in order to save and to invest in pursuit of these ends. With comprehensive brevity, Smith wrote:

---

7. *Ibid.*, pp. 6, 164; Cf. also his *Lectures on Justice, Police, Revenue and Arms,* (1896), delivered at the University of Glasgow. Reported by a student in 1763, and edited with an Introduction and Notes by Edwin Cannan, New York, 1956, pp. 157-61. Smith came very close to saying that in England technological changes were working to make nationally profitable a relative increase in urban population, a fact which has come true almost everywhere. Cf., on this point, Jacob Viner, *Canada and Its Giant Neighbour* (Alan B. Plaunt Memorial Lectures), Ottawa, 1958, pp. 39-42.

8. *Wealth of Nations,* pp. 247-50, 314, 332.

The poor man's son, whom heaven in its anger has visited with ambition, when he begins to look around him, admires the condition of the rich. He finds the cottage of his father too small for his accommodation, and fancies he should be lodged more at his ease in a palace.... It appears in his fancy like the life of some superior rank of beings, and, in order to arrive at it, he devotes himself forever to the pursuit of wealth and greatness. To obtain the conveniences which these afford, he submits in the first year, nay, in the first month of his application, to more fatigue of body and more uneasiness of mind, than he could have suffered through the whole of his life from the want of them.[9]

The drive of ambition continues:

He studies to distinguish himself in some laborious profession. With the most unrelenting industry he labours night and day to acquire talents superior to all his competitors. He endeavours next to bring those talents into public view, and with equal assiduity solicits every opportunity of employment. For this purpose he makes his court to all mankind; he serves those whom he hates, and is obsequious to those whom he despises.[10]

However, once great riches and power are achieved, Smith noted, they carry with them superstructures which are ready at any moment to burst into pieces and crush their possessor. They serve to avert minor adversities, not major ones. Their possessor remains as much, and sometimes more, exposed than before to anxiety, fear, sorrow, disease, danger, and death. People rarely regard these matters in a philosophical light. The external pleasures of wealth and greatness, Smith observed, strike the imagination as grand, beautiful, and noble. For their attainment, most people are willing to undergo all the labor and anxiety which are apt to be expended on them. Nevertheless, he said, it is fortunate that nature deludes us in this way.

It is this deception which rouses and keeps in continual motion the industry of mankind. It is this which first prompted them to cultivate the ground, to build houses, to found cities and commonwealths, and to invent and improve all the sciences and arts, which ennoble and embellish human life; which have entirely changed the whole face of the globe, have turned the nude forests of nature into agreeable and fertile plains, and made the trackless and barren ocean a new fund of subsistence, and the great high road of communication to the different nations of the earth.[11]

Smith's low view of the advantages of great personal riches, as expressed in the *Theory of Moral Sentiments,* is therefore not inconsistent with his analysis of the nature and causes of national opulence and the best methods of attaining such opulence, as expounded in the *Wealth of Nations.* He

9. Adam Smith, *The Theory of Moral Sentiments* (1759), London, 1880, pp. 259-60.

10. *Ibid.*, p. 260. With a touch of humor, Smith refers to the inscription on the tombstone of the man who had endeavored to mend a tolerable constitution by taking "physic." It may generally be applied, he says, with great justice to the distress of disappointed avarice and ambition: "I was well, I wished to be better; here I am." *Ibid.*, p. 211.

11. *Ibid.*, pp. 263-64.

regarded the advantages of great personal riches as largely illusory. But because men have persisted in thinking otherwise, they have worked to make the earth "redouble her natural fertility, and to maintain a greater multitude of inhabitants."[12] Accordingly, Smith devoted attention to the enduring problem of discovering those social arrangements under which the free pursuit of self-interest would promote the general interest of mankind. He demonstrated that under certain conditions it is possible to reconcile personal liberty and economic growth with peaceful social coexistence in a large area of man's life. Avarice and ambition could thus be channeled within a system of free social organization for the achievement of wealth and power of great nations. He applied this principle to economics and politics in his *Theory of Moral Sentiments.* Its refinement and elaboration, in the *Wealth of Nations,* constitutes Smith's major claim to fame: He endeavored to show that the detailed application to the economic world of the concept of a unified natural order–operating according to natural law, and left to its own course under freely competitive conditions–would produce results beneficial to mankind.

For the achievement of such results, the development of an environment conducive to economic progress was indispensable. Smith was not a doctrinaire advocate of laissez faire. He recommended at least four major programs of reform: the removal of impediments to free choice of occupation; to free trade in land; to internal free trade; and to free trade in foreign commerce. Moreover, he recognized the need for government activity in such fields as public education and hygiene, public works, regulation of currency and coinage, progressive (in effect, proportional) taxation, patents, copyrights, and even moderate export and import taxes for the purposes of revenue and development.[13]

The government of Smith's day was corrupt and incompetent; it often peddled monopoly privilege. Probably as a consequence, Smith was convinced that in general there was a strong indication against government activity, beyond its fundamental duties of justice and security. On grounds of *a priori* reasoning and experience, he maintained that individual initiative, applied in competitive ways to promote individual ends, would best serve the general interest. He was fully aware that the economic interests of different occupational groups were bound to conflict with one another, and with the interests of society as a whole. But he thought they could be

12. *Ibid.*, p. 264.

13. *Wealth of Nations*, pp. 101-102, 120-23, 134, 361-72, 420-39, 472-90, 595-96, 844. Cf. also Jacob Viner, "Adam Smith and Laissez Faire," republished in *The Long View and the Short*, Glencoe, Ill., 1958, pp. 213-45; and Lionel Robbins, *The Theory of Economic Policy*, London, 1952, chaps. 1 and 2. Robbins rightly maintained, I believe, that Smith regarded national advantage as the criterion of policy, though it was conceived in a cosmopolitan setting. He used the terminology of *Naturrecht*, but his arguments were consistently utilitarian in character.

restrained and partially reconciled by the operation of impersonal, competitive markets and, wherever necessary, by the activity of government under law. In effect, Smith laid the foundation of political reform for all classical economists in stressing the need for a stable, responsible government and an impartial system of laws to protect property. His approach to government was functional: government activity is natural and good when it promotes the general welfare; it is unnatural and bad when it injures the general interests of society. Smith was strongly prejudiced in favor of laissez faire; but he also had strong prejudices against the powerful and the grasping. He consistently spoke of the laboring classes in approbative terms and championed their cause. He was among the earliest economists to deal sympathetically with the human welfare problems of the masses. Although he did not foresee the Industrial Revolution, and the hardships incident to it, the *Theory of Moral Sentiments* and the *Wealth of Nations* were imbued with understanding tolerance–in a time of great intolerance.

Britain's economic progress up to the 1770's does not appear to have been inconsistent with Smith's eclectic explanation of it. Clearly, the *Wealth of Nations* contained much that was relevant to Britain's further economic growth, as well as that of other developing nations. By 1800, the book had run nine English editions; appeared in the United States, Ireland, and Switzerland; and had been translated into Danish, Dutch, French, German, Italian, Spanish, and Russian (1802-1806). Since then, it has also been translated into Japanese (1884-1888), Chinese (1902), Polish (1927), Czechoslovakian (1928), Finnish (1933), and probably other languages.[14]

The reforms which Smith had recommended were slowly achieved in Britain, and, as far as such things can be traced to their source, the *Wealth of Nations* was important in influencing policy both at home and abroad. We shall have occasion to observe that it still has relevance today to some problems facing developed and underdeveloped countries; but it must be borne in mind that Smith lived in an age when Britain was already undergoing economic progress. He was not analyzing nascent conditions prior to, or prerequisite for, economic development. As he pointed out, wages had "indeed" risen in Britain during the course of the eighteenth century. This seems to have been the effect not so much of inflation in the European market, as of an increase in the demand for labor in Britain, "arising from the great, and almost universal prosperity of the country."[15] In short, the real wages of labor had increased considerably; and this was both the necessary result and the natural symptom of *increasing* national wealth.[16]

14. See the *Vanderblue Memorial Collection of Smithiana*, Cambridge, 1939, pp. 1-31. This excellent collection is housed in the Kress Room of Baker Library at Harvard.

15. *Wealth of Nations*, p. 200.

16. *Ibid.*, p. 69: "It is not the actual greatness of national wealth, but its continual increase which occasions a rise in the wages." And again, p. 81: "The liberal reward of labour, therefore, as it is the effect of in-

Smith was not without vision. In dealing with Britain's future economic growth, and her relations with newly developing countries, he presented fresh analysis and radical recommendations. In theory and practice he struck a strong frontal attack against colonialism. The exclusive trade of mother countries with their colonies, he wrote, tends to reduce the aggregate level of world real income, or, at least, to diminish its rate of growth—and especially that of the American colonies. Their agricultural output was kept down, the price of their imports increased, their industrial output was held in check. The total amount of investment of all countries in the colonies was curtailed. Although British merchants made great profits, the mother country generally suffered. Primarily, the trade monopoly brought about a *diversion* of British trade away from Europe toward the colonies, rather than a *creation* of new trade. Specialization for the colonial market became so great that industry and commerce incident to it became overextended; they were bound to suffer from lack of product and geographic diversification. High profits in the mercantile trade led to profligate spending. Efficiency and the tendency to save were reduced. Incentives to invest in improvements for British agriculture declined. Expenditures on colonial defense and administration drained British resources.[17]

Smith considered the discovery of America and the discovery of a passage to the East Indies the most important events recorded in the history of mankind. They provided immeasurable opportunities for complementary trade with Europe, and for advance in human progress as well. But the superiority of force happened to be so great on the side of the Europeans that they committed grave injustice. The government of India, Smith wrote, was composed of a council of foreign merchants. "The plunderers of India," he called them in one passage; "military and despotical," in another.[18]

Regarding the American colonies, Smith observed that British trade policy was comparatively libertarian, even in the mercantilist period. Those newly developing countries which had plenty of good land, and the freedom to manage their own affairs in their own way, showed the most rapid progress. Wherever the trade monopoly of the mother country was least oppressive, the new lands prospered most. Fortunately, this was the case with the American colonies. The trade monopoly did much mutual harm, but the beneficial effects of the trade itself more than counterbalanced the ill effects of the monopoly. Nonetheless:

---

creasing wealth, so it is the cause of increasing population." Cf. also Smith, *Lectures*, pp. 256*ff*. The available evidence suggests that per capita national income of England and Wales more than doubled between 1688-1695 and 1770; it rose from approximately £8.7 to £18.5. See Phyllis Deane, "The Implications of Early National Income Estimates for the Measurement of Economic Growth in the United Kingdom," *Economic Development and Cultural Change*, IV, 1955, Table 8, p. 36.

17. *Wealth of Nations*, pp. 557-65, 570-80.

18. *Ibid*., pp. 603, 605.

To prohibit a great people, however, from making all that they can of every part of their own produce, or from employing their stock and industry in the way that they judge most advantageous to themselves, is a manifest violation of the most sacred rights of mankind. Unjust, however, as such prohibitions may be, they have not hitherto been very hurtful to the colonies. Land is still so cheap, and, consequently, labour so dear among them, that they can import from the mother country almost all the more refined or more advanced manufactures cheaper than they could make them for themselves. Though they had not, therefore, been prohibited from establishing such manufactures, yet in their present state of improvement, a regard to their own interest would, probably, have prevented them from doing so. In their present state of improvement, those prohibitions, perhaps, without cramping their industry, or restraining it from any employment to which it would have gone of its own accord, are only impertinent badges of slavery imposed upon them, without any sufficient reason, by the groundless jealousy of the merchants and manufacturers of the mother country. In a more advanced state they might be really oppressive and insupportable.[19]

In what way then, asked Smith, had the policy of Europe contributed to the establishment, the form of internal government, and the subsequent prosperity of the American colonies? Above all, it had produced men who were capable of laying the foundations of a great republic. They benefited from the equal and impartial administration of justice, which, by securing to every man the fruits of his own industry, gave the greatest and most effective encouragement to every sort of development.[20] The colonies owed to the policy of Europe the education and views of their enterprising founders; but some of the most important ideas on which their internal government was based were natively developed.[21]

Smith warned his readers that they were wrong in flattering themselves that the colonies would be conquered easily by force. He recommended that independence be granted by voluntary separation. If it were adopted, Britain would not only be freed from the expense of providing security for the colonies, but might also sign with them a treaty of commerce which would secure to her complete free trade. This would be more advantageous

19. *Ibid.*, p. 549.

20. *Ibid.*, p. 576. Furthermore, Smith drew attention to the need to establish a system of general principles which "ought to run through, and be the foundation of, the laws of all nations" *(Theory of Moral Sentiments,* p. 503). He concludes this book with a bid for further work on the principles of law and government, with respect to conditions of peace, as well as war. But he knew that the preservation of international peace would depend on the balance of power more than on legal principles and moral concepts. Hence, he warned: "The inhabitants of all the different quarters of the world may arrive at that equality of courage and force which, *by inspiring mutual fear,* can alone over-awe the injustice of independent nations into some sort of respect for the rights of one another" *(Wealth of Nations,* p. 591 [italics added]).

21. *Wealth of Nations,* p. 556. For his time, Smith attached considerable importance to the role of public education in promoting economic, and noneconomic, growth. Even in a civilized society, he pointed out, ignorance and stupidity benumb the understanding of the common people: "The more they are instructed, the less liable they are to the delusions of enthusiasm and superstition, which, among ignorant nations, frequently occasion the most dreadful disorders. . . . They are more disposed to examine, and more capable of seeing through, the interested complaints of faction and sedition." *Ibid.*, p. 740.

to the vast majority of the people, though less so to the merchants, than the monopoly which she currently held. By thus parting good friends, he hoped the affection of the colonies for the mother country would be revived. Not only might they then respect this treaty of commerce for centuries to come, but they might even become Britain's most faithful and generous allies.[22] Realizing, however, that the granting of such independence would be unacceptable to the pride of Britain—and to the private interests of those who wielded power and delegated positions of trust, distinction and profit—Smith suggested a more practicable solution, although still radical for the times. He proposed the formation of a federated Empire, granting the colonies representation in the British Parliament in proportion to their contribution to the public revenue. In compensation, they would be granted the same freedom of trade as all fellow subjects. The number of their representatives to Parliament would be increased through time in proportion to the rise in their contributions.[23]

Drawing on his analysis of the *Theory of Moral Sentiments,* Smith observed that a new method of acquiring importance, a new and more dazzling object of ambition would be presented to the leading men of each colony. With humorous sarcasm, he pointed out that instead of piddling for the little prizes which were to be found in the "paltry raffle of colony faction," they would hope, with the faith which men naturally have in their own ability and good fortune, to draw some of the great prizes which come from the "wheel of the great state lottery of British politics."[24] On the other hand, he reminded his countrymen that the unjust oppression of colonial industry usually falls back upon the heads of the oppressors, and ultimately crushes their industry more than it does that of the newly developing countries. As to the prospects of American development, he said:

> The persons who now govern the resolutions of what they call their continental congress, feel in themselves at this moment a degree of importance which perhaps the greatest subjects in Europe scarce feel. From the shopkeepers, tradesmen, and attornies, they are become statesmen and legislators, and are employed in contriving a new form of government for an extensive empire, which, they flatter themselves, will become, and which, indeed, seems very likely to become, one of the greatest and most formidable that ever was in the world.[25]

Smith attached paramount importance to the future of Anglo-American

22. *Ibid.*, p. 518.

23. *Ibid.*, p. 587. One authority refers to this vision of a federated Empire in poetic terms: "A conception of grandeur is worked out in its representative, fiscal and social aspects with the careful minuteness of the Dutch genre painter" (W. R. Scott, *Adam Smith as Student and Professor,* Glasgow, 1937, p. 99). Cf. also the careful study by Klaus E. Knorr, *British Colonial Theories 1570-1850,* Toronto, 1944, pp. 190*ff.*

24. *Wealth of Nations,* p. 587.

25. *Ibid.*, pp. 587-88. Cf. also G. H. Guttridge, "Adam Smith on the American Revolution: An Unpublished Memorial," *American Historical Review,* XXXVIII, 1933, pp. 714-20; the original essay was entitled, "Smith's Thoughts on the State of the Contest with America. Febry 1778."

relations. Trade policy, he realized, was the crux of British economic foreign policy. Hence, in modern terms, his views on mutual economic assistance between more and less developed economies can best be expressed as aid through free trade.

II
David Ricardo

One must turn to David Ricardo for the first reasonably rigorous classical theory of economic growth. In effect, a synthesis of "classical dynamics" characteristically purports to represent his views.[26] Basically, his argument rests on the Malthusian population principle and the law of historically diminishing returns. Briefly, it runs as follows: In an early stage of the classical economy, the population is small, compared to natural resources; consequently, profits, the rate of accumulation, and wages are all relatively high. The high level of accumulation serves to increase production, but it also serves to keep up the demand for labor. Hence, wages are high. This leads to a rising population. Since land is assumed to be fixed in quantity, there are diminishing average returns to additional units of labor in production. Therefore, as population increases, wages will tend to eat up more and more of the total product after rent payment, and thereby reduce the amount left over for profits. The inducement to invest will decline, and the demand for labor will be reduced. Wages will be forced toward a "subsistence level," and profits will tend to rise again. As long as total product after rent is greater than the total wage bill, there will be profits. Capital accumulation will be further induced, driving wages up, increasing population, and so leading to a new round in the process of growth. Once the working population rises to the point where total wages equal total product minus rent, there will be no more profits, even with wages at the "subsistence level." Accumulation will cease, and the stationary state will have been reached. An increase in productivity brought about by inventions and discoveries, the argument concludes, can only postpone the day of judgment.

This generally accepted model of "Ricardian economics" is not inconsistent with many passages to be found in Ricardo's writings. I think, however, that the most interesting aspects of Ricardo's discussions on growth are not to be found in the model *per se,* but in the way in which he uses his general analysis.

26. See, e.g., William J. Baumol, *Economic Dynamics,* New York, 1951, chap. 2. Following our survey of the usually accepted "Ricardian model," we shall have occasion to show that it does not satisfactorily represent Ricardo's position.

The really important long-run problems facing Britain, according to Ricardo, were those involving organization and efficiency: how to reorganize a growing economy with a rising population in which the key industries —manufacturing and agriculture—were developing at drastically different rates of productivity growth. He posed a timeless question: What rate of economic development is compatible with the resources, technology, and institutions of a country at a given time in its history? Ricardo endeavored to show that if the British economy is organized efficiently, if adaptations to potentialities are made—including essential reforms—its progress will be satisfactory; if not, it will suffer decline. The widespread view that Ricardo was a "pessimist" is either irrelevant or incorrect. If anything, he was over-optimistic as to the long-run prospects for English labor, provided certain conditions were met.[27]

To be sure, again and again, Ricardo reverts to his main theme: Economic growth is contingent upon capital formation. This depends primarily upon the productive powers of labor. Such productive powers are generally greater when there is an abundance of fertile land. If an increase in capital occurs, it raises the demand for labor and wages, and lowers profits. But the permanency of the rise in wages depends upon what happens to produce prices, and this depends upon the relationship between the growth in numbers and the fertility of the land.[28]

Ricardo suggested that in younger countries with an abundance of fertile land, so-called excess population is the *result,* rather than the cause, of backwardness and poverty: For if ignorance and indolence were reduced, productivity in agriculture would be raised, and, as Smith had shown, economic progress would have the effect of decreasing the population in agriculture and increasing it in industry. In older countries, on the other hand, where diminishing returns in agriculture are pronounced, excess population may be the *cause* of backwardness and poverty: For, under such conditions, the population may suffer from a lack of more productive occupations. In the case of the younger countries:

> . . . the evil proceeds from bad government, from the insecurity of property, and from a want of education in all ranks of the people. To be made happier they require *only to be better governed and instructed, as the augmentation of capital, beyond the augmentation of people, would be the inevitable result.* No increase in the population can be too great, as the powers of production are still greater.[29]

27. See *Works and Correspondence of David Ricardo,* Piero Sraffa and M. Dobbs, eds., Cambridge, 1951, I, pp. 98-99, 391-92; V, p. 180; X, p. 197. Cf. also Jacob Viner's review of *Works and Correspondence of David Ricardo,* republished in *The Long View and the Short,* pp. 434-36.

28. See *Works and Correspondence of David Ricardo,* I, esp. chaps. 5 and 6, and IV, pp. 10-44; George Stigler, "The Ricardian Theory of Value and Distribution," *Journal of Political Economy,* LX, 1952, pp. 187-207; and Mark Blaug, *Ricardian Economics,* New Haven, 1958, esp. chaps. 2, 9, 10, and 12.

29. *Works and Correspondence of David Ricardo,* I, p. 99 (italics added). This formulation is from the third edition of the *Principles,* a position which had been "watered

In the case of the older countries, however:

. . . the population increases faster than the funds required for its support. Every exertion of industry, unless accompanied by a diminished rate of increase in the population, will add to the evil, for production cannot keep pace with it.[30]

Since Britain was not an extensive country with an abundance of fertile land, Ricardo assumed that more and more land of inferior quality would have to be taken up and, other things being equal, the real price of agrarian products would rise, whereas the real price of manufactures would fall. Rent per unit of labor and capital on comparatively fertile land would rise, and so would money wages. Profits, consequently, would fall. England would hence be unable to feed itself and, at the same time, to generate a sufficiently large volume of profits to sustain sufficient capital formation for economic growth.

There could be no accumulation, wrote Ricardo, without a motive. The farmer and the manufacturer could no more live without profit than the laborer without wages. Their motive for accumulation would diminish with every diminution of profit, and would cease altogether when their profits were so low as not to afford them an adequate compensation for their "trouble" and "risk," which they must encounter in using their capital productively.[31]

Ricardo emphasized that the effects of accumulation would vary in different countries:

However extensive a country may be where the land is of a poor quality, and where the importation of food is prohibited, the most moderate accumulations of capital will be attended with great reductions in the rate of profit, and a rapid rise in rent; and on the contrary a small but fertile country, particularly if it freely permits the importation of food, may accumulate a large stock of capital without any great diminution in the rate of profits, or any great increase in the rent of land.[32]

These propositions, I believe, were fundamental in Ricardo's deliberations on Britain's future economic growth; they underlie virtually all his theoretical constructs and policy formulations. It was critically important to reor-

down" to meet the criticism of Mr. Ensor. (See Ricardo's letter to James Mill, Nov. 23, 1818, *ibid.*, VII, p. 334.) In the first edition Ricardo had written at this point that "the misery proceeds from the inactivity of the people. To be made happier, they need only to be stimulated to exertion; with such exertion, no increase. . . ." *(ibid.*, I, p. 99). He also applied this reasoning to the conditions of Poland and Ireland, which he thought similar to those of the South Seas: "Give to the Irish labourer a taste for the comforts and enjoyments which habit has made essential to the English labourer, and he would be then content to devote a further portion of his time to industry that he might be enabled to obtain them" *(ibid.*, I, p. 100, note). Otherwise, states Ricardo, a mere reduction in population would increase the evil, for wages would rise, and effort be reduced (i.e., a backward-sloping supply curve of labor). Cf. also Ricardo's incisive letter to Hutches Trower, January 25, 1822, *ibid.*, IX, p. 153.

30. *Ibid.*, I, p. 99.

31. *Ibid.*, I, p. 122.

32. *Ibid.*, I, p. 126.

ganize the British economy, so that rent per unit of labor and capital would not rise, and profits would not fall. The law of comparative advantage provided the principle whereby these objectives might be achieved: For it showed how an economy could most efficiently allocate its resources among industries developing at differential rates of productivity growth.

Following the tenets of comparative advantage, the adoption of free trade would lower agricultural prices, money wages, and rents; it would raise real wages and profits, and thereby bring about greater investments in the progressive manufacturing industries. Improvements in agricultural production might also occur. A country such as England would thus be able to experience a gradual increase in capital which was larger than the gradual increase in population, and enjoy a lasting growth in real income. But this could only be achieved, said Ricardo, if the distribution of income among landlords, laborers, and capitalists moved in favor of capital; only thereby would an expansion in profits generate sufficient savings to be invested in capital equipment for the production of manufactured goods.

Consequently, Ricardo opposed taxes on capital, wages, raw materials, and necessities. He also opposed the poor laws. All these levies, he believed, would raise money wages and lower profits. This would bring about a distribution of income in favor of consumption at the expense of capital accumulation, lowering the rate of economic growth and deteriorating the condition of the poor as well as the rich.[33]

Confident, on the other hand, that in the long run the opportunity to invest in English manufacturing was unlimited, Ricardo argued that there could be no limit to the amount of capital employed in producing commodities needed at home, except that which "bound" England's power to maintain the workmen who were required to produce them. He even disagreed with Smith that foreign trade might be necessary to provide sufficient outlets for investment.[34] Assuming no hoarding, he wrote:

> ... there is no limit to demand—no limit to the employment of capital while it yields any profit, and that however abundant capital may become, there is no other adequate reason for a fall of profit but a rise of wages. . . .[35]

He apparently believed that continual improvement in technique would prevent a decline in the long-term productivity of capital as its supply increased. Nonetheless, Ricardo became increasingly concerned that investment in capital would be labor-saving, and as a consequence bring about short-term unemployment. However, he did not believe in the probability of long-term technological unemployment. I therefore interpret him to mean that, in the long run, the expanding demand for capital would so increase

33. *Ibid.*, I, pp. 105-109, 150-55, 159-72, 205-14, 243-56, 257-60.

34. *Ibid.*, I, pp. 294-95.

35. *Ibid.*, I, p. 296.

the *total* demand for labor—the amount required to build the capital, plus the amount required to use it—that the combined effect of these forces would counteract the tendency toward long-term technological unemployment.[36]

Few men have appreciated more than Ricardo the fact that the problems of importance confronting a nation continually change their character. He knew that if the British economy was to take advantage of its potentialities, fundamental reforms and readjustments were required: free trade, resource mobility, free competition, monetary stability. Not only did he realize that a high level of capital formation was essential for economic growth, but he warned that if its gains were permanently to improve the condition of the poor, the expansion in their number would have to be kept in strict control. He was at pains to point out that the laboring classes, or their legislature, would have to make strong efforts if this control were to be achieved.[37] Insofar as the intellectual decencies of the times would permit, in his correspondence Ricardo seems to have expressed himself in favor of birth control.[38]

III

Appraisal

In the main, Ricardo's vision of Britain's early economic development was correct, although the Malthusian principle and, to some extent, the "law" of historically diminishing returns upon which his *alleged model* rests were not. His prediction in *Principles* of the form in which diminishing returns in agriculture would manifest themselves was partially incorrect, as were his predictions concerning the demand for goods and capital, the relationship between wages and profits, and, probably, the course of rents.

Clearly, England's comparative advantage in manufacturing became

36. *Ibid.*, I, pp. 386-97.

37. *Ibid.*, I, pp. 106-107.

38. Bentham appears to have been the first person to propose birth control as a measure of economic reform. See J. Bentham, "Situation and Relief of the Poor," *Annals of Agriculture*, XXIX, 1797, pp. 422-23. Speaking in Parliament on wages and machinery, Ricardo said: "But the people had the remedy in their own hands. A little forethought, a little prudence, . . . a little of that caution which the better educated felt it necessary to use, would enable them to improve their situation" (*Works and Correspondence of David Ricardo*, V, p. 303; cf. also VII, p. 219, and IX, p. 18). Among other classical writers, J. S. Mill went further, mentioning the possibility that a comparatively large, discontinuous rise in real income might change the saving and size of family patterns of the population, and hence induce a higher rate of economic growth. Cf. John Stuart Mill, *Principles of Political Economy*, W. J. Ashley, ed., London, 1909, pp. 710-24. ". . . The permanent remuneration of the labourers," he wrote, "essentially depends on what we have called their habitual standard; the extent of the requirements which, as a class, they insist on satisfying before they choose to have children. If their tastes and requirements receive a *durable* impress from the sudden improvement in their condition, the benefit to the class will be permanent" (*ibid.*, p. 719). Cf. also Abram L. Harris, *Economics and Social Reform*, New York, 1958, chap. II; and Joseph J. Spengler, pp. 3-64 in this volume.

overwhelmingly strong. The tremendous decline in British export prices from 1798 to 1850 can be attributed primarily to the rapid application of cost-reducing machine methods in textiles—the major export field. In no export industry did prices fall more rapidly than in cottons, where the new techniques were most extensively applied. The decline in export prices resulted also from extensive development in the growth of raw cotton in the United States during the 1820's and 1830's. Cotton costs, however, were only about 20 per cent of the total cost of finished fabrics. Since the price of finished fabrics fell by much more than 20 per cent, the decline in Britain's textile prices must be accounted for principally by the technological revolution.[39]

Thus, Ricardo correctly predicted that England's comparative advantage in manufacturing would be brought about "by the improvements in machinery, by the better division and distribution of labour, and by the increasing skill, both in science and art, of the producers."[40] He had correctly anticipated that for England, at the margin, the gain from international specialization would exceed the possible gain from more "balanced" domestic growth which might be brought about through tariff protection. He espoused more balanced international economic growth, even though it meant more "unbalanced" domestic growth. Ricardo believed that in a setting of reasonable international equilibrium, free trade would bring about a more efficient use of *both* domestic and international resources, and a more rapid rate of progress of *both* more, and less, developed economies.

As regards the "law" of historically diminishing returns, the real cost of producing wheat in England (in terms of inputs per unit of output) does not seem to have risen much, if at all, between the time of Waterloo and the adoption of free trade. The price of wheat actually fell during this period, but not as much as that of other commodities.

Diminishing returns in the production of grains appear to have manifested themselves in two ways. First, there was a tendency toward reduced output per unit of input, as production expanded and natural resources of lower quality were brought into use. This, however, was not of major significance. Technological advance apparently offset somewhat the deterioration in the quality of marginal agricultural resources, as rising output pressed on available land. Much more important was the second impact of diminishing returns: It had the effect of restricting the expansion of crops whose output could be increased only at sharply rising costs. The tendency toward historical diminishing returns revealed itself, not so much in absolute lower efficiency, but in relatively lower expansion of output. For

39. Cf. E. Baines, *History of the Cotton Manufacture*, London, 1835, p. 353; and W. W. Rostow, "The Historical Analysis of the Terms of Trade," *Economic History Review*, 2nd Series, IV, 1951, pp. 59-62.

40. *Works and Correspondence of David Ricardo*, I, p. 94.

Britain, in other words, the relative mechanization of industry had made further expansion of agriculture less profitable than that of manufacturing.

After the repeal of the corn laws, wheat imports increased substantially, but for many reasons there was no sharp drop in wheat prices. The *tendency* for the real cost of producing wheat to rise was checked by the gradual substitution of external for domestic grain supplies. British agriculture was compelled to reorganize, and in the process its productivity greatly increased. The contraction of tillage to best soils, technical improvements, increase in the proportion of capital to other inputs, expansion of livestock, dairy, and fruit production—all helped to raise productivity.[41] The period between 1846 and the 1870's is known, in fact, as the golden age of British agriculture. Throughout these years real wages rose both in agriculture and industry. But the prices of agricultural imports continued to fall relative to money wages, and productivity and real wages in nonagricultural production rose more rapidly than those in agriculture. Consequently, the pressure to economize on labor in agriculture became more powerful. The *efficient* contraction of British agriculture as a proportion of national income freed a comparatively larger proportion of savings for capital formation, and thereby contributed to Britain's long-term economic growth.

Developments in agriculture were therefore not entirely in accord with Ricardo's long-term analysis. It must be borne in mind, however, that he was not unaware of the possibility of important qualifications to his general discussion in the *Principles*. Because of fixed capital in agriculture, he observed, output might remain the same—rather than decline—after tariff reductions; and agricultural prices might decline for some time after a war, owing to overexpansion.[42]

41. See E. M. Ojala, *Agriculture and Economic Progress*, London, 1952, pp. 129-53; and Colin Clark, *Conditions of Economic Progress*, London, 2nd ed., 1951, pp. 225-26.

42. *Works and Correspondence of David Ricardo*, I, pp. 270-72. In the *Essay on Profits* (1815) and in *Principles* (1st ed., 1817), Ricardo strongly emphasized the fact that England would be obligated "to cultivate at disadvantage our poor lands, if the importation of corn is restricted or prohibited," and that freer trade would bring about lower agricultural prices and rents (see, e.g., *ibid.*, IV, p. 266). In this period Ricardo appears to have been stressing the unfortunate consequences that would result from a failure to gradually abolish the corn laws. However, on October 4, 1821, he wrote to Hutches Trower that if trade were left perfectly free, English growers would be able to compete with those abroad and imports of corn would be only "a few weeks consumption" (*ibid.*, IX, p. 86). In his essay *On Protection to Agriculture* (April 1822), Ricardo wrote that freer trade would bring about more steady agricultural prices, and this would be to the landowner's interest, although he insisted that rents would be lower as compared to protection (*ibid.*, IV, p. 266). Speaking in Parliament on May 9, 1822, Ricardo said: "Nations grow old, as well as individuals; and in proportion as they grow old, populous, and wealthy, must they become manufacturers. If things were allowed to take their own course, we should undoubtedly become a great manufacturing country, but we should remain a great agricultural country also. . . . There would always be a limit to our greatness, while we were growing our own supply of food; but we should always be increasing in wealth and power, whilst we obtained part of it from foreign countries, and devoted our own manufactures to the payment of it." *Ibid.*, V, p. 180. In this period Ricardo appears to have been stressing that British agriculture would not be gravely affected by the gradual adoption of free trade.

With respect to capital, its demand for home use in Britain did not rise rapidly after the mid-1870's. Domestic net capital formation amounted to approximately 9 per cent of net national product in the 1870's, and declined to approximately 7.5 per cent in the 1880's and 8 per cent in the 1890's.[43] It was indeed a fortuitous historical circumstance that Britain was able to invest much of her excess savings abroad whenever plans to invest at home declined relative to the level of total savings. For, around 1870, an important interrelated phenomenon occurred in Britain: a turning point from a high to a lower rate of capital formation, and from a high to a relatively low rate of increase of industrial output. From 1865 to 1875, physical industrial capital per head rose by as much as 35 per cent, but the rate of growth of industrial output had already begun to decline. It seems that a disparity developed in some major industries between the growth in physical capacity to produce and the growth of the current output of their mines and factories. Industries had expanded production capacity beyond the need of current operations. Profits as a *percentage of national income* were lower in 1872 and 1873 than in almost any other year during the period from 1871 to 1913. Savings as a per cent of national income reached a major peak between 1872 and 1874, a peak which was not surpassed in the pre-World War I era.

As the rate of growth of industrial output declined in the early 1870's, relative to the rate of growth of productive capacity, the net export of capital greatly increased. An examination of the data for the period from 1870 to 1895 reveals that in practically every year when the volume of domestic investment fell or remained the same, the volume of foreign investment rose. Both in absolute terms and as a percentage of net national product, Britain's foreign investment and home investment moved in opposite directions over the long period. Recurring declines (and probably reduced elasticity) in the marginal efficiency of capital schedule at home impelled investors to seek better opportunities for the supply of their savings abroad.

Fortunately, as regards the demand for savings, throughout the period from 1870 to 1913 foreign investment offered higher returns than most home investment, and the difference in returns was more than sufficient to compensate for extra risk. One can infer from the evidence that, *inter alia*, the growth of domestic investment as a percentage of net national product periodically generated a rate of growth in income, which, in turn, generated a rate of growth in savings (as a percentage of net national product) larger than that of planned investment; and, at the going or anticipated rates of return, these excess savings could be invested more profitably overseas.

So far as Britain was concerned, it was the same set of domestic forces

43. See J. M. Letiche, *Balance of Payments and Economic Growth*, New York, 1959, pp. 253-54 and sources cited therein.

that often, on the one hand, brought about a reduction in the volume of domestic investment, and, on the other, provided the incentives for an expansion in the volume of foreign investment, migration, and exports. The growth in Britain's capital stock would lower the marginal efficiency of capital schedule, as insufficient innovations were introduced to raise it. The returns on capital and expected returns on new investment would thus decline, the growth process would be interrupted, full capacity supply would be in excess of the total demand for the net national product, output would be reduced, and labor become unemployed. Concurrently, with higher levels of return on investment abroad, the decline in the marginal efficiency of capital schedule at home would bring on spasms of foreign lending.

Clearly, these developments do not correspond with Ricardo's vision of Britain's long-term economic growth. He foresaw the impact of differential rates of productivity growth on the British economy during the first half of the nineteenth century. However, understandably, he could not foresee the way in which continued technological improvements and changing demands would keep altering the relation between its economic development, fixed domestic investments, and resource base, on the one hand, and the composition and direction of its foreign trade and investments, on the other. Consequently, he could not foresee the emerging importance of rapid, flexible adjustments to "wrong" investments resulting from changing demands at home and abroad. In effect, from the middle of the nineteenth century to the outbreak of World War I, Britain's exports of manufactured goods showed a considerable decline as a proportion of her total exports. Britain's most important manufactures–textiles–began to face increased tariffs abroad at the very time when they were becoming less competitive in world markets. Furthermore, a process of fundamental change took place in the nature of her imports. The proportion of imported raw materials to be used in the manufacture of producer goods increased, in comparison with the proportion to be used in the manufacture of consumer goods. Many of the raw materials required to produce new goods which were increasing in world demand either were not produced in Britain or were produced in inadequate amounts, whereas other emerging industrial countries were better supplied with them domestically.[44]

Considering the role of the Malthusian principle in Ricardo's thinking, it is not surprising to find that his *customary* analysis of the relationship

44. After returning from a tour on the Continent in 1822, Ricardo wrote to Hutches Trower that he had previously held an exaggerated view of the wealth and greatness of England, "which is slowly subsiding to a more sober and just estimate" (*Works and Correspondence of David Ricardo*, X, p. 197). He did not foresee, however, that possible difficulties of adjustment might arise as a result of the industrialization of Western Europe, believing that the process of economic growth would be a comparatively smooth phenomenon (*ibid.*, IX, p. 246). As to his views on the role of capital exports in Britain's economic growth, he wrote: "It can never be allowed that the emigration of capital can be beneficial to a state" (*ibid.*, III, p. 269; see also IV, p. 16, note).

between agricultural prices and money wages (and hence profits) was incorrect. To wit: between 1815 and 1850 (i.e., including the period before the repeal of the corn laws) the price of grain fell, but, contrary to Ricardo's customary views, money-wages remained comparatively stable, and real wages rose.[45] Similarly, in the second half of the nineteenth century, the causal relationships between British agricultural prices, money-wages, and real wages were not those predicted by Ricardo. It was the rise in productivity of labor and capital in industry as well as agriculture—usually, but not always, associated with capital accumulation and fluctuations in terms of trade—that was chiefly responsible for the rise in wages *and* profits. Ricardo's basic vision of Britain's economic growth, say, until about 1870, was substantially validated, but, to some extent at least, by way of different *modus operandi.*

Rent per acre generally did not fall in England after the repeal of the corn laws. But this may not have been inconsistent with Ricardo's analysis, for his formulation ran in terms of rent per unit of labor and capital, not per acre. As to the Malthusian principle *per se,* comment here is probably unnecessary,[46] except to note that Ricardo did not stress the decline in death rates associated with industrialization—a decline which historically has been of primary importance in the transitional stages of economic development, and manifestly is a critical factor today in many newly developing countries. Improved health measures have rendered it important even in backward areas which have undergone virtually no economic progress as yet.

In discussing economic growth, both Adam Smith and David Ricardo emphasized the importance of knowledge, responsible government, protection of private property, social capital, healthy agriculture, entrepreneurial ability, specialization of labor, technological improvements, capital accumulation, and free trade. In short, they emphasized the efficient organization of the economy through "correct" allocation of resources by the operation of the pricing mechanism in competitive markets. They primarily analyzed

45. Although Ricardo believed that the price of food "regulates" the rate of wages, he did not believe that a decline in the price of food would necessarily bring about an *equivalent* decline in money-wages. As we have had occasion to observe, he maintained that with a healthy agriculture and/or the free importation of corn, real wages could rise permanently as long as the accumulation of capital increased more rapidly than the supply of labor. See, e.g., *ibid.*, II, p. 98, note. However, Ricardo's basic theoretical explanation of the determinants of wages was, of course, erroneous. For some evidence on the actual trend of prices and wages, see T. S. Ashton, "The Standard of Life of the Workers in England, 1790-1830," *Journal of Economic History*, IX, 1949, pp. 19-38; A. D. Gayer, W. W. Rostow, A. J. Schwartz, and I. Frank, *The Growth and Fluctuation of the British Economy*, Oxford, 1953, II, pp. 625-26, 950; and W. W. Rostow, *British Economy of the Nineteenth Century*, New York, 1948, chaps. I-IV.

46. Cf. the provocative discussion by J. A. Schumpeter in *History of Economic Analysis*, New York, 1952, pp. 250-76.

problems of growth in this way, as an application of economic principles, demonstrating what may, or may not, be done to achieve stated or recognized objectives. Their policy considerations were consistent with their general liberal outlook, and were in tune with the political, social, and business institutions of the time.

Not having formulated an adequate theory of growth, employment, or fluctuations, they did not realize, however, that free trade would not necessarily engender much economic development in some backward economies. But they did realize that economic growth is a unique historical process, usually unbalanced, and a process which gives rise to different problems requiring different analyses and solutions, both in time and space.

Smith, in particular, appreciated the fact that any theory of growth which places great reliance on a few simple relationships does not deserve serious consideration as an explanation of so vastly interdependent a phenomenon. He further recognized that economic development requires not only certain catalysts of growth, but a satisfactory "balance" between ego-centered and community-centered incentives for the effective utilization of economic potentialities.

Among Smith's important contributions was his recognition that a new situation had developed as a result of the social and technical advances of his time; consequently a new form of economic organization was required for its implementation. The restrictions arising from mercantilist discrimination and monopolization had to be swept away, if private enterprise and representative institutions were to help generate economic growth. It was for these reasons that he devoted particular attention to specialization and technological change, realizing that these were the most effective available means of "freeing" resources for further advance.

Ricardo wrote in Smith's tradition, despite the fact that during the period between the appearance of their major works the world had undergone the American, French, and Industrial Revolutions, as well as the Napoleonic Wars. It would be surprising indeed, if even when they used similar terminology, the similarity were not more apparent than real. When Smith wrote on "specialization of labor," he stressed literally the importance of labor. In his celebrated illustration of the manufacture of pins, the focus of attention was on the craftsman; in his discussion of the development of agriculture, he focused on the "improving landlord" and the efficient farmer. Ricardo, on the other hand, dealt to an increasing extent with the problems of capital, for the character of manufacturing had undergone radical change. He discussed specialization in more general, and in somewhat more modern, terms; one of his essays, was in fact entitled, "On Machinery." As the importance of England's foreign trade had greatly increased, and its structure changed, he developed the law of comparative advantage to explain the new emergent form of Britain's *international* specialization.

Herein, I believe, lies the major contribution of both Smith and Ricardo to the analysis of economic growth: a keen perception that new facts and/or new objectives call for a reconsideration of obsolete premises and outworn institutions. But even in the hands of so great a man as David Ricardo, when propositions whose validity depended merely upon certain institutional conditions were assumed to be "self-evident truths," they soon seriously distorted reality. The analytical power and policy implications of "Ricardian economics" so chloroformed a substantial segment of the profession that it failed to adjust its thinking to the conditions that were developing in England in the latter half of the nineteenth century. If the character of the problems of economic growth had undergone such rapid change during that period, one would expect them to be scarcely recognizable today. Nevertheless, most of the issues which Smith and Ricardo raised have remained relevant to the present—albeit nearly always in a different form.

Thus, with respect to an impartial system of laws for the protection of property, newly developing countries are now able to attract considerable public and private investments from abroad to supplement their domestic savings. Regardless of the political complexion of their institutions, failure to protect such "property" from unreasonable discrimination cannot help but adversely affect their credit for foreign capital and, hence, the rate of economic growth.

Concerning the importance of foreign *versus* domestic trade, Smith and Ricardo had occasion to caution that unless there is evidence to the contrary—and research on this problem is long overdue—foreign trade is neither superior nor inferior to domestic trade, as long as each is permitted to develop within the dimensions determined by free market forces. Regrettably, some developed countries have displayed a perverse tendency to press their exports artificially, while some underdeveloped countries have been disposed to exaggerate the importance of certain branches of domestic trade.

Much of the current literature on economic development notwithstanding, there is no fundamental conflict between the tenets of comparative advantage and more "balanced" economic growth.[47] It is true that under-

47. Interesting facets of this problem are analyzed by Ragnar Nurkse, *Problems of Capital Formation in Underdeveloped Countries*, New York, 1953, chaps. 1 and 2; Albert O. Hirschman, *The Strategy of Economic Development*, New Haven, 1958, chaps. 1, 3, and 4; and Tibor Scitovsky, "Growth—Balanced or Unbalanced," in *The Allocation of Economic Resources*, Essays in Honor of Bernard F. Haley, Moses Abramovitz, ed., Stanford, 1959, pp. 207-17.

developed countries may at times be caught in a vicious circle: The size of the market depends, *inter alia,* upon productivity; productivity depends primarily upon the amount of capital equipment used in production; the amount of investment in capital equipment depends upon the size of the market and its expected growth. Consequently, a limited market, an insufficient inducement to invest, and low productivity may be inextricably linked to one another. In such cases, only by moving forward on a broad front can the market be enlarged, risk reduced, incentives to invest in training and equipment at home increased, and higher productivity stimulated. However, this approach is not inconsistent with a dynamic conception of the law of "comparative cost" or "comparative income," given the economic horizon relevant to the decisions of private firms or planning agencies.

Smith and Ricardo discussed economic growth in terms of historical evolution; *viz.,* as a complementary process of interdependent development which was assumed to have long been under way. It occurred primarily under the aegis of private initiative, though with much government prodding, of the mercantilist variety. For England and many other Western countries —especially the United States—this outlook on economic growth has not been misleading, for these countries have been well supplied with private industrial and financial leadership, capable of, and motivated toward, economic progress. Many newly developing countries have not been as fortunate; hence, they require much more initiative on the part of their governments to induce economic development. For this very reason, the emphasis of the classical economists upon the need for a stable, responsible government has become markedly more relevant to the underdeveloped economies of the present time, than it was to the England and France of one hundred seventy-five years ago.

But are there any legitimate misgivings to which classical traditions and democratic institutions give rise? The answer is an emphatic affirmative. Underdeveloped countries will be greatly influenced by the respective performances of representative and authoritarian institutions. The strong emphasis placed by classical economists on free economic and political procedures has created in the Anglo-American literature an ideological bias against understanding the nature of authoritarian, especially communist, regimes. For an amazingly long period distinguished economists believed that such regimes would be unable to organize their economies efficiently. We now face a new danger which stems from the persistence of the same tradition: *viz.,* failure to appreciate sufficiently the over-riding importance that these regimes attach to releasing the forces of technological advance, a drive which has virtually nothing to do with their ideological dogma. These regimes are, in fact, better geared than are the democracies to make the necessary capital outlays for research in pure science, technical training, educational and "cultural" activities.

This poses a challenge for our age that strikes at the very roots of classical fundamentals. Smith and Ricardo painstakingly stressed that capital accumulation, viewed at present as investment in the human agent, natural resources, and reproducible capital, is a key factor in economic growth. It is an open question, however, whether democracies will be able to increase adequately their rate of capital formation and economic growth. To be sure, the classical writers never considered economic growth an end in itself, and repeatedly used the terms "economic growth" and "progress" interchangeably. Growth in per capita levels of well-being was considered to be indispensable to growth in human dignity. Economic growth was never confused with growth in national power or aggrandizement, to say nothing of the individual's right to question and challenge the objectives and policies of government. By usually analyzing economic growth in terms of long-run equilibrating mechanisms—assuming an ultimate approach toward the stationary state—the classical economists generally believed that with increased population, mass poverty was probably inevitable. The essence of the process of growth is now considered to be cumulative expansion—assuming that all parameters become variables—and in practice mass poverty is considered intolerable.

The problem is whether we shall be able to adjust anew the discrepancies which have arisen between the social aspirations and technical advances of our time, and the obsolete premises and institutions that require change. There is no need to belabor the issues at stake, or the uncertainty of the outcome; but if we succeed, our achievement will surely be in the philosophical spirit of Adam Smith and David Ricardo.

THE THEORY OF ECONOMIC GROWTH IN THE ENGLISH CLASSICAL SCHOOL

By Erskine McKinley

RICARDO AND MALTHUS are considered the major members of the English classical school, for they enunciated the fundamental theorems of classical dynamics. Because of their acknowledged obligation to Adam Smith, reference will be made to the Smithian theory of growth. The disciples may be called upon to testify, but by the time one gets to Senior, the epicycles have almost obscured the basic mechanics. A consensus appears to have emerged in the last decade as to the nature of the general classical system. A synthesis of this can be illustrated diagrammatically.[1]

1. W. J. Baumol has done this in his *Economic Dynamics,* New York, 1951, p. 18. See also Mark Blaug, *Ricardian Economics,* New Haven, 1958, p. 30. Since, as Blaug points out, one cannot deduce from Ricardo the behavior of the proportion rent, the slope of AP is only illustrative. Following Adolph Lowe's argument in "The Classical Theory of Economic Growth," *Social Research,* XXI, 1954, William O. Thweatt has presented a very ingenious diagrammatic interpretation in "A Diagrammatic Representation of Adam Smith's Growth Model," *Social Research,* XXIV, 1957. Dr. Herbert Geyer has carried this to its logical conclusion in the case of the Ricardian model by using difference equations. See *Untersuchungen über die Theorie des dynamischen makroökonomischen Kernprozesses,* Berlin, 1958.

But having so imposed an agreement upon the two, it would seem only just, and might prove illuminating, to indicate the points at which they may have protested this violent forcing of their ideas into a consistent whole.

On the horizontal axis of Figure 1, below, are shown units of labor equipped with capital, defined as wage goods in the classical manner, applied to a fixed quantity of land; on the vertical axis is output, also most conveniently thought of as wage goods.

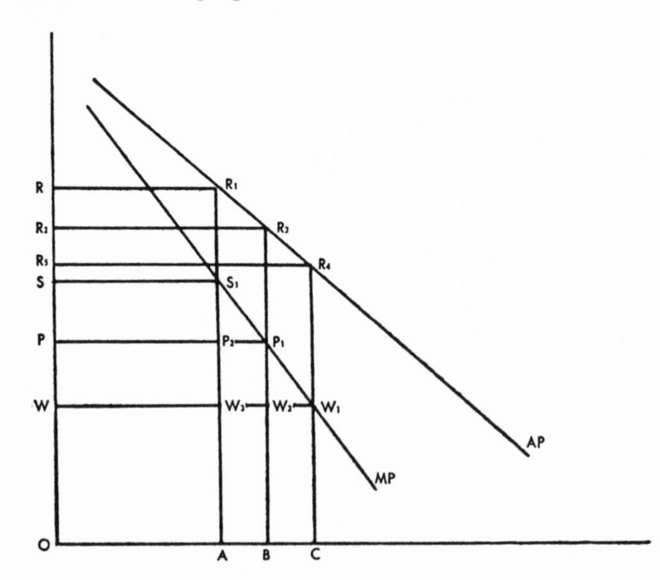

Figure 1

Thus, the average return to OA units of labor plus capital is AR_1 and the total product of the economy with a labor force of this size is OAR_1R. The marginal return to the Ath unit of labor plus capital is AS_1. The height of the schedule of average returns may be regarded as technologically fixed. Its negative slope is to be attributed to the fixity of the land factor. To the degree that division of labor is regarded as a technological change, the function represents net average product after the consideration of economies from this source. Hence, only innovation, other than increased division of labor, will shift the curve upward. The function thus shows the classical prediction that the economies obtained from increasing division of labor will be more than offset by the fixity of land as additional capital-equipped laborers are brought into existence.

If we define the "subsistence wage," OW, as the necessary supply price of a given unit of labor, the maximum labor force that can be supported by an economy characterized by the functions shown is at C. With the marginal, hence average, wage at subsistence, the wages and the rent payment to the landlord, $WW_1R_4R_5$, exhaust the total product. If there is no necessary supply price of capital maintenance, this point may be described as the stationary state into which the economy is destined to evolve.

If capital maintenance does have a necessary supply price, say WP, a return in excess of depreciation charges, equal at least, let us say, to the subsistence of the capitalist (as, for example, in Wicksell), the stationary state is defined at B. OBW_2W is distributed as wages, WW_2P_1P as the payment necessary for maintaining capital, and $PP_1R_3R_2$ as the pure rent which is the competitive, but not socially necessary, supply price of the fixed land factor. These payments exhaust the total product. In such a situation if the wages bill is infringed upon, the labor force will be diminished; and if the profits claim is infringed upon, capital will not be maintained.

Some members of the classical school regarded the arrival of the stationary state as a remote historical necessity, some as a pressing condition whose yearly postponement depended upon free trade, appropriate tax levies, etc. But all of the classicists used the concept analytically. They reasoned, for example, that England had a population of, say, OA. They then asked, "what are the necessary payments for the continuance of the economy at the size it has already reached?" Total product is OAR_1R. If all necessary payments, as defined above, are made to maintain this total product, then there is seen to be a residual, PP_2S_1S. This they regarded as the social dividend. Upon its disposition depended the economy's development, whether it would be stationary or growing.

For analytical purposes, total product was regarded as being in the hands of the entrepreneur at the beginning of the period of production. From this total product, he earmarked the necessary payments defined above. These payments were regarded as the *normal* prices of the factors. Normal, in other words, meant only that the price would insure a continuation of the stationary circular flow. Whether market prices of the factors would be equal to normal prices depended on whether the capitalist desired to expand his output. Assuming that he did, part of his profits (the social dividend) from the last period would be used to obtain more labor. Competitive bidding among capitalists for a given supply of labor would, in effect, raise the market rate above the normal rate by the amount of the social dividend that was "invested" in this fashion. The market rate of wages at A would then be equal to AW_3, plus some quantity equal to or less than P_2S_1; the former, if the sticking point of the capitalist were zero; the latter, if it were greater than zero. Investment from the social dividend now becomes a part of the wages bill, and a new equilibrium is reached when the increase in population (this being induced by the existence of a differential between the market rate of wages and the normal rate) has restored the per capita wage to the subsistence level. To the degree that the subsistence level is psychologically determined, the subsistence wage may fall, not to the pre-existing level, but to a somewhat higher level. This is equivalent to describing the subsistence level of wages as having a secular upward drift, and, to the degree that it so drifts, stationariness can be anticipated short of B.

As suggested, it might be worthwhile to examine in greater detail the difference in attitude of Smith, Ricardo, and Malthus toward the elements of the system described.

(1) *Population and wages.* Adam Smith's theory of population growth anticipated the Malthusian theory. At least, he said that "the demand for men, like that of any other commodity, necessarily regulates the production of men, quickens it when it goes on too slowly, and stops it when it advances too fast."[2] The more doctrinaire young Malthus might have denied that the production of men ever requires "quickening," and Smith agreed that however high the level of investment (i.e., however far above the subsistence level the market rate of wages might be), if this level should cease to rise since "the value of children is the greatest of all encouragements to marriage," the result would be that ". . . the number of labourers employed every year could easily supply, and even more than supply, the number wanted the following year. . . . The hands . . . would . . . naturally multiply beyond their employment."[3] Even if high wages or the "value of children" did not increase the number of marriages, indeed, even if one supposed that poverty or a low level of market wages was *not* a positive deterrent to marriage, this same poverty must still be extremely "unfavourable to the rearing of children."[4]

Malthus explicitly drew upon the suggestions of Adam Smith, among others, when he formulated his population "principle" in the *Essay.* However, he couched the principle in terms which were as dramatic as they were meaningless, when he enunciated the doctrine of comparative ratios.[5] In his *Principles* Malthus never completely abandoned a much weakened version: that the supply of labor is perfectly elastic at the subsistence wage level. He did admit that the subsistence wage rate might have a secular upward drift, but he never could be brought to agree that such a drift is an automatic consequence of economic growth. Malthus said that if the habits of the people (the standard of living) remain constant, the growth of population is an increasing function of the real wage, the "funds for the maintenance of labour." On the other hand, should these funds be held

2. Adam Smith, *An Inquiry into the Nature and Causes of the Wealth of Nations,* New York, 1937, p. 80. Alexander Gray (*The Development of Economic Doctrine,* London, 1948, p. 135) regards this as a terse and incisive summary of Malthus.

3. *Wealth of Nations,* p. 81.

4. *Ibid.,* p. 79.

5. Cf. Kenneth Smith's study, *The Malthusian Controversy,* London, 1951.

constant, the level of living and ultimately, though resisting, the standard of living, is a decreasing function of the population increase to be expected from the procreative habits of the people. He then added:

It rarely happens, however, that either of them remains fixed for any great length of time together. The rate at which the funds for the maintenance of labour increase is, we well know, liable to great variations; and the habits of people, though not so liable, or so necessarily subject to change, can scarcely ever be considered as permanent. In general, their tendency is to change together. When the funds for the maintenance of labour are rapidly increasing . . . he will acquire a taste for . . . conveniences, and his habits will be formed accordingly. On the other hand, it generally happens that, when the funds for the maintenance of labour become nearly stationary, such habits, if they have existed, are found to give way; and before the population comes to a stop, the standard of comfort is essentially lowered.[6]

All this could be interpreted to mean that wages, being more flexible upward than downward, must have a secular upward tendency, though hardly a rapid one.

Another important aspect of Malthus's wages and population theory in *Principles* is his explicit acknowledgement that an interval of time–he reckoned sixteen or eighteen years–must elapse before there is a noticeable change in the labor supply, as the result of an increase in the real wage rate. He recognized, to be sure, that there is scope for some expansion and contraction of the number of hours of labor expended through increasing intensity of effort and through the entry into the labor force of "marginal labor."[7] But this may only dampen the tidal-wave effect of the lag, and may even increase the amplitude of the ultimate shock, if the given population manifests inelasticity in their demand for income in terms of effort; if, in other words, there is a backward-rising supply schedule of labor. Will not, however, the laborer who has time left after producing necessaries utilize this time to acquire luxuries? Malthus feared that the workman might very well "consider indolence a greater luxury than those which he was likely to procure by further labour. . . ."[8] Thus, Malthus considered it not outside the realm of possibility that the owner of wage goods, seeking to invest them, might encounter "full employment" of the labor force, or

6. T. R. Malthus, *Principles of Political Economy Considered with a View to Their Practical Application* (1820), New York, 2nd ed., 1951, pp. 224-25.

7. Thus he explained that a "slack demand for labor is not sufficient perhaps to throw the actual labourers out of work but . . . is sufficient to prevent or diminish task work, to check the employment of women and children, and to give but little encouragement to the rising generation of labourers" *(ibid.,* p. 232). This cuts both ways, of course.

8. *Ibid.,* p. 133. Richard B. Simons attributes to Malthus the belief that " 'most' men are incorrigibly lazy. If they were not forced to work they would remain idle and soon 'sink to the level of brutes.' Curiously enough the 'upper classes' seem to have been free from this corruptibility . . ." ("T. R. Malthus on British Society," *Journal of the History of Ideas,* XVI, 1955, p. 61).

that an increased rate of real wages might result in a reduction of the number of hours or the intensity with which a given number of hours are spent.

Malthus defined a subsistence wage as "a certain portion of . . . necessaries . . . required to maintain a stationary population."[9] Yet, curiously enough (curious, that is, for the author of the *Essay*), he called a "most unnatural price" the Ricardian natural price of labor, "that price which is necessary to enable the labourers one with another to subsist, and to perpetuate their race without either increase or diminution."[10] Its unnaturalness resides in the fact that it is the wage that could exist only in the stationary state, and "could not permanently occur in any country, till the cultivation of the soil, or the power of importation had been pushed as far as possible."[11] Consequently, he considered it an analytical error to regard market price as a deviation from a wage which is "really rare, and in an ordinary state of things, at a great distance in point of time."

Ricardo's natural wage rate, as mentioned above, is the rate "which is necessary to enable the labourers, one with another, to subsist and perpetuate their race, without either increase or diminution." Although it may have appeared "unnatural" to Malthus when he was arguing with Ricardo, it does lend itself to purely analytical use, however difficult to isolate quantitatively from the market rate, as the wage which constitutes the "necessary" payment to labor; necessary, that is, to maintain the circular flow at the level of output which it is already producing.

But it is a variable rate of wages, even in Ricardo's presentation. Like Smith and Malthus, Ricardo seems to have believed that ordinarily the actual wage rate would be higher than the necessary rate. This upward displacement of the actual from the equilibrium rate presented the possibility and the mechanics whereby the equilibrium rate might rise. Thus, the social dividend is paid out by capitalists as wages in the investment process. While Smith had argued that the higher "wage" might lead to an increase in per capita output, Ricardo assumed, in general, that the technical input coefficient between labor and wage capital is fixed: A higher wage will not lead to an increase in per capita output. But the coefficient can vary over time. If the labor force did not increase during the "high-wage" period, but became habituated to the higher wage, so that in the next investment period a lower wage would lead to a reduction in the labor force, we might say that the normal or subsistence wage rate had risen to the market rate of the previous period, and that the technical coefficient had increased as between the two periods. However, the Ricardian assumption was that

9. *Principles*, p. 218.

10. Quoted in *ibid.*, p. 223 (original source: *The Works and Correspondence of David Ricardo*, Piero Sraffa, ed., Cambridge, 1951-1952, p. 93).

11. *Principles*, p. 223.

labor's reaction to an increase in wages would be an increase in numbers.

For Ricardo, the profit in any period of production could not be computed until labor had received the payment necessary to keep its numbers intact in the next period. This is the natural rate of wages. Having now seen what the rate of profits is, the capitalist may then decide to invest these profits. If he does so, profit from the last period becomes an "unnecessary" wage payment in the next period. The payment out of profits into the wages bill now becomes necessary in the following period if (a) the increase in the number of laborers drives the per capita real wage back to the old subsistence level, but the increase in hands means there is no reduction in the total payment that must be made in the next period; or (b) there is no increase in the size of the labor force, but any reduction in the real wage rate will induce a reduction in its size; or (c) it can remain a non-necessary payment from the social, but necessary from the competitive, point of view. In the last case it would actually be better to call it "profit received by the wage-earner," since it is, and continues to be, a part of the social surplus and is disposable.[12]

Certainly, Ricardo thought that where the custom-decreed subsistence standard of living remained the same (and he did not deny the possibility when it lagged, but was rising to a higher level of living), the market rate could continue above the natural rate for an indefinite period of time. In an improving society,

> . . . no sooner may the impulse which an increased capital gives to a new demand for labour be obeyed, than another increase of capital may produce the same effect; and thus, if the increase of capital be gradual and constant, the demand for labour may give a continued stimulus to an increase of people.[13]

Here is Smith's theorem: Competition among capitals will cause the rate of wages to be bid up, and for an indefinite period. It is paradoxical that when Ricardo analyzed the course of the rate of profit and the trend of rent, he virtually ignored this possibility.[14]

But whatever probability value Ricardo may have assigned to a rising wage level, caused by the outstripping by capital accumulation of a numerical increase in an incontinent population, he was sure that the laboring class could ameliorate its living conditions by reducing its rate of increase to zero. This might come about through the development of a taste on

12. *Works and Correspondence of David Ricardo,* I, p. 347 and 347*n.;* also VI, p. 147.
13. *Ibid.,* I, p. 95.
14. Cf. Ricardo's remark, quoted by J. H. Hollander in his introduction to Ricardo's *Notes on Malthus' "Principles of Political Economy,"* Baltimore, 1928, p. lxxxiii: "How then can it justly be said of me that the only cause I have recognized of high or low profits is the facility or difficulty of providing food for the labourer. I contend that I have also recognized the other cause, the relative amount of population to capital which is another of the great regulators of wages."

their part "for comforts and enjoyments," and he even suggested that "they should be stimulated by all legal means in their exertions to procure them."[15]

Granted that Ricardo's theory of wages can comfortably house a rise in the standard of living and the contingency that the laboring class will increase its preference for comforts over procreation, it would seem that analytically at least and in his policy recommendations as well, Ricardo did not pay much attention to the possibility. In general, he seems to have assumed that population growth would swallow up any gains from technological innovations fairly quickly—quite in the spirit of the early Malthus. Thus, in the Ricardian scheme, labor, though it *need* not be, and in the future *might* not be, was, in that time and place (and for the purposes of his analysis), considered an essentially passive factor, perfectly elastic in supply at the subsistence level of wages.[16]

(2) *Investment and the rate of profits.* If, in the classical model, economic growth depended on the response in the size of the labor force to the market rate of wages, while the market rate of wages depended on the willingness of the capitalist to invest the social dividend, some theory of investment behavior is required. All of the members of the classical school agreed to the proposition that the rate of profits must fall as the economy grows.[17] They were not in complete agreement, however, as to the reason for the fall, and where they agreed as to the reason, as did Smith and Malthus, they did not predict the same investor response to the decline.

Smith's theory of profits is not easily extricated. It does not seem completely erroneous, however, to ascribe to him the belief that if one regards an economy as a stationary going concern, the surplus can be isolated by subtracting from total output the costs necessary to reproduce it. Such costs include subsistence wages,[18] the subsistence of the capitalist,[19] and the price exacted by the owner of capital for not consuming it. After

15. *Works and Correspondence of David Ricardo*, I, p. 100.

16. E.g., *ibid.*, p. 16, 78.

17. But a dissenting voice: "The other question remains a practical question, and carrying along with it a sting of anxiety to whole generations. It is this:—Amongst all men (even those who pretend no scientific economy) there is a misgiving that profits, and by consequence, interest, must be under a fatal necessity of gradually sinking, until at length they touch the point of extinction. Even Ricardo has too much authorized this false idea. There is no *essential tendency* downwards in profits, more than upwards . . . the rate of interest is under no immutable law of declension. During these two centuries it has not uniformly declined: on the contrary it has oscillated in all directions: and by that one fact, so abundantly established, we are released from all apprehensions of a downward *destiny*" (Thomas de Quincey, "Logic of Political Economy," in *Collected Writings*, D. Masson, ed., London, 1897, IX, pp. 293-94). McCulloch, (*The Principles of Political Economy*, Edinburgh, 1825, p. 381) too, spoke of the beneficial effect of a high rate of profits. He seems properly to have felt that both wages and profits could rise if technological innovation were sufficiently rapid.

18. *Wealth of Nations*, p. 67.

19. "His profit, besides, is his revenue, the proper fund of his subsistence . . ." (*ibid.*, p. 55).

the payment of rent, there remains a disposable surplus which is the major source of investment.[20] It must be added that rent, too, is a source of investment, but was regarded by Smith as yielding interest to the rentier-lender, a payment that could be met from profits obtained by the entrepreneur-user of the borrowed capital.[21] The motive to invest was the increased return afforded by the greater division of labor as more workmen were employed. Smith seems to have thought that accumulation or the investment of the social surplus as wages would constantly outstrip the growth of the labor force so that investors would have increasing difficulty in obtaining new hands. To do so, they would have to pay higher wages and accept a lower rate of profit.[22] Smith's investor is undeterred by the fall in the rate of profits. Above some undefined minimum, he will "naturally" invest his profits for the sake of the pecuniary rewards.[23] Indeed, the number of entrepreneurs will probably increase as the rate falls, since the falling rate of profit pushes down the rate of interest, compelling the rentier to turn entrepreneur. Thus does the "natural" become the "necessary."[24]

---

20. But cf. J. J. Spengler, "Adam Smith's Theory of Economic Growth, Part I," *Southern Economic Journal,* XXV, 1959, p. 410: "Smith did not specifically identify undertakers and landlords as the main suppliers of capital, nor . . . did he define net revenue, as Ricardo later did, to make it essentially identical with the supposedly main source of savings and tax revenue, namely profits-plus-rent." Yet, as Spengler goes on to say, he certainly did this implicitly.

21. "That revenue derived from stock, by the person who manages or employs it, is called profit. That derived from it by the person who does not employ it himself but lends it to another, is called the interest or the use of money. It is the compensation which the borrower pays to the lender, for the profit which he has an opportunity of making by the use of the money. Part of the profit naturally belongs to the borrower, who runs the risk and takes the trouble of employing it: and part to the lender, who affords him the opportunity of making this profit. The interest of money is always a derivative revenue, which, if it is not paid from the profit which is made by the use of the money, must be paid from some other source of revenue" (*Wealth of Nations,* p. 52).

22. "When the stocks of many rich merchants are turned into the same trade their mutual competition naturally tends to lower profit; and when there is a like increase of stock in all the different trades carried on in the some [*sic*] society, the same competition must produce the same effect in them all" (*ibid.,* p. 87). Also, "The demand for labour increases with the increase of stock whatever be its profits; and after these are diminished, stock may not only continue to increase, but to increase much faster than before. . . . A great stock, though with small profits, generally increases faster than a small stock with great profits" (*ibid.,* p. 93). I do not defend Smith's arithmetic here.

23. "When an independent workman, such as a weaver or shoemaker has got more stock than what is sufficient to purchase the materials of his own work, and to maintain himself until he can dispose of it, he *naturally* employs one or more journeymen with the surplus in order to make a profit by their work" (*ibid.,* p. 69). Also, "As soon as the stock has accumulated in the hands of particular persons, some of them will *naturally* employ it in setting to work industrious people . . ." (*ibid.,* p. 58). "But when he possesses stock sufficient to maintain him for months or years he *naturally* endeavours to derive a revenue from the greater part of it . . ." (*ibid.,* p. 262 and *passim*). All italics supplied.

24. In Holland it is "unfashionable not to be a man of business. Necessity makes it usual for almost every man to be so, and custom every where regulates fashion" (*ibid.,* p. 96). Also, ". . . as the ordinary rate of clear profit would be very small, so the usual market rate of interest which could be offered out of it, would be so low as to render it impossible for any but the very wealthiest people to live upon the interest of their money. All people of small or middling fortunes would be obliged to superintend themselves the employment of their own stocks. It would be necessary that almost every man should be a man of business, or engage in some sort of trade" (*ibid*).

Thus, it is not, I believe, a complete violation of Smith's theory of profits to express it as follows: If an economy is progressing, then, *ex definitione,* capital is increasing, as is population. But also *ex definitione,* capital is increasing faster than population. These comparative rates of increase imply competition among capitalists for relatively scarce labor and, to the degree that this intensifies, the rate of profits will decline.[25] This at least seems to have been the construction placed on Smith's theory by Malthus and Ricardo.

Although Ricardo agreed with Smith as to the historical tendency of the rate of profits[26] to fall, he not only assigned a different reason for the decline, but assumed a different reaction to it on the part of the entrepreneur.

Smith, it will be recalled, holding no rigorous idea of *gradually* diminishing returns in agriculture,[27] saw the decline of profits as the result of "competition among capitals." Ricardo, on the other hand, while he admitted this as a cause, held that there is no permanent force making for lower profits other than the increasing cost of "producing" additional units of labor.[28] Under what assumptions was Ricardo justified?

25. It would be a relief to be able to say with any assurance that Smith also entertained some idea of the principle of diminishing returns to labor plus capital when applied to land. One cannot, but Smith at least pointed out that "when the most fertile and best situated lands have been all occupied, less profit can be made by the cultivation of what is inferior both in soil and situation, and less interest can be afforded for the stock which is so employed. In the greater part of our colonies, accordingly, both the legal and the market rate of interest have been considerably reduced during the course of the present century" *(ibid.,* p. 93).

26. Edwin Cannan (in *A History of the Theories of Production and Distribution,* London, 3rd ed., 1924, p. 206) points out that "Ricardo, who knew very well what profits meant in the concrete, was little interested in the abstract question of their nature and origin. He gives no definition of the term, and nowhere formally expresses any opinion on the subject." This is a curious construction, indeed, especially since the Ricardian theory in a very real sense *hinges* on the behavior of the rate of profits.

It might be well to indicate, also, that the Ricardian entrepreneur does not maximize money income so much as "net advantage." Thus, "a capitalist, in seeking profitable employment for his funds, will naturally take into consideration all the advantages which one occupation possesses over another. He may therefore be willing to forego a part of his money profit in consideration of the security, cleanliness, ease, or any other real or fancied advantage which one employment may possess over another" *(Works and Correspondence of David Ricardo,* I, p. 90).

27. I stress the *gradually.* Smith's concept of "maximum opulence" is, of course, incompatible with the idea of indefinitely increasing returns. Returns might not diminish gradually, but they must ultimately drop to zero.

28. "With the progress of society the natural price of labour has always a tendency to rise, because one of the principal commodities by which its natural price is regulated has a tendency to become dearer from the greater difficulty of producing it" *(Works and Correspondence of David Ricardo,* I, p. 93). Also: "From the account which has been given of the profits of stock, it will appear that no accumulation of capital will permanently lower profits unless there be some permanent cause for the rise of wages. If the funds for the maintenance of labour were doubled, trebled, or quadrupled, there would not long be any difficulty in procuring the requisite number of hands to be employed by those funds; but owing to the increasing difficulty of making constant additions to the food of the country, funds of the same value would probably not maintain the same quantity of labour. . . . Adam Smith, however, uniformly ascribed the fall of profits to the accumulation of capital, and to the competition which will result from it, without ever adverting to the increasing difficulty of providing food for the additional number of labourers which the additional capital will employ. . . . Adam Smith speaks here of a rise of wages, but it is of a temporary rise, pro-

Let us visualize again an economy at the end of a period of production, with the total product in the hands of the capitalist. After the payments necessary to insure a duplication of this product are made, there remains in the hands of the capitalist a surplus. Net profit for the period past would be computed by taking this surplus as a proportion of the total payments in the last period.[29] We consider that this surplus now is invested by the process described above. If there is no increase in the size of the labor force, since there need be no recourse to poorer land, neither gross product nor rent will increase. And at the end of the production period there will be a surplus identical with that generated in the last period. Necessary duplication payments are again made. If the payment required by labor has now increased (i.e., if the subsistence level has risen), then the net surplus remaining to the capitalist is smaller than in the previous period. Indeed, it may be zero. But, Ricardo would say, the physical surplus has not diminished, only now it is in the hands of the laborer. The cost of maintaining the labor force intact has risen, and profits have diminished by that amount. If the disposable surplus in the hands of the capitalists has fallen to zero, the economy has entered into the stationary state (unless the laborer, *qua* capitalist, invests). It is not, however, competition among capitals that has caused the rate of profits to fall, but an increase in the necessary wages of labor. Nevertheless, Ricardo would agree that it is the competition among capitals which raises the "market rate" sufficiently for the natural rate to rise (in real terms) over the course of time. But, as we concluded with respect to wages, population response was essentially passive in the Ricardian analysis. Consequently, while he would not rule out completely the possibility of a situation such as that sketched above, he would have considered it most unlikely.

ceeding from increased funds before the population is increased and he does not appear to see at the same time that capital is increased the work to be effected by capital is increased in the same proportion" (*ibid.*, p. 289). And of Smith's having given Holland as an example of an economy where competition of capitals had greatly reduced the rate of profits, Ricardo said: ". . . Holland was obliged to import almost all the corn which she consumed, and by imposing heavy taxes on the necessaries of the labour she further raised the wages of labour. These facts will sufficiently account for the low rate of profits and interest in Holland" (*ibid.*, p. 290*n*).

29. Although it remained for Senior to make it explicit, this concept of profit as the return uniquely to circulating capital seems to me strongly implied by Ricardo. I think it is clear that the social dividend was envisioned by the classical school as wage goods which could be used to support labor in the production of luxury goods, fixed capital, or more wage goods. Ricardo did not address himself to the question of the factors determining the division of labor into these three sectors until the third edition of the *Principles.* Cf. J.-B. Say, *A Treatise on Political Economy,* translated from the 4th ed. of the French by C. R. Prinsep, New American Edition, Philadelphia, 1857, pp. 305-306: ". . . the general and eternal law . . . is . . . that the more abundant is the disposable capital, in proportion to the multiplicity of its employments, the lower will the interest of borrowed capital fall. . . . But it is essential to pay strict attention to the meaning of the term *supply of disposable capital;* for this alone can have any influence upon the rate of interest; it is only so much capital, as the owners have both the power and the will to dispose of, that can be said to be in circulation. A capital already vested and engaged in production or otherwise, is no longer in the market, and therefore no longer forms a part of the total circulating capital. . . ."

In the normal course of events, according to Ricardo, the paying out of net profits from one period as wages above subsistence in the next would induce an increase in the labor force. If new land is taken into cultivation, there is a double pressure on profits: rents will rise on inframarginal land and the necessary wage payments to duplicate the now-larger gross product will be larger than those of the previous period. It seems to be true that Ricardo considered a stationary population to *depend* on the arrival of zero net investment. Thus, he said: "The tendency of the population to increase is, in our state of society, more than equal to that of capital to increase."[30]

Since the same result was arrived at by both Smith and Ricardo (and, to anticipate, by Malthus) and since, furthermore, any disagreement appears to be merely a terminological one, we might well inquire why the argument should be resolved. It would seem to matter in two essential ways. First, we have seen that Ricardo's system does not require a completely elastic labor supply. It is still workable if we assume a rising real wage, as long as we are careful to distinguish between the normal and the market rates of wages. Second, it is important when the speed of development is considered. It will be sufficient here to indicate that Ricardo conceded that competition among capitals could lead to a temporary drop in the rate of profits. However, he usually would have said "*only* a temporary drop." And, in his discounting of the time period required for population growth to restore the rate of profits to a higher (though not so high as the previous) level, there resides a world of difficulty when it comes to making policy proposals. If capital were quadrupled, Ricardo said, "there would not long be any difficulty in procuring the requisite number of hands."[31] Yet, rather than discounting, he magnified this lag when he arrived at the point of discussing the effect of cheaper food on the level of rents. Some of the implications of this will be discussed below.

In another sense, with respect to the reaction on the part of the capitalist to the secular fall in the rate of profits, Ricardo took exception to Smith's model of economic progress. Some difficulty is experienced in deciding whether Smith implied that a lower rate of profits is a *cause* of a greater quantity of savings, or whether a low rate of profits is the reflection of so high a level of wealth that *despite* the lower rate of profits a greater

30. He said this in a letter to Malthus in 1816 (*Works and Correspondence of David Ricardo*, VII, p. 72), having first acknowledged as logically sound Malthus' query as to "whether, if population were miraculously stopped while the most fertile land remained uncultivated, profits would not fall upon the supposition of an increase of capital still going on . . ." (*ibid.*, p. 69). In a new country, population may be incapable of as rapid an increase as capital, owing to the introduction of "arts and knowledge of countries far advanced in refinement." This might lead to a situation in which the competition of capitals appears as the sole force in the reduction of profits "if the deficiency of labourers were not supplied by more populous countries . . ." (*ibid.*, I, p. 98).

31. *Ibid.*, I, p. 289.

quantity of savings would be forthcoming. Smith might have meant that while profits are high, men can afford to be extravagant; but as the rate falls, they are forced to reduce their consumption in order to maintain a given level of income. Ricardo seems to have interpreted Smith in the former or causal sense, which he rejected: "While the profits of stock are high, men will have a motive to accumulate."[32]

There is room, however, to feel that Ricardo thought that, given income, the quantity of saving is an increasing function of the rate of profits, but that, given the rate of profits, saving is an increasing function of the level of income. (Smith, if we disregard his concept of "Sargant man" as typical in his analysis, simply considered income and the rate of interest as necessarily inverse.) Of the means, as opposed to the motives, for saving, McCulloch said: "And the capitalist who can invest capital so as to yield a profit of 10 per cent has it equally in his power to accumulate twice as fast as the capitalist who can obtain 5. . . ." Ricardo remarked on this: "This is understated–he could do more than accumulate twice as fast. Out of two loaves I may save one, out of four I may save three."[33]

It seems, then, a pity that Ricardo never clearly distinguished between the two concepts of the motive and the means for saving. At the same time, it must be conceded that current theory is little better off with respect to the distinction, since there is still empirical uncertainty as to whether saving is an increasing or decreasing function of the rate of interest, or whether it can properly be taken as a function at all, or whether it were not better solely related to the level of income.

It seems unnecessary to expound once again on the frequently discussed Ricardian use of the differential rent analysis. While in all production, except agricultural production, it was the low-cost firm whose unit of output was price-governing, in agriculture it was that of the high-cost firm. By this I mean to say that the natural course of price was downward for manufactured goods, and the firm which, by the use of innovations, was able to produce the most cheaply would capture the entire market unless firms which produced less efficiently followed its lead in innovation.[34]

32. *Ibid.*, p. 290. Victor Edelberg ("The Ricardian Theory of Profits," *Economica*, XIII, 1933, p. 63, note 29), in discussing the validity of this, says: "It may, of course, be argued against this that the rate of interest may fall indefinitely and that the incomes of investors may, nevertheless, continue undiminished; this is true provided that the amount of capital increases indefinitely in inverse ratio to the rate of interest–but such a supposition is extravagant." Far from extravagant, Smith apparently would have held that capital and interest *must* behave in precisely this inverse fashion.

33. In 1882 Ricardo also wrote to McCulloch (*Works and Correspondence of David Ricardo*, IX, p. 193) of "the abundance and cheapness of commodities" as affording "incentives to saving, and to the accumulation of capital," even where there is no rise in the profits of stock (*ibid.*, I, p. 133).

34. "The natural price of all commodities, excepting raw produce and labour, has a tendency to fall in the progress of wealth and population; for though, on the one hand, they are enhanced in real value, from the rise in the natural price of the raw material of which they are made, this is more than counterbalanced by the improvements in machinery, by the better division and distribu-

In agriculture, on the other hand, the "machines" or land that must be utilized as the demand increases because of population growth are poorer and poorer, and the differential between cost (not including rent) and price that ensues on higher-grade land as lands of inferior quality are taken under cultivation is competitively appropriated by the owners of the higher-grade land as rent.

One might very well object to this concept on the grounds that innovation can take place (and *has* taken place) in agriculture no less rapidly than in manufacturing. However, Ricardo assumed that while agricultural innovation might occur, it would not be sufficient to offset the poorer quality of the marginal unit of land; that is, the secular upward movement of the schedule of agricultural returns could not offset the downard movement caused by the increasing demand for food. And, of course, as viewed in retrospect, this was perhaps the chief weakness of the classical analysis, as formulated by and after Ricardo.

Malthus took specific note of–and rejected–Adam Smith's treatment of the obstacle to growth of a fall in the rate of profits by postulating such behavior on the part of the entrepreneur and rentier as would lead to increasing aggregate savings as the rate of return declined, resulting from their efforts to keep their incomes constant or to increase them. He agreed that high profits might lead to extravagant habits, but felt that "extravagant habits were a more frequent cause of a scarcity of capital and high profits, than high profits are a cause of extravagant habits."[35] Malthus found some justification, however, for Smith's presumption, in that "when a great revenue has once been created in a country . . . a considerable resistance will be made to any essential fall in its value."[36] But if income "in this way, by possibility be maintained, there is little chance of its increasing.[37] Malthus, like Ricardo, refused to admit that Smith's "Sargant man" is typical, and concluded that saving is an increasing function of the rate of profits.

Malthus defined capital as "that particular part of . . . accumulated wealth, which is destined to be employed with a view to profit in the production and distribution of future wealth. . . ."[38] The profits of capital are the difference between the price received for the commodity in whose production it is used and the cost of producing the commodity.[39] This cost

tion of labour, and by the increasing skill, both of science and art, of the producers" (*ibid.*, p. 94). Which is to say, diminishing returns would set in in manufacturing, as well as in agriculture (or better say *because* of diminishing returns to agriculture), were it not for the fact that this tendency will be overbalanced by increasing returns to scale (including innovation).

35. *Principles*, p. 192*n*.

36. *Ibid.*, p. 355.

37. *Ibid.*, p. 356. Since Malthus is discussing foreign trade when he makes this statement, I am guilty of quoting "out of context." I should not do so did I not consider the application of the sentiment in this context justified.

38. *Ibid.*, p. 262.

39. "In the employment of capital therefore, in any business, the advances, whether

is the sum of the advances which "consist of accumulations generally made up of wages, rents, taxes, interest, and profits."[40] At first glance, it appears contradictory to treat profits both as a cost and as a residual after costs. It is not, I think, because Malthus was considering the cost item "profit" as the non-outlay cost or "normal profit," the amount of profit required to maintain capital intact; the rate, that is, which would prevail in the stationary state.[41] Indeed, Malthus defined the natural rate of profits as the rate "which would just keep up the capital without increase or diminution. This is in fact the rate to which profits are constantly tending."[42] But it seems that we should interpret him here as we did in the matter of the natural price of labor. At any time, the normal level will be that level appropriate to the point which the economy has reached in its path toward the stationary state. It will depend, that is, on the real productivity of the marginal unit of land. In this Malthus agreed with Ricardo, and referred to such determination of the normal rate of profits as the "limiting principle." He said that "this cause is indeed of such a nature, that, if its action goes on, it must finally overwhelm every other."[43] The additional application of capital and labor to a fixed quantity of land, Malthus would say, results in a declining "joint" marginal product. Labor's absolute share being determined by subsistence at the limit, it is the same for marginal and inframarginal outputs. Labor's relative share in the joint marginal product increases, and the share going to profits declines, both absolutely and relatively.

Malthus also shared with Ricardo the idea that agriculture is subject to decreasing returns, but that manufacturing is subject to increasing returns. In this he was quite explicit:

> The elementary cost of manufacture, or the quantity of labour and other conditions of supply necessary to produce a given quantity of them, has a constant tendency to diminish; while the quantity of labour and other conditions of the supply necessary to procure the last addition which has been made to the raw produce of a rich and advancing country, has a constant tendency to increase.[44]

The question immediately arises as to why capital does not flow from agriculture, where the rate of profits is diminishing, into manufacturing, where it is increasing. Malthus admitted that it would, and he noted two equilibrating effects resulting from the flow. First, the competition

---

increasing or diminishing in value, may be known and measured *beforehand*, while the value of the product, and the proportion of that value which goes to replace the advances remains to be ascertained when the produce is sold" (*ibid.*, p. 266).

40. *Ibid.*, p. 262.

41. I do not think anything is to be gained from taking a position in the controversy over whether the rate of interest in a stationary state can lie above zero. I have the strong impression that the classical school considered that it would lie above zero, but only by some very small amount.

42. *Ibid.*, p. 224*n*.

43. *Ibid.*, p. 281.

44. *Ibid.*, p. 188. Cf. also pp. 273-74.

among capitals entering manufacture for opportunities in that field will tend to drive down the rate of returns to the level of agricultural profits. And, if employment be found for capital in manufacturing, the increased output attributable to its use will diminish in value relative to agricultural necessities. The terms of trade, that is, will turn increasingly in favor of agricultural output. This, too, was the Ricardian position, though Ricardo might have rejected the first effect.

In the face of such apparent accord between Malthus and Ricardo, how did it come about that in 1824 Malthus stated his conviction that Ricardo and his "school" were guilty of "an error equally fundamental and important . . . as that of the French economists. . . ."?[45] The fallacy, according to Malthus, was their "attempt to estimate the rate of profits in any country for ten or twenty years together with reference to this cause, diminishing returns to land, alone. . . ."[46] He felt this would lead "to the greatest practical errors," because the rate of profit, as will be recalled, is *actually* computed from the margin between the sales receipts of today's output and the costs of yesterday's input. Ricardo (at least in the *Principles*) would have denied that such a difference could exist. But Malthus insisted that not only could such a difference exist, but in all likelihood it would. Here Malthus followed directly in line with Adam Smith.[47] He spoke of

> . . . the varying value of the produce of the same quantity of labour occasioned by the accidental or ordinary state of the demand and supply, by which a greater or smaller proportion of that produce falls to the share of the labourers employed. This may be called the regulating principle of profits. . . .[48]

In a summary, Malthus held that the rate of profits can be driven down by the competition of capitals. He criticized Adam Smith for failing to take into account the "limiting principle" governing the trend in the rate of profits, but said that Smith's proposition of the practical dependence of profits on "the abundance and competition of capital" was "practically much nearer the truth" than the attitude of those who give unique effect to the limiting principle.

In the situation described, it is wage costs that would rise above their necessary level. Ricardo would have agreed to the possibility, denying, however, that the rate of profits (in the sense of social dividend as a proportion of total product prior to distribution) had fallen at all, but asserting rather that a portion of the wage was, in reality, profit.

Perhaps more important, Malthus emphasized a different case, one

45. Quoted by Bonar, *Malthus and His Work*, London, 1885, p. 275, from the *Quarterly Review*, LX, 1824, pp. 333-34.
46. *Principles*, p. 281.
47. "Even McCulloch conceded that Malthus was in the line of Adam Smith in this matter" (S. G. Checkland, "The Propagation of Ricardian Economics in England," *Economica*, XVI, 1949, p. 40).
48. *Principles*, p. 271.

in which, units costs remaining the same, an increase in output might not "command" the labor–more accurately, the necessary joint costs of production–it "embodies." In his analysis, Malthus distinguished between the wealth of a country (i.e., the mass of physical things it has produced) and the value of this wealth (i.e., the price that the quantity will command). He indicated that "the wealth of a country . . . does not always increase in proportion to the increase of value; because an increase of value may sometimes take place under an actual diminution of commodities."[49] In defense of this proposition, he made two arguments: First, the diminution in value of an increment to wealth may take place "because the various articles of which this quantity is composed may not be so proportioned to the wants and powers of the society as to give them their proper value." Ricardo, of course, agreed with the possibility of a temporary misallocation of resources, but would have attributed it to entrepreneurial miscalculation and considered it as incidental to the allocative process.[50] Capital would flow from the temporarily glutted industry into the area of scarcity. Malthus complained of this as the ascription of excessive mobility to capital. He doubted the possibility of a smooth transfer of unnecessary capital into an industry where the demand is elastic, because "in withdrawing capital, a part of which must necessarily be fixed, from one employment and placing it in another, there is almost always a considerable loss."[51] The Ricardian position on this is that the entrepreneur must simply take the loss on his sunk capital, and with all possible speed. Whereupon, Malthus again adverted to the inelasticity of the demand for income in terms of effort, but this time on the part of the entrepreneur. For experience had shown him that entrepreneurs retired from business when they could have continued to grow richer, and that "most men place some limits, however variable, to the quantity of conveniences and luxuries which they will labour for. . . ."[52] Here the crux of the dispute between Ricardo and Malthus begins to be clarified.

The basic argument between them can be reduced, as I see it, to a question of the shape of the demand schedule for wage goods. When Malthus said that an increase in value can take place with an actual diminution of commodities (and conversely, one supposes, a decrease of value with an augmenting of commodities), he very clearly implied that the aggregate demand for total output can be inelastic.[53] This is by no

49. *Ibid.*, p. 301.

50. *Works and Correspondence of David Ricardo*, II, p. 305.

51. *Principles*, p. 353. Ricardo would have argued that the rules of return to fixed capital, once it was constructed, were the rules of rent; it is the return to "free," that is, variable, capital that is the issue.

52. *Ibid.*, p. 355. While Malthus does not make it clear that it is the fall in the rate of profits that causes men to retire from business, I believe the inference is reasonable.

53. "If commodities were only to be compared and exchanged with each other, then indeed it would be true that, if they were all increased in their proper proportions to any

means the heroic assumption that it may appear. For, under the terms of the argument, total output is increasingly (and, in the strongest case, totally) composed of wage goods. This follows from the fact that entrepreneurs, landlords, and other rich persons ". . . by the supposition, have agreed to be parsimonious, and by depriving themselves of their usual conveniences and luxuries to save from their revenue and add to their capital."[54] This has the initial effect of increasing the demand for wage goods. Let us trace the process. First, there is a shift in demand away from luxury goods toward wage goods, a sufficient increase, let us say, in the production of the latter to absorb the workers displaced from the luxury-goods industries. The owners of the output of the wage-goods industries enter the market with their capital, seeking labor to equip with it for the further production of wage goods. The initial effect of the "competition among capitals" for relatively scarce labor will be to drive up the real wage of labor. (Ricardo's insistence that the increased wage is actually the profits of capital will do little to buoy up the spirits of the capitalists as their incomes fall. There is compensation, of course, to the degree to which the wage-earners, now with a higher potential level of living, forego it to turn entrepreneur themselves.) This produces an impulse toward increase in the population which, however, will not be felt in the labor market for sixteen to eighteen years. So far, Ricardo would agree. But this, he maintained, is a temporary situation.[55] Malthus might well be indulged a certain impatience with Ricardo if he is disposing of a sixteen-to-eighteen-year period as "immediate" and the effect as "temporary." It is to be said in Ricardo's defense that per capita income *will* decrease, though income per family will remain the same. This may serve to lower the level of living; but will not increase profits until output increases, and for output to increase more hands are needed, and a

---

extent, they would continue to bear among themselves the same relative value; but, if we compare them, as we certainly ought to do, with the means of producing them, and with the numbers and wants of the consumers, then a great increase of produce with comparatively stationary numbers or with wants diminished by parsimony, must necessarily occasion a great fall of value estimated in labour, so that the same produce, though it might have *cost* the same quantity of labour as before, would no longer *command* the same quantity; and both the power of accumulation and the motive to accumulate would be strongly checked" *(ibid.*, p. 317).

54. *Ibid.*, p. 315. If this seems to house poorly with the assumption of an elastic demand for income, let us make it sequential. First the agreement to be parsimonious, then the effects of this agreement, among which are to be numbered a reaction on the demand for income.

55. "There is only one case, and that will be temporary, in which the accumulation of capital with a low price of food may be attended with a fall of profits; and that is, when the funds for the maintenance of labour increase much more rapidly than population; —wages will then be high and profits low. If every man were to forego the use of luxuries and be intent only on accumulation, a quantity of necessaries might be produced for which there could not be any immediate consumption. Of commodities so limited in number, there might undoubtedly be an universal glut; and consequently there might neither be demand for an additional quantity of such commodities, nor profits on the employment of more capital. If men ceased to consume, they would cease to produce" (quoted, *ibid.*, pp. 318-19).

child must mature before he can work.[56] But Malthus went further than scoring Ricardo's "temporary," for he implied that the economy will be unable to emerge from the slump once it has got into it; that, rather, the slump will be a self-perpetuating condition. That is to say, he maintained that even when the population increase manifests itself on the labor market, the consequent fall in the rate of wages and rise in the rate of profits will not serve to reactivate the abandoned habit of parsimony. How does he make his case?

We have, first, simply the assertion that "the pressure of population hard against the limits of subsistence, does not furnish an effective stimulus to the continued increase of wealth. . . ."[57] This proposition is "confirmed by universal experience." While the case is by no means universal today, we must admit that there are examples in point. Malthus also said, however, that his proposition is also "evident in theory." And it is this that remains to be shown. He attempted to do so by treating several objections that might be made to his point that the slump will be self-perpetuating. We have already suggested the first objection. Will not the competition among the labor force, now approaching the level of subsistence, by driving down the rate of wages, raise the rate of profits sufficiently to bring about the utilization of any redundant capital and, indeed, to induce the creation of more by way of parsimony? No, said Malthus. Perhaps, this may happen temporarily, but only temporarily, because "the fall of real wages cannot go beyond a certain point without not only stopping the progress of the population but making it even retrograde."[58] Here we have a most interesting case. The necessary price of capital can be obtained only by the acceptance on the part of labor of a negative price (in the sense of being below the subsistence requirement).[59] Disregarding, for a moment, Ricardo's challenge that this *defines* a stationary state and cannot come about so long as resources are still available, Malthus does provide us with a possibly useful model of an underdeveloped economy.[60]

56. It is by this line of reasoning that Say quoted with disapproval the remark of a French general who, surveying the littered battlefield after a particularly bloody engagement, is reported to have said, "*Une nuit de Paris réparera tout cela*" (*op.cit.*, p. 334 note).

57. *Principles*, p. 311.

58. *Ibid.*, p. 312.

59. Turning the case around, cf. Joan Robinson, "Mr. Harrod's Dynamics," in *Collected Economic Papers*, Oxford, 1951, pp. 166-67: "Mr. Harrod suggests that . . . the ruling rate of interest is below or above the rate required for steady progress, but this way of putting the matter is somewhat artificial, for it may be that the influence of the rate of interest is so weak that no conceivable rate of interest would do the trick, so that the 'required rate of interest' has no meaning; and even when there is a definite value for the required rate it may well be one which could not conceivably obtain (for instance, it might be negative)."

60. "But how capital and population should be both redundant while you can increase the supply of necessaries I am at a loss to conceive. It is a contradiction in terms, it is saying there is a capital unemployed because its owner cannot find labourers, and there are people unemployed because there is no one having a capital to employ them"

We might find such a situation prevailing either in an economy whose members were all at the level of subsistence or in an economy, the bulk of whose members were at subsistence, and for those members who were not, the supplying of capital was not rewarded in sufficient value terms, though it might be great enough in real terms so that it was more than sufficient to pay the wages of labor. Here we would have the problem of increasing the effective demand for wage goods, or of making it more elastic. The next logical query then is: Will not the population increase, by intensifying the demand for consumption goods, raise their price above cost and so elevate the rate of profits to the necessary height? Malthus admitted that the population will have a *desire* for consumption goods, but denied that this desire can show itself as effective demand, since there is no labor available to begin with and no demand for it as it becomes available. No farmer will advance capital as wages to labor, if the return from the sale of the product of the additional labor is just equal to the wage outlay. As Malthus put it,

There must be something in the previous state of the demand and supply of the commodity, antecedent to and independent of the demand occasioned by the new labourers, in order to warrant the employment of an additional number of people in production.[61]

With the most sympathetic interpretation possible, we might believe Malthus to be saying something like this: Given an economy in stationary equilibrium with wages at subsistence, the investment of a unit of capital may, indeed, result in a positive return in real terms. But the reinvestment of this return will serve only to raise wages and will not therefore be undertaken.[62] This is not without theoretical credibility and might conceivably characterize an underdeveloped economy, particularly if, on the part of the property-owning class, parsimony is engaged in only for the sake of parsimony. This seems to be the presumption, for the next objection is: Why do not the capitalists increase their consumption sufficiently to furnish the necessary increase in demand? Because, Malthus said, they have agreed not to spend on "conveniences and luxuries," but "to add to their capital."[63] (This is, of course, of little interest to us, but I think we might substitute for it the supposition that the only available objects for expenditure are desired in no greater quantity.) It will be recalled, as it

---

(*Works and Correspondence of David Ricardo*, II, pp. 426-27). But cf. Joan Robinson, *op.cit.*, p. 165, ". . . in the slump, there is unused capacity, as well as unemployed labour."

61. *Principles*, p. 312.

62. Although not in this specific connection, Mrs. Robinson makes a comment of some interest here: "It may be that this is a mare's nest. It is hard to imagine investment being deterred by a prospective scarcity of labour" (*op.cit*, p. 170). It is not, I think, so hard to imagine under the classical restriction of investment as meaning the outpayment of wages, and with the further assumption of a fixed input coefficient between variable capital and labor.

63. *Principles*, p. 315.

was by Malthus, that this is the case in which Ricardo acknowledged the possibility of a glut. This being true, let us accept the Malthusian model with the following proviso: If it is true that the demand for the output of secondary and tertiary industry is virtually nonexistent in an economy characterized by private property and a skewed income distribution, the economy may come to rest in equilibrium short of the maximum population its land resource is capable of feeding. In the case as imagined, equalizing incomes would have the effect only of increasing the population. For, according to Malthus, the recipients of the transferred income would have no desire for a great quantity of luxuries and conveniences.[64]

We might summarize Malthus' position as follows: (a) An increase in the output of wage goods, since it will raise the real wage, encountering, as it does, an inelastic labor supply, will lower the rate of profits. (b) The increased wage may well result in diminished effort on the part of the labor force, just as the declining rate of profits may lead to diminishing entrepreneurial activity. These reactions, mutually reinforcing, may well result in a stationary equilibrium. (c) If the increased wage to labor results, not in diminished effort, but in an increase in population, when the population hump finally does enter the labor market (the gain in real wage having been dissipated by an increase in mouths prior to hands), it may be of such magnitude that a below-subsistence wage is necessary to raise the rate of profits to a level sufficient to induce further accumulation. (d) Whether the economy will now return to an equilibrium, with maximum resource utilization, will depend, as I see it, on the oscillation of wages around the subsistence level. The curtailment of the labor force that is necessary to keep the rate of capital accumulation and population in the proper balance is itself painful and may be disastrous.

The points at issue between Ricardo and Malthus are partly matters of definition, or they are customarily resolved by saying (e.g., in the case of the possibility of a "universal glut") that Malthus emphasized the step-by-step short-run adjustments, while Ricardo, slighting this aspect,

64. This I deduce from his statement: "Few indeed and scanty would be the portion of conveniences and luxuries found in society, if those who are the main instruments of their production had no stronger motives for their exertions than the desire of enjoying them. It is the want of *necessaries* which mainly stimulates the labouring classes to produce luxuries; and were this stimulus removed or greatly weakened, so that the necessaries of life could be obtained with very little labour, instead of more time being devoted to the production of conveniences, there is every reason to think that less time would . . ." (*ibid.*, p. 334). This presumption, if it is supportable and it may very well be, more or less invalidates Bonar's criticism, in that it denies the protasis: "If the workmen themselves had the wants and supplied them with their own labour, all the results that Malthus desires would be obtained without invidious distinction of classes, and with distinct improvement in the condition of the workmen" (*op.cit.*, pp. 300-301). But cf. W. D. Grampp, "Malthus on Money Wages and Welfare," *American Economic Review*, XLVI, 1956. Grampp's conclusions are less startling when one recalls what Malthus meant by "unproductive expenditures." So does R. L. Meek's moral indignation over Malthus's system as requiring a "vast horde of idlers" seem a trifle highly colored ("The Decline of Ricardian Economics in England," *Economica*, XVII, 1950, p. 51).

talked in terms of the long-run equilibrium.[65] I have no argument with this except that, while it should emphasize, it may instead conceal, one of Malthus' main points: the events of the short run govern, and can thus modify, the long-run developments. For with Smith's picture of indefinitely rising wages in his mind, he feared that Ricardo's blackest forecast might come about prematurely as the immediate result of short-run lags. Thus, Malthus feared that, as the result of these "temporary" gluts, and the premature drop in the rate of profits which they entailed, accumulation might come to a halt with the result that there might evolve a self-perpetuating slump, an economy stagnant before the available resource potential had been utilized. His argument, in the final analysis, stands or falls on the condition that the demand for wage goods is inelastic.

One of the other sources of argument between Ricardo and Malthus was the inconsistent fashion in which the former "distributed lags." It will be recalled that Ricardo asserted that wages could not long remain above the subsistence level, nor could profits be long reduced by the competition of capitals. His reasoning hinged on the elasticity of the labor supply or its reflection, the demand for wage goods. Malthus, whose *Essay* was written to prove this quality of high elasticity, but whose *Principles,* if nothing else, examined the conditions under which the supply of labor might be, or turn, inelastic, charged:

> It is a little singular that Mr. Ricardo, who has in general, kept his attention so steadily on permanent and final results . . . has always, in treating of rent, adopted an opposite course, and referred almost entirely to temporary effects.[66]

He was justified. Ricardo, treating of rent specifically, insisted that "labour is a commodity which cannot be increased and diminished at pleasure."[67] Yet, in speaking of an increase of capital, he had said that

65. For a pre-Keynes example of interest, see H. L. McCracken, *Value Theory and Business Cycles,* New York, 1933. For somewhat more recent essays which typify the acceptance of this explanation as a datum, see Omar Pancoast, "Malthus Versus Ricardo: The Effects of Distribution on Production," *Political Science Quarterly,* LVIII, 1943, pp. 47-66. In this essay, whose provocative title is a trifle misleading, we find: "Malthus may be said to have been stressing short-run effects under imperfect competition; Ricardo was considering long-term results in a more ideally fluid society" (p. 61). See also J. J. O'Leary, "Malthus's General Theory of Employment and the Post-Napoleonic Depression," *Journal of Economic History,* III, 1943, p. 191. Hla Myint's fine study, *Theories of Welfare Economics,* Cambridge, 1948, enters into the question in some detail, but I find no discussion there of why the demand for wage goods should not grow increasingly elastic when the population increase, induced by a higher real wage, begins to come into the labor market—no discussion, that is, of whether or not the stagnation will perpetuate itself. It is quite possible, of course, that the point is made but has escaped me. See especially chap. 3, p. 51. Myint's remark there is of interest: "Malthus's concept of Economic Progress is of a negative character. It does not offer a solution for increasing the standard of living of the masses of the people at least in the immediate future. It seems to be concerned mainly with the prevention of economic retrogression in the form of gluts and mass unemployment."

66. *Principles,* p. 210.

67. *Works and Correspondence of David Ricardo,* p. 165.

there would not long be any difficulty in procuring hands. Ricardo acknowledged that the long-run effect of an agricultural innovation (or, what was really the point at issue between him and Malthus, the repeal of the Corn Laws) would be increased accumulation, increased population, and a restored level of rent, but in this case he emphasized, rather than discounted, the time lag. Thus: "A *considerable* period would have elapsed, attended with a positive diminution of rent."[68]

R. L. Meek very generously says that "Ricardo was never particularly concerned to defend the interests of any single social class. . . ."[69] W. C. Mitchell explains Ricardo's inconsistent treatment of population lags in various problems as an ingenious kind of "imaginary experiment."[70]

I confess that I must take the side of Malthus here; I consider Ricardo's shift in emphasis not only "singular," but simply special pleading.[71] The adjustment to an improvement in machinery, Ricardo said, would be "in no long time," and expanded this to mean "a very few years."[72] But, unaccountably, after an agricultural innovation, the population increase can occur only after "a considerable period would have elapsed."[73] This period is rendered ambiguously "for a time" ten pages later. The adjustment "will not be till after a great addition has been made to the population," or "most speedily effected," depending on whether population is to increase after an innovation or in a "given state of the arts."[74] An increase in real wages taken as luxuries is "temporary," since the laborer will marry and need more food instead of luxuries.[75] Yet, population increase can take place only after a "considerable interval."[76] Even so, as we have seen, if capital were tripled or quadrupled, there would "not long be any difficulty in procuring . . . hands."[77] Consequently, Adam Smith is describing only a "temporary" effect. Small wonder an occasional impatience on Malthus' part!

After surveying the differences of opinion among Smith, Ricardo, and Malthus, one might question whether the synthesis described in the first part of this paper is, after all, a useful exposition of the classical growth model. It would seem to be, if only in displaying their unanimity in the selection of the variables they regarded as crucial to a theory of growth, whatever their disagreement as to the most likely behavior of these vari-

68. *Ibid.*, p. 80.
69. Meek, *op.cit.*, p. 50.
70. Wesley C. Mitchell, *Lecture Notes on Types of Economic Theory* (mimeographed), New York, 1949, I, pp. 157-59, 162. But cf. J. A. Schumpeter for whom this sort of "imaginary experiment" is no virtue, but rather the "Ricardian Vice" ("Review of the Troops," *Quarterly Journal of Economics*, LXV, 1951, pp. 160-61).
71. G. J. Stigler (in "The Ricardian Theory of Value and Distribution," *Journal of Political Economy*, LX, 1952, pp. 187-202) extols Ricardo for his clarity of logic. Logical he was, if we confine that to meaning "if A, then B." But logical he was not, if that term implies any consistency in "if A, when B?"
72. *Works and Correspondence of David Ricardo*, p. 16.
73. *Ibid.*, p. 80.
74. *Ibid.*, p. 96.
75. *Ibid.*, p. 163.
76. *Ibid.*, p. 165.
77. *Ibid.*, p. 289.

ables.[78] The recent concern over the problem of the economically underdeveloped areas of the world has vindicated the selection of investment and population as vital determinants of growth.

One must agree that "Seen exclusively through the lenses of the 'marginal revolution,' Classical political economy takes on the character of a graveyard of elementary blunders; nothing survives, not even the questions which were raised."[79] But it is necessary to pause before assenting to the further comment that ". . . the Ricardian approach was marked by an excessive emphasis upon population growth and natural resource scarcities."[80] While the economic history of nineteenth-century England would confirm that this emphasis was indeed excessive, it remains to be confirmed for large areas of the world today. The question remains open as to whether in the process of economic growth there will evolve automatically a "cultural pattern suited eventually to bring population growth to a stand."[81] Another open question is whether an economy is able to marshal sufficient variable capital to provide its labor force with the mobility necessary to take advantage of technological changes. One must have at least an adequate living income before one can begin to invest in growth stocks.

Part of the critical hostility the classical theory met at the hands of the more passionate marginalists probably comes from the classical school's positing the existence of a surplus. Include rent with the social dividend and one is as close to Marxian surplus value as he wishes to squeeze the necessary price of capital maintenance. Yet, the price one must pay for eliminating the concept of a surplus by assuming it away is a high one.[82]

Baumol describes classical dynamics as "magnificent" and as "a shrewd and courageous approach largely absent from present-day analysis."[83] This appraisal seems eminently just.

78. It would be unbecoming of most economists today to criticize them for this disagreement. While even now there is frequently professional agreement as to the proper course of action to relieve an actual or threatening economic disorder, any prediction of exact timing or of precise quantitative response rarely commands consensus.

79. Blaug, *op.cit.*, p. 4.

80. *Ibid.*, p. 5.

81. J. J. Spengler, "Malthus's Total Population Theory," *Canadian Journal of Economics and Political Science*, XI, 1945, p. 100.

82. If an economy is generating more output than is absolutely necessary to enable it to continue at the level which it has reached, then a "surplus" exists. This is true whether "necessary" prices are established by the decree of an absolute government, or by factor response in a free market. The concept of a surplus which is so useful in a theory of growth is surely fatal to the formal theory of pricing in static equilibrium, except under assumptions which destroy any bridge between the two theories.

83. Baumol, *op.cit.*, p. 19.

JOHN STUART MILL ON ECONOMIC DEVELOPMENT*

By Joseph J. Spengler

It is the perilous privilege of really eminent men, that their errors, as well as their wisdom, should be fertile in consequences.

Richard Jones, in *Essay on . . . Distribution of Wealth, p. ix.*

He had been brought up in the straitest sect of the abstract economists, and his method was formed before his mind was matured.

T. E. C. Leslie, in *Essays in . . . Moral Philosophy*, p. 221.

The imbecile flatness of the present bourgeoisie is measured by the altitude of its greatest intellects.

Karl Marx, in *Capital* (Kerr ed., Chicago, 1906), I, p. 568.

THIS PAPER has to do with John Stuart Mill's theory of economic development. In Section I, Mill's concern with economic development and his role in the development of economic theory are touched upon; in Section II, his treatment of the role of noneconomic phenomena and of differences between developed and backward countries are dealt with. In Sections III and IV, respectively, I take up Mill's treatment of population

*I am indebted to the Rockefeller Foundation for financial assistance in the preparation of this paper.

and the role of land, natural resources, and capital. In Section V, his analysis of those factors that improve the quality of requisites of production, or of the efficiency with which they are used, is examined; and in Section VI, I discuss his concept of the developmental role of the state. Mill's theory is contrasted with current thought in Section VII, and with the theories of some of his contemporaries in Section VIII.

I

Economists have differed greatly with respect to the position to be assigned John Stuart Mill (1806-1873) in the history of economic thought. In the opinion of his latter-day contemporaries, "the hegemony of Mill lay heavy on the science" of economics; yet, some believed that it was this very hegemony that was responsible for the lack of progress in political economy during the third quarter of the nineteenth century.[1] Certainly, he did not keep abreast of improvements in economic theory, or of accessions to relevant empirical information; and he failed to appreciate the contributions that statistical and mathematical tools might make, probably because he had been molded (as had many of his latter-day contemporaries) in a moral-philosophical tradition that was distrustful of measurement and "overmuch precision in theorising about society."[2] Yet, this modest man originated at least a half dozen contributions in the course of his efforts to improve the Ricardian system;[3] and to this day he is much cited and widely regarded as both a seminal and an integrative thinker. Believing that "sound action is possible only on the basis of sound theory,"[4] Mill was one of the first to distinguish clearly between the role of science, which determines how given ends may be produced, and the role of "art," which suggests ends, together with rules (based on the findings of science), for

1. See S. G. Checkland, "Economic Opinion in England as Jevons Found It," *The Manchester School*, XIX, 1951, pp. 143-69, esp. pp. 149, 159, 167. Checkland concludes that "English economics languished between Mill's *Principles* of 1848, and Jevons' *Theory* of 1871, largely because the academics had gained authority before they had developed competence" *(ibid.*, p. 168). See also Checkland, "The Advent of Academic Economics in England," *The Manchester School*, XIX, 1951, pp. 43-70; also Marx's sarcastic comment, quoted at the beginning of this paper.

2. Checkland, "Economic Opinion . . . ," *loc.cit.*, pp. 150, 168, also pp. 162, 166. See also H. S. Foxwell, "The Economic Movement in England," *Quarterly Journal of Economics*, II, 1887-1888, pp. 84-85, 88, where Foxwell attributes Mill's adherence to "the older forms of expression" to his regard for the authority of earlier classical economists, and to the fact that his education was much more literary than scientific. He never wholly emancipated himself from his father's philosophical influence. E.g., see Reginald Jackson, *An Examination of the Deductive Logic of John Stuart Mill*, London, 1941, p. viii; also the statement by Leslie, quoted at the beginning of this paper.

3. See G. J. Stigler, "The Nature and Role of Originality in Scientific Progress," *Economica*, XXII, 1955, pp. 296-99.

4. See Ernest Nagel, *John Stuart Mill's Philosophy of Scientific Method*, New York, 1950, p. xxvii.

their realization.[5] Some of this distinction enters into his attempt to advance the theory of economic development.[6]

Mill's treatment of economic development reflected both his conception of economic science and of the impact of divers economic changes, e.g., growth of the factory system and the working class, the diffusion of political power, the waning of confidence in laissez faire. His approach to economic development, though less overtly historical in his *Principles* than was Smith's approach, upon which it was patterned, is essentially a culmination of that mode of economic analysis which Smith had foreshadowed, and Ricardo had structured. It also took into account political and economic changes, to most of which Mill was quite sensitive; and it incorporated various non-Ricardian philosophical influences, especially those of Comtean origin–influences that were more conspicuous in the *System of Logic* than in the *Principles*. Mill's conception of economic method is somewhat difficult to characterize because his considerable and explicit treatment of method in *Logic* was never, to my knowledge, wholly transformed, if that be possible, into terms of method, implicit and explicit, in *Principles*. He looked upon political economy as a nonexperimental moral science, and hence as one in which recourse to the *a priori*, or deductive, method (which embraced three stages: induction, deduction, and verification) was essential. This science had to do with the study of phenomena arising from man's "pursuit of wealth." While these phenomena constituted a comparatively autonomous subset within the set of all social phenomena, their interpretation was often made difficult by their complexity and by the presence of both acting and counteracting causes. The ultimate basis of political economy, as of other social sciences, had therefore to be found in psychology, the science of the mind; its generalizations could not be depended upon until, as Kubitz puts it, they had been verified empirically and "confirmed and explained by the laws of human character which in turn were based upon psychological laws."[7] Similarly, the "Empirical Laws

5. J. S. Mill, *System of Logic*, London, 6th ed., 1865, VI, chap. 12. Throughout this paper, my references are to this edition. Nassau Senior had sought to distinguish between the art and the science of economics as early as 1826. See Marian Bowley, *Nassau Senior and Classical Economics* (1937), New York, 1949, pp. 54-55. Senior was in the praxeological tradition; Mill, in the positive.

6. On Mill's life, see his *Autobiography*, J. J. Coss, ed., New York, 1924; Michael St. John Packe, *The Life of John Stuart Mill*, London, 1954; Ruth Borchard, *John Stuart Mill the Man*, London, 1957. Walter Bagehot testifies to Mill's modesty and kindliness, in his *Works*, F. Morgan, ed., Hartford, 1889, V, pp. 412, 416.

7. *System of Logic* (hereinafter cited as *Logic)*, II, pp. 412, 433*ff.*, 508, 443-58 and 490-98 on ethology (i.e., the science of character which Mill derived from psychology, the science of the mind); Oskar A. Kubitz, *Development of John Stuart Mill's System of Logic*, Urbana, 1932, pp. 38-39, 177-78, 208-11, 216, 222-24, 233, 252-58; also Alburey Castell, *Mill's Logic of the Moral Sciences*, Chicago, 1936, pp. 30-82; also Bowley, *op.cit.*, pp. 58-64, for Senior's comments on Mill's hypothesis of the economic man. F. A. Hayek believes that A. Comte's influence upon the sixth book of Mill's *Logic* was very great (see *The Counter-Revolution of Science*, Glencoe, 1952, pp. 140, 186). See also Castell, *op.cit.*, pp. 74*ff.*; Mill, *Autobiography*, pp. 146-49, 156, 174*n*. Kubitz (*op.cit.*, p. 41) considers the influence of the

of Society," expressing uniformities of "coexistence" or "succession," even when supported by mass statistics, do not become highly dependable until they are connected "with the laws of human nature." As a rule, therefore, the generalizations of political economy (as of social science in general) could only be described as affirming tendencies.[8]

Mill's concern with economic development, evident as early as 1843 in his *System of Logic*[9] and in occasional essays, stands out prominently in his *Principles* (though much less so than did Smith's similar concern in *Wealth of Nations*), since Mill, writing after Ricardo, had to deal at length with value and distribution. Mill's concern is manifest in the declared purpose of the *Principles*,[10] in its chapter-composition, in his discussion of custom and institutions, in the distinction he makes between sets of institutions, and in the attention he gives to socio-economic develop-

Saint-Simonians to have been greater than that of Comte. See also works cited in footnote 17 below; also footnote 13 and text on "consensus" below.

8. *Logic*, II, pp. 508-11, 528-30; Kubitz, *op.cit.*, pp. 212-13, 254-56. The grounds for Mill's neglect of statistical data, suggested in his early writings (see *Essays on Some Unsettled Questions of Political Economy*, London, 1844, esp. pp. 137*ff*.), are most fully discussed in Book VI of *Logic* (pp. 490-500), wherein he described the "physical, or concrete deductive method" as the one most adapted to economic analysis, and asserted that one must be "well acquainted with the remoter causes" of man's economic behavior, if one would utilize and interpret statistical matter correctly. See also *ibid.*, pp. 509-11, 527-32, on "the inverse, deductive, or historical method" and the use of statistics. See also M. Blaug, *Ricardian Economics*, New Haven, 1958, pp. 185-88, 227-28; Jean Ray, *La méthode de l'économie politique d'après John Stuart Mill*, Paris, 1914. Lord Houghton reported, in the *Journal of the Royal Statistical Society*, XXXIV, 1873, p. 528, that Mill was interested in the Society's activities, but did not attend its meetings. According to P. R. Senn, Mill was the first to use the term "social science," in 1836, in which year S. de Sismondi used its French equivalent. See Senn, "The Earliest Use of the Term 'Social Science,'" *Journal of the History of Ideas*, XIX, 1958, pp. 568-70. See also R. Vaysset-Boutbien, *Stuart Mill et la sociologie française contemporaine*, Paris, 1941.

9. See VI, chap. 10, secs. 3-6, where he writes of French efforts to infer from the "general facts of history . . . the law of progress," which would permit prediction of future events. Mill considered such efforts misplaced; they could disclose only "empirical" laws, since they could not uncover underlying determinants; they could not project a course of events flowing out of cumulative cultural change. On "progressive effects" and "empirical laws" see also *ibid.*, III, chaps. 15-16. Mill's views have been assessed by Karl Popper in "The Poverty of Historicism," *Economica*, XI, 1944, pp. 124-26, 130; XII, 1945, pp. 71-75, 86-88. Aspects of Mill's view of social progress have been treated by A. L. Harris in *Economics and Social Reform*, New York, 1958, chap. 2.

10. *Principles of Political Economy With Some of Their Applications to Social Philosophy* (hereinafter cited as *Principles*), edited with an introduction by Sir W. J. Ashley, New York 1921. It is in *Principles* that the whole of Mill's theory of economic development may be found. His other published works sometimes elaborate and illustrate his views, but do not add to them substantially. Some of Mill's comments on current issues may be connected with his theory of economic development; some even have a seemingly timely ring (e.g., see his remarks on England's "almost insane blunder" regarding "the Suez Canal," and on the delivery of the "Hungarians, bound hand and foot, to their exasperated oppressors, in *Dissertations and Discussions* (hereinafter cited as *Dissertations*), London, 1867, III, pp. 162, 177. Mill's considerable correspondence, together with his own and other accounts of his life, when it relates to progress and development, sometimes clarifies the account and analysis presented in the *Principles*. Mill's writings, together with a brief indication of their contents, are listed in *Bibliography of the Published Writings of John Stuart Mill*, Ney MacMinn, *et al.*, eds., Evanston, 1945. In his review of this work (*Economica*, XII, 1945, p. 183), F. A. Hayek, the distinguished and well-informed student of Mill's period and life, lists several additional items. J. C. Rees reasons convincingly that *On Social Freedom* was not written by Mill (see *Mill and His Early Critics*, Leicester, 1956, pp. 38-54).

nent and the prospective course of man's history. In his preface to the irst edition (1848), Mill, much of whose philosophy was rooted in the ighteenth century, remarks that what is needed is "a work similar in its object and general conception to that of Adam Smith, but adapted to the more extended knowledge and improved ideas of the present age." It must be a work which recognizes, as did Smith's, that "there are perhaps no practical questions . . . which admit of being decided on economical premises alone." Mill went on to say, after having reported the "remarkable differences" in man's lot to be found in the world, that the economist must trace the "derivative laws" which govern the production of wealth and find therein "the explanation of the diversities of riches and poverty in the present and past, and the ground of whatever increase in wealth is reserved for the future."[11]

Large portions of the *Principles* are devoted to economic development. In Book I, on "Production," one finds, besides Mill's account of the division of labor and the requisites of production, and his emphasis upon the physical and cumulative character of the results of production, chapters dealing with the "laws" of increase of labor, capital, and "production from land," and the implications of these "laws" for man's economic prospects. Book IV has to do largely with circumstances underlying the progress of societies in wealth, the growth of capital and population, and improvements in the production and the procurement of commodities. Scattered here and there, particularly in Book V on the role of the state and in his discussion of trade and protectionism, one finds additional observations relating to economic growth. Mill did not make extensive reference to non-European countries, other than India (which he knew well), in part perhaps because he believed that a developed capacity to analyze economic situations could be applied to any country; and in part because he looked upon some hinterland areas as components of the European economy.[12]

11. *Principles,* p. 21. Ashley reported and dated all important changes introduced by Mill into the second and later editions. By "derivative laws," Mill meant "middle principles," which could be derived from the "highest generalizations" and which thus were intermediate between ultimate laws and "empirical laws resulting from simple observation." See *Logic,* II, pp. 453-55; also Kubitz, *op.cit.,* pp. 223-28. Mill defined "wealth" to embrace "all useful or agreeable things except those which can be obtained, in the quantity desired, without labour or sacrifice." See *Principles,* p. 9, also pp. 46*ff*., where he justifies his exclusion (from the category, "wealth") of immaterial services. Production, not consumption, is stressed in Mill's early *Essays,* cited in footnote 8, above.

12. *Principles,* pp. 685-87; see also footnote 15, below. Generalizations relating to "material and industrial phenomena" must "necessarily be relative to a given form of civilization and a given stage of social development." Nonetheless, whoever understands "the political economy" of a "complicated" and civilized European country "can deduce without difficulty the political economy of any other state of society, with the particular circumstances of which he is equally well acquainted." See *The Positive Philosophy of Auguste Comte,* Boston, 2nd ed., 1867, pp. 75-76; *Logic,* II, pp. 494-95; also "Representative Government," in *Utilitarianism, Liberty & Representative Government,* New York, 1920, pp. 376-93, on difficulties attending the extension of European principles of government to less advanced and dependent areas. See also *Chapter and Speeches on the Irish Land Question,* London, 1870, p. 118, where Mill says that the correct application

II

Countries differed greatly with respect to their degree of economic development, and the ease with which it might be carried forward. They differed not merely with respect to one or several, but with respect to many, interdependent social phenomena. "Consensus," a condition observed by Comte, and emphasized by Mill in his *Logic* (though not explicitly in *Principles*), ruled in the domain of social phenomena; every such phenomenon influenced every other such phenomenon, with the result that every cause had its effect spread through a society. Furthermore, randomness did not dominate the assembly of phenomena. "Not every variety of combination of these general social facts is possible, but only certain combinations"; only some kinds of "features of society" could coexist with given other kinds.[13] Economic phenomena arising from man's "desire of wealth" were relatively autonomous and free of the impact of "consensus," and hence subject to hypothetical isolation and fruitful analysis under *ceteris paribus* conditions. They were not wholly free of this impact, however; and Mill assigned it greater weight in his later writings than he had in his early years. He emphasized that one could not generalize and apply conclusions which were valid for one state of society to different states, unless differentiating conditions were adequately taken into account. Thus, one could not suppose that, because certain processes (say, intense "competition") and "empirical laws of human nature" were operative in highly developed countries (e.g., Great Britain, the United States), they would be equally operative in Asia and other underdeveloped regions, or even in Continental Europe.[14] Nor could one suppose that a policy appropriate for one country would always be appropriate for another.[15]

Mill believed that noneconomic factors played an important role in

---

of economic principles presupposes knowledge of a country's "circumstances"; see also R. D. C. Black, "The Classical Economists and the Irish Problem," *Oxford Economic Papers*, V, 1953, pp. 36*ff*.

13. *Logic*, II, pp. 487-90, 504-505; also footnote 18, below. Compare T. Parsons, *The Social System*, Glencoe, 1951, chap. 5.

14. *Logic*, II, pp. 494-98; "Civilization" (1836), in *Dissertations*, pp. 164-65, 188-89.

15. E.g., "There are . . . conditions of society in which a vigorous despotism is in itself the best mode of government for training the people in what is specifically wanting to render them capable of a higher civilisation." There are also conditions in which despotism has "no beneficial effect"; and, finally, there are conditions in which various other kinds of government are indicated. See "Representative Government . . . ," *loc.cit.*, pp. 198-99, 204-10, 382-83; "On Liberty," *ibid.*, pp. 118-19. Again, the institution of absolute ownership of land, though it functioned well in England, was not suited to Ireland, where men had no alternative to agriculture as a source of sustenance. See *England and Ireland*, London, 1868, pp. 14-15. Yet again, Mill, though an advocate of "the Religion of Humanity," and unable to discover much utility in other religions (see *Three Essays on Religion*, New York, 1884), noted that there were times (e.g., in the Middle Ages) when it was to society's advantage to have the clergy ascendant. See *The Spirit of the Age* (1831), with an introduction by F. A. Hayek, Chicago, 1942, pp. 78-81. See also footnote 12, above.

uman affairs, which involved economic progress. Among these factors e included beliefs, habits of thought, customs, and institutions.[16] Hence, e stressed the need for a new moral science, namely, ethology or group sychology. It would be the role of this science to bridge the gap between sychology and empirical generalizations regarding human nature; to llumine how human character is formed; and to make clear both how eliefs, customs, institutions, and other international cultural differences ame into being, and how they might be modified.[17] The "fundamental roblem" of social science was "to find the laws according to which any tate of society produces the state which succeeds it and takes its place."[18] Despite his belief that the science of society remained quite undeveloped, Mill believed that enough was known to supply guidance in many particuars, and that enough would be known in time to advance the "Political Art" greatly.[19]

Mill's discussion of the role of noneconomic factors assumed two orms. First, a number of times he observed that the backwardness of various countries was closely associated with the despotic and anti-progressive

---

16. Mill sometimes treated certain conditions as concomitants, rather than causes, f economic development: presence of midlle and laboring classes; relatively wide difusion of property and intelligence; great ower of cooperation; etc. E.g., see "Civilizaion," in *Dissertations,* I, pp. 163-65; also *bid.,* pp. 399-401, II, pp. 62-67. In "Coleidge," *ibid.,* I, pp. 415-25, Mill mentioned hree preconditions to political stability (and ence to economic development): Citizens nust be educated to subordinate their imulses and aims to what are "considered the nds of society"; they must share loyalty to ome fixed principles; and they must be ound together by a feeling of membership n the community. See also *Logic,* II, pp. 16-19. Mill thus recognized the importance f the kind of cohesive force signified by . Toennies' term *Gemeinschaft.*

17. *Logic,* II, pp. 443-58, 496-503, 527. ee also Castell, *op.cit.,* pp. 48-56; Kubitz, *p.cit.,* pp. 249-58; M. Ginsberg's Foreword o A. Löwe, *Economics and Sociology,* Lonlon, 1935. Mill's emphasis upon the role of ustoms, institutions, etc., reflected the influnce of his wife, the Saint-Simonians, A. Comte, Richard Jones, and T. B. Macaulay. ee *Autobiography,* pp. 174-76; Jones, *An Essay on the Distribution of Wealth and on he Sources of Taxation,* London, 1831, p. xv; Iris W. Mueller, *John Stuart Mill and French Thought,* Urbana, 1956, pp. 77, 121; Iayek's introduction to *The Spirit of the Age.* While Macaulay's essays were directed gainst James Mill's treatment of politics, hey indicated the inadequacy of postulating nly a fictional economic man (see Kubitz, *op.cit.,* pp. 31-37, 42, 176*ff.*) For the Mill-Comte correspondence, see L. Lévy-Bruhl, *Lettres inédites de John Stuart Mill à Auguste Comte,* Paris, 1899. See also R. Maduit, *Auguste Comte et la science économique,* Paris, 1929, chap. 10; R. K. Pankhurst, *The Saint Simonians, Mill, and Carlyle,* London, 1957; and footnote 7, above.

18. *Logic,* II, p. 506. By "a state of society," Mill meant "the simultaneous state of all the greater social facts or phenomena. Such are, the degree of knowledge, and of intellectual and moral culture, existing in the community, and in every class of it; the state of industry, of wealth, and its distribution; the habitual occupations of the community; their division into classes, and the relations of those classes to one another; the common beliefs which they entertain on all the subjects most important to mankind, and the degree of assurance with which these beliefs are held; their tastes, and the character and degree of their aesthetic development; their form of government, and the more important of their laws and customs" *(ibid.,* pp. 504-505).

19. *Logic,* II, pp. 135, 428, 462, 525-26, 552-53, also pp. 411*ff.,* 424*ff.,* and 459*ff.* Unlike his classical predecessors, Mill was not averse "to regarding individuals as instruments to be improved and manipulated in the hands of a wise and beneficent government." See W. D. Grampp, On the Politics of the Classical Economists," *Quarterly Journal of Economics,* LXII, 1948, p. 745. See also L. Robbins, *The Theory of Economic Policy,* London, 1952, *passim.*

character of their customs, especially when re-enforced (e.g., as in India and Turkey) by religious beliefs that made for uniformity of opinion, itself a great deterrent to improvement.[20] Second, Mill described the impact of custom and institution in relatively advanced economies, noting in particular that they might affect distribution (which was subject to social laws) but not production (which was subject to physical laws).[21] Thus, there might, or might not, be private property; and when private property prevailed, agricultural produce might be distributed through the agency of competition, or in accordance with prevailing custom.[22] Even the formation of prices other than rent, though more subject than rent to the regulative force of competition, was sometmies affected by custom.[23]

In part because he was so impressed with the preponderantly ankylotic influence of custom, Mill emphasized the importance of countervailing factors, particularly the change-producing role of creative individuals and the circumstances in which they flourish, but he did not effectively integrate his various treatments of this subject. In *Logic* he described "the state of the speculative faculties of mankind" as "predominant, and almost paramount, among the agents of the social progression," and he referred to "the state of knowledge at any time" as the "limit of the industrial improvements possible at that time." He particularly stressed the creative role of "remarkable" individuals (e.g., Newton, Aristotle), but he did not greatly play up the role of the entrepreneur, though he was always aware of the importance of persons of originality or genius.[24] These could flourish only if they were free of the trammels of the opinions and customs of the masses, only if non-

20. See *The Spirit of the Age*, pp. 76-77; "On Liberty," *loc.cit.*, pp. 69, 116-17, 123-24, 127-31; "Representative Government," *loc.cit.*, pp. 179, 190, 197, 201, 210, 214. Mill recognized that customs performed a necessary role, his concern being the persistence of a custom after it had ceased to serve the general welfare. See "Utilitarianism," *loc.cit.*, p. 59; "On Liberty," *loc.cit.*, pp. 116-17, 125-26. "The despotism of custom is everywhere the standing hindrance to man's advancement" *(ibid.*, p. 127). Mill would have approved C. E. Ayres's inference that salutary change is continually opposed by "the static force of ceremony—status, mores, and legendary belief." See *The Theory of Economic Progress*, Chapel Hill, 1944, p. 176.

21. *Principles*, pp. 200*ff*.

22. *Principles*, II, chaps. 4-8. When produce was distributed according to custom, laws of distribution which political economy might investigate were not operative. *Ibid.*, pp. 242, 304; also *Socialism*, W. D. P. Bliss, ed., New York, 1891, pp. 131-37, which includes Mill's papers on socialism. J. R. Hicks *(Value and Capital*, Oxford, 2nd ed., 1948, pp. 6-7) has discussed how difficult it is to allow for imperfectness of competition. Mill did not consider pricing under socialism "insurmountable" (in a review in *Westminster Review*, LVI, 1851, p. 89).

23. Mill mentioned professional fees, wages (upon which custom's influence was "slight") and retail prices and mark-ups (see *Principles*, pp. 245-48, 343, 403-404, 415-16, 440-41). Some of the examples which he gave of the influence of custom on prices were really examples of situations in which "monopolistic," rather than perfect, competition ruled. He noted that competition was most effective in "great centres of business," and he implied that the prevailing degree of competition was an index of industrial progress *(ibid.*, pp. 246, 415).

24. *Logic*, II, pp. 521-22, 533-35. In "On Liberty," when expressing concern at the supposed decline of individuality, Mill observed that "there is now scarcely any outlet for energy in this country except business," but he did not discuss the significance of this fact for England's economic development. See *loc.cit.*, p. 127. On the entrepreneur, see Section V, below.

conformity, individuality, and "diversity of character and culture" were guarded against the intolerant and leveling spirit of the mediocre. "Human development" presupposed "freedom" and "variety of situations," as well as considerable individual participation in public affairs. Mill was concerned, therefore, lest these various preconditions be weakened in civilized lands by the ascendency of public opinion, now that society had gotten "the better of individuality," and by the intensification of forces making for progress-retarding cultural homogeneity.[25]

Economic progress depended, as did the augmentation of human welfare, upon two sorts of improvement–upon the extension of man's "knowledge of the laws of nature," and his capacity to remove barriers imposed by an unbeneficent Nature;[26] and upon the removal of barriers imposed by men on themselves (in the form of beliefs, customs, opinions, and habits of thought), together with the sustenance of forces that made men strive to "improve and elevate human nature and life."[27] It was essential, of course, when seeking to augment human welfare by modifying customs (e.g., those affecting distribution), to proceed in such manner so as not to affect adversely the growth and application of knowledge. Mill assumed, because what men were had been largely determined by "the whole previous history of humanity," that much might be accomplished through efforts to modify customs and institutions, even though one could not be sure that men's "opinions and feelings" and rules of conduct would change sufficiently to make the new customs and institutions work. On the whole, however, the tendency was "towards a better and happier" state, though the rate of progress, even when accelerated through conscious intervention, was likely to be slow, variable, and unpredictable.[28] In *Principles,* Mill expressed himself more optimistically at times.

25. See "Representative Government," *loc. cit.,* pp. 188, 193, 199-201, 205, 208, 210-18; "On Liberty," *loc.cit.,* pp. 115-31. Only in "some early states of society" had there been an excess of "the element of spontaneity and individuality," and hence a need "to induce men of strong bodies or minds to pay obedience to any rules which required them to control their impulses" (*ibid.,* pp. 118-19). See also "Representative Government," *loc. cit.,* pp. 198-99, on the need to compel the uncivilized to acquire habits of industry. Mill's concern had been expressed much earlier. See Rees, *op.cit.,* pp. 5-10, 56.

26. Mill was devastatingly critical of the opinion of expositors of natural theology, etc., to the effect that "Nature" was beneficent. It was quite the contrary: "Nature" was unjust and merciless; man's virtues were cultural products; it was his duty to amend "Nature," not to follow her. See his essay, "Nature," in *Three Essays on Religion,* pp. 28-36, 51, 54, 56.

27. See "Representative Government," *loc. cit.,* pp. 190-91, 214-17. "A very small diminution of those exertions" to improve would not "only put a stop to improvement, but would turn the general tendency of things towards deterioration" (*ibid.,* p. 191).

28. This paragraph is based upon Mill's statements in *Logic,* II, pp. 507, 509, 519*ff.*, 523, 533-38, also pp. 461*ff.*, 496-98, 540-41; *Principles,* pp. 3, 21, 199-201; also *The Subjection of Women,* London, 1869, pp. 29, 187-88. Mill's belief in the provisional character and the improvability of man's institutions prompted him to attack the intuitionist theory of knowledge, which, he believed, gave "great intellectual support" to "false doctrines and bad institutions." See *Autobiography,* pp. 158-59, 192-93, and the focus of this attack, his *Examination of Sir William Hamilton's Philosophy,* London, 1865. On Mill's changing attitude toward institutions, see *Autobiography,* pp. 161-68; also *Socialism.*

Because he believed man's economic condition to be "undergoing progressive changes" at "all times," and because therefore "economical laws of a stationary and unchanging society" (of the sort contemplated in Books I-III of *Principles*) were not always applicable, Mill adopted Comte's distinction between statics and dynamics, redefined it, and incorporated it in his discussion of development in *Principles.* Statics had to do with conditions of political or economic stability, and dynamics, with "progressive movement," a sequence that depended mainly on "the progress of knowledge and the changes in the opinions" and "beliefs" of mankind. Thus, there was need for a "dynamics of political economy," for "a theory of motion," as well as for a "theory of equilibrium." Mill did not believe it possible, however, to reduce economic or social change to terms of invariable and prediction-yielding laws. Social phenomena were too complex.[29]

Mill distinguished between those countries which were susceptible to economic development and those which were not, given prevailing institutions. The nondeveloping countries differed from the developing ones principally because, in the former, the "surplus of food," beyond the "necessary consumption" of the cultivators, was "torn from the producers, either by the government, . . . or by individuals, who by superior force, or by availing themselves of religious or traditional feelings of subordination, have established themselves as lords of the soil." This surplus was then wasted by its appropriators. He pointed, in particular, to Asian countries which were undisturbed "by foreign influences," where the ruler, together with his retainers and employees, upon obtaining control of this surplus, exchanged what was not consumed for unproductive edifices and easily transported wealth (e.g., gold), with the result that little capital was formed, or could be formed, by any one.[30] The resulting indisposition to form capital was accentuated by the insecurity of both producers and those dependent upon the ruler[31] as well as by the apparently consequential weakness of the desire to accumulate capital.[32]

Europe and Asia were contrasted. Conditions were so bad in many parts of Asia that adverse effects could not be traced to excessive population growth; numbers "were kept down by actual starvation."[33] In Europe, capital was increasingly formed, after the fall of the wealth-wasting Roman

29. *Principles*, pp. 695-99; *Logic*, II, pp. 509-11, 521-23, 532-33; *The Positive Philosophy of Auguste Comte*, Boston, 1867, pp. 82*ff.*, 93*ff.* Mueller (*op.cit.*, p. 115) states that Mill came to appreciate that progress entailed the sacrifice of stability. In "Representative Government," *loc.cit.*, *pp.* 186-91, Mill rejected Comte's manner of distinguishing between "Order and Progress" and redefined "Order" to signify permanent net gains which formed a part of "Progress." On Comte's conception of economic statics and dynamics see H. Marechal, *Les conceptions économiques d'A. Comte*, Paris, 1919 chaps. 4-5.

30. *Principles*, pp. 12-14. In 1836 Mill called these countries "backward countries" (see *Dissertations*, I, p. 164).

31. *Principles*, p. 18, also p. 113, where "the poverty of many fertile tracts of Asia" is attributed to lack of "security," of "protection against" the rapacity of government

32. *Ibid.*, pp. 175, 408-409, 730.

33. *Ibid.*, p. 159, also pp. 704-705.

empire and the successive emergence of serfs, emancipated serfs, and burghers, together with the gradual replacement of wastrel landowners by bourgeois investors in land. Those who commanded a surplus found themselves increasingly secure in its possession. In consequence, there now existed several regions where agriculture was so productive that less than half the population could furnish abundant and varied produce for the whole population; as a result, half or more of its members could provide conveniences and luxuries and transport and productive power utilizable in the supply of military requirements and of public and private capital.[34] Mill had principally the European countries in mind, though America, too, answered to his description.[35]

Mill did not consider impossible the ultimate improvement of Asia and similarly situated or conditioned lands, given a congenial natural environment, rather than one which was apparently conducive to timidity and spiritlessness as in the tropics.[36] Even so, he believed that despotic custom, homogeneity of culture, ignorance, misgovernment, and perhaps other barriers to economic progress, would probably delay it for many generations.[37] However, Asian institutions might possibly be improved, and subsequently rendered effective; the presently very weak principles of accumulation would then be strengthened and made to furnish contrivances wherewith to ease the great drudgery characterizing labor in those lands. Were these changes made, the industry of the population was likely to increase.

The means are, first, a better government: more complete security of property; moderate taxes, and freedom from arbitrary exaction under the name of taxes; a more permanent and more advantageous tenure of land, securing to the cultivator as far as possible the undivided benefits of the industry, skill, and economy he may exert. Secondly, improvement of the public intelligence: the decay of usages or superstitions which interfere with the effective employment of industry; and the growth of mental activity, making the people alive to new subjects of desire. Thirdly, the introduction of foreign arts, which raise the returns derivable from

---

34. *Ibid.*, pp. 16-20. 113, 170, 731; also p. 687 on Venice. Whether population growth might terminate this happy situation is discussed below.

35. *Ibid.*, pp. 731, 761. Even these countries were in a "very early stage of human development" *(ibid.*, p. 749).

36. *Dissertations*, I, p. 415; *Logic*, II, p. 515. Friedrich List, to whom Mill never referred, believed the tropics unsuited to industrial development. See *National System of Political Economy* (1841-1844), translated by S. P. Lloyd, London, 1885, pp. 212-13.

37. *Principles*, p. 701; also p. 408 on insecurity, and p. 20 on unchanging "Oriental society," what was then still feudal Russia, and other more primitive societies. Despotic custom was one of the curses of Asia, everywhere hindering progress, producing the subjection of women, etc. (see also *Socialism*, pp. 210-11; "On Liberty," *loc.cit.*, pp. 127*ff)*. In *Three Essays on Religion*, p. 57, Mill refers to the voluptuous cruelty found in the "East, and Southern Europe." He attributed the progressive character of Europe (whose population was the "only one" yet to show "any capability of spontaneous improvement beyond a certain low level"), so unlike the stationary and unprogressive condition of "the whole East," to the "remarkable diversity of character and culture" of Europe's peoples and the variety of paths they had pursued. See *Dissertations*, II, pp. 71-72; "On Liberty," *loc.cit.*, pp. 128-30; *Westminster Review*, LVI, 1851, p. 101, on improvement-retarding effects of "provincial spirit"; also footnote 25 and text, above.

additional capital, to a rate corresponding to the low strength of the desire of accumulation: and the importation of foreign capital, which renders the increase of production no longer exclusively dependent on the thrift or providence of the inhabitants themselves, while it places before them a stimulating example, and by instilling new ideas and breaking the chains of habit, if not by improving the actual condition of the population, tends to create in them new wants, increased ambition, and greater thought for the future. These considerations apply more or less to all the Asiatic populations, and to the less civilized and industrious parts of Europe, such as Russia, Turkey, Spain, and Ireland.[38]

One gets the impression that the improvements Mill foresaw in Book IV of *Principles* would be enjoyed principally in the sphere of European civilization and in underpopulated parts of the world whither European peoples, capital, and culture migrated. Thus, he anticipated great increases in man's knowledge and command over nature; in his security of person and property, and hence in man's inclination to save and invest productively; in the relative number of individuals with business capacities, and in the formation of joint stock companies which could realize economies of scale.[39] In particular, he expected man's capacity for voluntary cooperation to grow. He supposed that this capacity would be manifested especially in profit-sharing cooperative associations. These associations would be large enough to realize economies of scale, and, by substituting profit-sharing for an earlier and often exploitative form of employer-employee relationship, would generate interest and incentive in work and improve human relations.[40] Mill expected that the real wages and economic condition of many worker groups would continue to rise as they had been doing, at least since the 1820's,[41] and that even mechanical invention might be made to confer the benefits it could make possible.[42]

38. *Principles,* pp. 189-90, and p. 701 on the long-run prospect. Mill recognized Asian cultures to be traditional. He reasoned, as did P. T. Bauer, when criticizing the opinion of R. Nurkse, that what here amounts to an international demonstration effect will stimulate individuals as producers more than enough to offset increases in their propensities to spend, with the result that saving increases. See Bauer, *Economic Analysis and Policy in Underdeveloped Countries,* Durham, 1957, pp. 64*ff.*

39. *Principles,* IV, pp. 695-99, 730, 762. One is unwarranted in inferring that he foresaw in Asia the subsequent achievements of Japan, begun about the time of his death. Some of the improvements noted are examined below.

40. *Ibid.*, pp. 763-64, 788-92. It was possible that in time such associations would absorb most work-people, despite the admitted innovative superiority of privately managed joint stock companies *(ibid.*, pp. 790-91). The cooperative movement would reduce distribution costs, which because of imperfectness of competition, remained excessive *(ibid.*, p. 789).

41. *Ibid.*, pp. 161, 193, 735; *Socialism,* pp. 94-95, 107. In one place Mill suggests that the remuneration of labor is derived from its product *(Principles,* pp. 29, 32), but he never attempts to convert this inference into a productivity theory. "It is unmeaning to say," he remarked, how much either of two cooperating agencies (e.g., the halves of a pair of scissors) produces, "or which of the factors, five or six, contributes most to the production of thirty" *(ibid.*, p. 26).

42. He first wrote in 1848 that "hitherto it is questionable if all the mechanical inventions yet made have lightened the day's toil of any human being" *(ibid.*, p. 751). The amount of labor required of the average worker had not been reduced, presumably because their numbers had increased so rapidly. *Ibid.*, p. 751; also p. 208, where he says that remuneration is almost "in an inverse ratio" to the hardness of the work done. E. J. Hobsbawm supports the view that living standards improved very little, if at all, be-

III

As has been shown, Mill attributed to unsalutary customs, beliefs, etc., the ultimate cause of economic backwardness in Asia and similarly situated parts of the world. These same forces were operative in the more developed parts of the world, but in much less intense measure. Even so, if these forces continued to operate, even in currently developed lands, they could prevent man's realizing his two correlated *quaesita*—a sufficiently high per capita income, and a combination of "just distribution" with "the greatest personal freedom."[43] At least the first of these *quaesita* could be realized if the quantity and/or the effectiveness of two of the three requisites of production—land and capital—increased more rapidly than the third—labor—and if the forces making for qualitative improvements in these factors and in the manner of their use were sufficiently powerful. If, however, numbers kept nearly abreast with, or even tended to outstrip, the requisites of production at man's disposal, and the forces making for improvement were not sufficiently powerful, it would be impossible to advance man's situation appreciably. Hence, fear that population growth might largely offset income-increasing forces lurked in much of Mill's discussion of economic progress.[44] In this section, therefore, I shall examine Mill's treatment of population, and in the next, his discussion of the developmental role of land, capital, and natural resources. In Sections V and VI, I shall examine his discussion of such dynamic forces as enterprise (which is not included among the three requisites of production), education, division of labor, etc., and his analysis of the role of the state.

In the absence of objective or subjective barriers, population grew rapidly, tending to double, under "most favorable circumstances," in twenty years or less. It was difficult to increase the means of production much more rapidly, if as rapidly. Consequently, positive or preventive checks came into operation. Thus, if a society were backward (as in Asia or medieval Europe) numbers were kept down by want and starvation. If however, a society were advanced, its population growth was restrained by fear of want and the desire for improved circumstances. The check then consisted not in an excess of deaths, but in a limitation of births prompted by "pru-

---

tween the 1790's and the middle 1840's, in "The British Standard of Living, 1790-1850," *Economic History Review*, X, 1957, pp. 46-68. But see footnote 45, below.

43. *Principles*, pp. xxix, 752, also pp. 748-50, on the ideal state, referred to again below.

44. Writing of the adherence of Mill and others to the wages-fund doctrine, F. W. Taussig remarked: "It was the exaggerated importance attached to the Malthusian theory which accounts for the stress laid on the wages fund doctrine." See *Wages and Capital*, New York, 1898, p. 224*n*. "The evils of over-population," Mill wrote in 1849, are not in some distant future; "they are, and have been throughout history, almost everywhere present, and often in great intensity." See *The Letters of John Stuart Mill*, H.S.R. Elliot, ed., London, 1910, I, p. 142.

dence and forethought" and "conscientious self-restraint." These motives were operative in the middle class, among the peasants as a rule, and among some skilled artisans, but very rarely among agricultural and unskilled workers. Even so, the habitual standard of the laboring classes was "gradually, though slowly, rising in the more advanced countries of Western Europe." Presumably, it would have risen faster had workers been better educated, had they experienced greater intellectual and moral improvement, and had they been freer to move from one occupational class to another.[45]

What really troubled Mill was the reproductive behavior of the working classes, not that of other classes, nor even that of advanced peoples considered as wholes. For while he remarked that "population almost everywhere treads close on the heels of agricultural improvement, and effaces its effects as fast as they are produced," with the result that improvement often served only to relax temporarily "the bonds which confine" population growth, he also observed that the rate of growth had declined in England and France.[46] This decline, however, reflected an increase in prudence on the part only of some, but not all, quantitatively important elements in the population. Of these imprudent elements, agricultural and unskilled workers were numerically most significant; they, in particular, were not prompted to control their numbers by the (supposed) fact that their economic condition depended ultimately upon their exercise of such control.[47] Thus, even in England, had it not been for the growth of towns and of urban capital wherewith to employ in-migrants from the countryside, the almost unrestricted breeding of England's hired agricultural labor would have reduced their condition to that of the rural Irish before 1846.[48]

---

45. *Principles*, pp. 158-61, also pp. 347, 353-57; pp. 393-94 on noncompeting groups; pp. 351-52 on evidence of the increasing importance of the prudential check. In England and France the condition of the worker had improved for forty years and the rate of population growth had fallen *(ibid.*, p. 161, also pp. 193, 735). For a less optimistic comment, see footnote 42, above. When referring to the distressed state of members of the laboring class, Mill usually had in view agricultural and unskilled workers. T. S. Ashton reports that, although more than half the English working population experienced improvement in its economic condition in 1790-1830, a large fraction, comprising mostly "unskilled or poorly skilled" agricultural and textile workers, did not. See F. A. Hayek, ed., *Capitalism and the Historians*, Chicago, 1954, pp. 151-59. Data assembled by Mill's contemporary, D. Chadwick, indicated that in 1859 real wages were appreciably higher in most branches of manufacture than they had been in 1839 *(Journal of the Royal Statistical Society*, XXIII, 1869, pp. 1-36). Charts on p. 950 of Volume II of *The Growth and Fluctuation of the British Economy, 1790-1850* (Oxford, 1953), by A. D. Gayer, *et al.*, reveal no strong upward wage movement. The apparent decline in per capita real income in the "hungry forties" is not specifically referred to by Mill. During the whole period, from 1800 to 1850, real per capita income increased about 14 per cent per decade; in 1850-1900, about 20 per cent per decade. See Phyllis Deane, "The Industrial Revolution and Economic Growth: The Evidence of Earlier British National Income Estimates," *Economic Development and Cultural Development*, V, 1956-1957, pp. 170-71. On changes in Mill's lifetime, see Asa Briggs, *The Age of Improvement*, London, 1959.

46. *Principles*, pp. 161, 721-22. Positive checks kept the rate low in backward countries *(ibid.*, pp. 704-705).

47. *Ibid.*, pp. 376-78; also pp. 190-91, 287-300, 353, 357-60; also section V, below.

48. *Ibid.*, p. 357. Among the peasantry of Western Europe, population growth usually

Mill took it for granted, therefore, that "due restriction of population" constituted the only means of preventing population growth from consuming the fruits of technical progress and capital formation and the "only safeguard of a labouring class." It was essential in general to avoid stimulation of population growth through governmental or other measures. It was essential in particular to decrease the relative numerical importance of the laboring class, and/or to modify its habits and customs appropriately and reshape and elevate its aspirations adequately.[49] For if most of the workers did not become prudent, the burden of population pressure, already chronic in many parts of the world, would weigh heavily upon the laboring class, even in Western Europe. In that event, although there were "a great increase of aggregate wealth, and even, in some respects, a better distribution of it," the "great class at the base of the whole might increase in numbers only, and not in comfort nor in cultivation."[50] Mill believed that prudential restraint would be strengthened if women were freed of subjection,[51] and that the imposition of legal restraints was permissible when the behavior affected was motivated by factors other than self-regard.[52] While Mill was circumspect in his public expression, he approved the use of contraceptive measures.[53]

In part perhaps because of his theory of "consensus," Mill did not believe that it would be easy to change the habits and aspirations of workers, and place a rising barrier of wants in the way of their natural increase.[54] For acquisition of the required higher standard of living, together with supporting habits, presupposed a large and sufficiently prolonged

---

was controlled. *Ibid.*, pp. 287-301, esp. pp. 290-93, and p. 296, where "the great power exercised over the minds of the people by the Catholic priesthood" is held partly responsible for the fact that the Belgian peasants did not effectively control their numbers. While Mill looked upon the peasant form of landownership as best suited to restrain population growth under existing conditions (e.g., see *England and Ireland*, p. 39; *Principles*, pp. 286*ff*., 762), he indicated that as the rural people became more enlightened, they might introduce large-scale modes of agricultural organization, when these were more efficient, and still duly regulate their numbers. See *ibid.*, pp. 762-64.

49. *Ibid.*, pp. 357-60, 363-66, 372, 374-81, 747, 751. See also pp. 353*ff*. on the fact that the prudential motives underlying the "restraining principle" greatly affect the conduct of the "middle class and skilled artisans," but not that of laborers, and on the further fact that custom sometimes "insensibly" molds the conduct of propertyless workers in such manner as to make them put off marriage or refrain from "over-rapid multiplication." In 1849 Mill described the "*droit au travail*" as endorsable, were it not for the "principle of population." See *Dissertations*, II, p. 385; also *Principles*, p. 364.

50. *Ibid.*, p. 699, also pp. 761, 704-705. Mill's contribution to optimum population theory is discussed in section V, below.

51. *Ibid.*, pp. 378, 760. See also Elliot, ed., *Letters*, I, p. 171, on the degradation of women by unrestricted childbearing and on the absolute necessity of child-limitation even when subsistence was available.

52. In 1865 Mill described restrictions upon marriage as not necessarily expedient, but permissible, inasmuch as marriage affected others than the parties concerned. See Elliot, ed., *Letters*, II, pp. 48-49. The underlying philosophy is expounded in "On Liberty," *loc.cit.* Mill treats of legal and customary restraints on marriage, etc., in *Principles*, pp. 353*ff*.

53. See N. E. Himes, "The Place of John Stuart Mill and of Robert Owen in the History of English Neo-Malthusianism," *Quarterly Journal of Economics*, XLII, 1927-28, pp. 627*ff*.

54. *Principles*, pp. 347, 360, 372, 374, 377-81, 384, 689, 719, 762.

improvement in the condition of the laboring class. A powerful and sustained force was needed.

To produce permanent advantage, the temporary cause operating upon them must be sufficient to make a great change in their condition—a change such as will be felt for many years, notwithstanding any stimulus which it may give during one generation to the increase of people. When, indeed, the improvement is of this signal character, and a generation grows up which has always been used to an improved scale of comfort, the habits of this new generation in respect to population become formed upon a higher minimum, and the improvement in their condition becomes permanent. Of cases in point, the most remarkable is France after the Revolution.[55]

Thus, it was the Revolution which had permanently modified the habits and morality of much of France's population, with the result that it alone of Europe's national populations had become nearly stationary. A similar sequel would attend the introduction of employer-worker cooperation and profit-sharing, since the resulting improvement in the condition of the working class could not be used up "in less than a generation," during which interval "the moral and intellectual influences of co-operation" (including its making palpable the "necessity of regulating population") would have had its effects. These effects would be intensified as more and more women entered industrial occupations and acquired economic and social independence.[56]

Unlike Malthus and his classical contemporaries, but in the manner of Torrens and Wakefield, Mill found in emigration an effective, though impermanent, counterbalance to unduly rapid natural population growth in countries such as England. Moreover, this efflux, as is explained in Section V below, would not only remove excess numbers; it would also facilitate the exportation of excess capital and the development of lands whence produce might be gotten on favorable terms. There were rich and as yet unexploited lands in the world, particularly in the United States, but also on other of the recently occupied continents. Potential migrants living in heavily peopled Europe could remove to these lands; develop their agricultural resources, and thereby ease land scarcity in Europe; and in the

55. *Ibid.*, pp. 348-49; see also *ibid.*, pp. 292-93, 371, 383-84, 719. As early as 1836, Mill reasoned that a person's rate of expenditure would be partly governed, when money was to be had, by the level of expenditure previously attained, but he did not apply his reasoning to the population problem. "The inheritors of immense fortunes . . . always live at least up to their incomes when at the highest," and go ever deeper into debt to maintain expenditure at this level when income actually received falls below the level of the highest (*Dissertations*, I, p. 169). Cf. *Principles*, p. 736, on a sometime rising marginal propensity to save.

56. On France, see *Principles*, pp. 293-95, 348; Elliot, ed., *Letters*, I, p. 153. On the probable effects of "co-operation" see Mill's letter of 1862 to M. Kyllman of Manchester, in *ibid.*, p. 269; *Principles*, pp. 759-64. He listed "among the probable consequences of the industrial and social independence of women, a great diminution of the evil of overpopulation" (*ibid.*, p. 760). In 1869 he declared that "the emancipation of women and co-operative production are . . . the two great changes that will regenerate society" (see *Letters*, II, p. 172).

process investment outlets would be provided for European capital.[57] In England and some European countries there were continually being accumulated large amounts of capital which, because domestic rates of return were low, were always ready to flow abroad and facilitate the settlement of Europe's excess population in underpeopled lands, and there bring about agricultural and industrial development. Hence, given a growing and free international trade, relatively cheap provisions could long be kept available to England and the continent, even though their numbers continued to grow. The advantages older countries got from this trade might be accentuated also by a considerable "extension of science and the industrial arts."[58] Eventually, of course, this developmental process would encounter limits arising out of population growth, given fixity in the supply of land.[59]

Ultimately, though the time might be far in the future, the state of every economy would become stable and stationary. The advent of this state depended, of course, upon what happened within a country and upon its relations with other countries. This state would be at hand when, as a result of the encroachment of wages and/or rent upon profits, the return on capital had fallen to the level at which the existing stock was merely kept intact but no longer added to.[60] Given a closed economy, the date of the advent would be governed principally by the nature and the amount of technological progress achieved; by the strength of the desire to accumulate capital, even at very low rates of return; and by the movement of the wage bill under the impact of rising food costs and/or rising real wages. Because the coming of the stationary state was compatible for a time either with nongrowth, or with continuing growth, of population, life in such a state might be pleasant or unpleasant (as Smith had described it). If the advent of this state had been largely consequent upon the practice of prudential restraint, then it would approximate the "best state for human nature," one "in which while no one is poor, no one desires to be richer, nor has any reason to fear

57. Apparently Mill had been impressed by Ireland's recent migratory history. He noted that enough migrants had gone from Ireland to the United States to reduce the Irish population by two million in 1841-1861, and to bring some relief to Ireland's misery-ridden people. The Irish had gone to "that flourishing continent which for generations will be capable of supporting in undiminished comfort the increase of the population of the whole world." *Principles,* p. 330. (In 1850 the world's population was growing about seven million per year.) Ireland was still suffering from population pressure in 1864 *(ibid.,* pp. 339-40). See also, on the great opportunities for growth and settlement in North America and Australia, *ibid.,* pp. 194, 350, 420, 721-22, 761, and p. 681 on high American productivity and wages.

58. *Ibid.,* p. 701, also pp. 715, 742, 744-45, 750; also, on abundance of capital, *ibid.,* pp. 173*ff.;* 731-33.

59. *Ibid.,* pp. 193-98. These limits are discussed in Sections IV and V, below. Mill apparently hoped that, during the period when emigration afforded relief, "a sounder morality on the subject of over-population" would be acquired. See his letter of 1850 in which emigration is described as ineffective unless the habits of the population improve *(Letters,* I, p. 153).

60. Mill was obsessed with the opinion that in advanced countries the rate of profit was "habitually" very close to the minimum. As Blaug remarks *(op.cit.,* p. 187), Mill did not even refer, in a laudatory review of a work of his disciple, Thomas de Quincey, to the latter's assertion that for two centuries profits had shown no tendency upward or downward, but had merely oscillated.

being thrust back by the efforts of others to push themselves forward," and one in which there "would be as much scope as ever for all kinds of mental culture, and moral and social progress."[61]

With the economy open, a larger population would be compatible with this ideal state. For, given investment opportunities in the underpeopled continents, capital could continually flow abroad, its quantity augmented by the stimulus to saving, occasioned in turn by the consequently higher rate of return. This outflow would finance, almost costlessly, an outflow of migrants who would develop foreign sources of produce and raw materials, and thereby defer the steady increase at home of food and raw-material costs, which continuing population growth, particularly at points of supply, would finally bring about.[62] In the end, however, since relevant improvements were limited, the state of a country's economy would become stationary, even though it remained open.[63] A society's preferred objective presumably ought to be the most satisfactory or agreeable of the stationary states realizable.[64]

IV

While "deficiency of capital, or of land," set a "limit to the increase of production," land was the more completely limitational factor in Mill's system, since, by putting limits upon man's capacity to increase agricultural output, it set bounds directly to capital formation and both directly and indirectly to population growth.[65] It thus made the advent of a stationary state inevitable. Because land, together with its products, was limited in amount, domestic support could be found for only a limited number of people; and capital accumulation itself became subject to restraint, as also did population insofar as its growth was conditioned by that of capital. For,

61. *Principles,* pp. 748-49, 751.

62. In the absence of such outflow, relatively excessive capital, being without much, if at all, superior alternative employment, might assume unproductive or quite fixed forms, without occasioning much, if any, disadvantage to the economy or to the working classes (*ibid.,* pp. 741-44). In a note on Senior's *Political Economy,* which was reprinted in 1836, Mill observed that until "emigration" was made "to facilitate further emigration," it would not be in sufficient volume to contribute significantly to the population growth of newly settled lands. "This could only be done by national arrangements, & emigration has never till now been a national concern." See J. S. Mill, "Notes on Senior's *Political Economy," Economica,* XII, 1945, p. 135. See footnote 80, below, on the influence of Wakefield.

63. *Principles,* pp. 736-42, 746-51; also pp. 193-98.

64. Of course, Mill did not specifically suggest a social welfare index in terms of which the choice might be made. Had he contrived one, it would have reflected the interests of the vast majority, since he recognized that the interest of some (e.g., landowners) might be at variance with that of most individuals.

65. *Ibid.,* pp. 189, also pp. 63-68. Mill sometimes used the term "land" to represent all "natural agents" (i.e., land, mines, fisheries, water, air), some of which (e.g., coal) were exhaustible (*ibid.,* pp. 26-27, 155-56, 176, 188, 477). Mill urged in Parliament that England pay off her national debt before her coal supplies were exhausted (see *Autobiography,* p. 202).

with land limited, an increase in the aggregate amount of capital tended to be accompanied, especially in a closed economy, by a decline in its rate of return, until this rate had descended to a level compatible merely with holding the stock of capital intact.[66] Furthermore, the cost of raw materials tended to rise, since, before the limits to the exploitation of "natural agents" were reached, they yielded "to any additional demands on progressively harder terms." This "law" of diminishing returns might "however be suspended, or temporarily controlled, by whatever adds to the general power of mankind over nature; and especially by any extension of their knowledge, and their consequent command, of the properties and powers of natural agents."[67] The impact of this law was heavier in the nonindustrialized sector of the economy. However, insofar as the marginal cost of raw materials rose in consequence of population growth, the cost of manufactures into which these materials entered tended to rise *ceteris paribus*. But other conditions did not stay put. Various forces (e.g., extension of division of labor, improvements, etc.) were at work, as a rule, reducing the cost of production of manufactures, only a small fraction of whose total cost reflected the input of raw materials. Hence, the real costs and prices of almost every manufacture had fallen, and would continue to fall "beyond any limit which it would be safe to specify."[68] It had to be through setting practical limits to food production and capital formation, therefore, that the tendency to diminishing return in primary industry could set limits to the growth of a country's numbers and aggregate output, provided, of course, that international trade was unable to overcome domestic shortages.

Deficiency of capital also served to limit output, since capital, always "the result of saving," was formed only when conditions were sufficiently favorable, and since it set limits to the amount of "industry" or employment realizable at any time.[69] Mill's emphasis upon the distinction between pro-

66. *Principles*, p. 189, also pp. 155-56, 417-21, 741. Mill's analysis of the role of land is patterned on Ricardo's in the latter's *Principles of Political Economy and Taxation*, E. C. K. Gonner, ed., London, 1903, chap. 6, also pp. 41, 112-13, 280.

67. *Principles*, p. 188. Even if population did not increase, coal, iron, and various metals would be exhausted in time, and before that time their costs would rise, as recourse was had to poorer and less tractable ores (*ibid*., p. 702). This argument appeared in the first edition, before Jevons wrote. Mill believed that if capital were used economically in British agriculture, and existing knowledge were put into effect, a great increase in output under conditions of constant return to capital would be possible (*ibid*., p. 180). In Britain, so great had been the improvements in agriculture, that the real cost of agricultural produce had fallen since the 1820's (*ibid*., p. 704). Typically, however, agricultural progress was slow (*ibid*., pp. 719, 721). On this trend, cf. C. Clark, *Conditions of Economic Progress*, London, 3rd ed., 1957, pp. 300-301.

68. *Principles*, pp. 184-86, also pp. 418, 702-703. It was "probable," but not "necessary," that the real cost of manufactures would fall; hence one could not declare this probability to be a law, as had Senior (*ibid*., p. 703).

69. *Ibid*., pp. 61-73. Capital included that part of man's possessions *intended* for "carrying on fresh production" (*ibid*., pp. 55-56), but not inventories (*ibid*., pp. 99-100). Saving consisted in consuming less than was produced (*ibid*., p. 70); it was necessary because a people's wants were met out of the produce of "past" labor. "There can be no more industry than is supplied with materials to work up and food to eat," that is, with wage goods

ductive and unproductive labor, and upon the distinction between productive and unproductive consumption, probably reflects the importance he attached to capital formation, at least in countries other than the advanced and well-settled, since only productive labor gave rise to material wealth, and since only productive consumption eventuated in the "permanent enrichment of society."[70] Moreover, capital formation might long offset population (or labor-force) formation, and could, in the more advanced countries, proceed at a rate rapid enough to push up real wages and average output, even though population and the number of "those who work for hire" were growing.[71]

How fast capital was formed in a country depended upon two circumstances: (a) the magnitude of "the net produce of industry," or "the amount of the fund from which saving can be made"; and (b), "the strength of the disposition to save," since (as John Rae had observed) capital was "the product of saving, that is, of abstinence from present consumption for the sake of the future good." The "strength of the disposition to save" depended, in turn, upon two conditions, one external to the individual, the other internal. It depended upon the rate of profit or return to be made or to be had upon savings, and upon "the effective desire of accumulation," or inclination to save at given rates of return, which reflected the underlying degree of willingness of individuals or nations to sacrifice "a present, for the sake of a future good." Whatever augmented the "net produce," or increased the return on capital or savings, or intensified the "effective desire of accumulation," served to increase the absolute and the relative amount of capital formation; whatever had an opposite effect occasioned a diminution in this amount.

---

and raw materials *(ibid.*, p. 64). The demand for labor thus depended upon circulating capital, particularly upon that part expended in the "direct purchase of labour" *(ibid.*, p. 343). Mill did not reason, as did Cairnes *(Some Leading Principles of Political Economy*, New York, 1874, pp. 170-80), that the supposedly falling ratio of circulating to total capital would be to labor's disadvantage. Though Mill abandoned his wages-fund doctrine in 1869 (see *Dissertations*, IV, pp. 42*ff*.), he did not remove it from the last edition (1871) of *Principles* to appear before his death in 1873. For modern interpretations of Mill's theory of the demand for labor, see A. C. Pigou, "Mill and the Wages Fund," *Economic Journal*, LIX, 1949, pp. 171-80; H. G. Johnson, "Demand for Commodities Is *Not* Demand for Labour," *ibid.*, pp. 531-36; F. A. Hayek, *Pure Theory of Capital*, London, 1954, pp. 273*ff*., 433*ff*. See also Pigou, *Industrial Fluctuations*, London, 1927, pp. 108, 111; E. Hahn, "The Share of Wages in the National Income," *Oxford Economic papers*, III, 1951, pp. 156-57; H. P. Neisser, " 'Permanent' Technological Unemployment," *American Economic Review*, XXXII, 1942, pp. 50-71; also Taussig, *op.cit.*, pp. 22-25.

70. *Principles*, I, chap. 3; also *Essays on Some Unsettled Questions of Political Economy*, pp. 75-89. Some of this "enrichment" must have been in the form of wealth not used in production, since fixed capital requirements were limited at any time. Output per worker depended upon fixed capital per worker in part (see *Principles*, pp. 107-108). Despite his emphasis upon education, Mill did not assign an important productive role to personal capital or investment in man's improvement. See also Hla Myint, "The Welfare Significance of Productive Labour," *Review of Economic Studies*, XI, 1943, pp. 20-30.

71. When discussing wages, Mill used the term "population" to refer to those "who work for hire" and capital to denote circulating capital expended directly upon the "purchase of labour." See *Principles*, p. 343, also pp. 342-43 on his formulation of the wages-fund theory.

Savings came out of a country's "net produce," consisting largely of profits and rent,[72] whence issued also governmental revenue,[73] together with private indulgence and the subsistence of persons not engaged in production. With given rates of return to be had on capital, the amount of saving depended largely upon the strength of the widely varying desire to accumulate capital.[74] This amount was correlated positively also with what enlarged the "net produce" and profits and, usually, with what increased the rate of profit or the rate of return on capital. Of great importance was whatever factor cheapened articles of consumption and industrial materials; for this enlarged net produce and increased profits, at least so long as habitual standards of consumption did not rise commensurately.[75] The emigration of capital to newer countries where a higher rate of return was to be had, was important for this reason, as well as because it made capital scarcer at home, and elevated the domestic rate of return, at least for the time being, thereby further stimulating its formation.[76] Whatever else increased the

72. This "net" consisted in the "surplus of produce" that remained "after supplying [out of gross output] the necessaries of life to all concerned in the production: including those employed in replacing the materials, and keeping the fixed capital in repair." See *ibid.*, p. 163, also pp. 407-408, 425, 427. Mill believes that Ricardo underestimated the amount of capital that might be available (*ibid.*, p. 164). Mill did not inquire carefully whether profit- or rent-receivers were more prone to save and form capital, though he noted that in new countries where rent was unimportant and profits were high, capital was accumulated rapidly. On Mill's conception of the role of interest and prospective profit in savings and investment, see L. C. Hunter, "Mill and the Law of Markets: Comment," *Quarterly Journal of Economics*, LXXIV, 1960, pp. 158-62.

73. While taxes might finance investment, they usually absorbed what might have been capital, and, if arbitrary, discouraged both industry and saving (*Principles*, pp. 66, 697, 821-31, 878-79, 883-84). See Section VI, below.

74. *Ibid.*, pp. 167*ff*., 408. Mill's account of the determinants of the "effective desire of accumulation" is based largely upon John Rae's discussion. The strength of this desire is correlated positively with such conditions as degree of law and order prevailing; security of property or earnings; safety of occupation; life expectancy; interest in others (e.g., children); intelligence; civilization, which furnishes men with motives to make provision for future goods; etc. See *ibid.*, pp. 97-98, 166-75, 638, 728-30. Hoarding in Asia is attributed to insecurity, fear of governmental rapacity, and dearth of relatively safe investment opportunities (pp. 665-66); the high rates of return expected on investment and the risk involved, and the "bad faith" and "poverty" of the borrowers (*ibid.*, pp. 173-75). See my account of Rae's developmental theory in the *Quarterly Journal of Economics*, LXXIII, 1959, pp. 393-406.

75. *Principles*, p. 736, also pp. 736-38 on the role of cheap imports in counterbalancing British population growth and elevating profits.

76. *Ibid.*, pp. 685-86, 736-39, 745. The movement of capital to colonies and elsewhere elevated the domestic rate of profit, and augmented the "supply of cheap food and cheap materials of clothing" available as imports, thereby retarding the rise of costs at home. Since the movement of capital produced this double effect, thereby increasing profits and the profit rate and savings, one could say that "up to a certain point, the more capital we send away, the more we shall possess and be able to retain at home" (*ibid.*, pp. 736-39). Mill described the "admission of cheaper food" from abroad as "equivalent to an agricultural invention" which reduced the cost of producing food domestically; but he remarked on obstacles to the continuing availability of cheap imported produce: (a) as yet (1871), only those parts of the globe situated near the sea or on navigable rivers could export produce, since internal transport remain so underdeveloped in most regions; (b) in food-exporting countries, with a strong effective desire to accumulate capital, population growth was rapid and would eventually diminish the amount of food left over for export; and (c) in countries where this desire was weak, capital was in short supply, and there was relatively little incentive to work hard or invest, it was difficult to increase the output and exportation of produce. He added, however, that, if high-yielding maize should ever become the "staple

domestic scarcity of capital, and hence its rate of return also tended to augment both savings and the number of savers.[77] For example, improvements had this effect, as did the emergence of new investment opportunities (e.g., railroads), and so did war loans and misuse and waste of capital, arising out of its misinvestment and mislocation, or out of "over-trading and rash speculation."[78]

Despite his emphasis upon the importance of capital accumulation, Mill believed that profits tended to a minimum, zero-saving level, given diminishing returns in agriculture and the consequent check to population growth.[79] This tendency became pronounced in the absence of improvements, and where there was a continuation of population growth at a rate exceeding that of capital. So great was this tendency in old and "opulent" countries (e.g., England and Holland) that, in the absence of countervailing forces, the current rate of accumulation could in "a short time...reduce profits to the minimum," below which "persons in general" would "not find sufficient motive to save."[80] When this limit was reached, capital formation, numbers, and output would become approximately stationary. This limit was the point of destination of industrial progress; its concrete locus was

food of the poor," the cost of producing food and maintaining a family would be "so diminished, that it would require some generations for population, even if it started forward at an American pace, to overtake this great accession to the facilities for its support" (*ibid.*, pp. 193-97, also p. 720). Alfred Marshall later emphasized the role of importation in keeping down British food and raw-material costs (*Principles of Economics*, London, 1920, pp. xv, 322, 691-92). Ricardo, while emphasizing international factor-immobility, had said that foreign trade could augment profits and capital formation by holding down the cost of wage goods (*Principles*, Gonner, ed., secs. 46-47, p. 116); he, like Marshall and unlike Mill, put predominant emphasis upon imports (*ibid.*, sec. 23, pp. 45-46).

77. Mill noted particularly those who saved to become richer or to leave others better off (see *Principles*, pp. 728-29). He remarked also that the "amount of capital permanently in existence" was not increased by persons who saved "at one period of life what they purpose to consume at another, or what will be consumed by their children before they can completely provide for themselves" (*ibid.*, p. 729).

78. *Ibid.*, pp. 642-43, 734-44, esp. pp. 733-35. The ratio of the rate of interest to that of profit was affected by the "proportion between the class of interest-receiving and that of profit-receiving capitalists"; it had been lowered by the gold discoveries, and raised by the legalization of joint stock companies and the "increasing willingness to send capital abroad." See *ibid.*, p. 642, also p. 647.

79. Mill's term, "rate of profit," usually denoted gross return on investment with interest included therein; at the minimum, this return, together with the associated rate of interest, just sufficed to keep the stock of capital intact (*ibid.*, pp. 407-408, 728-30). Sometimes, Mill used this term to denote the ratio of profits to wages-plus-profits at the no-rent margin (*ibid.*, pp. 419-20). Under the conditions assumed, a decline in this ratio was accompanied by a decline in the "rate of profit."

80. "The cause of this decline in profit is the increased cost of maintaining labour, which results from an increase in population and of the demand for food, outstripping the advance of agricultural improvement" (*ibid.*, p. 561, also p. 427, and IV, chaps. 3-4). See on the behavior of profits under different conditions, *ibid.*, pp. 173-75, 190, 350-51, 407, 729-35. Mill referred particularly to the works of E. G. Wakefield and William Ellis, and, following the former, noted that (a) "on a limited extent of land, only a limited quantity of capital can find employment at a profit," and that, therefore, (b) this limit having been attained, profit could "only be restored through an extension of the field of employment, either by the acquisition of fertile land, or by opening new markets in foreign countries, from which food and materials can be purchased with the products of domestic capital" (*ibid.*, p. 727). Elsewhere, as has been noted, Mill indicated that recourse (b) finally encountered limits. See *ibid.*, pp. 737-39, and footnote 76, above.

not fixed, however, shifting with changes in the actual rate of profit and in the strength of men's desire to accumulate at given schedules of rates of return.[81]

Mill's imperfect understanding of the role of fixed capital, rather than his estimate of the strength of the effective desire of accumulation, was responsible for his belief in the strength of the tendency of profits toward a zero-saving minimum of perhaps 1 per cent (net of risk) in England. In England enough circulating capital was readily formed to keep a growing labor force employed, given existing conditions favorable to saving, such as prolonged peace, puritanical values, good political institutions, freedom of enterprise, great prestige attaching to business, and the disposition of "the most enterprising and energetic characters" to enter business.[82] It was not likely that investment in fixed capital would "impair materially the funds for the maintenance of labour"; there tended to be enough capital for all purposes, most capital being short-lived and easy to replace.[83] While this opinion reflected Mill's stress on the fact that a nation's stock of capital was being continually replaced, as well as added to, it also reflected his underestimate of how much fixed capital might be economically combined with a worker, on an average, and how greatly such capital might increase his productivity.[84] It must also have resulted in his underestimate of the quantitative importance of fixed capital, and it may have led him to underestimate its effect upon the amplitude of the trade cycle, which he expected to become more moderate (despite the tendency of a low rate of return to encourage speculation).[85]

81. *Ibid.*, IV, chap. 6, also pp. 172, 728-30.

82. *Ibid.*, pp. 74, 173-75, 731, 742-44. In Mill's England the rate of profit was "habitually within . . . a hand's breadth of the minimum" *(ibid.*, p. 731).

83. *Ibid.*, pp. 74-78, 99. Thomas Chalmers, whose views Mill did not quite accurately represent (see R. O. Roberts, "Thomas Chalmers on the Public Debt," *Economica*, XII, 1945, p. 115), had pointed to the rapidity with which the "ravages of war" and catastrophe were repaired. "The greater part, in value, of the wealth now existing in England has been produced by human hands. A very small proportion indeed of that large aggregate was in existence ten years ago"; it had been kept in existence through repairs. Very few edifices "applied to industrial purposes" are of "great duration; . . . nor is it good economy to construct them of the solidity necessary for permanency." See *Principles*, pp. 73-79, 418; also pp. 51, 97, where (apparently following Rae) Mill noted that in capital-short countries too much labor sometimes was mistakenly invested in quite roundabout projects "in expectation of a distant return," when less roundabout projects would have yielded higher returns. Hayek *(Pure Theory of Capital*, pp. 47-48) indicates that Mill's emphasis upon the nonpermanence of capital goods and the perpetual reproduction of capital makes him partly "Austrian" in his capital theory. Capital invested in land was the most permanent, Mill noted *(Principles*, pp. 92-93).

84. On the productivity-increasing influence of machinery, etc., see *Principles*, pp. 107-108. Mill's neglect of Saint-Simonian investment-banking proposals may have been prompted in part by his conception of the role of fixed capital.

85. On Mill's theory of the trade cycle, and the role played therein by credit, speculation, and the lowness of the profit rate, see *ibid.*, pp. 653-65, 709, 734-35; also pp. 94-100 on the composition of investment and employment. See also B. A. Balassa, "Mill and the Law of Markets," *Quarterly Journal of Economics*, LXXIII, 1959, pp. 270-71; also Hunter, *op.cit.* What proportion of a nation's capital—i.e., wealth, "destined to be employed for reproduction," in which category inventories were not included—was fixed, in Mill's opinion, is not clear. He merely described fixed capital as constituting a "large portion of capital" and of increases in capital. *Prin-*

Mill did not believe, as did Wakefield and Torrens, that when the actual profit rate had reached a very low level, accumulation would still continue, with the result that slackness and unemployment would come into being.[86] For, as the profit rate, and hence the interest rate, fell, the demand for saving rose and its supply fell, until a minimum was reached at which "all further accumulation of capital would for the present cease."[87] Full-employment equilibrium would continue. Mill also rejected the view of Malthus and others that there could be "a general over-supply" of commodities or of capital until even "the working classes have also reached the point of satiety"; for men did not save "from mere habit" and they "consumed" what they "saved."[88] Even though the use of credit money, by dividing a transaction into two operations–buying and selling, made possible a temporary disequilibrium between money (commodity) demand and commodity (money) supply, such disequilibrium was soon corrected. It did, however, waste capital, thereby making it scarcer and elevating the profit rate.[89] Credit, of course, helped keep capital fully employed, and diverted it into the hands of relatively able undertakers.[90]

V

The principal forces which, according to Mill, made for improvement in the quality of the requisites of production, and in the efficiency with which they were used, included education, progress in science and the state of the arts, extension of specialization, and betterment of modes of economic organization. He also stressed enterprise and the contributions of creative thinkers, but he did not focus on the contribution of the entrepreneur as such. Mill's discussion of these forces often included discussions

ciples, I, chap. 6, also pp. 73-77. In his "Notes on . . . Senior's *Political Economy,*" *loc.cit.,* p. 135, Mill gave the "name fixed capital to all those portions of capital which are not consumed & reproduced within the year." Given this definition of fixed capital, circulating capital could have comprised only a quite minor fraction of all capital. In Mill's day the output of producer goods was growing about one-third faster than that of consumer goods. See Gayer, *op.cit.,* II, p. 625; also pp. 623, 647-51 on British investment and pp. 568-71 on the trade cycle.

86. *Principles,* pp. 727-28, 733. Mill's view of futurity was influenced by Ricardo, Sismondi, Wakefield, Torrens, and, according to H. Grossman, by William Playfair who even anticipated Veblen's view that late-developing nations would enjoy technological advantages over early-developing nations. See "W. Playfair, The Earliest Theorist of Capitalist Development," *Economic History Review,* XVIII, 1948, pp. 65-83, esp. pp. 80*ff.* Mill did not, however, adopt the view of Wakefield, Torrens, and others, that accumulation would continue in an essentially stationary society and generate slackness. See L. Robbins, *Robert Torrens and the Evolution of Classical Economics,* London, 1958, pp. 247-48.

87. *Principles,* pp. 562, 639, 733.

88. *Ibid.,* pp. 70, 560.

89. See *Essays on Some Unsettled Questions,* pp. 69-72; *Principles,* pp. 560-62, 653-56, 735. It was possible (e.g., in colonies) for capital to be unemployed because there were not "as many labourers obtainable, as the capital would maintain and employ" (*Principles,* p. 65). See also Balassa, *op.cit.,* pp. 263-74; this paper reveals the excellence of Mill's analysis.

90. *Principles,* pp. 413, 512, 638*ff.*

of changes in customs, habits, etc., but these changes are here treated as sequelae to education and progress in science.

In his account of the causes of international differences in output per head Mill mentioned, in addition to differences in specialization, availability of capital, and accessibility of natural advantages,[91] various subjective differences, among them differences in disposition to put forth energy, in skill and knowledge, in moral qualities, and in security of property. Thus, some peoples (e.g., the English) had, under the challenge of hardship, acquired a capacity to exert themselves greatly in the present, both to satisfy immediate wants and with "distant" objectives in view. They were industrious, and their time horizons were long. The state of the arts was more advanced in some countries than in others; workers and their superintendents were comparatively skilled and made their knowledge serve the purposes of industry; they were given to inventing and using machinery, to improving methods, to widening the range of technical possibilities, and to achieving economies in the use of labor and time. The moral qualities (e.g., trustworthiness) of some peoples were superior to those of others, enabling them to escape the costs of improbity. Finally, in some countries men were relatively more secure in the possession of the fruits of their industry, with the result that they had greater incentive to put forth effort.[92]

Education played a more important role in Mill's theory of economic development than did any other dynamic factor, because it generated or stimulated many of the forces making for socio-economic progress.[93] It played a double role, augmenting man's technical capacity to overcome the niggardliness of nature, and contributing to his moral progress by modifying the content of his mind. Mill considered the latter role the more important.[94] Education did or could shape, in important measure, the

91. Under the head of natural advantages, Mill included superiority with respect to soil fertility, climate and mineral supplies, and "maratime situation," adding that under many conditions possession of navigable rivers and good natural harbors offset almost all natural disadvantages (*ibid.*, pp. 102-103).

92. *Ibid.*, I, chap. 7, also p. 183 on agricultural progress; also p. 825 on tax-stimulated invention, and pp. 883-84 on incentive-reducing taxation. According to E. Cannan (*A Review of Economic Theory*, London, 1930, pp. 122-24), Mill, under the influence of John Rae, was the first British economist to stress the importance of cumulating knowledge and invention. Mill's follower, W. E. Hearn, wrote a chapter on invention (in *Plutology*, Melbourne, 1863, chap. 9), which Arnold Plant described in 1934 as still "the best" of its kind. See "The Economic Theory Concerning Patents for Inventions," *Economica*, I, 1934, p. 35.

93. In 1850 Mill said that he expected "very little from any plans which aim at improving even the economical state of the people by purely economical or political means. . . . Progress even of a political kind is coming to a halt, by reason of the low intellectual and moral state of all classes, and of the rich as much as of the poorer classes only. Great improvements in education (among the first of which I reckon dissevering it from bad religion) is the only thing to which I look for permanent good." See *Letters*, I, p. 153; also *ibid.*, II, p. 223.

94. He stressed the broadening role of education, its capacity for fostering inquiry and advancing human welfare and civilization, rather more than its narrow role as a utilitarian agent and diffuser of technical knowledge. See *Dissertations*, I, pp. 163*ff.*, 192-205; *The Positive Philosophy of Auguste Comte*, pp. 154-70; and "On Liberty," *loc. cit.*, pp. 159-63, where he approved the state's enforcing the education of children, but opposed the state's fixing the content of this

"opinions and habits" on which depended the economic progress of the community at large, and of the "laboring classes" in particular.[95] "All real amelioration in the lot of mankind depends on their intellectual and moral state."[96] "Successful production . . . depends more on the qualities of the human agents, than on the circumstances in which they work."[97] "There is hardly any source from which a more indefinite amount of improvement may be looked for in productive power, than by endowing with brains those who now have only hands."[98] Of the two tests of the merit of "any set of political institutions," one was the "degree in which they promote the general mental advancement of the community."[99]

As illustrating the impact of increasing knowledge, Mill signified England's agricultural revolution which had come in the wake of a marked increase in technical information.[100] At times, Mill wrote as if man's capacity to cumulate applied knowledge to overcome the niggardliness of Nature was without limit.[101] As was shown earlier, however, he recognized certain limitations, and these were incorporated into his theory of the stationary state. The "increase of wealth" was "not boundless," for the progressive movements underlying the growth of wealth were not "unlimited."[102]

Mill's account of the great importance of the division of labor reflects the fact that he wrote long after the Industrial Revolution began, whereas Smith's reflects his pre-industrial milieu. Following Wakefield's example,

---

education. It is possible that Mill's confidence in the capacity of education to improve mankind diminished in his later years. See *Autobiography,* pp. 75-76, 121, 125-26, and *Socialism,* p. 115; also F. A. Hayek, *John Stuart Mill and Harriet Taylor,* Chicago, 1951, pp. 77, 145-46, 148. On the views of Mill's father, see E. Halévy, *The Growth of Philosophical Radicalism,* New York, 1949, pp. 282*ff.*, 472.

95. The progress of per capita income "must depend on the opinions and habits of the most numerous class, the class of manual labourers." *(Principles,* pp. 752, 200*ff.)* Alteration of the "habits of the labouring people" called for an "effective national education of their children" and for a "system of measures which shall (as the Revolution did in France) extinguish extreme poverty for one whole generation." See *ibid.,* pp. 380-81, also pp. 954-56, on the manner in which the government was to make elementary education available. See also *ibid.,* pp. 285*ff.*, on the educational influence of the challenges which confronted the landowning peasant, sharpened his mental faculties, and supplemented his schooling, with the result that he acquired a middle-class point of view, made effective use of his practical knowledge, and restrained his natural increase. The anxieties of the English day-laborer, by contrast, had a deadening effect.

96. *Autobiography,* p. 167; also *Logic,* II, pp. 521-23, and *Principles,* pp. 108-11, 751.

97. *Ibid.,* p. 104. Mill did not wholly subscribe to current opinion that, as a rule, English workers were the most productive *(ibid.,* pp. 106-10) (e.g., see *Journal of the Royal Statistical Society,* XXV, 1862, pp. 508-10; XLI, 1878, pp. 93-103).

98. *Principles,* p. 187.

99. "Representative Government," *loc.cit.,* p. 195, also p. 193. He meant "advancement in intellect, in virtue, and in practical activity and efficiency" *(ibid.,* p. 195).

100. *Principles,* pp. 183-84, 715*ff.* Under the influence of Ricardo, Mill sought to distinguish between improvements which were merely labor-saving and improvements which were both labor- and land-saving. See Marshall's criticism of Mill's exposition *(op.cit.,* pp. 836-37).

101. The "growth of man's power over nature" is "perpetual, and so far as human foresight can extend . . . unlimited. Our knowledge of the properties and laws of physical objects shows no sign of approaching its ultimate boundaries; it is advancing more rapidly, and in a greater number of directions at once, than in any previous age or generation." The belief seemed justified "that our acquaintance with nature is still almost in its infancy" *(Principles,* p. 696, also p. 25).

102. *Ibid.,* p. 746.

Mill divided the division of labor into simple and complex "co-operation," that is, into intra- and inter-occupational specialization. Its effects at the national level, his account suggests, fell into two categories: those shaping the behavior of individuals, and those conditioning the behavior and size of firms. It increased the worker's dexterity, augmented the relative amount of time in which men and tools could remain uninterruptedly at work, stimulated invention, permitted individuals to be assigned to jobs in keeping with their particular capacities, and thus allowed nations to capitalize more efficiently on their differential advantages.[103] Capitalizing on these advantages in turn entailed recourse, as did the associated fact of input-lumpiness,[104] to larger-scale modes of organization, the relative importance of which would increase.[105] In many lines of activity, especially in the non-agricultural sector,[106] labor could be more advantageously subdivided in relatively large, than in relatively small, firms, and this advantage would increase.[107] In consequence, the joint stock company form of organization was proving relatively superior in industries characterized by notable economies of scale, since only this form permitted undertakers to assemble the large amounts of capital required.[108]

Division of labor, together with its beneficial effects, was affected in

---

103. *Ibid.*, pp. 124-30, 578. Mill was influenced by the views of Rae and Babbage *(ibid.*, pp. 128-29).

104. *Ibid.*, pp. 132-36. Mill mentioned overhead, or administrative expense; costly, but technologically efficient, machinery; and the capacity of highly skilled entrepreneurs. Optimum use of any one of these was not possible if a firm were too small.

105. *Ibid.*, pp. 142, 699, 760.

106. In agriculture relatively small-scale undertakings were often as productive, per acre, as were large-scale undertakings, if not more so, in part because small farmers, when they owned their land, worked longer and harder than did hired workers engaged in tilling large farms *(ibid.*, pp. 130-31, 144-50, 152-53, also pp. 324-27 on India). Well-cultured large farms were, however, "an important part of a good agricultural system," for they constituted a major source of agricultural improvements *(ibid.*, p. 334). Mill expected, furthermore, that as a society progressed, the greater efficiency of large-scale agriculture would bring about its spread *(ibid.*, pp. 762-63).

107. *Ibid.*, pp. 132, 762*ff*. Only a relatively large firm could keep all of its specialized employees fully occupied, Mill noted. For, with the degree of subdivision given, "there will be good economy in enlarging" a firm's operations "to the point at which" every person in a "special occupation, will have full employment in that occupation" *(ibid.*, p. 132). Mill, here following Babbage, seems to be saying that the firm-capacity required is the least common multiple of the capacities of the individual, specialized operating units.

108. *Ibid.*, pp. 137-39, 174, 902-903. See also *ibid.*, p. 142, where Mill indicates that capital tends to be available for investment in large firms when the supply of capital is increasing and when there are "large capitals in few hands"; and pp. 638*ff*., where he says that the joint stock company provided an outlet for savings of owners who were unable, or unwilling, to invest them. Publicity of corporate accounts tended to inspire confidence and keep management accountable *(ibid.*, pp. 138-39, 903). Mill believed that allowing managers a share of the profits would help to keep their zeal and fidelity enlisted, and that competition would normally guard the interests of the public *(ibid.*, pp. 138-42). When, however, efficiency could be secured only through restricting production to a single firm, it should be run by the government or made what we today call a public utility *(ibid.*, pp. 142-44, 960-63). Joint stock concerns were not suited to situations in which "small gains and small savings" were important, for they disregarded small sums *(ibid.*, p. 140). See also on Mill's views on joint-stock associations and monopoly, A. L. Harris, "J. S. Mill on Monopoly and Socialism: A Note," *Journal of Political Economy*, LXVII, 1959, pp. 604-611.

two ways by international exchange. First, it enabled every country to produce "the things in which it lies under the least disadvantage, if there be none in which it possess an advantage." It thus made possible for a set of trading countries to produce a larger aggregate output, and for each country (normally) to enjoy a larger income.[109] This source of advantage was especially significant, Mill's argument suggests, outside what might be called the larger English trading community, since outside this area the international mobility of factors, especially of capital, was quite low, though increasing.[110]

Within the English trading community, which embraced Britain's West Indian colonies, but not India, factors (at least capital) were mobile, profits were governed by the English rate, and commerce was of the town-country rather than of the international sort.[111] Second, international exchange enlarged the market for goods that were exported, as well as consumed at home, and thus extended the division of labor, made possible "greater use of machinery," and increased the likelihood of "inventions and improvements in the processes of production."[112] This last tendency was greatly strengthened by the international contacts to which trade gave rise, since these resulted in the introduction of superior foreign arts and practices.[113]

Complex cooperation was essential to a nation's economic development, in that it increased the elasticity of demand for income in terms of effort. Inter-occupational specialization made for variegatedness of output, and this in turn furnished men both with opportunities to sell their products and with motives to put forth effort, in the absence of which they would be without incentive to work as hard and efficiently. Thus, the development of towns was essential to both the agricultural and the economic progress of a country, at least so long as it lacked easy access to great export markets; for towns provided agriculturalists with markets and with incentives to augment output. When, as in India, the "stimulus" of a "large town population" was wanting, the impact of all other growth-retarding forces (e.g., minimum wants, governmental rapacity, unaspiring spirit) was intensified.[114] Foreign

109. *Principles*, pp. 578-79, 587-88, 701. Mill did not touch upon the possible effect of foreign trade upon income distribution within countries, though at times he noted that a cheapening of produce and raw materials of foreign origin might augment profits (see footnote 75, above).

110. *Ibid.*, III, chaps. 17-18, esp. pp. 575-76. Smith's view of trade as offering "a vent" for a country's produce is rejected. *Ibid.*, p. 579.

111. *Ibid.*, pp. 685-87. Mill's exposition of colonial trade, though essentially valid, was not adopted. See Ida Greaves, "The Character of British Colonial Trade," *Journal of Political Economy*, LXII, 1944, pp. 1-11; also Cairnes, *Political Economy*, pp. 305-307.

112. *Principles*, p. 581. Regarding Mill's assessment (*ibid.*, pp. 593-96) of the international impact of improvements in exporting countries, see M. C. Kemp, "Technological Change, the Terms of Trade and Welfare," *Economic Journal*, LXV, 1955, pp. 467-68.

113. *Principles*, pp. 581-82.

114. *Ibid.*, pp. 116-22, 195, 358. The sources of man's motives to work, etc., of so much concern to Mill, had received extended analysis at the hands of Malthus. See my "Malthus' Total Population Theory: A Restatement and Reappraisal," *Canadian Journal of Economics and Political Science*, XI, 1945, pp. 83-110, and "Malthus the Malthusian vs. Malthus the Economist," *Southern Economic Journal*, XXIV, 1957, pp. 1-12.

trade acted upon men's minds, much as did the presence of towns. This was particularly true when a country was in "an early stage of industrial advancement," and its people were in a "quiescent, indolent, uncultivated state, with all their tastes either fully satisfied or entirely undeveloped," and hence were indisposed "to put forth the whole of their productive energies." Foreign trade introduced new objects of desire, prompted new wants, and inculcated new tastes, with the result that men worked harder in order to be able to acquire these things and "even" undertook to "save and accumulate capital, for the still more complete satisfaction of these tastes at a future time."[115]

Mill found limitations to the income-increasing power of the division of labor, not only in the niggardliness of nature, as had Ricardo, but also in the organization of the economy as such; and for this reason, together with his conception of social welfare, he concluded that every country had an optimum population capacity which it was disadvantageous to exceed. He observed, as had Smith, that division of labor is limited by the extent of the market and by the "nature of employment" when, as was often the case in agriculture, this precluded the simultaneous pursuit of many different operations. In the absence of opportunity for heavy exportation, the extent of the market was restricted by the smallness or the scatteredness of the population, by its poverty, and by the "deficiency of roads and water carriage."[116] Mill did not expect, when these restrictions were overcome, that improvements in manufacture, consequent upon population growth and a resulting extension of division of labor, would always continue at a rate that was more than sufficient to offset increases in the cost of domestic produce; nor did he see a permanent way out in the exchange of exports for imported produce, though this recourse might long be available.[117] Even if rising food and material costs could be averted, advantages consequent upon division of labor made possible by population growth finally would become too small to further warrant such growth, particularly since these advantages would be offset by diminution in the amount of welfare realizable from noneconomic sources:

After a degree of density has been attained, sufficient to allow the principal benefits of combination of labor, all further increase tends in itself to mischief, so far

115. *Principles*, p. 581. Thus, as stated above (footnote 38), Mill did not accept Nurkse's interpretation of the impact of the demonstration effect. Twelve years earlier Mill had condemned the "puffing" of products and aggressive merchandising, at least as carried on in England (see *Dissertations*, I, pp. 182-84). At that time, however, he was apprehensive about the rise of "quackery" and the submergence of the individual; he was not dealing with the need for inculcating wants in certain classes or nations.

116. *Principles*, pp. 130-31.

117. *Ibid.*, pp. 701, 715, 736-37. Mill supposed that in time the cost of imported produce would rise (*ibid.*, pp. 194-97, 736-39), but he did not emphasize a prospective worsening of the terms of trade, as had Torrens (in his *Essay on the Production of Wealth*, London, 1821), pp. 96, 98, 286-89). See, however, footnote 76, above.

as regards the average condition of people; but the progress of improvement has a counteracting operation, and allows of increased numbers without any deterioration, and even consistently with a higher average of comfort.[118]

In the older advanced countries, however, density had become great enough to permit optimal use of resources and of whatever improvements were made.[119]

There is room in the world, no doubt, and even in old countries, for a great increase of population, supposing the arts of life to go on improving, and capital to increase. But even if innocuous, I confess I see very little reason for desiring it. The density of population necessary to enable mankind to obtain, in the greatest degree, all the advantages both of co-operation and of social intercourse, has, in all the most populous countries, been attained. A population may be too crowded, though all be amply supplied with food and raiment. . . . A world from which solitude is extirpated is a very poor ideal. . . . Nor is there much satisfaction in contemplating the world with nothing left to the spontaneous activity of nature; with every rood of land brought into cultivation, which is capable of growing food for human beings; . . .[120]

Mill did not play up the dynamic, developmental role of the entrepreneur, even though he usually viewed the governmental conduct of any set of industrial operations as a last resort.[121] He remarked on the importance of the contribution of private entrepreneurs to the process of innovation.[122] Mill also commented on the general scarcity of competent supervisory and managerial personnel, as well as that of entrepreneurs with technical education and proficiency, though he thought inter-occupational factor-mobility would minimize inter-occupational differences in the reward of skilled undertakers.[123] He even noted the absolute essentiality of that "striving, go-ahead character" which characterized England, the United States, and the "commercial class."[124] Yet, his personal values were such that he

118. *Principles*, pp. 191-92. Mill used the term "improvement" here, as elsewhere, to include "not only new industrial inventions, or an extended use of those already known, but improvements in institutions, education, opinions, and human affairs generally, provided they tend, as almost all improvements do, to give new motives or new facilities to production" (*ibid.*, p. 192).

119. *Ibid.*, pp. 750-51. Presumably Mill considered great population density inimical to "freedom," after the "primary necessities," the "first and strongest want of human nature." See *The Subjection of Women*, p. 178.

120. *Principles*, p. 750. At the time Mill wrote, population density in the more populous European countries (180 per square mile) approximated or exceeded that of the Northeastern United States in 1950. See my "Marshall on the Population Question," *Population Studies*, VIII, 1954-55, pp. 264*ff*.; IX, 1955-56, pp. 56*ff*.

121. *Principles*, pp. 137, 947, and p. 407 on the proverbial inefficiency of hired managers.

122. E.g., he commented on the "great perspicacity" of the "directing" heads of large companies and on their ability, because of "superior knowledge" and judgment, to guard "against blunders." He stated that private capitalist undertakers were much more disposed than was any cooperative "association to run judicious risks, . . originate costly improvements," and "commence things previously untried." See *ibid.*, pp. 141, 790-91; see also *Socialism*, pp. 103-107, 118.

123. *Principles*, pp. 108, 148-49, 409-12. Mill discusses profits in *ibid.*, II, chap. 15, but does not here emphasize innovation. He noted that increase in popular education would increase the supply of managerial and entrepreneurial personnel, and that making credit available would increase their effectiveness (*ibid.*, pp. 109, 413).

124. See "Representative Government," *loc.cit.*, pp. 191, 214; *Dissertations*, I, pp. 164-65, II, pp. 70-77.

could not find himself strongly sympathetic with a class, however strategic, whose energies were largely confined to money-getting; there was need also for the learned, the leisured, and for stable agriculturalists.[125] He was not enthusiastic, therefore, that in England there was "scarcely any outlet for energy . . . except business."[126]

Social and economic progress could not continue satisfactorily unless the existing employer-worker form of business organization was widely replaced by an "association of the labourers themselves, on terms of equality, collectively owning the capital with which they carry on their operations, and working under managers elected and removable by themselves."[127] Cooperation within associations was essential, if resources were to be used effectively and so as to realize economies of scale.[128] Such cooperation could not be achieved under the usual employer-worker relationship, which deprived workers of motives to be productive; made for inequity in the distribution of results; generated employer-worker hostility; and which did not, as would cooperation, induce the regulation of numbers, and increase the impact of the "improving influences of association."[129] Mill looked forward, therefore, to a time when, "through the co-operative principle," there would result "a change in society, which would combine the freedom and independence of the individual, with the moral, intellectual, and economical advantages of aggregate production."[130]

VI

Mill did not assign the state an important role in economic development, in part because the concentration of many economic functions in the hands of government would destroy men's individuality and liberty;[131] in part because governments (especially when routine-ridden) were less flexible and less effective and progressive, as a rule, than were private bodies;[132] and

125. *Dissertations,* II, pp. 73-75, I, pp. 177-78; *Principles,* 748-49. Mill objected in part to the ascendancy of any one class (see *Dissertations,* II, pp. 237-38).

126. "On Liberty," *loc.cit.*, p. 127.

127. *Principles,* p. 773. Mill expected the prevailing employer-worker relationship to be "gradually superseded" by: in "some cases, association of the labourers with the capitalist; in others, and perhaps finally in all, association of labourers among themselves." *Ibid.*, p. 764.

128. *Ibid.*, pp. 698-99. The spread of the joint stock form signified the importance of economies of scale.

129. *Ibid.*, pp. 760-61, 789; *Letters,* II, p. 269, on control of numbers, and I, p. 294, and II, p. 46, on the need of "co-operation" to remove worker-employer antagonism.

130. *Principles,* p. 791. Mill was under no illusion regarding mankind. He noted "the natural indolence of mankind," the necessity of "competition" *(ibid.,* pp. 792-94). The working class had no interest in the "preservation of natural beauty" (in the absence of suitable education), and it was likely to abuse political power, should it achieve such power. See *Letters,* II, pp. 45, 70, 122-23, 223.

131. "On Liberty," *loc.cit.*, pp. 165-68.

132. *Ibid.*, pp. 167-68; "Representative Government," *loc.cit.*, pp. 245-47. Representative governments were less immune to the rigidity that accompanied bureaucratization *(ibid.,* pp. 246-48, 216-18).

in part perhaps because, although the proper functions of government tended to be "much more extensive in a backward than in an advanced state," the governments found in such states might not be equipped to perform all these functions.[133] In principle, there was "scarcely anything really important to the general interest" that a government might not undertake if private enterprise failed to do so. In reality, however, Mill specified few such undertakings. Among his exceptions to the rule of laisser faire, governmental support of lower education and conduct of colonization stand out. He indicated also that the government must provide a milieu favorable to private enterprise; that it must establish or guard an incentive-producing system of land ownership; and that it must support the construction of necessary public works (e.g., irrigation, transport, etc.) when private enterprise was unable or unwilling to do so.[134]

The developmental role of government was limited by its particular qualities, some of which varied with time and place, and some of which were inherent in the governmental process. In less developed countries, large undertakings required governmental support.[135] Yet, the government in these countries might be lacking in probity and technical competence. In fact, where ignorance and misgovernment prevailed, the prospect for economic development was very poor, the incompetence of government being a major deterrent to economic growth.[136] It was only among morally advanced peoples that government was likely to be of a form and disposition suited to stimulate economic development.[137] Even in "the more advanced communities," however, there was little in the economic realm that government could do as well as private individuals. At the level of the firm and at the aggregate level, a government was inferior in "intelligence and knowledge"; at the administrative level, it was much more subject to want of efficient delegation and decentralization of responsibility for decision-making.[138] Regarding innovation, private management remained greatly superior to public management; and with regard to the regulation of economic activities in general, competition remained superior to all alternatives, and every extension of it was to the advantage of the vast majority

---

133. *Ibid.*, pp. 185, 200*ff.*; also *Logic*, II, pp. 514-15, on the correlation between state of civilization and type of government. On the recruitment of competent governmental personnel, see "On Liberty," *loc.cit.*, pp. 165-66; "Representative Government," *loc. cit.*, pp. 341-46.

134. *Principles*, V, chap. 2, esp. pp. 947-53, 969*ff.*, 977*ff.*; also II, chaps. 6-10 and p. 762 on land-ownership. Convenience might be a ground for having the state "assume powers and execute functions" (*ibid.*, p. 800).

135. "In countries where the practice of co-operation [e.g., as expressed in a joint stock company] is only in the earlier stages of its growth, the government alone can be looked to for any of the works for which a great combination of means is requisite." See *ibid.*, p. 137.

136. *Ibid.*, p. 701; *Socialism*, p. 95. Continental countries were "over-governed" (*Principles*, p. 961).

137. E.g., see *Principles*, pp. 209, 216-17; *Socialism*, pp. 114-16; *Logic*, II, pp. 514-15.

138. *Principles*, pp. 946-47.

of a society.[139] For these and other reasons, Mill expected that society would, "for a considerable time to come," be "founded on private property and individual competition."[140]

Mill endorsed the infant-industry principle, although with increasing reservation and on the supposition that employment was full. This was the only allowable exception—"on mere principles of political economy"—to freedom of trade. Having begun a particular industry relatively early sometimes accounted for a country's superiority therein, just as having acquired nationhood late sometimes accounted for a country's inferiority in certain branches of production. Hence "protecting duties can be defensible . . . when they are imposed temporarily (especially in a young and rising nation) in hopes of naturalizing a foreign industry, in itself perfectly suitable to the circumstances of a country." For, in the absence of such protection, or its equivalent, individuals would not undertake the costs and risks attendant on introducing a new manufacture, even though a country seemed potentially well adapted to it and "its trial under a new set of conditions" was likely to "promote improvements."[141] It was essential, however, that this protection be provided only for a definitely limited period of time, and be made to decrease gradually during the latter part of its existence.[142] Mill observed, incidentally, that some countries were unsuited, at least relatively, to economic development.[143]

Mill did not endorse the infant-stage-of-development argument for protection, because he thought its objective might better be accomplished other-

---

139. On innovating management, see *Socialism*, pp. 117-18, and *Principles*, pp. 790-91; on the advantages of competition, see *ibid.*, pp. 242-43, 343, 792-94, 950*ff*. Competition governed wholesale trade, manufacture, and banking; it was imperfect in retail trade outside cities and in the professions *(ibid.*, pp. 246-47, 411, 415-16, 440-41).

140. *Ibid.*, pp. 216-17; also pp. 208-209 on the need for improvement.

141. *Ibid.*, p. 922. Mill's view was influenced by John Rae's defense of infant-industry protectionism. Export taxes are described as "being contrary to the universal weal" *(ibid.*, p. 853). Protection of cottage industry did not give rise to opportunity costs, as did protection of other industries *(ibid.*, pp. 64-65*n*). Import duties were "partly paid" by foreigners who bought exports of the duty-levying country *(ibid.*, pp. 854-55).

142. *Ibid.*, pp. 922, 923, also p. 64. In 1868 Mill wrote that his endorsement of the infant-industry principle had been "greatly shaken" by his observation that protection, once granted, tended to become permanent. It would be better therefore to resort to an annual subsidy, since it was less likely to be continued than was a protective duty. See *Letters*, II, p. 149, also p. 299, where Mill denies that protection can raise wages. In the 1871 edition of *Principles*, Mill changed "will" to "might" in the sentence, "A protecting duty . . . might sometimes be the least inconvenient mode in which the nation can tax itself for the support of . . . an experiment" with a new manufacture; and he declared it "essential" that protection be confined to industries which would have need of it only a short time (see p. 922*n*). James Bonar has traced how Mill's faith in the temporary political practicality of protection was weakened by what he observed in Australia and the United States, namely, the extension of protection to industries without promise and its tendency to become permanent. See G. F. Shirras, "James Bonar," *Economic Journal*, LI, 1941, pp. 151-52.

143. *Dissertations*, I, p. 415; *Principles*, p. 578. "The labour and capital which have been sunk in rendering Holland habitable, would have produced a much greater return if transported to America or Ireland" *(ibid.*, p. 578, also pp. 686-87).

wise. There was much foundation for the argument that a nation should not engage almost exclusively in one or several pursuits, but in a variety of activities, that towns should abound, and that "a nation all agricultural" could not "attain a high state of civilization and culture." Whether the United States could overcome this difficulty remained to be seen. Protectionism was not a suitable solution, however, at least insofar as the object was "to check the excessive dispersion of the population."[144] E. G. Wakefield had "pointed out a better way," namely, to confer the advantages of cooperation by "securing that every colony shall have from the first a town population bearing due proportion to its agricultural, and that the cultivators of the soil shall not be so widely scattered as to be deprived by distance of the benefit of that town population as a market for their produce."[145] He would check "premature occupation of land, and dispersion of the people, by putting upon all unappropriated lands a rather high price," and utilize the proceeds to convey "emigrant labourers from the mother country."[146]

Mill found Wakefield's scheme, which in effect provided for self-supporting emigration and colonization within a framework of governmental regulation, to fall within the category of undertakings with respect to which state intervention was indicated. Society had a great stake in colonization and emigration, one involving the "future and permanent interest of civilization," and this stake could not be adequately guarded under laissez faire. Governmental intervention was essential, in order that emigration might not outstrip the capital available for its employment; to insure that settlers situated themselves suitably, and that new arrivals did not proceed too rapidly to take up land; to assure the advantages of urban and other cooperation; to prevent the individual from taking up more land than he could farm; and to see to it that the colony collectively bore the expenses of emigration to it. The mother country could make loans to colonies to get the flow of migrants started; the system, "once established, would increase in efficiency every year," its effect increasing "in geometrical progression" until the colony was "fully peopled." The Wakefield system, having been set in motion, would sustain the demand for Britain's growing supply of capital, ease population pressure in England, and enable the mother country to settle "unoccupied continents" at a satisfactory rate, and at little cost to itself or

144. *Ibid.*, p. 925. In 1871 Mill wrote that, while there had been force in the argument that America should not stay too agricultural, it had developed to the point where the argument was no longer applicable. See *Letters*, II, pp. 301-302. Mill referred to Henry Carey's works, but not to F. List's.

145. *Principles*, pp. 121, 925, also pp. 116-17, 144-45.

146. *Ibid.*, p. 965, also pp. 925, 972. On October 23, 1834, Mill published a letter in the *Morning Chronicle* (p. 3), objecting that the lowness of the price proposed for Australian land would make labor too scarce. See MacMinn, *op.cit.*, p. 42.

o the emigrants.[147] While Mill pointed to the disadvantages England was ınder in protecting and supporting her dependencies, he believed the ad-'antages to all concerned outweighed these disadvantages, at least as long ıs a dependency did not seek independence.[148]

Mill touched particularly upon at least four ways in which the state night influence the rate of capital formation: (a) He remarked that a ;overnment could "create capital" by laying on taxes and employing the 'evenue productively, or by taxing income or expenditure and using the proceeds to pay off "the public debts," since the fundholders would prob-ıbly use most of their receipts to support "productive employment."[149] (b) He noted that a tax on profits tended to reduce capital formation and ıe advocated exemption of saved income from taxes on income.[150] Mill vas not alarmed, however, at the capital-absorbing effect of taxation in :ountries in which capital abounded and "the spirit of accumulation" was strong, since he believed that the resulting capital scarcity would stimulate :ompensatory saving, and since he supposed that some taxpayers would :ndeavor to make up their tax payments by introducing income-increasing nventions.[151] (c) He feared that under socialism too little capital might ›e accumulated.[152] (d) He considered it fallacious to assert, with Hume or he Birmingham economists, "that an increase of the currency quickens ndustry," by setting idle capital to work, or otherwise. Capital did not tend o remain idle in a measure exceeding that required to support the prevail-ng division of labor. Depreciation of money could not, therefore, "benefit ınybody, except at the expense of somebody else."[153]

147. *Principles,* pp. 965-66, 970, 972-75; ılso pp. 382, 701; also Mill's "Notes on N. W. ;enior's *Political Economy,*" *loc.cit.,* p. 135. Aill's sanguine expectations were not real-zed (see Brinley Thomas, *Migration and Economic Growth,* Cambridge, 1954, chap. 13). H. O. Pappe writes, however, that 'Wakefield's role as an empire builder is oday beyond dispute" (see "Wakefield and Marx," *Economic History Review,* IV, 1951, ›. 88). Wakefield's scheme, together with Mill's support of it, rested upon the supposi-ion that voluntary and unregulated emigra-ion was unlikely to be both adequate and ›elf-supporting, though the heavy Irish emi-gration to the United States had been so, he "earnings of those who went before" supplying the "expenses of those who fol-owed." See *Principles,* p. 330. Cf. also W. S. Shepperson, "Industrial Emigration in Early Victorian Britain," *Journal of Economic His-'ory,* XIII, 1953, pp. 179-92.

148. "Representative Government," *loc. cit.,* pp. 379-81; *England and Ireland,* pp. 26-32. In 1867 Mill remarked that one way of solving "the Irish difficulty" would be for England, Scotland, and Ireland "to join the American Confederation as three states of the Union." See George O'Brien, "J. S. Mill and J. E. Cairnes," *Economica,* X, 1943, p. 275. Mill commented frequently on Irish af-fairs. See MacMinn, *op.cit.;* Black, *op.cit.*

149. *Principles,* pp. 66, 878-79.

150. *Ibid.,* pp. 826, 829. Mill held that every tax was "partly paid from what other-wise would be saved" *(ibid.,* p. 821). See also *ibid.,* p. 831, on expenditure taxes, and pp. 874-75 on the capital-absorbing effect of war loans. He did not, in his defense of inheritance taxes, analyze their effect upon capital formation, presumably because he be-lieved such taxes would result in a much better use of the property affected *(ibid.,* pp. 224-29).

151. *Ibid.,* pp. 697, 821-22, 825-26. Arbi-trary taxation discouraged saving and indus-try *(ibid.,* pp. 821, 857, 883-84).

152. *Socialism,* pp. 111-13.

153. *Essays on Some Unsettled Questions,* pp. 55-57, 65, 67-68; "The Currency Juggle," in *Dissertations,* I, pp. 50-54; *Principles,* pp. 65, 549-51, also pp. 488 and 579, on the

VII

In its broad outlines Mill's theory of economic development does not differ so greatly from comparable present-day theories. The movement of annual output depends upon the growth of capital and population (i.e., labor), upon the rate of scientific and technical progress, and upon the extent to which shortages of arable land and raw materials can be circumvented by improved methods or through importation. Capital formation and population growth, together with the growth of applied knowledge and the impact of shortages (if any) of land and sources of raw material, were conditioned by those of a society's institutions and values which affected natural increase, the inclination to form capital, or the disposition to accumulate and apply productivity-affecting knowledge. Although the role of the entrepreneur was not emphasized, that of private enterprise was, it being assumed that the aggregate economic role of the state, though possibly large under certain conditions, normally was quite small.

Mill made the population variable an element in his theory of development, treating it as essentially an endogenous, rather than an exogenous, variable. He was more concerned about the adverse influence of population growth than are many present-day writers. But he had basis for this concern, since population elasticity was close to unity in many parts of the world, and, he believed, not far below unity in the laboring classes of countries in which conditions were improving, and the over-all rate of population growth had fallen.[154] Mill's mistake consisted in his underestimate of the role of capital and of the productive influence of division of labor and in his overestimate of the adverse influence of the pressure of numbers on resources, an overestimate that arose out of his exaggeration of the prospective importance of organic products and his underestimate of both the productivity of labor and the rate of technical progress.[155] Although the example of France was at hand, he neglected the effects of changes in age composition, and the increase in the relative number of her people of work-

---

economic insignificance of money, the commodity form of which Mill preferred. See also Balassa's careful account *(op.cit.)*. On Hume, Malthus, T. Attwood, and the currency case (silenced by the gold discoveries), see S. G. Checkland, "The Birmingham Economists, 1815-1850," *Economic History Review*, I, 1948, pp. 1-19; also K. H. Niebyl, *Studies in the Classical Theories of Money*, New York, 1946, chaps. 7-8, 10; also R. G. Link, *English Theories of Economic Fluctuations 1815-1848*, New York, 1959, pp. 148-79.

154. Although, as Mill observed, natural increase fell early in France, it did not fall appreciably in Western Europe until after his death. Natality itself had not fallen in Asia (except for Japan), Africa, or most of Latin America eight decades later; the decline had been limited to Europe, Northern America, Australia, and a few Latin-American countries. Even in the European sphere of civilization, natural increase has been higher since Mill's death.

155. Lacking a productivity theory, and failing to use the statistical data at his disposal, Mill never attempted to estimate imputed output.

ıg age.[156] His emphasis upon the need for large, habit-breaking change oreshadowed modern views regarding means of escape from Malthusian raps.[157]

Even though Mill was the first British economist to stress the importance f applied knowledge, he greatly underestimated its role, in part because e implicitly attached so much weight to keeping up the supply of wage oods which he thought of largely in organic terms. Because he underesti- nated the importance of applied knowledge, he underestimated the role of nodern technical education and failed, in his account of education, to show hat, in light of his own principles, a great deal of state support was indicated.

Mill's analysis of the role of capital, essentially a corollary to his wages und theory, led him to underestimate greatly the contribution of increases n capital per head. Being without a productivity theory, and very imperfectly ware of the significance of fixed capital and its greatly augmentable com- inability with labor, he expounded a stagnation theory that had its basis n the supposedly rapid diminution of capital's usefulness in domestic in- estment in countries as densely populated as England.[158] At the same time Mill saw a way out in terms of capital exports which, along with emigration o underpeopled countries, would bring into being abroad, and at low cost, roduce and/or materials that might otherwise prove costly to supply at ome. He thus established a rationale for the foreign investment policy ursued by Britain during the fifty or sixty years preceding World War I. n so doing, Mill made of emigration what Malthus had refused to make f it—an important means of escape from population pressure in Britain nd Western Europe.

There is not much to be said of Mill's theory of institutions. He dealt in etail only with those relating to the use of land. He recognized, however, hat man's responses to variations in price reflect underlying noneconomic onditions, and that it may be feasible to modify these responses in an ppropriate direction. Moreover, unlike Marx, he appreciated the importance of education as a transformer of character and culture. His theory of develop- nent was therefore socio-economic, rather than economic, in character.

Mill did not integrate his theory of the trade cycle with what he said egarding population movements.[159] He said nothing of the impact of popu-

---

156. I do not recall having found a refer- nce in Mill to the papers in the *Journal of he Royal Statistical Society*, a rich reposi- ory of useful and/or interesting information.

157. E.g., see H. Leibenstein, *Economic Backwardness and Economic Growth*, New York, 1957, chaps. 8-10.

158. I have used the term usefulness since Mill did not express himself in terms of marginal productivity or marginal efficiency of capital. Nor did he suppose that the sup- ply of capital under conditions of full em- ployment would exceed what would be used; decline in the interest rate prevented this outcome. He could evade allocation problems because he relied upon competition and price changes to solve them.

159. He merely noted that the marriage rate varied with the trade cycle (*Principles*, pp. 161, 704), and that the cycle was asso- ciated with undue expansion and contraction of credit (*ibid.*, pp. 653-56, 709).

lation prospects upon the disposition of entrepreneurs to invest, to intro duce improved methods, etc. Those authors who developed this approac attached importance to fixed capital and subscribed in part to Say's Law Nor did Mill make much of other ways in which population growth o pressure might bring about salutary economic change.[160]

Mill believed land and natural resources to be more important than d contemporary writers. He underestimated the improvability of agricultur considering it much less than that of manufacture. He recognized, howeve that outlay for nonagricultural raw materials tended to form a very sma fraction of the total outlay for manufacture.

VIII

Having contrasted some of Mill's views with those current in presen day literature, I shall compare them now with the corresponding views o Smith, Malthus, and J. E. Cairnes. Smith and Malthus are selected becaus they, more than any other of the earlier English expounders of tenets o the classical school, concerned themselves with economic developmen Cairnes is selected because, while much less interested in economic growt than was Mill, he was the last outstanding proponent of the school's prin ciples. Thereafter, for several decades, the theory of economic developmen was dealt with principally in the writings of the historical economists, Mar shall's initially incomplete treatment not assuming rounded form unt 1890.[161]

(1) *Role of the state.* The political philosophy underlying Mill's con ception of the role of the state did not differ basically from that of Smith or Malthus, or Cairnes. It was the function of the state to provide an preserve a milieu within which economic individualism could flourish thereby accelerating economic progress, and to undertake or to facilitat the undertaking of activities involving indiscriminate benefits. Presumably the scope allowable to political liberty would expand with economic prog ress. The role of activities involving indiscriminate benefits might increas or decrease. Looking about him, Mill found need for this role to be large than had Smith or Malthus, just as he found need for the government t do more in its capacity as creator and preserver of an optimum milieu fo economic individualism.[162]

160. He did remark that when man lived in a semi-barbarous state, the pressure of numbers and want probably helped to break his habit of indolence *(ibid.*, pp. 358, 793).

161. See A. J. Youngson, "Marshall on Economic Growth," *Scottish Journal of Political Economy,* III, 1956, pp. 1-18; my "Marshall on the Population Question," cited in footnote 120, above; and Erskine Mc Kinley, "The Problem Of 'Underdevelopmen In The English Classical School," *Quarterl Journal of Economics,* LXIX, 1955, pp. 23 52.

162. See Lionel Robbins, *The Theory o Economic Policy in English Classical Politi cal Economy,* Lectures 2, 5-6; W. D. Gramp

(2) *Role of institutions.* Smith, Malthus, and Mill may be described as institutionalists, in that each found man's economic behavior to be conditioned by the complex of institutions embracing him. It was not supposed, therefore, that man's economic behavior was invariant, whatever his behavioral predispositions. Some classical principles, (e.g., Say's Law, determination by competition) received fullest expression in a developed economy, such as the British or American economy. In Asia institutional restraint denied full expression to competition and to other of these principles, as well as to man's salutary desire to better his condition, with the result that Asian economies were backward and poverty-ridden.

Two nineteenth-century sets of institutional arrangements connected with the rise of capitalism—trade unions and profit-sharing associations—were discussed at length by Mill and Cairnes, though they had had little or no attention from Smith and Malthus. Mill came to believe that trade unions (which he considered voluntary associations) might somewhat improve the wages of organized workers without correspondingly disadvantaging the earnings of the unorganized. Nonetheless, it was in profit-sharing cooperative associations of workers and employers or managers that he found the economically and ethically most suitable form of industrial organization, and hence "the true euthanasia of Trades' Unionism."[163] Cairnes, troubled by the supposedly slight improvement experienced in wages and profits, and with less faith than Mill in international cooperation, supported Mill's argument. Trade unionism was incapable of surmounting demographic and physical barriers to the augumentation of production, so long as the "industrial classes" were separated into "laborers and capitalists." It was essential that "the laborer cease to be a mere laborer," and that "profits" be "brought to re-enforce the Wages-fund," but this change must be accomplished in such way as to re-enforce the laborer's disposition to work and save, to modify his outlook, to inculcate prudence, and to check population growth. "Co-operation" was the only means to this set of ends.[164] In "co-operation," together with output and profit-sharing, therefore, lay the institutional answer to distributive struggles arising out of population growth and the limitedness of resources.

(3) *Distribution and growth.* Both Smith and Mill found distribution within the early nineteenth-century English economy more favorable to economic growth than was characteristic of feudal types of economy. Nonetheless, only Malthus emphasized the dependence of economic development

---

loc.cit., pp. 714-47. J. E. Cairnes (*Essays in Political Economy*, London, 1873, pp. 232-64, 312-43) was critical of laissez faire.

163. *Discussions*, IV, pp. 26, 67*ff.*, 83; *Principles*, pp. 116, 764-94, 934-939. See also Harris, *op.cit.*, pp. 91-98.

164. Cairnes, *Political Economy*, pp. 273-94, also p. 219 on the limited effectiveness of trade unionism. See also E. H. Phelps Brown's comments in his "Prospects of Labour," *Economica*, XVI, 1949, 1-10.

on a suitable "Union of the Powers of Production with the Means of Distribution."[165] Smith and Mill were cognizant of the defects of the distributive arrangements found in backward economies, and of the resulting paucity of incentive to work, but they supposed that the mechanisms underlying Say's Law would prove adequate in economies such as the British. At the same time, as already indicated, Mill and Cairnes considered recourse to cooperation essential, if a serious class struggle was to be averted.

(4) *Dynamic forces.* Apart from the influences flowing out of institutional change and capital formation, the dynamic forces–i.e., the forces occasioning changes in production functions–were two, division of labor and technological progress. While these forces were inter-related, they were of unequal importance. Mill, under the influence of John Rae, attached far more importance to education and to the accumulation of knowledge and technological progress than had Smith or Malthus, but much less than do twentieth-century economists. Even so, Mill shared Cairnes' opinion that this progress had not appreciably reduced the cost of wage goods, and therewith increased real wages and profits.[166] Greater weight was assigned by Smith and Mill, though not apparently by Malthus or Cairnes, to division of labor, viewed as an organizational and income-increasing principle. Mill also appreciated, in greater measure than did Cairnes or Smith, what Torrens had called the territorial division of labor.[167] Within a country, division of labor consequent upon population growth served to increase output per unit of input in manufactures;[168] at the international level, it might make available the products it could not evoke so efficiently at the domestic level. Accordingly, for some time to come there would exist a means of escape from the threat of population pressure, especially if international division of labor and factor movements were facilitated.

(5) *The factoral milieu.* Aside from the varied role that might be assigned to the undertaker, Smith, Malthus, Mill, and Cairnes envisaged a factoral milieu in which land and resources were fixed in amount; labor tended to increase, as circulating capital or wage-goods increased; and fixed and circulating capital tended to accumulate, until halted by shortage

165. *Principles of Political Economy,* London, 2d ed., 1836, pp. 361-71; the whole of the chapter, "On the Progress of Wealth," related to distribution and growth. See also my paper, cited in footnote 114, above.

166. *Principles,* pp. 278-79. Cairnes overlooked the fact that real wages were perhaps 20-25 per cent above the 1850 level at the time he was writing, wheat imports having steadily increased in previous decades and prevented the rise in marginal costs which might otherwise have taken place as population grew. See Ashley's notes, pp. 997, 999-1000, in his edition of Mill's *Principles;* also Colin Clark, *op.cit.,* pp. 300-301.

167. See Lionel Robbins, *Robert Torrens,* pp. 18-21.

168. Cairnes (in *Political Economy,* Part I, chap. 5) treats at length the changes in price structure that accompany economic and demographic development, in the tradition established by Smith, according to which the exchange value of primary products expressed in terms of manufactures steadily advances. See also *ibid.,* pp. 299-301; also Mill, *Principles,* IV, chap. 2.

f land, diminishing returns, and a consequent decline in profits, together ith an unwillingness to save at very low rates of return. Malthus, Mill, nd Cairnes, but apparently not Smith, were very apprehensive, lest an nrestricted population growth counterbalance the forces making for eco- omic improvement, even though they recognized that the movement of opulation was dominated by psycho-social, rather than physiological, rces. However, it was possible, Cairnes believed, as did Mill, that the ntroduction of a regime of cooperation might improve the worker morally nd prompt him to limit his numbers.[169] Mill, who rejected Malthus's opin- n that communism necessarily conduced to population growth,[170] found ossible solutions for the population problem in colonization and trade nd in pronounced economic change for the better which would eventuate a sufficient decline in fertility.

Smith having intimated that fixity of the land supply might, when com- ined with continuing population growth, occasion a fall in profits, Ricardo ook over this explanation and sharpened it into the proposition that in a osed economy the profit rate would decline as population grew and ultivation was extended, resulting in a rise in the marginal labor-cost of roduce. In consequence net capital formation might finally descend to ero. Mill, building particularly upon Ricardo and Wakefield, reasoned milarly, and concluded that a stationary state, free of unemployment and ith either high or low real wages, might ensue, Cairnes, following Mill, easoned in like manner.

(6) *Factor mobility*. Smith did not discuss factor mobility and immo- ility to any degree in the *Wealth of Nations*. What counted most was the ee international flow of goods, especially within a possible Atlantic nion. Ricardo, however, distinguished sharply between the intra-national obility and the international immobility of factors. Cairnes, having noted great increase in international migration and capital flow since Ricardo's ay, denied the latter's sharp distinction, but not in its entirety. It was a atter of degree. Political and cultural differences, together with distance, ade for greater immobility at the international level than at the national vel. Cairnes thererefore rejected both Mill's assumption of relatively igh international mobility and his proposal that mother country and col- nies be thought of as a single unit of space within which factors were obile.[171]

(7) *Migration, colonization, international commerce and investment.*

169. Cairnes, *Political Economy*, pp. 275- 4, also pp. 276-83 on the failure of techno- gical progress to reduce the cost of the orker's "consumption."

170. Under communism, Mill asserted, in d after 1852, "opinion might be expected declare itself with greatest intensity" against the "selfish intemperance" which gave rise to comfort-depressing population growth (see *Principles*, p. 207). Mill does not incor- porate this view into the argument presented in his later papers on socialism.

171. Cairnes, *Political Economy*, pp. 302- 307. Cf. Mill, *Principles*, pp. 685-86.

Whereas Smith had set great store by international trade as an extender of the division of labor, and hence as an antidote to population growth, Malthus had remarked on the dangers which might beset a country too dependent upon foreign markets and foreign sources of produce and raw materials. Cairnes's opinion resembled that of Smith, rather than that of Malthus, but he was less optimistic regarding the advantages to be derived from trade and colonization than were Wakefield, Torrens, Mill, and others. Mill, in particular, found in emigration, colonization, and foreign investment a set of mechanisms whereby population pressure might be alleviated in countries like England; the scope of division of labor and increasing return might be enlarged there and abroad; both markets for exports and sources of produce and raw materials might be established; and expanding outlets for capital might be provided. In consequence, the profit rate would remain above the zero-saving level, and the impact of diminishing productivity in agriculture would be largely cushioned. This set of mechanisms, Marshall later asserted, had freed the British economy of the drag of diminishing returns and released the forces of increasing return.

Not only did Mill's theory of economic growth extend and enlarge that of the classical school; it also afforded a partial bridge to Marshall, attempted to take noneconomic determinants into account, and gave consideration to many issues which are of concern to present-day growth theorists.

TOWARD A THEORY OF ECONOMIC GROWTH: THE NEOCLASSICAL CONTRIBUTION

By John Buttrick

THIS PAPER consists of four parts. First, a general survey of neoclassical approaches to the analysis of growth problems is presented. Essentially, this amounts to the construction of a frame of reference and the description of a point of view which is then used to organize neoclassical thought. The second part contains a relatively self-contained description of neoclassical methodology, inescapably presented in semi-mathematical terms. This section is important, if my contention is correct that the principal neoclassical contribution was methodological. Third, certain aspects of neoclassical thought are singled out for special consideration. While the major portion of the neoclassical contribution may be confined in a static model, certain growth-producing elements were isolated, and then placed in the category of "exogenous variables." It is the more important of these elements–from a neoclassical evaluation–that are considered in part three. Finally, a summary treatment of capital and interest is presented.

I

Introduction

THE FRAME OF REFERENCE

This essay is written with a particular, though widely held, view c theory construction in mind, namely, the synthetic mating of empirica generalizations and *a priori* assumptions for the production of theorem which are, in principle, capable of being tested. By an empirical generali zation is meant simply a correlation, together with a description of th variables which were held constant in making the observations, e.g., th relationship between inputs and outputs in a production process. An *a prio* assumption plays a duplicate role in theory construction: the specification c relationships which either cannot or have not yet been directly observec e.g., the relationship between utility and money income deflated, say, b some price index. Given a set of facts and assumptions, the next step i the production, through manipulation, of other relationships (theorems on which our interest—for whatever reason—focuses. If these deduction concern nonobservable variables, then an exceedingly tight logical con nection is required, e.g., between marginal cost = marginal revenue an Pareto Optimality.[1] This connection may be loosened, if an observable such as a particular price movement or even national income, is involve (so long as the direction of the deduction is not reversed). More ofte than not, our deductions will relate to observable variables. This is becaus economics is an empirical discipline, i.e., economists wish to explain o understand, in the sense of predict, some events in the real world.

Because of an interest in policy matters, as well as for purposes o testing, some empirical generalizations will take the form of statement that certain variables are "independent," e.g., a change in a tax rate wi alter national income, or rainfall will affect the wheat harvest, but no conversely. Because of unavoidable errors of measurement or observation or because economists (and everyone else) use "incomplete" models, o because they feel the real world contains intrinsically random component (it does not matter which, since there is no conceivable way of distinguish ing) the relationships used by economists must, in principle, contain ran dom variables. Hence, their hypotheses must be stated in probabilistic form

1. A "social state" such that any change will make at least one member of the society worse off in his own evaluation is Pareto Optimal. See, for example, Abram Bergson, "Socialist Economics," in *A Survey of Contemporary Economics,* Howard S. Ellis, ed. Philadelphia, 1948, I, p. 414; G. Debreu "Valuation Equilibrium and Pareto Optimum," *Proceedings of the National Academy of Science,* XL, 1954, pp. 588-92.

I can see no reason why the methodological position just outlined should not characterize the theory of economic growth—when such a theory is produced. Indeed, it seems to me that our present level of sophistication precludes a contradictory view. If this is granted, it follows that, in describing and evaluating the contributions made by neoclassical (or any other) economists, we should make use of these "theory requirements."

This does not mean, however, that work which falls short of this (ideal) objective should be belittled or ignored. Even though theorems relating to the manner in which theory is itself developed over time and space are hard to find, many have argued that a certain amount of messing around with data and vaguely held hunches is a necessary prelude to rigorous analysis. Although this notion may rest on the biological analogy that a child must crawl before he can walk or run, there is some (unspecifiable) probability that it is true. For this reason, it is well to keep on file a record of the hunches which were toyed with in the past, and which have been only partially exploited or even altogether ignored. It is possible, however, that looking into our antecedents may become sheer antiquarianism.

Since my purpose is to record and evaluate the neoclassical contribution to a theory of growth that has been only partially developed, and since I know of no adequate explanation of the process by which theory gets constructed, this essay will unavoidably contain assertions that certain neoclassical material will someday find a place in a theory of economic growth. Often, in essays on the history of thought, attempts are made to explain why some theorems or hunches (and not others) were developed at a particular point in history. Typically, attention is given to the social and economic milieu in which the theorem was produced and to its intellectual antecedents, as well as the particular psychological attributes of its creators. In the present instance this cannot easily be done, since our focus of interest is a theory which, as mentioned earlier, is remarkably incomplete. On the basis of our present "requirements" for theory, however, we can tautologically assert that its formal properties are already known, at least in part.[2] Furthermore, historical precedent suggests that it will contain some existing theorems from economics and other social sciences, together with part of the mechanisms (i.e., models) used to produce these theorems.

It is entirely possible to contend that the very idea of a theory of economic growth is empty. There will simply be economic theory couched in quite general terms, and then a vast number of applications in which parameter values are associated, more firmly than is customary, with given institutional patterns and historical sequences. Intellectually, this is the

2. See Trygve Haavelmo, *Toward a Theory of Economic Evolution*, Amsterdam, 1955.

position I maintain. Thus, for me, the "theory of economic growth" is simply a shorthand label to describe the work of those interested in one aspect of general economic theory, namely, that in which time is an explicit variable, in which "initial conditions" make a difference. It would therefore seem likely that "economic growth" will swallow up, and then replace, "business cycles" as a field of interest and, in so doing, provide a framework for much historical analysis.[3]

Moreover, I would guess that those who will develop the theory and its applications will find that mathematical and statistical equipment of a high level is essential (although obviously not sufficient) to their tasks.

AN OVERVIEW OF THE NEOCLASSICAL CONTRIBUTION TO GROWTH THEORY

For the purposes of this paper, the phrase "neoclassical economists" will refer to those who participated in the marginal breakthrough of the 1870's and to those who elaborated the various maximization rules which evolved from the model of pure competition, conceived of as both a normative and heuristic device. The beginnings of macro-analysis, displayed in the work of such men as Spiethoff, Hobson, Robertson, and Johannsen, will not be discussed; nor will I give attention to the miscellany of the "institutionalists," such as Veblen, Mitchell, and Commons. The men with whom we are concerned then is that group mainly responsible for what we now call micro-statics: Jevons, Menger, Edgeworth, Marshall, Clark, Walras, Pareto, Wicksteed, Fisher, Pigou, Wicksell are representative names. This group is both easier and harder to discuss than others dealt with in this volume. It is easier to discuss their contributions because my readers will be at least as familiar with their important works as I am; it is harder because each reader will bring to this essay judgments of his own which may differ from mine.

At first glance, the neoclassicists' concentration on the conditions required for equilibrium suggests that the complex, deductive micro-static model they produced is of little relevance to the analysis of economic change. It is my contention that such a view is, at best, misleading. First, consider the responses of the system of interrelated variables which they constructed under impact from the variables they labeled exogenous. Comparative statics under such circumstances is entirely appropriate, if the system of endogenous variables can be shown to have a unique, steady-state solution. Further, they made strenuous efforts in this connection to distinguish between stabilizing and destabilizing factors by

3. See, for example, John Buttrick, "A Note on Professor Solow's Growth Model," *Quarterly Journal of Economics*, LXXII, 1958, pp. 633-36.

excluding from their model as many of the latter as was feasible. In the process they succeeded in identifying and listing "growth producing" factors in a remarkably unambiguous manner. Their theory itself was formulated in terms of ranges of values for parameters, so that it was possible to describe clearly the differences between a stable and an internally unstable model. Moreover, they made strenuous efforts to describe the relationship between the conditions required for equilibrium and a number of possible socio-political environments. Indeed, they succeeded in demonstrating that their model was conceivably invariant with respect to changes in several important socio-political variables, e.g., private property and the profit motive.

Finally, the neoclassicists demonstrated conclusively that mathematical techniques could be employed in economics to produce theorems of empirical relevance. In this connection, they tidied up the terrain which earlier economists had plowed by either discarding previously held hunches or reformulating them in a more precise and useful manner; they also produced a number of new theorems and hypotheses. In short, they made considerable progress in transforming economics from a logical art to an empirical and normative science.[4] The fact that the typical neoclassical author made several empirical and theoretical mistakes should not overly detract from our estimation of his pioneering work–particularly since most of these errors were in the direction of over- rather than under-generalization.

Statements made by neoclassical authors concerning the objectives which motivated their work indicate that they believed what they were doing was essential to an understanding and ultimate control of the growth process. As Marshall put it: "Very little of my work [i.e., the problem of poverty] has been devoted to any inquiry which does not bear upon how to get rid of such evils in society as arise from a lack of material wealth."[5]

Given their emphasis on the production of short-run, micro-economic maximization formulae, and their disregard of time as an explicit variable, how are we to reconcile their end with their means? The answer is clear. Consider, for example, the use of their model building as a normative device to more nearly approach stated objectives. For the individual economic unit, achievement of greater utility can, without distortion, be

4. It is not our task here to explain the relatively high level of abstraction employed by neoclassical economists to make this transition, beyond suggesting the obvious relationship between the construction of the marginal edifice and the capture of economics by Academia, both of which occurred between 1870 and 1890.

5. F. Y. Edgeworth, "Reminiscences," in *Memorials of Alfred Marshall*, A. C. Pigou, ed., London, 1925, p. 70. See also Alfred Marshall, *Principles of Economics*, London, 8th ed., 1920, pp. 3-4; Knut Wicksell, *Lectures on Political Economy*, New York, 1935, I, pp. 3, 5; Irving Fisher, *Elementary Principles of Economics*, New York, 1912, p. 514; T. W. Hutchison, *A Review of Economic Doctrines*, London, 1953, pp. 7-12.

interpreted as "growth." Efforts to construct a social welfare function and attempts to derive rules for its maximization may be similarly interpreted. With this in mind, the neoclassicists felt that "growth" would in the main take care of itself if an appropriate socio-political environment were provided.[6] Furthermore, they believed that free competition, conceived of as a regulatory device used in conjunction with supplementary government controls, would assure such an environment. That we now tend to feel that at essential points these assertions rested on an act of faith may affect our judgment of the contributions made by neoclassical authors; it does not affect *their* view of matters.

In sum, then, to evaluate the contribution of the neoclassical authors to growth theory and policy, we must examine what they did not do and their reasons, either explicitly stated or easily inferred, for this neglect, as well as their positive achievements. They provide this information themselves by underlining the importance of exogenous variables, such as technology, tastes, and population, and speculating as to the behavior of these variables over time. (Incidentally, in a sense, doing this dates all their variables.) Furthermore, insofar as exogenous variables are capable of conscious control, e.g., by government, the neoclassicists devoted considerable space and attention to the invention of recipes which, if followed, would make for desirable economic change.

With the ideal requirements of growth theory in mind, it is true *ex post* that neoclassical authors did mislead ensuing generations of economists in important respects. The techniques taken from mathematics were so demanding of the data that the necessity of employing operationally defined variables and identifiable relationships was often forgotten. All too frequently, empirically meaningless theorems were produced. Largely for this reason, they were unable to incorporate uncertainty (and changes in expectations) into their theorems, or to reformulate their models so that, in principle, predictions could be dated. A model in the social sciences in which no stochastic elements are present, i.e., one in which relationships among variables are presumed to be exact and in which the variables themselves can be measured, is a model constructed for heuristic rather than "practical" (i.e., predictive) purposes. In a strict sense, a "certainty model" either will be incapable of refutation, or will be immediately refuted by the slightest appeal to evidence. Furthermore, the introduction of uncertainty and risk-preference functions is required to make sense out of even the simplest problems of asset-holding, i.e.,

6. Cf. Joseph A. Schumpeter, *History of Economic Analysis*, New York, 1954, pp. 892-93, where it is asserted that economic growth for neoclassical economists was "a continuous and almost automatic process that does not harbor any phenomena or problems of its own."

ıeories concerned with capital and investment on the part of business rms, households, or other economic units.

For an allied, but somewhat separate, reason, the models constructed y neoclassical authors possessed scant empirical applicability. These models laced extremely heavy intellectual demands on the potential user. Not nly was the level of mathematical sophistication required relatively high or a social science, but the computational difficulties imposed by their ıodels were extreme. Under these circumstances, it is not surprising to nd *a priori* assumptions being substituted for "facts." Indeed, it was in his period of the development of economics that the essentially expository roblem of "translation" arose. For the first time theorems were pro- uced, the proof of which was not within the competence of many ıembers of the profession.[7]

More important in a way was the somewhat Procrustean device used o attain the (important) results already mentioned. With limiting tech- iques and a legitimate fear of socio-historical reasoning, the neoclassical uthor "proved" many of his conclusions by using models of economies which were simplified well beyond bounds of realism. Thus, he achieved quilibrium, smoothness of transition, and stability by excluding from his nalysis known disequilibrating factors. That he was aware of this defect n approach is clear from the lengthy list of assumptions typically identi- ied as "necessary." The difficulty is that the list was so long and attempts o weaken assumptions so rare. Unfortunately, the impression was some- imes given that it was improper for the economist *qua* economist to veaken these necessary assumptions. This meant, by implication, that for everal decades important aspects of economic growth were deleted from he subject matter with which economists were concerned. However, by alling explicit attention to those factors which may prove disequilibrating, he neoclassical author did consciously present us with a remarkably com- lete list of growth-producing factors. He did not, however, give us xplicit help in constructing models with which these exogenous, dis- quilibrating elements could be handled systematically.

Especially with reference to long-period economic growth, the em- hasis placed by Marshallians on partial equilibrium models imposed major barrier to analytic understanding. Marshall's distinctions between ong and short run, and among firm, industry, and other industries, as vell as his reluctance to employ a general equilibrium model caused a vaste of literally thousands of man hours in needless controversy and

7. In 1838 Cournot offered proofs that ould not be understood by many who called ıemselves economists. Cournot, however, ould not be considered a member of the profession in any real sense until several generations after he wrote; few of his contemporaries knew of his work and fewer tried to read it.

"interpretation." In this connection, however, it must be recognized that part of this difficulty was expository rather than technical in origin. Particularly among English-speaking neoclassical economists, it was considered important to write for an audience of laymen and beginning students. Commitment to this high-minded educational imperative sometimes was used to justify the abandonment of work which could not be translated easily into everyday language. Consideration of more than two or three variables at a time was discouraged, and the use of mathematics for expository purposes (except for geometry) was frowned upon.

II

Neoclassical Methodology

The general remarks contained in the last section were, at several places, addressed to essentially methodological issues. Clearly, the neoclassical economist was convinced that his method of formulating explanations of events and the patterns of events (including growth phenomena) was by far the best available. That the neoclassical method, in essentials as well as in general outline, is still virtually unchallenged is mute testimony to its usefulness. Without much question it is *the* neoclassical contribution. To explore this method, to consider criteria by which it may be judged, and to document the assertions already made in this essay are our next tasks.

A SIMPLE THREE-VARIABLE MODEL

Perhaps the best way of explaining neoclassical methodology is to apply it to a simple, but concrete, problem. It is so complex and devious that other expository devices easily lead to misrepresentation and consequent misunderstanding. For these reasons, then, let me employ a simple model, involving three continuous, real variables: A, B, and C, each of which is related to the other two, i.e., $A = f(B,C)$; $B = g(A,C)$; $C = h(A,B)$. Let us assume that, as neoclassical scholars, we are interested in explaining possible (small) changes in these variables; and that, ultimately we wish to construct useful theorems regarding these changes. To see what is required, we compute:

$$dA = f_B \; dB + f_c \; dC$$
$$dB = g_A \; dA + g_c \; dC$$
$$dC = h_A \; dA + h_B \; dB$$

This shows that our assumptions must be stated at least in terms of the six parameters: f_B, f_C, g_A, g_C, h_A, h_B, while our hypotheses will relate to ratios between the variables, e.g., to dA/dB, dA/dC, dB/dC. Considering the first of these illustratively, we find, by manipulation:

$$\frac{dA}{dB} = \frac{f_C\, h_B + f_B}{1 - f_C\, h_A} = \frac{f_B\, g_C + f_C}{g_A\, f_C + g_C} = \frac{dA/dC}{dB/dC}$$

Suppose we have a hypothesis (or hunch) that $dA/dB < 0$, what is our next step, after noting that dA/dC and dB/dC must be of opposite sign? Clearly, we need to frame assumptions consistent with this hypothesis (i.e., assumptions from which this hypothesis can be derived). After pondering matters, we decide that, if we are not to shock our peers and ruin our professional reputations, we must limit each assumption about the size of a given parameter to one of the following statements:

(a) > 0, (*a*′) $\geqq 0$,
(b) < 0, (*b*′) $\leqq 0$,
(c) $= 0$,
(d) $\gtrless 0$.[8]

After all, these parameters are partial derivatives and so are not capable of *direct* observation, unless all but one variable is in our control, e.g., $dA/dB = f_B$ only if $f_C = 0$, and, in the social sciences, we believe this is virtually impossible to arrange experimentally.[9] So, being of academic temperament, we explore all the possibilities available, given this professional restriction. They are listed below in tabular form (see Table 1).

Any set of assumptions that conforms to one of these ten patterns will be both consistent with the hypothesis that $dA/dB < 0$ and sufficient for the job of deducing this hypothesis. Unfortunately, however, there is no way of narrowing this list without (a) committing ourselves to additional hypotheses; or (b) showing, through appeal to common sense and introspection, that several of these ten patterns are manifestly absurd. In short, the model is not "identified."[10] Being armchair theorists first and empiricists second, we will think about each parameter quite seriously and reach the conclusion that these assumptions make sense: $f_B < 0$, $f_C < 0$. Friends, colleagues, and students wholeheartedly agree. This narrows the field down to two sets of assumptions, numbers 5 and 6 in Table I. We are unable to choose between these until we go to the real world, so we

8. This somewhat curious hypothesis-restricting device is discussed below.
9. This point of view, strongly held by many neoclassical authors, is discussed below.
10. However, a "loose" theory, written in terms of all ten sets of assumptions, would be "identified."

Table 1

	f_C	h_A	g_C	f_B	h_B	g_A
1	$=0$	$\leqq 0$	<0	$\lessgtr 0$	$\gtreqqless 0$	$\gtreqqless 0$
2	$=0$	$\leqq 0$	>0	$\lessgtr 0$	$\gtreqqless 0$	$\gtreqqless 0$
3	<0	$\geqq 0$	<0	>0	$=0$	>0
4	<0	$\geqq 0$	<0	>0	$\leqq 0$	$=0$
5	<0	$\geqq 0$	>0	<0	$=0$	<0
6	<0	$\geqq 0$	>0	<0	$\geqq 0$	$=0$
7	>0	$\leqq 0$	>0	>0	$=0$	<0
8	>0	$\leqq 0$	>0	>0	$\leqq 0$	$=0$
9	>0	$\leqq 0$	<0	<0	$=0$	>0
10	>0	$\leqq 0$	<0	<0	$\geqq 0$	$=0$

design research to observe dA/dB and dA/dC. If we find that in some situations $dA/dB < 0$, then every one of the ten sets of hypotheses is wrong. As a matter of fact, however, investigation suggests very strongly not only that $dA/dB < 0$, but also that $dA/dC < 0$.

The question now arises as to how we can use this additional information. To find out, we compute equations for the two parameters which distinguish the fifth set of assumptions from the sixth:

$$g_A = \frac{dB}{dA} - g_C \frac{dC}{dA}$$

$$h_B = \frac{dC}{dB} - h_A \frac{dA}{dB}$$

It is obvious that the sign of g_A will still be indeterminant, no matter how much evidence we gather, so long as professional pride will only permit us to make the statement that $g_c > 0$. The story is different with respect to h_B, however. $dC/dB = \dfrac{dA/dB}{dA/dC}$ must be positive and $-h_A\ dA/dB \geqq 0$ in both assumption set 5 and 6 in Table I, so h_B is positive. Thus number six is our desired set of assumptions.

OBJECTIONS TO THE METHODOLOGY

Next, we may ask on what ground this theory, which appears to be both complete and sufficient, can be criticized. Essentially, there are five possible grounds for objection:

(1) We might argue that the variables manipulated in the model are, as defined, incapable of observation, e.g., B in the model might be "real income" including psychic components, while we observe national income as reported by the Department of Commerce and deflated with the BLS cost-of-living index.

(2) We might point out that if hypotheses which depend on the magnitudes, as well as the sign, of the parameters are included, the number of consistent hypotheses is manifestly greater than one. For example, f_C and h_A could be of the same sign, if $f_C\ h_A > 1$ and $h_B \leqq 0$, $f_B > 0$, $g_A < 0$, $g_C > 0$.

(3) We might question the *a priori* assumptions that $f_B < 0$ and $f_C < 0$.

(4) We might belittle the entire undertaking by pointing out that the theorems are obvious to any schoolboy. To illustrate, consider the force of the chosen assumptions with $h_A = g_A = 0$. In essence, our theory then becomes:

$$\begin{aligned} A &= f(B,C) = f[B,h(B)] \\ B &= g(C) = g[h(B)] \\ C &= h(B) \end{aligned}$$

which, perhaps, is not very interesting.[11]

(5) We might ask the perpetrator of this theory what would happen to dA, dB, dC in response to some change in the environment in which the model is imbedded. E.g., if technology, tastes, population, or simply "time" changed, would dA/dB, dA/dC, dB/dC also change as a consequence? This objection has two aspects: First, we feel a theory should be capable of explaining (in the sense of predicting), not only whether dA/dB, say, is $\gtreqqless 0$, but also whether it has a tendency to become larger or smaller over time; or second, we feel that many more variables than three must be considered before one should be permitted to offer an "explanation."

Objection (1) above is a serious one. If hypotheses are to be meaning-

---

11. Notice that, in this version of the model, B is transformed into an exogenous variable.

ful (i.e., conceivably refutable), they must concern observable variables. However, variables capable of direct, immediate observation relate to a single commodity (e.g., its price, or the quantity sold at a particular moment), or to a single economic unit (e.g., the production of a firm, or the expenditures by a governmental agency or a household over a specified time interval). Theory which employed only such variables would be either grotesquely complex or purely formal. Thus, aggregation becomes essential. But aggregation necessarily implies theorizing, e.g., construction of market supply and demand curves, computation of average profits for an "industry," measurement of the average (or marginal) propensity to consume.

Neoclassical authors recognized this; and, what is more important, they made strenuous efforts to deal with the aggregation problem on a conceptual level. Indeed, they were so bothered by possible divergence between manipulable (aggregate) variables and their real-world counterparts that many scholars, rationalizing their impotence, maintained in effect the essentially negativistic view that, in crucial cases, the specific nature of the relationship between systemically and operationally defined aggregate variables could never be specified.[12] As the more able neoclassical authors well realized, there is an obvious solution to this problem: while the specific relationship between a measurable variable and another crucial variable, not capable of definition in a manner permitting measurement, cannot be stated,[13] it may be both possible and sufficient to use observables so as to identify, without ambiguity, the class of functions into which the required relationship falls, i.e., an attempt may be made to construct theorems which do not depend upon the particular measuring instrument employed. The development of the concept of Pareto Optimality and the allied work on the "index number problem" are cases in point.[14] Some obvious implications of this work for the "measurement" of economic development will be considered later in this paper.

On examination the second objection turns out to be almost entirely a straw man, created for expository convenience. One way to view matters is to first consider a given set of assumptions, and then see whether these are sufficient to deduce hypotheses capable of being tested; another way is to consider the (known) relationships among the observable variables, and then, reasoning backward, to describe a set of assumptions

12. What is "crucial" in this context is, of course, largely a matter of taste. E.g., some economists are not concerned with questions relating to social welfare functions, but all social scientists encounter the problem at some point in their analysis.

13. In the present context, "measurement" means that the relationship between one way of measuring a given variable and every other way is, in principle, specifiable.

14. See Vilfredo Pareto, "Mathematical Economics," *International Economic Papers*, No. 5, 1955, pp. 73, 87; Paul A. Samuelson, "Evaluation of Real National Income," *Oxford Economic Papers*, II, 1950, pp. 1-29; Ragnar Frisch, "Annual Survey of General Economic Theory: Problem of Index Numbers, *Econometrica*, IV, 1936, pp. 1-38.

consistent with the evidence. Ideally, I suppose, if A and B are the two sets, then $A \cup B = A = B$. For many purposes, however, this is not essential. Certainly, if all theorems with which economists were concerned could be equally well derived from different assumptions, then which set one preferred would be purely a matter of taste. Adopting this point of view, the neoclassical economists placed emphasis on the minimum assumptions required. In other words, if, under these circumstances, $A \cup B \neq A \neq B$, the neoclassicist would redefine A and B until the equalities were fulfilled by concentrating on sufficient conditions; and he would point out the utter futility and stupidity of debating the matter further.[15] The austerity of this approach has much to recommend it, particularly in the context of cross-disciplinary research (e.g., in economic development). First, the problems of obtaining an identifiable model are minimized. Second, the greatest latitude is permitted those interested in explaining both economic and, say, sociological phenomena. Finally, this approach will minimize the chances of its being disproven later, when the validity of the assumptions may be directly checked, and is thus consonant with academic, competitive conservatism.

The third basis for objection, namely, the questioning of the *a priori* assumptions, touches on the essential weakness in the austere, minimum assumption approach. To illustrate, consider all sets of assumptions consistent with the known facts that $dA/dB < 0$ and $dA/dC < 0$. Eight major patterns and a considerably larger number of minor patterns, are possible, formed as set forth in Table 2 below. To delimit assumptions only to this

Table 2

$f_B g_A$	$f_B g_C$	$g_A f_C$	$g_C h_B$	$g_C h_A$	$g_A h_B$	$f_C h_A$	$f_B h_A$	$f_C h_B$
<1	$<-f_C$	$>-g_C$	>1	$>-g_A$	$>-h_A$	<1	$>-h_B$	$<-f_B$
						>1	$<-h_B$	$>-f_B$
			<1	$<-g_A$	$<-h_A$	<1	$>-h_B$	$<-f_B$
						>1	$<-h_B$	$>-f_B$
>1	$>-f_C$	$<-g_C$	>1	$>-g_A$	$>-h_A$	<1	$>-h_B$	$<-f_B$
						>1	$<-h_B$	$>-f_B$
			<1	$<-g_A$	$<-h_A$	<1	$>-h^B$	$<-f_B$
						>1	$<-h_B$	$>-f_B$

15. Indeed, so firmly held was this view that, in their search for minimum conditions, neoclassical authors erred frequently in the direction of over-generality, i.e., conditions asserted to be sufficient turned out, on closer examination, to be necessary, but not sufficient. Witness the additional restrictions imposed as a consequence of the "Keynesian revision."

extent is not particularly informative. Yet, there is no way of discarding any of these (in large part contradictory) theories unless (a) everyone agrees *a priori* to rule out some values for some parameters; and (b) the model which produced this muddle is revised. Thus, an objection to *a priori* theorizing on the neoclassical pattern is really a request for a new model. From what has been said, we can also see why the neoclassical authors were reluctant to accede to this request. In order to end up with only one set of assumptions, given an identification requirement, each basic relationship must differ from the rest with respect to at least one of the variables included. And this means that more variables must be added to the model. Furthermore, these additional variables must be exogenous, since otherwise the model would be incomplete. To avoid this *contretemps,* we add equations along with variables, and possibly end up in worse shape than we were in at the start. To illustrate the need for adding variables, consider a two-variable model in which $A = f(B)$ and $B = g(A)$. Then $dA/dB = f'$ and $dB/dA = g'$, i.e., $dA/dB = f' = 1/g'$, and there is no way of distinguishing one function from the other empirically. If, instead, $A = f(B,C)$ and $B = g(A)$, with C (and therefore also f_C) exogenous, this is no longer the case.[16]

There is another possibility, namely, we can hope that it may become possible to observe parameters directly through controlled experimentation, rather than indirectly through observation on the variables themselves.[17] The neoclassical approach was eclectic, in that a few well-chosen exogenous variables were introduced, *a priori* assumptions were made whenever "universal acceptance" seemed likely, and it was hoped that direct parameter observation would be possible in the future.

STABILITY

The last pair of objections, under (5) above, require amplification, since they are crucial to an understanding of the neoclassical approach to problems of economic change. For illustration, we shall use the three variable model discussed earlier, but we will add one more variable, *D*, which could be anything, so long as it is observable, e.g., population or the weather. Thus, we have:

$$A = f(B,C,D)$$
$$B = g(A,C,D)$$
$$C = h(A,B,D)$$

16. The fact that many neoclassical models lacked identification was pointed out long ago by Henry Schultz, among others. See, for example, his *Theory and Measurement of Demand*, Chicago, 1938, p. 72*ff*.; E. J. Working, "What Do Statistical Demand Curves Show?" reprinted in *Readings in Price Theory*, George J. Stigler and Kenneth E. Boulding, eds., Homewood, Ill., 1952, pp. 97-115.

17. To treat a parameter in one model as an intermediate variable in another model is, of course, equivalent to the construction of a single, larger model in which the parameter in question disappears under substitution.

With four variables and only three equations we are obviously in difficulty, so we add another equation $D = \phi(t)$, with t standing for "time" which is, presumably, an exogenous variable produced by some other (unspecified) model. We can now eliminate D by substitution, but that is all; we will still have more variables than equations. However, this may be useful: perhaps the relation between A and t is difficult to understand, while it is easier to think first in terms of A and D and then in terms of the exogenous "trend" connecting D and t. Notice further that an "intermediate" variable like D need not be defined operationally, since we will never have to observe it. With t exogenous we can now proceed to compute the ratios which are capable of observation: dA/dB, dA/dC, dB/dC are easy, e.g., $dA/dB = f_B + f_C\, dC/dB + f_D\, \phi'\, dt/dB = \frac{f_C\, h_B + f_B}{1 - f_C\, h_A}$. In short, dA/dB is exactly what we found it to be in the earlier model, since $dt/dB = 0$ by definition of the word "exogenous."

Whether or not we consider it worthwhile to compute changes in the variables over time (i.e., dA/dt, dB/dt, dC/dt) will depend, primarily, on the path taken by them. For example, if, following an exogenously produced change in f_C, we could be sure that dA/dt, dB/dt, dC/dt would become zero before too long, then we might well disregard time in making our analysis. Actually, there are three general possibilities: (a) the system may be "stable," e.g., dA/dt will become smaller and smaller as time passes; (b) the initiating change may just bounce around indefinitely without getting either larger or smaller, e.g., dA/dt will approach some constant number $\neq 0$; or (c) the system may be explosive, in the sense that dA/dt will ever increase in absolute size.

Since it was the first of these possibilities that the neoclassical authors explored most fully, we will do likewise. We therefore ask the question: Under what circumstances will dA/dt, dB/dt, and dC/dt all approach zero? Then, certainly, the model will be stable, and we can quite legitimately ignore the variables D and t altogether. Sufficient assumptions are not hard to state. There are three from which to choose:

$$(1)\quad f_B\, g_C + f_C = g_A\, f_C + g_C = 0$$
$$(2)\quad g_C\, h_A + g_A = g_A\, h_B + h_A = 0$$
$$(3)\quad f_C\, h_B + f_B = f_B\, h_A + h_B = 0$$

This, however, is a crude way of solving the problem, since acceptance of any of these assumptions, in effect, reduces our model to a pattern such as this:

$$A = f(B,D)$$
$$B = g[A,\ h(A,B,D)]$$
$$A = B$$

Nonetheless, the heuristic value of such a model is considerable, as generations of economists who learned that Savings = Investment and Supply = Demand can testify.

A more agreeable approach is to suppose that, while observation does not show $dA/dB = 0$, there is a "tendency" for it to become zero. To illustrate what is involved, let us consider the equation for dA/dt:

$$\frac{dA}{dt} = \left(\frac{f_B g_C + f_C}{1 - f_B g_A}\right) \frac{dC}{dt} + \phi' \left(\frac{f_B g_D + f_D}{1 - f_B g_A}\right)$$

If this expression is $\leqq 1$ in absolute value, as are the similar expressions for dB/dt and dC/dt (with one of them definitely < 1), then any exogenous shock to one of the variables will clearly bounce around the system with ever decreasing force until, finally, stability is achieved. To find the requisite conditions is, however, a formidable task, especially in the case of non-linear relationships. The difficulty is clear: We must eliminate dC/dt before we have a useful expression for dA/dt, but substitution will leave us with a relationship between dA/dt and dB/dt. And dB/dt will necessarily be expressed in terms of either dC/dt or dA/dt.

The next step, since we do not believe that even one of the triplet dA/dt, dB/dt, or dC/dt equals 0, is to compute d^2A/dt^2, d^2B/dt^2, d^2C/dt^2. (These ratios represent the rate at which our variables are changing over time, e.g., the magnitude of d^2A/dt^2 tells us how rapidly dA/dt is changing.) If at least two of these are zero, we can compute dA/dt in an unambiguous manner. Should we reject the notion that dA/dt is a constant, which is necessarily implied if $d^2A/dt^2 = 0$, we can continue our computations and then argue that d^3A/dt^3, d^3B/dt^3, and d^3C/dt^3 are all zero, i.e., that d^2A/dt^2, d^2B/dt^2, and d^2C/dt^2 are constants. Beyond this, we cannot go to higher derivatives, unless more endogenous variables are added to the system.[18] Until we make one of these alternative assumptions, dA/dt, dB/dt, and dC/dt cannot be computed, i.e., our model will be quite circular in the sense of "the chicken or the egg" and as such will be essentially meaningless.

At this point, a major methodological difficulty arises. Suppose we perform all the required computations and in the case of dC/dt, for example, find the requisite stability condition to be:

$$\frac{[f_B g_C + f_C + \phi' \ (f_B g^D + f_D)]^2}{1 - f_B g_A} + \frac{\phi'^2 \, g_{DD} + \phi'' \, g_D + g_{CC}}{g_{AA}} > 0$$

18. On the techniques of derivation employed, see, for example, R. G. D. Allen, *Mathematical Analysis for Economists*, London, 1938, esp. chap. 19. This book contains many examples of the methodology described above from the work of Edgeworth, Fisher, Marshall, Pareto, Wicksell, etc.

(This expression would be very much more complicated if, "for simplicity," we had not assumed $d^2A/dt^2 = d^2D/dt^2 = d^2C/dt^2 = f_{CB} = f_{DB}$ $f_{CD} = g_{CA} = g_{DA} = g_{DC} = h_{AB} = h_{AD} = h_{DB} = 0$.) Suppose, further, that we insert appropriate "empirical assumptions" about the parameters into the model. Now, we recognize immediately that in the real world it will be impossible to observe a "tendency toward stability" in an unambiguous manner. Nevertheless, we have derived this hypothesis from our model and would like to have it validated—at least in principle. In this extremity, we assert stability to be present in the real world, so long as the real-world counterparts of our parameters possess values which meet our required conditions. In evidence, we offer other hypotheses which can be empirically verified and which, when considered together, necessarily imply stability. For one instance, stability will clearly be present if $(1 - f_B g_A) > 0$ and if $(\phi'^2 g_{DD} + \phi'' g_D + g_{CC})$ is either opposite in sign from g_{AA} or zero. Consider just the first of these inequalities for purposes of illustration. If $1 - f_B g_A \not< 0$, what would our observable variables be doing in the real world? Simple manipulation will show the possibilities:

$$f_B\, g_A = \left(\frac{dA}{dB} - f_C \frac{dC}{dB}\right)\left(\frac{dB}{dA} - g_C \frac{dC}{dA}\right)$$

$$= \frac{dA}{dB}\frac{dB}{dA} - g_C \frac{dC}{dA}\frac{dA}{dB} - f_C \frac{dC}{dB}\frac{dB}{dA} + g_C\, f_C \frac{dC}{dB}\frac{dC}{dA}$$

$$= 1 - \frac{dC}{dB}(g_C + f_C) + g_C\, f_C \frac{dC}{dB}\frac{dC}{dA} \geqq 1$$

Thus, evidence that

$$\frac{dC}{dB}\left[g_c + f_c - g_c\, f_c \frac{dC}{dA}\right] \leqq 0$$

will disprove our hypothesis, and for this to happen, one of the following two patterns must appear:

$\frac{dC}{dB}$	g_C[19]	f_{CC}[19]	$\frac{dC}{dA}$
$\leqq 0$	$\geqq 0$	$\geqq 0$	$\leqq 0$
$\geqq 0$	$\leqq 0$	$\leqq 0$	$\geqq 0$

Perhaps it is now clear why neoclassical authors were so insistent on using a model which possessed stability, why, in fact, they removed many

19. For simplicity in exposition we assume that each of these parameters is capable of direct observation.

variables from their model and redefined others until they were sure of stability: Time (or whatever exogenous variables *t* represents) may legitimately be ignored if "stability" is present.[20] If stability is not present, the extremely sophisticated and intricate methodology they employed will simply break down when put to the task of deriving hypotheses. Or, more accurately, the methodology will, after time-consuming computations have been performed, produce a complete list of parameters, concerning which assumptions are required. Furthermore, once these assumptions are made, the methodology will produce theorems (i.e., testable hypotheses) with the accuracy and dispatch befitting the good machine it is. Unfortunately, however, even in a three-variable, non-linear model (with a fourth variable, time, exogenous), the number of assumptions required will place an intolerable burden on the most hardy investigator. Extreme computational difficulties and what he will be forced to admit is an appalling lack of data will soon force him to use a less refined model. He may decide to use only linear relations. But then the model will very likely explode under the slightest shock, and will, consequently, produce meaningful theorems for relatively short time periods only.

RATIONALIZING THE METHODOLOGY

Stability. By constructing a model so that it would be stable, the neoclassical author was able to use his remarkably precise methodology more fully—although he was forced to deal with a more limited range of phenomena, i.e., the *ceteris paribus* pound became worrisomely large. Thus, the neoclassical economist found himself trapped. His methodology not only drove him to employ stable models, but forced him to realize that, for a very long time indeed, he would be unable to make sensible statements about any other sort of a model. Yet, he wished desperately to discuss, and therefore incorporate, variables with obviously destabilizing properties.

Comparative statics offered one sop to his temporizing soul. The erection of firmly protected walls around his discipline provided another, i.e., if the theories propounded by workers in other disciplines could not be formulated in terms of his methodology, then, by definition, they were not theories at all. Comparative statics derived naturally from the method described above. Starting with a model that has reached equilibrium ($dA/dt = dB/dt = \ldots 0$), it is possible to change the value of one or more

20. The model, though stable, may not be capable of producing a unique solution. This, however, raises problems beyond the scope of this paper and the ability of the author. See Kenneth J. Arrow and Leonid Hurwicz, "On the Stability of the Competitive Equilibrium," *Econometrica*, XXVI, 1958, pp. 522-52, and the second part of this article to appear in a forthcoming issue of *Econometrica*.

parameters and then follow the adjustment process around the system until a new (stable) equilibrium is reached. If the adjustments are smooth, we will probably content ourselves with a simple statement concerning the differences between the values of the variables before and after; if they are more complex, we will probably try to describe the time paths of at least the more important variables. An illustration may serve to clarify: Suppose a model with $A = f_1(B) + f_2(C)$, $B = g(A)$, $C = h(t)$ which gives, setting $d^2A/dt^2 = d^2B/dt^2 = d^2C/dt^2 = 0$,

$$dA/dt = f_1' \, dB/dt + f_2'h' = -(1/g') \sqrt{f_2'' \, h'/f_1''}$$

$$dB/dt = g' \, dA/dt = -\sqrt{f_2'' \, h'/f_1''}$$

$$dC/dt = h'.$$

To see whether the system is stable, we compute $dA/dt - dB/dt = (1 - 1/g') \sqrt{f_2'' \, h'/f_1''}$. We suppose that, for stability, this must vanish which will occur either if $g' = 1$ or if $f_2''h' = 0$. Essentially, two choices are open to us: (a) We can use g' as a link between this and another model, and then arrange matters so that $g' \rightarrow 1$, e.g., the ratio of marginal cost to marginal revenue. (b) We can treat C as an exogenous variable–as indeed has been done here–so that $h' \rightarrow 0$, e.g., C could be the extra output caused by innovations, which dwindles until the next wave of innovation takes place. Once we have made one of these revisions, we can safely point out that the equilibrium is "meaningful," i.e., dA/dB has a "tendency" to become 1.

Exogenous variables. The use of exogenous variables has been mentioned at several points in this paper. We are now in a position to erect criteria by which to evaluate the neoclassical use of such variables. First, any variable to which the model being constructed is invariant can not only be placed in the exogenous category, but can be ignored altogether. As we have just seen, time is considered such a variable, if the system has stability properties and we are interested in the long run.

Second, any variable whose influence on the model is overwhelmingly unidirectional is an appropriate candidate. The weather is a good example of this sort of exogenous variable. While consumption and investment are both affected by changes in the weather, the reverse does not seem to be true empirically. Time, given an unstable system, would be another example. Traditionally, the point at which such a one-way linkage occurs is used to establish a boundary to the discipline under consideration. Thus, the economist is not expected to explain temperature changes or the passage of time; he can take these as "given" for his purposes, and need only show how the variables of his discipline (model) behave in response to changes in the exogenous variable. In cases of this sort, the neoclassical use of comparative statics is quite legitimate.

Finally, if a model is constructed with several variables which are exogenous in the above senses of "invariant to" and "independent of," this does not necessarily mean that these variables are either invariant to or independent of each other. Although exploration of the possible interconnections may not be the job of the economist, nonetheless, interconnections which in fact obtain must be recognized when he examines the behavior of his model in response to changes in variables he chooses to label exogenous. For example, to the extent that tastes and population are related, conclusions based on a change in population with tastes held constant would be suspect. Again, while the economic model may be invariant with respect to time, technology certainly is not.

Difficulties arise with respect to the classification of variables as exogenous only if they do not fit either of these two categories. Clearly, population or tastes, for example, not only affect the customary economic variables, but are also affected by them. Whenever this is so, the ground becomes treacherous. It may, for simplification, still be appropriate to make a variable exogenous (by treating it as an independently determined constant), or even to ignore it altogether (by setting the connecting parameter equal to zero), but this will depend upon the uses to which we will put the theory based on such assumptions. For example, if a prediction is required for only a relatively short period of time, tastes and the labor force may well be virtually constant and the obvious chain connecting

$$\text{income} \rightarrow \text{tastes} \rightarrow \text{population} \rightarrow \text{tastes} \rightarrow \text{labor force} \rightarrow \text{tastes} \rightarrow \text{output} \rightarrow \text{income}$$

may legitimately be broken. However, attempts to predict events over fifty or a hundred years, based on a model in which population, labor force, and tastes are all made exogenous, would be almost certainly proven wrong, unless remarkably good "guesses" were made as to the presumed time paths of these interrelated variables. And by definition, they would have to be "guesses," in the sense of nonrefutable, nondemonstrable assertions, since the variables in question are treated as if they were independent of economic variables when we are sure they are not independent.

Since the substance of these obvious remarks was the common property of neoclassical scholars, how did they justify treating as exogenous so many variables which clearly were not exogenous? In fact, only two answers are possible, namely, "stupidity" and "ignorance." Since this choice of words may seem unduly harsh, permit me to elaborate euphoniously. In place of "stupidity," read "for simplicity" or "for expository convenience." All too frequently, we, as well as our neoclassical forebears, simply do not have the imagination or the technical competence to construct and manipulate the more relevant, but more complex, models which ought to be employed. In place of "ignorance," substitute "because of the principle of insufficient reason." Often, we are sure that some variable is really quite important, but we cannot find out, through observation or introspection, how to restrict the connecting parameters, e.g., the effect of monopoly on innovation and investment, or the effect of the interest rate on saving. Under such circumstances, we typically appeal to ignorance and make the variable at issue exogenous. Indeed, there is a temptation to go even further and formulate our results as if they were invariant with respect to the vexacious variable. With these remarks in mind, it is scarcely fair to blame neoclassical authors for ignorance and stupidity–particularly since, in contrast to earlier economists, they made such strenuous efforts to delineate clearly the boundaries of their ignorance, and since they described in considerable and almost compulsive detail the content of their *ceteris paribus* pound.[21]

III

A Static Model and Growth

As has been emphasized earlier in this paper, the development of the neoclassical equilibrium-producing model required the elimination of destabilizing factors, either by a surgical removal of variables, i.e., by making them exogenous, or by the use of unrealistically restrictive *a priori* assumptions. In this section we will consider the content and force of both of these procedures.

JUSTIFYING THE MODEL

Starting with a policy orientation, and having inherited a crude competitive model, from which, it had been asserted, welfare propositions of the loosely stated, "invisible hand" sort could be derived, it was natural for neoclassical authors to give primary attention to revising received doctrine so that it could withstand leisurely scrutiny. To insure competition, the continuing presence of many independently controlled firms and house-

21. See, for example, Marshall, *op.cit.*, p. 366*ff.*; John B. Clark, *Distribution of Wealth*, New York, 1899, pp. 71-76, 400-404; Leon Walras, *Elements of Pure Economics*, London, 1954, pp. 256-57, 383-90.

holds was required. Furthermore, to be useful, the model built had to preclude indeterminancy and meaningless circularity. Both objectives were achieved by assumption. First of all, each economic unit was separated from the rest by supposing utility (subjectively defined) to be a function of the wealth (and income) owned by the economic unit in question. This was not sufficient, so the production (and utility) functions were restricted as to shape by fiat. Increasing returns to scale were ruled out of court and diminishing marginal utility was insisted upon. By way of added insurance, tastes (on the side of households) and technology (for firms) were shifted into the exogenous category. To insure a steady-state solution of the competitive process thus described, the neoclassical authors postulated continuous functions throughout; virtually eliminated ignorance and uncertainty; and insulated their model from changes in "exogenous" variables, such as population, government policy, and (initially) capital.

Having flaunted reality in this extreme manner, the neoclassical economist was forced into rationalization and pseudo-empirical justification. The grounds given were not only varied, but sometimes contradictory as well. Thus, the primary argument offered in support of his analysis was the short-run purpose for which the analysis was designed; yet, it was felt that the competitive mechanism under examination would require rather a long period before equilibrium was attained. A second line of defense was needed. This was provided by the socio-historical descriptive device of the Weberian Ideal Type. The impersonality of the mass market, the rampant individualism of a rapidly expanding, highly flexible industrial economy, the *anomie* produced in an urban setting under competitive pressure were noted, and discrete, emotionally insular economic units were postulated.[22] Robinson Crusoe was used as a convenient expository device; emulation was transformed into demonstration, and then deleted by an assumption of widely disseminated information; reliance on interpersonal comparisons was frowned upon, and questions concerning personal income distribution were formulated in ethical terms and then, insofar as pure theory was concerned, purposely ignored.[23]

The nonhuman, almost mechanistic, world created on this base was too much for all but the most introverted and compulsive members of the neoclassical school, so a third line of defense was erected. This was provided by first carefully marking out the boundaries of the discipline,

22. Cf. Schumpeter, *op.cit.*, pp. 887-89; Talcott Parsons, "Wants and Activities in Marshall," *Quarterly Journal of Economics*, XLVI, 1931, pp. 101-40; A. C. Pigou, *Economics of Welfare*, London, 4th ed., 1932, chap. 9.

23. See, for example, Walras, *op.cit.*, pp. 78-80; Clark, *op.cit.*, p. 8; the delightful statement by Jeremy Bentham, quoted in Lionel Robbins, *The Theory of Economic Policy*, London, 1952, p. 180; Enrico Barone, "The Ministry of Production in a Collectivist State," in *Collectivist Economic Planning*, F. A. von Hayek, ed., London, 1935, Appendix; Paul A. Samuelson, *Foundations of Economic Analysis, Cambridge*, 1947, pp. 204-207, 212-15.

and then arguing that, while economics appeared unrealistically depersonalized, it dealt only with one aspect of reality and could not be expected to do more. Thus, taste formation and population growth were tossed to the sociologists, innovations to the psychologists, and technology placed in the laps of the engineers.[24] It was hinted that if sister disciplines would only cooperate–presumably by taking their cues from economists and employing the same methodology–then economic models which conformed more closely to the real world would soon be forthcoming. This point of view was seductive, not only because it gave economists the illusion of goal achievement, but because it sanctioned somewhat irresponsible statements concerning noneconomic variables, e.g., an economist could be his own politician or his own sociologist without incurring the censure of his peers for lack of realism or rigor. Thus, for example, Marshall could praise the staunch, middle-class Victorian virtues without this affecting the esteem which he was (and is) accorded by fellow economists; Clark could endow marginal productivity theory with magically derived moral sanctions.

These several lines of defense were employed in various combinations to support deletion of variables and assumptions made about relationships. The specific set of justifications employed is not as important as is the underlying premise that sociological, technological, and political change would neither basically disrupt, nor long hinder, the operation of the underlying price mechanism. Innovation would occur, creating, by definition, a monopoly in the process. Soon, however, imitators would encroach, and competition would reassert itself. In response to changes in tastes and technology, workers and entrepreneurs would, albeit reluctantly, change their occupations and places of residence–with price variations playing the intermediate dual roles of signal and reward (and punishment). Similarly, changes in population or in the stock of capital would cause no real difficulties. Flexibility of prices (including interest rates), in general and in particular, would organize private maximizing efforts, so that Pareto Optimality would once again characterize the economic system.

It was recognized, of course, that competition (and the price mechanism in general) was a regulatory device of limited applicability. Situations in which, for example, important differences between social and private costs or benefits (including community goods) or an ethically unjustified income distribution occurred, however, were to be handled, by essentially ad hoc devices, as "exceptions."[25] In the course of time, needless to

---

24. Cf. Schumpeter, *op.cit.*, pp. 889-90; Walras, *op.cit.*, p. 386.
25. Cf. Hutchison, *op.cit.*, pp. 281-93.

say, the list of these exceptions grew in magnitude and extent, so that it became increasingly difficult to believe in the ultimate efficacy of the competitive mechanism. Nevertheless, until the late 1920's and the 1930's, it was still possible for most economists to uphold the essential realism of the liberal, individualistic postulates incorporated in their model; to believe that attempts to obstruct or sabotage the intricate, but immensely powerful, competitive mechanism, whether by organized monopolistic pressure groups or at the polls, would finally prove ineffective.

In summary, then, the neoclassical economists constructed a model on the basis of which they believed exogenous changes would be smoothly incorporated into the economy in such manner that welfare would be increased. Furthermore, they felt that a competitively impersonal society would be neutral toward–or possibly encourage–the initiation of growth-producing changes. For example, competition, they believed, was as likely as any other system of social control to encourage the production of an "optimum population," useful innovations, and a society with a presumably desirable liberal-individualistic political bias.

IMPLICATIONS FOR GROWTH

To evaluate this viewpoint, let us accept the theorem that a purely competitive, long-run equilibrium position will be both stable and Pareto Optimal.[26] (Pareto Optimality is the best we can do without a social welfare function to pick out *the* social optimum.) That neoclassical authors believed this theorem to be true without being able to offer rigorous proof speaks well for their intuition, or poorly for their prejudices–depending upon how we choose to view their efforts.[27] Certainly, however, they were not blinded into thinking that competition was the only way of attaining a Pareto Optimal position. Insofar as their model "explained" the real world then, this theorem suggests that they were quite right to treat economic growth–within their frame of reference–as a process which contains no special economic problems or phenomena of its own. Under this view, the rate of growth actually achieved by a given society will depend upon matters exogenous to the neoclassical model, e.g., rate of change in technology, in resources (including labor and capital), in tastes and numbers of consumers, and in the institutional setting (including government policy). Except for that portion of government policy which was treated as (independently) controllable, these growth factors were consciously placed outside the domain of the formal neoclassical economic model.

26. However, competition does not guarantee uniqueness.

27. In this connection, remember Walras' use of "prices cried at hazard in the market," and Edgeworth's device of recontracting.

The implications of this for the analysis of economic growth are fairly clear: We can ignore the intricate machinery of adjustment which is the competitive price system (or its socialist counterpart), and replace this entire mechanism by a dummy variable, e.g., "real national income per capita" or the "capital-labor ratio."[28] In other words, we need concentrate only on the connections between and among this dummy variable and those labeled exogenous, unless we are concerned with the path through time taken by the system in its approach to a Pareto Optimum position. If these neoclassical contentions are correct, the tasks of the economist interested in long-period growth are immensely simplified. He can legitimately pass on to others the problems of prediction and policy associated with short-period achievement and maintenance of Pareto Optimality.

RELEVANCE OF THE MODEL

Our task at this point is to go inside the neoclassical model to see (1) whether events in the real world can be explained by the "as if" competitive hypothesis which is spelled out in the model, and (2) whether the variables labeled exogenous are actually independent of the model and of one another. With respect to (1), we recognize, as did the neoclassical authors, the possible difficulties created by increasing returns to scale and other environmental features which permit or encourage noncompetition. We further recognize that, in any event, the path to equilibrium may be neither smooth nor rapid. We handle this last point in part by adopting a long-time perspective, and in part by presuming a set of independent government actions to insure that ignorance, uncertainty (and therefore expectations) will cause no difficulties. That is, we make these difficulties, along with those caused by divergences between private and social costs and benefits, exogenous *and* controllable.

We are now left with the possibility of increasing returns in production and consumption. The neoclassical authors gave serious consideration to these possibilities. Their approach was to turn to the real world to find out: (a) whether government actions were such that the sociopsychological environment created was in harmony with competition; and (b) whether the pattern of resources, technology, and population were such that competition was encouraged. In their attempt to check these matters, however, they ran into profound observational difficulties: the

28. See, for example, Paul A. Samuelson and Robert M. Solow, "Balanced Growth Under Constant Returns to Scale," *Econometrica,* XXI, 1953, pp. 412-24; Robert M. Solow, "A Contribution to the Theory of Growth," *Quarterly Journal of Economics,* LXX, 1956, pp. 65-94. The phrase "dummy variable" is used here because, while similar, the approach alluded to differs from Hicks's method of constructing "composite commodities."

neoclassical economists found (and it has been our experience as well) that it is impossible to directly observe tastes, uncertainty, ignorance, and expectations. An act of inference in these matters requires, of necessity, a theoretical framework which, in part, prejudges the results. Consumer behavior, for example, is consistent with the hypothesis of ordering relationships which are transitive, reflexive, and characterized by decreasing marginal utility. Moreover, such assumptions are reasonable *a priori*. However, observed behavior is also consistent with other postulates, e.g., parts of learning theory, which would render our Pareto Optimum conclusion vacuous, and we cannot select among these hypotheses without getting inside the minds and hearts of the members of our population. For predictive purposes, it is sufficient to say that people act "as if" they possessed certain ordering relations; for normative purposes, however, we have to presume that they actually possess (or actually ought to possess) the required socio-psychological makeup. On the normative side, then, there is no way to avoid an act of faith, i.e., we are forced to permit introspection as a research procedure, and this presupposes the possibility of something which smacks strongly of "interpersonal comparisons."

Direct observation appeared more promising with respect to the environmental assumptions required to eliminate the possibility of increasing returns and to achieve competitive markets. On closer examination, however, refutability proved difficult. If fewness of numbers was observed with respect to some given (physically described) commodity, it seemed frequently possible to point out many closely substitutable commodities, i.e., to question the boundaries of the market which the commodity defined. Furthermore, recognition of possible changes in tastes or technology rendered cross-section data suspect. In this connection, the effects of changes in population, transportation, and communication on the extent of the market seemed particularly important. Indeed, redefinition of the resources base occasioned by technological and taste changes made even geographically or geologically limited, nonreproducible resources a monopoly base of questionable strength. And, for long-period growth, quasi (i.e., transitory) monopoly could be ignored legitimately. Government-created monopoly also raised no problems, since government policy was presumed to be independently controllable. A controllable government policy also permitted banishment from the model of coalition-produced monopoly.

Similar problems of observation and significance arise with respect to the likelihood of pure increasing returns to scale. For each real-world firm, one or more factors of production are fixed over the typical period of observation (during which technology is constant). Under such circumstances, what appears to be increasing returns can easily be "explained" by an alternative assumption of indivisibilities. And, given the usual sorts of data, observation does not permit selection between these competing assumptions.[29] Over longer periods of time, changes in technology, organizational structures or skill of labor make the evidence inherently ambiguous. Thus, refutation of the assumptions of "constant returns to scale" and "many economic units," in any significant sense, again turn, in practice, on an article of faith. Certainly it does not seem intellectually dishonest to substitute "constant return to scale," plus "indivisibilities," for "increasing returns to scale." And, given exogenously-produced growth, indivisibilities cause, the neoclassical economist could argue, only transitory difficulties, unless these indivisibilities are really large. Viewing the growth process in historical perspective, however, indivisibilities (which I use here as a synonym for increasing returns) could, as the neoclassical authors pointed out, be most important: they could make for lumpy growth all by themselves, as was particularly manifest in the case of so-called social overhead items, e.g., massive public works. For similar reasons, monopoly elements (using the phrase in a generalized sense) could also constitute a significant barrier to the achievement of competition and Pareto Optimality at certain points in the growth process. Presumably, however, both are rendered less significant by a rising national income (widening of the market); thus, their importance is reduced by growth itself.

While the above is, I believe, a fair statement of the neoclassical view of production, several errors and ambiguities were committed, particularly by those neoclassical scholars who used the partial equilibrium approach. First, there was a tendency to confuse increasing returns to scale (technology constant) with a historical decline in costs (neither technology nor prices constant). Second, indivisibilities, in the sense of lumpy factors of production, were often confused with indivisibilities, in the sense of a finite number of efficient production activities or processes.[30] Third, in the earlier literature it was not always recognized that the phenomenon of decreasing returns, given a fixed factor, was not necessarily inconsistent with constant, or even increasing, returns to scale.[31]

The last two of these require no comment; the first may. Since it is quite obvious that indivisibilities in one sector of the economy will have repercussions elsewhere via both supply and demand, the single fact of historically decreasing costs (even with technology constant, as it must be for the analysis) is manifestly insufficient to locate the indivisibility. At

29. Hence, this selection may be made on the basis of analytical convenience. Cf. Tjalling C. Koopmans, *Three Essays on the State of Economic Science*, New York, 1957, pp. 151-54; Samuelson, *Foundations*, p. 84.

30. The mathematically simplifying assumption of continuity causes fewer difficulties, if a composite variable to represent national output and long-period changes is the focus of interest.

31. Phillip Wicksteed was among the first to get the distinction straight. See Schumpeter, *op.cit.*, p. 103*ff*. for a brief genealogy.

first glance, a separation of the economy into industries would seem to simplify the search. With this in mind, eight categories were constructed by combining the following in various ways.[32]

economies	external to the firm	external to the industry
diseconomies	internal to the firm	internal to the industry

The use of such a scanning device, however, presumes the possibility of distinguishing between firm and industry and of separating one industry from another on the basis of technology. But firms and industries are identified by the final commodities involved, and in the neoclassical view a commodity is defined in terms of consumer tastes via, e.g., cross-elasticities of demand. Furthermore, a production function, in the typical neoclassical meaning of the relation, is defined for a plant rather than a firm, and aggregation at the physical level is not possible.[33] Even if these problems could be solved, it is still doubtful whether the results would be useful for purposes of growth analysis. One of the hallmarks of growth is, after all changes in tastes and technology with respect to commodities, no matter how defined.

VARIABLES MADE EXOGENOUS

Our next task is to consider the several variables which were labeled exogenous in order to "solve" so many of the neoclassical economists' problems. If these variables are, for many practical purposes, really independent of the variables internal to the model, and also (relatively) independent of each other, then we may argue with force that the essentials of growth can be understood by examining in turn the relationships between each of these and the sort of dummy variable previously mentioned. Even superficial examination convinced the neoclassical authors that such simplification was not legitimate. Their procedure, however, did result in the identification of "growth-producing" elements, i.e., changes in tastes, technology, population, (natural) resources, and capital.

Although, for the most part, he was unable to include within the formal

32. Cf. Jacob Viner, "Cost Curves and Supply Curves," in *Readings in Economic Analysis*, Richard V. Clemence, ed., Cambridge, 1950, II, pp. 8-35; Allyn A. Young, "Increasing Returns and Economics Progress," *Economic Journal*, XXXVIII, 1928, pp. 527-42; Tibor Scitovsky, "Two Concepts of External Economies," *Journal of Political Economy*, LXII, 1954, pp. 143-51.

33. However, once the propriety of using a single dummy variable to represent all goods and services is established, it is possible to postulate a production relation using this variable. But the nature of the variable makes it impossible to use "natural" physical units for measurement, or to distinguish sharply this relation from a social welfare function.

model his hunches and educated guesses about the behavior of these exogenous variables, the neoclassical author filled his work with common-sense conclusions, offhand observations, and suggestive insights. With the viewpoint of a perhaps mythical statesman in mind, this material is intensely interesting. I would also point out that scrutiny of the history of ideas suggests that development of a set of vague, inadequately formulated hunches sometimes precedes the construction of scientifically useful theory.

With respect to specifically labeled growth-producing elements, the neoclassical authors were prolific in the production of hunches, as might be expected in view of their interest in the means whereby the lot of mankind could be improved. Simply to collect these hunches, besides being an encyclopedic undertaking, would not be particularly useful for our present purposes.[34] Instead, I propose to select a representative group and explore their meaning and applicability.

Let us begin with a statement of neoclassical views of the connections between population and per capita income. First, the neoclassical authors recognize, as has been suggested, that observable per capita income is an inappropriate measure of welfare, not only because of omissions and problems of distribution, but because, *cet. par.*, more people may be preferable to less. Second, the notion of an optimum population is defined systemically (although this definition is partially rejected by those whose search is for operationalism), and the likely effects of non-population variables on this optimum are listed in summary fashion, e.g., technology, tastes, capital, natural resources, allocative mechanism. Third, various attributes of population are distinguished, e.g., composition by age, sex, level of skill, occupation, socio-economic class, education, geographical location, value-attitude system, etc.; and, insofar as these attributes are considered independent, they are given a time dimension. Fourth, the neoclassical author is ready to talk about possible relationships among these variables, and between them, and variables already isolated in connection with the definition of an optimum population.[35]

So far, as can be readily seen, the neoclassical author is laying the foundation for an extension of his competitive model, and, in any event, he is building a model of the sort described earlier in this essay. After this preliminary work, however, he surveys the terrain and realizes that the requisite empirical generalizations and *a priori* assumptions are not available. There seems little point in constructing a host of empty boxes, i.e., listing

34. Although it might prove quite ego-deflating to many of those economists who believe that their particular set of hunches is new.

35. This and the next few paragraphs draw heavily on Joseph J. Spengler, "Marshall on the Population Question," *Population Studies*, VIII, 1955, pp. 264-87; and on his "Pareto on Population," *Quarterly Journal of Economics*, LVIII, 1944, pp. 571-601, and LIX, 1944, pp. 107-33.

parameters whose signs are even unknown. Instead, he tumbles in some disarray to a very much lower level of abstraction and decides to list those empirical generalizations and assumptions in which his confidence is high, in the hope that some day he, or some one else, will be able to complete the job. If he is of an optimistic frame of mind, he feels that even a partial model may be of some help, e.g., it may serve to demonstrate that some government policies are improper or useless. And it is true that the neoclassical author, simply by paying attention to definitions incorporating value judgments, was able to show the possible impropriety of some proposed government actions.

For example, there is no reason to suppose that the optimum population is near at hand. Clearly, technology will change and there seems no particular reason to assume that its rate of change will decline markedly in the near future. And the resource base is not invariant to technological change. Furthermore, with indivisibilities present, something we may call increasing returns may accompany population growth, at least for a time. Particularly noticeable in this connection are facilities for transportation and communication. Ultimately, decreasing returns, perhaps largely traceable to nonreproducible natural resources, will set in, but this will probably not happen, even in England, for, say, at least one hundred years, given foreign trade and present rates of population growth. For this reason, net inmigration and other signs of a growing population are not necessarily causes for alarm. This does not mean, however, that emigration should be restricted because, given a world view, skilled labor may well have higher productivity elsewhere. Even from the vantage point of an advanced country, emigration, like capital exports, may prove beneficial via foreign trade arguments. These judgments must, of course, be modified by "exigencies of military and commercial rivalries."

It was more difficult to formulate positive statements. With reference, for example, to the Malthusian connection between per capita income and the rate of natural increase, some authors felt that a small change in income would be soon vitiated by increasing numbers, and that a large, sudden change would be required before per capita income would rise permanently. Others asserted that an equivalent of Malthus' "moral restraint" was sufficiently strong so that sheer numbers of people would not become a problem, but both groups agreed that the argument turned on the value-attitude system of the population. While this was not observable, it could, with reference to population matters, be partly analyzed in terms of the cost of and benefit derived from raising children. This approach suggested that the size of families would decrease with urbanization.[36]

36. For a recent "neoclassical" population analysis, see Gary Becker, "Economic Aspects of Fertility," *Conference on the Interrelations of Demographic and Economic Change* (mimeographed), New York, 1958.

It was easier to reach agreement with respect to the death rate and the "vigor" of the population, and the obvious connections were commented upon in the obvious ways. The possibility of improvements in vigor, i.e., health, skill, and appropriate value attitudes, in some unspecified combination, were discounted too heavily by society. Education and the proper rearing of children, as well as a rising per capita income, were perhaps more important in terms of labor supply than sheer numbers. (Education is the academic man's infant industry.) In any event, there was obvious agreement on the assertion that the way people live is ultimately more important than what they consume. In this connection, several of the neoclassical authors felt that so long as a competitive market mechanism remained in use there was no cause for alarm, since those who "survived" under its operation would be those who "ought" to survive according to some absolute criteria of goodness, decency, and middle-class morality. There were dangers, however, that education and the teaching of morality might not proceed rapidly enough to counteract the inherent present-centered selfishness of man and the dysgenic influences of higher birth-rates among the poor and slothful. Positive action might also be required to regulate geographical mobility, so that a smaller portion of the benefits would go to the migrant-receiving sectors of the economy. ("The most enterprising, most highly gifted, those with the highest physiques and the strongest characters" appear to be those who move most readily.) And it will certainly require direct government intervention to handle problems of recreation space and general urban overcrowding. But this is just one example of divergence between social and private costs, although it is among the most important. In this connection, however, it is necessary to remember that increasing returns (loosely defined) are one product of urbanization, although if calculated solely in private terms they will probably be overstated.

Even on the basis of this brief and incomplete survey, the moralizing tendencies of many neoclassical economists is evident. Having left the confines of their rigorous methodology, it is almost as if they have to relieve inner tensions by surveying the firmament in panoramic fashion. In their eyes, there is little excuse for the obvious remark, unless it is placed in the context of a model or expanded in the direction of statesman-like advice. And after all, they feel (as do we) that these matters are terribly important, even if we are unable to say very much about them. Perhaps the neoclassical author thought that moralizing would underline this importance.

Once outside his theoretical structure, the neoclassical economist was forced to use a "naive model" in one or another of its several forms, and thus put himself in an essentially prescientific era of investigation. After all, it requires no special understanding to suppose that tomorrow will be like today, or that the change between yesterday and today will be the same as that between today and tomorrow, or that flipping a coin many times will produce as many heads as tails.

Neoclassical authors, as we have seen, replaced real-world firms and households for analytical purposes by relationships couched in mathematical language, e.g., by production functions and utility functions. In the case of the firm, they concentrated mostly on the technological conditions of production and weakened the "human element" by using a grossly oversimplified ordering relation, the profit function. In the case of the household, they omitted a production function and thus forced everything into the utility function. Their approach depended upon a grouping of factors, so that these crucial production and utility functions could be treated as relationships that were basically unchanging, i.e., they assumed "technology" and "tastes" were given. However, to underline the fact that they did not really believe that these functions were unchanging, most neoclassical authors offered a series of socio-psychological remarks concerning the manner in which tastes and technology might be expected to change. While the common-sense level of most of these observations prevents us from labeling them a contribution to growth theory, the treatment of changes in technology is worth some special attention.

Neoclassical authors recognize technological change as the end product of a process in which invention and innovation come first. To distinguish different steps in this process, we visualize *all* the known possibilities for combining inputs in order to produce outputs. The inventor then is conceived of as adding to the list of known possibilities, while the innovator has the task of selecting among these on the basis first of efficiency and second of profitability.

In an unchanging environment this task becomes almost a clerical matter, and therefore requires only a routine manager. As conditions of demand and supply (but not technological knowledge) change, the job of selection becomes more complicated and managers must consequently be more alert for profitable opportunities, i.e., they must scan a much larger range of possibilities. Neither the commodities being produced nor the methods of production employed can be considered permanent fixtures by the successful business decision-maker. Indeed, at this point, we begin to distinguish between managerial and entrepreneurial functions. When we move to the consideration of changes in the body of technological knowledge, i.e., into the area of invention and innovation, our somewhat fragile schema still enables us to handle matters with a semblance of ease. Innovation is not to be distinguished from other entrepreneurial tasks, except for the possibly greater amount of uncertainty involved. If we hold demand and supply conditions constant, and permit only technological possibilities o change, then the entrepreneurial function is nothing but innovation. nvention, of course, is placed among the "noneconomic" variables.[37]

From any long-run view of economic theory, this particular analytical ramework is unsatisfactory. In short, I question the usefulness of splitting he firm's decision-making center into clerical and risk-taking components, and then equating one with a dull and somewhat plodding manager and he other with the exciting, somewhat racy yet shrewd creature denoted by the word "entrepreneur." This split also created misgivings for our neo-classical economist. The truth is that the neoclassical economist's model was essentially unable to handle the costly gathering and processing of nformation, when the information is intrinsically and unavoidably incom-plete and uncertainty is an integral part of the world. Indeed, even today we do not know how to proceed, although techniques of statistical nference are now available to us. Moreover, and for the same sorts of easons, the neoclassical economist was unable to remold the *impersonal* decentralization of the competitive market, so that it would serve as a basis for understanding the *personal* decentralization displayed in the bureaucratic structure of firm or government agency. Instead, "organiza-tional ability" was lumped with the ability to innovate wisely. But, again, even today we have made little additional progress.

In spite of all these difficulties, we tend to think that competition, suitably modified by government action, will provide the sort of social environment in which appropriate technological changes will occur. The entrepreneurial personality should be encouraged; social mobility (perhaps enhanced by geographical mobility), coupled with pseudo-Darwinian selec-tion, is an obvious prerequisite, and an appropriate educational process will, if guarded, take care of the rest.[38] Even the frictions present in the real world may not be altogether deleterious, since in the process of over-coming them the spine will stiffen and too rapid change will be prevented. By and large, however, the process of technological change will be an easy one.

Competition will prove advantageous in another connection as well. It will compel imitation of successful entrepreneurs, and thus soon elimi-nate the pure profits of innovation. It will also provide a fairly automatic device by which the entire society will adjust to the new pattern required, now that production functions (or tastes) have changed. Since the inno-vator is more practical than the inventor, he will pay attention to the sig-nals transmitted by the price mechanism and introduce technological

37. In connection with this and the next few paragraphs, compare Richard V. Clem-ence and Francis S. Doddy, *The Schumpe-terian System*, Cambridge, 1950, esp. chaps. 5-8.

38. Cf. Guido Turin, *Der Begriff des Unter-nehmers*, Zürich, 1947; Arthur H. Cole, *Busi-ness Enterprise in its Social Setting*, Cam-bridge, Mass., 1959.

changes in response to changing prices wherever such changes occur. It may even be that invention is in part directed by innovators in response to social needs, as indicated by price changes. In this connection, there is reason to suppose, however, that small-scale enterprise may not prove as suitable for innovation as medium or large-scale enterprise (although more suitable for imitation). In any case, almost certainly the proportion of resources devoted to invention and innovation under competition will be smaller than seems socially desirable.[39] However, innate conservatism and the overvaluation of the present will see to this anyway. It will probably always be easier to get capital for purposes of duplicating existing production facilities than for new technology and products.

In this case, as with population and other socio-economic material, the dilemma faced by the neoclassical author is clear. Escaping from his special theoretical structure, he formulates some definitions, and then must appeal to common sense, a naive-type model, and statesman-like platitudes. Only in the field of government policy formation is the situation different. In this field he has through the years accumulated a lengthy list of independent variables, i.e., variables which, in his estimation, are or could easily be put under the control of government officials. Taxes, subsidies, and levies come in all sizes and shapes and can be applied to firms, commodities, or households, whether involved in domestic or in foreign trade. Similarly, possible variations in government expenditures for commodities and receipts from the sales of commodities are virtually without limit. Finally, although more difficult of manipulation, are laws and moral suasion with which the institutional framework and the climate of opinion may be altered directly.

With all these possibilities from which to choose, our problem as neoclassical authors is to prepare a book of recipes. For each important problem (in a historical sense), we will list the principal government remedies available. In inventing these remedies, however, we must be exceedingly careful not to create other problems, unless we are sure their order of magnitude will be relatively small. Given a general commitment to the fascinatingly intricate price mechanism, conceived as a control device, this is not an easy task, and our recipe book will have many empty pages. Attempts to design rules for recipe-making in any general sense we believe are doomed to failure.

The fact that we choose this normative-consultative role in relation to government does not mean that we believe the political task of persuading government officials, members of pressure groups, or the electorate to adopt our recipes is an easy one. Competition, education, and appeals to reason may ultimately work in a society of individuals who are unfettered

39. Cf. Frank Ramsey, "A Mathematical Theory of Saving," *Economic Journal,* XXXVIII, 1928, pp. 543-59.

by extreme egotism and imbued with the desirability of progress. In the meantime, however, we have few illusions. Ideally, we should view government itself as we do the economy, and transform our independent variables into intermediate variables, like the interest rate, but this seems an almost impossible task. Perhaps it is simpler to wait until our independent policy variables really are under the control of an enlightened government and hope that our writing and teaching will help to reduce this time interval. In our more pessimistic moods, however, we wonder whether the world displays any tendency to become a better place in which to live.

There is no need to dwell at length on specific suggestions regarding government policy. Many suggestions were offered to reduce ignorance, remove other barriers to mobility, and relieve uncertainty. Possible actions to cushion the shocks caused by changes in tastes, wealth, and technology, as well as those caused by events in other countries, were presented in detail. *Ad hoc* devices were suggested to handle situations in which private and social benefits and costs diverged, methods were invented by which a "competitive market" might be simulated to take care of problems created by indivisibilities (or increasing returns) in production or consumption and important "third-person" effects. Finally, ways of achieving various distributions of wealth were suggested, and (ethical) arguments offered in support of one or another distribution.[40] As is well known, however, this impressive deductive and inventive list of possible government actions was deficient with regard to direct controls over real saving, as well as either direct or indirect controls over variables exogenous to the model, such as population, tastes, technology, or value-attitudes of households or entrepreneurs.

IV

Capital as an Endogenous Variable

As a first approximation, it seemed entirely appropriate to employ a static world in which the stock of capital as well as the stock of natural resources was fixed. Soon, however, most neoclassical authors began to relax this critically unreal assumption and explore the conditions under which the rate of growth of capital stock would (and should) diverge from zero.

The normative aspects of the problem on the level of the competitive or monopolistic firm imbedded in a certain environment yielded easily, i.e., continue adding capital (investing) as long as expected profit increases

40. But it should be remembered that Pareto tried to show that a (particular) skewed income distribution was "natural." See H. S. Houthakker, "The Pareto Distribution and the Cobb-Douglas Production Function in Activity Analysis," *Review of Economic Studies*, XXIII, 1955-56, pp. 27-31.

as a consequence. Essentially the same rule worked for the household's similar problem regarding its real savings. In this case, however, difficulties created by the inherent fuzziness of the utility concept over time forced the use of significantly unreal assumptions about household wishes and desires. And, indeed, adequate formulation waited until the famous 1928 article by Frank Ramsey.[41] However, the underlying approach, namely, a comparison of present benefits lost (from consumption foregone) with future benefits gained (from spending accumulated savings), was a familiar one to neoclassical scholars.

With reference to the economy at large, capital theory soon ran into extreme conceptual difficulties. By definition, a capital good is valuable because of the uses to which it will presumably be put in the future. But the same physical object may be used solely for present enjoyment by one economic unit, while another will treat the object as capital, and still another will partly use and partly save it. In any event, the future is inherently uncertain, and statistical inference has only recently entered economics. Conceptualization was made even more difficult by the obviously heterogeneous nature of future goods and the fact that individual economic units can use money in place of an undifferentiated, divisible capital good. Yet, money is also used in other connections for other purposes. Treatment of capital as a productive factor necessarily implies a return which may be attributed to this factor; but, particularly in a "free enterprise," institutional setting, it is difficult to make empirically meaningful distinctions among interest, profits, rent (or quasi-rent), and the wages of management (conceived as a labor input). In this general connection, a Marshallian distinction between long and short run, which effectively tied the short-run production function to a particular type and amount of (fixed) capital, did not help. The forced separation of input and output markets, of households as buyers from households as sellers, and the concept of an industry associated solely with the output market also hindered adequate formalization.

Finally, some sorting out occurred. For the most part, this waited until after J. M. Keynes had exploited and propagandized the competitive one-commodity, one-firm world as a useful representation of reality, and P. A. Samuelson had forced us to consider carefully the differences between statics and dynamics. Indeed, only recently have we been able to appreciate what must have been the neoclassical-variable-capital-stock model.[42]

41. *Op.cit.,* Ramsey's conditions for an optimum, using a relatively uncomplicated neoclassical world, are: Optimum investment = (Bliss − present level of enjoyment) / marginal utility of present consumption.

42. See, in this connection, Solow, "A Contribution . . . ," *op.cit.;* Richard Stone, "Misery or Bliss," *Economia Internazionale,* VIII, 1955, pp. 72-93; James Tobin, "A Dynamic Aggregative Model," *Journal of Political Economy,* LXIII, 1955, pp. 103-15; Paul A. Samuelson and Robert M. Solow, "A Complete Capital Model Involving Heterogeneous Capital Goods," *Quarterly Journal of Economics,* LXX, 1956, pp. 537-62.

Conclusion

In more recent discussions of growth–particularly those which are policy oriented–we seem to have forgotten our neoclassical heritage. Having been reared in a social environment shaped by depression and war, our lack of confidence in competition as a device for social control represents an understandable desire to discard the past. Concentration on the shortcomings of competition has led us to emphasize the delineation of particularistic schemes that a willing and forceful (exogenous) government might employ to influence particular variables, e.g., the use of subsidies, taxes, direct investment by government, and the like. With this focus of interest, we find welfare criteria, e.g., the notion of Pareto Optimality, difficult of application. This is not surprising, since the neoclassical welfare theorems purposely did not refer directly to observable indicators. Instead, they were purely systemic deductions which, for "proof," depended on: (a) assumptions which, in principle, could not be checked directly; and (b) theorems of the "middle level" which did refer to observable variables. The assumptions were consistent with these middle-level theorems, and were also consistent with the welfare theorems. We now recognize, all too well, that an act of faith is required to bridge the gap between the two sets of theorems, i.e., we point to other assumptions with which the middle-level theorems could be supported, but from which the welfare theorems would not follow. Consequently, we find it necessary to invent pluralistic, observable, and grossly incomplete welfare indicators for policy purposes. In an important sense, welfare questions are transformed into political questions, and thereby placed in the category of questions to which only "arbitrary answers" can be given.

If we hold firmly to neoclassical methodology, there is an alternative approach which involves many fewer, although perhaps no less important, arbitrary decisions. We can attempt to discover or invent other devices for social control, parallel to those of competition, and then design "switching rules" to determine which device or combination of devices to employ. In this context, these switching rules would be related to the welfare implications of the available control devices and to ascertainable features of the environment, including the parameters which describe the behavior of the individuals contained. For example, a firm desiring to maximize profit (the welfare equivalent) could choose either a centralized or a decentralized network of communication and control. The choice might depend upon the cost of obtaining the requisite environmental information and the rapidity with which the unpredictable features of this environment changed over time. A decentralized mechanism, in which there were many decision makers, but in which the various decision rules were "built in," would probably be more efficient (i.e., more profitable), if the future shape of the physical environment were extremely uncertain. If the total environment were completely predictable, virtually any sort of network would probably also work equally well. The difficulties arise when the physical environment is predictable, but the human component is not, or when both are unknown.[43] The Lerner-Lange neoclassical variety of socialism recognized this difficulty, as does the extreme decentralization of a commodity market, or the relatively extreme centralization of a political party or army. Success in this sort of theorizing would permit assignation of the appropriate communication and control network to the various required decisions over time.

In the context of growth *cum* welfare, one unavoidably arbitrary decision must be mentioned. Following neoclassical reasoning, the issue may be stated as a paradox. If the tastes of this generation are to govern the composition of production (and therefore investment, including that devoted to research), the tastes of future generations are no longer independent (except for an error term). The force of decisions now made will unavoidably affect the decision-making power, given a finite time interval, of future generations. This is obvious and unavoidable, and particularly relevant when decisions regarding expenditures on "basic research" are being considered. The difficulty is that no statements can be made regarding the relative importance of different individuals; thus we cannot assign other than arbitrary weights to the tastes of different generations. Nor is the difficulty solved by pointing out that present members of society themselves have preferences regarding the preferences of future generations, without appealing to the vacuous "principle of insufficient reason."

At this stage in the development of growth theory perhaps our best bet is to concentrate on a few manipulable (by government) variables as did the classical economists. Then we can construct models which may enable us to predict the consequences on a set of welfare indicators of changes in such variables. Perhaps we had best leave to one side the problem of constructing an ordering relation by which to evaluate conflicting changes in these indicators. By focusing our primary attention on the development of maximization rules which may aid policy-makers in the performance of their (short-run) tasks, we may in time be able to combine a larger and larger number of particularistic models into a useful general model.

43. Lack of the appropriate invention may require centralization when the human element has attributes which, given the environment (certain or uncertain), are known to be antagonistic to the general (welfare) objectives.

THEORIES OF STAGES OF ECONOMIC GROWTH

By Bert F. Hoselitz

THIS PAPER is devoted to an analysis of those theories of economic growth which emphasize a series of stages in the evolution of economic systems and which explain the process of economic growth in terms of the successive development of these stages. Among economists who developed theories of economic stages, the members of the German historical school of economics were outstanding, and a substantial portion of this paper will be devoted to an analysis of their theories. But the consideration of theories of economic stages involves more than a discussion of their concepts and classifications. It has ramifications in the field of economic, and indeed general, history; it also touches upon some issues associated with theories of social evolution, in general; and, finally, in the economic realm itself, it leads to the consideration of a series of theories of growth in which the claim was made that there exist certain relationships between forms of occupational structure and stages of economic advancement.

I begin with a discussion of the theories of economic stages expounded by various German economists in the nineteenth century, particularly Friedrich List, Bruno Hildebrand, Karl Bücher, Gustav Schmoller, and Werner Sombart. Their writings have formed a basis for further discussion of problems of economic stages in Germany and, to some extent, elsewhere. Above all, there exists a considerable number of secondary writings in which the theories and classifications of these five writers, and especially the formulations of the last three, have been compared and critically analyzed. In spite of its bulk, much of this secondary literature is unoriginal and, what is more distressing, with few exceptions, devoid of recognition of the really crucial problems raised by the various theories of economic stages.

Above all, the proponents of economic stages themselves, as well as their critics, were often confused over the interpretation of their theories. This confusion centers around three main points. The first is the problem of whether the identification and classification of different economic stages is a means of studying the progressive development of a given economy, or whether it is a device for the comparative analysis of economic systems. The second is the question of whether these stages are essentially "ideal" constructs, designed to facilitate the analysis of economic systems and their dynamic aspects, or whether they are abbreviated and somewhat schematic presentations of actual historical developments. The third problem—and this interests us most in connection with the study of economic growth—is the question of identifying the factors which make for change, especially those which determine the transition of an economy from one stage to the next. Since we are interested primarily in theories of economic growth, I shall attempt to stress this last problem, and my evaluation of different theories will hinge not merely on the question of whether they establish useful types for purposes of comparison, but primarily on whether they present explicit statements on the forms of, and factors involved in, transitions from one stage to another, especially if subsequent stages are recognized as representing an advancement over previous ones. As we shall see later, the various authors of the systems of economic stages were not always explicit on this point, and some were not even aware of its significance. At the same time, it cannot be doubted that one of the objectives of all writers of the German historical school was the attempt to discover laws of development of national economies, though they differed on the methods to be used for the discovery of these laws, as well as on the expectation that such laws could be stated with any degree of precision.[1] In assessing the role assigned to laws of economic evolution, we may distinguish three approaches, each of which is characteristic of one of the main representatives of the older historical school: The first sees the principle of economic evolution as an analogue to organic life; economies grow, come to maturity, and decay. This was the position of Wilhelm Roscher. The second sees economic development as an aspect of the general trend of progress of human culture. This was the view of Karl Knies. The third sees economic growth realized in the succession of ever-higher stages of

1. A survey of the various theories of stages as implementations of laws of economic evolution has been presented by Gertrud Kalveram, *Die Theorien von den Wirtschaftsstufen,* Leipzig, 1933, pp. 73-117.

economic organization. This was the view of Bruno Hildebrand.[2] All three conceptions may be traced back to various interpretations of human progress in the writings of seventeenth- and eighteenth-century philosophers. But whereas the impact of the organismic analogy and the more or less naive belief in human perfectibility found few followers among later writers, the theory of stages reappeared in ever-new garb. For this reason, it appears more fruitful to devote this paper to an analysis of theories of economic stages of growth, rather than to the theories of economic evolution evolved by the members of the German historical school.

I

The first system of economic stages that we will examine was presented by Friedrich List in his work, *Das nationale System der politischen Oekonomie.*[3]

Before we examine List's classification of economic stages in detail, and their relation to his conception of economic growth, a few comments are in order. First, the idea of economic stages as such was not new in List's day. As Schumpeter has pointed out, he borrowed the general idea of progressive stages of development from the philosophy of enlightenment of the eighteenth century.[4] Second, List's book, although presented as a

2. Hildebrand's theory will be discussed at greater length below. The views of Roscher and Knies on laws of economic development have been discussed by Kalveram, *op.cit.*, esp. pp. 129*ff.*, but especially by Max Weber, "Roscher und Knies un die logischen Probleme der historischen Nationalökonomie," in *Gesammelte Aufsätze zur Wissenschaftslehre*, Tübingen, 1922, pp. 24*ff.*; Margret Hüter, *Die Methodologie der Wirtschaftswissenschaft bei Roscher und Knies*, Jena, 1928, pp. 33*ff.*; Gottfried Eisermann, *Die Grundlagen des Historismus in der deutschen Nationalökonomie*, Stuttgart, 1956, pp. 155-57, 198-99.

3. The first edition of this book was published in April 1841 in Stuttgart by J. G. Cotta. A second edition appeared in 1842, and a third edition with minor textual changes in 1844. Most later reprints of the work are based on this 1844 edition. The *editio princeps* of the work is contained in Volume VI of Friedrich List, *Schriften, Reden, Briefe*, Berlin, 1930. This edition, which bears the subtitle: Friedrich List, *Das nationale System der politischen Oekonomie*, was prepared by Artur Sommer. Though List's classification of economic stages contained in *Das nationale System* was his most widely known, it was neither his only, nor his first, classification. A more detailed series of economic stages was worked out by him in a prize essay which he composed in Paris in 1837, in response to a competition initiated by the Acádemie des Sciences Morales et Politiques. List's manuscript was published for the first time in Volume IV of the edition of his collected works (Friedrich List, *Das natürliche System der politischen Oekonomie*, Edgar Salin and Artur Sommer, eds.; Friedrich List, *Schriften, Reden, Briefe*, Berlin, 1927, IV). It thus remained unknown until 1927, and the classification of economic stages elaborated in that work had no influence on later writers. The prize essay has been given the title, "Le système naturel d'économie politique," by its editors; and it contains the rather extended discussion of three agricultural and three manufacturing stages or "periods." In addition, List stipulates a hunting and a pastoral stage antedating the earliest agricultural stage. List's various classifications of stages in the Paris prize essay, in his *National System of Political Economy*, and in a number of other essays published between 1839 and 1844 have been presented and discussed extensively by A. Sommer, "Friedrich List's Pariser Preisschrift von 1837, ihre Bedeutung und ihre Stellung im Gesamtwerke Lists," *Mitteilungen der Friedrich List Gesellschaft*, No. 3, 1926, esp. pp. 56-80.

4. Joseph A. Schumpeter, *History of Economic Analysis*, New York, 1954, p. 505. See also footnote 12, below.

general treatise on political economy, is, in essence, a critical comment on the economic policies of Adam Smith and his followers (usually referred to by List as the "School") and a discussion of the most appropriate economic policy designed to foster the productive forces (*Produktionskräfte*) of a nation. In other words, List's work was not an attempt to present a new economic theory merely for the sake of theorizing; it was an attempt to provide the theoretical underpinnings for a set of economic policies for economic development, or, rather, for industrialization. In its objective, List's work resembles much of the present literature on economic growth, which is also elaborated with the aim of providing guidelines for planned economic development. It is therefore not surprising that many of the ideas expressed by List are found again in contemporary literature on economic growth, or, conversely, that some passages in List's works have a thoroughly "modern" flavor.

Although List selects for special treatment alternative commercial policies, he does so because he was in substantial agreement with the proposition of the "School" that free competition within a country leads to optimum allocation of resources, and hence, he believed, to maximum stimulation of its productive forces. In part, this position was an outgrowth of the actual state of regulatory policies of his day; at that time, of all forms of governmental policies, the issue of free trade versus protection loomed largest. In part, it was an outflow of a particular situation which he had constantly in mind: the fact that the industry of the two countries whose economies he knew best and with whose advancement he was most concerned, i.e., Germany and the United States, was inferior to that of Britain. Hence, List must not be interpreted as favoring protection as such, but as favoring only protection of manufactures, and, indeed, protection of manufactures only in their initial infant stage. With reference to agriculture, List was a determined and unequivocal free trader, and the rationale for this position is implied in his theory of economic stages.[5]

Third, and this is implied by the title of his work and his pre-occupation with economic policy, List is not interested in economic relations in an abstract, closed system, but as aspects of a system of nations. List believes that progress in human welfare is a function of association.[6] He

5. See List's discussion of free trade for agriculture, both for agricultural countries, as well as those which also have manufacturing industry, in Frederick List, *National System of Political Economy*, translated by G. A. Mantle, Stephen Colwell, ed., Philadelphia, 1856, pp. 297-300. All further references to List's *National System of Political Economy*, unless specifically stated otherwise, will be made to this American translation, which will be cited as "*National System.*"

6. Similarly, Henry C. Carey considers the principle of association central to his theory (cf. *Principles of Social Science*, Philadelphia, 1875, I, 41*ff.*), and the question may therefore be raised as to the mutual influence exerted by the two men upon one another. It is impossible to ascertain any clear connection between List's and Carey's writings on this point, and the only writer who has compared their views on association comes to the conclusion that they diverge on this point. See Eduard Meuser, *List und Carey als wissenschaftliche Nationalökonomen*, Mainz, 1915,

describes how the individual in the state of nature is feeble and destitute. He states that the "highest association of individuals now realized, is that of the state, the nation and the highest imaginable, is that of the whole human race." But List believes that the unification of all men in a world state is utopian, and that, therefore, "to preserve, to develop, and to improve itself as a nation is . . . at present, and ever must be, the principal object of a nation's efforts. There is in that nothing false or selfish; it is a reasonable tendency, agreeing perfectly with the real interests of humanity; for it leads naturally to universal association, which is an advantage to men, so far as nations have reached the same degree of culture and power, and, consequently, so far as it may be realized by way of association or confederation."[7] Thus, the unit which List studies is the nation state, and his theory of economic stages must be understood as applying only to nation states. This is an important aspect of his theory, since it was one of the chief reasons why later writers rejected it. Bücher, for example, points explicitly to the fact that List and Hildebrand "assume that as far back as history reaches . . . there has existed a *national* economy based upon the exchange of goods. . . . They have no doubt whatever that the fundamental features of economic life have always been essentially similar."[8]

Fourth, and this does not so much concern an aspect of List's theorizing about economic stages as such, but an aspect of his views on the effectiveness of economic growth, he postulates that growth can occur only *in societies in which there is internal freedom,* i.e., freedom of political organization and freedom of the individual. He considers this viewpoint as capable of being derived from the "lessons of history." For example, he says that "it is vain that individuals are industrious, saving, intelligent, and inventive; these free institutions are still needful for the proper application of these qualities. History teaches, in fact, that individuals draw the greatest part of their productive power from the social conditions and

pp. 7-10. But it is likely that List did, in general, exercise an influence upon Carey, though the precise degree of List's influence is disputed. Some have held that the most characteristic views of Carey in his more mature works are derived from List. Among those who held this view are Eugen Dühring (*Kritische Geschichte der Nationalökonomie und des Sozialismus,* Berlin, 1875, p. 336), and Gustav Schmoller (*Zur Literaturgeschichte der Staats- und Sozialwissenschaften,* Leipzig, 1888, p. 109). Others, although they acknowledge that List exerted some influence on Carey, believe that the latter's views were worked out substantially independently. Among the writers who hold this view are Alfred Marshall, *Principles of Economics,* London, 8th ed., 1920, p. 767; Margaret E. Hirst, *The Life of Friedrich List,* London, 1909, pp. 118-21; and Meuser, *op.cit.,* passim. The whole issue is summarized by W. Notz, the editor of the second volume of List's collected works (see Friedrich List, *Schriften, Reden, Briefe,* Berlin, 1931, II, pp. 415-16).

Whatever connections may be traced between List and Carey, the latter did not adopt List's theory of stages, which were developed only after List had published his *Outlines of American Political Economy,* and it was this work, more than any other, which would have exerted an influence on Carey.

7. *National System,* pp. 70-71.

8. Karl Bücher, *Industrial Evolution,* S. M. Wickett, trans. and ed., New York, 1904, p. 86. (Italics added.)

the institutions of society."[9] There is a clear recognition of the interaction of the social and, above all, political conditions of a nation and the degree of development of its productive powers, i.e., its general economic advancement. List berates the "School" for trying to "persuade us that politics and the government of the State have nothing in common with political economy," i.e., for isolating economic variables, as such, for examination and analysis.[10] Although this charge overshoots the mark, even if applied to Ricardo, allegedly the most abstract thinker of the classical school, it is true that the classical economists who wrote before List paid but little attention to what we now would refer to as "cultural" factors, and that one can find in their works very few explicit, realistic discussions of economic relations in a social framework different from that of their own times. For that matter, it should be mentioned—and has been made quite clear by List's critics among his followers—that his own analysis of the social and political structures of societies which are different from those of the modern West is also lacking in realism and scientific accuracy; this was one of the chief grounds why this classification of economic stages was rejected by later writers.[11] But it remains true, nevertheless, that List raised an important point of criticism against the classical school, which later became one of the mainstays in the attack by the historical school against the classics: the essentially deductive character of classical theory and its lack of interest in deriving generalizations from the study and examination of empirical historical processes. It is in this context that List's theories of economic stages, and some later theories as well, must be understood.

If we now turn to a more detailed examination of List's classification, we find that he distinguishes the following five stages: (a) the savage stage, (b) the pastoral stage, (c) the agricultural stage, (d) the agricultural and manufacturing stage, and finally, (e) the agricultural, manufacturing, and commercial stage.[12] Although some of List's critics have taken exception

---

9. *National System*, pp. 178-79. The view expressed in this passage was widely held among the more enlightened intellectuals of Europe of that time. Cf., for example, John Stuart Mill, *Principles of Political Economy*, W. J. Ashley, ed., London, 1909, p. 940.

10. *National System*, p. 218.

11. Cf. Bücher, *op.cit.*, p. 86, and, above all, Werner Sombart, "Die gewerbliche Arbeit un ihre Organisation," *Archiv für soziale Gesetzgebung und Statistik*, XIV, 1899, p. 371 (hereinafter cited as "Gewerbliche Arbeit").

12. *National System*, p. 72. The classification of the first three stages, i.e., savagery or nomadism, pastoralism, and agriculturalism, is very old. The first distinction between peoples who make their living by different means may be traced back to Aristotle's *Politics*, Ernest Barker, ed., Oxford, 1946, I, viii, par. 6-13, pp. 20-21. In this work Aristotle distinguished, in a very general way, between pastoral, farming, freebooting, fishing peoples, and those who lived from the chase. Aristotle's disciple, Dicaearchus of Messene (fl. ca. 320 B.C.), was perhaps the first to introduce a sequence of stages. Though his own work on this problem has been lost, his views on successive productive stages has been preserved for us by the famous Roman writer Marcus Terentius Varro (*On Agriculture*, II, i, par. 3-5, translated by W. D. Hooper, London, 1934, pp. 312-15). Dicaearchus and, following him, Varro distinguished three stages. The first "was that state of nature in which man lived on those products which the virgin earth brought forth of her own accord"; the second stage was the

to his classification, primarily to the first three stages, he himself was relatively uninterested in them, and most of his discussion centers around the transition from stage (c) to stages (d) and (e). A critical examination of List's classification may give rise to three questions, in principle. First, are his distinctions the basis of a theory of economic growth? Second, how realistically do his stages describe the actual economic conditions prevailing in different societies on different levels of economic advancement? Third, what concepts did List hold about the process of economic growth, especially the conditions of transition from one stage to the next? We shall not take up the first two questions at this time, since they raise problems common to all theories of economic stages. But it may be fruitful to look somewhat more carefully into List's explanation of the processes of growth within a stage and the transition from one stage to another.

List's theoretical discussion of economic growth, even in slightly explicit form, relates only to a limited portion of his classification. Nothing is said about the progress from the savage to the pastoral stage, and from the pastoral to the agricultural stage. Moreover, there is little distinction between the last two stages: the agricultural and manufacturing, and the agricultural, manufacturing, and commercial stage.[13] The crux of his theory of growth centers on a description of the conditions under which a

---

pastoral stage; and then "by a third stage man came from the pastoral life to that of the tiller of the soil."

A very similar classification of stages can be found in the work of Adam Smith (*Wealth of Nations*, Edwin Cannan, ed., New York, Modern Library, 1937, pp. 653*ff.)*. Though Smith does not present an explicit theory of economic stages, he distinguishes between "nations of hunters, the lowest and rudest state of society"; "nations of shepherds, a more advanced state of society"; "a yet more advanced state of society . . . those nations of husbandmen who have little foreign commerce, and no other manufactures but those coarse and household ones which almost every private family prepares for itself"; and a still more advanced state caused by "the progress of manufactures, and the improvement in the art of war." This can scarcely be called a stage theory deserving of that name, yet, Joseph Cropsey has seen in it almost a statement of Smith's "philosophy of history," an interpretation which I am reluctant to accept. See J. Cropsey, *Polity and Economy*, The Hague, 1957, pp. 56*ff*.

All these discussions have in common the fact that stages are regarded as a natural, obvious sequence, which requires no explanation. The factors causing transition from one stage to the next are unexplained, or assumed to be associated essentially with the general advancement of the human mind. Thus, these theories are not theories of economic stages in the strict sense, but reflections on the economic aspects of theories of human progress in general. Some such theories were common in classical Greece and Rome, but they came to high florescence in Western Europe in the eighteenth and nineteenth centuries. Cf. on this point J. B. Bury, *The Idea of Progress*, London, 1920, esp. chaps. VII-XIV.

There is no question in my mind but that List's own theory is originally an outflow of the general intellectual vogue in which theories of progress were held in his formative years.

13. It appears that List himself placed no great importance on this latter distinction. He lists his stages again in a later publication and there distinguishes only between four stages. The last two are combined into one stage. Cf. *National System*, p. 265. It may perhaps be interesting to note that in an essay, published in 1839, List presented a classification of three stages corresponding to the ages of man. In the article, "L'èconomie politique devant le tribunal de l'histoire" (F. List, *Schriften, Reden, Briefe*, E. v. Beckerath, *et al.*, eds., Berlin, 1928, V, 109*ff.)*, he presents the following stages: (a) childhood—hunters and pasturage; (b) adolescence—pasturage and then agriculture; and (c) manhood—agriculture, industry, and commerce. Here again, no distinction is made between the various later stages, and the main emphasis is placed on the transition

mature agricultural state can exist, under which it may progress, and how an agricultural state can be transformed into one on a higher level by the introduction of manufactures. It may perhaps be simplest to present the bare skeleton of List's theory in a number of rather crude and straightforward assertions, as follows:

(1) Whereas all countries have presumably passed through the early stages of development, only the countries in the temperate zone are suited for manufactures. "A country of the torrid zone would make a very fatal mistake, should it try to become a manufacturing country. Having received no invitation to that vocation from nature, it will progress more rapidly in riches and civilization if it continues to exchange its agricultural productions for the manufactured products of the temperate zone."[14]

(2) Countries which "by nature" are destined to be agricultural, or those which are not yet prepared for industrialization by a sufficiently developed state of agriculture, will advance optimally if they maintain free-trade relations with manufacturing countries. "The less agriculture has advanced the more external trade has had to do in exchanging the surplus of agricultural products and raw materials of the country for articles manufactured abroad; the deeper a nation is plunged into barbarism, the more it requires the regimen of absolute monarchy, the more free trade, that is, the export of agricultural products and the import of manufactured products, concurs in its prosperity and civilization."[15]

(3) Once a country in the temperate zone has attained a fairly high level of agricultural development, and if it possesses a relatively dense population and varied resources in addition, it can only progress further by introducing manufactures. This can occur in two ways: (a) it may either be accomplished "under the law of free trade, when the various nations engaged at the time in manufacturing industry shall be in the same degree of progress and civilization"; or (b), if some have outdistanced others in manufactures, commerce, and navigation, this can only be achieved by the introduction of protection of industry.[16]

(4) Once a country has established manufacturing industries, it may gradually dispense with protecting them, as they become stronger, but under no circumstances must it introduce agricultural protection. For agriculture to flourish in a mixed agricultural and manufacturing country, the exchange between urban industry and rural agriculture is sufficient.

---

from "barbarism" to a modicum of civilization [in the transition from stage (a) to stage (b)], and from a despotic, relatively uncivilized society to one fully developed in its political, social, and economic institutions [in the transition from stage (b) to stage (c)]. This last transition appears to be the focal point of List's theory of growth.

14. *National System*, p. 75.

15. *Ibid.*, p. 266.

16. *Ibid.*, pp. 72-73.

Moreover, the increase in productivity of agriculture in an industrialized country is assured by the extension of industrial practices to agriculture. "In no country are agricultural machines and implements more perfect, and in none is agriculture in so advanced a state, as where manufacturing industry is flourishing. Under the influence of the latter, husbandry becomes itself a manufacture, a science."[17]

From this it appears that, basically, List recognizes only one dynamic element in the process of economic growth, the introduction of manufacturing. Agriculture is doomed either to remain stagnant or to increase in productivity, either by the stimulus exerted upon it by export demand or by its interaction with industrial growth, in which latter case a double influence is exerted upon agriculture. Its increased productivity is stimulated, on the one hand, by the growing demand for its output by the nonfarm (i.e., manufacturing) population and, on the other, by the transfer of more rational and efficient methods of production through the application

17. *Ibid.*, p. 286. The general process of economic development along the lines presented in the text has been summarized by List in a short paragraph *(ibid.*, p. 77), and more extensively in the classification of stages in his essay of 1837. There he presents the following list of stages: three agricultural stages, i.e., (1) agriculture uninfluenced by trade (this resembles approximately Bücher's category of "independent domestic economy"); (2) agriculture associated with foreign trade, i.e., export of agricultural raw materials against imports of manufactures; and (3) agriculture in equilibrium with manufacturing industry in the same country, These three stages of agriculture are counterbalanced by three corresponding stages of manufactures, i.e., (1) manufactured commodities are produced primarily by farmers and landowners, as well as "ordinary artisans" (this stage resembles strongly Bücher's category of "town economy"); (2) sizable manufactures arise in some fields which can withstand foreign competition "through the low level of wages or some other special local conditions"; (3) a stage of manufacturing in which virtually the entire domestic demand for industrial commodities is supplies from home production. Finally, both sets of stages are followed by a fourth, in which a country is in the position of importing agricultural raw materials and exporting, in return, manufactures. See F. List, *Schriften, Reden, Briefe*, IV, 236*ff.*, esp. 326-28. Cf. also the editor's comments, *ibid.*, pp. 580-81.

Now, it is clear that these seven stages are not thought of as successive stages, but as two sets of parallel developments which partly overlap. The conclusion that clearly arises from this classification is that the dynamic force in the process of development is industry. As far as agriculture is concerned, it progresses to the extent to which contact with industry becomes closer and more frequent. In the isolated agricultural stage, the distance between agriculture and manufacturing is "infinite"; in the second stage, some contact is established, but agriculture and manufacturing are located in different countries; and in the third stage, contact is closer and more frequent, because agriculture and industry are located in the same country and interact fully with one another. As concerns the second series, that of industrial growth, it is determined by the development of the relative and absolute amount of resources devoted to manufacturing within a given country, and hence represents the "purest" system of progressive stages developed by List.

Although most earlier writers were concerned with the lower end of the classification of stages, i.e., the transition from savagery to pastoralism and agriculture, Sir William Petty, like List, looked at the upper end. Petty did not stipulate stages, but he considered the productivity of different types of production, and he expressed himself on this point in his *Political Arithmetic*, which was first published in 1691. Like List, too, Petty stresses the overbearing importance of liberty of conscience and argues that this was one of the causes for the rise of the Dutch economy. But he also says that the economic success of the Dutch was due to their capturing a large part of the trade of Europe, since "there is much more to be gained by Manufacture than Husbandry, and by Merchandize than Manufacture." William Petty, *Economic Writings*, C. H. Hull, ed., Cambridge, 1899, I, 256.

of technical procedures developed in manufacturing. It should be noted, moreover, that the impact of manufacturing is not confined to the purely economic field, i.e., through affecting the demand for agricultural products and imparting new productive methods to agriculture. Its influence is also exerted in the field of social structure and culture. List emphasizes repeatedly the association between agriculture and despotism, on the one hand, and manufacturing and political and personal liberty, on the other. This noneconomic dimension of the growth of manufacturing is a necessary ingredient of List's theory, for it explains why industry provides an impetus for growth. On this point, List differs from other protagonists of industrial protectionism, who merely regard industry as superior in "productive power" to agriculture.[18] But what List has in mind is not a comparison between one industry and one branch of agricultural production, or between industry in general and agriculture in general, but a comparison between a society based primarily upon agriculture, and inhabited by an indolent, tradition-oriented population with a narrow horizon and lack of a spirit of innovation, and a society based upon manufacture and industry and the associated branches of production called forth by them, and peopled by a free, inventive, and forward-looking population. In other words, the basis for the superiority of industrial production over agriculture does not lie only in its economic superiority, i.e., its higher productivity, but in the social and cultural features by which industrial and agricultural countries differ.

Despite the fact that List's theory of stages, and particularly his interpretation of the superiority of an industrial over an agricultural state, bears only superficial similarities to later protectionist theories, there is a clear resemblance between List's three last stages and the concept of primary, secondary, and tertiary production, developed in the 1930's by A. G. B.

18. See, for example, Mihail Manoilesco, *The Theory of Protection and International Trade*, London, 1931, pp. 36*ff*. In one passage (p. 59), Manoilesco criticizes List for having put forward a doctrine of protection "more or less unconnected with strictly economic factors." This critique is based on a misunderstanding of List's theory. Though it is true that List favored industrialization, in part for noneconomic, i.e., chiefly political and sociological, reasons, he had a clear insight into the possibility of external economies which industrialization would call forth. The first work in which his later, more mature theory of industrial protectionism is expounded is *Outlines of American Political Economy*, which appeared in 1827 and which is reprinted in *Schriften, Reden, Briefe*, II. There, in one place, he speaks of the greater part of productive power promoted by industrialization as being "the intellectual and social conditions of the individuals, which I call capital of mind" (p. 119). In another place (p. 133), he says: "Every new business is connected with great losses by want of experience and skill for a considerable time. The advancement of every kind of manufactories, depends *upon the advancement of many other kinds*, upon the proper construction of houses and works, of instruments and machinery." This comes very close to the postulate of external economies to an industry, as expounded in the recent literature. Cf. for example, P. N. Rosenstein-Rodan, "Problems of Industrialization of Eastern and South-Eastern Europe," *Economic Journal*, LIII, 1943, pp. 202-11; K. Mandelbaum, *The Industrialization of Backward Areas*, Oxford, 1947, pp. 1-4; and Hans Singer, "Economic Progress in Underdeveloped Countries," *Social Research*, XVI, 1949, pp. 1-11.

Fisher and propagated further by Colin Clark.[19] In Colin Clark's formulation of this theory, a relationship is seen to obtain between economic progress, i.e., the growth of average real income (or one of its derivatives), and the progressive increase in the proportion, first, of persons engaged in manufacturing and mining (i.e., secondary production), and later, service (i.e., tertiary), industries.[20]

Now, it clearly follows from the labels by which List designated his last three stages that if the agricultural stage is transformed into an agricultural-manufacturing stage, the relative "center of gravity" of the economy shifts to secondary industry; and if the manufacturing-agricultural stage is transformed into an agricultural-manufacturing-commercial stage, a growth of service industries, or tertiary production, is implied. This becomes even clearer if we analyze more carefully List's description of "commerce." He includes under this category not only wholesale and retail trade, but also navigation and overland transport; and he would doubtless have included such other service industries as advertising and other forms of salesmanship, the operation of communications media, various forms of banking and insurance, and similar kinds of economic activity if they had been sufficiently developed in his day to call for explicit treatment. Moreover, it should not be forgotten that in List's time the concept of commerce or trade had a much wider meaning than it does today. Only a very short time before List wrote, manufacturers were still quite commonly designated as merchants, and there was little separation as yet of commercial activities, in the narrow sense, from banking and financial activities, especially in many of the more backward parts of Central Europe.

The similarity of List's view and that held by Fisher and Clark is enhanced if we compare its extension to the field of noneconomic aspects, which the transition from agriculture to manufacturing implies. The best comparison of this aspect of the two sets of theories can be made if we look at the first statement of the theory of primary, secondary, and tertiary production, which was published in 1933 by Allan G. B. Fisher.[21] Fisher begins this essay by proposing to present a "short not too imaginary sketch of world economic history." He then shows that "in the first stage of development . . . effort is concentrated mainly on primary production, on agricultural and pastoral and similar occupations." This is followed by a second stage in which "secondary or manufacturing production and the activities associated therewith began to predominate." Finally, there follows a tertiary stage in which increasing resources are allocated to the

19. See Allan G. B. Fisher, *The Clash of Progress and Security*, London, 1935, pp. 25-43; *idem*, "Production, Primary, Secondary and Tertiary," *Economic Record*, XV, 1939, 24-38; and Colin Clark, *The Conditions of Economic Progress*, London, 2nd ed., 1951, pp. 395*ff*.

20. See Colin Clark, *op.cit.*, pp. 420*ff*.

21. Allan G. B. Fisher, "Capital and the Growth of Knowledge," *Economic Journal*, XLIII, 1933, pp. 379-89.

provision of "facilities for travel, amusements of various kinds, personal and intangible services, flowers, music, art, literature, science, philosophy and the like."[22] What is significant is that Fisher, like List, attributes the superiority of the manufacturing and the manufacturing-commercial stage over the purely agricultural stage to the development of science and knowledge. He argues that the transition from agriculture to secondary production took place mainly because of extensions of knowledge; and the roster of activities characteristic of tertiary production which are cited are evidence that he, like List, holds that economic progress is associated not merely with increasing material welfare, but that it also provides an impetus for science, art, and various forms of the pursuit of knowledge.

But it is precisely this aspect of List's theory that derives its inspiration from the general notions about the progress of the human mind which were so popular in the eighteenth and nineteenth centuries. It is, of course, an incontrovertible fact that in the last few centuries there has been a great increase in scientific knowledge and, in the more advanced countries, leisure for the pursuit of arts, hobbies, and other spontaneous activities. But a simple parallel between the growth of science and economic progress is a very poor and barren theory on the noneconomic or meta-economic implications of economic advancement. List introduced one important connecting link which may properly be considered an aspect of the wider social structure, i.e., the distinction between the despotism of agricultural states and the freedom of manufacturing and commercial states. This is, in itself, an insufficient interpretation, and probably an incorrect one. The approach is correct, in that List recognized that the substantiation of a classification of progressive stages of economic systems by their major productive (or occupational) organization depends also upon the possibility of relating this organization to the over-all political and social structure of a society. Albeit on the basis of rather superficial historical analysis, it is easy to show that scientific and technical knowledge has grown more or less commensurately with increases in economic productivity; it is more difficult to demonstrate those generalized characteristics of social structure which will make possible, and perhaps even mutually reinforce, a simultaneous forward movement in these fields of human action. List did not solve this last problem, but even the contemporary literature on economic growth or industrialization has not produced insights into this process on a significantly more profound level.[23]

22. *Ibid.*, pp. 379-80. It is interesting to note that the somewhat heterogeneous character of tertiary production has recently been subjected to a more detailed analysis, and that further categories of "quaternary" and "quinary" industries have been proposed. See Nelson N. Foote and Paul K. Hatt, "Social Mobility and Economic Advancement," *American Economic Review*, XLIII, 1953, pp. 364-67.

23. An effort to determine the relationship between technological change and social change has been undertaken by Yale Brozen, especially in his essays, "The Social Impact

II

In view of the external similarity between List's theory of economic stages and that of Fisher and Clark, it is not surprising that both were criticized in a similar manner. The arguments which were raised against each theory partly disputed their analytical validity and partly their empirical applicability. In addition, the statistical evidence produced by Colin Clark was called into question by his critics. Since List does not publish statistics and does not base his argument on statistical evidence, the counter-argument could not be employed against him.[24]

Although, in addition to Hildebrand, other later proponents of theories of economic stages, among them Bücher and Sombart, have criticized List's theory, only Hildebrand's criticism is extensive and detailed enough to merit consideration. Sombart confines his critical remarks to the observation that "the theory employs too superficial characteristics of classification," and Bücher criticizes both List's and Hildebrand's theories by stating that they assume that "with the sole exception of the 'primitive state' there has existed a national economy based upon exchange of goods." In other words, Sombart accuses List of shallowness, and Bücher accuses him of lack of recognition that the unit of economic activity in the less highly developed societies is not a national state, but a smaller, less integrated group.[25] Neither of these criticisms need detain us. Sombart's remark betrays his unwillingness to penetrate more than superficially into List's reasoning, and, in view of Sombart's preoccupation with total eco-

of Technological Change," *Journal of Engineering Education,* XLI, 1950, pp. 148-54; "Adapting to Technological Change," *Journal of Business of the University of Chicago,* XXIV, 1951, pp. 114-26; and "The Value of Technological Change," *Ethics,* LII, 1952, pp. 240-65; and on a more strictly economic level by Adolph Lowe (*Economics and Sociology,* London, 1935, pp. 107-15). But in all these essays technological change is assumed to be given, and its implications are traced through. It would also be interesting to analyze the patterns of social structure which impinge differentially on both economic and technical change. Though this is one of the declared purposes of the sociology of science and technology, scarcely any valid results have been published as yet; but see Robert K. Merton, "Science, Technology and Society in Seventeenth Century England," *Osiris,* IV, part II, 1938, pp. 360-62; G. N. Clark, *Science and Social Welfare in the Age of Newton,* Oxford, 1937; and Bernard Barber, *Science and the Social Order,* Glencoe, Ill., 1952.

24. For criticism of the Fisher-Clark theory, see P. T. Bauer and B. S. Yamey, "Economic Progress and Occupational Distribution," *Economic Journal,* LXI, 1951, pp. 741-55; and Simon Rottenberg, "Note on 'Economic Progress and Occupational Distribution'," *Review of Economics and Statistics,* XXXV, 1953, pp. 168-70. For criticism of List's theory, see Bruno Hildebrand, *Die Nationalökonomie der Gegenwart and Zukunft,* Frankfurt-am-Main, 1848, pp. 73*ff.;* and *idem,* "Naturalwirtschaft, Geldwirtschaft und Creditwirtschaft," *Jahrbücher für Nationalökonomie und Statistik,* II, 1864, pp. 2-3. Both of Hildebrand's works, together with four other essays, were republished in 1922 in Jena, under the editorship of Hans Gehrig, with the title, *Die Nationalökonomie der Gegenwart und Zukunft and andere gesammelte Schriften.* All further references to Hildebrand's work will be made to this edition, which will be cited as *Nationalökonomie.* The references cited in this footnote can be found on pp. 61-62 and pp. 326-27 of *Nationalökonomie.*

25. See Sombart, *op.cit.,* p. 372; Bücher, *op.cit.,* p. 86.

nomic systems, List's emphasis upon industrialization must indeed have appeared as superficial and as a refusal to come to terms with "real issues." Bücher's comment is not so much a genuine criticism of List's theory as it is the expression of a different point of view, which we will explore in greater detail below.

Hildebrand, on the other hand, argues that the distinction between the emphasis on agriculture, as against commerce or manufactures, depends not on a general invariable law of progress, but rather on the socio-economic needs and cultural conditions existing at a given time and place. He agrees that logically primary production, i.e., the production of raw materials, must precede further processing and exchange of goods, but he holds that the specific form of economic organization and the over-all direction of economic and occupational specialization of a people depend upon the resources and soil available to it, its forms of political organization, and its general culture. For example, he argues that under the conditions of political division and economic specialization in classical Greece, navigation, trade, and even manufactures were substantially more important than they were under the manorial regime in medieval Europe. Therefore, the particular sequence of productive or occupational stages which a people passes through cannot be said to conform to a general invariant principle, but is affected by the particular environmental, i.e., political and cultural, conditions under which it exists.[26] In a very similar vein, Bauer and Yamey take Fisher and Clark to task when they argue that the Fisher-Clark generalization "seems to be based on the view that tertiary production is less essential than primary or secondary production; and that its products are in the nature of luxuries which cannot be afforded in economies with low real incomes." Here, again, the criticism is implied that whether primary, secondary, or tertiary production is stressed depends upon factors determining the over-all "environmental" conditions under which an economy functions. Under certain circumstances, tertiary industries may weigh heavily in the economies of peoples with very low incomes, simply because the over-all technical conditions of production and distribution in such economies require a heavy concentration on trade and other forms of tertiary production.[27]

With reference to the empirical applicability of List's theory, on the one hand, and the Fisher-Clark theory, on the other, criticisms are also parallel. Bauer and Yamey cite a number of instances from West Africa to illustrate that in these societies tertiary occupations, especially trading,

26. Hildebrand, *Nationalökonomie*, pp. 59-61, 326-27.

27. Bauer and Yamey, *op.cit.*, pp. 747-48.

are widespread, and that this great extension of trading activities is a necessary outflow of economic conditions, i.e., relative prices and available resources. This observation is further elaborated by Rottenberg, who provides a compelling economic rationale for this proliferation of petty services. Not only does he adduce evidence for the large amount of various forms of services, especially petty trading in some islands of the Caribbean, but he also shows that this is due to the general value orientation, prevalent in many parts of the world, which permits a laborer to sell his services on his own account at a price close to zero, or even at zero, whereas it prohibits anyone else from hiring him at such a wage. Now, in a society with very low productivity of labor, employment may not be offered because the productivity of the laborer does not meet the socially (or legally) maintained minimum wage. But in such a situation, a person may sell his own labor by offering various services at a price which will yield a total income lower than the acceptable minimum wage income. This, Rottenberg argues, is the economic rationale for the large number of persons occupied in service industries in many underdeveloped countries.[28]

Similarly, Hildebrand takes List to task because he did not look closely enough at the empirical world to which his system of stages was supposed to apply. For example, he argues that, at best, List's sequence of stages fits only the economic history of Britain, and he adds that "if List had made a simple comparison with the history of the formation of present-day Holland, he would have been persuaded of the fact that his theory was not tenable."[29] He implied that the Dutch were much more important as traders than as manufacturers, and that trade even overshadowed agriculture at the time of Holland's greatness. Only with the decline of Dutch superiority in trade did Holland turn to the encouragement of manufactures and agriculture. Hildebrand thus arrives at the conclusion that, on analytical as well as empirical-historical grounds, a theory of economic stages which employs spheres of production or occupations as the principle of classification is inadequate, and that it must be replaced by one which employs forms of distribution as the criteria for classification. Johann Plenge has characterized this shift in emphasis as the replacement of a *"Berufsstufentheorie"* (theory of occupational stages) by an *"Organisationsmitteltheorie"* (theory of means of organization).[30]

What Hildebrand was after was to find some aspect of economic ac-

---

28. See Rottenberg, *op.cit.*, p. 169. A further reason for the prevalence of services in relatively underdeveloped economies may be derived from the fact that most kinds of craftsmanship or manufacturing require either more skill or more capital, whereas many services, e.g., domestic service or even petty trading, can be exercised without capital or skill.

29. Hildebrand, *Nationalökonomie*, p. 58.

30. Cf. Johann Plenge, *Die Stammformen der vergleichenden Wirtschaftstheorie*, Essen, 1919, p. xv.

tivity which was invariant with respect to the environmental conditions of a society.[31] He found that production, and hence the occupations, in a society depended upon the resources available to it; he found that, similarly, differences in consumption depended on those goods which emerged from the production process. Following the old division of economic analysis into production, consumption, and distribution, only the last field of activity was left, and Hildebrand attached his theory of stages to this last field because, as he says of the system of distribution, "the material which is distributed by it is irrelevant. What man achieves by it is not tied to an object determined by nature. Hence the process of distribution is independent of climate and soil, and uninfluenced by local conditions of nature. It is the most universal, the most generally human process. For this reason, the distribution of goods is that sphere, in which we find the same common forms of development among all peoples, and which we observe to follow one another in the same order."[32]

Although Hildebrand claims that his theory presents successive stages, his three types of economy—natural, or barter, economy (*"Naturalwirtschaft"*), money economy, and credit economy—must be regarded merely as comparative forms of economic organization, rather than as real steps in development. For Hildebrand does not indicate how and why one stage evolves out of the previous one, and some of his critics have charged that, instead of explaining really distinctive basic features of each stage,

31. In stressing the purely social role which a stage theory should fulfill, Hildebrand set himself an ambitious and very exacting task. As we shall see, he did not succeed in developing a genuine theory of economic evolution, and his discussion of stages points more to limitational factors than to factors making for economic change. But in general conception, as well as in methodological penetration, Hildebrand's theory of stages is superior to that of other members of the older historical school. As pointed out at the beginning of this paper (see p. 194), Knies did not develop a stage theory, and Roscher's theory of stages is extremely simple and would more properly be considered an analogue than a theory.

The closest approximation of a theory of stages contained in Roscher's writings is a passage in his essay, "Ueber das Verhältnis der Nationalökonomie zum klassischen Altertum" (in *Berichte über die Verhandlungen der königlichen sächsischen Gesellschaft der Wissenschaften*, Leipzig, 1849, p. 123), where he says that all more highly civilized people pass through three stages which correspond to the "three factors which must be combined in all production: nature, labor, and capital. In the earliest period the factor, nature, predominates strongly. Forest, pastures, and streams feed a sparse population almost voluntarily. . . . In the second period, as was experienced by the majority of present-day states during the last half of the middle ages, the factor of human labor becomes increasingly important. Finally, in the third period the factor of capital comes to the fore: the productivity of the soil is immeasurably enriched by the application of capital; also in manufacturing the manual labor of each craftsman is gradually overshadowed by machine and factory industry; all this contributed to a constant increase of national wealth." Roscher repeats this classification in his comprehensive treatise on economics (*Principles of Political Economy,* with an Introduction by L. Wolowski, translated by John L. Lalor, Chicago, 1882, I, pp. 165-66). There, however, this classification is not viewed in terms of successive stages, but rather as a principle for comparison of different economies. It is not necessary to dwell at greater length on Roscher's stages, since they are based on largely nonoperational conceptualizations, and were, moreover, never used by him or anyone else as a principle by means of which a secular process of economic advancement could be explained or described.

32. Hildebrand, *Nationalökonomie,* p. 329.

he has merely paid attention to "symptoms" or special "aspects."[33] On the one hand, Gustav Cohn points out, the difference between money economy and credit economy is only a superficial one, because money plays an analogous role in both; the only difference consists in the physical form money takes. On the other hand, the distinction between a barter economy and a money economy cannot be made sharply, because empirically there exist too many instances in which part of exchanges is mediated by money and part consists in direct barter. Moreover, even in economies in which barter transactions are the rule, many valuations, e.g., fines or taxes, are quoted in money, and money or coins circulate as objects partly with commodity and partly with proper monetary functions.[34]

Though the justice of these arguments is granted, the distinction between economies in which transactions are exclusively or predominantly

33. This criticism was raised first by Sombart, *op.cit.*, p. 373. It is repeated by J. G. van Dillen, *Het economisch Karakter der middeleeuwsche Stad,* Amsterdam, 1914, p. 9; by Georg von Below, "Ueber Theorien der wirtschaftlichen Entwicklung der Völker," *Historische Zeitschrift,* LXXXVI, 1900, p. 17; and by Gustav Schmoller, *Grundriss der allgemeinen Volkswirtschaftslehre,* Leipzig, 1904, II, p. 1117. It is repeated again, in a somewhat different form, by Eli Heckscher, "Natural Economy and Money Economy," *Journal of Economic and Business History,* III, 1931, pp. 2-3.

34. For the criticism by Cohn, see Sombart, *op.cit.*, p. 373*n;* also Below, *op.cit.*, pp. 17-19, and esp. p. 18*ff;* but the most extensive proof of the joint presence of barter, money transactions, and even occasional instances of self-sufficiency was presented by Alfons Dopsch (in *Naturalwirtschaft und Geldwirtschaft in der Weltgeschichte,* Vienna, 1930).

In all fairness to Hildebrand, however, it should be pointed out that he was himself aware of the difficulties in distinguishing sharply between a barter and a money economy. Twelve years after the appearance of his first essay on this topic, he published another paper, which has attracted little attention. Since it is only a slight piece, of little scientific interest, this is not surprising. But though it contributes little of substance, it is evidence that Hildebrand tried to solve the complex problem of drawing a sharper distinction between a barter and a money economy. In this paper, "Die Entwickelungsstufen der Geldwirtschaft," *Jahrbücher für Nationalökonomie und Statistik,* XXVI, 1876, pp. 15-26 (and reprinted in *Nationalökonomie,* pp. 359-73), Hildebrand distinguishes three stages within the barter economy and two stages within the system of money economy. The three stages of the former are only listed, viz., (a) nomadism, implying absence of property in the soil; (b) predominance of communal property in the soil; and (c) predominance of private property in the soil. It seems reasonable to assume that this classification was inspired by the researches of Maurer on the early *Markgenossenschaft,* which enjoyed considerable popularity in Germany at that time.

The classification of sub-stages in the money economy is apparently unfinished. Hildebrand lists two stages, but this brings him only to the end of the middle ages, and he does not deal with the modern forms of money economy. The two stages which he distinguishes are the stage of monetary circulation of ingots and rings, and monetary circulation in the form of coins. The former state represents a mixed system in which money metal is still regarded as an object of barter; the second stage is the earliest form of a genuine money economy. Hildebrand explains the transition from the first to the second stage as arising out of the needs and privileges of rulers. Some empirical substantiation of this view of the role of precious metals in the early middle ages is provided by Marc Bloch, "Economie-nature ou économie-argent," *Annales d'histoire sociale,* I, 1939, p. 11.

It is unfortunate that Hildebrand did not complete his discussion of sub-stages and in this way fill out his classification of stages. He might have pointed to a series of political or cultural aspects of the deveolpment of economic institutions which would have made the very crude and almost barren distinction of barter, money, and credit economy take on a more useful guise. Lacking this more extensive discussion of sub-stages, his theory consists merely of more or less convenient labels for different forms of exchange, rather than of a theoretical explanation of changes in economic organization.

mediated by barter, those in which they are principally mediated by cash, and those in which an increasing amount of credit money is used has the merit of pointing to decreasing rigidities in exchange and the gradual removal of limitations to the most efficient allocation of resources. For it is clear that the possibility for specialization and the division of labor is seriously limited in an economy in which barter is the only, or the predominant, means of exchange, and that, compared with the wide availability of credit and the extension of a market for securities of all kinds, an economy which requires that all payments be made in hard cash has serious limitations. Moreover, as has been shown, the prevalence of barter, cash, or credit as means of exchange tends to produce different institutional patterns which, in turn, influence the form of economic organization and the development of productivity. Barter economies rely upon institutions for redistribution of reciprocity, and only cash economies develop genuine markets as the norm for distributive transactions. The prevalence of credit requires the development again of new institutions, such as, for example, corporate forms of enterprise, commercial and investment banks, and a government debt which is raised by means of freely salable securities. Some primitive forms of all these institutions were developed more than two hundred years ago, but they have become widely generalized and endowed with far-reaching impact only during the last two centuries.[35]

Renewed attention to Hildebrand's concepts and their usefulness was drawn by Johann Plenge and, following him, by Alfons Dopsch.[36] However, both of these men saw a connection between Hildebrand's classification of stages and others developed later by Karl Bücher and Gustav Schmoller. For this reason, the discussion of the reappearance of the debates on barter and money economy in German economic literature will be postponed until we have gained a greater familiarity with Bücher's doctrine, a theory which caused more stir and more debate than all previous classifications of economic stages taken together.

III

The most popular and probably the most widely discussed theory of economic stages is that elaborated by Karl Bücher. Though he made refer-

35. On the distinction between redistribution, reciprocity, and markets, see Karl Polanyi, *The Great Transformation*, New York, 1944, chaps. 4 and 5; on banks and related institutions and their role in economic development, the literature is too voluminous and too well known to require special references. See, however, Alexander Gerschenkron, "Economic Backwardness in Historical Perspective," in *The Progress of Underdeveloped Areas*, B. F. Hoselitz, ed., Chicago, 1952, pp. 3-29.

36. See Johann Plenge, *op.cit.; idem*, "Grundlegung der vergleichenden Wirtschaftstheorie," *Annalen für soziale Politik und Gesetzgebung*, V, 1917, pp. 492-518; and Dopsch, *op.cit.*

ences to it in earlier writings, it was first published in fully developed form in his essay, "Die Entstehung der Volkswirtschaft," which forms the main chapter of his collection of essays in a volume with that title. The first edition appeared in 1893; a second, somewhat revised and enlarged edition came out in 1897; the third edition, containing a short appendix with answers to the arguments of some of his critics, was published in 1900. Altogether, sixteen editions of the volume had appeared by the mid-1920's. Since that time, the book has declined somewhat in popularity, but its impact, especially before World War I, both within Germany and beyond, is attested to not only by its numerous German editions, but also by the fact that it was translated into English, French, Hungarian, Russian, and other languages.[37] As new editions appeared, Bücher appended further essays, so that the book, which began with six chapters, ended up as a two-volume work with more than twenty chapters. But Bücher's crucial contribution to the theory of economic stages is contained in a lecture which he delivered in 1890, and which was included in the very first edition of the book. Some supporting discussion of his theory, especially with respect to the economic conditions of primitive peoples, was added in later editions, but the English translation, which was made from the third German edition, contains Bücher's views in their final form. We will have occasion later in this essay to discuss Bücher's changing opinions, particularly with reference to the empirical applicability of his theory.[38]

In the final form of his classification, Bücher posits three stages: (a) the stage of the independent domestic, or household, economy; (b) the stage of town economy; and (c) the stage of national economy.[39] For each of his classes, he adds two further explanatory characteristics which constitute the criteria by which his classification has been achieved. Ideally, the domestic economy is characterized by the absence of exchange, and hence by production solely for the household. Goods are consumed at the place where they are produced. Bücher did not stipulate a stage at which division of labor was absent; what was lacking was an institutionalized system of market exchange. But this does not mean that at the stage of domestic economy certain paraphernalia of an extended system of trade were absent. Bücher specifically points to the existence of such paraphernalia of commerce as weights and measures; the carriage of

37. Two translations came out in 1901, one in French, under the title, *Etudes d'histoire et d'économie politique,* translated by A. Hansy, Paris and Brussels, 1901; and one in English, under the title, *Industrial Evolution,* translated by S. M. Wickett, New York, 1901. Hereinafter all references to Bücher's main essay will be made to the English translation edited by Wickett.

38. A very interesting discussion of the textual changes between the first and second German editions has been presented by Georg von Below, *op.cit.,* pp. 22-24, and by J. G. van Dillen, *op.cit.,* pp. 12-17.

39. Bücher, *Industrial Evolution,* chap. 3, esp. p. 89.

persons, news, and goods; hostelries; and the transference of goods and services. "In all, however, there is lacking the characteristic feature of economic exchange, namely, the direct connection of each single service with its reciprocal service, and the freedom of action on the part of the individual units carrying on trade with one another."[40]

The next stage, the town economy, is characterized by exchange; but exchange is limited to goods which pass directly from the producer to the consumer, i.e., ideally, all production is customer production. The transition to this stage arises out of the gradual dissolution of the domestic economy itself. In some of its manifestations, and "on the surface," elements of the town economy stage have already appeared under the general prevalence of the system of domestic economy. There are two types of transaction which Bücher stresses particularly. One is the distribution of commodities of high value, such as precious cloths, jewels, spices, and other commodities which are produced only in a small number of places, either because of the limited natural conditions under which they occur, or because of the scarcity of skills involved in their production. To the extent to which these commodities are distributed at all, they provoke some form of organized trade for their circulation. Bücher argues that though these objects get to places far from their place of origin, they often reach their destination, not in the course of organized trade, but rather as gifts, booty, or tribute. Nevertheless, a portion of these objects is traded by merchants who gradually tend to become specialized in this type of service. Apart from trade in rare and valuable commodities, the domestic economy tends to develop forms of exchange for the more common objects of use. Bücher exemplifies this transition by citing several examples, such as a slave-owner lending a neighbor a specially skilled slave for some time against the payment of a quantity of wine or wood. He gives another example of an artisan serf who is given the privilege of selling, on his own account, objects which he has produced during the time he was not under obligation to work for his lord. Nevertheless, exchanges are rare; the processes of exchange are cumbersome and complicated; and specialized traders constitute an almost negligible proportion of the population as a whole.[41]

This transition can last a long time; and, in fact, Bücher characterized the last centuries of the Roman empire and several centuries of the middle ages as a stage of domestic economy in which these symptoms of transition were present. Is the development of the town economy merely a gradual accumulation of the frequency of exchange transactions, or does some other force intervene to create a somewhat more discontinuous

40. *Ibid.*, pp. 106-107.

41. *Ibid.*, pp. 108*ff*.

change? It appears that Bücher sees such an extraneous force in the political constitution of the medieval town. While it would be difficult to prove this in detail, I believe that his conception of the social character of the medieval European town is similar to that elaborated more extensively by Max Weber.[42] Weber stressed the fact that the peculiar feature of the European city of the middle ages was its character as a corporate entity for defense, which required the economic cooperation of all its inhabitants and thus set them apart from the common people of the open country. This fact is also underlined by Bücher. But Weber stresses a further point, which Bücher probably would have accepted, although he does not mention it explicitly. I refer to the problem of how membership in the urban community was attained. This appears to be a characteristic which distinguishes the European city from cities both in antiquity and in non-western civilizations. The members of the medieval European city, according to Weber's view, formed not only a defensive community–such communities had existed in ancient cities and in cities elsewhere in the world–but one which was based upon a religious bond. Whereas elsewhere in the world different subgroups living together in an urban environment remained ceremonially alien from one another, and were thus unable to form ritualistic communities based on sworn compacts, the ecumenical character of the Christian religion, which admitted anyone who subscribed to the sacraments to membership, made possible the formation of a community in medieval Europe which was based on a sacred bond of brotherhood which embraced all members of the same faith. Thus, all Christians–and it is known that the Jews remained forever strangers in the medieval city–were admitted to communion and could participate as equal members in the *coniuratio* on which the urban constitution of the Western European town was ultimately based.[43]

The development of the stage of town economy is thus based upon the development of a very special institutional phenomenon, i.e., the development of the medieval Western European city. On the one hand, this implies a limitation of Bücher's theory of stages, by confining it to an attempted interpretation of the economic growth of Western and Central Europe, but, on the other hand, it also imparts some strength to the theory, by circumscribing a concrete, well-studied institutional framework within which the empirical content of the theory can be tested. The stage of the town economy, in particular, has been studied and restudied so extensively that it need not be discussed in detail. It may be said, without

42. See Max Weber, *Wirtschaft und Gesellschaft*, Tübingen, 1922, II, pp. 532-42; and idem, *General Economic History*, translated by F. H. Knight, Glencoe, 1950, pp. 315*ff*.

43. For a further discussion of this point, see my essay, "Cities in Advanced and Underdeveloped Countries," *Confluence*, IV, 1955, pp. 324*ff*.

exaggeration, that Bücher's system of stages received such widespread acceptance, especially in Europe, because of his description of the essential quality of the medieval town economy.[44]

Of greatest interest for us, however, is neither the detailed description of the town economy nor the transition from the domestic economy to the town economy, but rather the process of economic growth constituted by the transition from the town economy to the national economy. The stage of the national economy is characterized by Bücher as that in which goods are produced wholesale for a market which constitutes the characteristic institution through which they circulate. The producer and consumer are typically unknown to one another, and goods normally pass through many hands before they reach their ultimate destination. In other words, the stage of national economy corresponds in general to the economic system characteristic of the more highly industrialized nations of the last two or two-and-a-half centuries. How, according to Bücher, did the town economy become transformed into the national economy? Again, the major influence upon this transition is extraneous to the economic system in any narrow sense. Bücher explains this transition in its most crucial aspects when he says that the "final development of national economy is in its essence a fruit of the Middle Ages with the rise of territorial state organizations, and now finds its completion in the creation of the unified national State. Economic unification of forces goes hand in hand with the bowing of private political interests to the higher aims of the nation as a whole."[45]

Just as a political factor, i.e., the constitution of the city as a particular form of socio-political association, paved the way for further economic growth in the transition from the domestic economy to the town economy, so the transition from the town economy to the national economy is explained as being instigated by a political reorganization, the disintegration

---

44. Among the more comprehensive publications on the medieval town economy based in part on Bücher's discussion, see, above all, J. G. van Dillen, *op.cit.;* Fritz Rörig, *Die europäische Stadt im Mittelalter* (1932), Göttingen, 1955; Henri Pirenne, *Medieval Cities,* Princeton 1925; and Max Weber, *General Economic History,* chap. 28.

If this interpretation of the unique political role of the medieval European city is accepted, and if the peculiarity of the "town economy" is considered to be an outflow of the high degree of social solidarity and political self-determination of the medieval European city, the argument of some of Bücher's critics that he did not extend his analysis of the town economy to non-European cities is not only irrelevant but misleading. For example, Johann Plenge, in "Grundlegung der vergleichenden Wirtschaftstheorie," p. 98, says that it is to be regretted that Bücher did not understand how "to make correct use" of works on medieval Byzantium and Moslem cities, and urban conditions in China, in order to give his theory of stages "that universal-historical extension" it requires. Plenge was misled by certain superficial aspects of the operation of markets and by certain analogous functions of market supervision and the supervision of production by guild-like organizations. If he had looked at the deeper socio-structural relations in these non-Western European cities, he might have found profound differences which show the wisdom of Bücher's confining himself to the Occident as a first approximation.

45. Bücher, *op.cit.,* p. 134.

of medieval particularism in the socio-political, and consequently the economic, field and its replacement by the modern unified state. As an explanation of *economic* processes of growth, Bücher's theory must therefore be regarded as a retrogression, as compared with that of List. It may be empirically more accurate in describing various concrete forms of economic organization than either List's or Hildebrand's, but while its realism might prove an advantage in the study of economic history or economic anthropology, it is almost without value as a theory of economic processes. This raises two important questions. First, why was Bücher's theory so popular; second, what is the precise nature of its empirical relevance for economic history?

We cannot answer the first question merely by arguing that the generally unsatisfactory state of economic theory in Germany at the time Bücher wrote accounts for the wide acclaim his theory received. Nor can we say that, since he was close to the leaders of the so-called "New Historical School," Bücher's work was bound to be widely accepted. Bücher was a scholar of high integrity and great knowledge. His book on medieval Frankfurt is one of the best socio-economic studies ever written of a medieval city.[46] Similarly, several of his essays on special topics in economic history and organization are masterpieces of concise, clear, and ingenious analysis. Yet, his most important contribution to the theory of economic development, a field of enquiry which he prized above all and in which his main contribution was made, is essentially barren of analytical insights.[47] In any event, when Bücher's *Entstehung der Volkswirtschaft* appeared for the first time, he was already a well-known and highly respected scholar, and his work was bound to be read with interest and attention. I venture to say that its success was due to two facts: On the one hand, it summarized in able fashion some ideas that were widely current at the time, e.g., the description of the medieval town economy. On the other hand, it caused a stir by tracing back the development of modern economic systems to their most primitive antecedents. Both of these prob-

---

46. Karl Bücher, *Die Bevölkerung von Frankfurt am Main im vierzehnten und fünfzehnten Jahrhundert,* Tübingen, 1886.

47. It should be pointed out that in his volume, *Industrial Evolution* (pp. 154*ff.*), there is still another system of stages than the one discussed here. This is to be found in the fourth chapter, entitled, "A Historical Survey of Industrial Systems," in which five stages are listed. They are: domestic work; wage-work; handicraft; house industry, or putting-out system; and factory work. These five stages correspond roughly to the three over-all economic stages. Domestic work corresponds to the early domestic system; wage-work to the late domestic system and transition to the system of town economy; handicraft is the characteristic form of industrial organization in the town economy; and the last two stages correspond to the early phase and the later phase of the national economy. Thus, this classification of stages is merely a listing of some special aspects of the more general system of economic stages presented by Bücher. As a discussion of economic processes growth, it remains inferior to that presented earlier, and to the extent to which it explains successive systems of industrial organization as being based upon increasing division of labor, it remains far less sophisticated than what Adam Smith had said on this topic.

lems have relevance for the second question I stated earlier, e.g., the question of the empirical relevance of Bücher's work for the better understanding of economic history.

Let us first discuss the concept of town economy.[48] Bücher himself acknowledges that this concept and the description of the town economy as a special form of economic organization were not original. He says that he derived the concept from an essay by G. Schönberg, and Below later showed that substantially the same ideas had been published even earlier by Hildebrand and others.[49] In fact, the general concept of town economy and the analysis of its main economic forms had become a matter of common acceptance in the German economics of the time, and the special contribution of Bücher consisted in having given concise and clear expression to this body of ideas.

Nor did the concept of the closed domestic economy originate with Bücher. As he himself states, he derived this idea from the work of Rodbertus, who had, however, used a different term—"*oikos* economy."[50]

48. The discussion in the remainder of this section may be considered by some readers to be a side issue. Instead of testing the direct analytical validity of Bücher's "theory" of economic growth, we are about to discuss his views on the town economy and primitive economic conditions. But since the study of secular economic growth has an important historical dimension, and some problems of economic development can be better understood if we are aware of the differences and similarities—such as exist—between modern advanced and quite primitive forms of economic organization and their accompanying socio-political structures, a theory which stresses these points is of value for a better understanding of economic growth, even if it does not center around the purely economic processes of growth in particular.

49. See Karl Bücher, "Erwiderung," *Jahrbücher für Gesetzgebung Verwaltung und Volkswirtschaft im Deutschen Reich,* XVIII, 1894, pp. 318-19; Georg von Below, *op.cit.,* pp. 4-6; Gustav Schönberg, "Zur wirtschaftlichen Bedeutung des deutschen Zunftwesens im Mittelalter," *Jahrbücher für Nationalökonomie und Statistik,* IX, 1867, pp. 13-14; and Bruno Hildebrand, "Zur Geschichte der deutschen Wollenindustrie," *ibid.,* VII, 1866, pp. 85-86.

50. Cf. Bücher, *Industrial Evolution,* p. 97; also his "Erwiderung," *loc. cit.* The issue of whether Bücher's contribution was original or not had been raised in a review of the first edition of *Entstehung der Volkswirtschaft,* which Gustav Schmoller published in the *Jahrbuch für Gesetzgebung Verwaltung und Volkswirtschaft im Deutschen Reich,* XVII, 1893, pp. 1259*ff.* Schmoller had cited some of his own earlier writings and complained because Bücher had not referred to them. Bücher's reply was that the distinction of having discovered the concept of town economy belonged neither to himself nor to Schmoller, but to Schönberg. Below later traced the idea back to the work of Hildebrand and Perthes. As to the concept of closed domestic economy, Bücher acknowledged having borrowed the term from an obscure work by an E. Becher, and the descriptive aspects of it from Rodbertus.

Schmoller's attack against Bücher's claim that he was the originator of the theory of three stages of domestic economy, town economy, and national economy, was not the only one. His authorship of the theory was called into question a second time when Johann Plenge, in "Wirtschaftsstufen und Wirtschaftsentwicklung" *(Annalen für soziale Politik und Gesetzgebung,* IV, 1916, pp. 495-529), again questioned Bücher's authorship of the theory and attributed its invention to Gustav Schönberg. Plenge proceeded by collecting a series of paragraphs from Schönberg's early essay on medieval guilds, "Zur wirtschaftlichen Bedeutung des deutschen Zunftwesens im Mittelalter," pp. 1-72, 97-169, and then showed that Schönberg had used in that essay the concepts later included in Bücher's theory, and that he had presented approximately similar characteristics for each of the three stages. Bücher replied to Plenge's criticism in a sharp rejoinder, to which Plenge again answered ("Zum Prioritätsstreit über die Theorie der Wirtschaftsstufen," *Annalen für soziale Politik und Gesetzgebung,* V, 1917, pp. 248-62). The most important and ultimately convincing arguments raised by Bücher against Plenge's claim are the following: Bücher says that "Schönberg was not conscious of the fact that he had the parts of a uniform sequence of stages before his

But what Bücher had omitted to state was that Rodbertus had not merely described the *oikos* economy rather extensively and regarded it as the dominant form of economic organization of antiquity, but that in doing so he had also made a contribution to bridging the theory of economic stages of Hildebrand and that of Bücher himself. In fact, in some ways Rodbertus' discussion contains insights, especially on the nature and role of money, which in the later theorizing on economic stages have again been lost.[51] The bridge that Rodbertus builds between the theory of stages stipulated by Hildebrand and his own concept of the *oikos* economy rests on two pillars: One is the role of the medium of exchange; the other is the over-all social organization characteristic of each economic stage. Whereas Hildebrand had argued that the sequence of barter economy, money economy, and credit economy are successive stages in the history of one people, Rodbertus preferred to regard this sequence as descriptive of the entire economic development of the western world. In this view, the first stage of a barter economy thus becomes coincident with the domestic or *oikos* economy; the second stage of money economy becomes coincident with the medieval and post-medieval phase of economic growth (i.e., with the town economy and the national economy); and the third stage of a credit economy is a system of the future.

In support of this interpretation, Rodbertus analyzes first the social function of the medium of exchange in the three economic stages.[52] In the barter economy, any object which serves as a generalized means of exchange is a commodity which is distinguished from others only by its more general acceptability. The characteristic type of such a medium of exchange in a barter economy is cattle or bars of metal—objects which have an immediate use value for their possessor. Even in classical antiquity, when money circulated in the form of gold and silver, its trans-

---

eyes. He only gave descriptions of various situations which he compared with one another. When later in his life he discussed economic stages in his treatise, he made reference to the theory of F. List and also mentioned the theory of stages presented by myself. This fact cannot be explained—as Plenge has done—that he did not remember the theory of his youth. He never had such a theory" (p. 253).

Plenge did not reply to these points. Gertrud Kalveram *(op.cit.*, pp. 107*ff.)* has again raised the problem of whether or not Schönberg developed an original theory of stages, and she comes to an affirmative answer. She also points out that the main distinction between Schönberg's and Bücher's procedure is that the former presented his stages in more detail and with a greater number of "characteristic" variables than did either Bücher or Schmoller. If Miss Kalveram's reasoning is accepted, it appears that Schönberg's stages are described more nearly as "real types," and Bücher's more nearly as "ideal types."

51. See Karl Rodbertus, "Zur Geschichte der römischen Tributsteuern seit Augustus," *Jahrbücher für Nationalökonomie und Statistik,* VIII, 1867, esp. p. 106, note 51 on pp. 400-403, and pp. 408*ff.*

52. It should be stressed that we are concerned with the *social* and not the *economic* function of money. This latter is identical in all three stages, i.e., money serves as a generalized means of exchange and a store of value. But the social function of money—and as we shall see later, the social function of other institutions, e.g., markets or their equivalents—may vary considerably, since it does not depend on the purely economic effect of that institution, but primarily upon the general attitude held with regard to it by the members of a society.

formation into objects of use was obvious and actually took place ofter In a money economy, the medium of exchange still has intrinsic valu but it performs primarily a monetary function. In other words, thoug metallic money may circulate in a barter economy, this is regarde merely as a temporary form taken on by a commodity whose primary us is to serve needs other than the facilitation of exchange transactions. I a money economy, on the contrary, the transformation of metallic mone into plate or other objects, and its withdrawal from its primary functio as a medium of exchange, is an exception. The commodity aspect o metallic money has been a primary function in the barter economy stag and has become a subsidiary function in the stage of the money economy In the stage of the credit economy, the intrinsic value of money has becom irrelevant altogether; money is merely a token which, however, preserve its value because its social acceptability makes it an object enjoying genera confidence. Money in this stage is an object whose sole use is its function a a carrier of purchasing power.[53]

But the social function of money, in turn, is determined by the over-al social organization of a society and the form of economic relations existin in it. In the *oikos* economy, the differentiation of social roles is less comple than in the more highly developed societies with a developed money econ omy. Rodbertus expresses this quite clearly when he says:

If we compare, for example, the general social basis of the two orders with on another we find that in the one, as a consequence of slavery, the production o raw materials, their processing, and, at first, even commerce, are combined i one and the same household and productive unit, and hence separate classes o landowners, capitalists, entrepreneurs, and even workers do not exist and d not meet on a market. On the contrary, we find in the other order that, as consequence of free labor and the division of productive processes amon different owners, the production of raw materials, the processing of materials and trade are each carried on independently. In this situation workers an landowners, manufacturers and entrepreneurs make lively use of, and, indeed build up, a market through the free interchange of their varied services an other contributions to the productive process.[54]

To be sure, there is exchange in a barter economy; the very designatio

53. Rodbertus' view on the changing social function of money was developed much earlier than his writings on agrarian conditions in ancient Rome. In his first major work, *Zur Erkenntnis unsrer staatswirtschaftlichen Zustände* (Neubrandenburg, 1842, pp. 147*ff.*), he discusses the various forms a medium of circulation can take, and distinguishes between money with intrinsic commodity value (e.g., gold and silver coins) and the money of the future, which is a mere token without intrinsic value. In the course of this discussion, he examines the historical development of money and provides an explanation which bears a striking similarity to the ideas whic Hildebrand later incorporated in his essa of 1864. Although Rodbertus never claime that Hildebrand's classification of stages i derived from his earlier discussion, the simi larities are so great as to lead one to assum that Hildebrand may have had Rodbertus earlier work in mind when he composed hi essay of 1864. If this were so, then Rodbertu would have to be regarded not only as th original source of inspiration for a part o Bücher's theory, but also of Hildebrand' theory of economic stages.

54. Rodbertus, *op.cit.*, p. 401.

of this economic stage indicates this. But although there is exchange, it is not mediated by an institution which has common social characteristics with the market of the later town or national economy. Given this interpretation of Rodbertus, a unifying principle is found by which a necessary association between a barter economy and a domestic economy is established, and the main problem which remains to be answered is whether this analysis is an adequate interpretation of the socio-economic relations of that period to which it was alleged to apply, i.e., classical antiquity, especially the Hellenistic and imperial Roman period.

Both Rodbertus and, following him, Bücher had answered this question in the affirmative, but there were a host of writers who did not. Chief among them were a group of social and economic historians, led by such distinguished figures as Eduard Meyer, Alfons Dopsch, M. I. Rostovtzeff, and R. von Pöhlmann.[55] The main issue raised by these critics of the Bücher-Rodbertus theory was based on their conception of the essential similarity between the economy of the ancient world and the present. Perhaps the most extreme assertion of the "modernity" of the ancient world was made by Rostovtzeff, when he said that the economy of the Hellenistic and early imperial Roman period "was only quantitatively, not qualitatively different from the modern economy. This is, for me, a fact."[56] Yet, I believe that ordinary reflection should convince one that, owing to the profound differences in social structure, economic performance, and technological advancement between the societies of antiquity and the modern west, any such statement must be rejected as extreme. Rostovtzeff asks whether or not some form of economic progress occurred during the four thousand years of ancient history. He finds that such progress did occur, and that in the course of time, institutions and forms of organization were developed which externally resembled those of modern Europe. This last argument must be contested. It cannot be denied that there was progress in antiquity, at least that there was growth in the absolute number of population, in absolute wealth, and in technological and economic knowledge. However, the question is whether the presence of progress in itself necessarily leads to an economy which, in its basic structural features, is identical or even closely similar to the modern one. The clearly implied meaning of the argument expressed by men like Dopsch, Meyer, and Rostovtzeff affirms this proposition. But I think that in view of the differences in eco-

55. Eduard Meyer, "Die wirtschaftliche Entwicklung des Altertums," *Jahrbücher für Nationalökonomie und Statistik*, LXIV, 1895, pp. 696-743; Dopsch, *op.cit.;* M. I. Rostovtzeff, "Review of Johannes Hasebroek, *Griechische Wirtschafts und Gesellschaftsgeschichte*," *Zeitschrift für die gesamte Staatswisserschaft*, XCII, 1932, pp. 333-39; and R. von Pöhlmann, *Geschichte der sozialen Frage und des Sozialismus in der antiken Welt*, Berlin, 1925. See also G. Salvioli, *Der Kapitalismus im Altertum*, Stuttgart, 1912. And see Bücher's reply to the attack by Eduard Meyer in his article, "Zur griechischen Wirtschaftsgeschichte," (1901), reprinted in Karl Bücher, *Beiträge zur Wirtschaftsgeschichte*, Jena, 1922, pp. 1*ff*.

56. Rostovtzeff, *op.cit.*, p. 335.

nomic performance, and because of the greatly reduced resilience of ancient societies to economic crises and other forms of adversity, this view cannot be upheld. It may be, of course, that the description of the economy of antiquity as a closed domestic economy, or an *oikos* economy, is too narrow. It certainly does not describe adequately the variety of economic institutions that existed in the second century A.D. But it may be a very appropriate description of an ideal type which, with only relatively slight modification and divergences, may be the characteristic form of economic organization of the ancient world.[57]

But whereas the criticism of one group of writers was confined to the interpretation of the nature of Greek and Roman society, another group of historians, notably Alfons Dopsch, attacked the theory as such. Dopsch's argument is that since money is a means of exchange, any theory which stipulates the absence of money implicitly also asserts that all economic units of which the society is made up are self-sufficient and pursue a policy of autarchy. Hence, the concept of *Naturalwirtschaft* designates a situation in which no exchange takes place and in which each unit produces all it consumes. Dopsch maintains that this view is based on purely contrived situations, and that there exists exchange, even on the "lowest levels of civilization." Moreover, once these very low levels of primitive culture are passed, we find no societies in which either money or some commodity which serves as money is absent, nor do we find that any economy is composed of fully self-sufficient entities which live altogether without trade.[58]

Dopsch's criticism is in part a battle against strawmen of his own making, and in part betrays an unwillingness to give due regard to the qualifications introduced by Bücher in his account. He presents Bücher's

57. The controversy betwen the adherents of the Bücher-Rodbertus theory and its opponents has been subjected recently to two separate treatments. A summary of the controversy is presented in Edouard Will, "Trois quarts de siècle de recherches sur l'économie grècque antique," *Annales*, IX, 1954, pp. 7-19; and in a paper by H. W. Pearson, "The Secular Debate on Economic Primitivism," in *Trade and Market in the Early Empires*, K. Polanyi, C. M. Arensberg, and H. W. Pearson, eds., Glencoe, 1957, pp. 1-11. (See also the evaluation of the "*oikos* controbersy" by Max Weber, *Gesammelte Aufsätze zur Sozial- und Wirtschaftsgeschichte*, Tübingen, 1924, esp. pp. 8-12, 31-33.) The essay by Will contains a large number of footnote references to the pertinent literature. Will summarizes his discussion by characterizing the Greek economy as follows: "A socio-political structure oriented inward to a city, based ultimately on an essentially agricultural economy, and limited to an archaic handicraft production for the satisfaction of restricted needs. The growth of the city makes foreign commerce necessary in order to meet the needs of the *trophé*, and secondly (but concurrently) of the fisc. This produces an indispensable category of persons with the cosmopolitan outward orientation antagonistic to the basic archaic tendencies. The volume, complexity, and extension of this trade was very modest at the outset, but grew progressively, yet remained always extremely limited in comparison to our modern conceptions" (p. 19). Although this characterization seems on first blush to be a position in the "golden middle" between the two extremes, it lends considerable support to the interpretation by Bücher and Rodbertus, rather than the modernist view, since it stresses the predominantly agricultural and handicraft character of the Greek economy and the relatively limited scope of trade.

58. See Dopsch, *op.cit., passim,* but esp. chaps. 1 and 2.

theory in an extreme and absurd fashion. Moreover, Dopsch's work betrays his own weakness as a theorist, especially his inability to draw theoretical conclusions from the data which he himself adduces.[59] One example must suffice. In one place, Dopsch shows that throughout the Middle Ages many magnates paid their officials, in large part, not in money but *in natura,* i.e., by allocation of houses and the supply of food and other goods. He attributes this not to the scarcity of money, but to the fact that these lords owned large estates with houses on them, and that, moreover, these estates produced the food and other materials assigned as wages to the officials. Hence, he argues that under the conditions then prevailing, this form of payment without money was more economical, since the profit of the middleman was eliminated.[60] Dopsch is unaware that this argument defeats the core of his main thesis. The reason why this was a mutually beneficial form of remuneration in the early Middle Ages was due precisely to the absence of markets as institutions mediating exchange and because of the prevalence of a system of domestic economy. His confusion between domestic economy and economy without exchange *(Eigenwirtschaft),* and his over-simplified interpretation of the social function of money have misled him. There is no reason why ideal-typically, a system of domestic economy may not contain some exchange operations and have an object which performs monetary functions. Only someone who caricatures a theory can arrive at the critical conclusions Dopsch reached.[61]

IV

Although these attacks were directed chiefly against Bücher's formulation of economic stages, most of the criticism, as well as the praise, also applied to Schmoller's series of economic stages. For the two series were very similar, and their distinctive mark was not so much one of kind as of emphasis. I have already referred to the controversy between the two men regarding the question of who was entitled to the claim of priority with

59. This weakness of Dopsch was already castigated sharply and, in my opinion, quite accurately by Sombart with reference to Dopsch's *Die Wirtschaftsentwicklung der Karolingerzeit* (Weimar, 2 vols., 1912-1913); cf. Sombart, *Der Modern Kapitalismus,* Munich, 5th ed., 1922, I, pp. 53-55.

60. Dopsch, *Naturalwirtschaft und Geldwirtschaft in der Weltgeschichte,* pp. 253-54.

61. Dopsch's theoretical naivete is evidenced, moreover, by the argument *(ibid.,* p. 254) that the medieval system of payment in kind is identical with the truck system. But whereas, under the conditions prevailing in the middle ages, payment in kind was preferred by both parties, precisely because of the absence of organized markets, the truck system, to the extent to which it was practiced in economics in which well-developed markets were functioning, was not a mutually beneficial institution, but a means of exploitation of the worker. Hence, the two systems have only a superficial similarity and are basically different in their socio-economic role.

respect to the nomenclature employed in the sequence of stages. Schmoller's presentation, which was first published in 1884 and appears in more final form in his *Grundriss der allgemeinen Volkswirtschaftslehre,* includes the following five stages: village economy, town economy, territorial economy, national economy, and world economy.[62] In view of the similarity of the two classifications, it would be idle to enter into a lengthy critical analysis of Schmoller's point of view. Only three brief comments are in order at this time.

First, the classification of economic stages presented by Schmoller is clearly derived from the economic history of Germany. Whereas Bücher's stages, as he himself said, could be made applicable at least to Western and Central Europe, the validity of Schmoller's stages is even more limited.

Second, as can be seen from the labels of Schmoller's other stages, his village economy corresponds roughly to Bücher's closed domestic economy; as for the rest, he interposes the territorial economy between the town and the national economy and adds the stage of world economy at the end. Now, the problem which was, and could be, much discussed is whether Bücher's term, "domestic economy," is preferable to Schmoller's term, "village economy," and whether there is a separate niche for the territorial economy within the framework of the classification. If the stages are regarded as ideal types, or logical constructs, the particular form does not matter. It is different, however, if these stages are regarded as realistic descriptions, or even schematizations of actual historical periods of economic development. This same observation holds for the desirability of interposing the stage of territorial economy. Bücher's divergence from Schmoller on these points appears to me to be an indication of a difference in scientific approach. For Bücher, the strict historical relevance of the various categories was less important than their explanatory analytical content. But Schmoller made the obverse evaluation.

This interpretation also appears to conform to the third observation to be made about Schmoller's system. His general methodological approach to economics stressed the exposition of the historical development of economic institutions, rather than the deductive analysis of economic relations and an attempt to relate the principles so gained to empirical reality.[63] In view of Schmoller's preference for the historical approach, it is not difficult to see why he would regard his stages as schematic descriptions of episodes in the economic development of a society, rather than as logical categories

---

62. See Gustav Schmoller, *The Mercantile System* (a translation of a chapter from "Studien über die wirtschaftliche Politik Friedrich's des Grossen," first published in 1884), W. J. Ashley, ed. and trans., New York, 1895, pp. 3-6. For the later and more extensive exposition, see Gustav Schmoller, *Grundriss der algemeinen Volkswirtschaftslehre,* Leipzig, 1904, II, pp. 1126-31.

63. On Schmoller's method, particularly on his opinions with respect to analytical economics, see Schumpeter, *op.cit.,* pp. 809-15.

of forms of economic organization which could be subjected to comparative analysis.

The contrast between Bücher's and Schmoller's interpretation of the validity of economic stages consists less in the particular structure of the classification itself, but rather in the use to which economic stages are to be put. Whereas Schmoller saw in them cross-sections at various crucial intervals in the description of a historical process, Bücher saw in them patterns of characteristic forms of economic organization which, on the whole, were connected with one another by forming links in a chain of historical development. For Schmoller, the description of a process of historical development stood in the foreground; for Bücher, the comparison of economic relations on different levels of the developmental scale was of primary importance.[64]

The comparative use of economic stages was stressed increasingly by later authors. In fact, in Arthur Spiethoff's attempt to reinterpret the methodological foundation of theories of stages, the usefulness of economic stages —or "economic styles," as he prefers to call them—for comparison is stressed, above all.[65]

In the remainder of this paper, I shall try to trace briefly the development from Bücher's stages, by way of Sombart's "economic systems," to Spiethoff's "economic styles." As Lane and Riemersma point out in their introduction to Spiethoff's paper on the methodology of economic stages, which they include in their collection of economic essays on *Enterprise and Secular Change*,[66] in more recent work the theory of stages was intended to serve in the attempt to build a bridge between dynamic theory and economic history. In its most recent phase, this trend of analysis has led to such products as the essay by Bowman and Anderson on economic "types," which is introduced by the proposition that "by taking a comparative view of the world's economies we may gain fresh perspectives on the potentialities and limitations of modern economic theory and upon some of the points at which economic theory and history are mutually dependent." And in the summary of this paper, the observation is made that "while the . . . typology is not focused upon change, it contains many dynamic elements . . . [and] a whole set of hypotheses concerning eco-

---

64. This viewpoint is expressed with special emphasis in Karl Bücher, Volkswirtschaftliche Entwicklungsstufen," *Grundriss der Sozialökonomie*, Tübingen, 1924, I, Part I, esp. pp. 6, 17-18.

65. See Arthur Spiethoff, "Die allgemeine Volkswirtschaftslehre als geschichtliche Theorie: Die Wirtschaftsstile," *Schmollers Jahrbuch*, LVI, 1932, pp. 51-84; and *idem*, "Anschauliche und reine volkswirtschaftliche Theorie und ihr Verhältnis zueinander," in *Synopsis*, Edgar Salin, ed., Heidelberg, n.d., pp. 567-644. Parts of this last essay appeared in English translation under the title, "Pure Theory and Economic Gestalt Theory: Ideal Types and Real Types," in *Enterprise and Secular Change*, F. C. Lane and J. C. Riemersma, eds., Homewood, Ill., 1955, pp. 444-63.

66. See Lane and Riemersma, *op.cit.*, pp. 440-43.

nomic change may be derived from a comparison of observed associations of traits within these types."[67]

V

We have seen that throughout the work of Bücher and Schmoller a certain ambiguity prevailed as to whether the empirical-historical or the analytical-logical aspects of the stages were to be stressed. Unfortunately, this confusion was not resolved when Werner Sombart entered the field with his own theory of economic stages. Sombart tried to clear the ground for a new approach by distinguishing between economic stages *(Wirtschaftsstufen),* economic systems *(Wirtschaftssysteme),* and principles of economic activity *(Wirtschaftsprinzipien).* But instead of presenting a classification based upon distinctive principles of categorization, he combines the three series into a uniform one and assigns certain economic systems to particular economic stages, as well as to particular principles of economic activity. However, on the surface, economic stages and principles of economic activity do not overlap fully, so that a certain ambiguity in Sombart's classification results.[68]

In order to resolve this problem, let us follow Sombart's principles of classification. In order to find a *principium divisionis,* he attempts to find a phenomenon which has the following properties: it must be (a) a social phenomenon which permits (b) the comparison of various forms of economic organization, but which at the same time is (c) closely related to the most important fact of economic life, the development of productivity, and which also (d) most closely approximates the factual historical development of economic life. Sombart finds such criteria in the degree of social interaction *(Vergesellschaftung)* and concludes that there are three economic stages, depending upon the degree of social interaction. He calls the three stages individual economy, transitional economy, and social economy. The first is very close to Bücher's concept of the closed domestic economy. As Sombart explains, it is a stage in which social interaction exists primarily within a household, and in which only slight contact, rather than really full interaction, occurs with other economically active units. The transitional stage is one in which the total needs of a society are met through the cooperation of all members of that society, but where the degree of this interaction is still limited. In other words, the transitional

67. Mary Jean Bowman and C. Arnold Anderson, "Wirtschaftstypen," *Schmollers Jahrbuch,* LXXV, 1955, pp. 514, 532-33. I am citing from an English version circulated by the authors in mimeographed form.

68. See Sombart, "Gewerbliche Arbeit," *loc. cit.,* p. 402. For a discussion of the "economic stages," see *ibid.,* pp. 390-93, and for a discussion of "principles of economic activity," *ibid.,* pp. 395-96.

economy is a mixed stage in which part of the needs are met by individual production of each unit on its own and part by exchange with others. Finally, the social economy is a stage in which all needs are met by interaction with others. In other words, in the first stage of individual economy, the general principle is self-sufficiency of each household or similar unit. Some exchange exists in the transitional economy, but a considerable part of a household's needs are met by its own production; and in the social economy, division of labor has progressed to such a degree that each consumptive and productive unit is, in principle, dependent upon its becoming integrated into the society as a whole.

The economic systems which Sombart lists are merely examples of the concrete institutional arrangements that correspond to each of these three stages. For example, for the stage of individual economy, Sombart lists tribal economies, economies of large joint families, and so-called extended self-sufficient economies *(erweiterte Eigenwirtschaften),* of which the *oikos* is the best example. For the stage of transitional economies, Sombart lists the medieval manor, the village economy, and the town economy. For the third stage of social economy, he lists the slave economy of antiquity, the slave economy in modern colonial empires, the capitalist economy, and the socialist economy. From these examples it is clear that Sombart's economic stages were not designed to trace a uniform line of historical development. The ancient slave economy occurs in the third stage, and the medieval manor and the town economy occur in the second stage. Moreover, there does not seem to be a clearly corresponding second stage to the transition from the *oikos* economy (which is in the first stage) to the antique slave economy (which is in the third stage). With the inclusion of the ancient slave economy among economies in the third stage of "social economy," Sombart has, moreover, straddled the fence which involved Bücher in a dispute with Meyer and other historians on the nature of the economic system of antiquity and the degree of its "modernity."

Although Sombart's classification of stages appears to avoid some of the difficulties of earlier systems, it really does not push our insight much further. It is clear that one crucial problem is the extent of meaning of the concept of social interaction *(Vergesellschaftung).* In what sense is it true that the economic life of a primitive tribe is based on less social interaction than that of a modern capitalist society? On the one hand, the number of individuals involved in the process of interaction under capitalism is much larger than it is in the primitive tribe, and they are engaged in more diverse occupations. On the other hand, in their productive activity primitives are usually much more closely tied to the other members of their society than are economic actors in the relatively anonymous capitalist economy, although this tie exerts its effect mainly through magic and ceremonial, rather than rational, division of labor. Thus, the level of *Vergesellschaftung* is either inapplicable as a means of distinguishing between different economic stages, or becomes an indicator of the degree of economic specialization, commercialization of the economy, and division of labor. In this form, however, Sombart's theory would not be an advance over that of Bücher, though some specific distinctions would be spelled out more clearly and some characteristic variables defined more precisely.

But Sombart complicates his picture of economic stages by superimposing upon them his differentiation of principles of economic activity. He distinguishes two principles, which recur again in his later work. These principles, which in one place Sombart compares with the *Leitmotiv* of an economy, center around the main conscious purpose of productive activity. If production is carried on for the sake of satisfaction of needs, that is one thing; if it is carried on for the sake of gain as an end in itself, it is another thing.[69] Sombart distinguishes, therefore, between the principle of subsistence *(Idee der Nahrung)* and the principle of acquisition. The principle of subsistence characterizes the first two economic stages, i.e., the stages of individual economy and of transitional economy. With one exception—the socialist economy—the stage of social economy is dominated by the principle of acquisition. Although the socialist economy is clearly an economy belonging to the third stage of economies, with fully developed social interaction, its guiding principle is not acquisition, but the satisfaction of needs.

Although we cannot go into this aspect of the theory too deeply, it appears that in Sombart's reasoning two strands of historical economic and evolutionary theories have been welded together. One strand stems from the German historical school, and the other from Marxism. I have already pointed out that Sombart's three stages are essentially repetitions of Bücher's stages. However, whereas Bücher based his division on the interaction between consumer and producer, Sombart tries to "generalize" this principle of categorization by replacing it with the degree of *Vergesellschaftung*. This substitution of a more general principle is in itself a hint of Marxian influence. But the combination of economic stages and economic principles in Sombart's schema results in a dialectical sequence which, if not in content, certainly in spirit, is derived from the work of Karl Marx. As is well known, Marx regarded the history of human social development as a great dialectical process. For him, the world-historical triad was an initial stage of primitive communism, in which the producer is also the owner of the means of production, and in which, because of the low level of technological development, exploitation of man by man is

69. Cf. Sombart, "Gewerbliche Arbeit," *loc. cit.*, pp. 394-95. See also Sombart, *Der Moderne Kapitalismus*, I, *passim*, esp. pp. 14, 31*ff.*, 320, 327-30.

absent; hence no surplus value is available and no one can exploit anyone. This stage is replaced by the next stage, in which society is divided into classes: The worker is separated from the means of production and exploited under different forms (i.e., as a slave in antiquity, a serf in the medieval economy, and a salaried free proletarian under modern capitalism). The next step in the triad is the future socialist society, in which the highly developed productivity made possible under capitalism is combined again with the socialization of the means of production and the abolition of exploitation, and, hence, of social classes.[70]

Compare this schema with Sombart's. The first stage is the individual economy under the principle of subsistence. This gradually changes and is replaced by the transitional economy, still under the system of subsistence. But the latest "economic system" in the transitional stage is the town economy, in which manifold forms of the principle of acquisition begin to manifest themselves. This is finally replaced by the third stage, capitalism, a social economy under the principle of acquisition. And this, in turn, ultimately leads to a fully socialized economy under the principle of subsistence (or rather, satisfaction of needs); and that is socialism. The evolutionary processes are parallel, except that Sombart is somewhat less schematic than Marx and interposes the transitional stage, which corresponds roughly to the pre-capitalist forms of class societies of Marx.

In reality, Sombart's classification is also a grand evolutionary scheme of forms of socio-economic organization, and his claim that he presents comparative types, rather than a historical chain of economic stages, is supported more by the manner of his presentation than by the content of his discussion. Nevertheless, there are two aspects of Sombart's theory which constitute an innovation and which were, on the whole, overlooked by Sombart's critics and interpreters. One is his insistence on the principle of *Vergesellschaftung;* the other is his introduction of the concept of motivation of economic activity as an important aspect of an economic stage or system. In this way, Sombart lifted the discussion of economic stages from the realm of purely economic—and even purely economic-historical —analysis and placed it into a general sociological and socio-psychological framework. To be sure, the particular use he made of the principle of *Vergesellschaftung* was rather barren, as I believe I showed earlier, but in spite of its clumsiness, it contains one important kernel of insight. Sombart recognized clearly that any significant exposition of economic development by means of economic stages must regard these stages not merely as forms of economic organization, but rather as forms of social

70. A good summary of this schema is presented by Sombart himself. Cf. "Gewerbliche Arbeit," *loc.cit.*, pp. 379-82, esp. p. 380. But see also J. L. Gray, "Karl Marx and Social Philosophy," in *The Social and Political Ideas of Some Representative Thinkers of the Victorian Age*, F. J. C. Hearnshaw, ed., London, 1933, pp. 116-50, esp. pp. 135-38.

organization with different economic facets. An economic stage is significant, not because it describes different forms of economic behavior, but because it relates these forms of behavior to differences in social structure and socially relevant motivations. Thus, Sombart broadened the meaning of economic stages considerably, but the full implications of this remained largely unrecognized until recent years, when attention was drawn to this aspect of the theory.[71]

On the basis of the analysis of Sombart's system of economic stages presented so far, it should not be difficult to derive his view on the mechanism of the transition from one stage to the next. In his essay of 1899 Sombart paid little attention to that problem, but he explained this point at length in his later work on the development and growth of capitalism. We shall see that if this later analysis is applied to his classification of economic stages and their combination with economic systems and principles of economic activity, certain difficulties arise which point up the basic weakness of Sombart's scheme. In fact, we may assume that Sombart's exposition of an allegedly universal system of stages was a *tour de force,* which he undertook quite gratuitously while he was at work on his book on capitalism. What really mattered to him was an explanation of the rise of capitalism, and his analysis of transition from one stage to the next applies with full force only to the transition from the predominantly subsistence-oriented town economy to the acquisition-oriented capitalist economy. The difficulty in Sombart's general scheme of 1899 arises because, according to that scheme, another analogous transition must have taken place in antiquity, i.e., a transition from the subsistence-oriented *oikos* economy to the acquisition-oriented slave economy. Whereas Sombart presents an extensive discussion of the origin of capitalism, he completely omits any further discussion of the parallel process in antiquity. This may be interpreted either as his having given up his original system of economic stages, or as his having given up the designation of the ancient slave economy as one based on the principle of acquisition. But whatever may have been Sombart's intention, the fact that he never seriously returned to the problem of economic stages and never again took up the analysis of economic conditions of antiquity, but continued to write extensively on capitalism and its origins, entitles us to assume that the only important aspect of economic stages for him, like List and most others, was the explanation of the rise of modern capitalist economy and the reasons for its differences from all earlier forms of economic activity.

If the problem of Sombart's explanation of the forces determining the

71. See, for example, Bowman and Anderson, *op.cit.;* and my essays, "Social Structure and Economic Growth," *Economia Internazionale,* VI, 1953, pp. 52-72, and "Sociological Approach to Economic Development," *Atti del Congresso Internazionale di Studio sul Problema della Aree Arretrate,* Milan, 1955, II, pp. 755-78.

transition from the medieval "town economy" to the modern capitalist economy is posed in these terms, the answer becomes very simple. Since the earlier economic system is dominated by the principle of subsistence, and the later is dominated by the principle of acquisition, the major force in the development of this new stage of economic organization was a change in economic motivation. This is stated plainly by Sombart himself:

> Capitalism grew out of the deepest foundation of the European soul. The same spirit out of which was born the new state and the new religion, the new science and the new technology, also created the new economy. . . . This spirit which now begins to dominate economic life breaks through the barriers of a subsistence economy based on the quiet self-sufficiency of stationary, feudal-handicraft conditions of equilibrium. It drives men into the turmoil of an acquisitive economy.[72]

And in another place he summarizes his description of the development of this new spirit: "This new psychological state *(Seelenstimmung),* woven together of the bourgeois spirit and the entrepreneurial spirit, I call the capitalist spirit. It has created capitalism."[73] Sombart recognizes that such a categorical statement requires a twofold explanation. In the first place, it demands a detailed explanation of the derivation of the capitalist spirit from an earlier "spirit" or economic ethic; in the second place, it requires a clarification of whether an economic ideology can be regarded as determining the form of economic organization, or vice versa. Sombart is aware that in making the development of the capitalist spirit the ultimately determining influence of the development of capitalism, he is expressing an opinion diametrically opposed to historical materialism. His explanation of the process by which the spirit of capitalism evolved and why it should be regarded as determining the "material conditions of production" must, therefore, be understood not as an explanation of a social process as such, but primarily as a polemic against Marxism, and especially the Marxist interpretation of history.

It would lead us too far from the central core of this essay to follow Sombart's excursion into the field of the philosophy of history. His most pertinent remarks are contained in a book which he devoted to the sociological and historical analysis of the capitalist spirit and economic motivation in an acquisitive economy, as against a subsistence economy.[74] The very fact that Sombart's theory of historical development did not evoke very widespread attention is testimony to the fact that it may be regarded as the outcropping of a mind which was very well characterized by Schum-

72. Sombart, *Der Moderne Kapitalismus,* I, pp. 327-28.

73. *Ibid.*, p. 329.

74. Werner Sombart, *The Quintessence of Capitalism,* London, 1917. The German title of this book is *Der Bourgeois* (Munich, 1913); this title is more indicative of its content and general approach than the English title.

peter when he said that "Sombart's 'methodological' pronouncements followed fashion too closely to be interesting."[75]

What is more important for us, in the context of this essay, is that Sombart's interpretation of the transition from one stage to the next also requires the intervention of a *deus ex machina,* in this case, the alteration of an economic ideology. But since the relation between an economic ethic and the actual form of economic organization of a given economic stage is rather tenuous, and the interdependence of changes in the one and the other is left almost entirely unexplained, the usefulness of Sombart's contribution lies neither in his substantive assertions, nor even in his method. It lies chiefly in the fact that he insisted—as List and Bücher, and even Schmoller, had done before him, though much less forcefully and persuasively—that the full significance of the use of economic stages as a device to study economic development hinges upon the interrelation of forms of economic organization with corresponding socio-structural and political factors, and perhaps also with prevailing tendencies in economic motivation. But a full-fledged social theory which reveals this interdependence is still lacking.

VI

Sombart presented his theory of economic stages in an article which appeared in 1899. Although this particular date is accidental, it has an almost symbolic meaning, for with the end of the nineteenth century, there was also an end to the setting up of grandiose schemes of economic stages covering explicitly, or by implication, all human history and all forms of human culture. The work done in the twentieth century in the general realm of theorizing about economic stages was chiefly a continuation of the attempt to evaluate the empirical relevance of a given economic stage with historical or cultural reality and of the methodological dispute regarding the role of economic stages in the theory of economic growth. In addition, an attempt was made to classify different economies, not as representatives of various stages of development, but rather as entities described by some quantifiable magnitudes. I shall take up these three topics in the order presented.

There is little to be added to the first topic. I have already mentioned the debate on the degree of modernity of the economic institutions and form of economic organization of antiquity, which has been designated by

75. Schumpeter, *op.cit.*, p. 815. See also Schumpeter's general evaluation of Sombart's contribution to the study of capitalism, *ibid.*

some as the "*oikos* controversy." Other attemps to correlate the classifications of the stage theorists with long-run historical development were made by H. Spangenberg, who studied the German Middle Ages and the applicability of the concepts of town economy and territorial economy as descriptive labels for the economies of that period, and by Hans Geiss, who studied the usefulness of the dichotomy between natural and money economy for the economy of the early Middle Ages in Italy.[76] These monographs are perhaps the two ablest of a whole series of dissertations and journal articles which appeared on related topics in Germany during the 1920's and 1930's. Many of these works bring together valuable factual material, but on the whole, they neither confirm nor fully discount the sequence of stages they purport to analyze.

Another event which caused a widespread revival of interest in the validity of the classification proposed by Bücher, Schmoller, and Hildebrand was the publication of Dopsch's work on barter and money economy. In 1930, when this book appeared, Dopsch was at the peak of his reputation. It was inevitable that his work should be discussed and reviewed widely, and some of the most distinguished economic historians of the time participated in the discussion initiated by its appearance. Among the scholars who expressed opinions in this debate were Hans van Werveke, Henri Sée, Henri Hauser, Otto Hintze, Eli Heckscher, and Marc Bloch.[77] The general upshot of this discussion was a final re-evaluation of the usefulness of the concepts of barter economy and money economy, and a final determination of the historical conditions under which one or the other system may be said to have been in existence. Thus, although the general conclusion is reached that it is difficult, if not impossible, to find a pure barter economy, without any commodity which performs a monetary function, and that it is equally difficult to find a pure money economy in which no exchanges or payments *in natura* are performed, and although the claim of Dopsch as to the general prevalence of mixed systems is maintained, the extreme conclusions which Dopsch drew from this are rejected. For Dopsch had argued that, because of the mixture of monetary transactions and transactions in kind, the distinction of economic stages is false and misleading, from the point of view of economic history. Notwithstanding

---

76. H. Spangenberg, *Territorialwirtschaft und Stadtwirtschaft*, Munich, 1932; Hans Geiss, *Geld- und naturalwirtschaftliche Erscheinungsformen im staatlichen Aufbau Italiens während der Gotenzeit*, Stuttgart, 1931.

77. See Hans van Werveke, "Economie-Nature et Economie-Argent: Une discussion," *Annales d'histoire économique et sociale*, III, 1931, pp. 428-35; Henri Sée, "Review of Alfons Dopsch, *Naturalwirtschaft und Geldwirtschaft in der Weltgeschichte*," *Economic History Review*, IV, 1932-34, pp. 359-60; Henri Hauser, "Review of Alfons Dopsch, *Naturalwirtschaft . . . etc.*," *Révue Critique*, XCVII, 1930, pp. 476-78; Otto Hintze, "Review of Alfons Dopsch, *Naturalwirtschaft . . . etc.*," *Historische Zeitschrift*, CXLIII, 1931, pp. 524-27; Eli Heckscher, *op.cit.*, pp. 1-29; and Marc Bloch, "Les classifications économiques à la lumière des faits suédois," *Annales d'histoire économique et sociale*, III, 1931, pp. 435-40.

their agreement with much of Dopsch's factual account, his critics, notably van Werveke and Hintze, consider that this does not rob the theory of economic stages of its value in providing a framework for the analysis of economic history and economic growth. This point of view has been expressed most clearly perhaps by Hintze. He says, with regard to such stages as barter economy, domestic economy, money economy, and others:

They are not supposed to be adequate expressions for a historical reality, but heuristic principles, means of orienting research, and yardsticks for scientific judgments. It is, of course, a coarse methodological mistake if one uses them simply for the description of historical reality of an entire epoch. But this is not done, as a rule, and an epoch in economic history is only characterized *a posteriori*, depending upon the prevalence of barter or forms of money economy, or depending upon the degree of importance which a self-sufficient domestic economy has in a more or less developed system of exchange based on full social interaction.[78]

The very fact that this controversy as to the possible role of economic stages in historical interpretation could occur as late as the 1930's is evidence of the lack of intercommunication between history and the other social sciences. Even in Germany, where the historical approach in economics and sociology was so popular, especially in the period before 1914, the basic methodological reflections on the use of economic stages as ideal types in historical analysis, which derive ultimately from the work of Max Weber, found widely differing interpretations.[79] Although Weber had explicitly shown the applicability of ideal-type constructs for the analysis

78. Hintze, *op.cit.*, p. 525.

79. The classic exposition of the use of ideal-type constructs is Max Weber's essay on "Objectivity in Social Science and Social Policy," which was first published in 1904 and has been included in Max Weber, *The Methodology of the Social Sciences*, Glencoe, Ill., 1949, pp. 90*ff*. (This book will be cited hereinafter as *Methodology.)* In this essay, Weber makes explicit allusion to the town economy and designates it as an example of an ideal type. There is reason to believe that Bücher's own conception of his stages is very similar to the explanation given by Weber. This assumption comes from Bücher's statement in the preface to the second German edition of *Die Entstehung der Volkswirtschaft*, in which he says, with special reference to the two chapters containing his theory of economic stages, that "this work treats of economic theory, not of economic history. . . . In the first edition I expressed myself clearly enough, I think, regarding the *logical* character of the economic stages. In the present edition I have taken occasion, however, to give the passages in question such a form that in the future they cannot with good intentions be misunderstood." (*Industrial Evolution*, p. x [italics added].)

This argument was overlooked by most critics from the point of view of history. But Bücher's point was taken up by Below, who argued against this interpretation that whatever may have been the intention of Bücher, his stages imply a historical sequence of events, i.e., a more or less unbroken succession of stages (Below, *op.cit.*, pp. 22-24). In fact, Bücher's actual treatment of stages is somewhat ambiguous. When he mentions them explicitly, he designates them as logical constructs, but in the course of his essay, he treats them—as Below rightly recognizes—as focal points in a unilinear historical evolution. Moreover, he says in one place that he wishes to "divide the whole course of economic development, at least for the peoples of central and western Europe . . . into three stages"; and in another place, he writes of the "historical succession of industrial systems" (*Industrial Evolution*, pp. 89, 154). This manner of presentation may easily lead to misunderstanding.

After the end of the First World War, Weber's methodological teaching had, however, made sufficient headway among German social scientists, and gradually also among

of general theoretical relations in social science, as well as for historical reconstructions, there was still some doubt as to whether Spangenberg's opinion could be upheld that "economic history owes to the historical school of German economics the important methodological tool of measuring and representing the manifold phenomena of economic life by means of the construction of economic stages," or whether economic stages should be regarded as units in a comparative economic theory, as Johann Plenge had proposed.[80]

An attempt to resolve this problem once and for all, by using a "synthetic" approach, was made by Franz Oppenheimer.[81] Oppenheimer's approach is synthetic in two respects. On the one hand, he combines the stage theories of Hildebrand, Bücher, and Schmoller, and adds a fourth "dimension" of his own based on gradually more complex forms of the division of labor. On the other hand, he states explicitly that, starting from the standpoint of economic theory, he will construct ideal types, in order to show the "general evolution of a social economy undisturbed by political forces," so that the economic historian may recognize which "facts of the actual historical trend of development must be regarded as disturbances, abnormalities, or retarding forces." But Oppenheimer admits that, even then, any one of the ideal types cannot be found to have existed as a universal form of economic activity during any given stage, but that "earlier" and "later" stages can, and do, coexist. For example, the designation, "town economy," merely means that during a certain period, an economic system predominated which was characterized by the prevalence of artisan production; direct producer-client relations in exchange; the use of coined metallic money; and a division of labor according to occupations, but not yet with specialization within occupational groups. This form of economic organization coexisted with other, earlier forms, e.g., the village economy. but it "outshone all the others."[82]

Oppenheimer's approach, unfortunately, contributes as little to the solution of the problem as did Bücher's, since it suffers from the same ambiguity. Like Bücher, Oppenheimer states at the outset that he is interested in economic theory, in ideal types, presumably for comparative purposes, but, like Bücher, he treats his stages as more or less accurate

others, so that the interpretation of economic stages as ideal types was quite generally accepted, and only some diehards refused to concede this viewpoint. Among those who had given currency to Weber's views on method in the social sciences was, above all, Alexander von Schelting. Cf. his "Die logische Theorie der historischen Kulturwissenschaft von Max Weber und im besonderen sein Begriff des Idealtypus," *Archiv für Sozialwissenschaft und Sozialpolitik*, XLIX, 1922, pp. 701-26. Cf. also the Foreword by Edward A. Shils to the American edition of Weber's *Methodology*, pp. iii-x.

80. See Spangenberg, *op.cit.*, p. 1; and Johann Plenge, "Grundlegung der vergleichenden Wirtschaftstheorie," *Annalen für soziale Politik und Gesetzgebung*, V, 1917, pp. 52*ff*.

81. Franz Oppenheimer, *System der Soziologie*, Jena, 1923, III, Part I, pp. 275-300.

82. *Ibid.*, pp. 277, 300.

descriptions of a historical general trend of economic evolution. Though his stages are "multidimensional," whereas those of his predecessors (save, perhaps, Sombart) were "uni-dimensional," his treatment is not a real advance, substantively or methodologically, beyond Sombart's. The combination of several strands in a composite or synthetic picture is no substitute for genuine progress in scientific method, or for more accurate insights into social reality.

VII

Economists have, on the whole, seen little usefulness in the various theories of economic stages. They have listed the concepts of men like List, Hildebrand, Bücher, and Schmoller, but have regarded them as either aberrations or curious classifications which have little importance for economic analysis. Even J. A. Schumpeter, an economist with great sympathy for history, considers the use of economic stages "most primitive."[83]

The question of the usefulness of the economic stage approach as a bridge between economic history and economic theory has been raised several times in the last thirty years. Since each economic stage may be regarded as describing an economy in the neighborhood of an equilibrium position, the question was raised as to whether the analysis of economic development by means of stipulated economic stages may provide us with a model whereby the variables leading to successive levels of economic advancement may be described. Clearly, the stages stipulated by List and his followers do not lend themselves to such a task, since the major difference in the stages postulated by the members of the German historical school consists in institutional and other noneconomic arrangements, rather than in different combinations of economic variables. Therefore, Giersch is correct when he says that the stage approach of the German historical school is of little value for the study of economic growth, especially in societies whose basic institutions are assumed to be constant.[84] But although most writers of the German historical school hoped to be able to provide an explanation for the secular development of economies by means of the stage approach, they were aware that the process of growth that occurred within one stage required a different type of analysis. Hence, they soon recognized that any model of stages could be applied, not so much to the study of dynamic equilibrium within an economy in which the basic institutional framework was considered to be constant, but rather to

83. Schumpeter, *op.cit.*, p. 442.

84. Herbert Giersch, "Stages and Spurts of Economic Development," in *Economic Progress*, Leon H. Dupriez, ed., Louvain, 1955, p. 194.

the study of the alteration of the institutional, i.e., socio-political, framework within which an economy operated.

For this reason, such theories as that formulated by Predöhl of the phases or periods of capitalist development, or that of Walter Hoffmann of stages of industrialization, or even a narrower interpretation of Colin Clark's view of changing patterns of occupational distribution of the working population, have different objectives from the theories of stages promulgated by earlier writers.[85]

Predöhl is concerned mainly with an empirical description of the expansion of capitalist industry over the world and a subsequent creation of several industrial "gravitation fields"; Hoffmann's work centers on the empirical determination of different weights assignable to consumers and capital goods industries at different periods of maturity of industrial societies. Although neither Predöhl nor Hoffman give explicit attention to the institutional framework, it is clear from the context of their writings that they are concerned only with processes of growth in what List would call the agricultural-industrial-commercial stage, or what Bücher would have designated as the stage of national economy. Hence, the more recent theories of Predöhl and Hoffmann are not stage theories in the sense of the nineteenth-century writers and, whatever their merit for a better understanding of growth processes within industrial societies, they do not throw any light on the problem of how a pre-industrial or nonindustrial society becomes industrialized, a problem which, as we have seen, stood at the center of interest of the older theories and still forms a major aspect of the theorizing on economic growth.[86]

In contrast to the work of Hoffmann and Predöhl, Spiethoff attempted to rehabilitate the theory of stages from the viewpoint of economic history.[87] These writings are an attempt at clarification, both as to method and the legitimacy of use of stages or styles of economic activity. I shall not go into a detailed exposition and analysis of Spiethoff's contribution; it would be superfluous in view of the excellent introduction Lane and Riemersma have provided to his essay, reprinted in *Enterprise and Secular Change,* and in view of Lane's concluding essay in the same volume.[88] For our purposes, the major issue raised by Spiethoff is the stipulation that there exists some intermediate level of social science analysis between the extreme ideographic approach of the historian, interested in the explana-

85. Andreas Predöhl, *Aussenwirtschaft,* Göttingen, 1949, esp. pp. 46-136; Walter Hoffmann, *Stadien und Typen der Industrialisierung,* Jena, 1931; and Colin Clark, *op.cit.,* pp. 395*ff.*

86. Cf., for example, W. W. Rostow, "The Take-Off into Self-Sustained Growth," *Economic Journal,* LXVI, 1956, pp. 25-48; and my article, "Noneconomic Factors in Economic Development," *American Economic Review,* XLVII, 1957, pp. 28-41.

87. See the writings of Arthur Spiethoff, cited in note 65.

88. See Lane and Riemersma, eds., *op.cit.,* pp. 431-43; and F. C. Lane, "Conclusion," *ibid.,* pp. 522-34.

tion of unique events, on the one hand, and the generalizing, abstract theory of economic analysis, with its strictly nomothetic approach, on the other. This intermediate level is termed "economic Gestalt theory," and its vehicle is the "economic style," which is a more realistic, and an empirically more valid, form of an economic stage. What is important about Spiethoff's economic styles is that each is an ordered complex of variables whose interdependence is as clearly elucidated as possible. Whereas Spiethoff did not place much emphasis on problems of economic development, Bowman and Anderson have shown that a careful delineation of economic types (which are closely related to economic styles and, incidentally, to certain forms of economic stages as well) implicitly contains a great deal of material which makes them useful constructs in the analysis of economic growth.[89] It seems that this viewpoint is shared by a fairly

89. Cf. Bowman and Anderson, *op.cit., pp.* 533-34. Nor has Spiethoff's work remained without critics. Perhaps the sharpest attack against it and against economic stages) has been delivered by Walter Eucken (in *The Foundations of Economics,* Chicago, 1951, pp. 64-102). Many of Eucken's arguments are repetitions of earlier criticisms against the theories of economic stages, e.g., that stages are arbitrary; that they do not apply empirically to the situations for which they are stipulated; that they are not true ideal types, but concoctions of ideal and real elements; that they postulate different economic theories for different institutional arrangements; and that they are the outcome of a historicist viewpoint. Eucken argues that instead of constructing stages or styles of economic development, the bridge between history and economics can only be built by taking from history economically relevant "facts" and studying the forms of economic activity and organization characteristic of these facts. In this manner, Eucken studies a characteristic medieval monastery and the economic relations in which it is involved, or a representative medieval craftsman, or a middleman in trade or industry, or a practitioner of the putting-out system. Eucken believes that by this method, one can arrive at isolating a "certain limited number of basic forms which may be combined in different ways in actual economic structures" (p. 116). Out of these structures, ideal types may be built up which may be systematically classified and examined. As a consequence, Eucken arrives at a series of ideal types of economic systems, or "economic orders," which become the subject of comparative analysis.

In spite of Eucken's criticism of the methods of his predecessors, it is difficult to see that his positive proposal amounts to anything other than an alternative method of stipulating economic types. His main interest is in developing contemporary types of economic systems for comparative purposes. Clearly, there is no indication of developmental threads leading from one type to the next. The types are placed, as it were, in completely watertight compartments. But there is nothing in Spiethoff's exposition which would make this procedure inapplicable. To be sure, Eucken calls his types, "ideal types," whereas Spiethoff would call them "real types"; but this is merely a minor terminological discrepancy, and as Alexander von Schelting *(op.cit.,* pp. 726-31) has shown, even Max Weber had two "ideal-type" concepts, one of which designated a specific combination of historical action systems (e.g., medieval town economy), and the other a purely abstract pattern of variables which has no counterpart in reality and hence forms a pure "utopia" (e.g., some propositions in economic theory, such as the concept of economic man). To the extent to which Weber intervened in the discussion of the applicability of stage theories to the problems of economic history, he alluded to the first class of his ideal types, as we will see below. Also, Hintze's view, cited earlier (see above, p. 232), must be understood as implying the concept of "ideal type" in the first of Weber's senses, i.e., in a sense which Spiethoff would have labeled "real type."

In my opinion, the whole conflict between Eucken and the writers whom he criticizes boils down to two points. First, Eucken uses his types for a different purpose than Bücher or Schmoller had in mind for their stages. Eucken is interested purely in a typology made up exclusively of economic variables for comparing systems; Bücher and Schmoller were interested in typologies for the purpose of tracing through institutional changes as they occurred in a process of historical development. The second difference is that Eucken is opposed to the historicism which he finds in the writings of the German historical school. Here Eucken's position re-

large number of economic historians and also tends to gain more general acceptance among British and American economic historians.

A good summary of the usefulness of economic stages, particularly in western economic history, has been presented by N. S. B. Gras.[90] Gras not only lists those economic historians who have and those who have not used stages as tools in their exposition of economic history, but he also discusses in detail the role of stages in the work of economic historians.[91] Although Gras's exposition is not as sharp and clear-cut as that of Weber, he comes to the same conclusion, i.e., the economic stage, as an abstract paradigm of variables, forms the connecting link between theoretical economic analysis and economic history as an empirical study. In other words, since the economic stage is an ideal-type construct, it may be set up in such a fashion as to present a systematic interrelation of relevant variables. These variables are not, of course, those of economic theory, but rather relate to social institutions (e.g., mechanisms facilitating exchange, institutions concerned with the granting of credit or the disposition of accumulated savings, and, above all, institutions determining the distribution and use of authority and decision-making power in society). In such a system the change brought about by one variable may be traced through and related to change in other variables in the system. Moreover, it may be possible to identify change in certain variables which will bring about change in the system as a whole, or at least magnitudes of changes in certain variables may have this effect. That is, a well-constructed economic stage may be regarded as a methodological tool, by means of which the generalized aspects of institutional economic change, and hence of economic growth, can be analyzed. At the same time, the construction of an economic stage will have a certain, though limited, relevance for empirical historical research.

To be sure, it is extremely difficult to avoid confusion between theory and history by the use of this method. This has been stressed by Weber.

---

sembles that of Karl Popper in his volume, *The Open Society and Its Enemies* (London, 1945). We cannot follow this line of argument, since it would involve us in a philosophical digression beyond the limits of this paper. It should be pointed out, however, that the historicism of the writers of the German historical school of economics bears a closer resemblance to that described by Morton White *(Social Thought in America: The Revolt against Formalism,* Boston, 1957, p. 12) than that so bitterly combatted by Popper.

90. N. S. B. Gras, "Stages in Economic History," *Journal of Economic and Business History*, II, 1930, pp. 395-418.

91. Although not specifically pertinent to this discussion, the list given by Gras is interesting. Among writers who have not made use of stages, and whom he designates as "economic historians, not historical economists or genetic economists," he mentions Levasseur, Cunningham, Bolles, Hauser, Lipson, and Bogart. A second group, who uses stages "in moderation," includes Ashley and Heaton (both of whom were influenced by Schmoller), Heckscher, and Posthumus, who is singled out as regarding stages as ideal types. The third group, who "make stages the skeletons of their historical flesh," includes Unwin and Gras himself. (Cf. *ibid.*, pp. 414-15.) A recent example of the use of classification by stages in economic history is the essay by Arthur H. Cole, "A New Set of Stages," *Explorations in Entrepreneurial History*, VIII, 1955, pp. 99-107.

After asserting that developmental sequences can be constructed into ideal types, he warns:

Whether the empirical-historical course of development was actually identical with the constructed one can be investigated only by using this concept as a heuristic device for the comparison of the ideal type and the "facts". . . . This procedure gives rise to no methodological doubts so long as we clearly keep in mind that ideal-typical developmental *constructs* and *history* are to be sharply distinguished from each other, and that the construct here is no more than the means for explicitly and validly imputing an historical event to its real causes while eliminating those which on the basis of our present knowledge seem impossible.[92]

Thus, in order to be of maximum usefulness for a theory of economic growth, economic stages must be constructed in such a way as to minimize the likelihood that in the processes of economic change illuminated by these constructs, the merely "possible," rather than the "true," change-generating variables are included. It is on this basis, rather than any other, that the various theories produced by German economists and economic historians of the nineteenth century must be judged; and in applying this yardstick, they make a poor showing indeed. We have had repeated occasion to observe that whatever else may be said of the various classifications presented by the different protagonists of economic stages, they all fail to contain models including the main variables which may be made accountable for a transition from one stage to the next. In this sense, they are not genuine developmental sequences of ideal-type constructs.

The reasons for this failure are not difficult to see. Some stage constructs include variables of doubtful significance and often completely omit institutional variables arising from noneconomic sources, so that their impact is, as it were, purely contingent. Others, e.g., Werner Sombart's system, are more inclusive in their choice of variables, but they lack a systematic interrelation of all variables, or combinations of variables, which would permit the generalized treatment of successive stages as uniform, functionally interrelated systems of social action. Only in the last few years has some definite progress been made in this direction, notably by Talcott Parsons and his associates. This may be the time to construct a new theory of economic stages—or, rather, a theory of stages of social systems—which might provide some genuine explanation of situations of economic change, which the older theories failed to do. But such a theory would require a major research effort; this must be postponed for the present.[93]

92. Weber, *Methodology*, pp. 101-102 (italics in original).

93. Some indication of the direction such a theory of stages might take is contained in my essay, "Economic Policy and Economic Development," in *The State and Economic Growth*, Hugh G. J. Aitken, ed., New York, 1959, pp. 325-52.

Contemporary Theorizing on Economic Growth*

By Henry J. Bruton

THERE IS no body of thought or set of principles that may confidently be called the "modern theory of economic growth." Current and recent literature abound with seminal ideas, revealing insights, penetrating bits and pieces of analysis, loose ends, and unrealistic assumptions. There are elegant and rigorous models, concerned with explaining a very narrowly conceived phenomenon; there are general discussions, which introduce, in an ambiguous, imprecise fashion, all the factors that may conceivably be related to the economic process; and there are contributions at every point between these extremes. Correspondingly, there are writers who believe that all a theory of economic growth can hope to achieve is the establishment of a loose framework consisting of a number of general propositions, held together by intuition and *ad hoc* theorizing; and there are those who feel it may be possible to devise a theory of growth comparable in elegance and precision to, say, the modern short-run theory of income determination.

Despite this characterization of the state of, and thinking about, theoriz-

*Except for minor stylistic changes and the addition of a few footnote references, this paper was completed in April 1957.

ing on economic growth, an essay purporting to report on this theorizing must have some kind of order. To establish this order, it is necessary to take a particular point of view as to the scope of growth theory, and then to try to formulate a cohesive and unified description of the thought falling within this arbitrarily delimited area. This introductory section is devoted to this delimiting process, and to establishing the point of view from which we shall examine current thinking on our subject.

Modern concern with problems of growth cannot be attributed to a building up of a received body of thought which in recent years has required as its next layer of bricks a long-run theory.[1] Rather, current interest in the problems involved in explaining the behavior of an economy over an extended period has resulted from three major events which have characterized the world economy since 1920.

In the first place, evidence accumulated which led many economists to believe that the Western European countries and the United States had reached a state of maturity such that large-scale unemployment was a chronic problem, rather than a periodic nuisance. To a very significant degree, Keynes's *General Theory* may be considered to constitute a theoretical explanation of the proposition that it is possible for an economy to run down and be unable to generate a sufficiently high level of activity to avoid involuntary unemployment. Thus, although Keynes's theory is "static and short-run," it was describing a phenomenon with numerous long-run implications. Therefore, the effort to "dynamize Keynes" led to an interest in the formal properties of a growth theory.

The second event referred to above as provoking interest in growth economics has to do with the recognition that a large part of the world's population is forced to live in conditions of extreme economic poverty. Out of this awareness, and out of the great difficulties created for these so-called underdeveloped countries by the depressed conditions of the 1930's and World War II, grew a demand for programs and policies that would improve the economic well-being of the populations of such countries. To formulate such programs and policies requires an understanding of the processes of economic growth, which is to say a theory of economic growth.

The third event responsible for current interest in economic growth is the rise of the Soviet Union as a world power, and the conflict between it and the Western countries. Political considerations have therefore led to questions concerning rates of growth for an economy as a whole, and for specific sectors, over the recent past, and the prospects for growth in the future. It is to be noted that the issues raised by such considerations are

1. This is Simon Kuznets' view, expressed in his comments on Moses Abramovitz's essay, "Economics of Growth," in *A Survey of Contemporary Economics*, B. F. Haley, ed., Homewood, Ill., 1952, II, p. 180.

concerned not only with the capacity of a given society to wage war, but with every aspect of a country's productive system.

Given these varied origins of interest in growth economics, it is not surprising that there exist a wide variety of approaches to the problem of explanation. But rather than examine contemporary contributions to the growth literature in isolated groups, it would seem more useful—and more interesting—to attempt to examine them in the context of a single general framework. I propose therefore to examine modern growth theory in the following way: I shall begin with the simplest, and most formal, theory available—the capital stock adjustment theory, associated with the names of Harrod and Domar—and then, step by step, deepen, widen, and disaggregate, in an effort to include in the analysis the arguments and hypotheses of as many contemporary writers as seems warranted. Each section of this paper will therefore be an extension, in one way or another, of the theory described in the first section. I shall maintain the formal framework of the Harrod-Domar analysis throughout. This will not only provide a theme to hold the essay together, but has the additional merit of showing how various components, isolated and emphasized by the several authors, fit together (or do not fit together) and act on each other.

As the length of the paper must be finite, several difficult problems are solved by simple fiat. In the first place, I concentrate on the behavior of per capita real income. This means that I limit the problem of a theory of growth to explaining the time path of per capita income over a long period of time. Per capita income is chosen as the main measure of growth for two simple reasons: One, almost all writers direct attention to this variable; two, despite some obvious weaknesses in its use, there does not seem to be a practical alternative.[2]

Secondly, it is necessary to take an explicit position with respect to short-period fluctuations. In discussions of short-period phenomena, most authors assume that it is possible to ignore the slower changes going on in the economy. In an analysis of long-run growth, these slower changes must, of course, be examined and worked into the explanatory system. But then, can the short-run fluctuations—frequently called cycles—be ignored? It is evident that the long-period behavior of an economy is not at all independent of what happens in the short run, but the nature of such interdependence is far from clear, and no simple assumption seems to be appropriate from all points of view. However, it is possible to recognize the interdependence of cyclical fluctuations and longer-run phenomena,

2. It is to be emphasized that giving prime attention to per capita income is a limitation on the scope of the survey. Several writers are strong in their criticism of the use of per capita income as the strategic variable, but for the most part these writers offer no alternative. An exception is the work of Adolph Lowe, "Structural Analysis of Real Capital Formation," in *Capital Formation and Economic Growth,* Moses Abramovitz, ed., Princeton, 1956, pp. 581-635.

while concentrating our attention on the latter, and to consider the former only in terms of how it affects the behavior of the system over a long period of time, without giving detailed examination to the *modus operandi* of the cycle itself. This is the procedure followed in this essay.[3] I have therefore ruled out discussion of the formal properties of the several types of cycle models currently extant, but I do recognize that the growth process is likely to generate fluctuations, and that these fluctuations act on the growth process in turn. I shall seek then to introduce into the analysis of the determinants of growth the effect of this interdependence on these determinants and hence, to some extent at least, on the long-run behavior of the economy itself.

Thirdly, attention is limited herein to the "real" aspects of growth, at the expense of the "financial" aspects.[4] And, except for minor deviations, the discussion is limited to a closed economy, and little attention is given to the growth process in a centrally planned economy. Omission of the international section seems reasonable, in light of the limited extent to which international relations have been introduced into the formal theories of economic growth.[5] I have excluded consideration of centrally planned systems simply because of space and time limitations.

Finally, it should be noted that although there has been a healthy emphasis on noneconomic aspects of growth in much of recent literature, discussion of this material is also omitted. This is to be regretted; in those countries where growth seems most essential for human welfare, problems outside the conventional limits of economics are surely paramount. Indeed, a strong argument can be made that the problem of underdevelopment will not be solved until economics has achieved a more compatible marriage than now prevails with other social sciences.

---

3. Some such procedure is implied in much of the literature. Perhaps the best discussion is contained in William Fellner, *Trends and Cycles in Economic Activity*, New York, 1956, chaps. 1 and 2. Evidently, those theories—chiefly Schumpeterian in orientation—which find the origin of growth in the cycle itself, would not fit into this approach.

4. Professor Fellner (*op.cit.*, chaps. 5 and 9) has a good discussion of the role of the price level in growth. Robert Solow ("A Note on the Price Level and Interest Rate in a Growth Model," *Review of Economic Studies*, XXI, pp. 74-79), and S. S. Alexander ("The Accelerator as a Generator of Steady Growth," *Quarterly Journal of Economics*, LXIII, 1949, pp. 174-98), also give some attention to the effects of price-level behavior. Economic historians have, of course, long been concerned with price-level behavior over substantial periods of time. For a recent examination of some of the hypotheses arising from these historical inquiries, see David Felix, "Profit Inflation and Industrial Growth: The Historic Record and Contemporary Analysis," *Quarterly Journal of Economics*, LXX, 1956, pp. 441-63. A specific discussion of some of the financial aspects of growth may be found in J. G. Gurley and E. S. Shaw, "Financial Aspects of Economic Development," *American Economic Review*, XLV, 1955, pp. 515-38.

5. Useful discussions of some aspects of the role of the international sector in growth may be found in Harry G. Johnson, "Equilibrium Growth in an International Economy," *Canadian Journal of Economics and Political Science*, XIX, 1953, pp. 478-500, and Trygve Haavelmo, *A Study in the Theory of Economic Evolution*, Amsterdam, 1954, Part V.

I

The Capital Stock Adjustment Theory

By limiting his analysis to the short-run, Keynes was able to impound into *ceteris paribus* all those phenomena and characteristics of an economy that change more slowly than the immediate determinants of income. The short-run mechanism is assumed to work itself out in a setting in which capital stock, technology, market structure, saving habits, social and cultural environment, population, etc., remain unchanged. With all these given, the problem was to determine the equilibrium level of income.

It is possible by a comparative static technique to examine the effect on the equilibrium level of income of a once-and-for-all change in any of the occupants of the *ceteris paribus* pound. And, of course, this has been done. For example, much attention has been given to the effect of changes in income distribution on the consumption-income relationship, and to the effect of a change in the extent of monopoly on the rate of investment. But such changes in these "underlying" or "basic" characteristics are exogenous to the equilibrium conditions of the "static" Keynesian model. This statement is true, or approximately true, with respect to each member of the group in the preceding paragraph, except one—capital stock. Depending on the way the short-run system is established, if there is net positive saving, there is also net positive investment, and if there is net positive investment, the capital stock must be changing. Thus, the capital stock—surely a relevant determinant of the level of income—is not exogenous to the short-run mechanism, but changes in a way which is directly dependent upon how that mechanism works. Therefore, the first effort to extend Keynesian short-run theory into a growth problem was essentially to examine the effects of changes in the capital stock on the behavior of income.[6]

Since it is capital stock that is changed by investment, it appears reasonable to define equilibrium so that it involves the capital stock. Keynesian equilibrium requires equality between desired savings and desired investment, while the growth form of the model requires for equilibrium the continuing maintenance of the desired ratio between capital stock and the rate of output. In the early formulations, this ratio seems to be determined

6. The pioneering papers are R. F. Harrod, "An Essay in Dynamic Theory," *Economic Journal*, XLIX, 1939, pp. 14-33; E. D. Domar, "Capital Expansion, Rate of Growth and Employment," *Econometrica,* XIV, 1946, pp. 137-47; and S. C. Tsiang, "Rehabilitation of Time Dimension of Investment in Macrodynamic Analysis," *Economica,* XVI, 1949, pp. 204-17.

solely by technological considerations, i.e., it is a technological constant. It is convenient and helpful to label this kind of theory the capital stock adjustment theory.[7]

THE AGGREGATE MODEL

The capital stock adjustment theory may be stated in a variety of ways, but we may content ourselves with a single, simple form.[8] It was stated above that the central proposition of this theory is the explicit recognition that investment is capacity-creating as well as income-generating; it is therefore useful to develop the capacity effect and the demand effect separately, and then equate them to show the requirements for equilibrium.

The supply equations may be formulated in the following way: Let O_t be the capacity rate of output during period *t;* let K_t be the capital stock available to the system during period *t;* and let k be the relationship between capital and output, a technological constant. Therefore:

$$O_t = \frac{1}{k} K_t$$

and:

$$O_t - O_{t-1} = \frac{1}{k}(K_t - K_{t-1}) = \frac{1}{k} I_{t-1}$$

where I_{t-1} is investment during the $t-1$ period which becomes producing capital in the tth period. Then:

$$\text{(1)} \qquad \frac{O_t - O_{t-1}}{O_{t-1}} = \frac{\frac{1}{k} I_{t-1}}{O_{t-1}} = \frac{v}{k}$$

where v is the ratio of net investment to capacity output in the previous period. Equation (1) states that capacity will grow at a constant percentage

7. R. C. O. Matthews, "Capital Stock Adjustment Theories of the Trade Cycle and the Problem of Policy," in *Post-Keynesian Economics,* Kenneth K. Kurihara, ed., London, 1955, chap. 7.

8. D. Hamberg *(Economic Growth and Instability,* New York, 1956), discusses the numerous forms the theory may take and the implications of these several forms. Professor Hamberg also makes extensive references to the literature on this general body of theory. The reader interested primarily in exploring the details of the Harrod-Domar model should consult the Hamberg volume; our problem is something else. In particular, it might be noted that much depends upon the pattern of lags that is assumed.

A word on references is appropriate here. It is impossible to refer to every item in the literature worthy of note, and I shall follow the practice of noting only what seems to me to be the earliest or clearest formulations and/or those sources that do present extended bibliographies on the subject under discussion. Professor Fellner's book, cited in footnote 3, above, contains the most useful general list of references that I have seen.

rate, determined by the productivity of the additions to capital stock, k, and the proportion of the capacity devoted to the creation of new capital.

For the effect of investment on demand, we need an equation for consumption expenditures and one for investment expenditures. In an effort to maintain simplicity, we may write consumption as a function, $1-s$, where s is average and marginal propensity to save of current income, and investment as a function, b, of the change in income over the immediately preceding periods, all in constant prices. Thus:

$$C_t = (1-s)\,Y_t$$

and:

$$I_t = b\,(Y_t - Y_{t-1})$$

then:

$$Y_t = (1-s)\,Y_t + b\,(Y_t - Y_{t-1}) \tag{2}$$

and by simple algebraic manipulation:

$$\frac{Y_t - Y_{t-1}}{Y_{t-1}} = \frac{s}{b-s} \tag{3}$$

Equation (3) asserts that income will grow at a constant percentage rate, determined by the propensity to save and the extent to which changes in income induce investment.

Assuming that in period 0 equilibrium prevails, i.e., $O_0 = Y_0$, equilibrium growth requires that $\frac{v}{k} = \frac{s}{b-s}$. If $O_0 = Y_0$, then, since total savings equals total investment and the saving-income ratio is assumed to be constant, v must equal s, and the achievement of equilibrium growth depends upon the equality $k = b - s$. Under these assumptions as to relationships and (especially) as to lags, b must exceed k by the amount of the saving ratio. For this reason and for others to be discussed later, it is of considerable importance to distinguish carefully between k, a supply parameter, and b, a demand parameter.[9]

Given these assumptions, the economy can achieve equilibrium growth; but if k, b, and s are constants, the equilibrium path may be difficult to maintain. Suppose, for example, that the system is growing smoothly, but because of a shock of some sort, income suddenly fails to grow at the required rate, and excess capacity appears. Entrepreneurs may then seek to reduce their capital stock by reducing investment, but a reduction in

9. Cf. A. Kervyn, "A Note on the Accelerator and Constant Growth," *Review of Economic Studies*, XXII, 1954-55, pp. 61-66.

investment leads to further reductions in the income, and the desired ratio between capital and output cannot be re-established. If income happens to grow faster than expected, entrepreneurs, finding themselves shy of capital, may seek to add to their capital stock, but this act leads to further increases in income, and the capital-output ratio remains less than that desired. This extreme instability obviously depends upon entrepreneurial expectations. For example, if decision-makers reacted to the sudden appearance of an undesirably large capital-output, not by reducing their rate of investment, but by increasing it, then the above result would not follow. And the way entrepreneurs react will depend upon what they think the future holds, i.e., upon their expectations. Thus, an expectation function could be introduced that would make the equilibrium growth path stable.[10] Unhappily, little is known about the expectation functions of entrepreneurs, and results that depend in a significant way upon a particular function must be interpreted with caution. It would seem that most discussions of capital stock adjustment theory assume it to be unstable, and since the theory, as described to this point, does not indicate what happens when equilibrium is disturbed, it cannot explain the time path of per capita income without further elaboration. Since it has been assumed that the purpose of a theory of economic growth is to explain the time path of per capita income, it is necessary to introduce some hypotheses that will either stabilize the equilibrium path, or that will indicate the route that instability imposes on the system. This is done at the end of this section, after some comments on the theory as it now stands.

It was stated earlier that the only modification made in Keynes's theory in its metamorphosis from a static, short-run theory into a dynamic, long-run theory was the recognition that net investment cannot occur without a change in the capital stock. This means that other strategic Keynesian concepts were retained, and are presumed to be appropriate in the long-run context. For example, the linear saving-income relationship that Keynes could draw fairly confidently as applicable for his static, timeless model was, without modification, plugged into a model designed to explain the long-run growth of an economic system.[11] It is useful, then, to begin the discussion of the capital stock adjustment theory of growth by an examination of the concepts of this theory with respect to their suitability as parameters of a growth model. Since we are interested in explaining—that

10. The role of expectations in this growth model are discussed in some detail by Diran Bodenhorn, "The Stability of Growth Models," *American Economic Review*, XLVI, 1956, pp. 607-31. See also W. J. Baumol, "Formalization of Mr. Harrod's Model," *Economic Journal*, LIX, 1949, pp. 625-29.

11. The fact that the early forms of this model were all linear has led to the frightening result that income has to grow throughout eternity at a constant percentage rate or all is lost. Surely, in a long-run model the linearity assumptions are difficult to justify. See Solow, "A Note on the Price Level . . . ," *loc.cit.*, p. 75.

is, in accounting for—the behavior of per capita income, the criterion of suitability is the effectiveness with which a given parameter contributes to this explanation.

The key new parameter in this formulation is the supply parameter, the capital-output ratio. In the simplest form of the theory it is assumed to be a technologically fixed constant. The conceptual problems involved in defining capital are made much more intricate than usual when the term is used to define the capital-output ratio. The most satisfactory approach to follow in computing the value of a stock is to discount the future stream attributable to that stock back to the present time. But to measure the capital stock in this way reduces the capital-output ratio to a tautological constant, devoid of explanatory significance. Moreover, of course, two accumulations of capital stock, although alike in every respect, may have different values simply because the discount factor is not the same in each case, and this leads to undesirable results when one attempts to determine capital needs. It is therefore necessary to rule out defining and measuring the numerator of the capital-output ratio in this way, despite the fact that this procedure has the most appeal in many other problems.

Thus, we must resort to the less satisfactory technique of defining investment as the difference between total output and consumption, and capital as the accumulated value of investment (with all variables measured in constant prices). Under ideal circumstances, this method is satisfactory. It implies that a quantity of resources are devoted to producing commodities that are not consumed, and that these commodities add to the capacity of the system to produce more commodities. Since all measurements are in "real" terms, investment may be assumed to measure resources allocated to the production of capital goods. Capital is thus thought of in terms of the resources (chiefly labor) required to reproduce the existing stock of machines, equipment, plants, buildings, etc. A capital-output ratio, technologically fixed, would then mean that production of a given increment in capacity will always require the application of an unchanging quantity of inputs to the production of the necessary capital equipment. In practice, this method results in valuing capital formation in each period at cost to the investor, and only in a perfectly competitive system with no uncertainty will such valuation equal that arrived at by use of the discounting procedure. Difficulties in deflating, in computing depreciation, and in evaluating the "initial" capital stock introduce additional problems of measurement and conceptual ambiguities which make the use of the capital stock notion troublesome.[12]

---

12. These problems are discussed in some detail by Joan Robinson, "The Production Function and the Theory of Capital," *Review of Economic Studies*, XXI, 1953-54, pp. 81-106, and in her recent book, *The Accumulation of Capital*, London, 1956, *passim.*

There is the further conceptual difficulty of the period of gestation with respect to capital goods whose productivity is indirect, at best. It is a simple matter to see that the production of one hundred new looms will have a specific and measurable effect on the capacity of the textile industry, which effect will be evident immediately upon the completion of the construction of the looms. But it is not as clear what the effect on the capacity of the economy will be if the new capital creation is in the form of schools, hospitals, highways (or government monuments). The capacity of the system to supply school, hospital, and highway services is of course increased immediately (assuming the availability of necessary labor), but, evidently, this is not the total effect of these activities. The total effect on capacity of such forms of capital will not be apparent until sufficient time has elapsed for the full effects of the new capital to be felt throughout the system. In a similar category with schools, highways, and so on, is investment in research facilities, an area which is currently attracting considerable quantities of funds in the United States.[13]

Not only does the choice of the time interval affect the capacity-creating effects of a given investment outlay, but so also does the composition of the new capital. Evidently, a capital stock is not a homogeneous whole; it has a structure, and the productivity of newly created capital depends in part upon how the new capital fits in with the existing structure. If capital is viewed as a heterogeneous composite of many types of capital services, an appraisal of the capital-output ratio requires consideration of potential complementarities which may have significant consequences for the capacity of the system. Especially relevant in this respect are external economies and "social overhead facilities." Both of these concepts are difficult to handle, but they are surely highly relevant in understanding the growth process, and the use of an aggregative capital-output ratio conceals, rather than reveals, the problem. More will be said on this point below, in the section on the disaggregated form of this model.

A final point on the capital-output ratio concerns noncapital inputs. The equilibrium rates of growth were determined above solely in terms of the behavior of capital stock. If input coefficients are assumed to be constant, there is not much more that can be said, since then the rate of growth of total output is limited by the rate of growth of the input, whose supply is growing at the slower pace. With constant input coefficients, the equilibrium rate of growth will be the full employment of labor rate

13. Another aspect of this same problem has to do with the life of the capital that is accumulated. This problem and the associated one of the effects of depreciation decision on growth are not considered in this essay. This, too, is a serious lacuna in the discussion. On the effects of depreciation decision on growth, see, for example, E. D. Domar, "Depreciation, Replacement and Growth," *Economic Journal*, LXIII, 1953, pp. 1-32, and Robert Eisner, "Depreciation Allowances, Replacement Requirements and Growth," *American Economic Review*, XLII, 1952, pp. 804-19.

of growth only if the rates of growth of capital and labor are equal. Thus, the assumption of the fixity of input coefficients is important in our attempts to explain what happens to the level of employment, as well as in our efforts to account for the instability of the equilibrium growth path.

The other supply parameter—the saving function—has, of course, been the subject of countless articles and books. Conceptually, it poses fewer problems than the capital-output ratio, but there is one point to which reference should be made in the present context. Interest in saving arises out of the fact that it is necessary in order to release resources from producing for current consumption, so that they may be used to create products which will increase the capacity of the system in the future. But, evidently, many forms of expenditure have an effect on the future capacity of the economy. This is especially true of expenditures for education and health services, but it is also true of other consumption. In effect, this means that saving and investment, as they are usually computed, do not measure the total amount of resources devoted to increasing the capacity of the economy. It appears that one of the major differences between consumption expenditures in high-income countries and in low-income countries is that only a very small proportion of total consumption outlays in the latter countries affects capacity, while in the high-income countries the percentage is of considerable magnitude. There are real difficulties here in separating net from gross expenditures, i.e., in separating out those expenditures which merely maintain capacity from those which augment it. Furthermore, expenditures on health and education may well reduce the incentive to save out of remaining income. Nevertheless, such considerations do introduce an ambiguity with respect to saving—for the growth problem—which may be expected to contribute to the unpredictability of the capital-output ratio, and consequently to the behavior of the capacity of the economy through time.

On the demand side of the problem, little need be said about the consumption function. Conceptually, it is unambiguous, although of course many writers question its use as a parameter in any kind of a model. With respect to the demand for capital accumulation, the chief conceptual problems are concerned with the appropriateness of the accelerator and the distinction between induced and autonomous investment.[14] A detailed account of the accelerator is unnecessary for our purposes here, and we need mention only one point.

The literature seems to concentrate on the technological relationship

---

14. Autonomous investment was omitted from the equational system outlined above simply for ease of exposition, and because I later rule out the concept entirely. The literature on the accelerator is vast indeed, and specific references are hardly necessary: see Hamberg, *op.cit.* Many writers, of course, are reluctant to use autonomous investment as an acceptable theory of investment.

between output and capital. Thus, the equation is usually written as:

$$(4) \qquad I_t = b'(Y_t - Y_{t-1})$$

or:

$$(5) \qquad I_t = b''(Y_{t-1} - Y_{t-2})$$

where b' and b'' refer solely to the technological requirement of capital in the productive process. These relationships express the concept that income has increased, and this increase then induces investment. In order for such equations to be meaningful, it is necessary to assume that it is possible to increase output briefly with no increase in capital stock. Firms maintain a higher rate of output than is desirable, given their capital stock, for a period or two, then increase capital accumulation to re-establish the desired relationship between stock and output. The argument is based on purely technological considerations: A given rate of output requires a given stock of capital; therefore, if output rises, new capital must be created. This kind of argument implies that investment demand is an automatic response to technological needs.

The other way of looking at the accelerator involves something more. One of two changes may be made. Rather than thinking of investment as responding to a previous change in output, it may be argued that entrepreneurs estimate demand for output in the next period, and invest according to their expected needs. We would then write:

$$I_t = B''' \ (\hat{Y}_{t+1} - Y_t)$$

where $\hat{Y}_{t+1}$ is estimated income in the $(t + 1)^{th}$ period.[15] Or we may argue that the change in income between periods results in entrepreneurial activity, but that behavior is induced by many factors in addition to technological considerations. Thus, we could write $I_t = b\,(Y_t - Y_{t-1})$, where the b is the relation measuring investment response to changes in output, which response would depend chiefly upon expectations created by the difference between Y_t and Y_{t-1}. These last two equations are, therefore, quite similar with respect to the kind of phenomenon they represent. They both make it clear that the investment decision is something more than an automatic technological response.

Earlier, we stated the capital stock adjustment theory in such a way that the capital-output ratio and investment demand parameter had to be different, if equilibrium growth were to be attained. Under this form of the

---

15. This is the way the accelerator is written by Paul G. Clark, "The Telephone Industry: A Study in Private Investment," in Wassily Leontief, *et al.*, *Studies in the Structure of the American Economy*, New York, 1953, chap. 7.

model, it is possible to interpret the *b* as a technological parameter, although there must be an assumption, explicitly stated, as to entrepreneurial expectations. However, it seems much more rewarding, in spite of the increased difficulty, to consider the *b* as a behavioristic parameter, with certain technological limitations, and not merely as a technological coefficient handed to the economist by the engineer. If we do this, we are also required to say something more about the determinants of investment decisions. This we do later. The point here is that there must be a clear indication in the investment equation as to whether the accelerator is a purely technological parameter, or whether it is a behavioristic parameter as well; and, as just noted, it seems more acceptable to assume that it is a behavioristic parameter with certain technological limitations.[16]

A brief remark on "autonomous" investment may prove useful here. The concept of "autonomous" investment was introduced by authors who gave the investment coefficient–the accelerator–a rigid technological interpretation. Autonomous investment was that part of investment that was not technologically required to create the capital stock necessary to produce the changed output in the desired fashion. As such, the concept had meaning. But if the investment coefficient is interpreted as a behavioristic, as well as technological, parameter then it is difficult to find justification for a separation of total investment into "induced" and "non-induced." Autonomous investment, even if it is justified by the model, means that some part of total investment is outside the explanatory mechanism, and if such investment constitutes a large–but not fixed–proportion of total investment, then evidently the explanatory system is of little use. Thus, it would seem that autonomous investment should play only a very small role, or none at all, in the investment equation in a theory of growth.

The final point in this section concerns the constancy of the relationships defined in the capital stock adjustment model. It was observed earlier that the chief innovation that turned Keynes' timeless theory into a growth theory was the explicit recognition that investment results in increases in capacity. The maintenance through time of a Keynesian kind of equilibrium then required that demand grow so as to match the growing capacity. But now, with respect to each parameter, the further question must be asked as to whether the process of growth itself results in its changing in a systematic, predictable fashion. If it could be shown that a growing income did itself produce forces that resulted in systematic changes in the values of the parameters, then it would become necessary to explore further and to try to find the path of change that will be traced out. That is to say, if we are to understand the behavior of per capita income over time, it

16. This interpretation seems to be consistent with most of the literature. See, for example, Joan Robinson, *The Rate of Interest and Other Essays*, London, 1952, and Fellner, *op.cit.*

becomes necessary to deepen the explanatory system to the extent that these immediate determinants of growth are themselves explained, at least to the extent that these changes are functions of the growth process. This occupies our attention in Part III of this paper, but first, it may prove helpful to introduce some modifications into the above discussed model.

SOME MODIFICATIONS

The Keynesian setting of the capital stock adjustment theory has been emphasized, and it has been shown that several important results obtained are due to assumptions which are part of the Keynesian heritage. However, it is possible to change the setting from Keynesian to neo-classical, and when this is done it is not surprising that some of the more startling results obtained disappear. Such a resetting has been accomplished with great elegance by Professor Robert Solow.[17]

The strategic new assumptions are (a) at each instant of time all existing capital stock and all labor are thrown on the market; and (b) quasi-rents and wage rates adjust immediately to clear the market. With such a flexible productive system, the perfectly adjusting input prices would assure—under a wide range of conditions—that the capital output ratio, which did in fact obtain, was the desired one. The system could then always adjust to a given labor supply in such manner that the full employment of labor and the satisfying of entrepreneurs are achieved at the same time, not accidentally, but by a substitution of inputs responding to changed factor prices.

It is, of course, unlikely that factor prices and productive processes are such that the above assumptions can be considered realistic. However, it does seen reasonable to assume that, though not occurring instantaneously, such adjustments do tend to take place over a long period of time. In all countries which have experienced long periods of continued growth of per capita income, the evidence is strong that capital accumulation has proceeded at a faster pace than the labor supply has grown. Since the capital accumulated has been used—except for short interruptions, adjustments in the capital-labor ratio have evidently occurred. It is conceivable, of course, that such adjustments should be explained solely in terms of technological change, but this puts a burden on the rate and direction of technological change, a burden it seems incapable of supporting—for reasons to be discussed later. Further evidence that substitution takes place lies in the fact that it is possible to observe that different processes are being used by different firms to produce very similar products.

17. Robert Solow, "A Contribution to the Theory of Economic Growth," *Quarterly Journal of Economics*, LXX, 1956, pp. 65-94. See also H. Pilvin, "Full Capacity vs. Full Employment Growth," *Quarterly Journal of Economics*, LXVII, 1953, pp. 545-52.

It therefore appears meaningful to accept the proposition that at all times there is an optimum input mix, which optimum is a function of technology and the relative prices of the inputs. When deviations from such an optimum combination develop, relative prices and productive processes begin to change in such fashion as to restore the optimum conditions. Since neither prices of inputs nor the productive process can adjust immediately, the system will not be constantly in equilibrium, but neither is it uselessly unstable. In particular, the knife-edge equilibrium path disappears, as do also the problems created by it. Especially important is the fact that it now becomes meaningful to consider the equilibrium path as tracing out the actual time path of income for the economy.[18]

The introduction of flexibility into the system has another advantage as well. The above formulation of the capital stock adjustment theory stated the equilibrium conditions in terms of the continued maintenance of the desired relationship between the stock of capital and the flow of output. Under assumptions of fixed input coefficients, there is not much more to say on this subject (nor indeed is there much meaning to the notion of a "desired" capital output ratio). A more satisfactory approach appears to be to assume that the entrepreneur thinks in terms of achieving a satisfactory rate of return on his capital stock. What constitutes a satisfactory return depends upon many things, and the absolute magnitude of such a rate surely varies from time to time and from industry to industry. To facilitate the analysis, it is convenient to introduce the simplifying assumption of a constant equilibrium rate of return, and to assume that, if this rate is maintained, entrepreneurs will feel that their investment is justified. This means that continuing equilibrium growth requires that the capital-accumulating process generate a total supply and a total income to enable the rate of return on capital to remain about constant through time.

The rate of return on capital is the ratio between the share of output going to capital (call this q) and the capital-output ratio (k), i.e., it is q/k.[19] Therefore, a constant k, along with an unchanging distribution of income, will produce a constant rate of return on capital. Thus, with fixed coefficients, the rate of return will tend to remain constant, and the growth path defined earlier meets this new equilibrium condition.

However, the situation is different when a more flexible system is assumed, and when it is also assumed—as is necessary—that capital accumu-

18. There has been considerable discussion of the role of the fixity of input coefficients and the behavior of factor prices in accounting for the underemployment found in many underdeveloped countries. A recent useful discussion of this particular problem may be found in R. S. Eckaus, "Factor Proportions in Underdeveloped Areas," *American Economic Review*, XLV, 1955, pp. 539-65. For a detailed discussion of the process by which the technique of production becomes more capital intensive see Mrs. Robinson's *The Accumulation of Capital (op.cit.)*.

19. If Q is the total return to capital, and K is the capital stock, then Q/K is the rate of return on capital. If we then divide both numerator and denominator by output, we get q/k.

lation is proceeding more rapidly than the labor supply is growing. These assumptions make impossible the conclusion that the rate of return remains constant through time, without specific reference to the comparative rates of growth of capital and labor and the behavior of technological change. This means then that the conditions for equilibrium growth require specification of those conditions to which reference has already been made, and to innovation behavior as well. In other words, the requirements of steady and continuous growth must include a specific innovational pattern. The exact nature of these requirements will be examined in a later section.[20]

SOME IMPLICATIONS OF DISAGGREGATION

The formulation up to this point has been a highly aggregated one. In effect, the economy has been viewed as one giant firm which produces a single product for one giant consumer. The firm anticipates a market for an increased output, and in order to meet the growing demand, it invests; by so doing, it increases capacity at the same time that it generates the necessary increment of income. But apparently such aggregation, although it simplifies the analysis, masks many problems, and it is helpful to reduce the level of aggregation in order to explore the intersectoral conditions—as opposed to the aggregative conditions–that must be met if growth is to continue relatively smoothly.

The most widely known multi-sectoral model available is Professor Leontief's input-output system, and we shall make use of this system, with some slight modifications as to form and interpretation.[21]

Accordingly, a_{ij} represents the technical coefficient determining the amount of the product of industry "i" absorbed by the industry "j" per unit of output of "j." The "a's" are measured in terms of per dollar's worth units; i.e., for every dollar of output of "j," "a" dollars of output "i" are used. And x_j is the total output of the jth sector, measured in money units. If we assume given and unchanging prices, $a_{ij}\, x_{jt}$ represents the total payments of industry j to industry i for a given interval of time, for a given flow of output x_j.

If the jth industry wishes to increase its capacity, this may require purchase of i's products to increase j's capital stock. Let b_{ij} be the investment demand coefficient of industry j for i's products, indicating how an increase

20. The role of innovations, both as to rate and direction, has been discussed in detail by Fellner *(op.cit.)*. Further discussion of the Fellner argument here is postponed until the section on technological change.

21. See Leontief, *et al., op.cit.*, Part I. See also two papers by R. M. Goodwin: "The Multiplier as a Matrix," *Economic Journal*, LIX, 1949, pp. 537-55, and "Static and Dynamic Linear General Equilibrium Models," in *Input-Output Relations*, Leiden, Holland, 1953, pp. 68*ff*. I would emphasize that we are using this system for a specified purpose, and therefore I do not discuss many complex and intricate problems that arise in the use of such a high-powered machine. In fact, we are using the formal apparatus itself in a purely descriptive manner.

in the rate of output of the jth sector affects the demand of that sector for i's products as capital stock. The b's are measured in the same terms as the a's. If x_{jt} represents the capacity output rate, then we may write b_{ij} $(x_{jt} - x_{jt-1})$ to represent the total payments of industry j to industry i for a given increase in capacity of j. Thus b_{ij} is the equivalent of the economy-wide b, except here it is applicable to a single sector.

The total receipts of the ith sector is simply the sum of the a_{ij} x_{jt}'s and the b_{ij} $(x_{jt} - x_{jt-1})$'s, while its total outlay is the sum of the a_{ji} x_{it}'s and the b_{ji} $(x_{it} - x_{ti-1})$'s. Thus, we may describe the economy divided into n sectors in terms of a set of balance equations as follows:

$$x_{it} = \sum_{j=1}^{n} a_{ij} x_{jt} + \sum_{j=1}^{n} b_{ij} (x_{jt} - x_{jt-1}) \qquad (6)$$

Written in this way we have a closed system, that is one with no given final bill of goods. This means that included in the n sectors is the household sector, and that we assume that the input of consumption is a necessary requisite for the output of labor. If this is accepted, then we may look upon all the a's not only as input requirements per unit of output–technological relationships–but also as indicating the amount of output which must be "consumed" in order to produce the total output. Thus $|a|$ x_j "consumption" is required for the production of the remaining $|I - a|$ x_j output.[22] In effect, we are saying that just as we may interpret the household sector in terms of an input of consumption and an output of labor, so we may interpret the other sectors' inputs in terms of consumption. The system of equation (6) may then be considered a disaggregated version of equation (2) in the previous section.

We may then think of the a_{ij} as the marginal and average propensity to "consume," and $|I - a|$ as the proportion of output of the ith sector not required to produce the flow of output of the jth sector. If x_i exceeds Σ a_{ij} x_j, then evidently not all of x_i is being used as inputs for the flow of x_j, and equilibrium in the ith industry requires the condition:

$$|I - a| x_{jt} = \Sigma b_{ij} (x_{jt} - x_{jt-1}) \qquad (7)$$

This is to say that the amount of x_i, not consumed in the flow of output of x_j must be used by x_j in addition to the capacity of the latter industry. The equilibrium condition expressed by equation (7) is the disaggregated

22. The $|a|$ is the matrix of a_{ij}'s, and x_j is a vector. The I is an identity matrix, corresponding to unity in scalar algebra. Solow (see footnote 4) discusses the rationale of interpreting the a's in terms of consumption, and of writing the Leontief system as identical with the Harrod model.

equivalent of the equilibrium expressed earlier for the economy as a whole;[23] i.e., "saving" in each sector equals investment demand brought to bear on that sector. Now, instead of a single coefficient representing some kind of average behavioristic and technological relationships in the economy as a whole, there are matrices of coefficients indicating these same relationships for individual sectors of the economy. This greater detail is useful in several respects.

The solution to equations (6) may be written as:[24]

$$(8) \qquad x_{it} = c_1 h_{i1} e^{\lambda_{t1}} + c_2 h_{i2} e^{\lambda_{t2}} + \ldots\ldots + c_n h_{in} e^{\lambda_{tn}}$$

A numerical solution would involve estimating the value of the roots λ_1, λ_2, ... λ_n, the coefficients h_{i1}, h_{i2} . . . . h_{in}, and c_1, c_2, ... c_n. The λ's and the *h*'s depend on the *s*'s and *b*'s, and the *c*'s reflect the initial conditions of the system. The path of x_i will be dominated by the largest root, and after a sufficient period of time the equation may be written simply in terms of the expression containing this largest root. The ratio of the outputs of any two sectors would be the same through time, and therefore the rates of growth of all sectors would be the same. This is common sense, of course. With constant *a*'s and *b*'s over a long period of time, no industry can grow more rapidly than the rest of the system, as all sectors must keep pace in order to supply the inputs necessary for the given industry to grow at a specified pace. If the *a*'s and *b*'s remained constant long enough for the dominant root to assert itself, the economy will be getting larger and larger while all sectors maintain their position relative to other sectors and to total output. If it is further assumed that no innovations are taking place, that capital and labor are growing at equal relative rates, and that all sectors are characterized by constant returns to capital and labor, then capital accumulation must proceed at a constant relative rate in each sector (but this rate will not be the same in all sectors). Employment of labor in each sector will grow in a similar fashion. Under these assumptions, the profit rate is constant (at the equilibrium level) in each sector, and the conditions for entrepreneurial satisfaction are therefore met.[25]

On the basis of these assumptions, the growing economy may be en-

23. It seems unnecessary to introduce a specific supply equation. One is implied, of course, in equation (7).

24. The equation here is written as if 6 were a differential equation. This is simply for convenience; no change of interpretation is involved.

25. Cf. John von Neuman, "A Model of General Economic Equilibrium," *Review of Economic Studies*, XIII, 1945-46, pp. 1-9; Robert Solow and Paul A. Samuelson, "Balanced Growth Under Constant Returns to Scale," *Econometrica*, XXI, 1953, pp. 412-24; and the two volumes by Mrs. Robinson, cited in footnotes 12 and 16.

visaged as an expanding circular flow. Only the size of each sector and the size of the total change. Entrepreneurial decision-making under these conditions is very simple: Each period is merely a repeat performance of the preceding one, including the expansion of capacity. To this extent, little more is required of entrepreneurial activity than is required in a stationary circular flow, and it seems that little is revealed under present assumptions that is not revealed by the aggregated form of the theory. But the introduction of somewhat more realistic assumptions does lay bare further aspects of the growth process and further requirements which must be met if growth is to be sustained.

Evidently, in a growing economy, over a long period of time, the a's and b's will change, changing the roots and coefficients of equation (8). And, more important, over a given short period the effects of the a's and b's may be washed out by a high rate of growth in a single sector of the system. For example, suppose that because of a shock to the system–in the form, say, of a change in tastes–sector g begins to grow at a rate much higher than other sectors. Even though the a_{ig}'s and b_{ig}'s are relatively small, the high rate of growth of x_g would overcome the effect of the a's and b's, with the result that the growth of the others tends to be affected by the behavior of x_g itself, rather than the set of a's and b's appropriate to it. We may say then that under these circumstances x_g tends to "carry" the system for a given interval of time. This hypothesis leads to further aspects of growth which are of considerable significance.

In the first place, it suggests a point that several writers have emphasized, namely, that periods of sustained growth can usually be found to be dominated by one or, at the most, a few industries which are experiencing a rate of growth greatly in excess of that of the economy as a whole. The hypothesis then is that growth is characterized not so much by the movement forward of the whole economic system, in response to some general inducement which is equally effective on all fronts, but rather that growth results from the response of the system to the pull exercised by a few industries which are achieving an unusually rapid rate of growth due to new demand, new technology, etc.[26] This in turn suggests that a theory of economic growth must contain as an essential component a theory of the behavior of individual sectors, and an investigation of the implications of this behavior for the economy as a whole. Further remarks in this area are contained in the following section of this essay. An additional comment on the adjustment process is in order at this point, however.

26. Walt W. Rostow (*The Process of Economic Growth*, New York, 1952, esp. chaps. 5 and 6) has given specific attention to the role of individual sectors in the growth process. He has also emphasized this point in other of his writings as have Hansen, Robertson, Schumpeter, and others.

If the investment equation in the jth industry is written as:

$$I_{jt} = \Sigma \, b_{it}' \, (x_{jt} - x_{jt-1})$$

where the b_{ij}' is a purely technological coefficient, then we have ruled out disturbances in the system because of investment in the "wrong" sector. This equation states—as did the aggregative equation in the previous section (equation [4])—that entrepreneurs act *after* the increase in demand for their product has already occurred, and therefore we may expect the new capital to be created in that sector where the demand increase has become effective. If, however, we recognize here, as we did earlier, that b_{ij} is a behavioristic, as well as a technological, coefficient, then clearly mistakes and miscalculations are not at all unlikely. This kind of argument implies that if the capital-accumulating projects were allocated in one particular way, total savings would be offset and the equilibrium profit rate earned in all sectors. However, in a society where tastes are changing, innovations are being effected, expectations are jumping around, and numerous other things are happening, it is doubtful whether this precisely correct pattern of investment will be found with no delay and no errors. In any event, independent of mistakes and miscalculations, investment may turn out to be malallocated because of changed conditions between the time the investment is initiated and the time the increased output results. This may be due to many things, not the least of which is the fact that investment in the same industry is being undertaken by different entrepreneurs, and the result may be overproduction in a given area. Thus, we may conclude that the fact that the system may deviate from equilibrium cannot be attributed solely to the inappropriate level of total investment in the "wrong" sector.[27] This in turn suggests that equilibrium requires not only the aggregative equality between intended savings and intended investment, but that it also requires a "balance" among the several sectors of the economy with respect to the demand, supply, and the technological relationships prevailing in the growing system. Since the required balance is unlikely to be achieved at each moment of time—no matter how bright the entrepreneurs—mobility and adaptability would appear essential for continuing uninterrupted growth.

Obviously, the problem is not limited to entrepreneurial foresight and behavior. Labor's mobility and adaptability to a changing economic structure are vital factors. It is not uncommon to find in the literature a reluctance to attach much importance to labor supply as a ceiling on the over-all rate of growth of the economy. However, the point here is not the overall rate of growth, but rather the extent to which labor can and will shift

27. Cf. Rostow, *op.cit.*, chap. 5.

from occupation to occupation in response to changing demand. Indeed, it seems rather clear that inadequate labor mobility may be the major problem in preventing unemployment without first producing inflation in a growing economy. To assume "perfect mobility" is of course to assume the problem away, but it seems exceptionally difficult to formulate specific hypotheses which can be introduced into the argument.[28]

Similar observations are appropriate with respect to finance; although possibly they may be made with less emphasis. There would appear to be a stronger tendency for the supply of finance to move with the demand for it than there is in the case of labor. But there are difficulties here too, especially with respect to new firms and/or small firms, where substantial obstacles to the necessary finance may present themselves to potential entrepreneurs seeking to exploit an available market. A serious bottleneck to growth may develop in an economy dominated by old, large firms which have access to finance—where continuation of growth requires new products produced by new firms which have difficulty in achieving such access.[29]

A final point in this connection may be noted: In addition to resource mobility, appropriate adjustment to changing structure also requires price adjustment. Moreover, for an examination of price behavior as it affects the efficiency with which the economy adapts to such changes, a dynamic process analysis is required—as contrasted to the simpler comparative statics. Thus, it may be said that once the set of ideas developed in Part I of this essay are placed in a disaggregated setting, it is necessary to introduce into the argument what might be called a dynamic value theory. Such a theory is essential in several respects, perhaps the most important of which has to do with the stability of individual sectors and therefore the stability of the economy as a whole. But it is also relevant in terms of explaining entrepreneurial expectations, profit rate behavior, and the speed with which a system may eliminate non-optimum allocation conditions. For the most part, the literature available in this area has been limited to single markets, and has not been concerned specifically with the problem in a growing economy.[30]

The expanding circular flow is unrealistic in another respect; as noted earlier, it seems clear that in all economies which have experienced rising per capita income, capital has grown more rapidly than the labor supply. This means that it becomes necessary to introduce innovations into the

28. A useful and informative quantitative study of labor mobility is provided by William H. Miernyk, *Inter-Industry Labor Mobility*, Boston, 1955.

29. Further discussion of the role of finance in this connection may be found in Joan Robinson, *The Rate of Interest and Other Essays*, London, 1952, pp. 80-86, and in W. Arthur Lewis, *The Theory of Economic Growth*, London, 1955, *passim*.

30. A convenient discussion of the problem referred to here may be found in Baumol's *Economic Dynamics*, Part II. Baumol's comments are based chiefly on the work of Paul A. Samuelson, *Foundations of Economic Analysis*, Cambridge, 1947, and J. R. Hicks, *Value and Capital*, Oxford, 1946.

model to maintain the profit rate. For the disaggregated economy, each sector must achieve the appropriate rate of innovations in order to keep the pace. Thus, not only do we require an explanation of some over-all rate of innovation, but also of the distribution of innovation through the system. This imposes a further burden on the theory of technological change, a burden which, unhappily, that theory is ill-equipped to bear.

Another factor of great relevance to our understanding of economic growth is brought to the surface by disaggregation. We are confronted with the fact that "capital" is not a homogeneous resource, but, rather is quite heterogeneous and is therefore a structure.[31] This then suggests that not only are changes in the total quantity of capital important; so also are changes in composition in accounting for the behavior of the profit rate and the rate of investment. Once we allow for heterogeneity, we must also allow for complementarity among the several varieties of capital stock, and complementarity may produce results quite unlike those achieved from a routine application of the variable proportions argument. Capital structure then implies that, in addition to the way it was considered in the aggregated form of the model, "capital" must be considered as a who's who of items, with each such item performing a function essential to the rest (or some of the rest) of the productive capital items. Lachmann has suggested that just as the division of labor was to Adam Smith a strategic factor in economic growth, so too is the division of capital. Capital accumulation does not mean a mere multiplication of the existing who's who; some items will increase, others will remain constant, and new items will appear. And whether a given capital accumulation project will or will not be profitable frequently depends upon the availability of complementary capital items. But if complementary goods are available, there is no necessary reason to assume that newly created capital will earn a lower return than the previously existing capital earned. And, in addition to the complementarities that may be found, there also may be found in a capital structure the source of external economies. Here again, however, we run into a phenomenon, which, although it is of recognized importance in the understanding of a growing economy, has yet to be formalized in such a manner that it can be included simply and easily into the kind of growth model discussed here. The question is particularly pertinent with regard to underdeveloped countries, where it is necessary to assess the role of "social overhead facilities"—highways, communication, etc.—in increasing the productivity of the economy. Such assessment requires a conclusion as to complementarities and external economies, which assessment for the most part

31. See L. M. Lachmann's recent study of capital theory which emphasizes the importance of considering the structure of capital, as well as its total (*Capital and Its Structure,* London, 1956).

must come from an on-the-spot inquiry with little aid from existing theoretical arguments.

CONCLUSION

How can this body of thought regarding economic growth be evaluated? At the aggregative level it was found that the concepts supporting the theory are defective in several respects; furthermore, the basic relationships of the theory—as with all economic theory—are also open to numerous doubts. When the theory is disaggregated, it becomes more realistic, at the expense, however, of introducing several new and intractable problems. It would seem that the usefulness of the theory depends not so much on any specific, rigorously demonstrated conclusion, but rather on the fact that the model does suggest some important requirements which an economy must meet if it is to enjoy smooth and continuing growth. In this respect, this set of ideas is of value.

Three characteristics of the theory are of particular importance. First, it is a short-run theory. It was emphasized earlier in this essay that the aggregative theory arose from a single alteration of the Keynesian model. And Keynes' model is of course short-run. This characteristic is especially apparent in the rigid form in which the model—aggregative and disaggregative forms—was first introduced. The assumption of fixed production coefficients, for example, can hardly be defended except in the very short run. When this and similar assumptions are relaxed—as they must be when the analysis includes a long interval of time—then it is evident that those items assumed constant in the theory (as presented up to this point of our discussion) are indeed strategic to the growth process, and must therefore be included in the explanatory framework. It then becomes profitable to explore somewhat the literature on these more slowly changing factors of growth in an effort to determine what light has been thrown on their behavior through time, and to inquire further as to how the short-run model responds to this behavior.

This approach is suggested by a second characteristic of the theory as outlined herein. The extension of the Keynesian model pointed up the fact that investment is capacity-creating as well as income-generating. It has also been shown that in those systems where growth is taking place, innovations are necessary to maintain the profit rate at the equilibrium level. Innovations have virtually unlimited ramifications in an economy; in particular, they may be expected to change the a's, the b's, and the k's, i.e., change the structure of the economic system. Thus, economic growth results in rising income and rising capacity *and* in structural changes. These structural changes, in turn, change the environment within which the short-run mechanism functions. It then becomes necessary to examine the nature of these structural changes and the resulting effect upon the growth-generating powers of the economy. Thus both of the points mentioned here lead to the conclusion that the analysis, as presented up to this point, must be deepened, if it is to throw any light at all upon the truly long-run performance of an economy. The remaining sections of this essay are devoted to this purpose.

The third characteristic of the set of ideas under discussion shall be cited here, but not discussed. In effect, the theory jumps into the middle of an economy that is already in motion. But in many economies in the world, growth is about to begin, and in such economies the problems focus on establishing the appropriate preconditions for growth, rather than maintaining an already established growth rate. Thus, one can conceive of the problems of an underdeveloped world in terms of creating an economy whose routine functioning produces growth. These problems bring us into contact with a whole host of difficulties distinct from those considered here; to attempt even a cursory review of current thinking on this subject would take us well beyond the time and space available.

II

Structural Changes

Let us suppose that an economy has overcome the barriers to initiating growth just referred to, and is embarking on a period of sustained upward movement from a situation previously characterized by a relatively low (about subsistence) per capita income. The problem at this point is to indicate in broad outline the major changes that take place as this economy continues its growth over a period of substantial length. Given this broad outline as background, an attempt will then be made to examine more specifically changes in the structure of the economy and the consequences of such changes on the ability of the system to continue to grow.

The work of Kuznets, Burns, and Hoffmann provides the basic source of data for the theoretical discussion of this general problem, and heavy reliance is placed on the findings of these authors.[32] For those countries and industries for which data are available over an extended period of time,

32. Simon Kuznets, "Quantitative Aspects of Economic Growth of Nations. II. Industrial Distribution of the National Product and Labor Force," *Economic Development and Cultural Change*, Supplement, V, 1957; Arthur F. Burns, *Production Trends in the United States Since 1870*, New York, 1934; and Walter G. Hoffmann, *British Industry 1700-1950*, Oxford, 1955.

it seems reasonably clear that no one narrowly defined industry will continue to grow at a constant percentage rate; rather, it may be expected to grow strongly in the period immediately after its inception, and then to taper off as it catches up with the rest of the economy. This means that at any given period of time, a few industries are experiencing vigorous and rapid development and are, as it were, pulling the rest of the economy along. However, this rate of growth does not continue indefinitely. It begins to taper off toward the level of the rate of growth of the economy as a whole; eventually it will fall below the rate, and possibly decline in absolute terms. This in turn suggests that if total income is to grow at a fairly constant rate, some industries must be growing more rapidly than total output, while others are growing at a rate less than that of total output.

The supporting argument for this empirical material runs somewhat as follows: The initial period of rapid growth is possible because the new industry must "catch up" with the rest of the economy. For example, in the early days of the tractor, as farms became mechanized, tractor output in the United States could grow very rapidly. But once horses and mules were (almost) completely replaced, tractor demand began to depend upon things other than the mere fact that tractor power was recognized as being more economical than animal power. When an industry has "caught up," its future growth rate usually depends on one or more of three factors: the behavior of population, demand, and technology.

As for the population factor, it is suggested simply that the demand for a product follows population changes. Since, for the period covered by the earlier investigators of this problem, the rate of population growth for most western countries had fallen, it has been held that this decline contributed to the decline in the growth rate of individual sectors. But when per capita income is rising, any such population effect may be washed out by the income effect, and therefore something must be added about the behavior of the Engel curves. The simplest hypothesis we can formulate in this connection is that the Engel curve for any single product will at some level of per capita income flatten out (and possibly even turn down). If the Engel curves do behave in this manner, then as per capita income approaches the level where the income effect on demand becomes negligible, the rate of growth of demand for the product will begin to tail off to that promoted by population growth. Therefore, if the extent of the population effect is declining, and the income effect has run its course, the rate of growth of demand for the product will tend to fall.[33]

33. Such a hypothesis about the shape of Engel curves can hardly be said to be firmly based upon empirical findings, but it does seem to be appealing on theoretical grounds, and at least it is not inconsistent with the data. See Herman Wold, *Demand Analysis*, New York, 1953, chap. 1, and Richard Stone, *The Measurement of Consumers' Expenditure and Behavior in the United Kingdom 1920-1938*, Cambridge, 1954, I, chap. 23.

This hypothesis with regard to changing income elasticities of demand has been used to account for the change in the composition of output which seems to be characteristic of an economy in which per capita income is rising. In particular, this argument has been used to explain the decline in the size of agricultural output, relative to total output, as an economy emerges from a very low and constant per capita income status into a situation where per capita income is increasing. This is to say, the income elasticities of agricultural products begin to decline at an early stage of the growth process and, if income continues to rise, an increasing proportion of it will be devoted to the purchase of nonagricultural products.[34] The decline in the rate of the growth of demand for agricultural products also releases resources from this sector and these resources become available for the production of products which are beginning to enjoy an increasing demand. The changing pattern of consumer demand therefore results in tendencies toward industrialization accompanying rising per capita incomes. To the extent that this process succeeds, and the economy changes from an essentially agricultural to an industrialized society, additional growth-affecting events may be expected to occur. Two of these are of particular importance.

In the first place, as the composition of output changes, so also will the flow and capital (supply) coefficients, the *a*'s and *k*'s. It is especially important to note that as capital accumulation finds its way into manufacturing activities, the capital-output ratios may be significantly different from those which obtained when the economy was primarily agricultural. If the saving-income ratio remains constant, then such changes in the *k*'s will produce changes in the over-all rate of growth of output. The question of whether or not some order can be found in the changes in the *k*'s will be considered in a later section of this essay. At this time, I would merely call attention to the fact that the changes in the composition of output which are assumed to accompany growth, produce not only the problems of internal adjustment discussed earlier, but may also effect changes in the rate of growth the system can achieve at a given propensity to save.

A second factor has to do with the general social and cultural patterns which characterize the system. In particular, evidence has been produced to suggest that industrialization tends to be accompanied by

34. The income elasticity of the demand for agricultural products does not decline immediately consequent to rising per capita income. Indeed, this elasticity is likely to remain relatively high for a considerable time as income rises from a near subsistence level. This is especially relevant in countries where the increased income results from the fact that very low income groups in the society enjoy the major part of the rising income. Therefore, either because of a change in income distribution, or because growth begins from such a very low base, the argument in the text may not be applicable for a substantial period after growth is initiated.

urbanization; and, to some extent, it may indeed be argued that urbanization is a necessary concomitant to industrialization. The new social and economic conditions required for the successful change-over of a pre-industrial society into an industrialized one, although not uniquely urban, are more likely to thrive in an urban environment than elsewhere. For example, the management of a manufacturing enterprise with any degree of success requires a labor force fully committed to earning its livelihood by industrial activity, and it would appear that only urban workers fit this description. In the operation of many manufacturing techniques, it is also useful to have a group of firms supply the needed raw materials, the needed finance, the needed skills, etc. It is therefore to be expected that as the level of per capita income reaches the point where demand forces resources into areas other than agriculture, the extent to which the population is concentrated in urban areas is increased, and, in particular, the extent to which it is concentrated in other than small agricultural villages is greatly increased.

In turn, this industrialization-urbanization movement produces further consequences of relevance to the growth process. Workers come into contact with new and different ideas, with new ways of thinking and doing things; and such new contacts may be expected to contribute to the increased flexibility and fluidity of the social system within which the economic system functions. Such changes facilitate and indeed encourage the adaptation—and possibly the creation—of improved economic processes. Thus, the growth of cities seems to take place in a cultural climate favorable to economic change, and the industrial city then tends to become a leading force in strengthening the tendencies toward an economy based on "rational" economic behavior. On this basis, it may be argued that industrialization results not merely in a change in the composition of output, but also, and more importantly, in the emergence of an environment which, rather than impeding technical and social innovations, makes change a part of the routine of the economic process.[35]

---

35. A series of papers on urbanization and economic growth has been published in *Economic Development and Cultural Change,* III, October 1954 and January 1955. See also two papers by Bert Hoselitz: "Role of Cities in Economic Growth," *Journal of Political Economy,* LXI, 1953, pp. 195-208, and "The City, the Factory, and Economic Growth," *American Economic Review,* XLV, 1955, pp. 166-84. The importance to growth of a flexible and adaptable social system is discussed by numerous authors. See especially W. Arthur Lewis, *The Theory of Economic Growth,* London, 1955, chaps. 3 and 4, and H. G. Barrett, *Innovations: The Basis of Cultural Change,* New York, 1953, *passim.* Hoselitz, in the second of his articles referred to above, found that urban centers in modern underdeveloped countries do not follow the description in the text. This may be explained by noting that the increased rate of urbanization that apparently has taken place recently in such areas has not been in response to attractive economic advantages in the cities. Rather, this increased urbanization is the result of unemployment and other severe economic pressures in rural areas. The cities then become a reservoir of demoralized and unemployed workers of little or no use in any industrial movement that may get under way.

A final factor may be introduced to account for the behavior of individual sectors–innovations. Earlier, the expanding circular flow was seen to require that the rate of innovations–i.e., the rate of increase in output that would occur with no increase in inputs–be the same in each sector of the system; and if this were true, the innovations would have no effect on the changing relative position of the several industries. Such an assumption is hardly reasonable. Both Burns and Kuznets suggest that within a single industry the rate of technological change must decline.[36] The argument is very simple: In the infancy of the industry, there are wide areas which are amenable to technological improvement; but as the obvious improvements are made, it becomes more and more difficult to maintain a constant rate of innovations unless a major revolution–e.g., atomic power–occurs. If this hypothesis were accepted, it would provide another explanation for the observed behavior of individual industries. There are difficulties with this hypothesis, and these are examined later in this essay. I would point out, however, that any hypothesis formulated with respect to technological change is more likely to be subjected to criticisms than accolades.

At this point, we can be satisfied merely with the observation that innovations will undoubtedly proceed at divergent rates among the several industries. Such divergencies will produce changing relative costs, which, in turn, produce incentives to alter input combinations and consumption patterns. These innovation-induced changes then tend to have an effect similar to that produced by the changing composition of demand, in the sense that demand necessitates shifts in the flow of products. Such shifts require structural changes throughout the system, and these structural changes then become relevant in explaining the changing functioning of the short-run dynamic model.[37]

It was indicated above that the source of the changes in the structure and institutions which have been described as part of the growth process is the changing composition of output and changing technology. Evidently, there are additional sources of such changes within the economic system, and, of course, from the noneconomic sphere. But surely the behavior of demand and technology are most strategic. For example, it is frequently pointed out that considerable investment takes place in agriculture in underdeveloped countries which is not included in the statistics. But this type of investment is unlikely to produce changed structure or changed institutions, and therefore is likely to contribute less to growth than capital accumulation, which does produce such changes. Thus, a country whose

36. Burns, *op.cit.*, chap. 4, and Kuznets, "Quantitative Aspects . . . ," *loc.cit.*, *passim*.

37. To the sources mentioned it is necessary to add "autonomous" factors, for example, "autonomous" changes in tastes that seem to occur simply because people are people.

economy has long been dormant has undoubtedly developed an institutional and structural framework which is alien to the growth process. When an economy begins growth after a long period of non-growth, the existing institutions and social organization may well constitute a more fundamental bottleneck to the growth process than will simply a low rate of capital accumulation. It must therefore be emphasized that the growth process must be viewed in a larger context than simply the arithmetic of capital-output ratios, saving-income ratios, and population growth rates. Of greater relevance is an understanding of the mechanism by which the general environment, within which the economy functions, changes in response to those forces immediately responsible for a rising per capita income.

CONCLUSION

This section has had as its purpose a brief examination of, or more accurately, a brief reference to, the sources and nature of structural and institutional changes which obtain in a growing economy. An effort was also made to suggest the general nature of the structural and institutional changes which are likely to be generated by these sources.

Up to this point in this paper, then, two general aspects of the growth process have been defined. The first section emphasized the capacity and income-generating aspects of growth, and the conditions which must be met if these two facets of the growth process are to be kept in reasonable balance. This section, as just noted, has emphasized—albeit somewhat briefly and inadequately—that the very conditions necessary, in order that the economy maintain this balance in a growing system, also create structural changes, and that these changes, in turn, affect the "parameters" that govern the functioning of the capacity-creating, income-generating mechanism. In reducing the rigidities of the Harrod-Domar model, and in introducing structural changes into the discussion, considerable departure from a "Keynesian-type" world has been achieved. And, as stated earlier, attention must be focused on those factors which seem to determine the extent to which an economy is able to generate growth over a continuing interval. This means it is necessary to examine population behavior, technological change, and the like—problems more Ricardian than Keynesian. I shall attempt to do this in the following section, despite the difficulties involved in formulating such an analysis. The current literature contains little in the way of formal analysis, and few empirical hypotheses can bear up under the heavy artillery of facts. Nevertheless, such an inquiry is an essential step in an investigation of the growth problem, and our efforts in this direction may prove interesting.

III

The Long-Run Behavior of the Short-Run Parameters

POPULATION

In the preceding discussion it was assumed that the rate of growth of population and the ratio of the labor force to total population remain constant. However, once the interval of time, included within the analysis, is stretched out, neither assumption is valid. Since population behavior is strategic to the growth process in several ways, we must seek an explanation of this behavior. Specifically, the problem is to indicate the time paths of population growth and the labor force-population ratio which prevail as an economy changes from a non-growth into a growing society.[38] The consequence of such time paths for the growth of per capita output will be examined in various contexts below.

Most non-growth, pre-industrial economies were—and are—characterized by high birth and death rates. The high death rate is explained by the inadequacy of diet, shelter, sanitation facilities, preventative medicine, etc. Given the high death rate, a high birth rate is essential for the survival of the society. Under such conditions, it is not surprising that the institutions, cultural patterns, and social customs characteristic of such societies are of a type to encourage a high birth rate.[39] The result of this combination is a stable, or very slowly growing, population, and, what is more important, neither mortality nor natality are under very secure control. Thus, the time path of population growth evidently depends on the response of natality and mortality rates to economic growth.

The problems are simpler with respect to mortality, and agreement is much more widespread here than it was regarding the explanation of changes in the fertility rate. The death rate may be expected to decline very rapidly as per capita income grows from a low level. In simple terms, as per capita income rises, more resources may be devoted to health, sani-

38. The literature on population problems is surely without end. Happily, the United Nations has recently published a useful review of much of this literature, both old and new, in *The Determinants and Consequences of Population Trends,* New York, 1953. This is an exceedingly impressive work, and a very sad one. It is impressive in that it includes such a tremendous number of authors and treats their work in a well-organized coherent fashion. It is sad because it reveals so clearly our lack of understanding and agreement with respect to a problem which has been attracting the attention of men ever since they became aware that there was population. Economists, of course, are indebted to Professor J. J. Spengler for his work in the area of economic demography; see especially his essays in Harold F. Williamson and John A. Buttrick, eds., *Economic Development,* New York, 1954, chap. 3, and in Haley, *op.cit.,* chap. 3. See also the collection of readings, edited by Spengler and Otis D. Duncan, entitled *Population Theory and Policy,* Glencoe, 1956.

39. "High" death and birth rates would be in the neighborhood of forty per thousand.

tation, and medical facilities, plus the fact that the population has a more satisfactory diet and lives in more comfortable houses. As a result, death (particularly among infants) attributed to malnutrition, epidemics, exposure, and lack of medical care is reduced; moreover, improved transportation and communication help to eliminate the local famines that resulted in huge loss of life so often in the past. There seems to be no instance in the world where this effect of rising per capita income on the mortality rate has not been operative.

The major reduction in the mortality rate that growing countries have experienced has been due to curative medicine only to a very small degree; rather, it may be attributed to the control of infection and contagion and improved environmental conditions. It seems clear, however, that the impact of such factors on the death rate approaches a maximum as income continues to rise; further reductions in mortality in high income countries must depend upon major advances in medicine. The results to date suggest that such medical advances work relatively slowly once the most destructive diseases are conquered.[40] Therefore, the decline in the death rate may be expected to taper off as the advantages of sanitation, etc., are more fully exploited, and reliance for further reduction then begins to rest on increased medical knowledge. Hence, it is expected that the death rate will fall rapidly, but at a decreasing rate, and finally will fall very slowly as a system progresses from a very low per capita income to a very high per capita income.

One further point is appropriate in this connection. It is apparent that it is now possible to reduce the death rate with insignificant changes in the level of income. Previously, the death rate responded to improvements in the means of subsistence and living conditions, but measures are now available that eliminate the source of many diseases with no prior rise in income. For example, DDT may be used in many places to wipe out virtually all malaria, with a consequent reduction in the death rate, and the low price of DDT makes it available almost anywhere in the world. This point will be referred to again in connection with the particular problem of underdeveloped countries.[41]

As indicated above, the causes and effects of natality are less clear, and opinion is much more diverse in this respect. I would begin this discussion with one general, but revealing, statement. It was pointed out above that the death rate responds to a rising income as such, but it seems clear that the birth rate does not respond to rising incomes so much as it does to the structural and institutional changes which accompany rising incomes. This fact is of importance in at least two connections. In

40. See the J. J. Spengler, in Williamson and Buttrick, eds., *op.cit.*, pp. 98*ff*.

41. See Kingsley Davis, "The Amazing Decline of Mortality in Underdeveloped Countries," *American Economic Review*, XLVI, 1956, pp. 305-18.

the first place, structural and institutional changes occur more slowly than do simple changes in capacity and income. For this reason, we expect birth rates to react more slowly than death rates to changes in the level of income. In the second place, structural changes are much more uncertain and much more intractable to economic analysis than are income and capacity changes. This, added to the fact that the birth rate response to the changes which do occur is also subject to considerable doubt, means that birth rate behavior through time is difficult to explain and even more difficult to predict.

Indeed, the literature does seem to concentrate upon a relatively small number of explanatory factors. The existence of a negative relationship between the birth rate and the development of the "values associated with modern urban life" is frequently emphasized. It was observed in the previous section of this contribution that such values are likely to develop as an economy experiences the pangs of industrialization. From this, then, it is concluded that income growth produces industrialization, which, in turn, tends to destroy those institutions that encouraged a high birth rate and replace them with institutions that encourage a low birth rate.

Several aspects of modern urban life are usually referred to as contributing to this result. Almost all authors concentrate attention on the development of the importance of the individual, his health and personal comfort. Furthermore, it is argued that the urban community tends to produce a population in which a more rationalistic attitude toward decision-making prevails, and deliberate control of fertility becomes common practice. Thus, as it becomes obvious that having more children means reduced living standards, family size is likely to decline. This is particularly true in the light of the evidence that children remain an economic liability for a much longer period in urban, industrial society than they do in rural, agricultural areas. Geographical and class mobility, commercial recreation, and female employment are also assumed to contribute to an atmosphere which is conducive to small families. Evidently, however, the changes referred to in this paragraph come about slowly and unevenly, and birth rate response must also be expected to be slow and uneven. In this connection, most writers seem to believe the birth rate will respond, albeit slowly, to the changes that accompany economic growth, and that it will eventually follow the mortality rate downward.

With respect to the labor force-population ratio, two factors may be noted. First, the decline in the mortality rates at the outset of growth is likely to be concentrated among the children in the society. The result, of course, is an immediate fall in the labor force-population ratio, i.e., an immediate fall in the productive proportion of the population. Second, as the birth rate falls, and population growth drops very low, the labor force-population ratio will at some point tend to rise as the average age of the population rises. Indeed, this could continue until the size of the labor force relative to the population begins to fall because such a large part of the population is in the retired category. Thus, if medical science increases life expectancy from sixty-five to ninety years, without increasing the interval during which an individual is able to work at the same time, a very low birth rate may result in a declining labor force-population ratio.

These remarks suggest the general evolutionary pattern of population growth and age composition which seems to accompany the growth of real per capita income. The population tends to pass from a high growth rate, characterized by a constant birth rate and a rapidly falling death rate, to a situation with a low growth potential, where both the birth rate and the death rate are very low, with the former slightly higher, but falling. The labor force-population ratio tends to be relatively low in a high growth-potential population, will fall even lower as the mortality rate drops, and then will begin to rise as the birth rate falls, possibly only to fall again as the population achieves greater life expectancy.[42]

Two problems worthy of particular emphasis emerge from such an analysis. First, the high growth-potential of the population in many low income areas which are already densely populated creates a major obstacle to the achievement of a growing economy. Huge investment outlays would be necessary, if growth of income is to outrun population, for a sufficiently long period to establish an atmosphere conducive to reduced birth rates. Contemporary high income areas did not face this problem; not only was it impossible a century ago to reduce the death rate at the current rate, but, too, no country now classified as highly developed was as densely populated when it began its growth as are some of the modern underdeveloped countries. It becomes increasingly apparent that methods must be found to limit the quick upsurge in population, if some of the more heavily populated countries are to emerge from their stagnant, low income status.[43]

The second problem it might be well to keep in mind has to do with the fact that over any given short-run interval of time, the birth rate-death rate argument stated above may be submerged by other considerations. For example, population growth in the United States in the 1930's fell exceedingly low, presumably as a result of the prolonged depression of this period. Since about 1940, however, population growth has been

42. This behavior of the L/P ratio may be complicated by an increase in the number of women in the labor force. This number—in terms of the total labor force—probably rises along with per capita income.

43. Two discussions of this problem have been published recently: R. R. Nelson, "A Theory of the Low-Level Equilibrium Trap," *American Economic Review*, XLVI, 1956, pp. 894-908, and Harvey Leibenstein, *A Theory of Economic Demographic Development*, Princeton, 1954.

higher than "normal"; apparently, an effort is being made to make up for the 30's. It would appear that neither the experience of the 30's nor that of recent years represents a fundamental change in the reproduction habits of United States citizens. Nevertheless, such shocks to the system are of importance in explaining the actual growth path followed by an economy, and create difficulties in establishing any general set of principles that may be assumed to govern a phenomena. Despite such reservations, in the following sections it will be assumed that the propositions of this sub-section have reasonable validity.

THE SAVING-INCOME RATIO

In Section I the saving function was described as simply as possible; saving was made to depend upon current income, and the marginal and average propensity to save were assumed to be equal and constant through time. The problem in this section is to treat the saving ratio as a variable, and to seek to isolate those factors that determine its time path. However, it is convenient at this point to write the saving-income relationship as $S = s\ (Y - m)$. The m indicates the income at which there is zero net saving; $Y - m$ would be the income out of which positive saving took place. This is a useful formulation, because it would seem that the behavior of m is of considerable relevance in accounting for the behavior of total saving through time.

The statistical evidence for the United States and the United Kingdom suggests that the proportion of income saved has remained relatively constant for the interval from 1875 to 1950. Much of the literature is concerned with the examination of hypotheses which would account for this particular phenomenon.[44] The discussion here will not seek to defend a given empirical hypothesis, but rather to examine some of the arguments currently extant with respect to changes in the propensity of an economy to save.

The population pattern outlined above may have some effect. If, in a society with a constant total income and a constant age distribution of income, all individuals saved solely for retirement, a stable population with an unchanging age distribution would have zero net saving, as the dissaving of retired members of the society would be matched exactly by the saving of employed people. There would be net saving with either

44. As might be expected, the literature on the consumption and/or saving function is vast. The particular question asked here has not been discussed directly to the same extent as more "static" or "comparative static" questions. Raymond W. Goldsmith (*A Study of Saving in the United States*, Princeton; 1956, III) provides a lengthy list of references, as well as a general survey of recent efforts, to find "the" saving function discussed in Part IV, below. See also James S. Duesenberry, *Income, Saving and the Theory of Consumer Behavior*, Cambridge, 1954, and the literature cited therein.

a rising population or a rising per capita income because the number of savers would exceed the number of dissavers, or because the income of current savers would exceed the income of past savers. But complications arise even in this simple situation because accumulated savings and present assets are not necessarily equal; and there are further difficulties as well, since the age distribution of a growing population is also changing.

Children under fifteen, for example, and adults over about sixty-five are generally not earners, and the larger these groups become, the lower will aggregative saving tend to be. Therefore, the increase in population growth due to a decline in child mortality will tend to produce a reduction in aggregative saving. If income per capita continues to rise, and population responds as indicated earlier, then the proportion of the population in the labor force will also rise and savings will tend to increase. However, within the working-age group, it seems that workers over forty-five or fifty save more than younger workers in the labor force. The argument is simply that by middle age most families are established–houses and furniture are bought and paid for, children are educated, and other major expenditures have been made–and retirement begins to loom well within the time horizon. Under these conditions, the incentive to make consumption expenditures falls, and the incentive to save rises. If the proportion of retirees does increase, then the tendency produced will be in the direction of reduced saving.

The effect of population on saving would appear to result in a falling capacity to save at the outset of growth, followed by a steadily rising capacity, which reaches a peak when the age distribution is such that the proportion of the population in the fifty to sixty-five age groups is a maximum; from this point it declines. Such a population effect is undoubtedly small in magnitude, and the effect of population behavior on the composition of output may be more important. In the high growth-potential situation, with children comprising a relatively large proportion of the population, a major share of expenditure on what is usually classified as consumption may have a significant effect on the capacity of the system to produce. Similarly, in a population with an age structure which yields a large proportion of the population over, say, sixty-five, expenditures on health and welfare services will have no effect on the capacity of the economy. Thus, even though a society with a relatively high percentage of the population in the under-fifteen age group may save less out of a given income than a population with an older age structure, resources devoted to increasing capacity may be as large or larger. It is important, however, to bear in mind that the gestation period of such outlays is likely to be unusually long.

The structural changes outlined in Section II, above, have also been used to explain saving behavior. In particular, the difference between the propensity for rural and urban residents to save and the saving capacity of employees, as compared with the self-employed, has attracted attention. Generally, the rural farmer has less contact with new products and new ideas than his urban counterpart, and perhaps he is also under less pressure to match his neighbors in consumption habits. For the self-employed, the argument is usually stated in terms of incentives to save: The self-employed achieves greater professional and social prestige from capital accumulation than from consumption expenditures, and this in turn induces a greater effort to save. If increased urbanization and a relative decrease in the self-employed is characteristic of a growing economy, then counteracting effects on total national saving are produced. The net effect depends then upon the relative strength of the two forces and the time when they become effective. Little information seems available in this regard. Of course, hypotheses have also been formulated with respect to the effect of income and its distribution on total saving.

The available data show rather clearly that at a given level of national income, persons in the higher income brackets save a larger proportion of their income than do those in the lower income groups, and from this empirical evidence it is tempting to go on to the proposition that as per capita income rises all along the line, total saving will rise relative to income. But this is a questionable leap. If we rule out cyclical effects and lags, then, in effect, this proposition means that "wants" are more nearly satisfied at higher income levels than they are at lower levels. But surely within the range of income that now appears attainable, this proposition has little to recommend it. Rather, historical experience suggests that "wants" vary with the power to satisfy them, and tend to increase with knowledge of new products and new services. This in turn implies that "wants" do not constitute a definite, finite quantity, but are a function of the extent of our capacity to exploit our economic resources.

Persons in the higher income brackets at a given level of income do save a larger share of their income than do those in the lower income groups, but this is explained in terms of sources of income, lags in the development of new consumption outlets, relative income position, etc., rather than in the mere height of the absolute magnitude of income.

However, if, at any level of income, the higher income groups tend to save a larger proportion of their income than do the low income groups, the larger the share of income going to a given percentage of the population, the larger will be the over-all saving total. And if, as the system develops, there is a more unequal distribution of income, then this will contribute to a rising proportion of income saved. Unhappily, there is little evidence as to the behavior of income distribution in a growing economy.[45] The two factors mentioned most frequently are: the behavior of innovations and monopoly. Further comments on innovations may be postponed until the following section of this essay. As to monopoly, despite the considerable literature on the subject, it seems safe to say that economists have yet to make up their minds as to whether or not monopoly increases with economic growth. Several hypotheses exist on both sides, but until further empirical evidence is available little headway is likely. And then, even if it is concluded that monopoly increases with growth, this conclusion may be undermined by development of antidotes to monopolistic effects on income distribution—e.g., labor unions.

Other factors may be mentioned, but these are probably less important. Urban income is more unequal than farm income, and so the trend toward urbanization may result in increased inequality of the distribution of income. Personal services which earn a high income are difficult to bequeath to one's heirs, and therefore this kind of income does not accumulate. Taxing policies may be such that inequality is decreased. And other factors might be cited, but the results are quite inconclusive.

Our inquiry is further thwarted by the fact that it is possible to make a good case that saving will increase with an equalizing of income. If much of consumption is of the imitative variety, then the elimination of consumption leaders in the upper income groups may mean that the lower income groups would save a higher proportion of their incomes. Thus, it is not clear what the time path of income distribution in a growing economy will be, and even if it were known, the effect on saving would still remain doubtful.

More recently, it has been argued that though the factors listed above may have some effect on aggregative saving, that effect is slight (or it has been in the United States at least). Rather, it is assumed that if income grows smoothly and without interruption, then the saving-income ratio remains about constant.[46] In cyclical fluctuations—from one peak income, through depression, to recovery, to the level of the preceding peak—saving falls and then rises more than proportionately to income. When income proceeds beyond the level of the preceding highest peak, then saving rises about in proportion to income, and the assumption of equality between the average and the marginal propensity to save is valid. This hypothesis

45. Kuznets recently published a study on income distribution: "Economic Growth and Income Inequality," *American Economic Review*, XLV, 1955, pp. 1-29.

46. This argument was first stated by Duesenberry, *op.cit.*, and Franco Modigliani, "Fluctuations in the Saving-Income Ratio: A Problem in Economic Forecasting," in *Studies in Income and Wealth*, New York, XI, 1949. See also R. C. O. Matthews, "The Saving Function and the Problem of Trend and Cycle," *Review of Economic Studies*, XXII, 1954-55, pp. 75-95. Richard M. Goodwin ("Problems of Trend and Cycle," *Yorkshire Bulletin of Economic and Social Research*, V, 1953, pp. 89-98) argues that fixed expenditures of the firm rise more easily during a boom than they fall during a downturn. Thus, a firm's "consumption" behaves very similarly to an individual's.

rests on the argument that a family tends to make its consumption standard correspond to its position on the Lorenz income distribution curve. As income rises, it is necessary to increase consumption expenditure, in order to maintain consumption at the standard required of one's income group. As a result, the short-run saving function would be moving to the right, i.e., the value of income at which there is zero saving, m in the earlier equation, would rise. For the United States, this hypothesis appears reasonably appropriate as an explanation of the secular constancy of the saving-income ratio since about 1870.

Nor is this explanation of saving behavior necessarily inconsistent with the hypotheses offered earlier. Indeed, it seems appropriate to argue that the Duesenberry-Modigliani theory requires for its validity the institutional and structural changes that accompany economic growth. In particular, it seems essential to emphasize the role of new products and new ways of living that occur in a growing economy. If the Engel curve of each individual product does in fact level off at some level of per capita income, then evidently new products must be forthcoming constantly, if the saving-income ratio is to remain about constant.[47] Thus, here again it would appear that the growth of income is not the key to the behavior of a short-run parameter; rather, that key is to be found in the structural changes which are part of the growth process.

With respect to corporate saving, available hypotheses are even less precise and trustworthy than they are for personal saving. Professor Hansen has suggested that since corporations seek to maintain a fairly reliable dividend policy, they are reluctant to cut dividends in the face of falling income and hesitate to raise them even if income is rising, as long as it remains below the previous highest level.[48] If income continues to rise, stockholder pressure may be expected to produce rising dividends approximately in proportion with income. This would produce the same ratchet effect as is found in individual saving. The evidence that corporations seek to maintain a relatively constant dividend payment in money terms is fairly clear-cut, but it is necessary to recognize at the same time that investment plans are also a determining factor. Thus, corporation saving is not completely independent of demand for investment. The latter is especially relevant, since many large enterprises tend to finance much of their capital expansion from internal accumulation. It would appear that over a given short period the effort to maintain a particular size dividend payment would be the over-riding consideration, and that saving would be simply a residual. Over a longer period of time, however, it would

47. Cf. Alvin H. Hansen, *Business Cycles and National Income*, New York, 1951, pp. 164*ff*.

48. *Ibid.*, p. 169.

seem more valid to assume that corporate saving is not independent of corporate investment plans.[49]

Is any sort of general conclusion possible with respect to the behavior of the saving propensity in a growing economy? Perhaps it is legitimate to assume that the level of income at which saving equals zero rises as income grows. Possibly, it is also meaningful to assume, as a first approximation, that a relatively low saving propensity will tend to prevail in the earlier stages of the growth process, and then slowly rise as the system becomes more completely "modernized." This hypothesis may be defended on the grounds that structural changes making for a low saving propensity–urbanization, new products, young age composition of the population, and so on–are stronger at this early stage in an economy's growth process than they are later. After such major structural adjustments have worked themselves out, the ratchet principle, supplemented by the new product assumption, may become more nearly appropriate. Although here institutionalized saving may alter this effect, and it is not yet clear whether (in the United States) social security, extended pension coverage, etc., are having a secular effect on saving behavior.

With respect to corporate saving, it seems useless to attempt to evolve a set of hypotheses which would define a time path. One interesting argument suggested by Professor Lewis and Mrs. Robinson,[50] among others, concerns the distribution of saving among firms: Savings are made by old and cautious firms and here reserves accumulate, while young and enterprising firms suffer from a lack of access to funds. Since new firms seem essential to continuing growth, such a development may be an obstacle of some magnitude. This is largely a question of the study of finance rather than saving, but the problem arises–or is said to arise–due to assumptions regarding corporation saving behavior. However, the evidence is far from clear in this area, and firm conclusions must await additional data.

THE CAPITAL-OUTPUT RATIOS

We turn now to the set of problems involved in explaining the time path of the productivity of capital, i.e., the time path of the capital-output ratios, the k's in the model. The convenient assumption of constancy of this coefficient, or matrix of coefficients, was made in both the aggregative

49. For a discussion of the difficulties entailed in applying the Duesenberry-Modigliani hypothesis to corporation saving behavior, see John Lintner, "The Determinants of Corporation Savings," in *Savings in the Modern Economy*, Walter W. Heller, Francis M. Boddy, and Carl L. Nelson, eds., Minneapolis, 1953. This article also contains a number of useful references.

50. See footnote 29, above.

and the disaggregative form of the short-run model. However, it was further assumed that the capital coefficients were not fixed technologically, but, instead, responded to changing relative prices of factor inputs. This latter assumption tended to remove the stability problem, which has been of concern to several writers in this field, and also made it necessary to discuss briefly the way the k's may change as the system grows. It is appropriate at this point to identify three major factors as influencing the behavior of the productivity of capital: availability of other inputs, technological change, and the composition of output. These will be considered below in the order listed.

With a given technology, it is usually assumed that the productivity of a given factor is greater, the more abundant the supply of other factors. Therefore, if a two-input production function is assumed, and capital is growing more rapidly than labor, there should be a tendency for the marginal product of capital (and at some point the average product) to decline. If population follows the pattern outlined earlier, then the rate of growth of the labor supply will rise significantly only after growth has been proceeding for some time. This is due to the concentration of the reduction of the death rate among pre-working age groups; and though population shoots up rapidly, labor force changes may lag behind until the older age groups begin to increase. At this point, the growth rate of the labor force will begin to increase more rapidly and will approximate the growth rate of population until the post-working age group begins to grow relative to the rest of the population. Under the usual assumptions, it is expected that the lower the growth rate of the labor supply, the greater the rate of increase of the (incremental) capital-output ratio. Per capita output will grow at a rate which will also move in direct opposition to population growth, and which will lie at some value between the rate of growth of population and that of capital.

This simplified diminishing returns argument ignores the possibilities of complementarities, external economies, and increasing returns to scale, that is, it ignores the point, made earlier, that capital has a structure and cannot be treated as a homogeneous input. It is clear that the existence of such phenomena may prevent diminishing returns from becoming effective, but little else is clear. Perhaps the safest procedure is to say that each situation must be diagnosed separately, that conclusions will depend upon a given set of circumstances. Nevertheless, one hypothesis seems worthy of mention, at least. In the early stages of growth, it may be argued, the "complementarity effect" on the newly created capital is sufficiently great that any tendency toward diminishing returns is outweighed. Thus, even though capital accumulation proceeds at a rate greater than the corresponding rate of the labor supply, the capital-output ratios will tend to remain about constant. It is especially important to emphasize that the capital created is not a reproduction of already existing capital goods. However, as the economic system continues to grow and to acquire a larger and larger capital stock–i.e., a longer and longer list of capital goods–the "complementarity effect" becomes less powerful, and, in turn, the simple diminishing returns argument becomes increasingly applicable. The conclusion then would be that for an economy just beginning to emerge from a low income, non-growth status, diminishing returns to capital would not be a damaging factor to the rate of growth of output for a considerable period of time.[51]

However, the productivity of capital is affected, not only by the quantity of other inputs, but also by the quality of such inputs. The major change in the quality of labor is likely to be concentrated in the period immediately after the industrialization process begins–perhaps capitalization process is a better term. At the very outset of growth, labor may well be untrained (and possibly untrainable) and may not have adapted to new routines and new tools. During this period, the capital-output ratios will tend to be higher and the rate of increase in output lower, irrespective of the relative supplies of capital and labor. As the new forms of economic activity become more widespread and accepted, as younger workers become more educated and better trained, and as improved food and housing facilities become available, it may be expected that the productivity of capital will rise because of the application of more effective labor. At the same time, it would appear that the extent of change in labor's role is not without limit, and that after the economy achieves a reasonably high degree of capitalization, this force will no longer be a significant contributing factor in explaining changes in the *k*'s.

If natural resources are introduced into the production function, the argument which emphasizes diminishing returns to capital is strengthened. If there are rich and abundant resources, obviously this factor will tend to increase the productivity of capital and facilitate the maintenance of growth. As resources become depleted, we would expect more capital to be required to create the same rate of output, therefore raising the *k*'s. The difficulty with this approach is that "natural resources" are not a datum, but depend upon the state of technology. Objects of no economic value may become valuable because of a new invention; similarly, objects of great economic value at one point may be worthless at another time because of a change in technical knowledge. In a system where innovations are more or less regular events, it is not possible to predict what will

51. Thus, Mrs. Robinson, for example, speaks of an economy that has "long since laid the basis of the economic overhead," where population is of sufficient density to "have realized the most important economies of scale." (*The Accumulation of Capital*, p. 343).

happen to inputs of natural resources without giving careful prior consideration to the behavior of innovations.[52] Of course, on the other hand, the relationship between innovations and natural resources is so obscure that little can be said beyond recognition that a relationship does exist. The simplest possible hypothesis is that there are constant (or nondecreasing) returns to labor and capital combined, due to the effects of innovation on natural resources and capital equipment. Perhaps the only thing in favor of such an hypothesis is that it is simple and facilitates theory-making. Even if one is dissatisfied with this hypothesis, the key point is worth keeping in mind: In any analysis of the growth process, natural resources are augmentable and must be so considered.

If it is assumed that capital is growing more rapidly than labor, then the above analysis indicates that at some point the incremental capital-output ratio will begin to rise. Therefore, in order to maintain growth with a constant rate of capital formation, innovations must be introduced into the analysis. An innovation is usually defined as a change in the relationship between inputs and output, i.e., a change in the production function. Therefore, innovations have three effects. First, they evidently affect the rate of output obtainable with given inputs. It is convenient to speak of the rate of innovations as the percentage rate of increase in output that would occur, if inputs remained constant. Second, innovations also affect the coefficients in the production function; and, third, by virtue of the effect on the input coefficients, they also produce changes in the distribution of the total product and the profit rate.

At this point we are concerned with the effect of changes in technical knowledge on the behavior of the capital-output ratios. Other problems will be discussed below. By ignoring possible unfavorable effects on the profit rate, the requirement for technology may be simply stated: If capacity is to grow at a constant rate (with a given rate of saving), innovations must be such that they offset the rise in the k's due to the rising capital-labor ratio. That is, with no innovations, output will grow at a slower rate than will capital; how much slower depends upon the production function and the rate of growth of labor. Innovations must then compensate for labor's failure to grow at the same rate as capital. On the basis of the earlier discussion of the behavior of the rate of growth of the labor force, it would seem unlikely that the capital-labor ratio will behave in a very regular fashion; therefore, if innovations are to compensate exactly, they too must follow a rather complex pattern. It seems reasonable, however, to assume that by the time innovations become essential—to prevent the k's from rising—the rate of growth of labor will have

52. This point is discussed in a helpful way in the first four chapters of the revised edition of Professor A. P. Usher's *History of Mechanical Inventions*, Cambridge, 1954.

become more or less constant at a fairly low level. Even with this simple assumption it is not completely clear what behavior innovations must follow in order to keep the capital-output ratio constant. If k would rise at an increasing rate without innovation, then the effect of innovation on output must grow through time. Or if k should rise only at a constant rate, then the innovation effect need but be constant. It is also necessary for innovations to be such that they facilitate the use of increasing quantities of capital relative to labor. This is necessary because it seems impossible for input price changes alone to accomplish this over an indefinite interval during which capital growth exceeds labor growth. Unless innovations are forthcoming in the prescribed fashion, the assumption of a constant rate of capital formation will result in a declining rate of growth of output. Later in this essay it will be shown that further requirements are imposed on innovation behavior in order to keep the profit rate from falling.

To achieve the expanding circular flow, the required rate of innovation must take place in all sectors. Unless this occurs (or there is a counteracting change in the rate of capital accumulation), some adjustment in the input-output routine is necessary, since the rates of growth of output in the various sectors will no longer be the same. Although little is known about the invention and innovation process, it seems safe to assume that innovations have not, and will not, occur evenly throughout the economy. But, as will be indicated at greater length below, it is difficult to find hypotheses in the literature that suggest how innovations will take place throughout the economy.

Finally, let us consider the effects of the composition of output on the nation's capital requirements. To some extent, it is dangerous to talk about the capital-output ratio of a single industry in isolation, for the capital requirements for a given output depend, in part at least, on what other products are being produced simultaneously. Furthermore, evidently technical advances may be such that they alter capital requirements in varying ways throughout the system, and thus make any sort of discussion of the effect of composition of output on the capital requirements of doubtful value. Nevertheless, it does appear useful in this connection to point out a few rather conspicuous factors.

The available data[53] suggests that in non-growth areas, where agricul-

53. Data in this area are limited in both volume and accuracy. Furthermore, once again, most data pertain to the United States and the United Kingdom. See especially the following Occasional Papers of the National Bureau of Economic Research: Daniel Creamer, *Capital and Output Trends in Manufacturing Industries, 1880-1948,* New York, 1954; A. S. Tostlebe, *The Growth of Physical Capital in Agriculture, 1870-1950,* New York, 1954; T. Borenstein, *Capital and Output Trends in Mining Industries, 1870-1948,* New York, 1954; also Raymond Goldsmith's contribution in *Income and Wealth of the United States,* Cambridge, 1952; E. H. Phelps Brown and B. Weber, "Accumulation, Productivity, and Distribution in the British Economy, 1870-1938," *Economic Jour-*

ture is the dominant activity, little capital is used in the productive process.[54] And, similarly, it has been argued that under these conditions agricultural output may be increased with little capital outlay. When such an economy begins to devote its resources to manufacturing activity, it is likely to experience an increase in capital requirements to produce the composition of output. If saving remains constant, the result will be a slowing down in the rate of growth of output, as the economy begins to reduce its concentration on agricultural output produced with primitive techniques. And for reasons referred to earlier—chiefly, population behavior—this may create difficulties.

Moreover, it seems that some (not all) social overhead facilities are likely to require substantial capital outlays no matter what technique is used. Furthermore, these types of projects are usually indivisible, and substantial building ahead of the market is not uncommon. This, too, will produce an upward pressure on capital requirements. But it may well be that the building of such facilities creates economies in the use of capital in other parts of the system, and that capital requirements are reduced in the economy as a whole. Such economies may not accrue immediately, however, and for a not insignificant period, capital requirements would be increased, due to the effect of these social overhead facilities. Nor is it unreasonable to assume that construction of such capital will constitute a larger proportion of total capital in the earlier, than in the later, phases of growth, and here again is a possible reason why the initial stages of growth may provide the most difficulties in achieving sustained growth. But this is conjecture of a rather radical type, since "social overhead facilities" are rarely built by private undertaking, and governments may build them when they please. However, it may be argued that until these facilities become available, growth will not continue without costly interruption.[55]

Another hypothesis frequently encountered concerns the capital requirements of the so-called tertiary industries. It is frequently argued that,

nal, LXIII, 1953, pp. 263-88; the Leontief volume cited in footnote 15, above; and K. Martin, "Capital-Output Ratios in Economic Development," *Economic Development and Cultural Change,* VI, 1957, pp. 24-31. The United Nations has published some estimates of capital stock and output for a number of "underdeveloped" countries, but these estimates are extremely rough.

54. Not infrequently, agricultural activity in highly developed countries is very intensively capitalized.

55. A number of economists (see, especially, two books by Harvey Leibenstein, *A Theory of Economic Demographic Development,* and *Economic Backwardness and Economic Growth,* New York, 1957) have argued that, because of the particular nature of the problems of underdeveloped areas, growth can be initiated only by a "crash program" of investment. This "big push" is necessary in order to break through the "low level equilibrium trap" in which many of these countries find themselves. Several problems raise doubts as to the appropriateness of this argument and the policy conclusions that flow from it. However, these problems are primarily concerned with initiating growth, and we have ruled this set of problems beyond the scope of this paper (see p. 262, above). I would call the reader's attention to the fact that the remarks in the text do not have reference to this particular argument.

as income continues to rise, income elasticities are such that the demand for services increases at the expense of other, more tangible output. It is then argued that the capital requirements are smaller in service industries than they are in manufacturing. If this argument is correct, it would mean that as per capita income reaches higher levels, it is possible—so far as capital requirements are concerned—for the economy to grow at an increasing rate. However, labor may prove a bottleneck at this point for two reasons. First, by the time the economy reaches this point, the rate of growth of the labor supply may be very low; second, the substitutability of capital for labor may be more difficult in the service industries than for manufactured products.[56] But here again caution is called for, not only because the hypothesis regarding the demand for "services" as income rises is open to a number of objections, but also because there may be considerable indirect capital costs associated with service activities.[57]

After the system has become fairly advanced, perhaps the most important composition of output effect on capital requirements is the extent to which construction dominates total investment activity. Construction in all forms seems to require great amounts of capital per unit of output (and it is an industry that is unreceptive to technological change); therefore, where this activity is conducted on a large scale, the rate of growth of capacity will tend to be less than it would be if resources were devoted to, say, textile machinery. Housing needs are related primarily to population growth and the internal movement of the population, particularly of farmers to urban areas. It may be expected, therefore, that construction is more important in a system where population is growing rapidly than it is in a system with a slowly growing population; and that construction is of greater consequence where the process of change from a largely rural, to a largely urban, economy is under way than where the urbanization process has been resolved. For reasons already referred to, both population growth and urbanization movement may make construction important in the earliest periods of growth. Subsequently, construction—and especially housing—may be said to depend on the shocks to the system, as these are reflected in changes in the rate of population growth.

Does any sort of general hypothesis emerge to suggest the time pattern of capital requirements in a growing economy? To begin with, any such general hypothesis must itself rest on specific hypotheses regarding technology and demand, and it is difficult to muster much confidence with

56. The decreased substitutability is difficult to substantiate in an effective manner. Examples are available on both sides. Thus, it is unlikely that robots will replace actors and actresses, but television may well make obsolete the college lecturer.

57. Martin Wolfe recently published an article which examines the hypotheses on changes in the composition of demand as per capita income rises ("The Concept of Economic Sectors," *Quarterly Journal of Economics*, LXIX, 1955, pp. 402-20). This article also contains several references to other writings concerning this issue.

respect to any hypothesis concerning technology and demand. With the proper qualifications in mind—due to the inadequacy of our understanding of technical change and demand behavior—it is perhaps justifiable to suggest the following general argument: For several reasons—indicated earlier—the output stream during the earliest stages of growth would appear demanding of capital to a greater extent than can be forecast for later stages. However, as population growth subsides, and as the construction of social overhead capital is completed, it would seem that the output stream produced will decline in capital intensity. After this point, economies in capital use may be present, due to the existence of a base of capital (including knowledge), and this will tend to reduce capital-output ratios throughout the system. Similarly, the quality of labor inputs may improve as the system continues to grow. Unless there are counteracting diminishing returns because of the failure of innovations to live up to expectations, these results will produce declining capital requirements, and, therefore, enable the rate of growth to rise if the saving-income ratio remains unchanged. However, it was suggested earlier that economies of the type referred to are, in effect, used up at some point. The same is true for improved labor, and therefore these two possible sources of reduced capital requirements are exhausted. If the arguments concerning tertiary industry are accepted, they may become applicable at approximately this point to contribute further to preventing most of the *k*'s from rising. But, surely, beyond this point, the greatest burden rests on innovations.

IV

The Problem of Aggregate Demand

INVESTMENT, INNOVATION, AND ENTREPRENEURSHIP

Up to this point, it has been assumed that the system will grow at the rate permitted by the growth of capacity. Analysis of the behavior of aggregative demand has, of course, been discussed in countless books and articles over the last twenty years, but despite the voluminous literature on the subject, there does not seem to have emerged a common set of ideas which may be plugged into the analysis. Since this problem has been discussed at such length,[58] it would appear most useful in this context to concentrate on those aspects of the problem of most relevance in a long-run context. For the most part, all of these aspects can be included under one

58. Moses Abramovitz's essay on "Economics of Growth" in B. F. Haley, ed., *A Survey of Contemporary Economics*, Homewood, Ill., 1952, II, pp. 132-78, is concerned very largely with this problem.

of the following headings: population growth, invention and innovation, and entrepreneurship.

Clearly, the dominant opinion is that investment demand is the crucial factor and provides the mainspring to growth, while consumption is passive and simply responds to income changes. Keynes assumed investment to be autonomous and entirely decisive in moving the system. In a recent survey article on growth theory, Professor Domar also assumed investment to be exogenous.[59] In the light of these opinions, it would appear appropriate to begin this discussion assuming the key problem to be investment.

The investment function for a sector was written earlier as $I_{it} = b_i (X_{jt} - X_{jt-1})$, where b_i is assumed to be a behavioristic and technological parameter, rather than merely a technological parameter. It is recalled that the primary behavioristic assumption governing entrepreneurial action is assumed to be the equating of the actual rate of return on his capital with a rate that is thought to be appropriate for a given social and economic environment. For reasons of simplification, this equilibrium rate of return is assumed constant. Since capital accumulation is by its very nature a forward-looking phenomenon, it will take place only if investors expect a return which will match their requirements for equilibrium. As noted earlier, analysis of expectations poses elusive and difficult problems which await solution, and the most satisfactory approach would appear to lie in an inquiry into the conditions necessary to keep the rate of return reasonably constant for a rate of investment required to match savings in a fully employed, growing economy. In view of the indecision with respect to saving behavior, it is not unreasonable to assume, for the purposes of this discussion, that the saving-income ratio will remain approximately constant as the economy grows. The assumption is then made that if the profit rate maintains itself over a long period, investors will be provided with the incentive necessary to continue the going rate of capital accumulation.[60]

Once again, it is appropriate to begin with a few comments on population.[61] If there are constant returns to capital and labor, the equality

59. Evsey D. Domar, "Economic Growth: An Econometric Approach," *American Economic Review*, LXII, 1952, pp. 479-95.

60. It can easily be seen that the pure accelerator theory of investment will fit in this argument as a special case, under specific assumptions as to expectations. If entrepreneurs expect the rate of growth in demand for their product in the succeeding periods to be equal to the demand they have just experienced, and that their share of return will remain unchanged, and if they expect no diminishing returns, they will invest in such a way that the pure accelerator model will hold. But, also, the assumptions in the text emphasize what it is surely necessary to emphasize, namely, the fact that investors think in terms of expected rates of return, rather than in terms of achieving a specific capital-output ratio. It is recalled that the profit rate is equal to the share of output going to capital over the capital-output ratio.

61. References in this connection are seemingly endless. See the United Nations review, cited in footnote 38, above, esp. Part III, and Spengler and Duncan, eds., *op.cit.*, esp. sections 5 and 6. The reader will find in these sources abundant references to additional publications on the subject.

of the growth rate of these two inputs would result—under a variety of production functions—in a capital widening process which would keep the rate of return on capital constant. The case would be the same in those areas where there was a surplus of labor to draw on (e.g., the often referred to disguised unemployment in underdeveloped areas). If capital accumulation is proceeding at a faster rate than population, and there are no innovations, the capital-output ratio will tend to rise for reasons referred to above. With no change in the (functional) distribution of income, the rate of return on capital will vary inversely with the capital-output ratio. It is unnecessary to repeat here the discussion contained in the previous section of this essay on the relation between population growth and the capital-output ratio.

The literature also emphasizes the necessity of population growth in order to achieve economies of scale in given areas of production. High per capita income alone may not do this, because the composition of demand could well be such that it would provide a market for only limited quantities of individual products. Similarly, it has been suggested that the composition of demand accompanying a growing population (and income) is more likely to be concentrated on the essentials and staples of living, and therefore to be more dependable, than the demand for less necessary items that accompanies merely a rise in per capita income. For the same kind of reasons, it is sometimes argued that mistakes are less likely to result in permanent damage in a rapidly growing economy (growing in population and income) than in one which is growing slowly. Temporary oversupply of a particular type is quickly eliminated, and exercises little or no negative effects on investment plans. Finally, it may be observed that a young and growing population contributes to the flexibility and adaptability of the labor force to the changes necessarily imposed by a growing income. It is maintained that as a result of these several population effects, entrepreneurs are more optimistic, and so maintain a higher rate of investment than would be the case in the absence of a population growth.

These remarks suggest that population growth acts upon investment demand in two ways: First, it affects the time path of the capital-output ratio, and thereby the rate of return on capital through time. Second, a rising population seems to help to create an atmosphere which is encouraging to capital accumulation and which justifies capital accumulation to some extent.[62] It hardly appears necessary to point out that in

62. One further point is worthy of mention. It is frequently argued that the greater the capital requirement per unit of output, the less the problem of total demand. Obviously, if the increased output is given, the larger the capital requirement for this output, the greater the amount of saving that is offset. However, the larger the capital requirement, the lower the rate of return, given the income distribution. Unless a redistribu-

those areas with a large excess of population, the key problem is population control, and the advantages referred to above are surely swamped many times over by weight of numbers, as compared to available resources.

At this time, let us consider innovations once again. It was suggested earlier that if capital grows more rapidly than labor, the diminishing returns argument would lead to a rising capital-output ratio. The rising capital-output ratio, in turn, would produce not only a decline in the rate of growth of output (with a given saving-income ratio), but also a decline in the profit rate. In our earlier discussion of the capital-output ratio, the only requirement imposed upon innovations was that they be such that output would grow as rapidly as capital. But now a further requirement seems necessary. It would appear that as capital continues to grow, the more advantageous applications will be used up. At some time, then, the elasticity of substitution of capital for labor will begin to fall, and finally the relative share of capital must also fall.[63] Thus, even though innovations occur in a sufficient amount to keep the capital-output ratio constant, the profit rate may still fall because of the decline in the elasticity of substitution. If this assumption about the elasticity of substitution is made, it follows that innovations must not only be of a magnitude sufficient to keep output growing at a rate equal to capital, but that they must also be such that the share of capital does not decline indefinitely. In other words, innovations must be "slanted" in the manner dictated by the behavior of relative factor supplies. In this case this means that the marginal product of capital must be raised relative to that of labor, i.e., innovations must be capital-using. Continuing growth under these hypothesized conditions imposes two obligations which innovations must meet: They must be of sufficient magnitude, and they must be the kind that respond appropriately to divergent movements in relative factor supplies.[64]

It would appear clear then that innovations are strategic to the growth process, and therefore that any theory of economic growth must contain an explanation of their behavior. Contemporary economics does not offer a "theory of innovations," in the sense of a systematic theory accounting for the rate and "slant" of innovations through time. Thus, perhaps it

tion of income is forthcoming, the change in composition of output from products requiring large quantities of capital per unit to that requiring smaller quantities would encourage investment rather than discourage it. It would appear that some of the "mature economy" literature is misleading in this respect.

63. The elasticity of substitution was the subject of a number of articles in the 1930's. It was introduced, of course, by J. R. Hicks in his *Theory of Wages*, New York, 1932. See also A. P. Lerner, *The Economics of Control*, New York, 1946, chap. 13.

64. The discussion of the role of innovations in the growth process is most clearly elaborated by Professor William Fellner in his previously cited *Trends and Cycles in Economic Activity*. Professor Fellner also emphasizes that innovations must not be so labor saving that they result in increasing unemployment. Moses Abramovitz provides a rough measure of the influence of technological change on the growth of output in the United States since 1870 in his "Resource and Output Trends in the United States since 1870," *American Economic Review*, XLVI, 1956, pp. 5-23.

would be reasonable to say nothing more on this subject and to pass on to the next topic. However, it seems useful to point out a few things, if for no other reason than to show how much work needs to be done in this area.[65]

It is necessary to keep separate two distinct phenomena: invention and innovation. If we think of an invention as the *creation* of a new technique or new product, and an innovation as the *putting it into effect,* then evidently inventions are a necessary prerequisite to innovations. The necessity for this distinction is pointed up, since the factors contributing to the achievement of a rapid rate of invention are not always the same as those which contribute to a rapid rate of innovation. I shall consider first the process of invention.

Historical evidence among currently advanced countries suggests that as an economy becomes more and more developed, it allocates an increasing quantity of resources to the search for improved techniques and products. Entrepreneurs, managers, and engineers learn all the time, and continuously put into effect the results of their newly acquired knowledge. Many firms maintain research and development departments, whose primary purpose is to provide a constant stream of inventions eligible to be turned into innovations by the policy-makers. Under these circumstances, the inventive (and innovational) process is as much a part of the economic process as is adjustment to a given technology, and it is therefore subject to the maximization scheme governing the firm's policy decisions. Indeed, in many instances, expenditures on research are treated as an outlay which results in revenue, just as any other outlay made by the firm.[66]

The result seems to be that economic growth is accompanied by a regularization of inventions, or, perhaps more accurately, by an attempt at regularization. It suggests also that the patterns of invention become less subject to chance and luck as these patterns become more and more a strategic part of the firm's effort to maintain its profit rate. If this kind of argument is accepted, it would appear that the firm's activities contribute to a behaviorial pattern of inventions which is consistent with the requirement regarding direction stated previously. That requirement, it will be

65. W. W. Rostow, in his *Processes of Economic Growth,* explicitly recognizes the necessity of making innovations endogenous. See also the writings of Yale Brozen, for example, his "Entrepreneurship and Technological Change," in Williamson and Buttrick, eds., *op.cit.* Brozen's paper also contains a number of references. Mrs. Robinson *(The Accumulation of Capital,* and *The Rate of Interest and Other Essays)* issues some interesting dicta on the subject, and W. Arthur Lewis' *Theory of Economic Growth* includes a chapter on the accumulation of knowledge. Further references are cited later in this essay.

66. Further discussion of this point may be found in Gordon F. Bloom, "Wage Pressure and Technological Discovery," *American Economic Review,* XLI, 1951, pp. 603-17; W. Rupert Maclaurin, "Technical Progress in Some American Industries," *American Economic Review,* XLIV, 1954, pp. 178-89; Carolyn Shaw Solo, "Innovations in the Capitalistic Process," *Quarterly Journal of Economics,* LXV, 1951, pp. 417-28; and United States National Resources Committee, *Technological Trends and National Policy,* Washington, 1937, *passim.*

recalled, was that innovations must be capital-using in the long run. Capital-using innovations will tend to raise the profit rate, and if inventions are a part of the routine of business enterprise, it is to be expected that inventive efforts will be directed toward this end.

As for the rate of inventions, little can be said with confidence even in purely formal terms. It seems generally agreed now that inventions do not constitute a major and sharp break with the past, but rather evolve out of an existing situation.[67] It would appear not unreasonable to expect that purposeful and directed research programs would tend to speed up this evolutionary process. At the same time, however, there is evidence that the policy of devoting resources to inventive activity is itself haphazard in relation to the requirements outlined above, and also that the effect of such a policy varies widely in relation to "inputs." Indeed, it seems impossible to specify, by definition, an exact relation between inputs and outputs where the latter is "knowledge." Therefore, even if it were acknowledged that business enterprises or governments did direct a given percentage of their resources to "inventive activity," there is no assurance that the results will be equally constant. Even though more and more firms consider technology a variable and, to some extent, subject to control, the application of the customary rules of production theory do not seem applicable. And until the inventive process is understood more clearly it is doubtful that technical knowledge can be made much of a control variable.[68]

With respect to innovations, the situation is somewhat different. Since innovating consists of introducing a new process, it presumably will take place when the policy-maker thinks the potential effect on his profit rate warrants such action. In the case of inventing, the decision to devote resources to research is filled with uncertainty as to the possible rewards obtainable from such an investment. However, effecting an innovation is much less of a blind act, and to an even greater extent than is the case with respect to invention, may be brought within the limits of the profit maximization scheme of the individual firm. In this way, then, the analysis of innovations is essentially an analysis of those market situations which provide incentive to the introduction of technical change.

The most frequently discussed relationship is of course that which

67. Cf. H. G. Barnett, *Innovation: The Basis of Cultural Change*, New York, 1953; the essay by A. P. Usher in *Capital Formation and Economic Growth*, Moses Abramovitz, ed., Princeton, 1956; S. C. Gilfillan, *The Sociology of Inventions*, Chicago, 1935; and John Jewkes, David Sawers, and Richard Stillerman, *The Sources of Invention*, New York, 1958.

68. Perhaps it is possible to do the most useful work in this connection at present in the area of case studies of the history of inventions and innovations in given industries. See, for example, A. A. Bright, Jr., *The Electric Lamp Industry: Technological Change and Development from 1800 to 1947*, New York, 1949, and W. R. Maclaurin, *Invention and Innovation in the Radio Industry*, New York, 1949.

obtains between innovations and monopoly. Even in this widely discussed area there seem to be few propositions that can safely be said to be part of the current thinking of the modern economist.[69] Unhappily, like almost all of the other problems with which we are concerned, much can (and has been) said on both sides.

On the negative side, fears of excess capacity and/or losses in sunk capital seem to be of primary concern. Since a monopolist exercises control over the market, by virtue of his control over supply, he seeks to maintain a market structure which permits him to earn a satisfactory rate of return on his invested capital. In an oligopolistic situation, it is difficult to expand at the expense of competitors, and the tendency is therefore to create a reluctance to experiment with a new technique or new product. The monopolist, by virtue of his control over the market, seeks to prevent innovations which will result in existing capital being made obsolete,[70] while in a competitive situation the entrepreneur (to a greater extent) must innovate in order to protect himself from competitors who will innovate. Therefore, an economy dominated by large monopolistic enterprises tends to be slower in introducing changes in technique than an economy–with an equivalent flow of inventions–dominated by competitive firms.

Independent of the monopolistic aspects of large-scale enterprises, frequent mention is made of the fact that large corporations are necessarily run by a bureaucracy. And one of the characteristics of a bureaucracy is conservatism and a tendency to try to achieve security at the expense of progress–and uncertainty. Management decisions are aimed therefore at maintaining the *status quo,* at trying to avoid "risky" undertakings, rather than yielding to the lure of possible profits due to innovations. Under these circumstances, the very nature of corporate enterprise militates against the introduction of new techniques and ideas.[71]

On the positive side, the arguments are usually one of two types. In the first place, large-scale–and hence monopolistic–enterprises are deemed necessary to supply inventions. The assumption that the flow of invention is the same in a competitive economy as it is in a monopolistic economy is therefore untenable. In the second place, it has been argued that monopoly profits are a necessary incentive to innovation. The possibility of a temporary gain, lost through competition, is not sufficient inducement; rather, it is necessary to allow the prospects of a permanent gain in profit

---

69. A recent survey of the literature on this subject is contained in the article by P. Hennipman, "Monopoly: Impediment or Stimulus to Economic Progress," in *Monopoly and Competition and Their Regulation,* E. H. Chamberlin, ed., London, 1954.

70. Further discussion of these points may be found in J. Steindl, *Maturity and Stagnation in American Capitalism,* Oxford, 1952, and Evsey D. Domar's essay, "Investment, Losses, and Monopolies," in *Income, Employment, and Public Policy,* New York, 1954.

71. Cf. Hamberg, *op.cit.,* pp. 129*ff.,* and W. E. Moore, *Industrial Relations and the Social Order,* New York, 1951, chap. 4 and the references cited therein.

or market position to take hold before firms will take the trouble to introduce innovations.

This list of pros and cons leaves us nowhere. Perhaps the key point that can be made with confidence is with respect to inventions, rather than innovations. If it could be shown that technical knowledge can be advanced only in the research laboratories of large-scale firms, then all the arguments against such firms must fall to the ground. Since inventions are a necessary prerequisite to innovations, it does not matter how conducive the market structure may be to innovations; if there are no available inventions, no innovations will be possible. Surely, over the long-run, the invention problem is of greater concern, and, as was stated above, little formal analysis has been applied to the process involved.[72]

Perhaps one further possible conclusion of considerable importance can be reached. With respect to both inventions and innovations, it seems that the rate is likely to be higher in new industries and new firms than in old established ones. This is reasonable for several reasons: New firms are much more interested in finding a place in the market than in maintaining the *status quo*. Thus, they may have greater incentive to seek new inventions and to put them into effect immediately. We may also expect that business leaders in new industries will be more optimistic and more alert as to the advantages of a dynamic policy with respect to innovations and investment, and so more willing to assume the risks involved in following such a policy. Both Burns and Kuznets suggest that the possibilities for technical progress in a single productive activity are limited.[73] The greater the improvement in the technical aspects of a given process, the less scope there may be for further improvement; therefore, the rate of technical progress in old industries will tend to taper off. To a large extent, the validity of such a hypothesis depends upon how an industry is defined. An industry may be defined narrowly enough, so that this is surely an acceptable hypothesis, but whether this is a reasonable definition for other purposes is open to question. Nevertheless, it would appear that a market and social structure that encourages the entry of new firms, with new blood and new ideas, is more likely to generate a satisfactory flow of innovations than is a structure where economic activity is limited to old and established firms.[74] But the technique by which such a market (and social) structure is created is not clear.

It is clear that a fluid economic and social atmosphere is a major

72. Although there may be some doubt—as noted—with respect to the development of monopoly through time, there seems little doubt that large-scale industry increases as an economy grows. To the extent that the degree of monopoly does not increase as the economy develops, the problems—or advantages—accompanying that increase would not be present.

73. See footnote 32, above.

74. Further discussion of the importance to the economy of new firms and new men may be found in J. A. Schumpeter, *Business Cycles,* New York, I, 1939, pp. 94*ff*.

inducement to the discovery and exploitation of new techniques and new ideas. It has already been suggested that as a country changes from a rural, non-growth agricultural community to an urban, industrial society, there appears to be less reluctance to accept change. This suggests then that the fluidity of the economic structure would tend to increase as the economy develops. However, older economies also show evidences of solidification, not so much because of social barriers as because of financial and technological barriers.[75] Thus ease of entry of new firms is reduced because of the magnitude of initial outlays; the ease of entry of new men is reduced because of the bureaucratization of large-scale corporate organization. Somewhere in between "infancy and maturity" a growing society would achieve the greatest receptivity to new ideas of all kinds. However, there is little available in this area in the way of analytically supported conclusions, and projected historical generalizations are, of course, open to any number of questions. Furthermore, it is not unlikely that the development of well-organized research departments in the larger business firms counteracts any negative effects of excess bureaucratization insofar as technical innovations are concerned.

The remarks in the preceding paragraphs, suggesting the importance of "new men" in the investment process, provide a convenient stepping stone to a brief discussion of entrepreneurial activity. Recognition that the investment demand parameter is a behavioristic coefficient indicates that the investment decision process is not a completely objective act. Indeed, an appraisal of future profit opportunities can hardly be independent of the personality of the individual doing the appraising. An economy may lag, not because there are no resources or profit opportunities, but simply because there is no one around to provide the driving force essential to exploit these latent advantages. The entrepreneur then may be conceived of as the instrument by which investment plans are made and put into effect. Since, under rather general assumptions, the actions of entrepreneurs justify themselves to some extent, a society blessed with a large group of dynamic, optimistic leaders may be able to grow rapidly, despite a lack of "objective" profit opportunities. In other words, not only do entrepreneurs exploit the profit opportunities generated by the system, but by their own action may create such opportunities, and therefore move the system. Obviously, the supply conditions of entrepreneurial talent is a strategic element in the growth process.

It is difficult to discuss this topic at any length within the limits of this essay. Most of the available literature is concerned with tracing out the implications of assumed entrepreneurial behavior, or with examining the

75. See for example, J. A. Schumpeter, *Capitalism, Socialism, and Democracy,* New York, 1947, *passim.*

behavior of a particular entrepreneur in narrative form.[76] And it seems safe to generalize to the effect that little is known about the source of supply of entrepreneurial talent. Indeed, the *modus operandi* of the entrepreneurial role is such that it is difficult to isolate sufficient and necessary conditions required to produce entrepreneurs, for they can emerge under a wide variety of circumstances. The key factors surely lie within the domain of the socio-cultural aspects of growth, and such aspects have been largely excluded from consideration in this essay. But even these discussions are usually not revealing from the standpoint of analysis. The importance of precedence, of vertical mobility, of a strong middle class which supplies a constant stream of new men, and of a set of values in which material gain and economic achievement rank high are usually emphasized. But such a list hardly serves the purpose of a theory. Our problem is to define the specific relationships which produce these conditions, and then relate these conditions in a specific way to the emergence and continuing supply of a well-defined and identifiable entrepreneurial input. When the problem is defined in this way, its solution is evidently a matter for the future. However, the mere statement of the problem is useful, as a reminder that this is an aspect of the growth problem which is at once intractable to the economist's tools and also essential to our understanding of a process which has been defined as an economic process by economists.

THE ROLE OF CONSUMPTION

The aggregative demand problem is almost always discussed solely in terms of investment, and consumption is assumed to be passive. But again, this assumption is more appropriate for a short-run analysis than for a long-run inquiry, and a brief comment as to the type of questions which arise in this connection is in order.

Two relevant points were made in the earlier discussion of saving. The Duesenberry-Modigliani hypothesis that the floor under consumption tends to rise as income rises means that it is consumption—and not investment—which prevents the economy from falling back to previous levels during cyclical downturns. The Goodwin hypothesis,[77] as to business firm "consumption" outlays over the cycle, contributes to the same end. It was also pointed out that it is unlikely that the average saving-income relationship will rise to, say, .5 or .6; this means that the burden placed on investment demand will not reach unmanageable proportions. Furthermore, if the hypothesis about the importance of new products and new men to

76. Perhaps the best source of material on entrepreneurial activity and talent is the journal, *Explorations in Entrepreneurial History*. The articles and bibliographical material in the successive issues of this journal will provide the interested reader with a clear picture of the kind of work being done in this area.

77. See footnote 46, above.

entrepreneurial and innovational activity is accepted, the assumed declining income elasticities of demand gains added pertinence. Thus, changes in the composition of demand facilitate–indeed, require (if the propensity to save remains constant)–the establishment of new industries and new firms to produce new products.

Now these and other possible conjectures regarding consumer behavior are hardly consistent with a simple function relating consumption to income. Such consumption activity is related to the structural changes which accompany growth, rather than to simple changes in income; and, in turn, this growth produces structural changes which affect the further growth of the economy, especially the profit-ability of new capital accumulation. In this sense, consumer activity is not only not "passive," indeed, it is "autonomous" and creates a situation that "induces" investment.[78]

It is not necessary to seek a definitive answer to the question as to whether it is the entrepreneur or the consumer who produces the spark necessary to move the system. In fact, perhaps the question itself is not a meaningful one. Clearly, it is correct to think in terms of entrepreneurial behavior as the strategic factor in the short-run and of consumption as passive. It is equally clear that over a long period of time it is misleading to think simply in terms of a "long-run consumption function," and to believe that nothing more remains to be said on the subject.[79]

CONCLUSION

Again my conclusion is hardly a conclusion in the true sense of the word. One can say very little about the behavior of investment demand over a long period of time. Population has neither a dependable effect on investment demand, nor is it a factor over which significant control is possible. The requirements imposed upon inventions and innovations can be specified with reasonable confidence, but so little is known about the process of invention and innovation that it is possible to specify only the very general conditions that are necessary to produce this required behavior. And only truistic generalizations are available to account for the supply of entrepreneurial talent. However, one conclusion may be justified: Early in the growth process the outlets for investment seem bountiful: new industries are being established, the static social order is breaking down, new ideas are becoming available, and so on. Thus, all the factors which (apparently) affect investment decisions are favorable. But then, as growth continues,

78. Simon Kuznets discusses this point briefly in Simon Kuznets, W. E. Moore, and J. J. Spengler, eds., *Economic Growth: Brazil, India, Japan,* Durham, 1955, pp. 13-14.

79. It is frequently observed that the chief motivating force in low-income countries is changed consumer attitudes and behavior. Especially, it is noted that a large proportion of consumers have become convinced that unhappy economic plights are not a necessary condition, and that something can and must be done to remedy such situations.

some of these factors are, in effect, used up. That is, as a society begins to grow, barriers to new enterprises are reduced; but once such barriers are cleared away, this growth-affecting force is no longer present. Similarly, a society can become more receptive to new ideas, and so facilitate technical change; but it will surely reach a stage at which this receptivity is no longer a bottleneck, and further changes cannot be relied upon to affect the rate of innovation. So too, it was suggested earlier that "external economies" are not without limit. At some point, then, the full weight of the responsibility for continuing investment, at a rate sufficient to maintain full employment, will fall exclusively upon innovations.

The contribution to an atmosphere favorable to the maintenance of demand, due to consumption habits, should also continue. It is probably true that a low-income country is less likely to experience an oversaving problem than is a highly developed one, simply because of consumption expenditure. But the consumer effect, referred to in the last paragraph of the previous sub-section of this paper, should be as strong in a mature country as it is in an immature one. Evidently, however, this does not remove much pressure from the role innovations are required to play.

V

Conclusion

This essay began with the observation that growth theorizing varied, ranging between neat, rigorous models and loose, historical generalizations. The preceding discussion reflects this characteristic. In my discussion of what was referred to as the short-run theory—the capital stock adjustment theory—it was defensible to introduce assumptions which made it possible to reach fairly reliable conclusions with respect to the requirements for consistent growth in a given short-run period. This applies to both the aggregative model or the multi-sectored model. These results were possible for two reasons: First, the Keynesian heritage for the aggregative model and the Walrasian heritage for the multi-sectored model were both a stationary equilibrium sort, and a growth theory within this heritage could limit itself to a very narrowly defined process and "assume constant" everything else. Second, the ambiguity of the tools—the capital-output ratios, the saving functions, etc.,—was not of great consequence, as long as growth was limited to a short period of time.

When the period of time is lengthened—as it evidently must be, if the formulation of a growth theory is the aim—difficulties multiply rapidly. Here the *ceteris paribus* pound must be emptied of a large number of items, and the economist is forced to consider as variables population growth, technological change, entrepreneurial supply, and the like. Specification as to the requirements for continued growth over a long period then involves some investigation of how these "variables" must behave. But there are so many "combinations of behavior" which will enable growth to continue—or prevent it from continuing—that precise specifications (as opposed to truistic generalities) are almost impossible. Perhaps the most reliable, and the most important, requirement along these lines is the conclusion with respect to innovations. Even here, it was necessary to be content with the statement that innovations must be of a "certain" magnitude and of a "certain" slant. Further discussion would involve a knowledge of production functions, rates of growth of capital and labor, demand conditions, and the effect of innovations on natural resources. And when an attempt was made to probe deeper and establish the conditions necessary to produce this innovation behavior, little could be said that was analytically satisfying. But beyond this, conclusions were elusive. How much "entrepreneurial talent" is necessary for continuing growth? It is not very helpful to say that a minimum is required, because, for one thing, it is difficult to define entrepreneurial inputs with any degree of rigor. How much saving is required depends on innovations and population growth. And so on.

Earlier, the growth process was divided into three categories: capacity-creating, income-generating, and structure-changing processes. It was then argued that the capacity and income creation took place in a given structure, but that the process of growth would itself produce changes in that structure which in turn act on the income- and capacity-creating power of the system. It would seem that the above remarks may be summarized by saying that considerably more confidence is allowable with respect to the requirements of the capacity-creating and income-generating processes than is permissible with respect to structural changes.

When one attempts to outline an actual time path, the problems are even more severe, and the results must be interpreted with caution. The following points, however, do seem to emerge clearly.

(1) The major obstacles to growth are to be found in the earliest stages of the process. An economy which tries to emerge from a quagmire of poverty and hopelessness finds itself handicapped by the fact that it must operate in a society which finds the very notion of change alien. It is here that the social obstacles to growth are at their maximum. Furthermore, there is no base of capital from which to proceed with further accumulation, and no precedence for saving and capital creation. The forces making for technical change are also absent. Moreover—and in some cases this is the major factor—population growth may well be such that any output increase is more than matched by an increase in the number of mouths to feed.

There is thus a discontinuity–a hump–which must be hurdled in order to get the growth process off the ground, and this hurdle may be of such magnitude that it prevents growth from *ever* beginning in some areas of the world.

(2) If, however, this initial hurdle is cleared, the economy is likely to find easier going for a while. For in this "second phase," external economies and economies of scale will begin to be realized. Also, the loosening up of the social structure, brought about by higher incomes, urbanization, and industrialization will facilitate the adjustments necessary for continuing growth. It is also likely that at this point there is no problem as to diminishing returns, due to the exhaustion of natural resources.

(3) By the same token, it does not seem unreasonable to assume that at some point the factors mentioned in the previous paragraph will be "used up." External economies will not materialize indefinitely, and economies of scale may well turn into diminishing returns. More confidently, it may be assumed that such contributions as a "loosening up" in the social structure are of a "one-shot" variety; once this loosening up has occurred, they become permissive, rather than contributory to growth.

(4) When the "once and for all" factors are used up, further growth is dependent to a very large extent upon innovations and capital accumulation. And possibly the most important single aspect of the evolutionary process of an economic system is the development of a force in the economy which will produce a constant stream of technological innovations. It may well be the case, too, that the failure of a highly developed area to continue to grow may be attributed to its failure to find the secret of technical change. Perhaps the most important deficiency–among a host of deficiencies–in the body of thought examined in this essay is the lamentable state of our understanding of the origin and process of technical change.[80]

(5) At the outset of the essay, it was stated that no specific attention would be given to "socio-cultural" matters. Yet, throughout the essay, it was impossible not to flirt constantly with factors usually considered in the noneconomic category. For example, it is impossible to discuss entrepreneurial activities or the behavior of innovations in a meaningful way without including in the discussion analyses of the institutional complex in which such phenomena occur. This leads us to an exceedingly important conclusion. It must be recognized that in a long-period analysis the distinc-

80. It is worth pointing out that it is more or less meaningless to try to identify any specific growth curve which per capita income might follow. To do this requires much more empirical material and theoretical understanding than the contemporary literature provides. It would also require the introduction of the effects of shocks to the time path of the system, and this leads to many extremely difficult problems. With regard to a model with shocks specifically introduced, see Part V of the Haavelmo monograph, cited in footnote 5, above. But the fact that no growth curve emerged from this discussion is surely the least of the problems confronting the growth theorist at this time.

tion between "economic" and "noneconomic" factors loses significance, and it becomes necessary to acknowledge that economic growth must be seen as a special aspect of general social evolution, rather than as a process which can be factored out of the social system and studied in isolation. This suggests not only that more empirical and analytical inquiries are necessary, but possibly also that the tools and method of the economist must be altered if the problems are to yield.[81]

This essay cannot claim to have isolated either the key to growth or the *modus operandi* of the growth process. Indeed, it would seem to be a list of questions, rather than a list of answers, and a list of things to look for rather than an elegant piece of machinery to apply to all places at all times. At this point, it is comforting to recall that someone once said that he who asks questions is frequently more useful than he who answers them.

81. The most straightforward attempt at new tool-making is found in W. W. Rostow's *The Process of Economic Growth*. Rostow frames his analysis here in terms of six propensities: the propensity to develop fundamental science, to apply science to economic ends, to accept innovations, to seek material advance, to consume, and to have children. All of the processes contained in these propensities are, of course, pertinent and were discussed above in terms other than propensities. Until it becomes possible to give a clearer meaning to the concept of propensity, in Rostow's sense, it would seem that this is simply another way of asking the right questions.

APPENDIX TO CHAPTER I

By Joseph J. Spengler

IN THIS APPENDIX I shall present summaries of the developmental programs of representative mercantilists. Italian, French, Spanish, German and English programs will be considered in that order. A certain amount of background and supplementary material is included.

(1) The spirit of mercantilist growth theory made its appearance in Italy long before Antonio Serra supplied it with a rationale in 1613. As early as the 1470's, just after Machiavelli's birth, D. Carafa, though he believed that commerce (the principal source of wealth) should be free, was indicating ways in which the prince might help industry and agriculture.[1] G. Botero, who believed that wealth consisted of goods, and who was not essentially a monetary mercantilist,[2] declared the strength of the state

1. In *De regis et boni principis officio,* republished in 1668. Carafa supposed that the prosperity of the state might be affected by the mode of expenditure and system of taxation in effect, but he did not provide a rationale for a particular system of taxation, as did M. Palmieri (1405-1475) for proportional taxation (in *Della vita civile,* Florence, 1529). L. Zecchi (1532-1610) recommended princely support of agriculture, promotion of manufactures, and prohibition of both the exportation of raw materials and the emigration of skilled artisans. A critic of usury, as was Botero, Zecchi was somewhat aware of the dependence of the growth of population upon the growth of subsistence. Earlier, F. Patrizii (1412-1494) had endorsed protection for merchants and tradesmen.

2. See *Della Ragione di Stato,* 1589. I have used the translation by P. J. and D. P. Waley (New Haven, 1956). In Book VII Botero, after noting that the prince must accumulate funds to meet the needs of peace, prestige, defense, and war (since money moves resources to where they are needed), stated that accumulation must be limited. It must not be carried to the point where it interferes with the ordinary course of trade and traffic, and thereby impoverishes a prince's subjects by whom his funds are supplied. Accord-

to consist in population, provided (apparently) that it is of good enough quality; and he approved of measures conducive to population growth. It followed that the prince should promote agriculture, because it is the foundation of population growth.[3] Botero considered industry even more essential than agriculture to the growth of the state, for industry, by giving innumerable forms to raw materials, occupied many more inhabitants and produced a much greater product than did agriculture, or agriculture together with the other extractive industries. Hence, a prince, bent on making his state populous, must introduce every kind of industry and skill and enable his people to export labor in the form of wrought goods for raw materials and produce. This he might do by attracting skilled foreign artisans and providing them with suitable opoprtunities, by esteeming inventions and the works of the naturally talented, by rewarding excellence, and by prohibiting the exportation of raw materials, thereby preventing the loss of artisans to foreign lands. It was not desirable, however, that the prince himself engage in trade, this activity being reserved to private individuals, except when these individuals lacked the necessary means or could not trade in a manner conducive to the good of the state.[4]

Serra, writing at a time when Naples supposedly had almost reached the limit of its economic capacity, did not submit a program of development. Instead, he described the sources of wealth, rejected M. de Santis's thesis that the scarcity of coin in Naples was traceable to the high rate of exchange, and criticized various measures advanced at the time as cures for the penury of money (e.g., prohibition of the export of precious metals; arbitrary fixation of exchange rates, or of the exchange value of domestic or foreign money). Serra's point of departure was the state of the balance of trade.

The rate of exchange, Serra contended, depended upon a country's balance of trade. In a country lacking mines, as did Naples, the state of

ingly, the prince should add to his holdings at any time no more than the amount of money that comes in from abroad when the sale of merchandise abroad exceeds its purchase abroad. In the event that sales fall short of purchases abroad, it is desirable that the prince make his subjects more industrious. In Book VIII (chap. 2) he advised the ruler not to send money abroad except for essentials. Botero's approach reflects his scholastic training and the influence of both Bodin and Machiavelli.

3. In *Delle cause della grandezza delle città* (Rome, 1588), Botero concluded that, since the generative force is more powerful than the nutritive force, it is the latter, as expressed in the supply of subsistence, which limits population, and that, therefore, immediate checks to population have their origin in lack of subsistence. Again, in *Della Ragione,* he indicated that the size of various Italian cities was limited by their inability to procure more than a limited amount of provisions from the surrounding countryside or abroad; and that while colonies need not depopulate the mother country, it was preferable that they be peopled largely with those in surplus and who were burdensome to the mother country (see *ibid.*, VIII; *Delle cause,* III. R. Peterson's translation of *Delle Cause* is included with that of *Della Ragione* in the edition cited in footnote 2, above). Botero attributed Spain's decline to her neglect of agriculture and manual arts for military activity *(ibid.*, p. 146).

4. See *Della Ragione,* VIII, also the passage at the close of Book III in the first two editions.

this balance depended solely upon those economic conditions that governed that country's capacity to develop and export a surplus of goods and services and convert this surplus into gold and silver or its equivalent. Among these conditions, he included the industrial composition of a country, its situation, the quality of its population, and the regulations of its sovereign. With respect to industrial composition, he indicated that manufacturing was superior to agriculture, because the physical output of agriculture was limited. The output of manufactures, on the other hand, was both unlimited and subject to decreasing unit-costs, because manufacturing was free of the uncertainties of agriculture; because manufactured products (unlike agricultural produce) were immune to spoilage, and hence could be distributed throughout a geographically larger and much more extensible market; and (apparently) because the demand for manufactured products, and hence the profits realizable through their sale were much more expansible than were agricultural sales and profits. With respect to the geographical situation of a country, Serra indicated that a country could engage in carrying the goods of other nations only if it were favorably situated (as was Venice), but he added that when a country's manufactures are many and variegated, its attractiveness as a practitioner of the carrying trade was enhanced. Regarding the quality of a country's population, he pointed out that, if a people were industrious, diligent, watchful for opportunity, and ingenious in building up trade abroad as well as at home (as were the Genoese), their commerce would flourish much more than if they were unenterprising (as were the Neopolitans).

Having treated the circumstances described, Serra turned to the regulatory role of the sovereign. He emphasized the difficulties confronting a sovereign (e.g., that a given effect may have several causes, just as a given measure may produce diverse effects; that requisite information is hard to come by; that regulations must be effectively administered; etc.). And he indicated specifically that it was not advisable to have recourse to monetary measures (e.g., prohibit the export of money; overvalue and utilize foreign money), though he believed that the government might influence the exchanges to stimulate exports if it could thereby accomplish this objective. At the same time, Serra regarded governmental regulation as an efficient and powerful cause, provided it removed impediments to industry and trade, stimulated the development of manufactures and commerce, appropriately improved the quality of the population, and otherwise augmented its productivity and capacity to generate an export surplus; but he made no specific recommendations.[5]

5. See *Breve Trattato delle Cause che Possono Far Abbondare li Regni d'Oro et d'Argento, dove non sono Miniere. Con Applicazione al Regno di Napoli*, Naples, 1613, esp. Parts I and III. Serra indicated that it was not practicable to expropriate foreign owners of Neapolitan rentes and industries, or even to reduce imports, since these were

One is hard pressed to find a rounded mercantilist program in the writings of Italian economists who followed Serra. There was always considerable sentiment in Italy for freedom of internal trade and for substantial freedom in both trade in corn and external trade in general, with the result that the policies advocated by Italian mercantilists were usually moderate. Very rarely was prohibition of the export of money endorsed. The principle of a favorable balance of trade was endorsed a number of times, however, and attention was sometimes given to methods by which it could be attained, such as the prohibition, or the taxing, of raw-material exports and/or finished-goods imports, at least until manufacturing had become firmly established.[6]

(2) While French mercantilist theory and policy are identified primarily with the name of Colbert, mercantilist growth theory was expressed much earlier. Even before Bodin had formulated a quantity theory, and thereby contributed to the eventual dissolution of monetary mercantilism,[7] it had been recommended that luxury be repressed and the export of bullion be prohibited. It had also been recommended that commerce, manufactures, and internal development be fostered by preventing the exportation of raw materials, and working them up in France instead; by interdicting the importation of finished goods and producing them in France instead; by giving governmental and other support to shipping; by compelling the unemployed poor to work; and by reserving employment opportunities for Frenchmen.[8] Similar recommendations were made by Barthélemy de Laffemas in and after 1596, by Antoyne de Montchrétien in 1615, and subsequently by their disciples.[9] Setting as his goal the development of a favorable balance of trade and an influx of gold and silver, Laffemas, a protectionist, sought to establish manufactures, above all silk, that

---

largely essential in character. Serra was unfamiliar with international trade theory and ignored the quantity theory of money, though he considered an abundance of precious metals to be of benefit to a country and believed that a prosperous country could acquire as much gold and silver as it required. An English translation of portions of Serra's treatise is included in A. E. Monroe, *Early Economic Thought,* Cambridge, 1927. See also O. Doléjal, *Le milieu politique et économique du Royaume de Naples au XVI*[e] *et au début du XVII*[e] *siècle,* Ligugé, (Vienne), 1921.

6. Among the writers on whose works the above statement is based are G. B. De Luca, Leone Pascoli, G. B. Paolini, G. Palmieri, G. P. Pereira, F. M. Gianni, L. Muratori, P. Vergani, F. Galiani, A. Zanon, A. Genovesi, G. M. Galanti, and P. Verri. Shortly after Serra wrote, V. Lunetti, though an exponent of commercial freedom, recommended forbidding the export of coin.

7. See H. Hauser, ed., *La response de Jean Bodin à M. de Malestroit* (1568), Paris, 1932. On the significance of Bodin's finding that the great increase in prices was due principally to the influx of precious metals from the New World, see Hauser's introduction. Bodin, though a populationist, an exponent of import and export duties and of taxes on luxuries, and a defender of political absolutism (see *Les six lives de la république,* 1576), was not essentially a mercantilist or an expositor of economic growth theory. See C. W. Cole, *French Mercantilist Doctrines Before Colbert,* New York, 1931, pp. 47-62.

8. *Ibid.,* pp. 6-46.

9. Laffemas's views appear in a number of tracts; Montchrétien's are contained in his *Traicté de l'oeconomie politique* (1615), Th. Funck-Brentano, ed., Paris, 1889. Their views, and those of subsequent writers, are summarized by Cole, *op.cit.,* chaps. 2-4.

would work up French raw materials and set the many idle to work; and he favored the introduction of skilled foreign workers, but not foreign industrial and financial managers. He also brought about the establishment of a commission of commerce which sought to promote silk culture, horse breeding, linen and fustian manufacture, navigation, mechanical inventions, the training of apprentices, etc., and which approved the admission of foreigners under various conditions. Montchrétien, besides emphasizing the importance of agriculture and the degree of unemployment (for whose amelioration he proposed work schools and workhouses) to a greater extent than had Laffemas, recommended the establishment of metal (iron, steel, etc.) and clothing trades and of printing, urging the use of subsidies and of import and export duties and controls to accomplish his recommendations. He considered commerce good because it made possible the influx of gold and silver and because it contributed to French sea power, even as did the fisheries. He looked upon the colonies as markets and as sources of raw materials. Among the proposals of subsequent writers, one finds, apart from many of the recommendations already enumerated, prohibition of bullion exports, repression of luxury consumption, and encouragement of internal improvements.

Mercantilist opinion regarding economic development permeates Philippe de Béthune's *The Counselor of Estate*.[10] Tillage was neglected because it was carried on solely under the stimulus of the profit motive (which did not assure careful cultivation), because of absentee ownership, and because so many were ignorant of good husbandry. Manufactures might be expanded through the introduction of skilled foreign workers, through instruction of the poor in manufacturing techniques, and through setting to work monastics who were not suited to a life of contemplation. Though Béthune defined "riches" as consisting in "all things necessary for the life and service of Man," he recommended prohibiting the exportation of gold and silver (except when essential to the importation of necessities) and raw materials, and he proposed that foreign luxuries be excluded or heavily dutied. Although he condemned monopoly, he recommended that merchants trading abroad form companies, and thus avoid ruinous competition. He also recommended that more prestige be conferred upon merchants and that the nobility engage in commerce at sea.[11] Finally, Béthune noted that a state could become rich and make effective use of its resources only if private persons practiced "parcimony or sparing," though he later added that if a government drew much gold and silver from its subjects and did

10. Published in translation in London in 1634.

11. *The Counsellor of Estate*, Part I, chaps. 41-43. When discussing state revenues, Béthune indicated that raw-material imports and wrought-goods exports should not be taxed, and that only moderate duties should be imposed on imported necessities (*ibid.*, chap. 45). In Part III, chaps. 1-2, the growth of towns and of population in general is discussed, though not in a penetrating fashion.

not expend it, or lend it, "it may incommodate the commerce and traffique of the subjects . . . [and] dry up the spring of the Treasure."[12]

Because French mercantilism is so closely identified with Colbert, the principles underlying his developmental theory will be indicated, even though these appeared in the form of decrees, memoranda, letters, etc.[13] A bullionist, Colbert was interested in attracting money, in preventing its subsequent export, and in enabling the people to profit by its circulation. As a result, he favored prohibition of specie exports, decrease of imports, and increase of exports, and he undertook to foster the development of commerce and manufacturing in order that, among other things, a favorable balance might be generated and expanded. Among Colbert's measures intended to increase commerce, we may include efforts to negotiate favorable commercial treaties and secure the participation of the nobility in commerce; establishment of marine insurance and of protection against pirates and privateers; the creation of a powerful navy to guard France's commerce, to be constructed in part by newly established state-operated shipyards; augmentation of the nation's merchant marine through tonnage duties on foreign ships, bounties, subsidies, etc.; establishment of regulated and privileged trading companies (together with facilitation of their financing) to develop and exploit commerce in the colonies and in various parts of the world with which well-ordered trade had not yet been established; development of the colonies as a protected market for French goods and as a source of both raw materials and certain manufactures which the colonies could profitably produce.[14]

Industry played as important a role in Colbert's program as did commerce, for industry, by making for exports and self-sufficiency, both attracted bullion and checked its outflow as well. Moreover, industry provided employment, did away with idleness, and contributed to the revenue and strength of the crown and to the comfort of the people. Accordingly, Colbert resorted to

---

12. *Ibid.*, Part I, chaps. 41, 44, 49. It is suggested (*ibid.*, p. 181) that the prince ought to lay up yearly in his exchequer no more than the amount by which the money entering the country exceeds that leaving it. Cf. Botero, footnote 2 above.

13. For convenience we shall refer only to C. W. Cole's very detailed account of Colbert and Colbertism in *Colbert and a Century of French Mercantilism*, New York, 1939, and to Heckscher's extensive summary in his *Mercantilism* (New York, rev. 2nd ed., 1955). Concerning the role of the French state in France's economic development during the two centuries preceding the beginning of Colbert's ascent to power (1651), see, besides the two works just cited, P. Boissonnade, *Le socialisme d'état*, Paris, 1927. Throughout this period there was a great deal of state intervention.

14. See Cole, *Colbert*, I, pp. 337-38, 342*ff.*, 346, 351, 384-415, 438-72, 475; chaps. 8-9 on the various companies; and II, pp. 21*ff.*, 41-45, on efforts to supply the colonies with population. See also Heckscher, *Mercantilism*, I, pp. 345-51; II, pp. 279*ff.*; and *passim*. Colbert was especially interested in the Levant trade, which was marked by an "unfavorable" balance, and in the Spanish trade, through which a surplus of specie was gotten. See Cole, *Colbert*, I, pp. 392-93, 403-408. Conceiving the volume of world trade to be static and substantially fixed, and an increase in one country's share (especially if in excess of its "natural" quota) to be obtainable only at the expense of the shares of other countries, Colbert viewed French commerce as "a war of money against all the states of Europe." See *ibid.*, pp. 342-44; Heckscher, *Mercantilism*, II, pp. 25-28. Much of Colbert's program was colored by his hostility to the Dutch.

all methods, including various combinations of private and state enterprise, that appeared suited to rehabilitate and enlarge the industrial structure of the country. Among these methods, discriminatory protectionism was most important: Lower import duties on raw materials and other goods used in internal manufacture, and reduce export duties on domestic manufactures destined for foreign markets; impose high duties on raw-material exports and on manufactured goods coming from abroad, above all, on those that compete with domestic industries especially indicated for support; grant subsidies and refunds of export duties on goods whose foreign sale was being fostered. He granted tax reductions to localities that undertook to establish or enlarge industries, but he made the continuance of these reductions contingent on continuation of the industrial program in question. Subsidies, interest-free capital, and the vast orders by state agencies and the crown were extended to particular industries selected for support; and favors were granted to nobles, officials, and private persons who worked for industrial expansion. Municipal and provincial governments were induced to grant subsidies, tax exemption, rent-free premises, or pensions to entrepreneurs. Protestant manufacturers were supported, and honorific awards were employed. Efforts were made to recruit foreign industrialists and artisans, and to prevent the departure from France of skilled craftsmen and of those who possessed valued technical skill. Exclusive and restrictive privileges, together with favors and immunities, were granted to those who introduced new industries.[15] Manufactures were subjected to detailed regulations, often administered through the guilds, which were intended to insure the market-winning quality of the products and which reflected Colbert's partial distrust of entrepreneurial motives,[16] a distrust that sometimes induced Colbert to advocate recourse to state-operated industry.[17]

Colbert supported a variety of measures designed to increase national output; among them, he advocated stimulation of the growth and health of the population, setting the unemployed and the idlers to work, and reducing the number of holy days. He sought to regularize commercial law and practice, and to establish academies and journals to advance and

---

15. See Cole, *Colbert*, I, pp. 346-51, 415-36; II, chaps. 10-11, esp. pp. 132-41; Heckscher, *Mercantilism*, II, pp. 47, 146, 160, 253, 302. Colbert even sought, by his industrial and other policies, to support the money income of each province, and thereby keep money circulating throughout the whole kingdom (Cole, *Colbert*, I, pp. 352-55). The retaliatory measures that Colbert's methods inspired (*ibid.*, pp. 431*ff.*) caused some of his foreign disciples to take the possibility of retaliation into account. Cf. Uztáriz below; also Child.

16. See *ibid.*, II, chap. 12, esp. pp. 363-70; Heckscher, *Mercantilism*, II, pp. 158-66, 320.

17. Cole remarks that Colbert "regarded the typical bourgeois as a self-centered, narrow-minded, unpatriotic, profit-seeking individual" (*Colbert*, I, pp. 334-35) who must be regimented, if improvements are to be made and the larger interests of the community served (*ibid.*, II, pp. 363-64). Accordingly, while Colbert believed in using the lure of profit and reasonable state aid to encourage entrepreneurship, and supposed that individuals did better in manufactures than did the state or companies, he also believed that in the field of public works state enterprise was superior to private enterprise. See *ibid.*, I, pp. 349-50, 375.

diffuse technological knowledge and scientific discoveries. He set up a much more effective council of commerce than did Laffemas. At one time he put a 5 per cent ceiling on the interest rate. He attempted to reduce tolls and other barriers to internal trade, and to standardize weights and measures. He supported improvements of roads, waterways, and other media of internal transportation. He gave a limited amount of support to agricultural activities and considerable support to mining. He regarded with disfavor bullion-costing luxury consumption and the overcrowding of legal and financial occupations.[18]

Although the Colbertian mercantilist program for fomenting economic development was somewhat extended after his death, it gave way, early in the eighteenth century, to "paper money mercantilism," a product of English theory and continental practice, and this in turn was eventually swamped by forms of economic thought shot through with liberalism of the sort that received expression around the beginning of the eighteenth century.[19] There are no longer to be found, therefore, French exponents of what might be called programmatic, mercantilist growth theory. There are to be found, however, a number of spokesmen for the new mercantilism, which, though it played down the importance of specie and hence a favorable balance of trade (by proposing a paper substitute for specie), was an outgrowth of the earlier emphasis upon the importance of specie.[20] This view was given effective expression in France by John Law. He argued, in substance, that the level of domestic trade and employment, together with population and economic growth, depends on the extent to which money is available and in circulation.[21] If there is sufficient money in a country, enough people will be employed to give rise to an "overplus to Export"; but if "the Money lessens," unemployment and an unfavorable trade balance will ensue.

18. See *ibid.*, I, pp. 313, 318-19, 357-80; II, chap. 12; Heckscher, *Mercantilism*, II, pp. 155*ff.*, 160, 166.

19. See Heckscher, *Mercantilism*, I, pp. 106*ff.*, 458*ff.*, chap. 5; C. W. Cole, *French Mercantilism, 1683-1700*, New York, 1943, *passim;* also my *French Predecessors of Malthus*, Durham, 1942, *passim*. In a forthcoming study, Warren Scoville will present evidence showing that liberal opinion had become widespread in early eighteenth-century France.

20. See Heckscher, *Mercantilism*, II, pp. 231-37; Charles Rist, *History of Monetary and Credit Theory*, New York, 1940, pp. 31-67, 103-30; P. Harsin, ed., *John Law: Oeuvres Complètes*, Paris, 1934, Introduction. We shall cite only Law's *Money and Trade* (1705) in *ibid.*, I, which was written before he went to France. Many of Law's views, as E. J. Hamilton's forthcoming work reveals, were not original, having appeared earlier in the writings of Hugh Chamberlen and others. Law's views may therefore be looked upon as epitomizing much late seventeenth-century opinion regarding money and its institutional forms and role.

21. "A limited Sum can only set a number of People to Work proportion'd to it, and tis with little success Laws are made, for Employing the Poor or Idle in Countries where Money is scarce." Good laws can but maximize the circulation of a country's money, but they cannot enable a given amount, if insufficient, to set everybody to work, and the deficit of money cannot be met through credit "unless the Credit have a Circulation," in which event the "Credit is Money." See Harsin, ed., *op.cit.*, I, pp. 14-16, also pp. 132, 134. That the volume of trade depends upon the amount of money in circulation had been argued in various ways long before Law wrote. See Jacob Viner, *Studies in the Theory of International Trade*, New York, 1937, pp. 36*ff.;* also Chi-yuen Wu, *An Outline of International Price Theories*, London, 1932, pp. 54-62.

Scarcity of money is thus both the cause and the consequence of an unfavorable balance, the cure for which consists in adding "to the Money." If there is more than enough money and trade, immigrants will be attracted from places where unemployment prevails.[22] That Scotland and England had too little money was evident from the large amount of unemployment found there in those countries.[23] The answer consisted, therefore, in making land money, thereby making the quantity depend on the nation's own power, particularly since the issuer of the paper money could always adjust its supply to the demand for it.[24] Law doubted that interest could be made lower by legal prescription, and he attributed the historical decline in interest to the increase in money.[25]

Law's views were further developed by F. V. de Forbonnais, who, however, also supported limited protectionism, sought a favorable balance of trade, and stressed the restrictions to which the use of paper money was subject.[26] Forbonnais argued that once prices had become adjusted to the amount of money in circulation, a decrease in that amount would produce unemployment and misery. Although a rapid increase in the quantity of money tends to produce only a marked price increase, a *gradual* increase in the money supply, usually originating in a favorable balance of trade, is beneficial, since the ensuing initial increases in prices serve to increase both the labor force and production until the resulting competition, together with the associated diminution in profits and interest, offsets the tendency for prices to rise in response to an increase in money.[27]

---

22. Harsin, ed., *op.cit.*, pp. 16, 18, 24, 32, 62, 64, 160. On pp. 102 and 104 it is suggested that the increase in output consequent upon the increase in money would sell at a lower unit price, because the interest rate would be lower and apparently because Law believed that overhead costs per unit would be lower in manufacturing.

23. *Ibid.*, pp. 150, 158-60. Holland apparently had enough money. Money would not "fall in its value" unless there were a "greater Quantity than there was a Demand for" (*ibid.*, p. 160; also p. 120 where Law describes the value of paper money as more stable than that of silver).

24. *Ibid.*, pp. 120, 160, 124, 126, 136. Coining plate and regulating trade were likely to be ineffectual means of allaying the want of money (*ibid.*, p. 156, also p. 58).

25. *Ibid.*, pp. 26, 90. On the movement of the interest rate and some of the current explanations, see H. J. Habakkuk, "The Long-Term Rate of Interest and the Price of Land in the Seventeenth Century," *Economic History Review*, V, 1952, pp. 26-45.

26. There is not space here to discuss the views of Law's secretary, J. F. Melon (*Essai politique sur le commerce*, 1734), or C. Dutot's *Réflexions politiques sur le commerce et les finances*, both of which are included in E. Daire, ed., *Economistes financiers du xviii*[e] *siècle*, Paris, 1851, and the second of which was issued in a new edition, edited by P. Harsin, in Paris in 1935. Melon argued that it was in domestic, rather than in foreign, economic affairs that the legislator could, with certainty, affect scarcity, population, migration, etc., and encourage industry, to whose progress there were "no bounds" (so long, presumably, as men were excited by liberty and sureness of reward), just as there were no bounds to the wants of men. See E. Daire, ed., *op.cit.*, pp. 691, 775, chap. 9. Elsewhere Melon finds advantage in a favorable balance; indicates that although colonies may be useful, it may be better to develop unused land in the mother country; recommends limiting the operations of privileged companies to relatively unsettled areas; and, in a discussion of Petty, implies that the comparative importance of a given type of worker depends on the relative numbers found in different occupations. See *ibid.*, chaps. 4, 6, 8, 22.

27. See his *Principes économiques* (1767), in *Mélanges d'économie politique*, E. Daire and G. de Molinari, eds., Paris, 1847, I, pp. 195, 197, 202, 218-19, 223-28, 235-37. Earlier, in his *Elemens du commerce* (Leyden, 1754), Forbonnais had reasoned that a favorable

(3) Although traces of a somewhat growth-oriented mercantilism appeared several centuries before the Age of Discovery,[28] the economic literature of Spain, most of which was empiricist and more or less "mercantilist" in character, reflects, more perhaps than does the literature of any other country of Europe of the time, the effects of surrounding conditions on the views of authors of mercantilist works. The dominant theme came to be the arresting of the country's economic deterioration and the restoration of its earlier prosperity, rather than the continuing expansion of its economy. Presumably, because of their concern with Spain's economic survival, Spanish economists were sensible of the importance of economic balance; they gave less attention to the colonies than one might have anticipated; and, though most of them complained of the drain of precious metals out of Spain, they attached less importance to gold and silver, as such, than a cursory reading of their works might suggest. Even so, as E. J. Hamilton notes, Europe early found in Spain's experience a test of the validity of monetary mercantilism. For, just as the supposed correlation of the import of precious metals into Spain with her achievement of the hegemony of Europe in the sixteenth century supposedly gave support to Colbertian policies, so the decadence of Spain's industry, together with the growth of her poverty, served, after 1660, to demonstrate the powerlessness of prohibitions upon the export of specie, either to retain it or to insure prosperity.[29]

balance of trade would stimulate employment and numbers, and that, as the English believed, it was best to work up both domestic and imported raw materials into wrought form and export these, whilst avoiding the importation of finished goods except for re-export or because they were essential. The carrying trade was also described as useful to England. See *ibid.*, I, pp. 42-52, also chap. 4, and II, pp. 244*ff*. While he opposed the importation of foreign luxuries, for the reason indicated, Forbonnais described how important was luxury's role in the economy of his day (*ibid.*, II, chap. 11). The role of colonies is described as complementary, but subordinate, to that of the metropole (*ibid.*, I, pp. 371*ff*.; also *Principes*, pp. 200-201). Wealth consists of income-producing instruments; its volume depends, as does a nation's power, upon the industry of the population. It is the object of the state to maximize its sources of power. See *ibid.*, pp. 174, 176, 195. Mercantilist opinions appear in *Observations oeconomiques*, Amsterdam, 1767, wherein the views of the physiocrats are criticized. J. W. Angell describes Forbonnais's argument in *Principes* as "the best defense of Mercantilism ever advanced" (*The Theory of International Prices*, Cambridge, 1926, p. 218).

28. As early as the thirteenth century the use of Spanish ships was made compulsory in some branches of commerce, and consumption was made subject to various sumptuary controls. It was not until the close of the fifteenth century, however, that the central government sought to encourage commerce and manufacturing, and prevent the outflow of precious metals, in part through the regulation of consumption and efforts to attract foreign workers. Subsequently, the regulative structure was enlarged, colonial policy became mercantilistic, privileges and franchises were employed, etc. By 1623, a thoroughly prohibitive system had come into being. See H. Berindoague, *Le mercantilisme en Espagne, Paris,* 1929, pp. 18-77, 88*ff*., 146*ff*. See also D. M. Colmeiro, *Historia de la Economía Política en España,* Madrid, 1863; M. B. Amzalak, *Do estudo e da evoluçao das doutrinas ecónomicas em Portugal,* Lisbon, 1928; and R. Gonnard, *La Conquête Portugaise,* Paris, 1947. Gonnard (*ibid.*, p. 84) does not find Portuguese mercantilism fully developed until the first quarter of the seventeenth century. See also A. Ferreira, *Unbekannte portugiesische Merkantilisten,* Bern, 1952.

29. See E. J. Hamilton, "Spanish Mercantilism Before 1700," in *Facts and Factors in Economic History,* A. H. Cole *et al.*, eds., Cambridge, 1932, pp. 238-39. It was the price revolution, originating in Spain (as Bodin had observed in 1568), that gave support to the quantity theory, and eventually undermined the belief, apparently common among mercantilists, that specie could be accumu-

The views of Spanish mercantilists did not wholly coincide with those implicit in Spanish legislation, particularly after 1600.[30] Though they continued to emphasize the importance of treasure, they now looked upon prohibitions against specie exports as futile, and advocated instead the achievement of a favorable balance of trade through the imposition of restrictions on both the importation of manufactures and the exportation of raw materials, "paternalistic regulation of industry, and zealous application of arts and commerce."[31] Most seventeenth-century Spanish economists, of whom perhaps not more than two were essentially outside the Spanish tradition,[32] denounced the supposed causes of Spain's decadence: monetary

---

lated almost without limit. See *ibid.*, p. 239. Although Francisco López de Gómara, writing about 1557-58, observed that there was a great difference between prices in his day and prices in 1500, "caused, in my judgment, by the great quantity of silver which has come to us from the Indies" (in his *Annals of The Emperor Charles V*, R. B. Merriman, ed., Oxford, 1912, pp. ii, 2), Hamilton believes that it is first in the work of Martín González de Cellorigo (1600), who cites Bodin, that a Spanish explanation similar to Bodin's is to be found. Hamilton finds similar explanations in the works of Sancho de Moncada (1619), who also cites Bodin, Pedro Fernández Navarrete (1626), and D. Saavedra Fajardo (1640). See E. J. Hamilton, *American Treasure and the Price Revolution in Spain, 1501-1650*, Cambridge, 1934, pp. 293*ff*. The works of these authors, cited below, are: De Moncada, *Restauración Política de España*, (1619), Madrid, 1746; Fernández Navarrete, *Conservación de Monarquías y Discursos Políticos* (1626), Madrid, 1853; Diego de Saavedra Fajardo, *Idea de un Príncipe Político Cristiano* (1640), Milan, 1642. Alonso de Carranza attributed the flow of gold and silver from Spain to Holland to the fact that these metals had greater purchasing power in Holland than in Spain. See his *El Ajustamiento i Proporción de las Monedas de Oro, Plata i Cobre*, Madrid, 1629, p. 208. It is held by some that several of the jus-naturalist writers preceded Bodin in giving expression to the quantity theory. See José Larraz, *La Época del Mercantilismo en Castilla (1500-1700)*, Madrid, 2nd ed., 1943, chap. 3, and Marjorie Grice-Hutchinson, *The School of Salamanca*, Oxford, 1952, pp. 47-61; also B. W. Dempsey, "The Historical Emergence of Quantity Theory" and E. J. Hamilton's comments thereon, in *Quarterly Journal of Economics*, L, 1935, pp. 174-92.

30. Among the objectives of Spanish mercantilist legislation were the prohibition of gold and silver exports and the augmentation of their production in America, together with diminution of the exchange of foreign goods for Spanish gold and silver. This last objective, which was inspired in part by the desire to encourage domestic manufactures, was sought through navigation acts favoring the use of Spanish ships, through restriction of the export of raw materials, and through interdiction of the import of various finished goods. See Hamilton, "Spanish Mercantilism . . . ," *loc. cit.*, pp. 214-39. See also *ibid.*, pp. 228-29, 237-38, concerning the degree to which internal trade was obstructed by local duties and restrictions, and the extent to which use of the Seville monopoly to regulate and protect bullion imports operated to make Spanish prices higher. On Seville's role, see also R. S. Smith, *The Spanish Guild Merchant*, Durham, 1940, esp. chap. 6.

31. See Hamilton, "Spanish Mercantilism . . . ," *loc. cit.*, pp. 234-35. As early as 1558, a memorial incorporating a lucid formulation of the balance of trade doctrine was prepared by Luis Ortiz, but it exercised little subsequent influence. It was essential, if Spain were to increase her treasure, that her agriculture, animal husbandry, forestry, and industry be developed, and that she be thereby freed of dependence upon foreign products. Hence Ortiz recommended the gradual prohibition of both the export of raw materials and the import of finished goods, and the development of a skilled labor force through the introduction of skilled foreign workmen and the training of native workmen. See *ibid.*, pp. 230-31, and Larraz, *op.cit.*, pp. 159-66. Perhaps representative of the views of writers who typify the transition from a more static medieval state to a less static mercantile one are Miguel de Giginta's late sixteenth-century opinions on poor relief and Pedro Rivadeneira's views (in *Tratado de la Religión y Virtudes*, 1595) on trade and agriculture. On the persistence in Spain of medieval ideas and institutions, see R. S. Smith, *op.cit.*, p. 113.

32. In 1624, A. Struzzi, a naturalized Spaniard of Neopolitan birth, rejected the idea that it was desirable for Spain to accumulate gold and silver without limit. Furthermore, he favored freedom of occupational choice and substantially free trade, urged that wealthy Spaniards invest capital in industry and commerce instead of in real property and government obligations, sanctioned state help for domestic manufactures, and endorsed a low-wage apprentice system for orphans. He also criticized the banking schemes of his

chaos, "latifundia, primogentiture, mortmain, vagabondage, deforestation, redundance of ecclesiastics, contempt for manual labor and arts, indiscriminate alms, oppressive taxation, and excessive holidays." Still others condemned usury, favored restriction of celibacy and encouragement of marriage, advocated prohibition of the importation of many or all manufactures, and so on. Among the reforms these writers believed necessary were freedom of internal trade, "technological education, immigration of artisans, restoration of the coinage, extension of irrigation, and improvement of internal waterways."[33] Recommendations to the effect that "a single tax" should replace all other taxes, perhaps more common in Spain than in Italy, were designed to simplify, improve, and make more equitable the existing tax structure.[34]

Representative of the programmatic views in vogue in the early seventeenth century are those of de Moncada (who knew Botero's work).

---

day (see footnote 38, below). In 1684, Diego José Dormer, of Aragon, opposed embargoes, high tariffs, and duties; but he looked upon the importation of foreign goods as disadvantageous to Spain, and favored attracting foreign industrialists and skilled artisans, in order to establish manufactures in Spain and reduce idleness. See R. S. Smith, "Spanish Anti-Mercantilism of the Seventeenth Century: Alberto Struzzi and Diego José Dormer," *Journal of Political Economy*, XLVIII, 1900, pp. 401-11.

33. See Hamilton, "Spanish Mercantilism . . . ," *loc.cit.*, p. 237. Spanish mercantilists did not advocate artificial regulation of exchange rates as frequently as did mercantilists in other countries *(ibid.*, pp. 229-30). See also Berindoague, *op.cit.*, *passim.*

34. In 1646 a general income tax (of about 2 per cent) was recommended by Alcázar de Arriaga, and in 1651 a single and progressive poll tax was advocated by Bautista Dávila; finally in 1671 a single tax on land (to replace all existing taxes) was proposed by F. Centani. Juan de Cabrera placed considerable stress upon the easing of legal burdens and the moderation of taxes, charges, and duties incident upon trade. See his *Crísis Política*, Madrid, 1719, pp. 149-50, 158-60. Miguel de Zabala y Auñon was especially critical of the existing tax system, indicating that it constricted the internal market for farm products and made the costs of Spanish suppliers so high that they could not supply the Indies with goods at prices as low as those of other countries. The depressed state of manufacturing was further accentuated by depopulation, which was traceable to the ceiling-price and other regulations which had contracted agricultural production. Because of the depressed state of manufacturing and commerce, the backbone of an economy, Spain could not retain precious metals. Zabala therefore proposed that all other taxes be replaced by a single tax based upon fixed income and income-producing assets, by a tax, that is, that was not arbitrary, was not incident on the poor, and did not augment prices. He proposed further that various export duties be lowered and import duties be raised. Finally, he proposed that Spaniards make use of trading companies, which had proved so successful in other countries. He rejected, of course, arguments to the effect that Spaniards did not care to conduct commerce through companies (e.g., because, as Cabrera had noted [*op.cit.*, p. 159], nobles did not engage in commerce, on the ground that it was lacking in esteem; Spaniards were not inclined to work and trade diligently; the estate was unwilling to confer enough power on companies; Spaniards lacked faith in the company arrangement). See *Misceláñea Económico-Política* (1732), Madrid, 3rd ed., 1787. Earlier, somewhat similar views had been expressed by Miguel Alvarez Osorio y Redín, in *Celador General para el Bien Común de Todos* (1686) and in *Extensión Política y Económica*, both of which are included in Pedro Rodríguez, Conde de Campomanes, *Apéndice a la Educación popular*, Madrid, 1775, Parts I and III. Certain taxes on textiles are described as unfavorable to the industries concerned, and the formation of trading companies is proposed, in part perhaps because the author believed there were too many middlemen in some lines of activity. Given such measures, Spanish prices would be lower; and given lower prices, together with improvements in trade regulations, Spain's trade balance would become more favorable. On criticisms of tax burdens by Portuguese mercantilists, see Gonnard, *La Conquête Portugaise*, Part 2, *passim;* Ferreira, *op.cit.*, pp. 49, 72*ff.*, 90.

Moncada rejected the various alleged causes of Spain's decadence (e.g., her diverse character; the sterility of her agriculture; luxurious consumption [to which he attributed much demand for labor]; confusion in Spain's legal structure; the disposition of Spaniards to desert a life of economic activity for the unproductive occupation of rentier; the use of vellon money). He also criticized prevailing demographic opinion,[35] in that he enumerated the causes (e.g., excessive number of celibates, war, famine, plague, expulsion of the Moors) to which the dearth of Spain's population had been attributed, and then noted that some of these had not even been operative and that much of this dearth was attributable to mortality traceable to extreme want, to the emigration of individuals in search of better situations, and to the fact that so many Spaniards died without leaving heirs. Moncada did not mention colonization as a cause of depopulation. Spain's decadence had its principal cause, as did her depopulation, in her commercial intercourse with foreigners, since it was this intercourse that caused her to lose gold and silver whose utility was permanent. He therefore advocated enforcement of the legislation which prohibited removal of gold and silver from Spain, but added that if Spanish prices were kept low enough, the precious metals would be attracted to Spain. Furthermore, Moncada advocated that foreigners be deprived of the opportunity of working or trading in Spain and the Indies and earning income there; that the exportation of raw materials be prohibited, so that they might be worked up at home; that foreign manufactures be excluded, so that their production in Spanish factories might provide work for the idle (since the value of most manufactures consisted predominantly of labor), and so that foreigners might be deprived of the income they were getting for carrying goods to and from Spain; and that Spain's commerce be carried in Spanish ships.[36]

35. The views of Navarrete *(op.cit.,* 1853, ed., pp. 467-75) are somewhat representative. Navarrete attributed Spain's depopulation to war, the expulsion of the Jews and Moors, the discovery of the New World, and emigration to the colonies, the large number of unemployed, the excessive number of celibates, and the great number of holidays. He proposed that only certain of Spain's colonies be opened to settlement, so that the need for settlers would be kept commensurate with the number Spain could supply. Sixteen years later Saavedra Fajardo attributed Spain's depopulation to external causes (war; removal of population to the colonies) and to internal causes (i.e., burdensome taxes; lack of manufacturing and commerce; an excessive number of holidays; failure to cultivate the fields, a failure apparently attributable in part to absentee ownership and a consequent neglect of estates). Although he identified power with arms and precious objects, Fajardo suggested that a developed agriculture, together with industry and trade, would suffice to provide a state with needed gold and silver, and presumably to furnish it with population. See Fajardo, *op.cit., empresas* 66, 68-69.

36. He opposed the immigration of foreigners into Spain on grounds of religion and national security. See *op.cit.,* discourses i and iii and that on "Población." On Moncada's influence in Spain and Portugal, see Larraz, *op.cit.,* pp. 168-74, and Gonnard's account of the work of the Portuguese economist, Ribeiro de Macedo (in *La Conquête Portugaise,* pp. 141*ff.).* See also D. Juan Sempere y Guarinos, *Biblioteca Española Económico-Política,* Madrid, 1804, II, pp. clxxxv *ff.* Moncada's contemporary, Mateo Lison y Biezma *(Discursos y Apuntamientos,* 1622), an advocate of both autarky and the acquisition and retention of precious metals, attributed Spain's depopulation to the consumption of wasteful luxuries and to the importation of manufactures which deprived Span-

Among the writers influenced by Moncada, F. Martínez de la Mata[37] merits comment because of his discussion of finance and consumption. Martínez reprinted the royal decree of October 22, 1622, providing for the establishment of banks and pawnshops in 119 sales-tax districts,[38] and went on to argue that the royal banks would liquidate most of the national debt, earn enough profit to permit abolition of all but the ordinary sales tax, facilitate the collection of taxes and the deposit of governmental revenues, cope effectively with transient local grain shortages, provide manufacturers with raw materials and sales outlets, enable or compel the utilization of idle land and mineral resources, stimulate trade and agriculture, provide technical experts and financing for the development of irrigation works, handle domestic exchange, enforce legislation designed to keep precious metals in Spain, and channel capital (raised through taxes, fines, and donations) into fixed and/or risky investment.[39] Martínez rejected the view that excessive and superfluous expenditure was responsible for Spain's economic plight, since the expenditure of some is the income of others, and since, if men were dominated by "avarice" and purchased

---

iards of work and hence of support. See *ibid.*, folios 7, 7R, 7V, 8R, 11V, 12R. Ribeiro de Macedo, ambassador to France (1668-1677), proposed adapting Colbert's system to Portugal. He favored, above all, the establishment of lumber, paper, iron, and some textile industries, because labor, of which Portugal had a surplus, made up two-thirds or more of the value of the products of these industries. The products, he added, could readily be sold. See Ferreira, *op.cit.*, pp. 89-93.

37. His *Memoriales . . . en razon del remedio de la despoblación, pobreza y esterilidad de España* (n.p., 1650) was reprinted by Conde de Campomanes in *Apéndice a la Educación popular* (Madrid 1775-77). The *Epítome* (originally printed in 1699) of Martínez's *Memorial* appears in *ibid.*, I, pp. 433-500; the *Memorial*, an extension of the *Epítome*, comprises eight discourses and appears in Part IV of Campomanes' *Apéndice*. In his introduction to the *Memorial*, Campomanes observes (pp. lxxxviii, xc) that most seventeenth-century Spanish authors were strongly protectionist. See also Castillo, *op. cit.*, chap. 3.

38. See *Memorial*, disc. viii, art. 80. Banking schemes (exclusive of the banks of deposit, established at the beginning of the fifteenth century [see A. P. Usher, *The Early History of Deposit Banking in Mediterranean Europe*, Cambridge, 1943, Part II]), received attention in Spain in the sixteenth century, it being believed, among other things, that the establishment of banks would result in low interest rates, and that these in turn would greatly stimulate economic growth (cf. argument of the Englishman, J. Child, below) and solve many of the economic problems troubling the Spanish economy. See E. J. Hamilton, "Spanish Banking Schemes Before 1700," *Journal of Political Economy*, LVII, 1949, pp. 134-56, and "The Foundation of the Bank of Spain," *ibid.*, LIII, 1945, pp. 97-114. When the Bank of Spain finally was chartered in 1782, it did not live up to expectations. See E. J. Hamilton, "The First Twenty Years of the Bank of Spain," *ibid.*, LIV, 1946, pp. 17-37, 116-40. The Portuguese, Duarte Gomes Solis (1622), recommended the creation of banks to facilitate the handling of exchange and the prevention of loss of specie. See Gonnard, *La Conquête Portugaise*, pp. 119-21.

39. See *Memorial*, disc. viii; Castillo, *op. cit.*, pp. 67*ff.*; Hamilton "Spanish Banking . . . ," *loc. cit.*, pp. 152-54. The crown was extremely enthusiastic in the decree of October 22, 1622, asserting that the banks would increase production by supplying working capital; they would also cut costs and prices, both increase tax revenue and reduce taxes, pay off public debt, diminish specie exports and deflate fractional currency, permit Spaniards to underbid foreigners on governmental contracts, provide the poor with employment, eliminate vagabondage, and (through provision of opportunity in Spain) attract immigrants and ideas and reduce emigration. See *ibid.*, p. 145. Whereas many banking schemes were proposed during the century preceding 1650 (one of them by Navarrete, *op.cit.*), only a few were published during the next half century, of which three are discussed by Hamilton.

only what was strictly necessary, commerce and science would cease, and idleness, ignorance, and misery would prevail. Expenditure gave rise to difficulty only when it was directed toward foreign commodities and occasioned loss of treasure.[40]

Mercantilist thought, observes R. S. Smith, "reached its zenith in 1724 with publication of Gerónimo de Uztáriz's" well-known work. His program was neither very original nor economically analytical; yet, it incorporated most recommendations of earlier writers, and it greatly influenced Ward, Ulloa, and others.[41] A panegyrist of Colbertism and frequently an exponent, as were many of his contemporaries, of the view that the loss of specie was very detrimental to economic progress and political strength,[42] Uztáriz sought to establish conditions conducive to a favorable balance of trade, since he recognized the virtual futility of bullionist regulations and specie-export prohibitions. He therefore became primarily a proponent of industrialization, and looked for guiding principles in the legislation and experience of England, France, Holland, and Spain. While he deemed governmental action essential to the fomenting of manufacturing and trade, Uztáriz had indirect promotion in view, since he believed that manufacturing succeeded best under the management of competent, private entrepreneurs.

His program was relatively simple. An exponent of discriminatory protectionism, he favored low duties or no duties on Spain's wrought exports, since then far more could be sold abroad at the consequently lower prices. He also favored high duties on unwanted imports (i.e., imports other than needed raw materials) from abroad since outright import prohibitions might produce retaliation. He recommended extending protection to agri-

40. See *Memorial,* disc. v; also *Epítome,* pp. 433-34. While Martínez observed that the branches of an economy reciprocally assisted one another, and that their coordinate development was indicated, he stressed the strategic character of manufacturing, whose decline, attributable to the influx of foreign goods, was the cause of the decay of agriculture, of the extent of unemployment, and hence of depopulation. Excessive taxation, he added, caused poverty, but not depopulation. See *Memorial,* disc. i-iv, vi-vii. It was not so much the loss of treasure as the depression of manufacturing that concerned Martínez, since, although "power is an effect of riches," manufactures (consisting primarily of commodities) "are effects of the arts." See *ibid.,* disc. vi, also vii in which it is argued that the jobs of Spaniards are taken by foreign craftsmen who fill many positions in many occupations.

41. See Uztáriz, *Teórica y Práctica de Comercio y de Marina,* 1724. I have used the third edition, Madrid, 1757. An excellent summary of Uztáriz's program is given by E. J. Hamilton in a paper in *Economics, Sociology & the Modern World,* N. E. Himes, ed., Cambridge, 1935, pp. 111-29. See also A. Wirminghaus, *Zwei spanische Merkantilisten, Gerónimo de Uztáriz und Bernardo de Ulloa,* Jena, 1886; A. Mounier, *Les faits et la doctrine économique en Espagne sous Philippe V—Gerónimo de Uztáriz,* Bordeaux, 1919; A. V. Castillo, *Spanish Mercantilism. Gerónimo de Uztáriz—Economist,* New York, 1930; R. S. Smith, "The Wealth of Nations in Spain and Hispanic America," *Journal of Political Economy,* LXV, 1957, pp. 104*ff*. Hamilton remarks that Uztáriz's program included nothing new except proposals for the use of protective duties (after the manner of Colbert) and the introduction of model factories (of which there were already some in Spain). Uztáriz's discussion of the role of colonies was not extensive, perhaps because he never finished what he planned to write about colonial policy.

42. E.g., see Mounier, *op.cit.,* pp. 228*ff*., also chaps. 2, 4-5, on Spanish taxes, industry, and commerce; Hamilton, ". . . Gerónimo Uztáriz," *loc. cit.,* pp. 115-16.

culture, insofar as practicable, and facilitating the production of sugar and needed raw materials, but he failed to advocate removal of the various taxes and related burdens to which agriculture was subject. Although Uztáriz would have preferred to prohibit exportation of raw materials which were utilized domestically, his fear of retaliatory action led him to advocate only the imposition of heavy duties on most of Spain's raw-material exports. An exponent of internal freedom of trade, he favored the removal, in whole or in part, of the repressive taxes then being imposed on materials, finished goods, and consumables; for these imposts augmented the costs of production and (hence) the prices of goods Spain sought to export to the Indies or abroad, and thus curbed her industry and commerce. Although he opposed (on political grounds) chartering companies to carry on the colonial trade (with the exception of the East Indies trade), he endorsed the granting of franchises, privileges, and concessions to manufacturers. The objective of these various measures was the increase of exports, the decrease of imports, and the generation of a favorable balance of trade, as he pointed out in rejecting the arguments of those who advocated low import duties and high export duties, the latter on the ground that foreigners paid such duties. The greater circulation of money resulting from these measures would further stimulate industrial development; and with its progress, population would grow, along with the king's revenue and power.[43]

Aware that Spain's labor force was less skilled than that of several other countries, Uztáriz recommended the extension of attractive offers to foreign masters and artisans, particularly in Catholic countries whence he hoped to attract 200,000 skilled workers. He proposed further, after the manner of Colbert, the establishment of academies designed to provide instruction in navigation and branches of engineering, to facilitate invention and advance technology, to diffiuse technical knowledge, and so on. Indigent, able-bodied, unemployed persons were to be set to work and afforded training of sorts in workhouses already in existence. Though he attached great importance to a navy and a merchant marine, he gave little attention to ship subsidies, navigation acts, and other measures promotive of a merchant marine, neglecting even to encourage (as was the usual practice) development of the fishing industry. He did recommend, however, the establishment, in eighteen leading European cities, of Spanish factors, to be charged with promoting the sale of Spanish goods, gathering commercial

43. Uztáriz rejected the view then common (cf. Cabrera, *op.cit.*, p. 228), that depopulation had been caused by emigration to the colonies, remarking that the parts of Spain whence the emigrants had gone remained among the more heavily populated. He favored populousness, however, since then more workers would be available, but he held that Spain had enough people to establish trade and manufactures. See Mounier, *op.cit.*, pp. 14-26, concerning alleged causes of depopulation (e.g., colonization, excessive number of religious, war, holidays, unemployment and vagabondage) and some of the writers who advanced these causes. Uztáriz held, in effect, that if an economy were progressive, numbers and industry would grow, each stimulating the other.

intelligence, and facilitating necessary importation and bill negotiation. He hoped that, given low duties on American staples and discriminatory measures against foreign colonial wares, these staples would find ready markets. Uztáriz favored establishing a spice industry in the Philippines, a tobacco factory in Havana, and additional copper mines in the colonies. While he did not neglect to make recommendations with respect to internal improvements and the conservation of natural resources, he emphasized these less than had many of his predecessors.

Among Uztáriz's leading disciples were Bernardo de Ulloa and Bernardo Ward (who was quite familiar with English practices). Ulloa made few modifications in, or additions to, Uztáriz's argument. He favored development of the fishing industry and the establishment of trading companies, approved the principle of the navigations acts, and condemned the Cadiz monopoly of the Philippine trade. He reasoned that, since growth of population depended on expansion of employment, when depopulation was encountered (as in Spanish America) it was traceable to lack of employment.[44] Ward, a moderate mercantilist and an advocate of discriminatory protection, deprecated the wholesale prohibition of imports from abroad. He favored the introduction of industrious foreigners, and advocated the suppression of crafts and brotherhoods, of the privileges of the Mesta, and of exclusive privileges generally. Ward further recommended agricultural education, free inland trade in corn, and export bounties on corn (as in England). He proposed establishment by the state of a land bank which would take money on deposit at 4 per cent and lend it out on mortgage. He recommended improvements in American mining, careful inquiry into the state of actual and potential public works in Spain and America, and specification of works to be carried out by the state and by municipalities and private persons, respectively. He proposed creation of a *Junta de Mejoras,* or development board, whose function it would be to promote the nation's interests and supply the government with economic intelligence, and establishment of a financial institution, whose task it would be to bring together suppliers of money and credit and potential borrowers. Regarding the colonies, he went far beyond Uztáriz, suggesting (on the basis of natural law) that the mother country and the colonies be viewed as constituting one economic entity, requiring protection against foreign competition and freedom from duties and burdens upon internal trade. He therefore rejected the view that colonization had depopulated Spain, both on the general ground that population growth depended upon the availability of work and sustenance and on the specific ground that most of those who went to the colonies would have been idle had they remained

44. See Ulloa, *Restablecimiento de las Fábricas y Comercio Español,* Madrid, 1740. I have used a French translation published in Amsterdam in 1753. See *ibid.,* pp. 11, 50-52, 58, 67-68, 193, 204, and chap. 13.

in Spain. He argued further, on the basis of English writings and practice, that colonies, by providing markets and supplies, give rise to employment in the mother country, and hence stimulate population growth there. In general, though Ward held that a state's wealth and power depended on the union of "agriculture, arts, manufactures, and commerce," he looked upon manufacturing as the most strategic and dynamic of these four agencies.[45]

José del Campillo y Cosío was one of the few who, like Ward,[46] assigned an important role to the colonies.[47] A monarchist, who looked upon the function of colonies as the aggrandizement of the mother country, and who favored rigid control of commerce between the colonies and countries other than Spain, he concluded that if Spain were to derive optimum benefits from her colonies, she must either permit the establishment of industries in the colonies, or else pursue a policy of free trade between the colonies and the mother country. Campillo favored the latter course, for he anticipated an expanding colonial market. Accordingly, he recommended giving land to the Indians and establishing intendants in the colonies (much as in France). Their responsibilities would include education of the Indians, introduction among them of incentives to work, improvement of transportation and mining, and the development of suitable arts and forms of commodity production. It was desirable, in general, that the colonies produce what could not be produced in Spain, or what could be produced more cheaply in the colonies than in Spain. He believed that Indians, acting as individual producers, could supply some products (e.g., sugar, tobacco, cacao) at less cost than could Negro labor utilized under plantation conditions. He supposed that the shortage of population in the colonies would

45. See Ward, *Proyecto Económico,* Part I (written about 1762), Madrid, 1779. Reputedly, at least, Part II of the *Proyecto* was written by José del Campillo y Cosío (d. 1743). In his *Obra Pía,* (1750), Ward proposed changes in the Spanish treatment of the poor, whereunder the able-bodied poor and vagrants would be shut up in hospitals and made to work for their livelihood. The works of Ward and Ulloa and their relation to that of Uztáriz are treated by Castillo, *op. cit.,* chap. 8. In his *Modo de extender el Comercio de España en Alemania y el Norte* (a film of which has been used), Ward, after examining the possibility of Spain's supplying Germany with products gotten from England and France, remarks that the Spanish people "do not have the industry and activity of the other (peoples), nor the spirit of economy, nor the zeal for public well-being, nor the great maxims which great establishments require." It was necessary, therefore, that the government make up these lacks, and that a minister be appointed to accomplish this. But Ward implied that a merchant would not be suited to this task, since what a merchant prescribed was not likely to be in the public's interest. See *ibid.,* P442V, P443R, P444R. If, as some believe (e.g., see Hamilton, "... Gerónimo de Uztáriz," *loc. cit.,* p. 112*n.*), Ward plagiarized from Campillo, this would account for the similarity between Ward's view of the role of colonies in Part I of the *Proyecto* and that found in Part II, attributed to Campillo.

46. In his *Recreación Política,* Vitoria, 1779, Nicolás de Arriquibar, who was well informed on economic literature and legislation, who endorsed the principle of the navigation acts, and who appeared to appreciate the profit motive, observed that if the colonies had drawn people out of Spain, it was only because there had been a shortage of industrial occupations and employment in Spain. See *ibid.,* I, pp. 44, 210; II, pp. 89, 94-95, 145ff.

47. His work, *Nueva Sistema de Govierno Económico para la América* (Madrid, 1789) appeared to be Part II of Ward's *Proyecto;* it was written shortly before 1743. See footnote 45 above.

decline as a result of its natural growth in response to the introduction of industry; it could also be alleviated through immigration from Catholic countries.[48] Campillo's contention that the colonies and the mother country be treated as a single political entity within which trade would be free and unencumbered was supported by Conde de Campomanes, in some measure a liberal, who sought complete exploitation of all Spain's land and resources and the "useful employment" of her manpower, "first in farming, and afterwards in manufacturing, navigation, and commerce," but free of special privileges and regulations.[49]

The last half of the eighteenth century witnessed the emergence of an elite eager to embrace new ideas and apply rational methods to the solution of Spain's problems, and favorably disposed to reforms in agriculture, industry, education, and public administration. The country's persisting problems (e.g., taxation, monetary, and land reforms; idleness and unemployment; scientific agriculture and industrialization; expansion of foreign and colonial trade) were subjected to analysis by economists of liberal or physiocratic persuasion, as well as by those with mercantilist preconceptions. Commissions, institutes, and societies were established to study problems of economic development, with the most important role played by quasi-official economic societies, of which there were some sixty, which were usually interested in promoting applied science, technical and agricultural education, schools and institutes, experimental workshops and farms, and so on. Some change resulted, in a liberal direction, even the loss of Spain's colonies being predicted in 1786, but a revolutionary transformation of Spanish society did not take place.[50]

(4) Whereas French economic policy was subordinated to French dynastic aims, and Spanish economic policy was dominated by Spanish political aspirations, German economic policy was not particularly swamped by German political policy. German experience is somewhat more in

48. *Ibid.*, pp. 71-101, 164, 169, 177-86, 195-96, 223, 245, 262-63, 276, 280-87, and chap. 8.

49. See his "Discurso sobre el Comercio Activo de la Nación," in *Apéndice a la Educación popular*, Madrid 1777, Part IV, pp. xii-xiv, xx-xxv, xxxiii-xliii, liii, lxvii. On p. x he recommended the establishment of commercial schools in the principal ports of Spain, so that those carrying on her commerce might be well-informed. See footnote 50, below.

50. See R. S. Smith, "The *Wealth of Nations* in Spain . . . ," *loc. cit.;* and "Economists and the Enlightenment in Spain, 1750-1800," *Journal of Political Economy*, LXIII, 1955, pp. 345-48; also the important work of Jean Sarrailh, *L'Espagne éclairée de la seconde moitié du xviiie siècle*, Paris, 1954, Part II, esp. chaps. 4-5, and Part III, chaps. 1-5; also Don Luis García de la Huerta, *Discorso sobre la Obligación Que Tiene la Nación de Contribuir al Fomento de las Sociedades Económicas, Mallorca*, 1785. See Arriquibar, *op.cit.*, I, pp. 32-36, for proposals to establish a board or council to deal with agriculture, commerce, and manufactures, an academy to advance learning with respect to these essentially coordinate branches of the economy, and an institution for the study of public finance. On the dissemination of skills and industrial know-how, principally for the purpose of establishing manufacture in the home and giving employment to the many idle men, women, and children (especially in agricultural areas), see Conde de Campomanes, *Discurso Sobre el Fomento de la Industria popular*, Madrid, 1774, pp. vii-x. See also *ibid.*, pp. xxxiii-xxxviii, on agricultural and industrial academies, schools of design, and the importance of mathematics; p. cxix, on the industrial-educational role of

keeping, therefore, with Schmoller's interpretation of mercantilism as a system for transforming local and territorial economic policy into national economic policy.[51] German and Austrian mercantilists, believing political aims to be superior to economic aims, were much more interested in laying down rules for the guidance of economic policy than in inquiring analytically into the presuppositions underlying these rules. Von Hornigk is typical. Believing that Austria was well equipped with resources (possessing surpluses of most resources), raw materials, precious metals, and competent manpower, he supposed that if she developed her economic potential and became comparatively self-sufficient, she would become ascendant over other European powers. Moreover, he looked upon collective and individual aims as being in essential harmony, in part because he seems to have supposed that population growth would increase security and output per head, as well as augment the tax base (which depended upon both numbers and income per head).[52] He therefore lay down nine "self-evident" rules; given their observation, Austria would develop her potential.

1. Inventory the country's resources, in particular its prospective gold and silver deposits, and discover how to use each effectively.
2. Work up all commodities that cannot be used in their natural state,

---

the state; and pp. cix, cxviff., on the need to do away with guilds and closed societies of artisans. In *Discurso sobre la Educación Popular de los Artesanos y Su Fomento*, Madrid, 1775, pp. 385-404, he discusses certain principles whose observation makes for the expansion of commerce and manufactures.

51. *The Mercantile System*, p. 51; but cf. Heckscher, *Mercantilism*, I, pp. 56ff.

52. The state could intervene, of course, should individuals attempt to act contrary to the nation's common good. See Philipp W. von Hornigk, *Oesterreich über Alles, Wann Es Nur Will* (1684), Regensburg, 1717, pp. 5, 20-24, 27, 33, 43, 45, 49, 129, 187. Concerning the approach of the Cameralists to certain questions, the following may be consulted: Walther Focke, *Die Lehrmeinungen der Kameralisten über den Handel 1650-1750*, Erlangen, 1926; W. Dreissig, *Die Geld und Kreditlehre des deutchen Merkantilismus*, Berlin, 1939; A. Tautscher, "Die Dynamische Kredit-theorie der deutschen Merkantilisten," *Weltwirtschaftliches Archiv*, LVI, 1942, pp. 143-68. Heckscher *(Mercantilism*, II, p. 263) groups Hornigk, Becher (by whom he was influenced), and W. Freiherr von Schröder together, as the Cameralists who had most in common with West-European writers. While Schröder believed Austria and Germany to be equipped with the necessary resources, he did not endorse highly protectionist or prohibitive legislation. One of the earliest Cameralist exponents of a balance of trade theory (having been influenced by Mun and others), he stressed the importance of the volume of money and its manner of circulation and of low interest rates; yet he did not believe that Austrian monetary and interest conditions would become as favorable as the Dutch. The money supply could be increased, however, he indicated, through the establishment of banks (suited, among other things, to channel the unused savings of the nobility into trade) and the use of paper money and credit. Steps could also be taken, with and without the sovereign's assistance, to expand trade and manufacturing and thereby render the trade balance favorable. Recognizing the need of capital, he endorsed frugality and thrift (provided they did not entail hoarding) and lending at interest. Among the circumstances he described as favorable to the growth of trade and manufactures are: factors conducive to the immigration of foreign capitalists and artisans; training for young native workers; assignment of an important social role to merchants (upon whom he looked as dynamic agencies); removal of monopolistic guild and related arrangements; assembly and diffusion of commercial information; governmental sponsorship of trade and enterprise; facilitation of communication, marketing, and aggressive selling. See his *Fürstliche Schatz- und Rentkammer* (1686), Leipzig, 1713, pp. 23-30, 71-78, 95-125, 139-41, 148, 159-63, 182, 224, 228-38, 249, 267, 292-335, 343, 369, 374ff. An advocate of absolutism, he supposed that the interests of the sovereign and his subjects coincided. *Ibid.*, pp. 5-7, 371-74.

since the value of a manufactured good is worth 3 to 100 times the value of its raw-material content.

3. Make the population as large as the country can support, engaging everyone in a remunerative occupation and instructing him (through foreign instructors, if necessary) in some invention, art, or trade.
4. Prohibit the exportation of specie, keeping it in circulation and out of uses that absorb or destroy it.
5. Induce the inhabitants to get along with domestic products, consume domestic luxuries, and avoid foreign luxuries insofar as possible.
6. Purchase indispensable foreign wares, not with gold and silver, but with domestic products.
7. Import foreign wares in raw form and work them up in Austria, thereby using Austrian labor.
8. Seek markets everywhere for Austrian goods, and sell them for gold and silver.
9. Never import commodities of which there is a sufficient supply at home.[53]

Von Hornigk found the key to observance of these rules in adherence to the principle, use Austrian goods, however bad they be initially, and refrain from purchasing foreign goods. He wanted the fifth rule to be applied, in particular, to the importation of silk, wool, linen, and "French wares," remarking that, in time, if foreign manufactures were banned, these could be produced effectively in Austria, even for export. The money formerly spent on imports would then serve as a source of capital; domestic consumption would stimulate its formation; and foreign artisans, having lost access to the Austrian market, would immigrate to Austria.[54] Should domestic manufactures prove inferior to foreign manufactures, Austrians could be sent abroad to study both manufacturing and the construction of necessary machinery; standards could be fixed; competitions could be conducted, and so on.[55]

---

53. *Oesterreich über Alles*, pp. 29*ff*. To this list a tenth rule should be added: Confer high prestige and social recognition upon merchants. For von Hornigk believed that, so long as great social esteem was not attached to the role of the merchant, successful merchants would abandon commerce, become landholders, and shunt their children into the professions, with the result that commerce would be deprived of both capital and able practitioners. Much earlier (1622), Duarte Gomes Solis had attributed the poverty of Spain and Portugal in part to a shortage of merchants, these being most skilled in economic affairs. See Ferreira, *op.cit.*, p. 69.

54. Because of smuggling, etc., protective tariffs alone would not suffice. Von Hornigk rejected arguments against the prohibition of foreign imports out of hand, saying that requirements could be provided domestically, that adversely affected middlemen could undertake to handle domestic goods, that raw materials in short supply could be imported, that new fashions (if essential) could be devised or copied, that profiteering by domestic artisans and businessmen could be prevented through administrative controls, and that retaliatory action could be averted by purchasing needed supplies in open markets. He supposed that naval power and sea commerce were complementary.

55. *Oesterreich über Alles*, pp. 101-28. J. J. Becher pioneered ideas respecting colonies in Germany, arguing that Germany needed colonies to provide raw materials and should have access to the colonial areas monopolized by Holland and other Western powers. See H. Hassinger, *Johann Joachim Becher*

J. H. G. von Justi, proponent of enlightened despotism, incorporated into his developmental program much of what earlier writers had recommended.[56] A populationist, Justi anticipated no difficulty from population growth so long as local deficits of food and materials were offset by commerce, manufactures, and good administration; for progress in number, especially when suitably concentrated in space, made for prosperity and the growth of wealth, increase of any one part stimulating that of other parts of the population. Money played an important role in Justi's system, even though he looked upon wealth as consisting in goods and believed that paper money might meet a nation's domestic circulation requirements. Withdrawal of money abroad or into hoards caused unemployment. Additions to the money supply operated, not to increase prices, but to augment production, at least, apparently, as long as resources were not fully employed. It was desirable, therefore, that a country's stock of specie be augmented through mining (even at a loss) and a favorable balance of

---

1635-1682, Vienna, 1951, pp. 45-51. Becher, a populationist, believed economic stability depended upon the state's preserving a suitable occupational balance, in particular the right proportion between those engaged in professional services and the rest of the labor force (i.e., peasants, laborers, merchants). He looked upon the maintenance of consumption, especially that of merchants, as of strategic importance for a country's economic growth, adding that consumption would be adversely affected if there were too much or too little competition. He stressed the dynamic role of entrepreneurship, attributing Germany's backwardness to lack of enterprise and Holland's wealth to its abundance of enterprise and to the freedom prevailing there. Becher favored keeping living costs low, so that exports might be marketed at low prices. He advocated import duties to protect domestic industry and recourse only to such taxes as did not retard economic growth. He also advocated attracting immigrants and using workhouses to instruct people in new manufacturing methods. Believing easy availability of money to be essential to the spread of manufactures and economic development generally, he opposed the transfer of money abroad and suggested the creation of a land bank which might assemble the savings of the wealthy and lend them to traders. See *ibid.*, pp. 99-102; *Politischer Discurs* (1668), Frankfort, 1688, pp. 1-9, 99-116, 205*ff.*, 288*ff.*, and *passim*. J. Niehans (in *Der Gedanke der Autarkie im Merkantilismus . . .*, Zurich, 1945, p. 43) describes Becher as a mercantilist who conceived of the state in terms of a complete and fully planned autarky in which striving after profit would be at a minimum. I cannot reconcile this interpretation with Becher's arguments. Becher encouraged innovation in Germany, particularly as expounded in his *Narrische Weisheit und weise Narrheit* (1682), which in turn gave stimulus to the work of P. K. Marperger (1656-1730). The latter did not believe uneducated merchants to be capable of judging whether a project was practicable or not. See F. Redlich, "The Role of Innovation in a Quasi-Static World: Francis Bacon and His Successors," *Explorations in Entrepreneurial History*, VII, 1954, pp. 22-23.

56. In his emphasis upon public administration, V. L. von Seckendorf resembled Justi. Stressing the full and appropriate use of the nation's resources, he pointed to certain activities (e.g., grain, wool, wine, yarn, cloth, etc.) as deserving of discriminatory treatment; yet, he argued that most favor should be shown industries which were highly remunerative. It was desirable that Germany work up her raw materials instead of exporting them, and that her people consume home-produced commodities, thereby augmenting domestic employment. It was also desirable that the activities of merchants engaged in export trades be furthered in various ways. He condemned conspicuous consumption out of keeping with one's station, and advocated prevention of the importation of luxuries in exchange for money. A populationist, he stressed the importance of health and the need to attract talented immigrants. He would avoid usurious contracts, maintain a good coinage and monetary system, remove guild and other restrictions on the freedom of workers, reduce the period during which apprentices must undergo training, and support general education. See *Der teutsche Fürstenstaat* (1656), Leipzig, 1737, pp. 215-27, 329, Appendix; pp. 30, 214-21, on self-interest; p. 182 on money's role.

trade. It was similarly desirable that the needs of working capital be met adequately: through extension of credit by the sovereign to entrepreneurs; through the establishment of insurance and of mortgage, deposit, and exchange banks; through pawnshops, designed to meet the needs of artisans, etc.; and even through foreign borrowing, if necessary. Among the measures that might contribute to a favorable balance he included the following: light imposts or tolls upon manufactured exports, indispensable imports, and goods in transit or destined for re-export; heavy imposts upon dispensable imports and raw-material exports (should these not be prohibited); prohibition of the transfer of money abroad when not essential. Justi did not oppose luxurious consumption, believing that it afforded employment; and, like Becher, he noted the importance of occupational balance. He recommended many measures, in the belief that they were conducive to economic development: eliminate idleness and vagabondage; inculcate commercial spirit; provide industrial education; divert wealth from those who do not use it industriously, e.g., clergy; maintain a good monetary system and encourage saving; attract foreign merchants and craftsmen, by preserving religious and other freedoms, granting tax exemptions, subsidies, etc.; establish an active bureau of commerce and initiate suitable provisions for commercial litigation; give preference to those industries which support the most workers; maintain efficiency in wage-goods industries, and thereby keep down the cost of living and level of money wages and production costs; utilize large-scale companies in mining; surround the use of company organization in foreign commerce by suitable safeguards; remove monopolistic arrangements in commerce, together with government price controls; assemble and diffuse economic data and information; systematize taxation; negotiate favorable commercial treaties; appropriately channel the economic expression of self-interest and self-love.[57]

The program of Joseph Freiherr von Sonnenfels, based on the premise

57. Justi, *Staatswirtschaft; oder systematische Abhandlung aller ökonomischenund Cameralwissenschaften* (1755), Leipzig, 1758, I, pp. 208-10, 225*ff*., 246, 266, 275, 280, 292, 310, 316, 461, 469, 541. Volume II is devoted to questions of public finance, it being indicated that taxes stimulate industry and trade, since, when "taxes are too low, many subjects follow the tendency to indolence," considering "not working" preferable to "a larger income" *(ibid.*, p. 53). In *System des Finanzwesens* (1766) Justi sets down criteria for evaluating taxes, among them, the need to avoid trenching upon capital or upon requirements for minimum subsistence. He implies that taxes are excessive when they exceed 25 per cent of national income, as they sometimes did. In late eighteenth-century Austrian Galicia, the total "services the peasants owe to the government" exceeded "one half of the total product created" by their labor (R. Rosdolsky, "The Distribution of the Agrarian Product in Feudalism," *Journal of Economic History*, XI, 1951, p. 263). In parts of India, land revenue is still 50 per cent of net produce (Times of India, *Directory and Yearbook*, 1955-56, p. 92). The Moghul government took one-third of the gross product of agriculture. In Japan, as late as 1930, about two-thirds of the net product of agriculture was absorbed by rent, interest, and taxes (W. W. Lockwood, *The Economic Development of Japan*, Princeton, 1954, p. 57). See Small, *Cameralists*, pp. 285-480, on Justi; see also note 74 in Part I on Joseph II's tax reform.

that it was the function of the state to harmonize public and private interests, resembled that formulated by Justi. Sonnenfels, though aware that a state's population capacity was subject to limits, characterized policies as good (bad) when they stimulated (did not stimulate) population growth. Population growth was good because it enlarged and apparently differentiated a society, occasioned fuller exploitation of land and resources, increased security, and made for fuller use of its institutional structure, thereby reducing the cost per head of this structure. Because he believed the growth of population to be dependent upon the multiplication of occupations and the expansion of employment, Sonnenfels stressed this, rather than the increase of the money supply through establishment of a favorable balance of trade. Commerce was beneficial when exports provided more employment at home than imports occasioned abroad. Luxury was defensible so long at is provided employment, even foreign luxury being unobjectionable so long as it was gotten in exchange for domestically produced goods. Whether it was advisable to introduce labor-saving machinery depended on whether it would diminish employment; it was objectionable in agriculture, however, because it reduced the rural population. Manufacturing was advantageous because it consisted so largely of labor. Colonies served to generate employment in the mother country, so long as they remained dependent, providing the mother country with raw materials and affording a secluded market for its manufactures. Sonnenfels' preference for domestically produced raw materials rested on both employment and monetary grounds. The level of employment and the progress of population depended upon the degree to which the supply of money was adequate and there were no hindrances to its circulation (e.g., high interest rates, which caused hoarding), but Sonnenfels did not stress a favorable pecuniary balance of trade, in part, presumably, because he believed that monetary functions could be performed by credit and the securities of companies. His development program included support for agriculture (e.g., bounties on agricultural exports, exploitation of unused land), some of it apparently intended to aid manufacturing (e.g., internal improvements and agricultural education, designed to keep down the costs of subsistence). He also recommended removal of barriers to the expansion of manufactures (e.g., guild restrictions, monopolistic arrangements, etc., which prevented the production of goods that were varied, attractive, and of good quality, but of sufficiently low price to sell); idleness, due in part to indiscriminate almsgiving; and obstacles to internal trade. He favored granting subsidies, credit, etc., together with import quotas and duties, to promote domestic manufactures; bestowing honors on successful merchants, provided their children became merchants; shipping goods in domestically owned ships; granting financial assistance, if necessary, to companies engaging in foreign commerce. With the exception of such projects as road construction, Sonnenfels apparently supposed that private entrepreneurs could carry on most effectively, given suitable governmental support.[58]

(5) Because of its abundance and comparatively good quality, English mercantilist literature presents a sampler with problems. The programs of Mun, Child, and Petty, however, appear to be quite suitable to our purposes. For the flavor of mid-sixteenth-century growth theory we may turn to a work of John Hales and to a slightly older work by an anonymous author.[59] The latter promised to "declare how this realme . . . may be made Populus, the people wealthie the king riche and Realme without Cyvill Discorde: vitall plenty" (original punctuation) principally by utilizing labor time now being wasted by people on holidays, by members of religious orders, and by the very many persons wholly or partly idle. This time would be used to produce exports and goods heretofore imported, and to clear and cultivate waste lands and land presently given to pasturing sheep. He also proposed subsidies to facilitate the sale of surplus corn abroad and to enable British producers to turn out wrought goods heretofore purchased abroad. These measures, the author predicted, would produce a favorable overplus and, consequently, a heavy influx of bullion.[60]

Hales differs, as does Thomas Starkey, from the late medieval writers who continued to envisage social problems primarily in moral terms. For, while he did not wholly reject moral interpretations, he recognized both

58. *Grundsätze der Polizey, Handlung, und Finanzwissenschaft* (1765-67); Small, *op.cit.*, pp. 486-584. See *Grundsätze, passim*, esp. I, chaps. 1-3; II, chaps. 1-5, 7, 9-16. Volume III deals with finance. Sonnenfels favored a tax that was proportional to income-less-subsistence, rejecting a progressive tax because it tended to modify an income structure that was not accidental. See Small, *op.cit.*, pp. 583-84. M. Palmieri, an exponent of proportional taxation, had opposed progressive taxation in 1529 on the ground that it was intended to modify an income stucture that expressed the order of nature.

59. "Polices to Reduce the Realm of Englande Unto A Prosperous Wealthe And Estate," 1549, printed in that rich repository, *Tudor Economic Documents*, 3 vols., R. H. Tawney and Eileen Power, eds., London, 1924, III, pp. 311-44. In this collection, as in *English Economic History: Select Documents*, A. Bland *et al.*, eds. London, 1915, there appear a number of papers dealing with the encouragement of industry and trade. The argument that command at sea affords commercial, as well as political, advantages was nicely set forth long before Hales's time in the anonymous *The Libelle of Englyshe Polycye* (1436), Sir George Warner, ed., Oxford, 1926. The author complains, as had others before him, of Englishmen giving up gold for Italian luxuries *(ibid.*, pp. 21, 78). England's true interest lay, not in cross-Channel military successes, but in expanding her trade, an objective realizable if she became supreme at sea *(ibid.*, pp. 28-31, 42*ff.).* Ferguson ("Renaissance Realism in the 'Commonwealth' Literature of Early Tudor England," *Journal of the History of Ideas*, XVI, 1955, pp. 287-305) describes this work, and Sir John Fortescue's *The Governance of England* (C. Plummer, ed., Oxford, 1885) as the only two late medieval works to take underlying social forces significantly into account.

60. Other measures, including the introduction of free competition in victual markets, are proposed, but these do not have to do primarily with economic growth. He considered whether, because French living standards were appreciably below the British, they could produce various wrought goods more cheaply. Apparently inspired by Patricius of Siena, the author remarked *(op.cit.*, p. 328) that whereas fruitful lands produce "soloutheful and Idell people" those "people which inhabite the Barren countries, be mouche more Dilligent and Industrious." This version of the challenge theory is to be found also in von Schröder, *op.cit.*, p. 192, who observed that the inhabitants of fertile lands usually were lazy and poor. Hard lands constitute a Toynbeean challenge.

that social causation is complex and that the behavior of man can be manipulated through use of law and decree, provided that these laws are based upon man's psychology, predispositions, and aspirations. The formulation of effective policies and remedies presupposed knowledge of the "principall cause" of that being regulated.[61] Hales took it for granted that men, being governed largely by self-interest, undertook what seemed most profitable, and carried their goods and treasure to the markets where they were most highly valued. Policy-makers must take these tendencies into account. The rise in prices, with which Hales associated many of England's ills, was attributed (in 1565) to debasement of coinage, rather than to the presence of monopoly or the influx of specie. He supposed that the amount of employment to be had in England could be expanded by increasing the number of occupations that could be pursued and by developing a favorable balance of trade. A favorable balance would develop, provided grain could be exported freely and if duties were imposed upon wrought-good imports; for these goods could then be made out of British materials by British labor, and there would be employment even for those currently idle, as well as for foreign craftsmen who might be attracted to England by the new opportunities. As there is nothing of the infant-industry thesis in his argument, he probably had principally in mind setting the unemployed and the underemployed to work.[62]

61. See *A Discourse of the Common Weal of Thys Realm of England* (written in 1565; printed in 1581), E. Lamond, ed., Cambridge, 1929, pp. 97-100, 121*ff*. In order to illustrate how a principal cause produces its effects through the medium of superficial causes, he referred to the mechanism of a clock and the manner in which each wheel, "being stirred it drives the next." Cf. E. Zilsel on the rise of experimental science, in *International Encyclopedia of Unified Science*, Chicago, 1941, II, No. 8, pp. 60*ff*. On the plural character of social causation see also Thomas Starkey, *A Dialogue Between Reginald Pole & Thomas Lupset* (c. 1535), K. M. Burton, ed., London, 1948, pp. 69-70, and *passim;* also cf. Serra, treated near the beginning of this Appendix; also footnote 20 in chap. 1.

62. *Discourse,* pp. 46-47, 50, 56, 58-70, 89, 122-29. See also E. A. J. Johnson, *Predecessors of Adam Smith,* New York, 1937, chap. 2. Prenotions of mercantilism abound in Starkey's *Dialogue* (see preceding footnote), whose content, however, is shot through with values endorsed by medieval and/or Greek (i.e., Plato, Aristotle) philosophers. England was in a bad way; her people were poverty-ridden, in part because of extravagance, in part because of ill-use of manpower and resources; her economy lost money to foreign lands, because luxuries and labor-embodying wrought goods were imported; her population was too small, its growth was in need of stimulation through facilitation of marriage and the penalization of celibacy. Starkey's recommendations were directed largely to increasing the fullness with which England's productive powers were used, e.g.: utilize untilled land; develop animal husbandry; require all children to learn a craft or profession; inspire greater diligence in agriculturalists, artificers, etc.; reduce tax and other burdens, which, because excessive, were deterrent to the realization of desired objectives, or which augmented the cost of "vittle" and hence the prices at which craftsmen must sell their wares; provide useful employment for those who were "idle" or "ill-occupied" in unnecessary or overcrowded activities (e.g., clergy and other religious personnel; personal servants; caterers to man's pleasure, vanity, luxurious tastes, etc.); require English merchants to use English ships; restrict exports to what can be spared and imports to what is essential, since then England would use her idle and poor and "ill-occupied" to work up her raw materials, and these workers would in time become so skilled that England could export wrought goods to the very countries whence she had fetched them. See *ibid.,* pp. 6-15, 48, 75-89, 124, 135-60. Whereas Hales wrote at a time when England's population was growing, Starkey was writing at a time when England's population was growing very little, if at all. In England, as in other European countries,

The works of Thomas Mun and Josiah Child exemplify the better sort of growth theory being expressed at that time in English history when merchants and foreign trade were held in highest esteem.[63] Mun's program is set down in his *England's Treasure by Forraign Trade*,[64] a work prompted

population began to decline in the fourteenth century, apparently in the first quarter, after having grown for more than two centuries. Population apparently did not begin to grow again until the second half of the sixteenth century, numbers apparently varying little in the first half. The spread of pasture in fifteenth-century England is attributed in part to the decline in numbers. The increase that took place in and after the late fifteenth century gave rise, in the sixteenth in England, to the belief that England was overpopulated. Conceivably, the elasticity of supply of produce in response to increases in labor may have become low. See M. Postan, "Some Economic Evidence of Declining Population in the Later Middle Ages," *Economic History Review*, II, 1950, pp. 221-46; E. E. Rich, "The Population of Elizabethan England," *ibid.*, pp. 247-65; K. F. Helleiner, "Population Movement and Agrarian Depression in the Later Middle Ages," *Canadian Journal of Economics and Political Science*, XV, 1949, pp. 368-77, and his paper in *Cambridge Economic History of Europe*, III (forthcoming); J. C. Russell, *British Medieval Population*, Albuquerque, 1948; Wilhelm Abel, *Die Wüstungen des ausgehendes Mittelalters*, Stuttgart, 1955. See also paper by Brown and Hopkins, cited in footnote 42 in chap. 1.

63. On the importance of trade at this time, and on the changes that took place in English trade in the seventeenth century, See R. W. K. Hinton, "The Mercantile System in the Time of Thomas Mun," *Economic History Review*, VII, 1945-55, pp. 277*ff.*; R. Davis, "English Foreign Trade, 1660-1700," *ibid.*, pp. 150*ff.*; K. G. Davies, "Joint-Stock Investment in the Later Seventeenth Century," *ibid.*, IV, 1952, pp. 284-85; E. Lipson, *The Economic History of England*, London, 4th ed., 1947, II, chap. 2. Mun's enthusiasm for trade was shared by Lewes Roberts (see his *The Treasure of Traffike* [1641], reprinted in J. R. McCulloch, *Early English Tracts on Commerce*, London, 1856); he described trade as a superior alternative to planting colonies abroad, and as essential to a nation's deriving enrichment from its natural and its artificial (i.e., wrought) wares. The strategic importance of trade continued to be emphasized; for Defoe expressed common opinion when, in his *Plan of English Commerce* (1728), he represented trade as the father of manufacture and navigation, and hence as the ultimate source of employment. In his account of the growth of English shipping, R. Davis reports estimates to the effect that seamen constituted about 1 per cent of the English population and persons engaged in ancillary activities something like another 1 per cent; the former proportion is about five times the corresponding proportion today. Thus, shipping was "one of the three or four largest employers of wage labour in the country, and it was certainly the largest user of fixed capital other than buildings." See "Merchant Shipping in the Economy of the Late Seventeenth Century," *Economic History Review*, IX, 1956, pp. 59-73, esp. pp. 71-73. See also Violet Barbour's paper in *Essays in Economic History*, E. M. Carus-Wilson, ed., London, 1954, pp. 227-53.

64. Oxford, 1949. Apparently written in the late 1620's, it was first published in 1664. See J. D. Gould, "The Date of *England's Treasure By Forraign Trade*," *Journal of Economic History*, XV, 1955, pp. 160-61. In his earlier *A Discourse of Trade* (1621) Mun sought to refute the charge that the trade carried on by the East India Company cost England specie, and to demonstrate that England derived many advantages from the company's activities. Eighty years later, the author of *Considerations on the East-India Trade* (1701), again undertook to refute the charge that this trade cost England bullion, employment, and rental income. Both works are included in McCulloch's *Early English Tracts on Commerce*. (Defenders of the East India Company [e.g., Child, Davenant] found it necessary, as Johnson [*Predecessors*, p. 144] and others have suggested, to interpret trade in more "liberal" terms than did critics of this company, so as to give support to its operations; but their analyses were inferior to those of D. North and N. Barbon.) Charles Wilson has argued that the Baltic and the Oriental trade cost England specie. See his "Treasure and Trade Balances: The Mercantilist Problem," *Economic History Review*, II, 1949, pp. 156-57, and "Treasure and Trade Balances: Further Evidence," *ibid.*, IV, 1951, pp. 231-42; the latter is a reply to E. A. Heckscher's critique, "Multilateralism, Baltic Trade, and the Mercantilists," *ibid.*, III, 1950, pp. 219-28. Heckscher, however, endorses Wilson's opinion that augmentation of bullion supplies through increasing employment was the primary mercantilist objective, and not (as Lord Keynes had argued) solicitude for employment (*ibid.*, p. 228). See also B. E. Supple, "Currency and Commerce in the Early Seventeenth Century," *ibid.*, X, 1957, pp. 239-55; also note 63 in chap. 1.

by the trade depression of the 1620's, in which the point of departure is his notion of a favorable balance of trade,[65] and in which what Marx might consider to be the capitalist formula of circulation is emphasized.[66] Mun dismissed various conditions held somewhat responsible for the adversity of the trade balance, and specified various conditions making for a favorable balance and hence for a favorable rate of exchange. Among these conditions he included: bring waste land into cultivation, thereby reducing importation of produce; eliminate idleness; require consumers to purchase domestic products and luxuries, thereby giving rise to manufactures; adjust the asking price for particular exports to the elasticity of demand encountered, except when low prices are being offered in order to destroy foreign competition;[67] carry trade in England's own ships and supply insurance, etc. domestically;

---

65. In "The Trade Depression . . . ," *loc. cit.*, Gould reports complaint in the early seventeenth century of loss of bullion and shortage of coin; see also Hinton, "The Mercantile System . . . ," *loc.cit.*, pp. 284*ff*. The expression, "balance of trade," was used by Misselden in 1623; the idea of a balance is of earlier date, but the adjectives "favourable" and "unfavorable" were not applied thereto until 1767, and then by Sir James Steuart. It was recognized that invisible, as well as visible, items entered into the constitution of the balance, but major emphasis usually was put upon the latter. Whether the state of the balance was favorable or not was to be inferred from the state of the foreign exchanges and the direction of specie flow, rather than from the commodity balance. See F. W. Fetter, "The Term 'Favorable Balance of Trade,'" *Quarterly Journal of Economics*, XLIX, 1935, esp. pp. 621-28; Jacob Viner, *Studies in the Theory of International Trade*, New York, 1937, pp. 6-15; R. De Roover, *Gresham on Foreign Exchange*, Cambridge, 1949, pp. 250-66, also pp. 37-49 on medieval attempts to acquire or retain bullion. He rejects (*ibid.*, pp. 277-78, 281) the distinction sometimes made between bullionists and later mercantilists, and accredits Mun, together with the emergence "of deposit banking and the inland bill of exchange," with causing the earlier mercantilist interest in exchange regulation to give way to stress on "the need for securing a favorable balance of trade."

66. See K. Marx, *Capital* (Kerr edition), Chicago, 1906, I, Part 2, chap. 4, pp. 164-73. Let *C* designate commodities and *M* and *M'*, money, where $M' > M$. In the medieval period, it was supposed, the economic circuit was *C-M-C;* commodities were exchanged for money and this was again exchanged for commodities. In the mercantile period the circuit became *M-C-M'*, money *M* being exchanged for commodities *C* which were subsequently exchanged for a larger amount of money, *M'*. The contrast between these two modes of circulation helps to explain the much greater emphasis placed upon money by the mercantilists than by their medieval forbears. It is *M-C-M'* that Mun describes in *England's Treasure*, chap. 4. It is *C-M-C* that Thomas Wilson had in mind when he wrote (in *A Discourse Upon Usury* [1572], R. H. Tawney, ed., New York, 1925, p. 309), "And surelye merchauntes should not lyve by gayne of monye, but by gayne of wares."

67. Mun refers (in *England's Treasure*, pp. 8, 17) to an increase of 50 per cent in sales consequent upon a 25 per cent cut in price. Demand in given markets for particular British wares varied in elasticity, because of variation in the conditions under which foreign competitors were able to supply the good. Here Mun has in view what is the most profitable price in given situations, but he does not convert his argument into one about terms of trade, as did Malynes (some of whose views on exchange control Mun criticized). Malynes (as had Gresham earlier) indicated that a nation would reduce its wealth if it sold its products "too cheap" and bought foreign products "too dear." See De Roover, *Gresham*, pp. 186, 240-50; Viner, *Studies*, pp. 17, 35-36; and Tawney, ed., *Tudor Economic Documents*, III, pp. 348-49, 357 (cited by De Roover). On the controversy over the role of exchange rates and their control, see De Roover, *Gresham*, chap. 4, and Johnson, *Predecessors*, chaps. 3-4. That the supplies of goods were inelastic in Mun's day, and that demands may have been inelastic, is suggested by Gould, "The Trade Crisis . . . ," *loc. cit.*, p. 125. That demand might be elastic was not appreciated until later. See D. C. Coleman, "Eli Heckscher and the Idea of Mercantilism," *Scandinavian Economic History Review*, V, 1957, pp. 14, 20-21.

introduce frugality, so that less is consumed at home and more sold abroad; develop fisheries; facilitate and expand re-export trade; emphasize distant trade (e.g., pepper) since the margin of profit thereon is comparatively high; export money when it begets trade which begets more money; work up foreign materials and export finished goods custom-free; keep duties low on domestic goods, so their prices will be low enough to be salable abroad; make the most of the nation's natural and artificial commodities by developing the productive arts; keep the exchanges free; avoid both commercial legislation (e.g., the bullionist statutes of employment, dating from 1390) that prompts foreign retaliation and a too great insistence on frugality regarding purchase of foreign wares.[68] Mun observed that the prince should not add to his holding of treasure more than the net annual specie inflow, but indicated that the prince could invest this specie and thus keep it employing men and materials.[69] He noted that plenty of money made things more expensive, and commented on the dispersal of Spain's treasure; but he did not allow for the fact that rising prices, consequent upon a favorable balance, eventually would make its continuation impossible. Moreover, as Supple remarks, though Mun probably allowed for the short-run stickiness of the British economy, he overlooked relevant considerations and processes whereby balance might be restored.[70]

---

68. *England's Treasure,* chaps. 3-4, 6, 10, 11-12, 14-15, 19. On the statutes of employment which Mun successfully combatted, see De Roover, *Gresham,* pp. 38-49.

69. *England's Treasure,* chap. 18; cf. chap. 5. Armstrong and others (cf. Heckscher, *Mercantilism,* II, pp. 208*ff.*) expressed somewhat similar views.

70. *England's Treasure,* pp. 17, 21, 39, chaps. 4, 6. See Supple, *op. cit.,* esp. pp. 245-46, 252-55; also Rice Vaughn, *A Discourse of Coin and Coinage* (c. 1623-1625), included in McCulloch, ed., *Old and Scarce Tracts on Money,* London, 1856. Vaughn, Supple believes *(op.cit.,* pp. 254-55), best understood the situation to which Mun was responding. The failure of Mun and others to arrive at a conception of a self-regulating mechanism has been of interest to various economists (e.g., Viner, *Studies,* pp. 74*ff.;* Heckscher, *Mercantilism,* II, pp. 249-50; J. A. Schumpeter, *History of Economic Analysis,* New York, 1954, pp. 344*ff.,* 365*ff.*). In the early seventeenth century, Hinton finds, paper money substitutes for hard money had not yet come into widespread use, and business enterprises required relatively large amounts of working capital and only relatively small amounts of fixed capital. Mun supposed, Gould believes, that when foreign sales exceeded foreign purchases, the resulting influx of bullion would raise internal prices unless, as had happened in Holland and was happening in England, the increment in bullion were used to finance an increase in trade in such manner as to avert an increase in domestic prices. Hinton argues, similarly, that the mercantilists believed that the increment in bullion might finance an increase in trade, or occasion an increase in agricultural productivity, the amount of employment, etc., and thus augment output enough to counterbalance the increase in money. The rationale of the mercantilist argument is not carefully delineated by Mun and others, or by Gould and Hinton. It is not indicated, for example, whether only re-export trade is contemplated; or whether an increase in exports is envisaged, and, if so, whether there exist unemployed resources to transform into this increase in exports; or whether productive power is growing rapidly enough to offset such increases in bullion as take place; etc. It is not indicated whether the English and the Dutch situations are really comparable, or whether Mun's reasoning is generalizable to other countries. Eighteenth-century French mercantilists were influenced by Mun's and similar arguments; see Angell, *Theory of International Prices,* pp. 211*ff.;* also discussion of Law, above. See Gould, "The Trade Crisis . . . ," *loc. cit.,* pp. 124-33; Hinton, "The Mercantile System . . . ," *loc. cit.,* pp. 282-88. Cf. Steuart's approach, footnote 97, below.

Josiah Child's work is of interest because it reflects English opinion concerning the sources of Dutch economic strength[71] and the means whereby similar strength might be developed in England.[72] Among the circumstances responsible for Dutch success were: dominance of councils of state by informed merchants; equal division of property among children; Dutch concern for the quality and reputation of their products; the encouragement given inventors, new manufacturers, and discoverers of new occupations; economically operated ships; parsimony, e.g., a Dutchman with £100,000

71. See Heckscher, (*Mercantilism,* I, pp. 351-73, II, pp. 142, 181, 274, 315) on Dutch practices and their relation to the development of mercantilist thought in other countries. Many writers touched upon the supposed causes of Dutch prosperity. For example, in the late seventeenth century, Sir William Temple found confirmation of his economic views in the contrast between Holland and Ireland. In Holland, increase in the density of population had produced a spirit of frugality and industry, whereas in Ireland the ease with which bare subsistence was to be had ("two days labour may gain enough to feed" a man) had disposed the population to idleness. Because of banks, a favorable balance of trade, and an influx of immigrants (attracted by economic and religious liberty) and money, there was a sufficiency of money in Holland; and this sufficiency, together with parsimony, made possible low interest, quick trade, easy payments, and public improvements. There were also low customs, land registry, and careful management of trade. These conditions were not to be found in Ireland; there, however, horse breeding, linen manufacture, etc., might be established. Temple objected to all luxuries on the ground that they sapped the strength of an economy, and to imported luxuries on the ground that they reduced the magnitude of the balance (if any) of foreign sales over foreign purchases. See *Works,* Edinburgh, 1754, I, pp. 118-31, 146*ff.;* II, pp. 58*ff.* Davenant and Petty, among others, also contrasted Holland and Ireland. Roberts *(op.cit.,* pp. 88*ff.)* found in the lowness of Dutch customs an important cause of Dutch success. R. Coke, more liberal than mercantilistic, but envious of the Dutch, found in immigration and in the absence of prohibitions the most practical answer to the Dutch, and criticized the navigation acts as putting control of British foreign trade in the hands of a few. See Heckscher, *Mercantilism,* II, pp. 48*ff.,* 281, 295. The Dutch, like the Spaniards and the French, were attacked by various British authors (P. W. Buck, *The Politics of Mercantilism,* New York, 1942).

72. *A New Discourse of Trade* (1690), London, 1693, written largely in the 1660's, at which time the tariff and related policies of the French were being attacked, and a commercial treaty easing French duties and policies was being proposed (in consequence of a supposedly large unfavorable balance with France). See Margaret Priestley, "Anglo-French Trade and the 'Unfavourable Balance' Controversy, 1660-1685," *Economic History Review,* IV, 1951, pp. 37-52; Lipson, *op.cit.,* III, pp. 99-116.

The revised Navigation Acts (1651, 1660, and extended to Scotland in 1661), designed to keep the Dutch from exploiting Britain's colonial trade, and described by Child as a *Charta Maritima,* were followed by considerable investment in British trade and by some change in its composition; they embodied a principle expressed in Barcelona in 1227 and in England in 1381, 1485, 1489, 1541, and in 1646 (after having been rejected in 1558). As expressed in the Act of 1660, the principle of which dominated shipping policy until the 1820's, foreigners were denied the right to become merchants in the colonies; carriage of colonial trade was restricted to English ships, with crews made up at least three-fourths of Englishmen; the chief products of England's colonies could be shipped only to England, Ireland, or other colonies; and the coasting trade was restricted to English ship-owners. In 1663 the privileges of the Act were restricted to British-built ships. See G. Edmundson, *Anglo-Dutch Rivalry During the First Half of the Seventeenth Century,* Oxford, 1911; L. A. Harper, *The English Navigation Laws,* New York, 1929; Lipson, *op.cit.,* III, pp. 116-33; Davis, papers cited in footnote 63 above; C. W. Wilson's paper in *Essays in Economic History,* Carus-Wilson, ed., pp. 254-69; K. E. Knorr, *British Colonial Theories, 1570-1850,* Toronto, 1944.

A campaign against French imports was inaugurated by Samuel Fortrey *(England's Interest and Improvements,* [1663], in McCulloch, *Early English Tracts);* it was based upon the supposed existence of a trade balance markedly unfavorable to England. Later (1713), when a trade treaty with France was proposed, it was attacked in part on the ground that trade with France was not of the sort to give much employment to British labor. See E. S. Furniss, *The Position of the Laborer in a System of Nationalism,* Boston, 1920, pp. 52*ff.* The treaty proposal reactivated (see Johnson, *Predecessors,* chap. 8) a

spent no more than an Englishman with £1500; education of sons and daughters in writing, accounting, etc., with the result that all continue in trade, whereas the successful British businessman retires to a landed estate; low customs and imposts; provision for, and employment of, the poor; use of banks; toleration of divers religions; expeditious and inexpensive law merchants; a law enabling the transference of bills of indebtedness which permits the Dutch to turn over stock twice to three times as often as is usual in England; public registry of property transfers and mortgages; lowness of the interest rate (3 per cent, until war with England raised it to 4), the "causa causans of all the other causes" of Dutch riches.[73] Later, Child added that a decline in the interest rate would augment farm rents and values; multiply artificers and foster employment of the poor; increase foreign trade; and make for thriftiness and increase of the people's "stock."[74] He suggested

---

campaign against French imports, under the leadership of Charles King and *The British Merchant*. The spokesmen for this view criticized the position of those who emphasized England's "general balance," rather than her "particular balance" with any given country, and who favored (e.g., Defoe, Child, Davenant, N. Barbon, D. North, all defenders of the East India Company) freer trade with France. King, a protectionist, brought out, as a three-volume work (*The British Merchant* [1721, 1743]), essays contributed in 1713-14 by him and others to the propagandizing journal of the same name; and it remained influential for forty years. Fortrey's were the usual arguments: favor population growth and immigration; foster manufacturing, because it consists largely of labor; import what is not to be had in England, but can be further worked up; export agricultural and mineral products whose sale is highly profitable; hinder or prevent the importation of luxury goods; support the navigation acts, since they conduce to a favorable balance of trade and make for a lower interest rate. *The British Merchant* opposed the importation of luxuries and of goods that competed with domestic products in the English market; opposed emigration on the ground that it diminished England's main market, the domestic; condemned trade (e.g., the French) which cost England treasure, and thus reduced the demand for English labor, land, and enterprise; favored trade (e.g., the Portuguese) which supposedly increased the demand for these agents of production. (For an interesting account of Charles Davenant's political about-face on Franco-Dutch trade in 1705-10 see D. Coombs, "Dr. Davenant and the debate on Franco-Dutch Trade," *Economic History Review*, X, 1957, pp. 104-112.) The navigation acts were not approved by all seventeenth-century writers, of course; W. Petyt (like Coke) numbered them among the "cloggs on our Trade" which, given England's natural advantages, would flourish if it were freed of impediments (*Brittania Languens*, 1680, in *Early English Tracts*, McCulloch, ed., pp. 314, 326, 491-95). Petyt declared "People and Treasure the true Pillars of the National Strength," and emphasized the great labor content of manufactures (*ibid.*, pp. 298*ff.*, 457). See Barbour's paper in *Essays*, E. M. Carus-Wilson, ed., pp. 226-53; also Buck, *op.cit.*, pp. 56-59, 65, 70, 117, 179, 202-203; Heckscher, *Mercantilism*, *passim*. T. Wadell shows that Davenant, while opposed to some forms of protection, conceived of policy in terms of balance of trade. See "Charels Davenant (1656-1714)—a Biographical Sketch," *Economic History Review*, XI, 1958, pp. 279-88.

73. *New Discourse*, pp. 1-7. In the preface (n.p.) Child proposes lowering by law English interest to 4 per cent, and suggests that the resulting increase in trade will actualize "a great Progression in wealth and power." Low interest is described as the mother of frugality, industry, and the arts; and the excess of English over Dutch interest is declared responsible for England's losing trade to Holland, when this trade is not reserved to England by navigation acts. Child denied that England had lost trade to Holland because English wages were too high, for Dutch wages were higher, reflecting Holland's great wealth. Moreover, should English wages be reduced, skilled workers would move to Holland from England, just as they had moved to England from France when French wages were cut. In his preface Child charges that "bankering" by goldsmiths "advanced usury"; see also pp. 178*ff.*, for his tract on usury.

74. *Ibid.*, pp. 43-59. On p. 69 he remarks that when interest is low, rentier income is insufficient to support a family, with the result that its members continue in trade. This type of argument appeared in late nineteenth-

(though perhaps with rhetorical intent) that a reduction of the interest rate would be accompanied by removal of many trade-restricting regulations and by introduction of that economic freedom (i.e., absence of regulation) which had contributed to Holland's economic strength.[75]

Of the various other questions that engaged Child's attention, support of colonial development is most important in the context of the present paper. Though a populationist, who associated improvement with population growth, he rejected the view that her colonies tended to depeople England, and maintained that population depended upon employment (the potential availability of subsistence apparently being taken for granted), and that the development of colonies expanded employment in England and provided an outlet for poor persons who could not find employment in England. But he qualified the latter argument, saying that it did not hold for New England which was beginning to engage in activities competitive with, instead of complementary to, those carried on in England. Accordingly, whereas one English emigrant to the Barbadoes (together with his ten Blacks) would provide employment for four Englishmen, ten emigrants to New England (or to Ireland) would not provide work for one man in England.[76] With respect to the balance of trade, Child indicated that it could be rendered more favorable by increasing the nation's hands and stock, by making foreign trade more advantageous to foreign buyers and potential British sellers, by increasing the number of merchants and artificers, etc.[77]

Among the productive forces identified by Petty, besides such measures

---

century French literature on population (cf. my *France Faces Depopulation*, Durham, 1938, pp. 168-69). On pp. 15-16 Child states, as did Malthus later, that when provisions are expensive, rather than cheap, workers must labor longer to earn sufficient subsistence, with the result that the national product is greater (cf. Justi). See also Furniss, *op.cit.*, pp. 122*ff.*; Temple, cited in footnote 71, above.

75. *New Discourse*, pp. 71-74, also chap. 8. Among the restrictions were those on freedom to buy, sell, and price, to move coin, to hire apprentices, etc. As a spokesman for the East India Company, through whose trade some British industries suffered an intensification of competition, it was essential that Child defend substantially unregulated trade. Davenant (*Works*, I, pp. 86-123; II, pp. 77-162) recounted the advantages of this trade, and argued that it did not interfere with manufactures which it was in England's interest to promote. See also *Considerations on the East India Trade* (1701), in McCulloch, ed., *Early English Tracts*. This work, highly praised by McCulloch and T. B. Macaulay (*ibid.*, pp. xiii*ff.*) and by M. Arkin ("A Neglected Forerunner of Adam Smith . . . ," *South African Journal of Economics*, XXIII, 1955, pp. 299-314), may have been written by Henry Martin. P. J. Thomas still considered it a "high-water mark" of late seventeenth-century free-trade opinion in his account of the origins of the protectionist attack on the East India Company and of the ascendancy of protectionism around 1700 (in *Mercantilism and the East India Trade*, London, 1926). Among the formulators of protectionism, who sought the development of a strong English textile industry, were John Cary, Joshua Gee, Thomas Manley, and J. Pollexfen. See *ibid.*; also Heckscher, *Mercantilism, passim*. Concerning the attack upon the Irish woolen industry, initially launched by John Cary, see H. F. Kearney, "The Political Background to English Mercantilism," *Economic History Review*, XI, 1958, pp. 484-96.

76. *New Discourse*, pp. 91, 97*ff.*, 179*ff.*, 186*ff.*, 195*ff.*, 212-16; also chaps. 4, 7 on the navigation acts, naturalization, and the advantages of immigration. See Knorr, *op.cit.*, for the similar arguments of Brewster, Davenant, and others; also J. Cary, *Essay on Trade*, Bristol, 1695, pp. 69-71.

77. *New Discourse*, chap. 9, also chap. 3 on companies, and chaps. 5-6 on debt transference and the court merchant.

as abolishing idleness and setting the poor to work in industry or on public works, the following were most prominent: keep the money supply adequate; increase population and the labor force and the stock of wealth; modify the composition of the labor force, increasing the relative number engaged in more productive activities, and diminishing the relative number engaged in less valuable activities; augment the skill, art, and ingenuity of the labor force. Though coin made up scarcely 1/100 part of the national wealth, its role was extremely important, except insofar as this role was played by bank money. There was so much money needed to drive trade, with the precise magnitude of this amount conditioned by the velocity of money, the access of people to banks, and so on. If there were too much money, certain adverse effects would result, but the quantity could be appropriately reduced through the king's impounding the excess, or the excess could be sent abroad. If, on the contrary, there were too little money in circulation (e.g., if the king collected too much as taxes and disbursed too little), employment and trade would fall off; but the scarcity could be remedied through the establishment of banks, even though gold and silver were preferable.[78] Petty opposed prohibition of the exportation of money, noting that it would be futile, even as he opposed interdicting the export of wool and the regulation of interest,[79] observing that increase of money (and not legislation) had served to lower interest, and that an influx of skillful Dutch workmen could eliminate Dutch advantage in woolen manufacture.[80]

Remarking that about five-eighths of the national output was attributable to labor and about three-eighths[81] to wealth or stock (of which something like three-fifths is reportedly composed of land), much of which was the effect of past labor, Petty inferred that output would increase, at least in proportion to the increase in the labor force, since it was easy to increase stock other than land and since the fertility and yield of land could be increased indefinitely.[82] Moreover, increase in the density of population seemingly was accompanied by increase in net output per head, because the cost of government, etc., fell per head and perhaps because there was

78. *The Economic Writings of Sir William Petty*, C. H. Hull, ed., Cambridge, 1899, two vols. which are paged continuously. On money, see *ibid.*, pp. 32, 35-36, 112-13, 265, 268-69, 310, 439, 446.

79. *Ibid.*, pp. 57-60, 87, 445-48.

80. *Ibid.*, pp. 59-61, 304.

81. *Ibid.*, p. 108, though on p. 307 it is put at four-sevenths. In Joseph Harris's *An Essay upon Money and Coins*, London, 1757, Part I, chap. 1, the ratio of the product of labor to that of land is given, on the authority of the *British Merchant*, as 7 to 2. The ratio varies greatly, however, from country to country, Harris observes, labor's fraction being higher in wealthy than in poor countries.

82. *Economic Writings*, pp. 51-52, 108, 110, 249, 254-55; also pp. 307-309, where Petty stated that, were England's spare hands engaged in occupations that needed filling (e.g., fishing, shipping, producing goods presently imported), the national income could be increased two- to five-seventieths, much of which could be saved. On p. 259, gold and silver are described as universal, nonperishable wealth. On saving, see also *The Petty Papers*, the Marquis of Lansdowne, ed., London, 1927, I, pp. 210-14. See also, on transforming the labor force and shunting its members into useful occupations, W. L. Bevan, "Sir William Petty," in *Publications of the American Economic Association*, IX (4), 1894, pp. 410-12.

greater division of labor and greater stimulus to activity.[83] Apparently, Petty was not sure of his argument, however, for he indicated that 1.5-3 acres were required to feed a man, and that a country might, voluntarily or under compulsion, bring corn from foreign parts.[84] Yet, he concluded, on the basis of Holland's experience, that "A small Territory, and even a Few People, may by Situation, Trade, and Policy, be made equivalent to a greater; and that convenience for Shipping, and Water-carriage, do most eminently and fundamentally conduce thereunto."[85]

Whereas many mercantilists were content to say that some occupations were much more important than others, Petty based his arguments upon his observation that output per worker was much greater in some occupations than in others.

> There is much more to be gained by Manufacture than Husbandry, and by Merchandize than Manufacture. . . . Husbandmen, Seamen, Soldiers, Artizans and Merchants are the very Pillars of any Common-Wealth.

In capacity, as well as in earning power, a seaman was worth three husbandmen, and the seaman's labor had the further advantage of being always, as was shipping, of the "nature of an Exported Commodity." Trade was the way to wealth and the source of treasure. Holland's income was so high because its labor force avoided, largely or altogether, unprofitable trades (foot soldier, husbandman, cow-keeper) and engaged in better-paying activities (e.g., trade, merchandising).[86] Petty also observed that trade flourished more among the heterodox than among the orthodox, that Protestants possessed three-fourths of the world's trade, and that in consequence a country like Holland, where many Protestants lived, enjoyed a differential advantage.[87] He did not recommend a large degree of state intervention (other than expenditure upon education and the support of highways, riverways, ports, etc.), however, to modify the industrial structure.[88]

---

83. *Economic Writings*, pp. 22, 34, 249, 255-56, 260, 286, 289*ff*., 298-300. Like Wakefield, Petty held that it was essential that population not be too dispersed (*ibid.*, p. 300); cf. C. Davenant, *Works*, C. Whitworth, ed., London, 1771, II, pp. 1*ff*. Several times, Petty touches upon the role of the city, of urban agglomeration, in fostering technical and economic progress (e.g., see *The Petty Papers*, I, pp. 40-42). As early as 1608, Louis Mendes de Vasconcelos, in his *De sitio de Lisboa* (1608), a work influenced by Plato and Aristotle, noted both economies of transportation made possible by the large city and the essentiality of a great urban concentration to a country's development. See Ferreira, *op.cit.*, pp. 43*ff*.; also note 65 in chap. I.

84. *Economic Writings*, pp. 267-68, 287-88. In the case of Holland, such importation was advantageous, he suggests.

85. *Ibid.*, p. 268. The earlier discussion implies great population density. When discussing Ireland, Petty described it as underpeopled. *Ibid.*, pp. 6, 46, 217, 272, 445.

86. *Ibid.*, pp. 256, 259-61, 266-68. Nehemiah Grew believed many of the activities in which men engaged were useless or worse, but he did not translate this directly into terms of income. See Johnson, *Predecessors*, pp. 99, 133-37.

87. *Economic Writings*, pp. 263-64.

88. The structure of customs duties, he suggests, is slightly favorable to manufacture, in that duties on exports and unfinished imports are low, whereas those on imported consumables and superfluities are relatively

Petty attached great importance to human art and ingenuity, since these attributes, along with population and industry, formed the source of national power. In *Political Arithmetick* he points out that "one Man by Art may do as much work, as many without it" in both agricultural and nonagricultural undertakings.[89] He proposed establishing publicly supported advanced institutions of learning that would train the best minds in "the discovery of Nature in all its operations."[90] Even more strongly under the influence of Bacon than under that of Hobbes, Petty proposed the establishment of a college for tradesmen "for the advancement of all mechanical arts and manufactures" and preparation of a history of trades (embracing all that could be known about each trade), both of which were designed to educate practitioners and to improve the trades.[91] He was also interested in other aspects of education, but always on utilitarian grounds,[92] and in the development and application of invention.[93] Petty supposed that in these areas, as well as in those in which governments usually participated, the state might support an aggressive policy.[94]

Further English examples need not be provided, Law having been dealt with earlier, and Cantillon and others, though partly mercantilist, being without rounded growth-oriented programs.[95] In Joshua Gee, for example, one encounters a limited protectionism, animated by the desire to bring about full employment of the British labor force in industry and agriculture. Emphasis on the importance of exporting labor-oriented goods and importing raw material-oriented goods persists, it being supposed that thereby work is exported and enabled to earn foreign-paid income, with the result that the population and labor force and the strength of the country exporting

high (*ibid.*, pp. 55-56). Taxes may increase income, he wrote, when they discourage destructive or luxurious consumption and replace it with expenditure favorable to the formation of capital, or at least the accumulation of somewhat durable commodities (*ibid.*, pp. 268-70). Petty favored (as had Hobbes) a benefit theory of taxation (*ibid.*, p. 91).

89. *Ibid.*, pp. 21, 249-50, also p. 182 where he tries to establish an "Equation between Art and Simple Labour."

90. *Ibid.*, pp. 19-20.

91. See *The Petty Papers,* I, pp. 203-10; W. E. Houghton, Jr., "The History of Trades: Its Relation to Seventeenth-Century Thought," *Journal of the History of Ideas,* II, 1941, pp. 33-60.

92. E. Strauss, *Sir William Petty,* Glencoe, Ill., 1954, pp. 39, 137-42, 174*ff.*, chap. 19.

93. See G. N. Clark, *Science and Social Welfare in the Age of Newton,* Oxford, 1949, esp. chaps. 2-3. Nehemiah Grew's approach was similar to Petty's, in that he advocated a complete inventory of England's resources and their potential uses, and of the potentialities and applicability of invention (under government encouragement) to manufactures, since "Ingenuity" might do the work of many men. He proposed a protectionist approach to international trade. To augment the labor force, he proposed banishing idleness, minimizing unproductive occupations, and increasing the population through immigration and natural increase. On Grew, see Johnson, *Predecessors,* chap. 7.

94. In his account of the elements in Dutch policy that helped make Holland superior to France, he included mode of ship construction, liberty of conscience, registry of property titles, use of banks to increase money. See *Economic Writings,* pp. 261-67.

95. See my "Richard Cantillon: First of the Moderns," *Journal of Political Economy,* LXII, 1954, pp. 281, 406. On Cantillon's influence on late eighteenth-century liberal trends in Spain, see Fabián Estapé, "Algunos comentarios a la publicación del 'Ensayo sobre la naturaleza del comercio en general' de Cantillon," *Moneda y Crédito,* No. 39, 1951, pp. 38-77.

work grow, at the expense of the countries whence come the raw materials. This view, which appears even in the work of Harris,[96] was given most unqualified expression by Sir James Steuart, when he made the gain from trade turn on the extent to which work was exchanged for "matter" and a favorable balance in terms of "matter" (which helps to support "labor") was achieved. "It is therefore a general maxim, to discourage the importation of work, and to encourage the exportation of it"; and to discourage the export of "matter" and to encourage its import.[97] Of greater significance, however, is the fact that Steuart, with his emphasis upon "the importance of organized society" and the role of economic statesmanship, provided an approach and a philosophy which, while partly in the Cameralistic and mercantilistic traditions, foreshadowed the approach and philosophy of the middle third of the twentieth century.[98]

96. *Loc.cit.;* see Johnson, *Predecessors,* chap. 15.

97. See his *An Inquiry into the Principles of Political Economy* (1767), in *Works,* London, 1805, II, p. 2; also *ibid.*, II, chaps. 26-29, IV, Part 2, on Steuart's rejection of the simple quantity theory and his formulation of the balance of trade theory. Steuart's book was designed for the use of the "statesman," who, by applying its principles, makes the economy function effectively and provide as much well-being as is attainable. Through it runs a theory of employment, together with exposition of a policy suited to keep interest low, "low interest" being "the soul of trade." See S. R. Sen, "Sir James Steuart's General Theory of Employment, Interest and Money," *Economica,* XIV, 1947, pp. 19-36; also Johnson, *Predecessors,* chap. 11, W. F. Stettner, "Sir James Steuart on the Public Debt," *Quarterly Journal of Economics,* LIX, 1945, pp. 451-76.

98. See S. R. Sen, *The Economics of Sir James Steuart,* Cambridge, 1957. Steuart considered private interest and enterprise of fundamental importance, but most likely to function in accordance with the general welfare when appropriately channelled through recourse to the statesman's tools (i.e., sumptuary legislation, money, and, above all, taxation and public expenditure). See *ibid.*, pp. 134-35, 148-51, 183; also p. 122 where he is described as the original expositor of "functional finance." He observed (as had Mun, J. Houghton, and others) that taxes might be a spur to industry, that taxes on profits might check capital formation, and that a single tax on land (of the sort proposed by Locke) would be discriminatory, in that it would be incident upon but one component of a society's "taxable fund." See *ibid.*, pp. 113-21.

INDEX